iOS 12 App Development Essentials

iOS 12 App Development Essentials – First Edition

ISBN-13: 978-0-9600109-1-2

Rev: 1.0

Table of Contents

Chapter 1

1. Start Here

The goal of this book is to teach the skills necessary to create iOS applications using the iOS 12 SDK, Xcode 10 and the Swift 4 programming language.

How you make use of this book will depend to a large extent on whether you are new to iOS development, or have worked with iOS 11 and need to get up to speed on the features of iOS 12 and the latest version of the Swift programming language. Rest assured, however, that the book is intended to address both category of reader.

1.1 For New iOS Developers

If you are entirely new to iOS development then the entire contents of the book will be relevant to you.

Beginning with the basics, this book provides an outline of the steps necessary to set up an iOS development environment. An introduction to the architecture of iOS 12 and programming in Swift 4 is provided, followed by an in-depth look at the design of iOS applications and user interfaces. More advanced topics such as file handling, database management, graphics drawing and animation are also covered, as are touch screen handling, gesture recognition, multitasking, location management, local notifications, camera access and video playback support. Other features are also covered including Auto Layout, local map search, user interface animation using UIKit dynamics, Siri integration, iMessage app development, CloudKit sharing and biometric authentication.

Additional features of iOS development using Xcode are also covered, including Swift playgrounds, universal user interface design using size classes, app extensions, Interface Builder Live Views, embedded frameworks, collection and stack layouts and CloudKit data storage in addition to drag and drop integration and the document browser.

The key new features of iOS 12 and Xcode 10 are also covered in detail, including Siri shortcuts and the new iOS machine learning features.

The aim of this book, therefore, is to teach you the skills necessary to build your own apps for iOS 12. Assuming you are ready to download the iOS 12 SDK and Xcode 10, have an Intel-based Mac and ideas for some apps to develop, you are ready to get started.

1.2 For iOS 11 Developers

If you have already read the iOS 11 edition of this book, or have experience with the iOS 11 SDK then you might prefer to go directly to the new chapters in this iOS 12 edition of the book.

All chapters have been updated to reflect the changes and features introduced as part of iOS 12, Swift 4.2 and Xcode 10. Chapters included in this edition that were not contained in the previous edition, or have been significantly rewritten for iOS 12 and Xcode 10 are as follows:

- *Using iCloud Drive Storage in an iOS 12 App*
- *An Overview of Siri Shortcut App Integration*
- *Building Siri Shortcut Support into an iOS App*
- *An Introduction to Machine Learning on iOS*
- *Using Create ML to Build an Image Classification Model*
- *An iOS Vision and CoreML Image Classification Tutorial*

1.3 **Source Code Download**

The source code and Xcode project files for the examples contained in this book are available for download at:

https://www.ebookfrenzy.com/retail/ios12/

1.4 **Download the eBook with 20 Bonus Chapters**

Thank you for purchasing the print edition of this book. Your purchase includes a color copy of the book in PDF format which includes 20 additional chapters covering 3D Touch handling, notifications, audio playback and recording, voice-to-text transcription, background multitasking, state preservation and restoration, SpriteKit game development and in-app purchasing.

If you would like to download the extended eBook edition of this book, please email proof of purchase (for example a receipt, delivery notice or photo of the physical book) to *feedback@ebookfrenzy.com* and we will provide you with a download link for the book in PDF format.

1.5 **Feedback**

We want you to be satisfied with your purchase of this book. If you find any errors in the book, or have any comments, questions or concerns please contact us at *feedback@ebookfrenzy.com*.

1.6 **Errata**

While we make every effort to ensure the accuracy of the content of this book, it is inevitable that a book covering a subject area of this size and complexity may include some errors and oversights. Any known issues with the book will be outlined, together with solutions at the following URL:

https://www.ebookfrenzy.com/errata/ios12.html

In the event that you find an error not listed in the errata, please let us know by emailing our technical support team at *feedback@ebookfrenzy.com*.

Chapter 2

2. Joining the Apple Developer Program

The first step in the process of learning to develop iOS 12 based applications involves gaining an understanding of the advantages of enrolling in the Apple Developer Program and deciding the point at which it makes sense to pay to join. With these goals in mind, this chapter will outline the costs and benefits of joining the developer program and, finally, walk through the steps involved in enrolling.

2.1 Downloading Xcode 10 and the iOS 12 SDK

The latest versions of both the iOS SDK and Xcode can be downloaded free of charge from the Mac App Store. Since the tools are free, this raises the question of whether to enroll in the Apple Developer Program, or to wait until it becomes necessary later in your app development learning curve.

2.2 Apple Developer Program

Membership in the Apple Developer Program currently costs $99 per year to enroll as an individual developer. Organization level membership is also available.

Prior to the introduction of iOS 9 and Xcode 7, one of the key advantages of the developer program was that it permitted the creation of certificates and provisioning profiles to test your applications on physical iOS devices. Fortunately this is no longer the case and all that is now required to test apps on physical iOS devices is an Apple ID.

Clearly much can be achieved without the need to pay to join the Apple Developer program. There are, however, areas of app development which cannot be fully tested without program membership. Of particular significance is the fact that iCloud access, Apple Pay, Game Center and In-App Purchasing can only be enabled and tested with Apple Developer Program membership.

Of further significance is the fact that Apple Developer Program members have access to technical support from Apple's iOS support engineers (though the annual fee initially covers the submission of only two support incident reports more can be purchased) and membership of the Apple Developer forums which can be an invaluable resource for obtaining assistance and guidance from other iOS developers and for finding solutions to problems that others have encountered and subsequently resolved.

Program membership also provides early access to the pre-release Beta versions of both Xcode and iOS.

By far the most important aspect of the Apple Developer Program is that membership is a mandatory requirement in order to publish an application for sale or download in the App Store.

Clearly, program membership is going to be required at some point before your application reaches the App Store. The only question remaining is when exactly to sign up.

2.3 When to Enroll in the Apple Developer Program?

Clearly, there are many benefits to Apple Developer Program membership and, eventually, membership will be necessary to begin selling applications. As to whether or not to pay the enrollment fee now or later will depend on individual circumstances. If you are still in the early stages of learning to develop iOS applications or have yet to come up with a compelling idea for an application to develop then much of what you need is provided without program membership. As your skill level increases and your ideas for applications to develop take shape you can, after all, always enroll in the developer program at a later date.

If, on the other hand, you are confident that you will reach the stage of having an application ready to publish or know that you will need access to more advanced features such as iCloud, In-App Purchasing and Apple Pay then it is worth joining the developer program sooner rather than later.

2.4 Enrolling in the Apple Developer Program

If your goal is to develop iOS applications for your employer then it is first worth checking whether the company already has membership. That being the case, contact the program administrator in your company and ask them to send you an invitation from within the Apple Developer Program Member Center to join the team. Once they have done so, Apple will send you an email entitled *You Have Been Invited to Join an Apple Developer Program* containing a link to activate your membership. If you or your company is not already a program member, you can enroll online at:

https://developer.apple.com/programs/enroll/

Apple provides enrollment options for businesses and individuals. To enroll as an individual you will need to provide credit card information in order to verify your identity. To enroll as a company you must have legal signature authority (or access to someone who does) and be able to provide documentation such as a Dun & Bradstreet D-U-N-S number and documentation confirming legal entity status.

Acceptance into the developer program as an individual member typically takes less than 24 hours with notification arriving in the form of an activation email from Apple. Enrollment as a company can take considerably longer (sometimes weeks or even months) due to the burden of the additional verification requirements.

While awaiting activation you may log into the Member Center with restricted access using your Apple ID and password at the following URL:

https://developer.apple.com/membercenter

Once logged in, clicking on the *Your Account* tab at the top of the page will display the prevailing status of your application to join the developer program as *Enrollment Pending*. Once the activation email has arrived, log into the Member Center again and note that access is now available to a wide range of options and resources as illustrated in Figure 2-1:

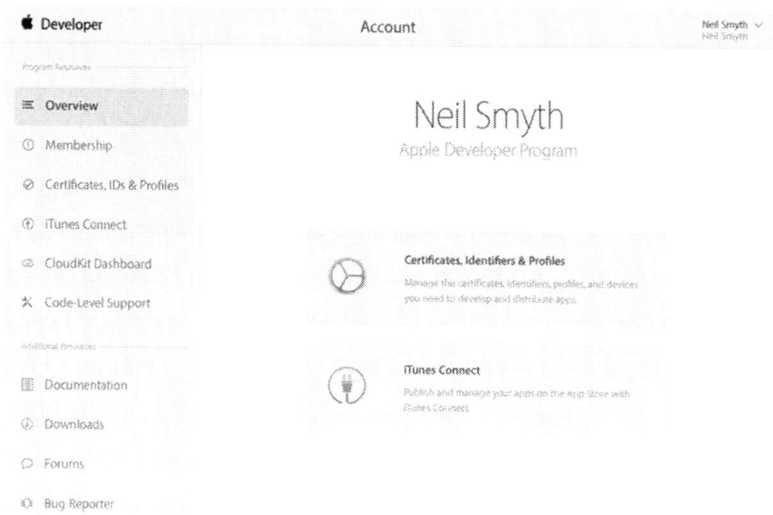

Figure 2-1

2.5 Summary

An important early step in the iOS 12 application development process involves identifying the best time to enroll in the Apple Developer Program. This chapter has outlined the benefits of joining the program, provided some guidance to keep in mind when considering developer program membership and walked briefly through the enrollment process. The next step is to download and install the iOS 12 SDK and Xcode 10 development environment.

Chapter 3

3. Installing Xcode 10 and the iOS 12 SDK

iOS apps are developed using the iOS SDK in conjunction with Apple's Xcode development environment. Xcode is an integrated development environment (IDE) within which you will code, compile, test and debug your iOS applications. The Xcode environment also includes a feature called Interface Builder which enables you to graphically design the user interface of your application using the components provided by the UIKit Framework.

In this chapter we will cover the steps involved in installing both Xcode and the iOS 12 SDK on macOS.

3.1 Identifying Your macOS Version

The Xcode 10 environment requires that the version of macOS running on the system be version 10.13.4 or later. If you are unsure of the version of macOS on your Mac, you can find this information by clicking on the Apple menu in the top left-hand corner of the screen and selecting the *About This Mac* option from the menu. In the resulting dialog check the *Version* line

If the "About This Mac" dialog does not indicate that macOS 10.13.4 or later is running, click on the *Software Update...* button to download and install the appropriate operating system upgrades.

Figure 3-1

3.2 Installing Xcode 10 and the iOS 12 SDK

The best way to obtain the latest versions of Xcode and the iOS SDK is to download them from the Apple Mac App Store. Launch the App Store on your macOS system, enter Xcode into the search box and click on the *Get* button to initiate the installation.

3.3 Starting Xcode

Having successfully installed the SDK and Xcode, the next step is to launch it so that we can create a sample iOS 12 application. To start up Xcode, open the Finder and search for *Xcode*. Since you will be making frequent use of this tool take this opportunity to drag and drop it into your dock for easier access in the future. Click on the Xcode icon in the dock to launch the tool. The first time Xcode runs you may be prompted to install additional components. Follow these steps, entering your username and password when prompted to do so.

Once Xcode has loaded, and assuming this is the first time you have used Xcode on this system, you will be presented with the *Welcome* screen from which you are ready to proceed:

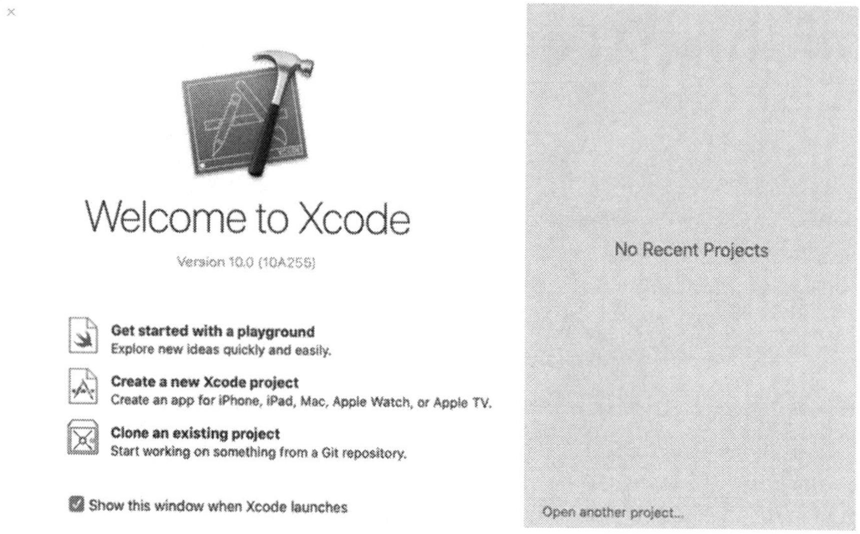

Figure 3-2

3.4 Adding Your Apple ID to the Xcode Preferences

Regardless of whether or not you choose to enroll in the Apple Developer Program it is worth adding your Apple ID to Xcode now that it is installed and running. Select the *Xcode -> Preferences...* menu option and select the *Accounts* tab. On the Accounts screen, click on the + button highlighted in Figure 3-3, select *Apple ID* from the resulting panel and click on the *Continue* button. When prompted, enter your Apple ID and associated password and click on the *Sign In* button to add the account to the preferences.

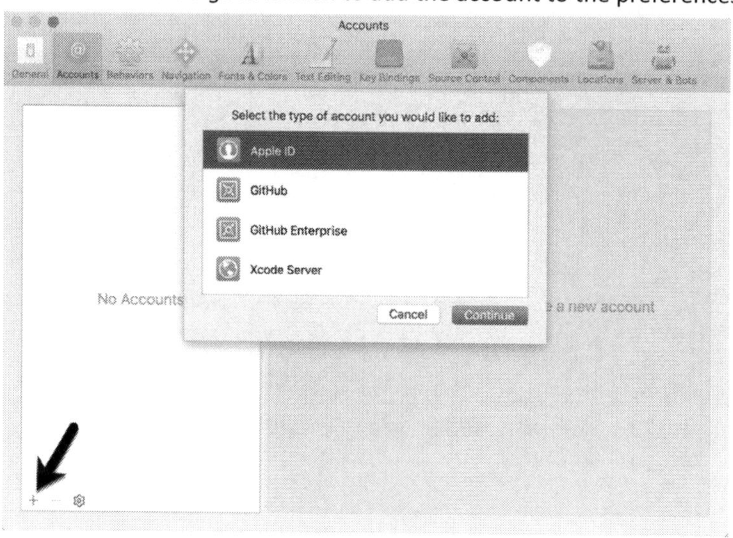

Figure 3-3

3.5 Developer and Distribution Signing Identities

Once the Apple ID has been entered the next step is to generate signing identities. To view the current signing identities, select the newly added Apple ID in the Accounts panel and click on the *Manage Certificates...* button at which point a list of available signing identities will be listed. If you have not yet enrolled in the Apple Developer Program it will only be possible to create iOS and Mac Development identities. To create the iOS Development signing identity, simply click on the + button highlighted in Figure 3-4 and make the appropriate selection from the menu:

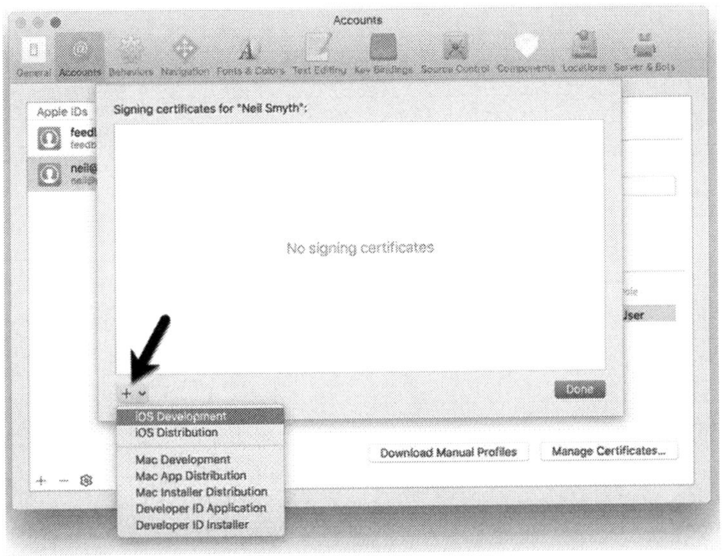

Figure 3-4

If the Apple ID has been used to enroll in the Apple Developer program, the option to create an *iOS Distribution* certificate will, when clicked, generate the signing identity required to submit the app to the Apple App Store.

Having installed the iOS SDK and successfully launched Xcode 10 we can now look at Xcode in more detail.

Chapter 4

4. A Guided Tour of Xcode 10

Just about every activity related to developing and testing iOS applications involves the use of the Xcode environment. This chapter is intended to serve two purposes. Primarily it is intended to provide an overview of many of the key areas that comprise the Xcode development environment. In the course of providing this overview, the chapter will also work through the creation of a very simple iOS application project designed to display a label which reads "Hello World" on a colored background.

By the end of this chapter you will have a basic familiarity with Xcode and your first running iOS application.

4.1 Starting Xcode 10

As with all iOS examples in this book, the development of our example will take place within the Xcode 10 development environment. If you have not already installed this tool together with the latest iOS SDK refer first to the *Installing Xcode 10 and the iOS 12 SDK* chapter of this book. Assuming that the installation is complete, launch Xcode either by clicking on the icon on the dock (assuming you created one) or use the macOS Finder to locate Xcode in the Applications folder of your system.

When launched for the first time, and until you turn off the *Show this window when Xcode launches* toggle, the screen illustrated in Figure 4-1 will appear by default:

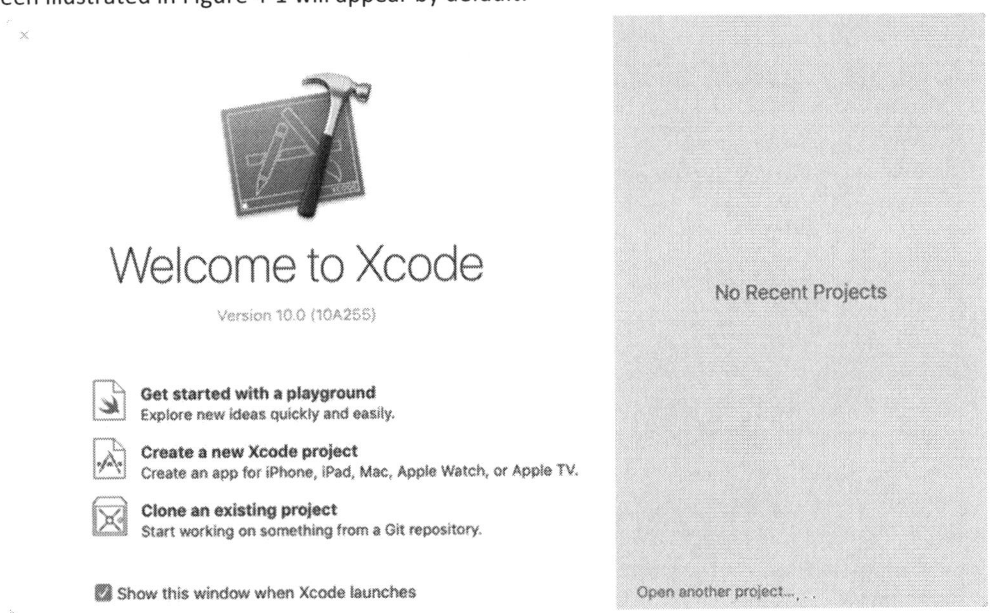

Figure 4-1

If you do not see this window, simply select the *Window -> Welcome to Xcode* menu option to display it. From within this window, click on the option to *Create a new Xcode project*. This will display the main Xcode project window together with the *project template* panel where we are able to select a template matching the type of project we want to develop:

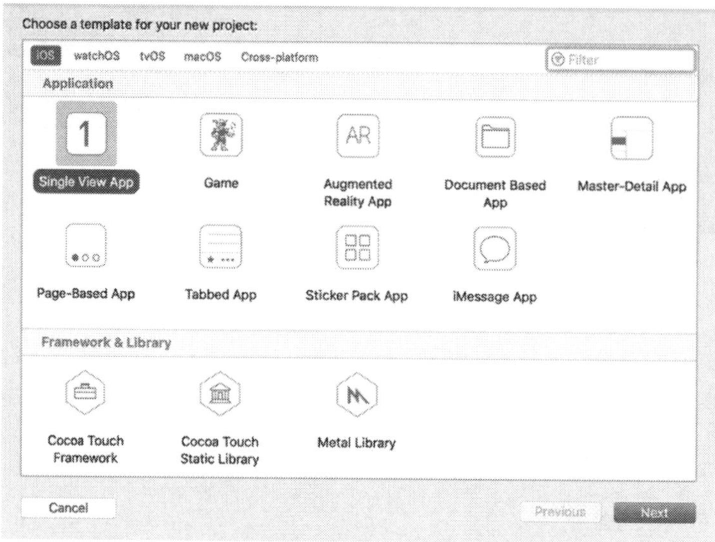

Figure 4-2

The toolbar located on the top edge of the window allows for the selection of the target platform, providing options to develop an application for iOS, watchOS, tvOS or macOS.

Begin by making sure that the *Application* option located beneath *iOS* is selected. The main panel contains a list of templates available to use as the basis for an application. The options available are as follows:

- **Master-Detail Application** – Used to create a list based application. Selecting an item from a master list displays a detail view corresponding to the selection. The template then provides a *Back* button to return to the list. You may have seen a similar technique used for news based applications, whereby selecting an item from a list of headlines displays the content of the corresponding news article. When used for an iPad based application this template implements a basic split-view configuration.
- **Page-based Application** – Creates a template project using the page view controller designed to allow views to be transitioned by turning pages on the screen.
- **Tabbed Application** – Creates a template application with a tab bar. The tab bar typically appears across the bottom of the device display and can be programmed to contain items that, when selected, change the main display to different views. The iPhone's built-in *Phone* user interface, for example, uses a tab bar to allow the user to move between favorites, contacts, keypad and voicemail.
- **Single View Application** – Creates a basic template for an application containing a single view and corresponding view controller.
- **Game** – Creates a project configured to take advantage of Sprite Kit, Scene Kit, OpenGL ES and Metal for the development of 2D and 3D games.
- **iMessage Application** – iMessage apps are extensions to the built-in iOS Messages app that allow users to send interactive messages such as games to other users. Once created, iMessage apps are made available for purchase through the Message App Store.
- **Sticker Pack Application** – Allows a sticker pack application to be created and sold within the Message App Store. Sticker pack apps allow additional images to be made available for inclusion in messages sent via the iOS Messages app.
- **Augmented Reality App** – Creates a template project pre-configured to make use of ARKit to integrate augmented reality support into an iOS app.

- **Document Based App** – Creates a project intended for making use of the iOS document browser. The document browser provides a visual environment in which the user can navigate and manage both local and cloud-based files from within an iOS app.

For the purposes of our simple example, we are going to use the *Single View Application* template so select this option from the new project window and click *Next* to configure some more project options:

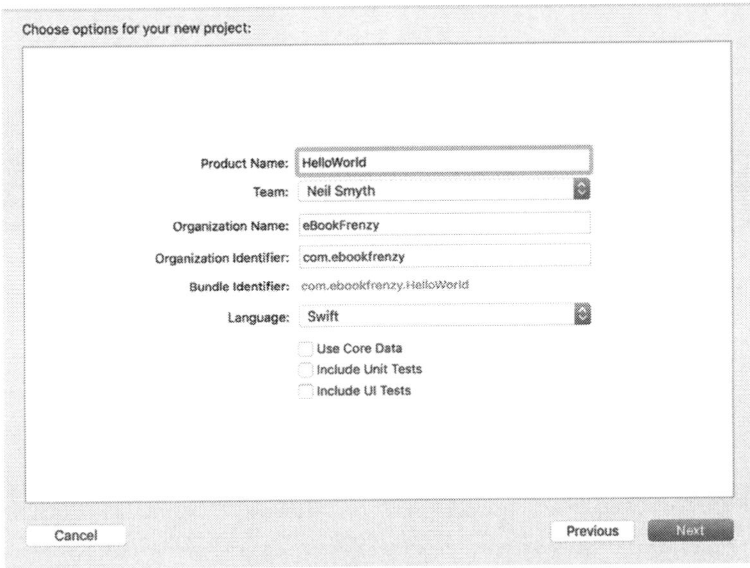

Figure 4-3

On this screen, enter a Product name for the application that is going to be created, in this case "HelloWorld" and then select the development team to which this project is to be assigned. If you have already signed up to the Apple developer program, select your account from the menu, otherwise leave the option set to None.

The text entered into the Organization Name field will be placed within the copyright comments of all of the source files that make up the project.

The company identifier is typically the reversed URL of your company's website, for example "com.mycompany". This will be used when creating provisioning profiles and certificates to enable testing of advanced features of iOS on physical devices. It also serves to uniquely identify the app within the Apple App Store when the app is published.

Apple supports two programming languages for the development of iOS apps in the form of *Objective-C* and *Swift*. While it is still possible to program using the older Objective-C language, Apple considers Swift to be the future of iOS development. All the code examples in this book are written in Swift, so make sure that the *Language* menu is set accordingly before clicking on the *Next* button.

On the final screen, choose a location on the file system for the new project to be created. This panel also provides the option to place the project under Git source code control. Source code control systems such as Git allow different revisions of the project to be managed and restored, and for changes made over the development lifecycle of the project to be tracked. Since this is typically used for larger projects, or those involving more than one developer, this option can be turned off for this and the other projects created in the book.

Once the new project has been created, the main Xcode window will appear as illustrated in Figure 4-4:

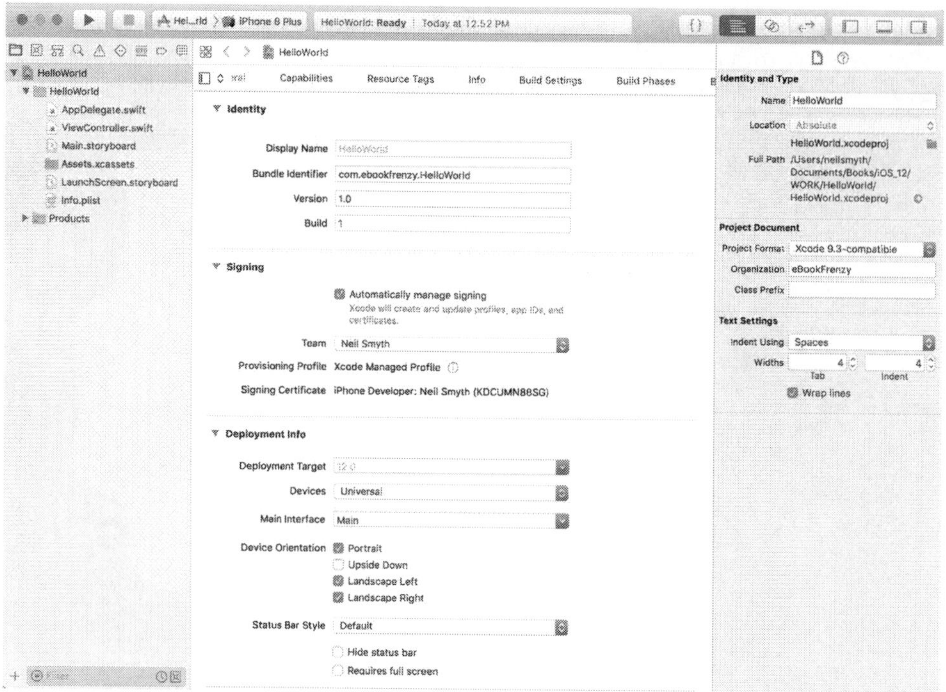

Figure 4-4

Before proceeding we should take some time to look at what Xcode has done for us. First, it has created a group of files that we will need to create our application. Some of these are Swift source code files (with a .swift extension) where we will enter the code to make our application work.

In addition, the *Main.storyboard* file is the save file used by the Interface Builder tool to hold the user interface design we will create. A second Interface Builder file named *LaunchScreen.storyboard* will also have been added to the project. This contains the user interface layout design for the screen which appears on the device while the application is loading.

Also present will be one or more files with a .plist file extension. These are *Property List* files which contain key/value pair information. For example, the *Info.plist* file contains resource settings relating to items such as the language, executable name and app identifier and, as will be shown in later chapters, is the location where a number of properties are stored to configure the capabilities of the project (for example to configure access to the user's current geographical location). The list of files is displayed in the *Project Navigator* located in the left-hand panel of the main Xcode project window. A toolbar at the top of this panel contains options to display other information such as build and run history, breakpoints and compilation errors.

By default, the center panel of the window shows a general summary of the settings for the application project. This includes the identifier specified during the project creation process and the target device. Options are also provided to configure the orientations of the device that are to be supported by the application together with options to upload icons (the small images the user selects on the device screen to launch the application) and launch screen images (displayed to the user while the application loads) for the application.

The Signing section provides the option to select an Apple identity to use when building the app. This ensures that the app is signed with a certificate when it is compiled. If you have registered your Apple ID with Xcode using the Preferences screen as outlined in the previous chapter, select that identity now using the Team menu. If no team is selected, it will not be possible to test apps on physical devices, though the simulator environment may still be used.

The Deployment Info section of the screen also includes a setting to specify the device types on which the completed app is intended to run as highlighted in Figure 4-5:

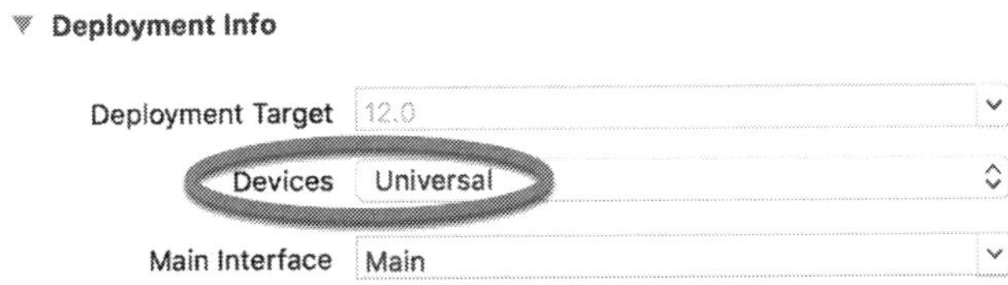

Figure 4-5

The iOS ecosystem now includes a variety of devices and screen sizes. When developing a project it is possible to indicate that the project is intended to target either the iPhone or iPad family of devices. With the gap between iPad and iPhone screen sizes now reduced by the introduction of the iPad Mini and iPhone Plus/Max range of devices it no longer makes sense to create a project that targets just one device family. A much more sensible approach is to create a single project that addresses all device types and screen sizes. In fact, as will be shown in later chapters, Xcode 10 and iOS 12 include a number of features designed specifically to make the goal of *universal* application projects easy to achieve. With this in mind, make sure that the *Devices* menu is set to *Universal*.

In addition to the General screen, tabs are provided to view and modify additional settings consisting of Capabilities, Info, Build Settings, Build Phases and Build Rules. As we progress through subsequent chapters of this book we will explore some of these other configuration options in greater detail. To return to the project settings panel at any future point in time, make sure the *Project Navigator* is selected in the left-hand panel and select the top item (the application name) in the navigator list.

When a source file is selected from the list in the navigator panel, the contents of that file will appear in the center panel where it may then be edited. To open the file in a separate editing window, simply double-click on the file in the list.

4.2 Creating the iOS App User Interface

Simply by the very nature of the environment in which they run, iOS apps are typically visually oriented. As such, a key component of just about any app involves a user interface through which the user will interact with the application and, in turn, receive feedback. While it is possible to develop user interfaces by writing code to create and position items on the screen, this is a complex and error prone process. In recognition of this, Apple provides a tool called Interface Builder which allows a user interface to be visually constructed by dragging and dropping components onto a canvas and setting properties to configure the appearance and behavior of those components.

As mentioned in the preceding section, Xcode pre-created a number of files for our project, one of which has a .storyboard filename extension. This is an Interface Builder storyboard save file and the file we are interested in for our HelloWorld project is named *Main.storyboard.* To load this file into Interface Builder simply select the file name in the list in the left-hand panel. Interface Builder will subsequently appear in the center panel as shown in Figure 4-6:

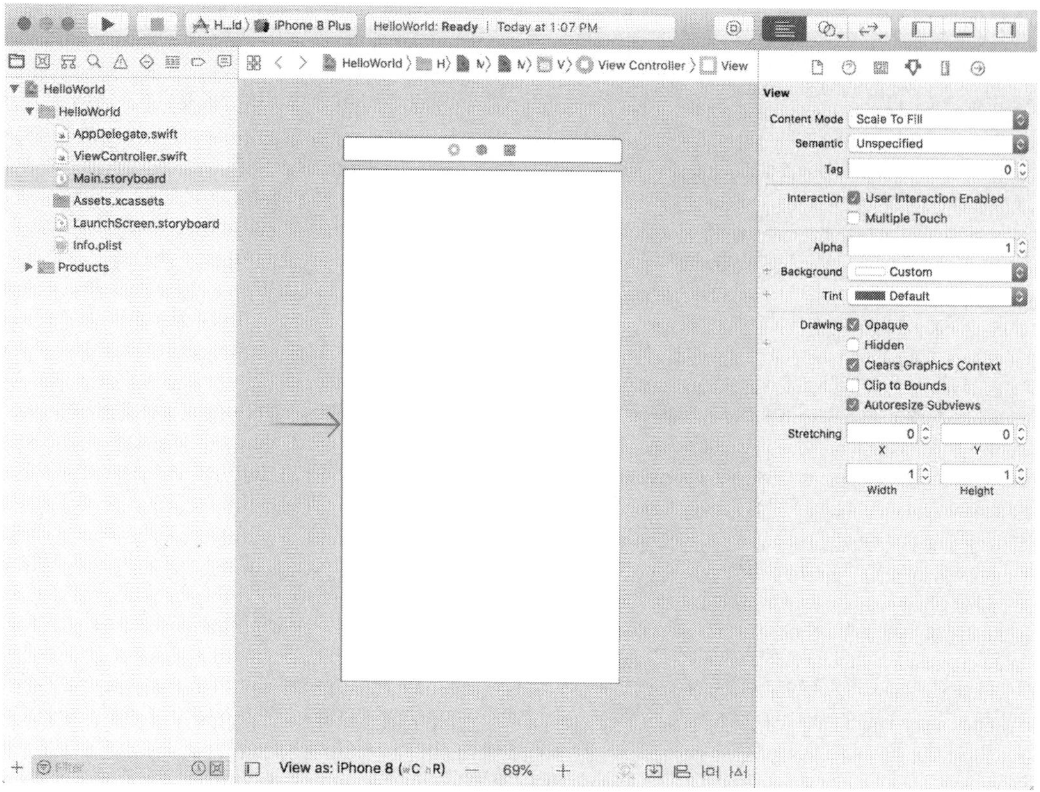

Figure 4-6

In the center panel a visual representation of the user interface of the application is displayed. Initially this consists solely of a *View Controller* (UIViewController) containing a single View (UIView) object. This layout was added to our design by Xcode when we selected the Single View Application option during the project creation phase. We will construct the user interface for our HelloWorld app by dragging and dropping user interface objects onto this UIView object. Designing a user interface consists primarily of dragging and dropping visual components onto the canvas and setting a range of properties. The user interface components are accessed from the Library panel which is displayed by clicking on the Show Library button in the Xcode toolbar as indicated in Figure 4-7:

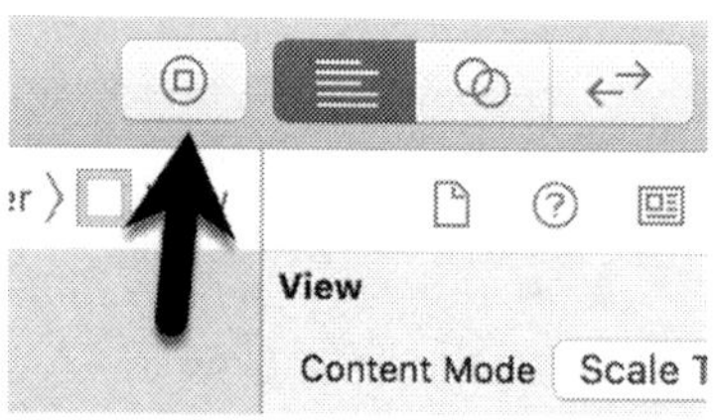

Figure 4-7

This button will display the UI components that can be used to construct our user interface. The layout of the items in the library may also be switched from a single column of objects with descriptions to multiple columns without descriptions by clicking on the button located in the top right-hand corner of the panel and to the right of the search box.

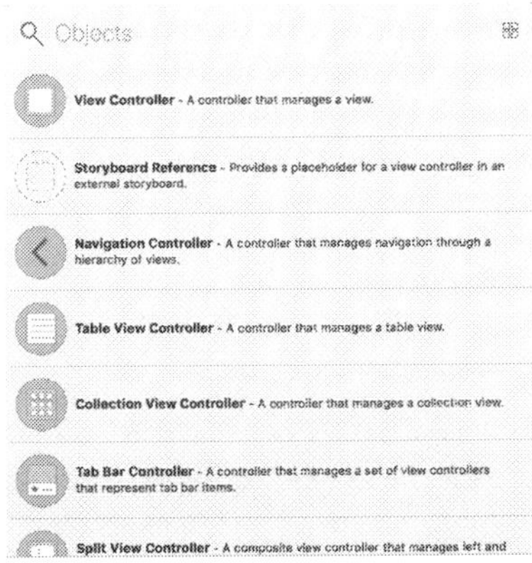

Figure 4-8

By default, the library panel will disappear either after an item has been dragged onto the layout or a click is performed outside of the panel. To keep the panel visible in this mode, hold down the Option key while clicking on the required Library item. Alternatively, displaying the Library panel by clicking on the toolbar button highlighted in Figure 4-7 while holding down the Option key will cause the panel to stay visible until it is manually closed.

In order to property settings it is necessary to display the Xcode right-hand panel (if it is not already displayed). This panel is referred to as the *Utilities panel* and can be displayed by selecting the right-hand button in the right-hand section of the Xcode toolbar:

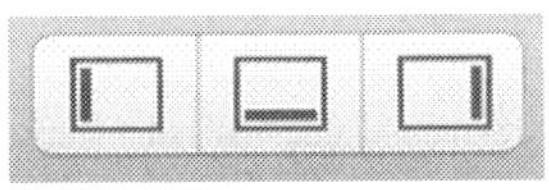

Figure 4-9

The Utilities panel, once displayed, will appear as illustrated in Figure 4-10:

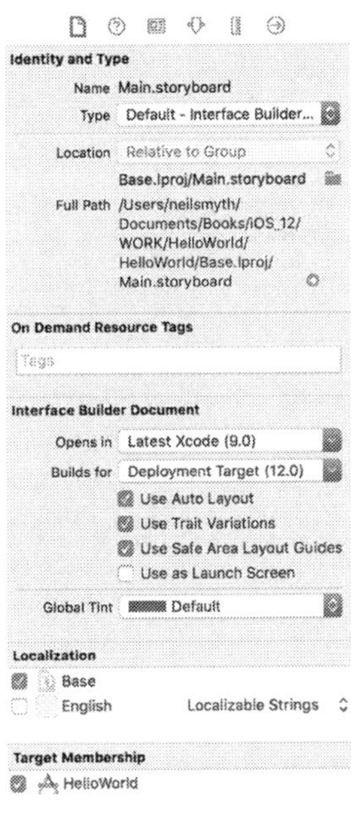

Figure 4-10

Along the top edge of the panel is a row of buttons which change the settings displayed in the upper half of the panel. By default the *File Inspector* is typically displayed. Options are also provided to display quick help, the *Identity Inspector, Attributes Inspector, Size Inspector* and *Connections Inspector*. Before proceeding, take some time to review each of these selections to gain some familiarity with the configuration options each provides. Throughout the remainder of this book extensive use of these inspectors will be made.

4.3 Changing Component Properties

With the property panel for the View selected in the main panel, we will begin our design work by changing the background color of this view. Start by making sure the View is selected and that the Attributes Inspector (*View -> Utilities -> Show Attributes Inspector*) is displayed in the Utilities panel. Click on the current property setting next to the *Background* setting and select the Custom option from the popup menu to display the *Colors* dialog. Using the color selection tool, choose a visually pleasing color and close the dialog. You will now notice that the view window has changed from white to the new color selection.

4.4 Adding Objects to the User Interface

The next step is to add a Label object to our view. To achieve this, display the Library panel as shown in Figure 4-7 above and either scroll down the list of objects in the Library panel to locate the Label object or, as illustrated in Figure 4-11, enter *Label* into the search box beneath the panel:

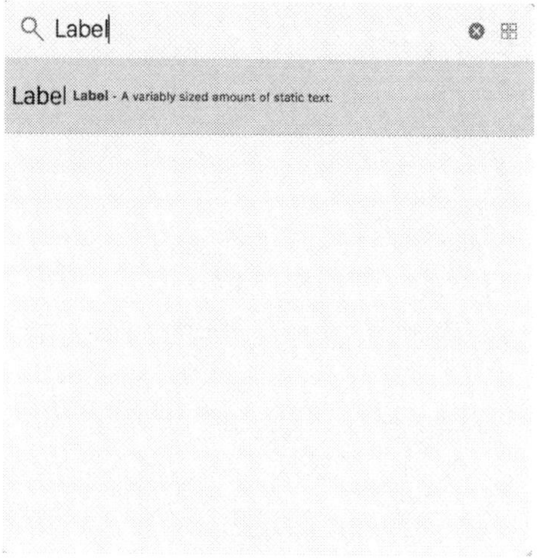

Figure 4-11

Having located the Label object, click on it and drag it to the center of the view so that the vertical and horizontal center guidelines appear. Once it is in position release the mouse button to drop it at that location. We have now added an instance of the UILabel class to the scene. Cancel the Library search by clicking on the "x" button on the right-hand edge of the search field. Select the newly added label and stretch it horizontally so that it is approximately three times the current width. With the Label still selected, click on the centered alignment button in the Attributes Inspector (*View -> Utilities -> Show Attributes Inspector*) to center the text in the middle of the label view.

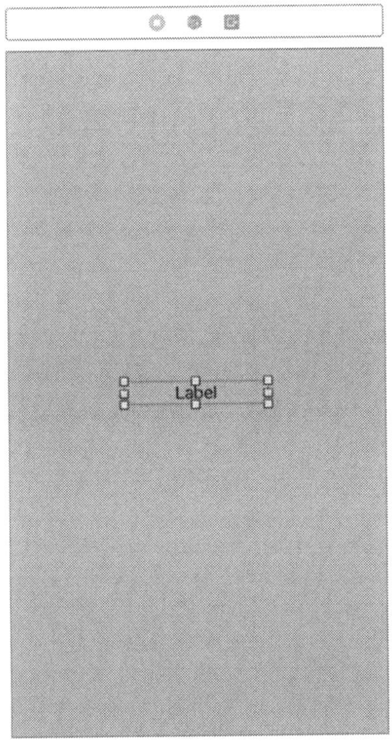

Figure 4-12

Double-click on the text in the label that currently reads "Label" and type in "Hello World". Locate the font setting property in the Attributes Inspector panel and click on the "T" button next to the font name to display the font selection menu. Change the Font setting from *System – System* to *Custom* and choose a larger font setting, for example a Georgia bold typeface with a size of 24 as shown in Figure 4-13:

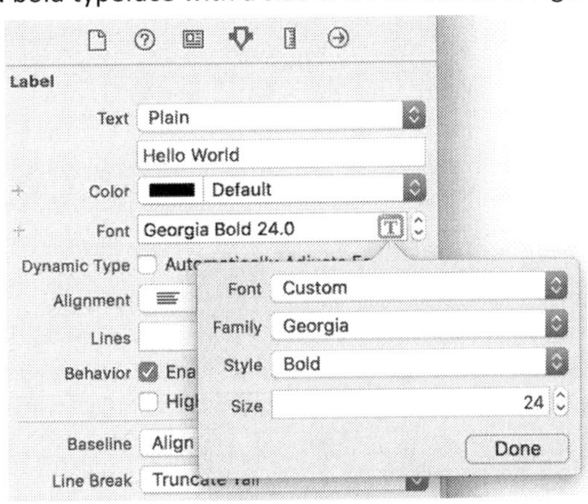

Figure 4-13

The final step is to add some layout constraints to ensure that the label remains centered within the containing view regardless of the size of screen on which the application ultimately runs. This involves the use of the Auto Layout capabilities of iOS, a topic which will be covered extensively in later chapters. For this example, simply select the Label object, display the Align menu as shown in Figure 4-14 and enable both the

Horizontally in Container and *Vertically in Container* options with offsets of 0 before clicking on the *Add 2 Constraints* button.

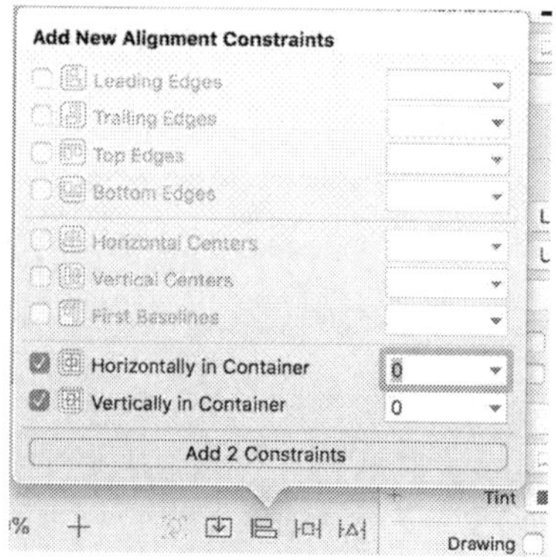

Figure 4-14

At this point, your View window will hopefully appear as outlined in Figure 4-15 (allowing, of course, for differences in your color and font choices).

Figure 4-15

Before building and running the project it is worth taking a short detour to look at the Xcode *Document Outline* panel. This panel appears by default to the left of the Interface Builder panel and is controlled by the small button in the bottom left-hand corner (indicated by the arrow in Figure 4-16) of the Interface Builder panel.

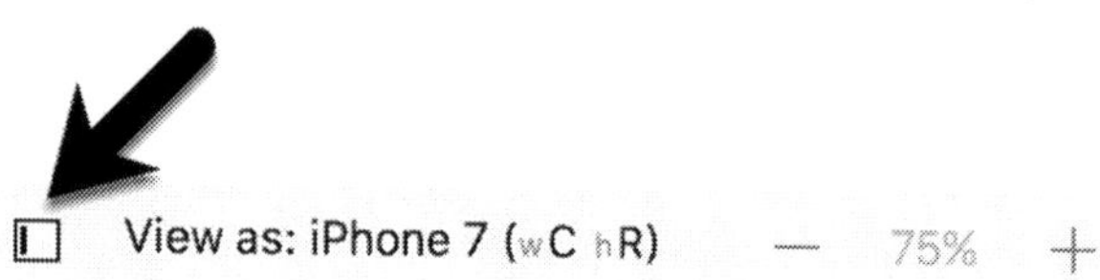

Figure 4-16

When displayed, the document outline shows a hierarchical overview of the elements that make up a user interface layout together with any constraints that have been applied to views in the layout.

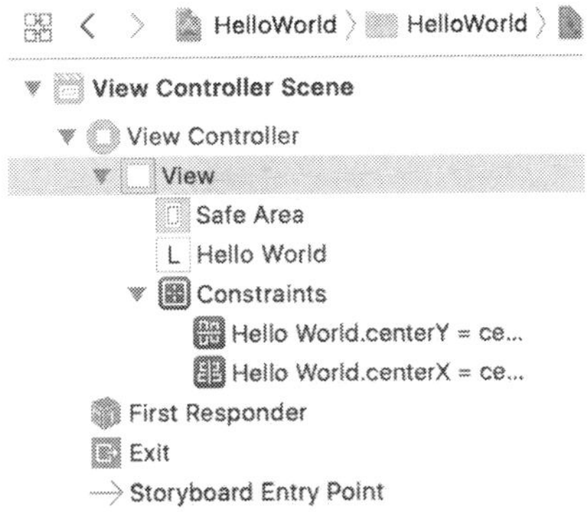

Figure 4-17

4.5 Building and Running an iOS 12 App in Xcode 10

Before an app can be run it must first be compiled. Once successfully compiled it may be run either within a simulator or on a physical iPhone, iPad or iPod Touch device. For the purposes of this chapter, however, it is sufficient to run the app in the simulator.

Within the main Xcode project window, make sure that the menu located in the top left-hand corner of the window (marked C in Figure 4-18) has the *iPhone 8 Plus* simulator option selected:

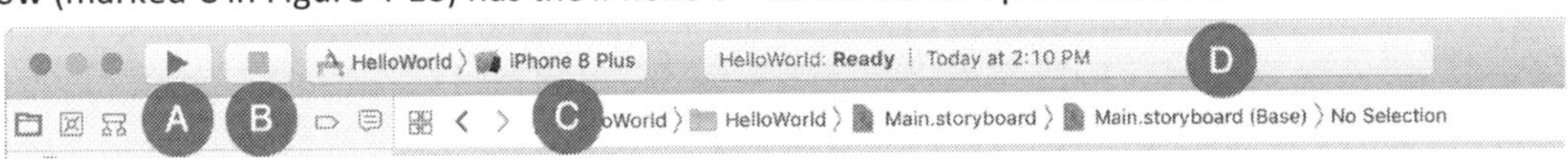

Figure 4-18

Click on the *Run* toolbar button (A) to compile the code and run the app in the simulator. The small panel in the center of the Xcode toolbar (D) will report the progress of the build process together with any problems or errors that cause the build process to fail. Once the app is built, the simulator will start and the HelloWorld app will run:

Figure 4-19

Note that the user interface appears as designed in the Interface Builder tool. Click on the stop button (B), change the target menu from iPhone 8 Plus to iPad Air 2 and run the application again. Once again, the label will appear centered in the screen even with the larger screen size. Finally, verify that the layout is correct in landscape orientation by using the *Hardware -> Rotate Left* menu option. This indicates that the Auto Layout constraints are working and that we have designed a *universal* user interface for the project.

4.6 Running the App on a Physical iOS Device

Although the Simulator environment provides a useful way to test an app on a variety of different iOS device models, it is important to also test on a physical iOS device.

If you have entered your Apple ID in the Xcode preferences screen as outlined in the previous chapter and selected a development team for the project, it is possible to run the app on a physical device simply by connecting it to the development Mac system with a USB cable and selecting it as the run target within Xcode.

With a device connected to the development system, and an application ready for testing, refer to the device menu located in the Xcode toolbar. There is a reasonable chance that this will have defaulted to one of the iOS Simulator configurations. Switch to the physical device by selecting this menu and changing it to the device name as shown in Figure 4-20:

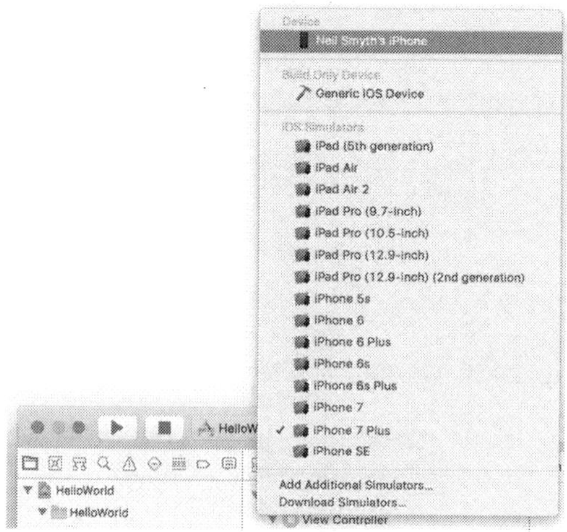

Figure 4-20

With the target device selected, make sure the device is unlocked and click on the run button at which point Xcode will install and launch the app on the device. As will be discussed later in this chapter, a physical device may also be configured for network testing, whereby apps are installed and tested on the device via a network connection without the need to have the device connected by a USB cable.

4.7 Managing Devices and Simulators

Currently connected iOS devices and the simulators configured for use with Xcode can be viewed and managed using the Xcode Devices window which is accessed via the *Window -> Devices and Simulators* menu option. Figure 4-21, for example, shows a typical Device screen on a system where an iPhone has been detected:

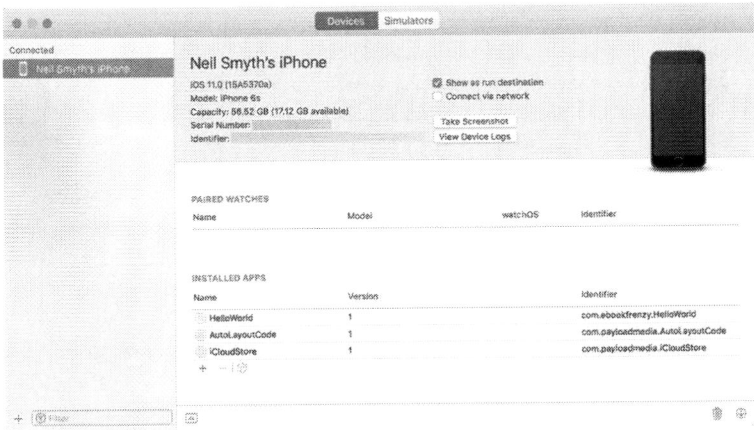

Figure 4-21

A wide range of simulator configurations are set up within Xcode by default and can be view by selecting the *Simulators* tab at the top of the dialog. Other simulator configurations can be added by clicking on the + button located in the bottom left-hand corner of the window. Once selected, a dialog will appear allowing the simulator to be configured in terms of device, iOS version and name.

The button displaying the gear icon in the bottom left corner allows simulators to be renamed or removed from the Xcode run target menu.

4.8 Enabling Network Testing

Earlier in this chapter, the example app was installed and run on a physical device connected to the development system via a USB cable. Xcode 10 also supports testing via a network connection. This option is enabled on a per device basis within the Devices and Simulators dialog introduced in the previous section. With the device connected via the USB cable, display this dialog, select the device from the list and enable the *Connect via network* option as highlighted in Figure 4-22:

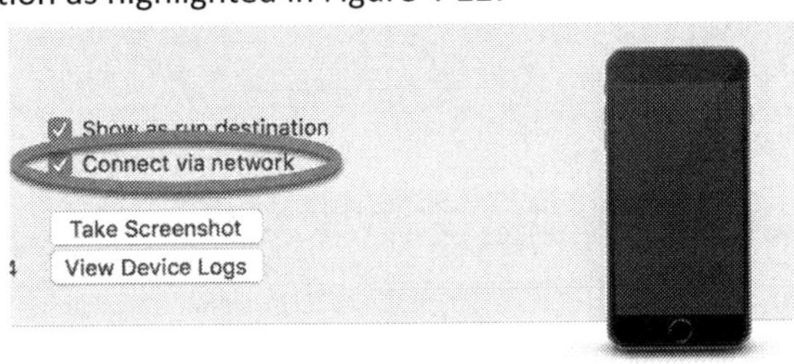

Figure 4-22

Once the setting has been enabled, the device may continue to be used as the run target for the app even when the USB cable is disconnected. The only requirement being that both the device and development computer be connected to the same Wi-Fi network. Assuming this requirement has been met, clicking on the run button with the device selected in the run menu will install and launch the app over the network connection.

4.9 Dealing with Build Errors

As we have not actually written or modified any code in this chapter it is unlikely that any errors will be detected during the build and run process. In the unlikely event that something did get inadvertently changed thereby causing the build to fail it is worth taking a few minutes to talk about build errors within the context of the Xcode environment.

If for any reason a build fails, the status window in the Xcode toolbar will report that an error has been detected by displaying "Build" together with the number of errors detected and any warnings. In addition, the left-hand panel of the Xcode window will update with a list of the errors. Selecting an error from this list will take you to the location in the code where corrective action needs to be taken.

4.10 Monitoring Application Performance

Another useful feature of Xcode is the ability to monitor the performance of an application while it is running. This information is accessed by displaying the *Debug Navigator*.

When Xcode is launched, the project navigator is displayed in the left-hand panel by default. Along the top of this panel is a bar with a range of other options. The sixth option from the left displays the debug navigator when selected as illustrated in Figure 4-23. When displayed, this panel shows a number of real-time statistics relating to the performance of the currently running application such as memory, CPU usage, disk access, energy efficiency, network activity and iCloud storage access.

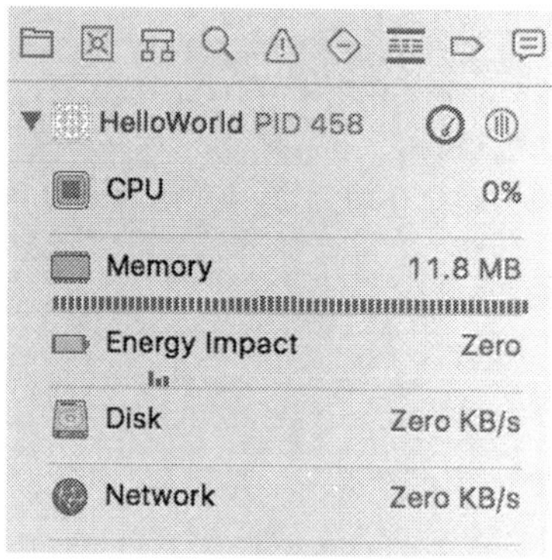

Figure 4-23

When one of these categories is selected, the main panel (Figure 4-24) updates to provide additional information about that particular aspect of the application's performance:

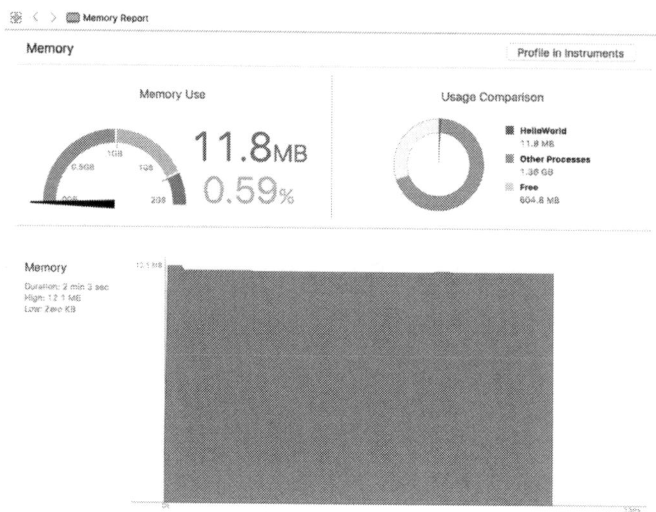

Figure 4-24

Yet more information can be obtained by clicking on the *Profile in Instruments* button in the top right-hand corner of the panel.

4.11 An Exploded View of the User Interface Layout Hierarchy

Xcode also provides an option to break the user interface layout out into a rotatable 3D view that shows how the view hierarchy for a user interface is constructed. This can be particularly useful for identifying situations where one view object is obscured by another appearing on top of it or a layout is not appearing as intended. To access the View Hierarchy in this mode, run the application and click on the *Debug View Hierarchy* button highlighted in Figure 4-25:

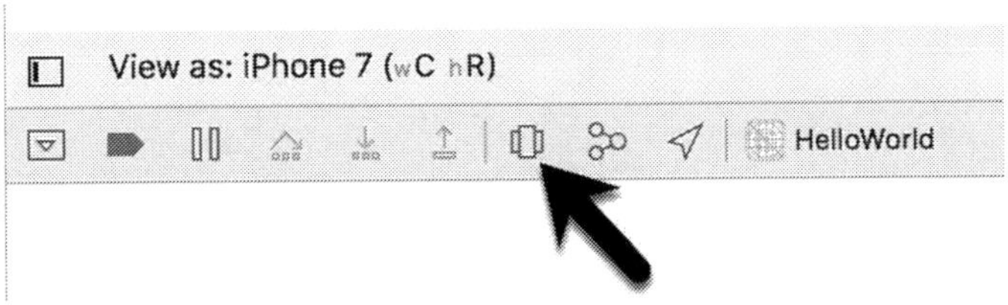

Figure 4-25

Once activated, a 3D "exploded" view of the layout will appear. Note that it may be necessary to click on the *Orient to 3D* button highlighted in Figure 4-26 to switch to 3D mode:

Figure 4-26

Figure 4-27 shows an example layout in this mode for a more complex user interface than that created in this chapter:

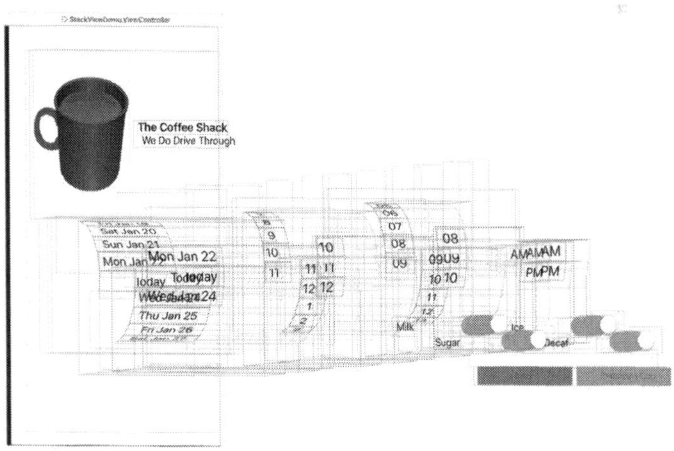

Figure 4-27

4.12 Summary

Applications are primarily created within the Xcode development environment. This chapter has served to provide a basic overview of the Xcode environment and to work through the creation of a very simple example application. Finally, a brief overview was provided of some of the performance monitoring features in Xcode 10. Many more features and capabilities of Xcode and Interface Builder will be covered in subsequent chapters of the book.

Chapter 5

5. An Introduction to Xcode 10 Playgrounds

Before introducing the Swift programming language in the chapters that follow, it is first worth learning about a feature of Xcode known as *Playgrounds*. Playgrounds are a feature of Xcode designed to make learning Swift and experimenting with the iOS SDK much easier. The concepts covered in this chapter can be put to use when experimenting with many of the introductory Swift code examples contained in the chapters that follow and will be of continued use in future when experimenting with many of the features of UIKit framework when designing dynamic user interfaces.

5.1 What is a Playground?

A playground is an interactive environment where Swift code can be entered and executed with the results appearing in real-time. This makes an ideal environment in which to learn the syntax of Swift and the visual aspects of iOS app development without the need to work continuously through the edit/compile/run/debug cycle that would ordinarily accompany a standard Xcode iOS project. With support for rich text comments, playgrounds are also a good way to document code as a teaching environment.

5.2 Creating a New Playground

To create a new Playground, start Xcode and select the *Get started with a playground* option from the welcome screen or select the *File -> New -> Playground...* menu option. Choose the iOS option on the resulting panel and select the Blank template.

The Blank template is useful for trying out Swift coding. The Single View template, on the other hand, provides a view controller environment for trying out code that requires a user interface layout. The game and map templates provide preconfigured playgrounds that allow you to experiment with the iOS MapKit and SpriteKit frameworks respectively.

On the next screen, name the playground *LearnSwift* and choose a suitable file system location into which the playground should be saved before clicking on the *Create* button.

Once the playground has been created, the following screen will appear ready for Swift code to be entered:

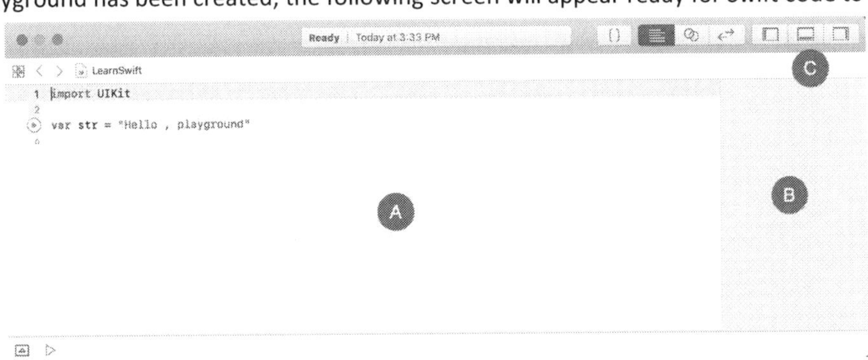

Figure 5-1

The panel on the left-hand side of the window (marked A in Figure 5-1) is the *playground editor* where the lines of Swift code are entered. The right-hand panel (marked B) is referred to as the *results panel* and is where the results of each Swift expression entered into the playground editor panel are displayed.

The cluster of three buttons at the right-hand side of the toolbar (marked C) are used to hide and display other panels within the playground window. The left most button displays the Navigator panel which provides access to the folders and files that make up the playground (marked A in Figure 5-2 below). The middle button, on the other hand, displays the Debug view (B) which displays code output and information about coding or runtime errors. The right most button displays the Utilities panel (C) where a variety of properties relating to the playground may be configured.

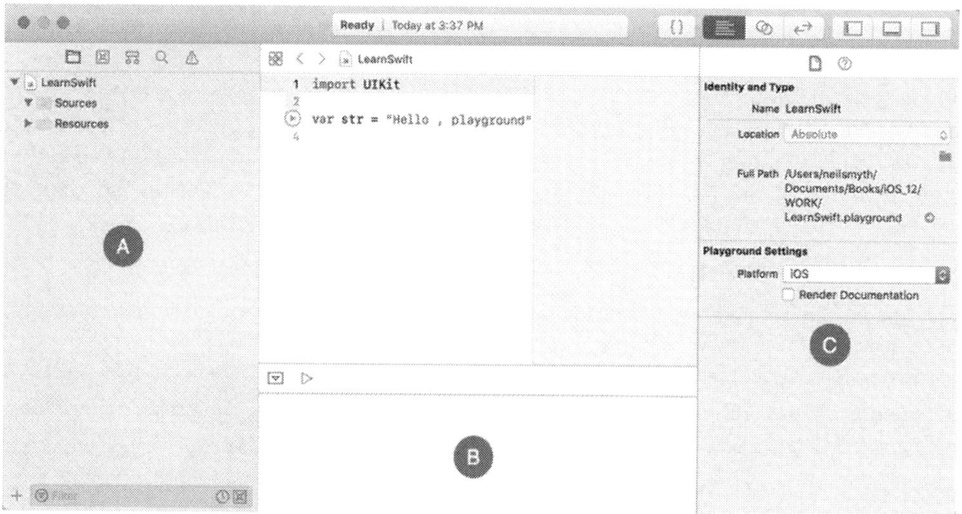

Figure 5-2

By far the quickest way to gain familiarity with the playground environment is to work through some simple examples.

5.3 A Basic Swift Playground Example

Perhaps the simplest of examples in any programming language (that at least does something tangible) is to write some code to output a single line of text. Swift is no exception to this rule so, within the playground window, begin adding another line of Swift code so that it reads as follows:

```
import UIKit

var str = "Hello , playground"

print("Welcome to Swift")
```

All that the additional line of code does is make a call to the built-in Swift *print* function which takes as a parameter a string of characters to be displayed on the console. Those familiar with other programming languages will note the absence of a semi-colon at the end of the line of code. In Swift, semi-colons are optional and generally only used as a separator when multiple statements occupy the same line of code.

Note that although some extra code has been entered, nothing yet appears in the results panel. This is because the code has yet to be executed. One option to run the code is to click on the Execute Playground button located in the bottom left-hand corner of the main panel as indicated by the arrow in Figure 5-3:

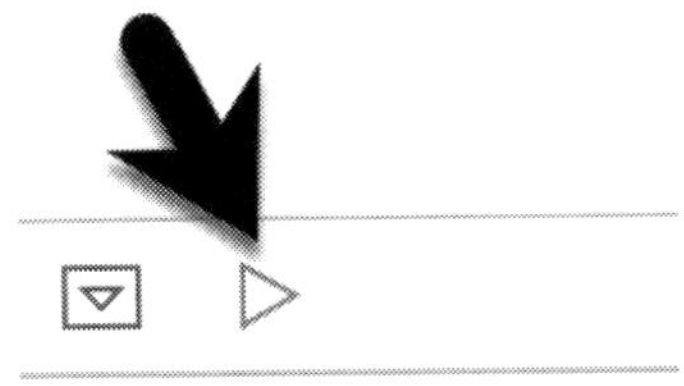

Figure 5-3

When clicked, this button will execute all of the code in the current playground page from the first line of code to the last. Another option is to execute the code in stages using the run button located in the margin of the code editor as shown in Figure 5-4:

Figure 5-4

This button executes the line numbers with the shaded blue background including the line on which the button is currently positioned. In the above figure, for example, the button will execute lines 1 through 3 and then stop.

The position of the run button can be moved by hovering the mouse pointer over the line numbers in the editor. In Figure 5-5, for example, the run button is now positioned on line 5 and will execute lines 4 and 5 when clicked. Note that lines 1 to 3 are no longer highlighted in blue indicating that these have already been executed and are not eligible to be run this time:

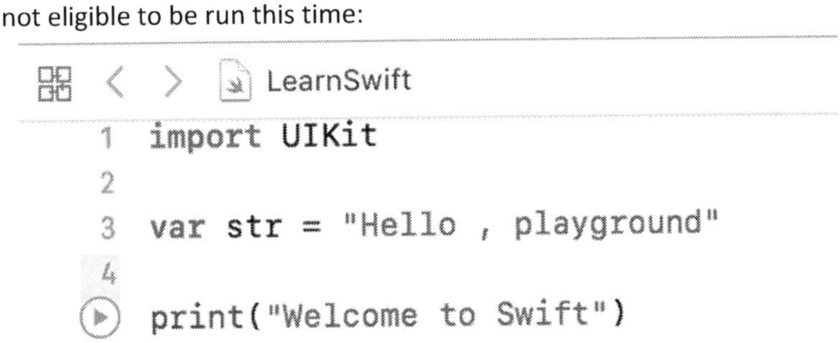

Figure 5-5

This technique provides an easy way to execute the code in stages making it easier to understand how the code functions and to identify problems in code execution.

To reset the playground so that execution can be performed from the start of the code, simply click on the stop button as indicated in Figure 5-6.:

Figure 5-6

Using this incremental execution technique, execute lines 1 through 3 and note that output now appears in the results panel indicating that the variable has been initialized:

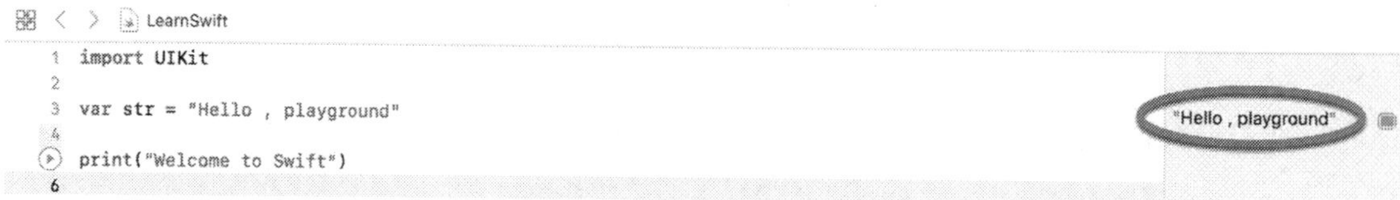

Figure 5-7

Next, execute the remaining lines up to and including line 5 at which point the "Welcome to Swift" output should appear both in the results panel and Debug panel:

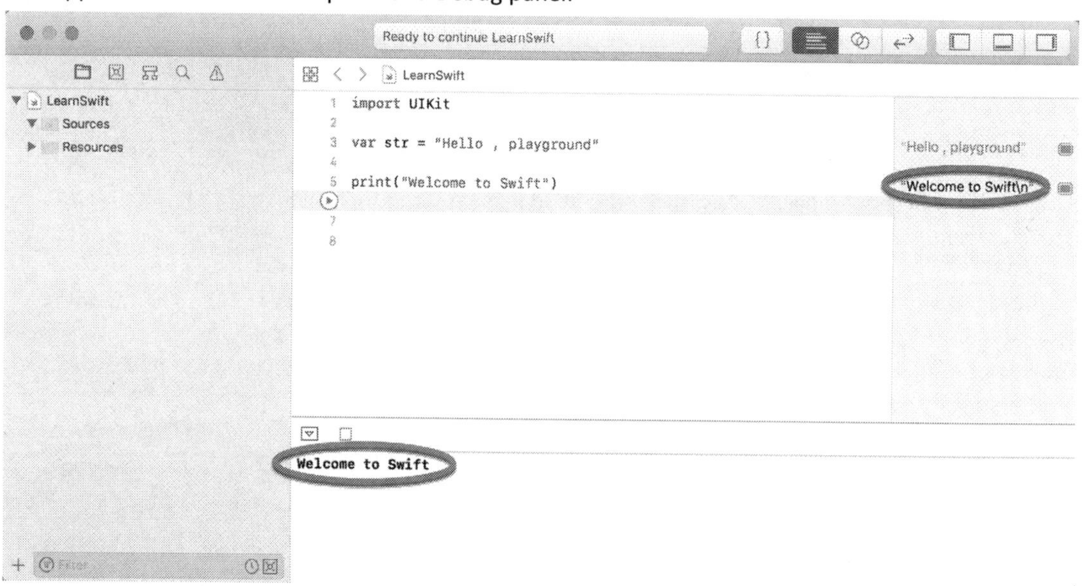

Figure 5-8

5.4 Viewing Results

Playgrounds are particularly useful when working and experimenting with Swift algorithms. This can be useful when combined with the Quick Look feature. Remaining within the playground editor, enter the following lines of code beneath the existing print statement:

```
var x = 10

for index in 1...20 {
    let y = index * x
    x -= 1
    print(y)
```

```
}
```

This expression repeats a loop 20 times, performing an arithmetic expression on each iteration of the loop. Once the code has been entered into the editor, click on the run button positioned at line 13 to execute these new lines of code. The playground will execute the loop and display in the results panel the number of times the loop was performed. More interesting information, however, may be obtained by hovering the mouse pointer over the results line so that two additional buttons appear as shown in Figure 5-9:

Figure 5-9

The left most of the two buttons is the *Quick Look* button which, when selected, will show a popup panel displaying the results as shown in Figure 5-10:

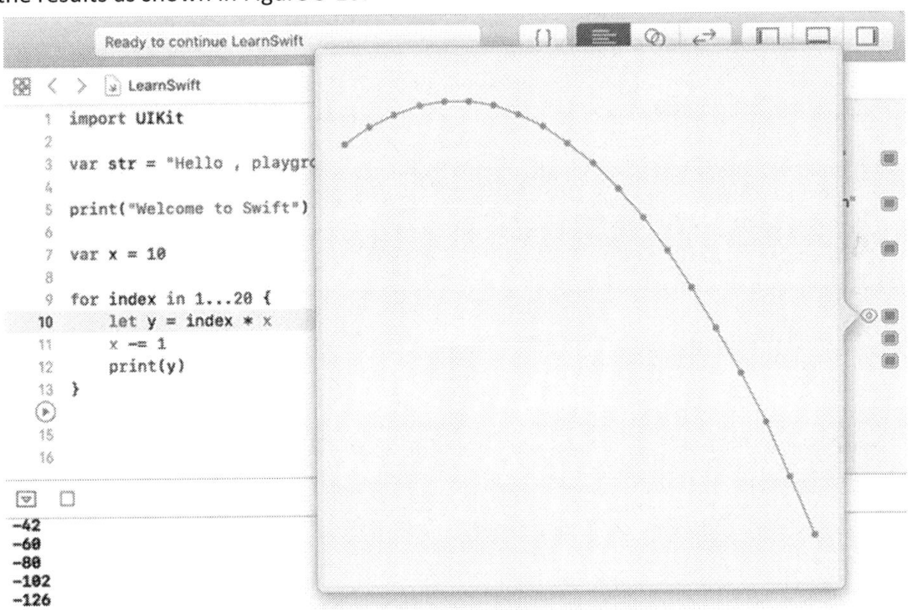

Figure 5-10

The right-most button is the *Show Result* button which, when selected, displays the results in-line with the code:

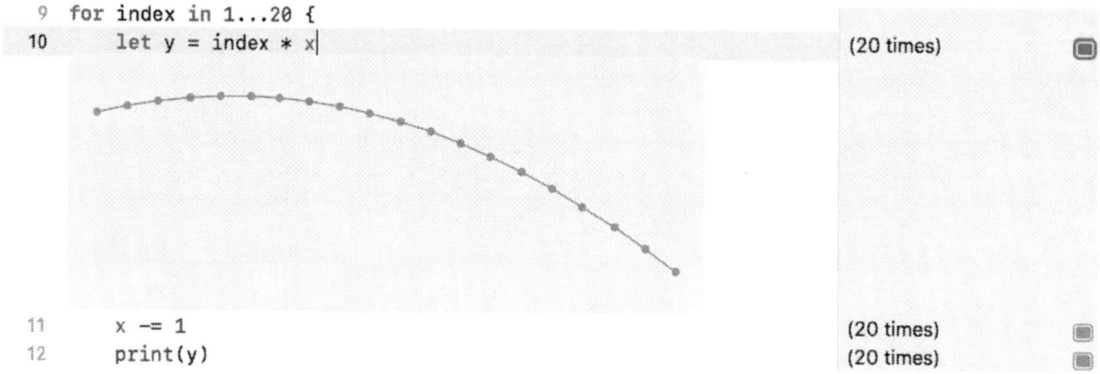
9 for index in 1...20 {
10 let y = index * x
(20 times)
11 x -= 1
12 print(y)
(20 times)
(20 times)

Figure 5-11

5.5 Adding Rich Text Comments

Rich text comments allow the code within a playground to be documented in a way that is easy to format and read. A single line of text can be marked as being rich text by preceding it with a //: marker. For example:

```
//: This is a single line of documentation text
```

Blocks of text can be added by wrapping the text in /*: and */ comment markers:

```
/*:
This is a block of documentation text that is intended
to span multiple lines
*/
```

The rich text uses the Markdown markup language and allows text to be formatted using a lightweight and easy to use syntax. A heading, for example, can be declared by prefixing the line with a '#' character while text is displayed in italics when wrapped in '*' characters. Bold text, on the other hand, involves wrapping the text in '**' character sequences. It is also possible to configure bullet points by prefixing each line with a single '*'. Among the many other features of Markdown are the ability to embed images and hyperlinks into the content of a rich text comment.

To see rich text comments in action, enter the following markdown content into the playground editor immediately after the *print("Welcome to Swift")* line of code:

```
/*:
# Welcome to Playgrounds
This is your *first* playground which is intended to demonstrate:
* The use of **Quick Look**
* Placing results **in-line** with the code
*/
```

As the comment content is added it is said to be displayed in *raw markup* format. To display in *rendered markup* format, either select the *Editor -> Show Rendered Markup* menu option, or enable the *Render Documentation* option located under *Playground Settings* in the Utilities panel (marked C in Figure 5-2). Once rendered, the above rich text should appear as illustrated in Figure 5-12:

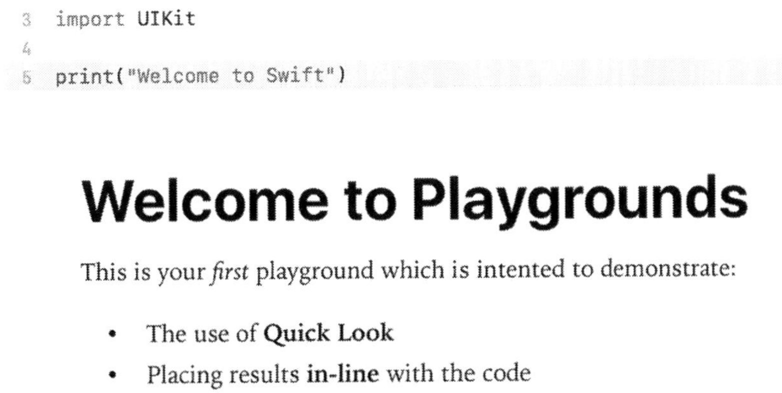
import UIKit
print("Welcome to Swift")
Welcome to Playgrounds
This is your first playground which is intented to demonstrate:
The use of Quick Look
Placing results in-line with the code

Figure 5-12

Detailed information about the Markdown syntax can be found online at the following URL:

https://developer.apple.com/library/content/documentation/Xcode/Reference/xcode_markup_formatting_ref/index.html

5.6 Working with Playground Pages

A playground can consist of multiple pages, with each page containing its own code, resources and rich text comments. So far, the playground used in this chapter contains a single page. Add an additional page to the playground now by selecting the LearnSwift entry at the top of the Navigator panel, right-clicking and selecting the *New Playground Page* menu option. Once added, click on the left most of the three view buttons (marked C in Figure 5-1) to display the Navigator panel. Note that two pages are now listed in the Navigator named "Untitled Page" and "Untitled Page 2". Select and then click a second time on the "Untitled Page 2" entry so that the name becomes editable and change the name to *UIKit Examples* as outlined in Figure 5-13:

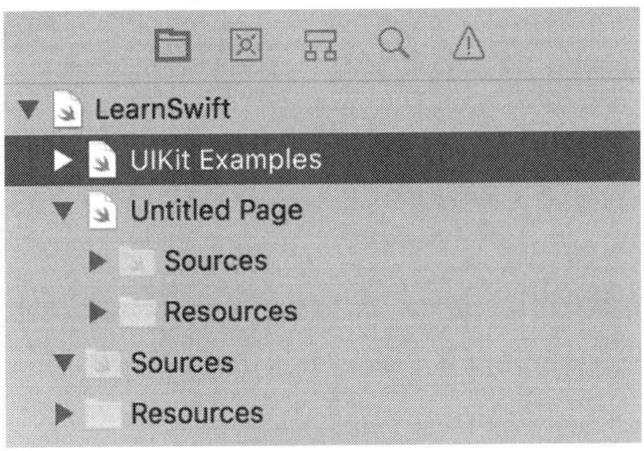
LearnSwift
UIKit Examples
Untitled Page
Sources
Resources
Sources
Resources

Figure 5-13

Note that the newly added page has Markdown links which, when clicked, navigate to the previous or next page in the playground.

5.7 Working with UIKit in Playgrounds

The playground environment is not restricted to simple Swift code statements. Much of the power of the iOS SDK is also available for experimentation within a playground.

When working with UIKit within a playground page it is necessary to import the iOS UIKit Framework. The UIKit Framework contains most of the classes necessary to implement user interfaces for iOS applications and is an area which will be covered in significant detail throughout the book. An extremely powerful feature of playgrounds is that it is also possible to work with UIKit along with many of the other frameworks that comprise the iOS SDK.

The following code, for example, imports the UIKit framework, creates a UILabel instance and sets color, text and font properties on it:

```
import UIKit

let myLabel = UILabel(frame: CGRect(x: 0, y: 0, width: 200, height: 50))

myLabel.backgroundColor = UIColor.red
myLabel.text = "Hello Swift"
myLabel.textAlignment = .center
myLabel.font = UIFont(name: "Georgia", size: 24)
myLabel
```

Enter this code into the playground editor on the UIKit Examples page (the existing code can be removed) and run the code. This code provides a good example of how the Quick Look feature can be useful. Each line of the example Swift code configures a different aspect of the appearance of the UILabel instance. Clicking on the Quick Look button for the first line of code will display an empty view (since the label exists but has yet to be given any visual attributes). Clicking on the Quick Look button in the line of code which sets the background color, on the other hand, will show the red label:

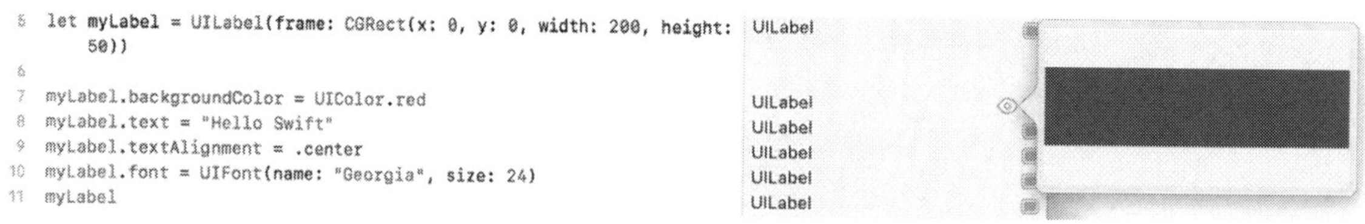

let myLabel = UILabel(frame: CGRect(x: 0, y: 0, width: 200, height: 50))
myLabel.backgroundColor = UIColor.red
myLabel.text = "Hello Swift"
myLabel.textAlignment = .center
myLabel.font = UIFont(name: "Georgia", size: 24)
myLabel
UILabel

Figure 5-14

Similarly, the quick look view for the line where the text property is set will show the red label with the "Hello Swift" text left aligned:

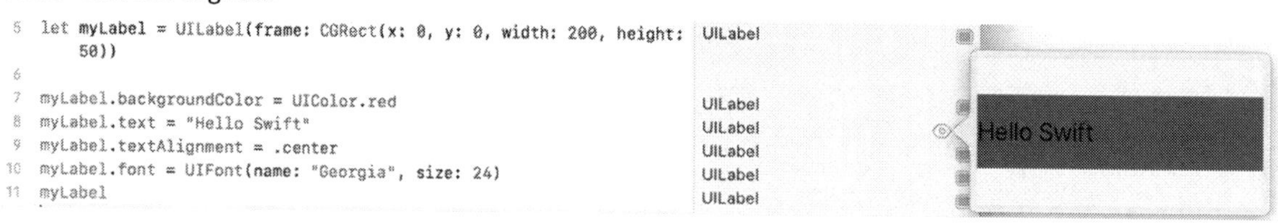

let myLabel = UILabel(frame: CGRect(x: 0, y: 0, width: 200, height: 50))
myLabel.backgroundColor = UIColor.red
myLabel.text = "Hello Swift"
myLabel.textAlignment = .center
myLabel.font = UIFont(name: "Georgia", size: 24)
myLabel
UILabel
Hello Swift

Figure 5-15

The font setting quick look view on the other hand displays the UILabel with centered text and the larger Georgia font:

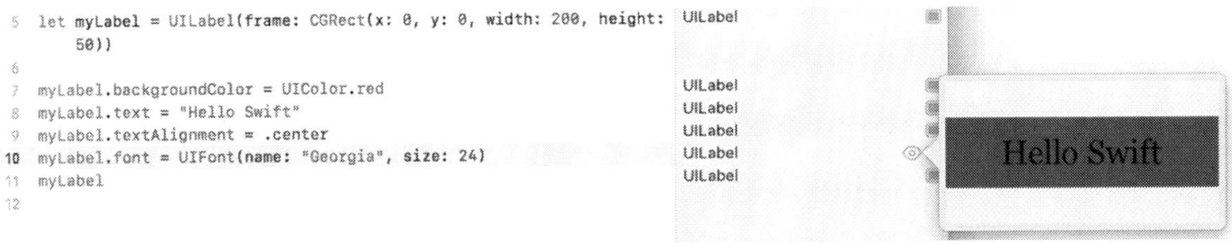

Figure 5-16

5.8 Adding Resources to a Playground

Another useful feature of playgrounds is the ability to bundle and access resources such as image files in a playground. Within the Navigator panel, click on the right facing arrow (known as a *disclosure arrow*) to the left of the UIKit Examples page entry to unfold the page contents (Figure 5-17) and note the presence of a folder named *Resources*:

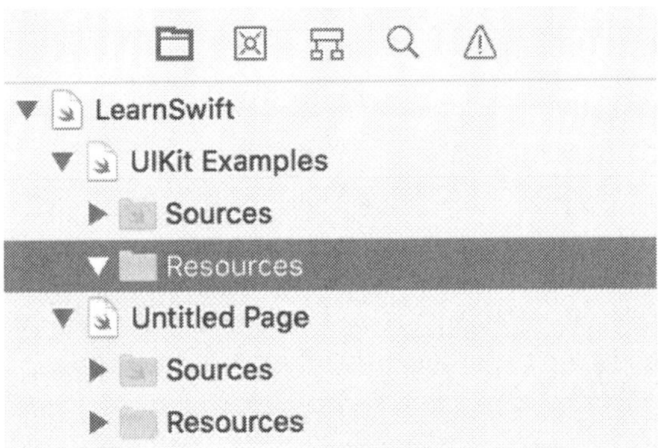

Figure 5-17

If you have not already done so, download and unpack the code samples archive from the following URL:

https://www.ebookfrenzy.com/retail/ios12/

Open a Finder window, navigate to the *playground_images* folder within the code samples folder and drag and drop the image file named *waterfall.png* onto the *Resources* folder beneath the UIKit Examples page in the Playground Navigator panel:

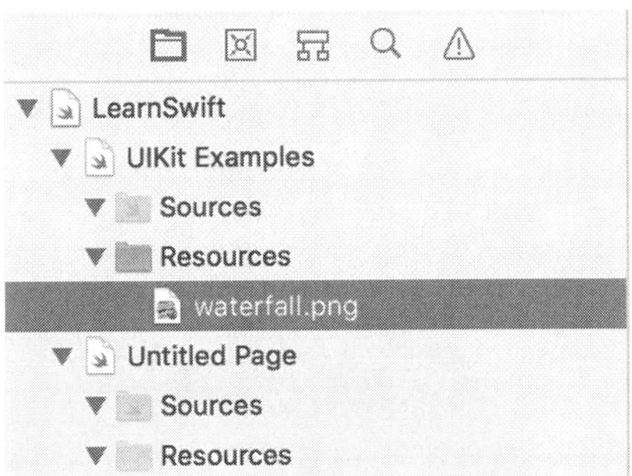

Figure 5-18

With the image added to the resources, add code to the page to create an image object and display the waterfall image on it:

```
let image = UIImage(named: "waterfall")
```

With the code added, run the new statement and use either the Quick Look or inline option to view the results of the code:

Figure 5-19

5.9 Working with Enhanced Live Views

So far in this chapter, all of the UIKit examples have involved presenting static user interface elements using the Quick Look and in-line features. It is, however, also possible to test dynamic user interface behavior within a playground using the Xcode Enhanced Live Views feature. To demonstrate live views in action, create a new page within the playground named *Live View Example*. Within the newly added page, remove the existing lines of Swift code before adding import statements for the UIKit framework and an additional playground module named PlaygroundSupport:

```
import UIKit
import PlaygroundSupport
```

The PlaygroundSupport module provides a number of useful features for playgrounds including the ability to present a live view within the playground timeline.

Beneath the import statements, add the following code:

```
import UIKit
import PlaygroundSupport

let container = UIView(frame: CGRect(x: 0,y: 0,width: 200,height: 200))
container.backgroundColor = UIColor.white
let square = UIView(frame: CGRect(x: 50,y: 50,width: 100,height: 100))
square.backgroundColor = UIColor.red

container.addSubview(square)

UIView.animate(withDuration: 5.0, animations: {
    square.backgroundColor = UIColor.blue
    let rotation = CGAffineTransform(rotationAngle: 3.14)
    square.transform = rotation
})
```

The code creates a UIView object to act as a container view and assigns it a white background color. A smaller view is then drawn positioned in the center of the container view and colored red. The second view is then added as a child of the container view. An animation is then used to change the color of the smaller view to blue and to rotate it through 360 degrees. If you are new to iOS programming rest assured that these areas will be covered in detail in later chapters. At this point the code is simply provided to highlight the capabilities of live views.

Once the code has been executed, clicking on any of the Quick Look buttons will show a snapshot of the views at each stage in the code sequence. None of the quick look views, however, show the dynamic animation. To see how the animation code works it will be necessary to use the live view playground feature.

The PlaygroundSupport module includes a class named PlaygroundPage that allows playground code to interact with the pages that make up a playground. This is achieved through a range of methods and properties of the class, one of which is the *current* property. This property, in turn, provides access to the current playground page. In order to execute the live view within the playground timeline, the *liveView* property of the current page needs to be set to our new container. To display the timeline, click on the toolbar button containing the interlocking circles as highlighted in Figure 5-20:

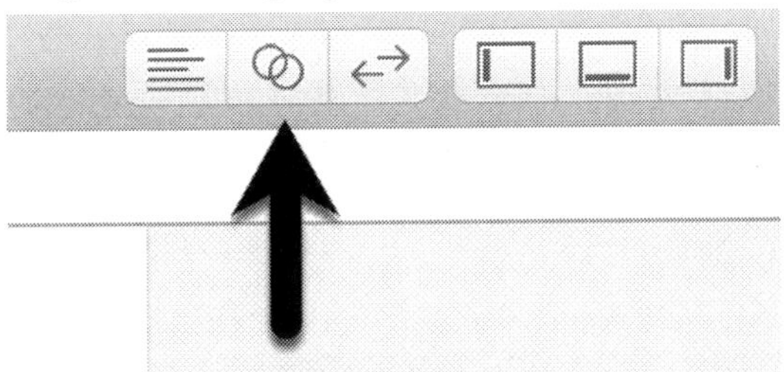

Figure 5-20

When clicked, this button displays the Assistant Editor panel containing the timeline. Once the timeline is visible, add the code to assign the container to the live view of the current page as follows:

```
import UIKit
import PlaygroundSupport

let container = UIView(frame: CGRect(x: 0,y: 0,width: 200,height: 200))

PlaygroundPage.current.liveView = container

container.backgroundColor = UIColor.white
let square = UIView(frame: CGRect(x: 50,y: 50,width: 100,height: 100))
square.backgroundColor = UIColor.red

container.addSubview(square)

UIView.animate(withDuration: 5.0, animations: {
    square.backgroundColor = UIColor.blue
    let rotation = CGAffineTransform(rotationAngle: 3.14)
    square.transform = rotation
})
```

Once the call has been added, re-execute the code at which point the views should appear in the timeline (Figure 5-21). During the 5 second animation duration, the red square should rotate through 360 degrees while gradually changing color to blue:

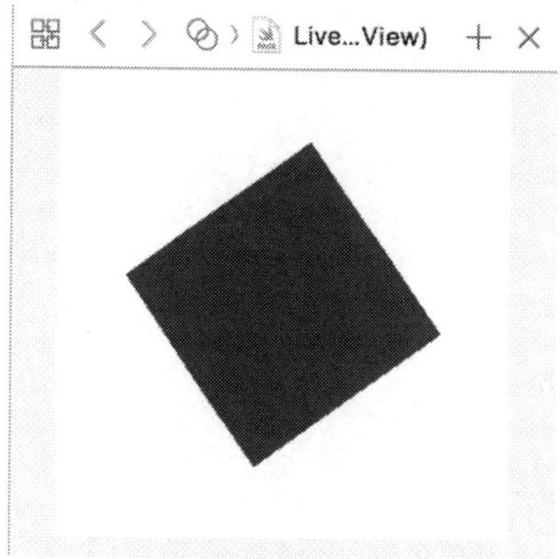

Figure 5-21

To repeat the execution of the code in the playground page, click on the stop button highlighted in Figure 5-6 to reset the playground and change the stop button into the run button (Figure 5-3). Click the run button to repeat the execution.

5.10 When to Use Playgrounds

Clearly Swift Playgrounds provide an ideal environment for learning to program using the Swift programming language and the use of playgrounds in the Swift introductory chapters that follow is recommended.

It is also important to keep in mind that playgrounds will remain useful long after the basics of Swift have been learned and will become increasingly useful when moving on to more advanced areas of iOS development.

The iOS SDK is a vast collection of frameworks and classes and it is not unusual for even experienced developers to need to experiment with unfamiliar aspects of iOS development before adding code to a project. Historically this has involved creating a temporary iOS Xcode project and then repeatedly looping through the somewhat cumbersome edit, compile, run cycle to arrive at a programming solution. Rather than fall into this habit, consider having a playground on standby to carry out experiments during your project development work.

5.11 Summary

This chapter has introduced the concept of playgrounds. Playgrounds provide an environment in which Swift code can be entered and the results of that code viewed dynamically. This provides an excellent environment both for learning the Swift programming language and for experimenting with many of the classes and APIs included in the iOS SDK without the need to create Xcode projects and repeatedly edit, compile and run code.

Chapter 6

6. Swift Data Types, Constants and Variables

Prior to the introduction of iOS 8, the stipulated programming language for the development of iOS applications was Objective-C. When Apple announced iOS 8, however, the company also introduced an alternative to Objective-C in the form of the Swift programming language.

Due entirely to the popularity of iOS, Objective-C had become one of the more widely used programming languages. With origins firmly rooted in the 40-year-old C Programming Language, however, and in spite of recent efforts to modernize some aspects of the language syntax, Objective-C was beginning to show its age.

Swift, on the other hand, is an entirely new programming language designed specifically to make programming easier, faster and less prone to programmer error. Starting with a clean slate and no burden of legacy, Swift is a new and innovative language with which to develop applications for iOS, macOS, watchOS and tvOS with the advantage that much of the syntax will be familiar to those with experience of other programming languages.

The introduction of Swift aside, it is still perfectly acceptable to continue to develop applications using Objective-C. Indeed, it is also possible to mix both Swift and Objective-C within the same application code base. That being said, Apple clearly sees the future of development in terms of Swift rather than Objective-C. In recognition of this fact, all of the examples in this book are implemented using Swift. Before moving on to those examples, however, the next several chapters will provide an overview and introduction to Swift programming. The intention of these chapters is to provide enough information so that you can begin to confidently program using Swift. For an exhaustive and in-depth guide to all the features, intricacies and capabilities of Swift, some time spent reading Apple's excellent book entitled "The Swift Programming Language" (available free of charge from within the Apple iBookStore) is strongly recommended.

6.1 Using a Swift Playground

Both this and the following few chapters are intended to introduce the basics of the Swift programming language. As outlined in the previous chapter, entitled *An Introduction to Swift Playgrounds* the best way to learn Swift is to experiment within a Swift playground environment. Before starting this chapter, therefore, create a new playground and use it to try out the code in both this and the other Swift introduction chapters that follow.

6.2 Swift Data Types

When we look at the different types of software that run on computer systems and mobile devices, from financial applications to graphics intensive games, it is easy to forget that computers are really just binary machines. Binary systems work in terms of 0 and 1, true or false, set and unset. All the data sitting in RAM, stored on disk drives and flowing through circuit boards and buses are nothing more than sequences of 1s and 0s. Each 1 or 0 is referred to as a *bit* and bits are grouped together in blocks of 8, each group being referred to as a *byte*. When people talk about 32-bit and 64-bit computer systems they are talking about the number of bits that can be handled simultaneously by the CPU bus. A 64-bit CPU, for example, is able to handle data in 64-bit blocks, resulting in faster performance than a 32-bit based system.

Humans, of course, don't think in binary. We work with decimal numbers, letters and words. In order for a human to easily (easily being a relative term in this context) program a computer, some middle ground between human and computer thinking is needed. This is where programming languages such as Swift come into play. Programming languages allow humans to express instructions to a computer in terms and structures we understand, and then compile that down to a format that can be executed by a CPU.

One of the fundamentals of any program involves data, and programming languages such as Swift define a set of *data types* that allow us to work with data in a format we understand when programming. For example, if we want to store a number in a Swift program we could do so with syntax similar to the following:

```
var mynumber = 10
```

In the above example, we have created a variable named *mynumber* and then assigned to it the value of 10. When we compile the source code down to the machine code used by the CPU, the number 10 is seen by the computer in binary as:

```
1010
```

Now that we have a basic understanding of the concept of data types and why they are necessary we can take a closer look at some of the more commonly used data types supported by Swift.

6.2.1 Integer Data Types

Swift integer data types are used to store whole numbers (in other words a number with no decimal places). Integers can be *signed* (capable of storing positive, negative and zero values) or *unsigned* (positive and zero values only).

Swift provides support for 8, 16, 32 and 64-bit integers (represented by the Int8, Int16, Int32 and Int64 types respectively). The same variants are also available for unsigned integers (UInt8, UInt16, UInt32 and UInt64).

In general, Apple recommends using the *Int* data type rather than one of the above specifically sized data types. The Int data type will use the appropriate integer size for the platform on which the code is running.

All integer data types contain bounds properties which can be accessed to identify the minimum and maximum supported values of that particular type. The following code, for example, outputs the minimum and maximum bounds for the 32-bit signed integer data type:

```
print("Int32 Min = \(Int32.min) Int32 Max = \(Int32.max)")
```

When executed, the above code will generate the following output:

```
Int32 Min = -2147483648 Int32 Max = 2147483647
```

6.2.2 Floating Point Data Types

The Swift floating point data types are able to store values containing decimal places. For example, 4353.1223 would be stored in a floating point data type. Swift provides two floating point data types in the form of *Float* and *Double*. Which type to use depends on the size of value to be stored and the level of precision required. The Double type can be used to store up to 64-bit floating point numbers with a level of precision of 15 decimal places or greater. The Float data type, on the other hand, is limited to 32-bit floating point numbers and offers a level of precision as low as 6 decimal places depending on the native platform on which the code is running.

6.2.3 Bool Data Type

Swift, like other languages, includes a data type for the purpose of handling true or false (1 or 0) conditions. Two Boolean constant values (*true* and *false*) are provided by Swift specifically for working with Boolean data types.

6.2.4 Character Data Type

The Swift Character data type is used to store a single character of rendered text such as a letter, numerical digit, punctuation mark or symbol. Internally characters in Swift are stored in the form of *grapheme clusters*. A grapheme cluster is made of two or more Unicode scalars that are combined to represent a single visible character.

The following lines assign a variety of different characters to Character type variables:

```
var myChar1 = "f"
var myChar2 = ":"
var myChar3 = "X"
```

Characters may also be referenced using Unicode code points. The following example assigns the 'X' character to a variable using Unicode:

```
var myChar4 = "\u{0058}"
```

6.2.5 String Data Type

The String data type is a sequence of characters that typically make up a word or sentence. In addition to providing a storage mechanism, the String data type also includes a range of string manipulation features allowing strings to be searched, matched, concatenated and modified. Strings in Swift are represented internally as collections of characters (where a character is, as previously discussed, comprised of one or more Unicode scalar values).

Strings can also be constructed using combinations of strings, variables, constants, expressions, and function calls using a concept referred to as *string interpolation*. For example, the following code creates a new string from a variety of different sources using string interpolation before outputting it to the console:

```
var userName = "John"
var inboxCount = 25
let maxCount = 100

var message = "\(userName) has \(inboxCount) messages. Message capacity
remaining is \(maxCount - inboxCount)"

print(message)
```

When executed, the code will output the following message:

```
John has 25 messages. Message capacity remaining is 75 messages.
```

A multiline string literal may be declared by encapsulating the string within triple quotes as follows:

```
var multiline = """

    The console glowed with flashing warnings.
    Clearly time was running out.
```

```
    "I thought you said you knew how to fly this!" yelled Mary.

    "It was much easier on the simulator" replied her brother,
     trying to keep the panic out of his voice.

"""

print(multiline)
```

The above code will generate the following output when run:

```
    The console glowed with flashing warnings.
    Clearly time was running out.

    "I thought you said you knew how to fly this!" yelled Mary.

    "It was much easier on the simulator" replied her brother,
    trying to keep the panic out of his voice.
```

The amount by which each line is indented within a multiline literal is calculated as the number of characters by which the line is indented minus the number of characters by which the closing triple quote line is indented. If, for example, the fourth line in the above example had a 10 character indentation and the closing triple quote was indented by 5 characters, the actual indentation of the fourth line within the string would be 5 characters. This allows multiline literals to be formatted tidily within Swift code while still allowing control over indentation of individual lines.

6.2.6 Special Characters/Escape Sequences

In addition to the standard set of characters outlined above, there is also a range of *special characters* (also referred to as *escape sequences*) available for specifying items such as a new line, tab or a specific Unicode value within a string. These special characters are identified by prefixing the character with a backslash (a concept referred to as *escaping*). For example, the following assigns a new line to the variable named newline:

```
var newline = "\n"
```

In essence, any character that is preceded by a backslash is considered to be a special character and is treated accordingly. This raises the question as to what to do if you actually want a backslash character. This is achieved by *escaping* the backslash itself:

```
var backslash = "\\"
```

Commonly used special characters supported by Swift are as follows:

- **\n** - New line
- **\r** - Carriage return
- **\t** - Horizontal tab
- **** - Backslash
- **\"** - Double quote (used when placing a double quote into a string declaration)
- **\'** - Single quote (used when placing a single quote into a string declaration)

- **\u{*nn*}** – Single byte Unicode scalar where *nn* is replaced by two hexadecimal digits representing the Unicode character.
- **\u{*nnnn*}** – Double byte Unicode scalar where *nnnn* is replaced by four hexadecimal digits representing the Unicode character.
- **\U{*nnnnnnnn*}** – Four byte Unicode scalar where *nnnnnnnn* is replaced by eight hexadecimal digits representing the Unicode character.

6.3 Swift Variables

Variables are essentially locations in computer memory reserved for storing the data used by an application. Each variable is given a name by the programmer and assigned a value. The name assigned to the variable may then be used in the Swift code to access the value assigned to that variable. This access can involve either reading the value of the variable, or changing the value. It is, of course, the ability to change the value of variables which gives them the name *variable*.

6.4 Swift Constants

A constant is similar to a variable in that it provides a named location in memory to store a data value. Constants differ in one significant way in that once a value has been assigned to a constant it cannot subsequently be changed.

Constants are particularly useful if there is a value which is used repeatedly throughout the application code. Rather than use the value each time, it makes the code easier to read if the value is first assigned to a constant which is then referenced in the code. For example, it might not be clear to someone reading your Swift code why you used the value 5 in an expression. If, instead of the value 5, you use a constant named interestRate the purpose of the value becomes much clearer. Constants also have the advantage that if the programmer needs to change a widely used value, it only needs to be changed once in the constant declaration and not each time it is referenced.

As with variables, constants have a type, a name and a value. Unlike variables, however, once a value has been assigned to a constant, that value cannot subsequently be changed.

6.5 Declaring Constants and Variables

Variables are declared using the *var* keyword and may be initialized with a value at creation time. If the variable is declared without an initial value it must be declared as being *optional* (a topic which will be covered later in this chapter). The following, for example, is a typical variable declaration:

```
var userCount = 10
```

Constants are declared using the *let* keyword.

```
let maxUserCount = 20
```

For greater code efficiency and execution performance, Apple recommends the use of constants rather than variables whenever possible.

6.6 Type Annotations and Type Inference

Swift is categorized as a *type safe* programming language. This essentially means that once the data type of a variable has been identified, that variable cannot subsequently be used to store data of any other type without inducing a compilation error. This contrasts to *loosely typed* programming languages where a variable, once declared, can subsequently be used to store other data types.

There are two ways in which the type of a constant or variable will be identified. One approach is to use a *type annotation* at the point the variable or constant is declared in the code. This is achieved by placing a colon after the constant or variable name followed by the type declaration. The following line of code, for example, declares a variable named userCount as being of type Int:

```
var userCount: Int = 10
```

In the absence of a type annotation in a declaration, the Swift compiler uses a technique referred to as *type inference* to identify the type of the constant or variable. When relying on type inference, the compiler looks to see what type of value is being assigned to the constant or variable at the point that it is initialized and uses that as the type. Consider, for example, the following variable and constant declarations:

```
var signalStrength = 2.231
let companyName = "My Company"
```

During compilation of the above lines of code, Swift will infer that the signalStrength variable is of type Double (type inference in Swift defaults to Double for all floating point numbers) and that the companyName constant is of type String.

When a constant is declared without a type annotation it must be assigned a value at the point of declaration:

```
let bookTitle = "iOS 12 App Development Essentials"
```

If a type annotation is used when the constant is declared, however, the value can be assigned later in the code. For example:

```
let bookTitle: String
.
.
if iosBookType {
        bookTitle = "iOS 12 App Development Essentials"
} else {
        bookTitle = "Android Studio Development Essentials"
}
```

It is important to note that a value may only be assigned to a constant once. A second attempt to assign a value to a constant will result in a syntax error.

6.7 The Swift Tuple

Before proceeding, now is a good time to introduce the Swift tuple. The tuple is perhaps one of the simplest, yet most powerful features of the Swift programming language. A tuple is, quite simply, a way to temporarily group together multiple values into a single entity. The items stored in a tuple can be of any type and there are no restrictions requiring that those values all be of the same type. A tuple could, for example, be constructed to contain an Int value, a Float value and a String as follows:

```
let myTuple = (10, 432.433, "This is a String")
```

The elements of a tuple can be accessed using a number of different techniques. A specific tuple value can be accessed simply by referencing the index position (with the first value being at index position 0). The code below, for example, extracts the string resource (at index position 2 in the tuple) and assigns it to a new string variable:

```
let myTuple = (10, 432.433, "This is a String")
let myString = myTuple.2
print(myString)
```

Alternatively, all of the values in a tuple may be extracted and assigned to variables or constants in a single statement:

```
let (myInt, myFloat, myString) = myTuple
```

This same technique can be used to extract selected values from a tuple while ignoring others by replacing the values to be ignored with an underscore character. The following code fragment extracts the integer and string values from the tuple and assigns them to variables, but ignores the floating point value:

```
var (myInt, _, myString) = myTuple
```

When creating a tuple it is also possible to assign a name to each value:

```
let myTuple = (count: 10, length: 432.433, message: "This is a String")
```

The names assigned to the values stored in a tuple may then be used to reference those values in code. For example to output the *message* string value from the myTuple instance, the following line of code could be used:

```
print(myTuple.message)
```

Perhaps the most powerful use of tuples is, as will be seen in later chapters, the ability to return multiple values from a function.

6.8 The Swift Optional Type

The Swift optional data type is a new concept that does not exist in most other programming languages. The purpose of the optional type is to provide a safe and consistent approach to handling situations where a variable or constant may not have any value assigned to it.

Variables are declared as being optional by placing a ? character after the type declaration. The following code declares an optional Int variable named index:

```
var index: Int?
```

The variable *index* can now either have an integer value assigned to it, or have nothing assigned to it. Behind the scenes, and as far as the compiler and runtime are concerned, an optional with no value assigned to it actually has a value of nil.

An optional can easily be tested (typically using an if statement) to identify whether or not it has a value assigned to it as follows:

```
var index: Int?

if index != nil {
    // index variable has a value assigned to it
} else {
    // index variable has no value assigned to it
}
```

If an optional has a value assigned to it, that value is said to be "wrapped" within the optional. The value wrapped in an optional may be accessed using a concept referred to as *forced unwrapping*. This simply means that the underlying value is extracted from the optional data type, a procedure that is performed by placing an exclamation mark (!) after the optional name.

To explore this concept of unwrapping optional types in more detail, consider the following code:

```
var index: Int?

index = 3

var treeArray = ["Oak", "Pine", "Yew", "Birch"]

if index != nil {
    print(treeArray[index!])
} else {
    print("index does not contain a value")
}
```

The code simply uses an optional variable to hold the index into an array of strings representing the names of tree types (Swift arrays will be covered in more detail in the chapter entitled *Working with Array and Dictionary Collections in Swift*). If the index optional variable has a value assigned to it, the tree name at that location in the array is printed to the console. Since the index is an optional type, the value has been unwrapped by placing an exclamation mark after the variable name:

```
print(treeArray[index!])
```

Had the index not been unwrapped (in other words the exclamation mark omitted from the above line), the compiler would have issued an error similar to the following:

```
Value of optional type Int? not unwrapped
```

As an alternative to forced unwrapping, the value assigned to an optional may be allocated to a temporary variable or constant using *optional binding*, the syntax for which is as follows:

```
if let constantname = optionalName {

}

if var variablename = optionalName {

}
```

The above constructs perform two tasks. In the first instance, the statement ascertains whether or not the designated optional contains a value. Second, in the event that the optional has a value, that value is assigned to the declared constant or variable and the code within the body of the statement is executed. The previous forced unwrapping example could, therefore, be modified as follows to use optional binding instead:

```
var index: Int?

index = 3

var treeArray = ["Oak", "Pine", "Yew", "Birch"]

if let myvalue = index {
    print(treeArray[myvalue])
```

```
} else {
    print("index does not contain a value")
}
```

In this case the value assigned to the index variable is unwrapped and assigned to a temporary constant named *myvalue* which is then used as the index reference into the array. Note that the myvalue constant is described as temporary since it is only available within the scope of the if statement. Once the if statement completes execution, the constant will no longer exist. For this reason, there is no conflict in using the same temporary name as that assigned to the optional. The following is, for example, valid code:

```
.
.
if let index = index {
    print(treeArray[index])
} else {
.
.
```

Optional binding may also be used to unwrap multiple optionals and include a Boolean test condition, the syntax for which is as follows:

```
if let constname1 = optName1, let constname2 = optName2,
      let optName3 = …, <boolean statement> {

}
```

The following code, for example, uses optional binding to unwrap two optionals within a single statement:

```
var pet1: String?
var pet2: String?

pet1 = "cat"
pet2 = "dog"

if let firstPet = pet1, let secondPet = pet2 {
    print(firstPet)
    print(secondPet)
} else {
    print("insufficient pets")
}
```

The code fragment below, on the other hand, also makes use of the Boolean test clause condition:

```
if let firstPet = pet1, let secondPet = pet2, petCount > 1 {
    print(firstPet)
    print(secondPet)
} else {
    print("insufficient pets")
}
```

In the above example, the optional binding will not be attempted unless the value assigned to *petCount* is greater than 1.

It is also possible to declare an optional as being *implicitly unwrapped*. When an optional is declared in this way, the underlying value can be accessed without having to perform forced unwrapping or optional binding. An optional is declared as being implicitly unwrapped by replacing the question mark (?) with an exclamation mark (!) in the declaration. For example:

```
var index: Int! // Optional is now implicitly unwrapped

index = 3

var treeArray = ["Oak", "Pine", "Yew", "Birch"]

if index != nil {
    print(treeArray[index])

} else {
    print("index does not contain a value")
}
```

With the index optional variable now declared as being implicitly unwrapped, it is no longer necessary to unwrap the value when it is used as an index into the array in the above print call.

One final observation with regard to optionals in Swift is that only optional types are able to have no value or a value of nil assigned to them. In Swift it is not, therefore, possible to assign a nil value to a non-optional variable or constant. The following declarations, for instance, will all result in errors from the compiler since none of the variables are declared as optional:

```
var myInt = nil // Invalid code
var myString: String = nil // Invalid Code
let myConstant = nil // Invalid code
```

6.9 Type Casting and Type Checking

When writing Swift code, situations will occur where the compiler is unable to identify the specific type of a value. This is often the case when a value of ambiguous or unexpected type is returned from a method or function call. In this situation it may be necessary to let the compiler know the type of value that your code is expecting or requires using the *as* keyword (a concept referred to as *type casting*).

The following code, for example, lets the compiler know that the value returned from the *object(forKey:)* method needs to be treated as a String type:

```
let myValue = record.object(forKey: "comment") as! String
```

In fact, there are two types of casting which are referred to as *upcasting* and *downcasting*. Upcasting occurs when an object of a particular class is cast to one of its superclasses. Upcasting is performed using the *as* keyword and is also referred to as *guaranteed conversion* since the compiler can tell from the code that the cast will be successful. The UIButton class, for example, is a subclass of the UIControl class as shown in the fragment of the UIKit class hierarchy shown in Figure 6-1:

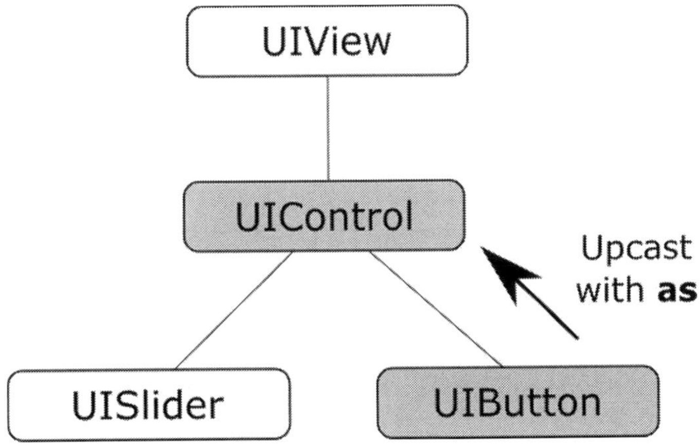

Figure 6-1

Since UIButton is a subclass of UIControl, the object can be safely upcast as follows:

```
let myButton: UIButton = UIButton()

let myControl = myButton as UIControl
```

Downcasting, on the other hand, occurs when a conversion is made from one class to another where there is no guarantee that the cast can be made safely or that an invalid casting attempt will be caught by the compiler. When an invalid cast is made in downcasting and not identified by the compiler it will most likely lead to an error at runtime.

Downcasting usually involves converting from a class to one of its subclasses. Downcasting is performed using the *as!* keyword syntax and is also referred to as *forced conversion*. Consider, for example, the UIKit UIScrollView class which has as subclasses both the UITableView and UITextView classes as shown in Figure 6-2:

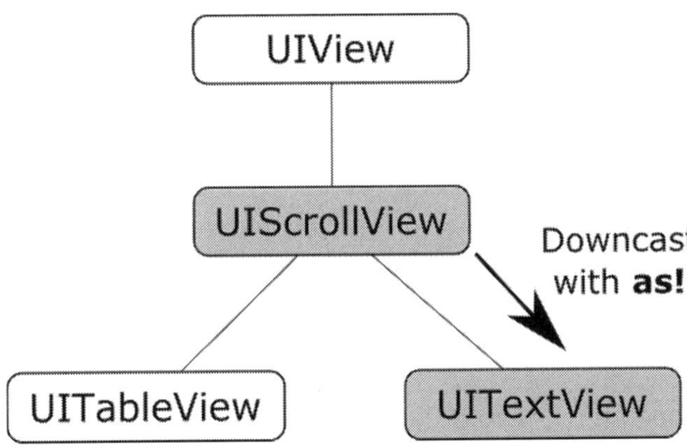

Figure 6-2

In order to convert a UIScrollView object to a UITextView class a downcast operation needs to be performed. The following code attempts to downcast a UIScrollView object to UITextView using the *guaranteed conversion* or *upcast* approach:

```
let myScrollView: UIScrollView = UIScrollView()
```

```
let myTextView = myScrollView as UITextView
```

The above code will result in the following error:

```
'UIScrollView' is not convertible to 'UITextView'
```

The compiler is indicating that a UIScrollView instance cannot be safely converted to a UITextView class instance. This does not necessarily mean that it is incorrect to do so, the compiler is simply stating that it cannot guarantee the safety of the conversion for you. The downcast conversion could instead be forced using the *as!* annotation:

```
let myTextView = myScrollView as! UITextView
```

Now the code will compile without an error. As an example of the dangers of downcasting, however, the above code will crash on execution stating that UIScrollView cannot be cast to UITextView. Forced downcasting should, therefore, be used with caution.

A safer approach to downcasting is to perform an optional binding using *as?*. If the conversion is performed successfully, an optional value of the specified type is returned, otherwise the optional value will be nil:

```
if let myTextView = myScrollView as? UITextView {
    print("Type cast to UITextView succeeded")
} else {
    print("Type cast to UITextView failed")
}
```

It is also possible to *type check* a value using the *is* keyword. The following code, for example, checks that a specific object is an instance of a class named MyClass:

```
if myobject is MyClass {
        // myobject is an instance of MyClass
}
```

6.10 Summary

This chapter has begun the introduction to Swift by exploring data types together with an overview of how to declare constants and variables. The chapter has also introduced concepts such as type safety, type inference and optionals, each of which is an integral part of Swift programming and designed specifically to make code writing less prone to error.

Chapter 7

7. Swift Operators and Expressions

So far we have looked at using variables and constants in Swift and also described the different data types. Being able to create variables is only part of the story however. The next step is to learn how to use these variables and constants in Swift code. The primary method for working with data is in the form of *expressions*.

7.1 Expression Syntax in Swift

The most basic Swift expression consists of an *operator*, two *operands* and an *assignment*. The following is an example of an expression:

```
var myresult = 1 + 2
```

In the above example, the (+) operator is used to add two operands (1 and 2) together. The *assignment operator* (=) subsequently assigns the result of the addition to a variable named *myresult*. The operands could just have easily been variables (or a mixture of constants and variables) instead of the actual numerical values used in the example.

In the remainder of this chapter we will look at the basic types of operators available in Swift.

7.2 The Basic Assignment Operator

We have already looked at the most basic of assignment operators, the = operator. This assignment operator simply assigns the result of an expression to a variable. In essence, the = assignment operator takes two operands. The left-hand operand is the variable or constant to which a value is to be assigned and the right-hand operand is the value to be assigned. The right-hand operand is, more often than not, an expression which performs some type of arithmetic or logical evaluation, the result of which will be assigned to the variable or constant. The following examples are all valid uses of the assignment operator:

```
var x: Int? // Declare an optional Int variable
var y = 10 // Declare and initialize a second Int variable

x = 10 // Assign a value to x
x = x! + y // Assign the result of x + y to x
x = y // Assign the value of y to x
```

7.3 Swift Arithmetic Operators

Swift provides a range of operators for the purpose of creating mathematical expressions. These operators primarily fall into the category of *binary* operators in that they take two operands. The exception is the *unary negative operator* (-) which serves to indicate that a value is negative rather than positive. This contrasts with the *subtraction operator* (-) which takes two operands (i.e. one value to be subtracted from another). For example:

```
var x = -10 // Unary - operator used to assign -10 to variable x
x = x - 5 // Subtraction operator. Subtracts 5 from x
```

The following table lists the primary Swift arithmetic operators:

Operator	Description
-(unary)	Negates the value of a variable or expression
*	Multiplication
/	Division
+	Addition
-	Subtraction
%	Remainder/Modulo

Note that multiple operators may be used in a single expression.

For example:

```
x = y * 10 + z - 5 / 4
```

7.4 Compound Assignment Operators

In an earlier section we looked at the basic assignment operator (=). Swift provides a number of operators designed to combine an assignment with a mathematical or logical operation. These are primarily of use when performing an evaluation where the result is to be stored in one of the operands. For example, one might write an expression as follows:

```
x = x + y
```

The above expression adds the value contained in variable x to the value contained in variable y and stores the result in variable x. This can be simplified using the addition compound assignment operator:

```
x += y
```

The above expression performs exactly the same task as *x = x + y* but saves the programmer some typing.

Numerous compound assignment operators are available in Swift. The most frequently used of which are outlined in the following table:

Operator	Description
x += y	Add x to y and place result in x
x -= y	Subtract y from x and place result in x
x *= y	Multiply x by y and place result in x
x /= y	Divide x by y and place result in x
x %= y	Perform Modulo on x and y and place result in x

7.5 Comparison Operators

Swift also includes a set of logical operators useful for performing comparisons. These operators all return a Boolean result depending on the result of the comparison. These operators are *binary operators* in that they work with two operands.

Comparison operators are most frequently used in constructing program flow control logic. For example an *if* statement may be constructed based on whether one value matches another:

```
if x == y {
      // Perform task
}
```

The result of a comparison may also be stored in a *Bool* variable. For example, the following code will result in a *true* value being stored in the variable result:

```
var result: Bool?
var x = 10
var y = 20

result = x < y
```

Clearly 10 is less than 20, resulting in a *true* evaluation of the *x < y* expression. The following table lists the full set of Swift comparison operators:

Operator	Description
x == y	Returns true if x is equal to y
x > y	Returns true if x is greater than y
x >= y	Returns true if x is greater than or equal to y
x < y	Returns true if x is less than y
x <= y	Returns true if x is less than or equal to y
x != y	Returns true if x is not equal to y

7.6 Boolean Logical Operators

Swift also provides a set of so called logical operators designed to return Boolean *true* or *false* values. These operators both return Boolean results and take Boolean values as operands. The key operators are NOT (!), AND (&&) and OR (||).

The NOT (!) operator simply inverts the current value of a Boolean variable, or the result of an expression. For example, if a variable named *flag* is currently true, prefixing the variable with a '!' character will invert the value to false:

```
var flag = true // variable is true
var secondFlag = !flag // secondFlag set to false
```

The OR (||) operator returns true if one of its two operands evaluates to true, otherwise it returns false. For example, the following code evaluates to true because at least one of the expressions either side of the OR operator is true:

```
if (10 < 20) || (20 < 10) {
        print("Expression is true")
}
```

The AND (&&) operator returns true only if both operands evaluate to be true. The following example will return false because only one of the two operand expressions evaluates to true:

```
if (10 < 20) && (20 < 10) {
      print("Expression is true")
}
```

7.7 Range Operators

Swift includes several useful operators that allow ranges of values to be declared. As will be seen in later chapters, these operators are invaluable when working with looping in program logic.

The syntax for the *closed range operator* is as follows:

x...y

This operator represents the range of numbers starting at x and ending at y where both x and y are included within the range. The range operator 5...8, for example, specifies the numbers 5, 6, 7 and 8.

The *half-open range operator*, on the other hand uses the following syntax:

x..<y

In this instance, the operator encompasses all the numbers from x up to, but not including, y. A half closed range operator 5..<8, therefore, specifies the numbers 5, 6 and 7.

Finally, the *one-sided range* operator specifies a range that can extend as far as possible in a specified range direction until the natural beginning or end of the range is reached (or until some other condition is met). A one-sided range is declared by omitting the number from one side of the range declaration, for example:

x...

or

...y

The previous chapter, for example, explained that a String in Swift is actually a collection of individual characters. A range to specify the characters in a string starting with the character at position 2 through to the last character in the string (regardless of string length) would be declared as follows:

2...

Similarly, to specify a range that begins with the first character and ends with the character at position 6, the range would be specified as follows:

...6

7.8 The Ternary Operator

Swift supports the *ternary operator* to provide a shortcut way of making decisions within code. The syntax of the ternary operator (also known as the conditional operator) is as follows:

```
condition ? true expression : false expression
```

The way the ternary operator works is that *condition* is replaced with an expression that will return either *true* or *false*. If the result is true then the expression that replaces the *true expression* is evaluated. Conversely, if the result was *false* then the *false expression* is evaluated. Let's see this in action:

```
let x = 10
let y = 20

print("Largest number is \(x > y ? x : y)")
```

The above code example will evaluate whether x is greater than y. Clearly this will evaluate to false resulting in y being returned to the print call for display to the user:

```
Largest number is 20
```

7.9 Bitwise Operators

As previously discussed, computer processors work in binary. These are essentially streams of ones and zeros, each one referred to as a bit. Bits are formed into groups of 8 to form bytes. As such, it is not surprising that we, as programmers, will occasionally end up working at this level in our code. To facilitate this requirement, Swift provides a range of *bit operators*.

Those familiar with bitwise operators in other languages such as C, C++, C#, Objective-C and Java will find nothing new in this area of the Swift language syntax. For those unfamiliar with binary numbers, now may be a good time to seek out reference materials on the subject in order to understand how ones and zeros are formed into bytes to form numbers. Other authors have done a much better job of describing the subject than we can do within the scope of this book.

For the purposes of this exercise we will be working with the binary representation of two numbers. First, the decimal number 171 is represented in binary as:

```
10101011
```

Second, the number 3 is represented by the following binary sequence:

```
00000011
```

Now that we have two binary numbers with which to work, we can begin to look at the Swift bitwise operators:

7.9.1 Bitwise NOT

The Bitwise NOT is represented by the tilde (~) character and has the effect of inverting all of the bits in a number. In other words, all the zeros become ones and all the ones become zeros. Taking our example 3 number, a Bitwise NOT operation has the following result:

```
00000011 NOT
========
11111100
```

The following Swift code, therefore, results in a value of -4:

```
let y = 3
let z = ~y

print("Result is \(z)")
```

7.9.2 Bitwise AND

The Bitwise AND is represented by a single ampersand (&). It makes a bit by bit comparison of two numbers. Any corresponding position in the binary sequence of each number where both bits are 1 results in a 1 appearing in the same position of the resulting number. If either bit position contains a 0 then a zero appears in the result. Taking our two example numbers, this would appear as follows:

```
10101011 AND
00000011
```

```
========
00000011
```

As we can see, the only locations where both numbers have 1s are the last two positions. If we perform this in Swift code, therefore, we should find that the result is 3 (00000011):

```
let x = 171
let y = 3
let z = x & y

print("Result is \(z)")
```

7.9.3 Bitwise OR

The bitwise OR also performs a bit by bit comparison of two binary sequences. Unlike the AND operation, the OR places a 1 in the result if there is a 1 in the first or second operand. The operator is represented by a single vertical bar character (|). Using our example numbers, the result will be as follows:

```
10101011 OR
00000011
========
10101011
```

If we perform this operation in a Swift example the result will be 171:

```
let x = 171
let y = 3
let z = x | y

print("Result is \(z)")
```

7.9.4 Bitwise XOR

The bitwise XOR (commonly referred to as *exclusive OR* and represented by the caret '^' character) performs a similar task to the OR operation except that a 1 is placed in the result if one or other corresponding bit positions in the two numbers is 1. If both positions are a 1 or a 0 then the corresponding bit in the result is set to a 0. For example:

```
10101011 XOR
00000011
========
10101000
```

The result in this case is 10101000 which converts to 168 in decimal. To verify this we can, once again, try some Swift code:

```
let x = 171
let y = 3
let z = x ^ y

print("Result is \(z)")
```

7.9.5 Bitwise Left Shift

The bitwise left shift moves each bit in a binary number a specified number of positions to the left. Shifting an integer one position to the left has the effect of doubling the value.

As the bits are shifted to the left, zeros are placed in the vacated right most (low order) positions. Note also that once the left most (high order) bits are shifted beyond the size of the variable containing the value, those high order bits are discarded:

```
10101011 Left Shift one bit
========
101010110
```

In Swift the bitwise left shift operator is represented by the '<<' sequence, followed by the number of bit positions to be shifted. For example, to shift left by 1 bit:

```
let x = 171
let z = x << 1

print("Result is \(z)")
```

When compiled and executed, the above code will display a message stating that the result is 342 which, when converted to binary, equates to 101010110.

7.9.6 Bitwise Right Shift

A bitwise right shift is, as you might expect, the same as a left except that the shift takes place in the opposite direction. Shifting an integer one position to the right has the effect of halving the value.

Note that since we are shifting to the right there is no opportunity to retain the lower most bits regardless of the data type used to contain the result. As a result the low order bits are discarded. Whether or not the vacated high order bit positions are replaced with zeros or ones depends on whether the *sign bit* used to indicate positive and negative numbers is set or not.

```
10101011 Right Shift one bit
========
01010101
```

The bitwise right shift is represented by the '>>' character sequence followed by the shift count:

```
let x = 171
let z = x >> 1

print("Result is \(z)")
```

When executed, the above code will report the result of the shift as being 85, which equates to binary 01010101.

7.10 Compound Bitwise Operators

As with the arithmetic operators, each bitwise operator has a corresponding compound operator that allows the operation and assignment to be performed using a single operator:

Operator	Description
x &= y	Perform a bitwise AND of x and y and assign result to x

x |= y	Perform a bitwise OR of x and y and assign result to x
x ^= y	Perform a bitwise XOR of x and y and assign result to x
x <<= n	Shift x left by n places and assign result to x
x >>= n	Shift x right by n places and assign result to x

7.11 Summary

Operators and expressions provide the underlying mechanism by which variables and constants are manipulated and evaluated within Swift code. This can take the simplest of forms whereby two numbers are added using the addition operator in an expression and the result stored in a variable using the assignment operator. Operators fall into a range of categories, details of which have been covered in this chapter.

Chapter 8

8. Swift Flow Control

Regardless of the programming language used, application development is largely an exercise in applying logic, and much of the art of programming involves writing code that makes decisions based on one or more criteria. Such decisions define which code gets executed, how many times it is executed and, conversely, which code gets by-passed when the program is executing. This is often referred to as *flow control* since it controls the *flow* of program execution. Flow control typically falls into the categories of *looping control* (how often code is executed) and *conditional flow control* (whether or not code is executed). This chapter is intended to provide an introductory overview of both types of flow control in Swift.

8.1 Looping Flow Control

This chapter will begin by looking at flow control in the form of loops. Loops are essentially sequences of Swift statements which are to be executed repeatedly until a specified condition is met. The first looping statement we will explore is the *for-in* loop.

8.2 The Swift *for-in* Statement

The *for-in* loop is used to iterate over a sequence of items contained in a collection or number range and provides a simple to use looping option.

The syntax of the for-in loop is as follows:

```
for constant name in collection or range {
        // code to be executed
}
```

In this syntax, *constant name* is the name to be used for a constant that will contain the current item from the collection or range through which the loop is iterating. The code in the body of the loop will typically use this constant name as a reference to the current item in the loop cycle. The *collection* or *range* references the item through which the loop is iterating. This could, for example, be an array of string values, a range operator or even a string of characters (the topic of collections will be covered in greater detail within the chapter entitled *Working with Array and Dictionary Collections in Swift*).

Consider, for example, the following for-in loop construct:

```
for index in 1...5 {
      print("Value of index is \(index)")
}
```

The loop begins by stating that the current item is to be assigned to a constant named *index*. The statement then declares a closed range operator to indicate that the for loop is to iterate through a range of numbers, starting at 1 and ending at 5. The body of the loop simply prints out a message to the console panel indicating the current value assigned to the *index* constant, resulting in the following output:

```
Value of index is 1
Value of index is 2
```

```
Value of index is 3
Value of index is 4
Value of index is 5
```

As will be demonstrated in the *Working with Array and Dictionary Collections in Swift* chapter of this book, the *for-in* loop is of particular benefit when working with collections such as arrays and dictionaries.

The declaration of a constant name in which to store a reference to the current item is not mandatory. In the event that a reference to the current item is not required in the body of the *for* loop, the constant name in the *for* loop declaration can be replaced by an underscore character. For example:

```
var count = 0

for _ in 1...5 {
    // No reference to the current value is required.
    count += 1
}
```

8.2.1 The while Loop

The Swift *for* loop described previously works well when it is known in advance how many times a particular task needs to be repeated in a program. There will, however, be instances where code needs to be repeated until a certain condition is met, with no way of knowing in advance how many repetitions are going to be needed to meet that criteria. To address this need, Swift provides the *while* loop.

Essentially, the *while* loop repeats a set of tasks while a specified condition is met. The *while* loop syntax is defined as follows:

```
while condition {
      // Swift statements go here
}
```

In the above syntax, *condition* is an expression that will return either *true* or *false* and the *// Swift statements go here* comment represents the code to be executed while the *condition* expression is *true*. For example:

```
var myCount = 0

while  myCount < 100 {
      myCount += 1
}
```

In the above example, the *while* expression will evaluate whether the *myCount* variable is less than 100. If it is already greater than 100, the code in the braces is skipped and the loop exits without performing any tasks.

If, on the other hand, *myCount* is not greater than 100 the code in the braces is executed and the loop returns to the *while* statement and repeats the evaluation of *myCount*. This process repeats until the value of *myCount* is greater than 100, at which point the loop exits.

8.3 The *repeat ... while* loop

The *repeat ... while* loop replaces the Swift 1.x *do .. while* loop. It is often helpful to think of the *repeat ... while* loop as an inverted *while* loop. The *while* loop evaluates an expression before executing the code contained in the body of the loop. If the expression evaluates to *false* on the first check then the code is not executed. The *repeat ... while* loop, on the other hand, is provided for situations where you know that the code contained in the body of the loop will *always* need to be executed at least once. For example, you may want to keep stepping through the items in an array until a specific item is found. You know that you have to at least check the first item in the array to have any hope of finding the entry you need. The syntax for the *repeat ... while* loop is as follows:

```
repeat {
       // Swift statements here
} while conditional expression
```

In the *repeat ... while* example below the loop will continue until the value of a variable named *i* equals 0:

```
var i = 10

repeat {
       i -= 1
} while (i > 0)
```

8.4 Breaking from Loops

Having created a loop, it is possible that under certain conditions you might want to break out of the loop before the completion criteria have been met (particularly if you have created an infinite loop). One such example might involve continually checking for activity on a network socket. Once activity has been detected it will most likely be necessary to break out of the monitoring loop and perform some other task.

For the purpose of breaking out of a loop, Swift provides the *break* statement which breaks out of the current loop and resumes execution at the code directly after the loop. For example:

```
var j = 10

for _ in 0 ..< 100
{
    j += j

    if j > 100 {
        break
    }

    print("j = \(j)")
}
```

In the above example the loop will continue to execute until the value of j exceeds 100 at which point the loop will exit and execution will continue with the next line of code after the loop.

8.5 The *continue* Statement

The *continue* statement causes all remaining code statements in a loop to be skipped, and execution to be returned to the top of the loop. In the following example, the print function is only called when the value of variable *i* is an even number:

```
var i = 1

while i < 20
```

```
{
        i += 1

        if (i % 2) != 0 {
            continue
        }

        print("i = \(i)")
}
```

The *continue* statement in the above example will cause the print call to be skipped unless the value of *i* can be divided by 2 with no remainder. If the *continue* statement is triggered, execution will skip to the top of the while loop and the statements in the body of the loop will be repeated (until the value of *i* exceeds 19).

8.6 Conditional Flow Control

In the previous chapter we looked at how to use logical expressions in Swift to determine whether something is *true* or *false*. Since programming is largely an exercise in applying logic, much of the art of programming involves writing code that makes decisions based on one or more criteria. Such decisions define which code gets executed and, conversely, which code gets by-passed when the program is executing. This is often referred to as *flow control* since it controls the *flow* of program execution.

8.7 Using the if Statement

The *if* statement is perhaps the most basic of flow control options available to the Swift programmer. Programmers who are familiar with C, Objective-C, C++ or Java will immediately be comfortable using Swift *if* statements.

The basic syntax of the Swift *if* statement is as follows:

```
if boolean expression {
    // Swift code to be performed when expression evaluates to true
}
```

Unlike some other programming languages, it is important to note that the braces ({}) are mandatory in Swift, even if only one line of code is executed after the *if* expression.

Essentially if the *Boolean expression* evaluates to *true* then the code in the body of the statement is executed. The body of the statement is enclosed in braces ({}). If, on the other hand, the expression evaluates to *false* the code in the body of the statement is skipped.

For example, if a decision needs to be made depending on whether one value is greater than another, we would write code similar to the following:

```
let x = 10

if x > 9 {
       print("x is greater than 9!")
}
```

Clearly, x is indeed greater than 9 causing the message to appear in the console panel.

8.8 Using if ... else ... Statements

The next variation of the *if* statement allows us to also specify some code to perform if the expression in the *if* statement evaluates to *false*. The syntax for this construct is as follows:

```
if boolean expression {
    // Code to be executed if expression is true
} else {
    // Code to be executed if expression is false
}
```

Using the above syntax, we can now extend our previous example to display a different message if the comparison expression evaluates to be *false*:

```
let x = 10

if x > 9 {
        print("x is greater than 9!")
} else {
        print("x is less than 9!")
}
```

In this case, the second print statement would execute if the value of x was less than 9.

8.9 Using if ... else if ... Statements

So far we have looked at *if* statements which make decisions based on the result of a single logical expression. Sometimes it becomes necessary to make decisions based on a number of different criteria. For this purpose, we can use the *if ... else if ...* construct, an example of which is as follows:

```
let x = 9;

if x == 10 {
        print("x is 10")
} else if x == 9 {
        print("x is 9")
} else if x == 8 {
        print("x is 8")
}
```

This approach works well for a moderate number of comparisons, but can become cumbersome for a larger volume of expression evaluations. For such situations, the Swift *switch* statement provides a more flexible and efficient solution. For more details on using the *switch* statement refer to the next chapter entitled *The Swift Switch Statement*.

8.10 The guard Statement

The guard statement is a Swift language feature introduced as part of Swift 2. A guard statement contains a Boolean expression which must evaluate to true in order for the code located *after* the guard statement to be executed. The guard statement must include an *else* clause to be executed in the event that the expression evaluates to false. The code in the else clause must contain a statement to exit the current code flow (i.e. a *return, break, continue* or *throw* statement). Alternatively the else block may call any other function or method that does not itself return.

The syntax for the guard statement is as follows:

```
guard <boolean expressions> else {
    // code to be executed if expression is false
    <exit statement here>
}

// code here is executed if expression is true
```

The guard statement essentially provides an "early exit" strategy from the current function or loop in the event that a specified requirement is not met.

The following code example implements a guard statement within a function:

```
func multiplyByTen(value: Int?) {

    guard let number = value, number < 10 else {
        print("Number is too high")
        return
    }

    let result = number * 10
    print(result)
}
```

The function takes as a parameter an integer value in the form of an optional. The guard statement uses optional binding to unwrap the value and verify that it is less than 10. In the event that the variable could not be unwrapped, or that its value is greater than 9, the else clause is triggered, the error message printed and the return statement executed to exit the function.

In the event that the optional contains a value less than 10, the code after the guard statement executes to multiply the value by 10 and print the result. A particularly important point to note about the above example is that the unwrapped *number* variable is available to the code outside of the guard statement. This would not have been the case had the variable been unwrapped using an *if* statement.

8.11 Summary

The term *flow control* is used to describe the logic that dictates the execution path that is taken through the source code of an application as it runs. This chapter has looked at the two types of flow control provided by Swift (looping and conditional) and explored the various Swift constructs that are available to implement both forms of flow control logic.

Chapter 9

9. The Swift Switch Statement

In *Swift Flow Control* we looked at how to control program execution flow using the *if* and *else* statements. While these statement constructs work well for testing a limited number of conditions, they quickly become unwieldy when dealing with larger numbers of possible conditions. To simplify such situations, Swift has inherited the *switch* statement from the C programming language. Those familiar with the switch statement from other programming languages should be aware, however, that the Swift switch statement has some key differences from other implementations. In this chapter we will explore the Swift implementation of the *switch* statement in detail.

9.1 Why Use a switch Statement?

For a small number of logical evaluations of a value the *if ... else if ...* construct is perfectly adequate. Unfortunately, any more than two or three possible scenarios can quickly make such a construct both time consuming to write and difficult to read. For such situations, the *switch* statement provides an excellent alternative.

9.2 Using the switch Statement Syntax

The syntax for a basic Swift *switch* statement implementation can be outlined as follows:

```
switch expression
{
     case match1:
          statements

     case match2:
          statements

     case match3, match4:
          statements

     default:
          statements
}
```

In the above syntax outline, *expression* represents either a value, or an expression which returns a value. This is the value against which the *switch* operates.

For each possible match a *case* statement is provided, followed by a *match* value. Each potential match must be of the same type as the governing expression. Following on from the *case* line are the Swift statements that are to be executed in the event of the value matching the case condition.

Finally, the *default* section of the construct defines what should happen if none of the case statements present a match to the *expression*.

9.3 A Swift switch Statement Example

With the above information in mind we may now construct a simple *switch* statement:

```
let value = 4

switch (value)
{
      case 0:
        print("zero")

      case 1:
        print("one")

      case 2:
        print("two")

      case 3:
        print("three")

      case 4:
        print("four")

      case 5:
        print("five")

      default:
        print("Integer out of range")
}
```

9.4 Combining case Statements

In the above example, each case had its own set of statements to execute. Sometimes a number of different matches may require the same code to be executed. In this case, it is possible to group case matches together with a common set of statements to be executed when a match for any of the cases is found. For example, we can modify the switch construct in our example so that the same code is executed regardless of whether the value is 0, 1 or 2:

```
let value = 1

switch (value)
{
      case 0, 1, 2:
        print("zero, one or two")

      case 3:
        print("three")
```

```
    case 4:
      print("four")

    case 5:
      print("five")

    default:
      print("Integer out of range")
}
```

9.5 Range Matching in a switch Statement

The case statements within a switch construct may also be used to implement range matching. The following switch statement, for example, checks a temperature value for matches within three number ranges:

```
let temperature = 83

switch (temperature)
{
    case 0...49:
      print("Cold")

    case 50...79:
      print("Warm")

    case 80...110:
      print("Hot")

    default:
      print("Temperature out of range")
}
```

9.6 Using the where statement

The *where* statement may be used within a switch case match to add additional criteria required for a positive match. The following switch statement, for example, checks not only for the range in which a value falls, but also whether the number is odd or even:

```
let temperature = 54

switch (temperature)
{
    case 0...49 where temperature % 2 == 0:
      print("Cold and even")

    case 50...79 where temperature % 2 == 0:
      print("Warm and even")
```

```
        case 80...110 where temperature % 2 == 0:
          print("Hot and even")

        default:
          print("Temperature out of range or odd")
}
```

9.7 Fallthrough

Those familiar with switch statements in other languages such as C and Objective-C will notice that it is no longer necessary to include a *break* statement after each case declaration. Unlike other languages, Swift automatically breaks out of the statement when a matching case condition is met. The fallthrough effect of other switch implementations (whereby the execution path continues through the remaining case statements) can be emulated using the *fallthrough* statement:

```
let temperature = 10

switch (temperature)
{
        case 0...49 where temperature % 2 == 0:
          print("Cold and even")
        fallthrough

        case 50...79 where temperature % 2 == 0:
          print("Warm and even")
          fallthrough

        case 80...110 where temperature % 2 == 0:
          print("Hot and even")
          fallthrough

        default:
          print("Temperature out of range or odd")
}
```

Although *break* is less commonly used in Swift switch statements, it is useful when no action needs to be taken for the default case. For example:

```
.
.
.
          default:
            break
}
```

9.8 Summary

While the *if.. else..* construct serves as a good decision making option for small numbers of possible outcomes, this approach can become unwieldy in more complex situations. As an alternative method for implementing flow control logic in Swift when many possible outcomes exist as the result of an evaluation, the *switch* statement invariably makes a more suitable option. As outlined in this chapter, however, developers familiar with switch implementations from other programming languages should be aware of some subtle differences in the way that the Swift switch statement works.

Chapter 10

10. An Overview of Swift 4 Functions, Methods and Closures

Swift functions, methods and closures are a vital part of writing well-structured and efficient code and provide a way to organize programs while avoiding code repetition. In this chapter we will look at how functions, methods and closures are declared and used within Swift.

10.1 What is a Function?

A function is a named block of code that can be called upon to perform a specific task. It can be provided data on which to perform the task and is capable of returning results to the code that called it. For example, if a particular arithmetic calculation needs to be performed in a Swift program, the code to perform the arithmetic can be placed in a function. The function can be programmed to accept the values on which the arithmetic is to be performed (referred to as *parameters*) and to return the result of the calculation. At any point in the program code where the calculation is required the function is simply called, parameter values passed through as *arguments* and the result returned.

The terms *parameter* and *argument* are often used interchangeably when discussing functions. There is, however, a subtle difference. The values that a function is able to accept when it is called are referred to as *parameters*. At the point that the function is actually called and passed those values, however, they are referred to as *arguments*.

10.2 What is a Method?

A method is essentially a function that is associated with a particular class, structure or enumeration. If, for example, you declare a function within a Swift class (a topic covered in detail in the chapter entitled *The Basics of Object-oriented Programming in Swift*), it is considered to be a method. Although the remainder of this chapter refers to functions, the same rules and behavior apply equally to methods unless otherwise stated.

10.3 How to Declare a Swift Function

A Swift function is declared using the following syntax:

```
func <function name> (<para name>: <para type>,
                      <para name>: <para type>, ... ) -> <return type> {
          // Function code
}
```

This combination of function name, parameters and return type are referred to as the *function signature*. Explanations of the various fields of the function declaration are as follows:

- **func** – The prefix keyword used to notify the Swift compiler that this is a function.
- **<function name>** - The name assigned to the function. This is the name by which the function will be referenced when it is called from within the application code.
- **<para name>** - The name by which the parameter is to be referenced in the function code.
- **<para type>** - The type of the corresponding parameter.

- **<return type>** - The data type of the result returned by the function. If the function does not return a result then no return type is specified.
- **Function code** - The code of the function that does the work.

As an example, the following function takes no parameters, returns no result and simply displays a message:

```
func sayHello() {
    print("Hello")
}
```

The following sample function, on the other hand, takes an integer and a string as parameters and returns a string result:

```
func buildMessageFor(name: String, count: Int) -> String {
      return("\(name), you are customer number \(count)")
}
```

10.4 Calling a Swift Function

Once declared, functions are called using the following syntax:

```
<function name> (<arg1>, <arg2>, ... )
```

Each argument passed through to a function must match the parameters the function is configured to accept. For example, to call a function named *sayHello* that takes no parameters and returns no value, we would write the following code:

```
sayHello()
```

10.5 Handling Return Values

To call a function named *buildMessage* that takes two parameters and returns a result, on the other hand, we might write the following code:

```
let message = buildMessageFor(name: "John", count: 100)
```

In the above example, we have created a new variable called *message* and then used the assignment operator (=) to store the result returned by the function.

When developing in Swift, situations may arise where the result returned by a method or function call is not used. When this is the case, the return value may be discarded by assigning it to '_'. For example:

```
_ = buildMessageFor(name: "John", count: 100)
```

10.6 Local and External Parameter Names

When the preceding example functions were declared, they were configured with parameters that were assigned names which, in turn, could be referenced within the body of the function code. When declared in this way, these names are referred to as *local parameter names*.

In addition to local names, function parameters may also have *external parameter names*. These are the names by which the parameter is referenced when the function is called. By default, function parameters are assigned the same local and external parameter names. Consider, for example, the previous call to the *buildMessageFor* method:

```
let message = buildMessageFor(name: "John", count: 100)
```

As declared, the function uses "name" and "count" as both the local and external parameter names.

The default external parameter names assigned to parameters may be removed by preceding the local parameter names with an underscore (_) character as follows:

```
func buildMessageFor(_ name: String, _ count: Int) -> String {
      return("\(name), you are customer number \(count)")
}
```

With this change implemented, the function may now be called as follows:

```
let message = buildMessageFor("John", 100)
```

Alternatively, external parameter names can be added simply by declaring the external parameter name before the local parameter name within the function declaration. In the following code, for example, the external names of the first and second parameters have been set to "username" and "usercount" respectively:

```
func buildMessageFor(username name: String, usercount count: Int) -> String {
      return("\(name), you are customer number \(count)")
}
```

When declared in this way, the external parameter name must be referenced when calling the function:

```
let message = buildMessageFor(username: "John", usercount: 100)
```

Regardless of the fact that the external names are used to pass the arguments through when calling the function, the local names are still used to reference the parameters within the body of the function. It is important to also note that when calling a function using external parameter names for the arguments, those arguments must still be placed in the same order as that used when the function was declared.

10.7 Declaring Default Function Parameters

Swift provides the ability to designate a default parameter value to be used in the event that the value is not provided as an argument when the function is called. This simply involves assigning the default value to the parameter when the function is declared. When using default parameters, it is important that the parameters for which a default is being declared be placed at the end of the parameter list so that the compiler does not become confused about which parameters have been omitted during a function call. Swift also provides a default external name based on the local parameter name for defaulted parameters (unless one is already provided) which must then be used when calling the function.

To see default parameters in action the *buildMessageFor* function will be modified so that the string "Customer" is used as a default in the event that a customer name is not passed through as an argument:

```
func buildMessageFor(_ name: String = "Customer", count: Int ) -> String {
    return ("\(name), you are customer number \(count)")
}
```

The function can now be called without passing through a name argument:

```
let message = buildMessageFor(count: 100)
print(message)
```

When executed, the above function call will generate output to the console panel which reads:

```
Customer, you are customer 100
```

10.8 Returning Multiple Results from a Function

A function can return multiple result values by wrapping those results in a tuple. The following function takes as a parameter a measurement value in inches. The function converts this value into yards, centimeters and meters, returning all three results within a single tuple instance:

```
func sizeConverter(_ length: Float) -> (yards: Float, centimeters: Float,
                                        meters: Float) {

    let yards = length * 0.0277778
    let centimeters = length * 2.54
    let meters = length * 0.0254

    return (yards, centimeters, meters)
}
```

The return type for the function indicates that the function returns a tuple containing three values named yards, centimeters and meters respectively, all of which are of type Float:

```
-> (yards: Float, centimeters: Float, meters: Float)
```

Having performed the conversion, the function simply constructs the tuple instance and returns it.

Usage of this function might read as follows:

```
let lengthTuple = sizeConverter(20)

print(lengthTuple.yards)
print(lengthTuple.centimeters)
print(lengthTuple.meters)
```

10.9 Variable Numbers of Function Parameters

It is not always possible to know in advance the number of parameters a function will need to accept when it is called within application code. Swift handles this possibility through the use of *variadic parameters*. Variadic parameters are declared using three periods (…) to indicate that the function accepts zero or more parameters of a specified data type. Within the body of the function, the parameters are made available in the form of an array object. The following function, for example, takes as parameters a variable number of String values and then outputs them to the console panel:

```
func displayStrings(_ strings: String...)
{
    for string in strings {
        print(string)
    }
}

displayStrings("one", "two", "three", "four")
```

10.10 Parameters as Variables

All parameters accepted by a function are treated as constants by default. This prevents changes being made to those parameter values within the function code. If changes to parameters need to be made within the function body, therefore, shadow copies of those parameters must be created. The following function, for example, is passed length and width parameters in inches, creates shadow variables of the two values and converts those parameters to centimeters before calculating and returning the area value:

```
func calcuateArea(length: Float, width: Float) -> Float {

    var length = length
    var width = width

    length = length * 2.54
    width = width * 2.54
    return length * width
}

print(calcuateArea(length: 10, width: 20))
```

10.11 Working with In-Out Parameters

When a variable is passed through as a parameter to a function, we now know that the parameter is treated as a constant within the body of that function. We also know that if we want to make changes to the parameter value we have to create a shadow copy as outlined in the above section. Since this is a copy, any changes made to the variable are not, by default, reflected in the original variable. Consider, for example, the following code:

```
var myValue = 10

func doubleValue (_ value: Int) -> Int {
    var value = value
    value += value
    return(value)
}

print("Before function call myValue = \(myValue)")

print("doubleValue call returns \(doubleValue(myValue))")

print("After function call myValue = \(myValue)")
```

The code begins by declaring a variable named *myValue* initialized with a value of 10. A new function is then declared which accepts a single integer parameter. Within the body of the function, a shadow copy of the value is created, doubled and returned.

The remaining lines of code display the value of the *myValue* variable before and after the function call is made. When executed, the following output will appear in the console:

```
Before function call myValue = 10
```

```
doubleValue call returns 20
After function call myValue = 10
```

Clearly, the function has made no change to the original myValue variable. This is to be expected since the mathematical operation was performed on a copy of the variable, not the *myValue* variable itself.

In order to make any changes made to a parameter persist after the function has returned, the parameter must be declared as an *in-out parameter* within the function declaration. To see this in action, modify the *doubleValue* function to include the *inout* keyword, and remove the creation of the shadow copy as follows:

```
func doubleValue (_ value: inout Int) -> Int {
    value += value
    return(value)
}
```

Finally, when calling the function, the inout parameter must now be prefixed with an & modifier:

```
print("doubleValue call returned \(doubleValue(&myValue))")
```

Having made these changes, a test run of the code should now generate output clearly indicating that the function modified the value assigned to the original *myValue* variable:

```
Before function call myValue = 10
doubleValue call returns 20
After function call myValue = 20
```

10.12 Functions as Parameters

An interesting feature of functions within Swift is that they can be treated as data types. It is perfectly valid, for example, to assign a function to a constant or variable as illustrated in the declaration below:

```
func inchesToFeet (_ inches: Float) -> Float {

    return inches * 0.0833333
}

let toFeet = inchesToFeet
```

The above code declares a new function named *inchesToFeet* and subsequently assigns that function to a constant named *toFeet*. Having made this assignment, a call to the function may be made using the constant name instead of the original function name:

```
let result = toFeet(10)
```

On the surface this does not seem to be a particularly compelling feature. Since we could already call the function without assigning it to a constant or variable data type it does not seem that much has been gained.

The possibilities that this feature offers become more apparent when we consider that a function assigned to a constant or variable now has the capabilities of many other data types. In particular, a function can now be passed through as an argument to another function, or even returned as a result from a function.

Before we look at what is, essentially, the ability to plug one function into another, it is first necessary to explore the concept of function data types. The data type of a function is dictated by a combination of the parameters it accepts and the type of result it returns. In the above example, since the function accepts a floating point parameter and returns a floating point result, the function's data type conforms to the following:

```
(Float) -> Float
```

A function which accepts an Int and a Double as parameters and returns a String result, on the other hand, would have the following data type:

```
(Int, Double) -> String
```

In order to accept a function as a parameter, the receiving function simply declares the data type of the function it is able to accept.

For the purposes of an example, we will begin by declaring two unit conversion functions and assigning them to constants:

```
func inchesToFeet (_ inches: Float) -> Float {

    return inches * 0.0833333
}

func inchesToYards (_ inches: Float) -> Float {

    return inches * 0.0277778
}

let toFeet = inchesToFeet
let toYards = inchesToYards
```

The example now needs an additional function, the purpose of which is to perform a unit conversion and print the result in the console panel. This function needs to be as general purpose as possible, capable of performing a variety of different measurement unit conversions. In order to demonstrate functions as parameters, this new function will take as a parameter a function type that matches both the inchesToFeet and inchesToYards function data type together with a value to be converted. Since the data type of these functions is equivalent to (Float) -> Float, our general purpose function can be written as follows:

```
func outputConversion(_ converterFunc: (Float) -> Float, value: Float) {

    let result = converterFunc(value)

    print("Result of conversion is \(result)")
}
```

When the outputConversion function is called, it will need to be passed a function matching the declared data type. That function will be called to perform the conversion and the result displayed in the console panel. This means that the same function can be called to convert inches to both feet and yards, simply by "plugging in" the appropriate converter function as a parameter. For example:

```
outputConversion(toYards, value: 10) // Convert to Yards
outputConversion(toFeet, value: 10) // Convert to Inches
```

Functions can also be returned as a data type simply by declaring the type of the function as the return type. The following function is configured to return either our toFeet or toYards function type (in other words a function which accepts and returns a Float value) based on the value of a Boolean parameter:

```
func decideFunction(_ feet: Bool) -> (Float) -> Float
{
    if feet {
        return toFeet
    } else {
        return toYards
    }
}
```

10.13 Closure Expressions

Having covered the basics of functions in Swift it is now time to look at the concept of *closures* and *closure expressions*. Although these terms are often used interchangeably there are some key differences.

Closure expressions are self-contained blocks of code. The following code, for example, declares a closure expression and assigns it to a constant named sayHello and then calls the function via the constant reference:

```
let sayHello = { print("Hello") }
sayHello()
```

Closure expressions may also be configured to accept parameters and return results. The syntax for this is as follows:

```
{(<para name>: <para type>, <para name> <para type>, ... ) ->
                                                <return type> in
        // Closure expression code here
}
```

The following closure expression, for example, accepts two integer parameters and returns an integer result:

```
let multiply = {(_ val1: Int, _ val2: Int) -> Int in
        return val1 * val2
}
let result = multiply(10, 20)
```

Note that the syntax is similar to that used for declaring Swift functions with the exception that the closure expression does not have a name, the parameters and return type are included in the braces and the *in* keyword is used to indicate the start of the closure expression code. Functions are, in fact, just named closure expressions.

Closure expressions are often used when declaring completion handlers for asynchronous method calls. In other words, when developing iOS applications it will often be necessary to make calls to the operating system where the requested task is performed in the background allowing the application to continue with other tasks. Typically in such a scenario, the system will notify the application of the completion of the task and return any results by calling the completion handler that was declared when the method was called. Frequently the code for the completion handler will be implemented in the form of a closure expression. Consider the following code from an example used later in the book:

```
eventstore.requestAccess(to: .reminder, completion: {(granted: Bool,
```

```
                    error: Error?) -> Void in
    if !granted {
        print(error!.localizedDescription)
    }
})
```

When the tasks performed by the *requestAccess(to:)* method call are complete it will execute the closure expression declared as the *completion:* parameter. The completion handler is required by the method to accept a Boolean value and an Error object as parameters and return no results, hence the following declaration:

```
{(granted: Bool, error: Error?) -> Void in
```

In actual fact, the Swift compiler already knows about the parameter and return value requirements for the completion handler for this method call, and is able to infer this information without it being declared in the closure expression. This allows a simpler version of the closure expression declaration to be written:

```
eventstore.requestAccess(to: .reminder, completion: {(granted, error) in
    if !granted {
        print(error!.localizedDescription)
    }
})
```

10.14 Closures in Swift

A *closure* in computer science terminology generally refers to the combination of a self-contained block of code (for example a function or closure expression) and one or more variables that exist in the context surrounding that code block. Consider, for example the following Swift function:

```
func functionA() -> () -> Int {

    var counter = 0

    func functionB() -> Int {
        return counter + 10
    }
    return functionB
}

let myClosure = functionA()
let result = myClosure()
```

In the above code, *functionA* returns a function named *functionB*. In actual fact functionA is returning a closure since functionB relies on the *counter* variable which is declared outside the functionB's local scope. In other words, functionB is said to have *captured* or *closed over* (hence the term closure) the counter variable and, as such, is considered a closure in the traditional computer science definition of the word.

To a large extent, and particularly as it relates to Swift, the terms *closure* and *closure expression* have started to be used interchangeably. The key point to remember, however, is that both are supported in Swift.

10.15 Summary

Functions, closures and closure expressions are self-contained blocks of code that can be called upon to perform a specific task and provide a mechanism for structuring code and promoting reuse. This chapter has introduced the concepts of functions and closures in terms of declaration and implementation.

Chapter 11

11. The Basics of Object-Oriented Programming in Swift

Swift provides extensive support for developing object-oriented iOS applications. The subject area of object-oriented programming is, however, large. It is not an exaggeration to state that entire books have been dedicated to the subject. As such, a detailed overview of object-oriented software development is beyond the scope of this book. Instead, we will introduce the basic concepts involved in object-oriented programming and then move on to explaining the concept as it relates to Swift application development. Once again, while we strive to provide the basic information you need in this chapter, we recommend reading a copy of Apple's *The Swift Programming Language* book for more extensive coverage of this subject area.

11.1 What is an Object?

Objects (also referred to as instances) are self-contained modules of functionality that can be easily used, and re-used as the building blocks for a software application.

Objects consist of data variables (called *properties*) and functions (called *methods*) that can be accessed and called on the object or instance to perform tasks and are collectively referred to as *class members*.

11.2 What is a Class?

Much as a blueprint or architect's drawing defines what an item or a building will look like once it has been constructed, a class defines what an object will look like when it is created. It defines, for example, what the methods will do and what the properties will be.

11.3 Declaring a Swift Class

Before an object can be instantiated, we first need to define the class 'blueprint' for the object. In this chapter we will create a bank account class to demonstrate the basic concepts of Swift object-oriented programming.

In declaring a new Swift class we specify an optional *parent class* from which the new class is derived and also define the properties and methods that the class will contain. The basic syntax for a new class is as follows:

```
class NewClassName: ParentClass {
   // Properties
   // Instance Methods
   // Type methods
}
```

The *Properties* section of the declaration defines the variables and constants that are to be contained within the class. These are declared in the same way that any other variable or constant would be declared in Swift.

The *Instance methods* and *Type methods* sections define the methods that are available to be called on the class and instances of the class. These are essentially functions specific to the class that perform a particular operation when called upon and will be described in greater detail later in this chapter.

To create an example outline for our BankAccount class, we would use the following:

```
class BankAccount {

}
```

Now that we have the outline syntax for our class, the next step is to add some instance properties to it.

11.4 Adding Instance Properties to a Class

A key goal of object-oriented programming is a concept referred to as *data encapsulation*. The idea behind data encapsulation is that data should be stored within classes and accessed only through methods defined in that class. Data encapsulated in a class are referred to as *properties* or *instance variables*.

Instances of our BankAccount class will be required to store some data, specifically a bank account number and the balance currently held within the account. Properties are declared in the same way any other variables and constants are declared in Swift. We can, therefore, add these variables as follows:

```
class BankAccount {
    var accountBalance: Float = 0
    var accountNumber: Int = 0
}
```

Having defined our properties, we can now move on to defining the methods of the class that will allow us to work with our properties while staying true to the data encapsulation model.

11.5 Defining Methods

The methods of a class are essentially code routines that can be called upon to perform specific tasks within the context of that class.

Methods come in two different forms, *type methods* and *instance methods*. Type methods operate at the level of the class, such as creating a new instance of a class. Instance methods, on the other hand, operate only on the instances of a class (for example performing an arithmetic operation on two property variables and returning the result).

Instance methods are declared within the opening and closing braces of the class to which they belong and are declared using the standard Swift function declaration syntax.

Type methods are declared in the same way as instance methods with the exception that the declaration is preceded by the *class* keyword.

For example, the declaration of a method to display the account balance in our example might read as follows:

```
class BankAccount {

    var accountBalance: Float = 0
    var accountNumber: Int = 0

    func displayBalance()
    {
       print("Number \(accountNumber)")
       print("Current balance is \(accountBalance)")
    }
}
```

The method is an *instance method* so it is not preceded by the *class* keyword.

When designing the BankAccount class it might be useful to be able to call a type method on the class itself to identify the maximum allowable balance that can be stored by the class. This would enable an application to identify whether the BankAccount class is suitable for storing details of a new customer without having to go through the process of first creating a class instance. This method will be named *getMaxBalance* and is implemented as follows:

```
class BankAccount {

    var accountBalance: Float = 0
    var accountNumber: Int = 0

    func displayBalance()
    {
       print("Number \(accountNumber)")
       print("Current balance is \(accountBalance)")
    }

    class func getMaxBalance() -> Float {
        return 100000.00
    }
}
```

11.6 Declaring and Initializing a Class Instance

So far all we have done is define the blueprint for our class. In order to do anything with this class, we need to create instances of it. The first step in this process is to declare a variable to store a reference to the instance when it is created. We do this as follows:

```
var account1: BankAccount = BankAccount()
```

When executed, an instance of our BankAccount class will have been created and will be accessible via the *account1* variable.

11.7 Initializing and Deinitializing a Class Instance

A class will often need to perform some initialization tasks at the point of creation. These tasks can be implemented by placing an *init* method within the class. In the case of the BankAccount class, it would be useful to be able to initialize the account number and balance properties with values when a new class instance is created. To achieve this, the *init* method could be written in the class as follows:

```
class BankAccount {

    var accountBalance: Float = 0
    var accountNumber: Int = 0

    init(number: Int, balance: Float)
    {
        accountNumber = number
        accountBalance = balance
    }
```

```
    func displayBalance()
    {
        print("Number \(accountNumber)")
        print("Current balance is \(accountBalance)")
    }

}
```

When creating an instance of the class, it will now be necessary to provide initialization values for the account number and balance properties as follows:

```
var account1 = BankAccount(number: 12312312, balance: 400.54)
```

Conversely, any cleanup tasks that need to be performed before a class instance is destroyed by the Swift runtime system can be performed by implementing the deinitializer within the class definition:

```
class BankAccount {

    var accountBalance: Float = 0
    var accountNumber: Int = 0

    init(number: Int, balance: Float)
    {
        accountNumber = number
        accountBalance = balance
    }

    deinit {
        // Perform any necessary clean up here
    }

    func displayBalance()
    {
        print("Number \(accountNumber)")
        print("Current balance is \(accountBalance)")
    }
}
```

11.8 Calling Methods and Accessing Properties

Now is probably a good time to recap what we have done so far in this chapter. We have now created a new Swift class named *BankAccount*. Within this new class we declared some properties to contain the bank account number and current balance together with an initializer and a method to display the current balance information. In the preceding section we covered the steps necessary to create and initialize an instance of our new class. The next step is to learn how to call the instance methods and access the properties we built into our class. This is most easily achieved using *dot notation*.

Dot notation involves accessing an instance variable, or calling an instance method by specifying a class instance followed by a dot followed in turn by the name of the property or method:

```
classInstance.propertyName
classInstance.instanceMethod()
```

For example, to get the current value of our *accountBalance* instance variable:

```
var balance1 = account1.accountBalance
```

Dot notation can also be used to set values of instance properties:

```
account1.accountBalance = 6789.98
```

The same technique is used to call methods on a class instance. For example, to call the *displayBalance* method on an instance of the BankAccount class:

```
account1.displayBalance()
```

Type methods are also called using dot notation, though they must be called on the class type instead of a class instance:

```
ClassName.typeMethod()
```

For example, to call the previously declared *getMaxBalance* type method, the BankAccount class is referenced:

```
var maxAllowed = BankAccount.getMaxBalance()
```

11.9 Stored and Computed Properties

Class properties in Swift fall into two categories referred to as *stored properties* and *computed properties*. Stored properties are those values that are contained within a constant or variable. Both the account name and number properties in the BankAccount example are stored properties.

A computed property, on the other hand, is a value that is derived based on some form of calculation or logic at the point at which the property is set or retrieved. Computed properties are implemented by creating *getter* and optional corresponding *setter* methods containing the code to perform the computation. Consider, for example, that the BankAccount class might need an additional property to contain the current balance less any recent banking fees. Rather than use a stored property, it makes more sense to use a computed property which calculates this value on request. The modified BankAccount class might now read as follows:

```
class BankAccount {

    var accountBalance: Float = 0
    var accountNumber: Int = 0;
    let fees: Float = 25.00

    var balanceLessFees: Float {
        get {
            return accountBalance - fees
        }
    }
```

```
    init(number: Int, balance: Float)
    {
        accountNumber = number
        accountBalance = balance
    }
.
.
.
}
```

The above code adds a getter that returns a computed property based on the current balance minus a fee amount. An optional setter could also be declared in much the same way to set the balance value less fees:

```
var balanceLessFees: Float {
    get {
        return accountBalance - fees
    }

    set(newBalance)
    {
            accountBalance = newBalance - fees
    }
}
```

The new setter takes as a parameter a floating point value from which it deducts the fee value before assigning the result to the current balance property. Regardless of the fact that these are computed properties, they are accessed in the same way as stored properties using dot-notation. The following code gets the current balance less the fees value before setting the property to a new value:

```
var balance1 = account1.balanceLessFees
account1.balanceLessFees = 12123.12
```

11.10 Using self in Swift

Programmers familiar with other object-oriented programming languages may be in the habit of prefixing references to properties and methods with *self* to indicate that the method or property belongs to the current class instance. The Swift programming language also provides the *self* property type for this purpose and it is, therefore, perfectly valid to write code which reads as follows:

```
class MyClass {
    var myNumber = 1

    func addTen() {
        self.myNumber += 10
    }
}
```

In this context, the *self* prefix indicates to the compiler that the code is referring to a property named *myNumber* which belongs to the MyClass class instance. When programming in Swift, however, it is no longer necessary to use self in most situations since this is now assumed to be the default for references to properties and methods. To quote The Swift Programming Language guide published by Apple, "in practice you don't need to write *self* in your code very often". The function from the above example, therefore, can also be written as follows with the self reference omitted:

```
func addTen() {
    myNumber += 10
}
```

In most cases, use of self is optional in Swift. That being said, one situation where it is still necessary to use *self* is when referencing a property or method from within a closure expression. The use of self, for example, is mandatory in the following closure expression:

```
document?.openWithCompletionHandler({(success: Bool) -> Void in
    if success {
        self.ubiquityURL = resultURL
    }
})
```

It is also necessary to use self to resolve ambiguity such as when a function parameter has the same name as a class property. In the following code, for example, the first print statement will output the value passed through to the function via the myNumber parameter while the second print statement outputs the number assigned to the myNumber class property (in this case 10):

```
class MyClass {

    var myNumber = 10 // class property

    func addTen(myNumber: Int) {
        print(myNumber) // Output the function parameter value
        print(self.myNumber) // Output the class property value
    }
}
```

Whether or not to use self in most other situations is largely a matter of programmer preference. Those who prefer to use self when referencing properties and methods can continue to do so in Swift. Code that is written without use of the self property type (where doing so is not mandatory) is, however, just as valid when programming in Swift.

11.11 Summary

Object-oriented programming languages such as Swift encourage the creation of classes to promote code reuse and the encapsulation of data within class instances. This chapter has covered the basic concepts of classes and instances within Swift together with an overview of stored and computed properties and both instance and type methods.

Chapter 12

12. An Introduction to Swift Subclassing and Extensions

In *The Basics of Object-Oriented Programming in Swift* we covered the basic concepts of object-oriented programming and worked through an example of creating and working with a new class using Swift. In that example, our new class was not derived from any base class and, as such, did not inherit any traits from a parent or super class. In this chapter we will provide an introduction to the concepts of subclassing, inheritance and extensions in Swift.

12.1 Inheritance, Classes and Subclasses

The concept of inheritance brings something of a real-world view to programming. It allows a class to be defined that has a certain set of characteristics (such as methods and properties) and then other classes to be created which are derived from that class. The derived class inherits all of the features of the parent class and typically then adds some features of its own.

By deriving classes we create what is often referred to as a *class hierarchy*. The class at the top of the hierarchy is known as the *base class* or *root class* and the derived classes as *subclasses* or *child classes*. Any number of subclasses may be derived from a class. The class from which a subclass is derived is called the *parent class* or *super class*.

Classes need not only be derived from a root class. For example, a subclass can also inherit from another subclass with the potential to create large and complex class hierarchies.

In Swift a subclass can only be derived from a single direct parent class. This is a concept referred to as *single inheritance*.

12.2 A Swift Inheritance Example

As with most programming concepts, the subject of inheritance in Swift is perhaps best illustrated with an example. In *The Basics of Object-Oriented Programming in Swift* we created a class named *BankAccount* designed to hold a bank account number and corresponding current balance. The BankAccount class contained both properties and instance methods. A simplified declaration for this class is reproduced below:

```
class BankAccount {

    var accountBalance: Float
    var accountNumber: Int

    init(number: Int, balance: Float)
    {
        accountNumber = number
        accountBalance = balance
```

```
    }

    func displayBalance()
    {
        print("Number \(accountNumber)")
        print("Current balance is \(accountBalance)")
    }
}
```

Though this is a somewhat rudimentary class, it does everything necessary if all you need it to do is store an account number and account balance. Suppose, however, that in addition to the BankAccount class you also needed a class to be used for savings accounts. A savings account will still need to hold an account number and a current balance and methods will still be needed to access that data. One option would be to create an entirely new class, one that duplicates all of the functionality of the BankAccount class together with the new features required by a savings account. A more efficient approach, however, would be to create a new class that is a *subclass* of the BankAccount class. The new class will then inherit all the features of the BankAccount class but can then be extended to add the additional functionality required by a savings account.

To create a subclass of BankAccount that we will call SavingsAccount, we simply declare the new class, this time specifying BankAccount as the parent class:

```
class SavingsAccount: BankAccount {

}
```

Note that although we have yet to add any instance variables or methods, the class has actually inherited all the methods and properties of the parent BankAccount class. We could, therefore, create an instance of the SavingsAccount class and set variables and call methods in exactly the same way we did with the BankAccount class in previous examples. That said, we haven't really achieved anything unless we actually take steps to extend the class.

12.3 Extending the Functionality of a Subclass

So far we have been able to create a subclass that contains all the functionality of the parent class. In order for this exercise to make sense, however, we now need to extend the subclass so that it has the features we need to make it useful for storing savings account information. To do this, we simply add the properties and methods that provide the new functionality, just as we would for any other class we might wish to create:

```
class SavingsAccount: BankAccount {

    var interestRate: Float = 0.0

    func calculateInterest() -> Float
    {
        return interestRate * accountBalance
    }
}
```

12.4 Overriding Inherited Methods

When using inheritance it is not unusual to find a method in the parent class that almost does what you need, but requires modification to provide the precise functionality you require. That being said, it is also possible you'll inherit a method with a name that describes exactly what you want to do, but it actually does not come close to doing what you need. One option in this scenario would be to ignore the inherited method and write a new method with an entirely new name. A better option is to *override* the inherited method and write a new version of it in the subclass.

Before proceeding with an example, there are two rules that must be obeyed when overriding a method. First, the overriding method in the subclass must take exactly the same number and type of parameters as the overridden method in the parent class. Second, the new method must have the same return type as the parent method.

In our BankAccount class we have a method named *displayBalance* that displays the bank account number and current balance held by an instance of the class. In our SavingsAccount subclass we might also want to output the current interest rate assigned to the account. To achieve this, we simply declare a new version of the *displayBalance* method in our SavingsAccount subclass, prefixed with the *override* keyword:

```
class SavingsAccount: BankAccount {

    var interestRate: Float

    func calculateInterest() -> Float
    {
        return interestRate * accountBalance
    }

    override func displayBalance()
    {
       print("Number \(accountNumber)")
       print("Current balance is \(accountBalance)")
       print("Prevailing interest rate is \(interestRate)")
    }
}
```

It is also possible to make a call to the overridden method in the super class from within a subclass. The *displayBalance* method of the super class could, for example, be called to display the account number and balance, before the interest rate is displayed, thereby eliminating further code duplication:

```
override func displayBalance()
{
       super.displayBalance()
       print("Prevailing interest rate is \(interestRate)")
}
```

12.5 Initializing the Subclass

As the SavingsAccount class currently stands, it inherits the init initializer method from the parent BankAccount class which was implemented as follows:

```
init(number: Int, balance: Float)
{
        accountNumber = number
        accountBalance = balance
}
```

Clearly this method takes the necessary steps to initialize both the account number and balance properties of the class. The SavingsAccount class, however, contains an additional property in the form of the interest rate variable. The SavingsAccount class, therefore, needs its own initializer to ensure that the interestRate property is initialized when instances of the class are created. This method can perform this task and then make a call to the *init* method of the parent class to complete the initialization of the remaining variables:

```
class SavingsAccount: BankAccount {

    var interestRate: Float

    init(number: Int, balance: Float, rate: Float)
    {
        interestRate = rate
        super.init(number: number, balance: balance)
    }
.
.
.
}
```

Note that to avoid potential initialization problems, the *init* method of the superclass must always be called *after* the initialization tasks for the subclass have been completed.

12.6 Using the SavingsAccount Class

Now that we have completed work on our SavingsAccount class, the class can be used in some example code in much the same way as the parent BankAccount class:

```
let savings1 = SavingsAccount(number: 12311, balance: 600.00,
                                                rate: 0.07)

print(savings1.calculateInterest())
savings1.displayBalance()
```

12.7 Swift Class Extensions

Another way to add new functionality to a Swift class is to use an extension. Extensions can be used to add features such as methods, initializers, computed properties and subscripts to an existing class without the need to create and reference a subclass. This is particularly powerful when using extensions to add functionality to the built-in classes of the Swift language and iOS SDK frameworks.

A class is extended using the following syntax:

```
extension ClassName {
  // new features here
```

```
}
```

For the purposes of an example, assume that we need to add some additional properties to the standard Double class that will return the value raised to the power 2 and 3. This functionality can be added using the following extension declaration:

```
extension Double {

    var squared: Double {
        return self * self
    }

    var cubed: Double {
        return self * self * self
    }
}
```

Having extended the Double class with two new computed properties we can now make use of the properties as we would any other properties of the Double class:

```
let myValue: Double = 3.0
print(myValue.squared)
```

When executed, the print statement will output the value of 9.0. Note that when declaring the myValue constant we were able to declare it as being of type Double and access the extension properties without the need to use a subclass. In fact, because these properties were added as an extension, rather than using a subclass, we can now access these properties directly on Double values:

```
print(3.0.squared)
print(6.0.cubed)
```

Extensions provide a quick and convenient way to extend the functionality of a class without the need to use subclasses. That being said, subclasses still have some advantages over extensions. It is not possible, for example, to override the existing functionality of a class using an extension and extensions cannot contain stored properties.

12.8 Summary

Inheritance extends the concept of object re-use in object-oriented programming by allowing new classes to be derived from existing classes, with those new classes subsequently extended to add new functionality. When an existing class provides some, but not all, of the functionality required by the programmer, inheritance allows that class to be used as the basis for a new subclass. The new subclass will inherit all the capabilities of the parent class, but may then be extended to add the missing functionality.

Swift extensions provide a useful alternative option to adding functionality to existing classes without the need to create a subclass.

Chapter 13

13. Working with Array and Dictionary Collections in Swift

Arrays and dictionaries in Swift are objects that contain collections of other objects. In this chapter, we will cover some of the basics of working with arrays and dictionaries in Swift.

13.1 Mutable and Immutable Collections

Collections in Swift come in mutable and immutable forms. The contents of immutable collection instances cannot be changed after the object has been initialized. To make a collection immutable, assign it to a *constant* when it is created. Collections are mutable, on the other hand, if assigned to a *variable*.

13.2 Swift Array Initialization

An array is a data type designed specifically to hold multiple values in a single ordered collection. An array, for example, could be created to store a list of String values. Strictly speaking, a single Swift based array is only able to store values that are of the same type. An array declared as containing String values, therefore, could not also contain an Int value. As will be demonstrated later in this chapter, however, it is also possible to create mixed type arrays. The type of an array can be specified specifically using type annotation, or left to the compiler to identify using type inference.

An array may be initialized with a collection of values (referred to as an *array literal*) at creation time using the following syntax:

var variableName: [type] = [value 1, value2, value3, …….]

The following code creates a new array assigned to a variable (thereby making it mutable) that is initialized with three string values:

```
var treeArray = ["Pine", "Oak", "Yew"]
```

Alternatively, the same array could have been created immutably by assigning it to a constant:

```
let treeArray = ["Pine", "Oak", "Yew"]
```

In the above instance, the Swift compiler will use type inference to decide that the array contains values of String type and prevent values of other types being inserted into the array elsewhere within the application code.

Alternatively, the same array could have been declared using type annotation:

```
var treeArray: [String] = ["Pine", "Oak", "Yew"]
```

Arrays do not have to have values assigned at creation time. The following syntax can be used to create an empty array:

```
var variableName = [type]()
```

Consider, for example, the following code which creates an empty array designated to store floating point values and assigns it to a variable named priceArray:

```
var priceArray = [Float]()
```

Another useful initialization technique allows an array to be initialized to a certain size with each array element pre-set with a specified default value:

```
var nameArray = [String](repeating: "My String", count: 10)
```

When compiled and executed, the above code will create a new 10 element array with each element initialized with a string that reads "My String".

Finally, a new array may be created by adding together two existing arrays (assuming both arrays contain values of the same type). For example:

```
let firstArray = ["Red", "Green", "Blue"]
let secondArray = ["Indigo", "Violet"]

let thirdArray = firstArray + secondArray
```

13.3 Working with Arrays in Swift

Once an array exists, a wide range of methods and properties are provided for working with and manipulating the array content from within Swift code, a subset of which is as follows:

13.3.1 Array Item Count

A count of the items in an array can be obtained by accessing the array's count property:

```
var treeArray = ["Pine", "Oak", "Yew"]
var itemCount = treeArray.count

print(itemCount)
```

Whether or not an array is empty can be identified using the array's Boolean *isEmpty* property as follows:

```
var treeArray = ["Pine", "Oak", "Yew"]

if treeArray.isEmpty {
    // Array is empty
}
```

13.3.2 Accessing Array Items

A specific item in an array may be accessed or modified by referencing the item's position in the array index (where the first item in the array has index position 0) using a technique referred to as *index subscripting*. In the following code fragment, the string value contained at index position 2 in the array (in this case the string value "Yew") is output by the print call:

```
var treeArray = ["Pine", "Oak", "Yew"]

print(treeArray[2])
```

This approach can also be used to replace the value at an index location:

```
treeArray[1] = "Redwood"
```

The above code replaces the current value at index position 1 with a new String value that reads "Redwood".

13.4 Random Items and Shuffling

A call to the *shuffled()* method of an array object will return a new version of the array with the item ordering randomly shuffled, for example:

```
let shuffledTrees = treeArray.shuffled()
```

To access an array item at random, simply make a call to the *randomElement()* method:

```
let randomTree = treeArray.randomElement()
```

13.5 Appending Items to an Array

Items may be added to an array using either the *append* method or + and += operators. The following, for example, are all valid techniques for appending items to an array:

```
treeArray.append("Redwood")
treeArray += ["Redwood"]
treeArray += ["Redwood", "Maple", "Birch"]
```

13.5.1 Inserting and Deleting Array Items

New items may be inserted into an array by specifying the index location of the new item in a call to the array's *insert(at:)* method. An insertion preserves all existing elements in the array, essentially moving them to the right to accommodate the newly inserted item:

```
treeArray.insert("Maple", at: 0)
```

Similarly, an item at a specific array index position may be removed using the *remove(at:)* method call:

```
treeArray.remove(at: 2)
```

To remove the last item in an array, simply make a call to the array's *removeLast* method as follows:

```
treeArray.removeLast()
```

13.6 Array Iteration

The easiest way to iterate through the items in an array is to make use of the for-in looping syntax. The following code, for example, iterates through all of the items in a String array and outputs each item to the console panel:

```
let treeArray = ["Pine", "Oak", "Yew", "Maple", "Birch", "Myrtle"]

for tree in treeArray {
    print(tree)
}
```

Upon execution, the following output would appear in the console:

```
Pine
Oak
Yew
Maple
```

```
Birch
Myrtle
```

13.7 Creating Mixed Type Arrays

A mixed type array is an array that can contain elements of different class types. Clearly an array that is either declared or inferred as being of type String cannot subsequently be used to contain non-String class object instances. Interesting possibilities arise, however, when taking into consideration that Swift includes the *Any* type. Any is a special type in Swift that can be used to reference an object of a non-specific class type. It follows, therefore, that an array declared as containing Any object types can be used to store elements of mixed types. The following code, for example, declares and initializes an array containing a mixture of String, Int and Double elements:

```
let mixedArray: [Any] = ["A String", 432, 34.989]
```

The use of the Any type should be used with care since the use of Any masks from Swift the true type of the elements in such an array thereby leaving code prone to potential programmer error. It will often be necessary, for example, to manually cast the elements in an Any array to the correct type before working with them in code. Performing the incorrect cast for a specific element in the array will most likely cause the code to compile without error but crash at runtime. Consider, for the sake of an example, the following mixed type array:

```
let mixedArray: [Any] = [1, 2, 45, "Hello"]
```

Assume that, having initialized the array, we now need to iterate through the integer elements in the array and multiply them by 10. The code to achieve this might read as follows:

```
for object in mixedArray {
    print(object * 10)
}
```

When entered into Xcode, however, the above code will trigger a syntax error indicating that it is not possible to multiply operands of type Any and Int. In order to remove this error it will be necessary to downcast the array element to be of type Int:

```
for object in mixedArray {
    print(object as! Int * 10)
}
```

The above code will compile without error and work as expected until the final String element in the array is reached at which point the code will crash with the following error:

```
Could not cast value of type 'Swift.String' to 'Swift.Int'
```

The code will, therefore, need to be modified to be aware of the specific type of each element in the array. Clearly, there are both benefits and risks to using Any arrays in Swift.

13.8 Swift Dictionary Collections

String dictionaries allow data to be stored and managed in the form of key-value pairs. Dictionaries fulfill a similar purpose to arrays, except each item stored in the dictionary has associated with it a unique key (to be precise, the key is unique to the particular dictionary object) which can be used to reference and access the corresponding value. Currently only String, Int, Double and Bool data types are suitable for use as keys within a Swift dictionary.

13.9 Swift Dictionary Initialization

A dictionary is a data type designed specifically to hold multiple values in a single unordered collection. Each item in a dictionary consists of a key and an associated value. The data types of the key and value elements type may be specified specifically using type annotation, or left to the compiler to identify using type inference.

A new dictionary may be initialized with a collection of values (referred to as a *dictionary literal*) at creation time using the following syntax:

var *variableName*: [*key type*: *value type*] = [*key 1*: *value 1*, *key 2*: *value2* ….]

The following code creates a new array assigned to a variable (thereby making it mutable) that is initialized with four key-value pairs in the form of ISBN numbers acting as keys for corresponding book titles:

```
var bookDict = ["100-432112" : "Wind in the Willows",
                "200-532874" : "Tale of Two Cities",
                "202-546549" : "Sense and Sensibility",
                "104-109834" : "Shutter Island"]
```

In the above instance, the Swift compiler will use type inference to decide that both the key and value elements of the dictionary are of String type and prevent values or keys of other types being inserted into the dictionary.

Alternatively, the same array could have been declared using type annotation:

```
var bookDict: [String: String] =
                ["100-432112" : "Wind in the Willows",
                 "200-532874" : "Tale of Two Cities",
                 "202-546549" : "Sense and Sensibility",
                 "104-109834" : "Shutter Island"]
```

As with arrays, it is also possible to create an empty dictionary, the syntax for which reads as follows:

var *variableName* = [*key type*: *value type*]()

The following code creates an empty dictionary designated to store integer keys and string values:

```
var myDictionary = [Int: String]()
```

13.10 Sequence-based Dictionary Initialization

Dictionaries may also be initialized using sequences to represent the keys and values. This is achieved using the Swift *zip()* function, passing through the keys and corresponding values. In the following example, a dictionary is created using two arrays:

```
let keys = ["100-432112", "200-532874", "202-546549", "104-109834"]
let values = ["Wind in the Willows", "Tale of Two Cities",
                        "Sense and Sensibility", "Shutter Island"]

let bookDict = Dictionary(uniqueKeysWithValues: zip(keys, values))
```

This approach allows keys and values to be generated programmatically. In the following example, a number range starting at 1 is being specified for the keys instead of using an array of predefined keys:

```
let values = ["Wind in the Willows", "Tale of Two Cities",
        "Sense and Sensibility", "Shutter Island"]
```

```
let bookDict = Dictionary(uniqueKeysWithValues: zip(1..., values))
```

The above code is a much cleaner equivalent to the following dictionary declaration:

```
var bookDict = [1 : "Wind in the Willows",
                2 : "Tale of Two Cities",
                3 : "Sense and Sensibility",
                4 : "Shutter Island"]
```

13.11 Dictionary Item Count

A count of the items in a dictionary can be obtained by accessing the dictionary's count property:

```
print(bookDict.count)
```

13.12 Accessing and Updating Dictionary Items

A specific value may be accessed or modified using key subscript syntax to reference the corresponding key. The following code references a key known to be in the bookDict dictionary and outputs the associated value (in this case the book entitled "A Tale of Two Cities"):

```
print(bookDict["200-532874"])
```

When accessing dictionary entries in this way, it is also possible to declare a default value to be used in the event that the specified key does not return a value:

```
print(bookDict["999-546547", default: "Book not found"])
```

Since the dictionary does not contain an entry for the specified key, the above code will output text which reads "Book not found".

Indexing by key may also be used when updating the value associated with a specified key, for example, to change the title of the same book from "A Tale of Two Cities" to "Sense and Sensibility"):

```
bookDict["200-532874"] = "Sense and Sensibility"
```

The same result is also possible by making a call to the *updateValue(forKey:)* method, passing through the key corresponding to the value to be changed:

```
bookDict.updateValue("The Ruins", forKey: "200-532874")
```

13.13 Adding and Removing Dictionary Entries

Items may be added to a dictionary using the following key subscripting syntax:

dictionaryVariable[*key*] = *value*

For example, to add a new key-value pair entry to the books dictionary:

```
bookDict["300-898871"] = "The Overlook"
```

Removal of a key-value pair from a dictionary may be achieved either by assigning a *nil* value to the entry, or via a call to the *removeValueForKey* method of the dictionary instance. Both code lines below achieve the same result of removing the specified entry from the books dictionary:

```
bookDict["300-898871"] = nil
bookDict.removeValue(forKey: "300-898871")
```

13.14 Dictionary Iteration

As with arrays, it is possible to iterate through the dictionary entries by making use of the for-in looping syntax. The following code, for example, iterates through all of the entries in the books dictionary, outputting both the key and value for each entry panel:

```
for (bookid, title) in bookDict {
  print("Book ID: \(bookid) Title: \(title)")
}
```

Upon execution, the following output would appear in the console:

```
Book ID: 100-432112 Title: Wind in the Willows
Book ID: 200-532874 Title: The Ruins
Book ID: 104-109834 Title: Shutter Island
Book ID: 202-546549 Title: Sense and Sensibility
```

13.15 Summary

Collections in Swift take the form of either dictionaries or arrays. Both provide a way to collect together multiple items within a single object. Arrays provide a way to store an ordered collection of items where those items are accessed by an index value corresponding to the item position in the array. Dictionaries provide a platform for storing key-value pairs, where the key is used to gain access to the stored value. Iteration through the elements of Swift collections can be achieved using the for-in loop construct.

Chapter 14

14. Understanding Error Handling in Swift 4

In a perfect world, a running iOS app would never encounter an error. The reality, however, is that it is impossible to guarantee that an error of some form or another will not occur at some point during the execution of the app. It is essential, therefore, to ensure that the code of an app is implemented such that it gracefully handles any errors that may occur. Since the introduction of Swift 2, the task of handling errors has become much easier for the iOS app developer.

This chapter will cover the handling of errors using Swift and introduce topics such as *error types, throwing methods and functions*, the *guard* and *defer* statements and *do-catch* statements.

14.1 Understanding Error Handling

No matter how carefully Swift code is designed and implemented, there will invariably be situations that are beyond the control of the app. An app that relies on an active internet connection cannot, for example, control the loss of signal on an iPhone device, or prevent the user from enabling "airplane mode". What the app can do, however, is to implement robust handling of the error (for example displaying a message indicating to the user that the app requires an active internet connection to proceed).

There are two sides to handling errors within Swift. The first involves triggering (or *throwing*) an error when the desired results are not achieved within the method of an iOS app. The second involves catching and handling the error after it is thrown by a method.

When an error is thrown, the error will be of a particular error type which can be used to identify the specific nature of the error and used to decide on the most appropriate course of action to be taken. The error type value can be any value that conforms to the ErrorType protocol.

In addition to implementing methods in an app to throw errors when necessary, it is important to be aware that a number of API methods in the iOS SDK (particularly those relating to file handling) will throw errors which will need to be handled within the code of the app.

14.2 Declaring Error Types

For the sake of an example, consider a method that is required to transfer a file to a remote server. Such a method might fail to transfer the file for a variety of reasons such as there being no network connection, the connection being too slow or the failure to find the file to be transferred. All of these possible errors could be represented within an enumeration that conforms to the Error protocol as follows:

```
enum FileTransferError: Error {
    case noConnection
    case lowBandwidth
    case fileNotFound
}
```

Once an error type has been declared, it can be used within a method when throwing errors.

14.3 Throwing an Error

A method or function declares that it can throw an error using the *throws* keyword. For example:

```
func transferFile() throws {
}
```

In the event that the function or method returns a result, the *throws* keyword is placed before the return type as follows:

```
func transferFile() throws -> Bool {
}
```

Once a method has been declared as being able to throw errors, code can then be added to throw the errors when they are encountered. This is achieved using the *throw* statement in conjunction with the *guard* statement. The following code declares some constants to serve as status values and then implements the guard and throw behavior for the method:

```
let connectionOK = true
let connectionSpeed = 30.00
let fileFound = false

enum FileTransferError: Error {
    case noConnection
    case lowBandwidth
    case fileNotFound
}

func fileTransfer() throws {

    guard connectionOK else {
        throw FileTransferError.noConnection
    }

    guard connectionSpeed > 30 else {
        throw FileTransferError.lowBandwidth
    }

    guard fileFound else {
        throw FileTransferError.fileNotFound
    }
}
```

Within the body of the method, each guard statement checks a condition for a true or false result. In the event of a false result, the code contained within the *else* body is executed. In the case of a false result, the throw statement is used to throw one of the error values contained in the FileTransferError enumeration.

14.4 Calling Throwing Methods and Functions

Once a method or function is declared as throwing errors, it can no longer be called in the usual manner. Calls to such methods must now be prefixed by the *try* statement as follows:

```
try fileTransfer()
```

In addition to using the try statement, the call must also be made from within a *do-catch* statement to catch and handle any errors that may be thrown. Consider, for example, that the *fileTransfer* method needs to be called from within a method named *sendFile*. The code within this method might be implemented as follows:

```
func sendFile() -> String {

    do {
        try fileTransfer()
    } catch FileTransferError.noConnection {
        return("No Network Connection")
    } catch FileTransferError.lowBandwidth {
        return("File Transfer Speed too Low")
    } catch FileTransferError.fileNotFound {
        return("File not Found")
    } catch {
        return("Unknown error")
    }

    return("Successful transfer")
}
```

The method calls the *fileTransfer* method from within a *do-catch* statement which, in turn, includes catch conditions for each of the three possible error conditions. In each case, the method simply returns a string value containing a description of the error. In the event that no error was thrown, a string value is returned indicating a successful file transfer. Note that a fourth catch condition is included with no pattern matching. This is a "catch all" statement that ensures that any errors not matched by the preceding catch statements are also handled. This is required because do-catch statements must be exhaustive (in other words constructed so as to catch all possible error conditions).

14.5 Accessing the Error Object

When a method call fails, it will invariably return an Error object identifying the nature of the failure. A common requirement within the catch statement is to gain access to this object so that appropriate corrective action can be taken within the app code. The following code demonstrates how such an error object is accessed from within a catch statement when attempting to create a new file system directory:

```
do {
    try filemgr.createDirectory(atPath: newDir,
                    withIntermediateDirectories: true,
                    attributes: nil)
    } catch let error {
        print("Error: \(error.localizedDescription)")
}
```

14.6 Disabling Error Catching

A throwing method may be forced to run without the need to enclose the call within a do-catch statement by using the *try!* statement as follows:

```
try! fileTransfer
```

In using this approach we are informing the compiler that we know with absolute certainty that the method call will not result in an error being thrown. In the event that an error is thrown when using this technique, the code will fail with a runtime error. As such, this approach should be used sparingly.

14.7 Using the defer Statement

The previously implemented *sendFile* method demonstrated a common scenario when handling errors. Each of the catch clauses in the do-catch statement contained a return statement that returned control to the calling method. In such a situation, however, it might be useful to be able to perform some other task before control is returned and regardless of the type of error that was encountered. The *sendFile* method might, for example, need to remove temporary files before returning. This behavior can be achieved using the *defer* statement.

The defer statement allows a sequence of code statements to be declared as needing to be run as soon as the method returns. In the following code, the *sendFile* method has been modified to include a defer statement:

```
func sendFile() -> String {

    defer {
        removeTmpFiles()
        closeConnection()
    }

    do {
        try fileTransfer()
    } catch FileTransferError.NoConnection {
        return("No Network Connection")
    } catch FileTransferError.LowBandwidth {
        return("File Transfer Speed too Low")
    } catch FileTransferError.FileNotFound {
        return("File not Found")
    } catch {
        return("Unknown error")
    }

    return("Successful transfer")
}
```

With the defer statement now added, the calls to the *removeTmpFiles* and *closeConnection* methods will always be made before the method returns, regardless of which return call gets triggered.

14.8 Summary

Error handling is an essential part of creating robust and reliable iOS apps. Since the introduction of Swift 2 it is now much easier to both trigger and handle errors. Error types are created using values that conform to the ErrorType protocol and are most commonly implemented as enumerations. Methods and functions that throw errors are declared as such using the *throw* keyword. The *guard* and *throw* statements are used within the body of these methods or functions to throw errors based on the error type.

A throwable method or function is called using the *try* statement which must be encapsulated within a do-catch statement. A do-catch statement consists of an exhaustive list of catch pattern constructs, each of which contains the code to be executed in the event of a particular error being thrown. Cleanup tasks can be defined to be executed when a method returns through the use of the *defer* statement.

Chapter 15

15. The iOS 12 Application and Development Architecture

So far we have covered a considerable amount of ground intended to provide a sound foundation of knowledge on which to begin building iOS 12 based apps. Before plunging into more complex apps, however, it is vital that you have a basic understanding of some key methodologies associated with the overall architecture of iOS applications.

These methodologies, also referred to as *design patterns,* clearly define how your applications should be designed and implemented in terms of code structure. The patterns we will explore in this chapter are *Model View Controller (MVC)*, *Subclassing*, *Delegation* and *Target-Action*.

It is also useful to gain an understanding of how iOS itself is structured in terms of operating system layers.

If you are new to these concepts this can seem a little confusing to begin with. Much of this will become clearer, however, once we start working on some examples in subsequent chapters.

15.1 An Overview of the iOS 12 Operating System Architecture

iOS consists of a number of different software layers, each of which provides programming frameworks for the development of applications that run on top of the underlying hardware.

These operating system layers can be presented diagrammatically as illustrated in Figure 15-1:

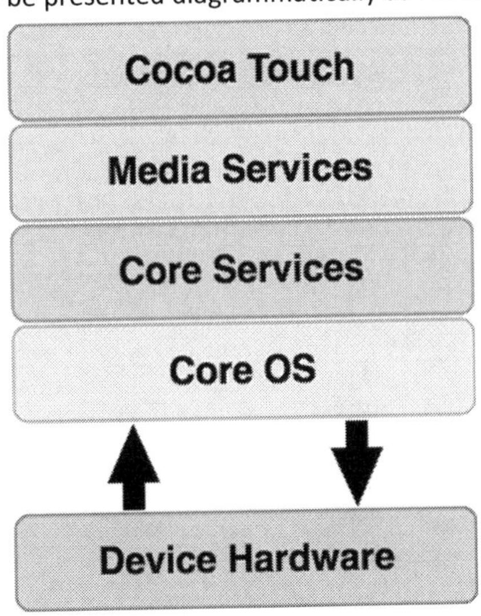

Figure 15-1

Some diagrams designed to graphically depict the iOS software stack show an additional box positioned above the Cocoa Touch layer to indicate the applications running on the device. In the above diagram we have not done so since this would suggest that the only interface available to the app is Cocoa Touch. In practice, an app can directly call down to any of the layers of the stack to perform tasks on the physical device.

That said, however, each operating system layer provides an increasing level of abstraction away from the complexity of working with the hardware. As an iOS developer you should, therefore, always look for solutions to your programming goals in the frameworks located in the higher level iOS layers before resorting to writing code that reaches down to the lower level layers. In general, the higher level of layer you program to, the less effort and fewer lines of code you will have to write to achieve your objective. And as any veteran programmer will tell you, the less code you have to write the less opportunity you have to introduce bugs.

15.2 Model View Controller (MVC)

In the days before object-oriented programming (and even for a time after object-oriented programming became popular) there was a tendency to develop applications where the code for the user interface was tied tightly to the code containing the application logic and data handling. This coupling made application code difficult to maintain and locked the application to a single user interface. If, for example, an application written for Microsoft Windows needed to be migrated to macOS, all the code written specifically for the Windows UI toolkits had to be ripped out from amongst the data and logic code and replaced with the macOS equivalent. If the application then needed to be turned into a web based solution, the process would have to be repeated again. Attempts to achieve this feat were usually found to be prohibitively expensive and ultimately ended up with the applications being completely re-written each time a new platform needed to be targeted.

The goal of the MVC design pattern is to divorce the logic and data handling code of an application from the presentation code. In this concept, the Model encapsulates the data for the application, the View presents and manages the user interface and the Controller provides the basic logic for the application and acts as the go-between, providing instructions to the Model based on user interactions with the View and updating the View to reflect responses from the Model. The true value of this approach is that the Model knows absolutely nothing about the presentation of the application. It just knows how to store and handle data and perform certain tasks when called upon by the Controller. Similarly, the View knows nothing about the data and logic model of the application.

Within the context of an object-oriented programming environment such as the iOS SDK and Swift, the Model, View and Controller components are objects. It is also worth pointing out that applications are not restricted to a single model, view and controller. In fact, an app can consist of multiple view objects, controller objects and model objects.

The way that a view controller object interacts with a Model is through the methods and properties exposed by that model object. This, in fact, is no different from the way one object interacts with another in any object-oriented programming environment.

In terms of the view controller's interactions with the view, however, things get a little more complicated. In practice, this is achieved using the *Target-Action pattern*, together with *Outlets* and *Actions*.

15.3 The Target-Action pattern, IBOutlets and IBActions

When you create an iOS app you will typically design the user interface (the view) using the Interface Builder tool and write the view controller and model code in Swift using the Xcode code editor. The previous section looked briefly at how the view controller interacts with the model. In this section we will look at how the view created in Interface Builder and our view controller code interact with each other.

When a user interacts with objects in the view, for example touching and releasing a button control, an *event* is triggered (in this case the event is called a *Touch Up Inside* event). The purpose of the *Target-Action* pattern is to allow you to specify what happens when such events are triggered. In other words, this is how you connect the objects in the user interface you have designed in the Interface Builder tool to the back end Swift code you have written in the Xcode environment. Specifically, this allows you to define which method of which controller object gets called when a user interacts in a certain way with a view object.

The process of wiring up a view object to call a specific method on a view controller object is achieved using something called an *Action.* An action is a method defined within a view controller object that is designed to be called when an event is triggered in a view object. This allows us to connect a view object created within Interface Builder to the code that we have written in the view controller class. This is one of the ways that we bridge the separation between the *View* and the *Controller* in our MVC design pattern. As we will see in *Creating an Interactive iOS 12 App*, action methods are declared using the *IBAction* keyword.

The opposite of an *Action* is the *Outlet*. As previously described, an Action allows a view object to call a method on a controller object. An Outlet, on the other hand, allows a view controller object method to directly access the properties of a view object. A view controller might, for example, need to set the text on a UILabel object. In order to do so an Outlet must first have been defined using the *IBOutlet* keyword. In programming terms, an *IBOutlet* is simply an instance variable that references the view object to which access is required.

15.4 Subclassing

Subclassing is an important feature of any object-oriented programming environment and the iOS SDK is no exception to this rule. Subclassing allows us to create a new class by deriving from an existing class and then extending the functionality. In so doing we get all the functionality of the parent class combined with the ability to extend the new class with additional methods and properties.

Subclassing is typically used where a pre-existing class does most, but not all, of what you need. By subclassing we get all that existing functionality without having to duplicate it and simply add on the functionality that was missing.

We will see an example of subclassing in the context of iOS development when we start to work with view controllers. The UIKit Framework contains a class called the UIViewController. This is a generic view controller from which we will create a subclass so that we can add our own methods and properties.

15.5 Delegation

Delegation allows an object to pass the responsibility for performing one or more tasks on to another object. This allows the behavior of an object to be modified without having to go through the process of subclassing it.

A prime example of delegation can be seen in the case of the UIApplication class. The UIApplication class, of which every iOS application must have one (and only one) instance, is responsible for the control and operation of the application within the iOS environment. Much of what the UIApplication object does happens in the background. There are, however, instances where it gives us the opportunity to include our own functionality into the mix. UIApplication allows us to do this by delegating some methods to us. As an example, UIApplication delegates the *didFinishLaunchingWithOptions* method to us so that we can write code to perform specific tasks when the app first loads (for example taking the user back to the point they were at when they last exited). If you still have a copy of the Hello World project created earlier in this book you will see the template for this method in the *AppDelegate.swift* file.

15.6 Summary

In this chapter we have provided an overview of a number of design patterns and discussed the importance of these patterns in terms of structuring iOS applications. While these patterns may seem unclear to some, the relevance and implementation of such concepts will become clearer as we progress through the examples included in subsequent chapters of this book.

Chapter 16

16. Creating an Interactive iOS 12 App

In the previous chapter we looked at the design patterns that we will need to learn and use regularly in the course of developing iOS 12 based applications. In this chapter we will work through a detailed example intended to demonstrate the View-Controller relationship together with the implementation of the Target-Action pattern to create an example interactive iOS 12 application.

16.1 Creating the New Project

The purpose of the application we are going to create is to perform unit conversions from Fahrenheit to Centigrade. Obviously the first step is to create a new Xcode project to contain our application. Start Xcode and, on the Welcome screen, select *Create a new Xcode project.* On the template screen make sure iOS is selected in the toolbar before choosing the *Single View App* template. Click *Next,* set the product name to *UnitConverter,* enter your company identifier and select your development team if you have one. Before clicking *Next*, change the *Language* menu to Swift. On the final screen, choose a location in which to store the project files and click on *Create* to proceed to the main Xcode project window.

16.2 Creating the User Interface

Before we begin developing the logic for our interactive application we are going to start by designing the user interface. When we created the new project, Xcode generated a storyboard file for us and named it *Main.storyboard.* It is within this file that we will create our user interface, so select this file from the project navigator in the left-hand panel to load it into Interface Builder.

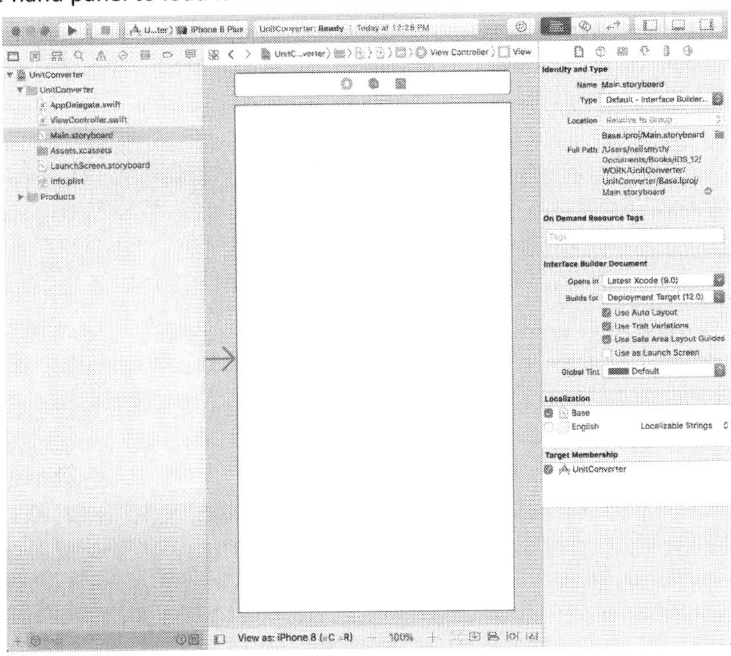

Figure 16-1

Display the Library panel by clicking on the toolbar button shown in Figure 16-2 while holding down the Option key and drag a Text Field object from the library onto the View design area:

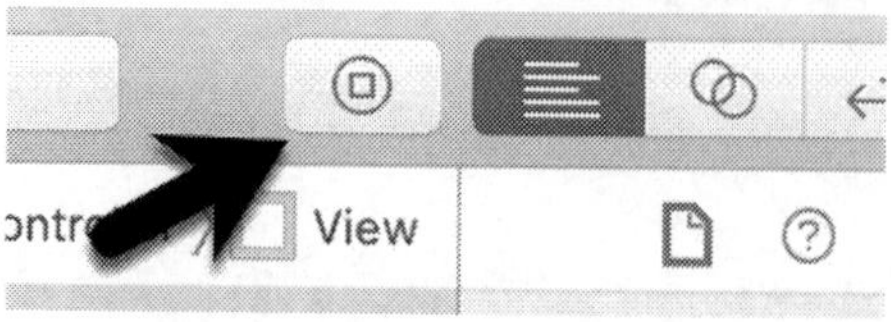

Figure 16-2

Resize the object and position it so that it appears as outlined in Figure 16-3.

Figure 16-3

Within the Attributes Inspector panel (*View -> Utilities -> Show Attributes Inspector*), type the words *Enter temperature* into the *Placeholder* text field. This text will then appear in a light gray color in the text field as a visual cue to the user. Since only numbers and decimal points will be required to be input for the temperature, locate the *Keyboard Type* property in the Attributes Inspector panel and change the setting to *Numbers and Punctuation*.

Now that we have created the text field into which the user will enter a temperature value, the next step is to add a Button object which may be pressed to initiate the conversion. To achieve this, drag and drop a *Button* object from the Library to the View. Double-click the button object so that it changes to text edit mode and type the word *Convert* onto the button. Finally, select the button and drag it beneath the text field until the blue dotted line appears indicating it is centered horizontally in relation to the containing view before releasing the mouse button.

The last user interface object we need to add is the label where the result of the conversion will be displayed. Add this by dragging a Label object from the Library panel to the View and position it beneath the button. Stretch the width of the label so that it is approximately two thirds of the overall width of the view and reposition it using the blue guidelines to ensure it is centered in relation to the containing view. Modify the Alignment attribute for the label object so that the text is centered.

Double-click on the label to highlight the text and press the backspace key to clear it (we will set the text from within a method of our View Controller class when the conversion calculation has been performed). Though the label is now no longer visible when it is not selected, it is still present in the view. If you click where it is located it will be highlighted with the resize dots visible. It is also possible to view the layout outlines of all the views in the scene, including the label, by selecting the *Editor -> Canvas -> Show Bounds Rectangles* menu option.

In order for the user interface design layout to adapt to the many different device orientations and iPad and iPhone screen sizes it will be necessary to add some Auto Layout constraints to the views in the storyboard. Auto Layout will be covered in detail in subsequent chapters, but for the purposes of this example, we will request that Interface Builder add what it considers to be the appropriate constraints for this layout. In the lower right-hand corner of the Interface Builder panel is a toolbar. Click on the background view of the current scene followed by the *Resolve Auto Layout Issues* button as highlighted in Figure 16-4:

Figure 16-4

From the menu, select the *Reset to Suggested Constraints* option listed under *All Views in View Controller*:

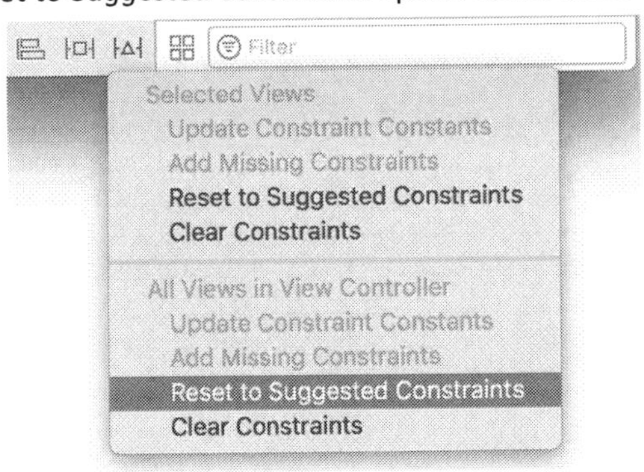

Figure 16-5

At this point the user interface design phase of our project is complete and the view should appear as illustrated in Figure 16-6. We now are ready to try out a test build and run.

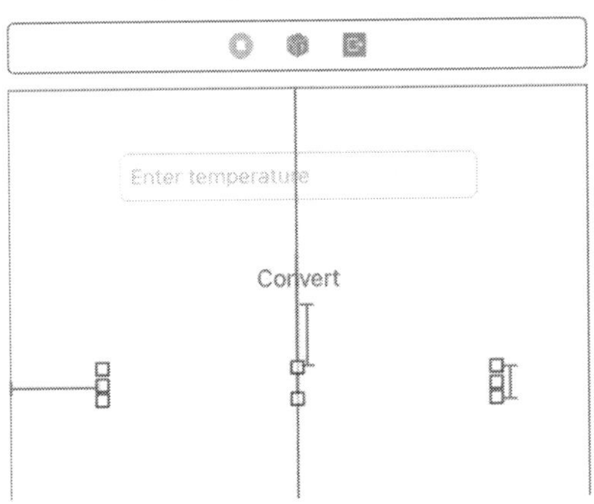

Figure 16-6

16.3 Building and Running the Sample Application

Before we move on to implementing the view controller code for our application and then connecting it to the user interface we have designed we should first perform a test build and run of the application so far. Click on the run button located in the toolbar (the triangular "play" button) to compile the application and run it in the simulator or a connected iOS device. If you are not happy with the way your interface looks feel free to reload it into Interface Builder and make improvements. Assuming the user interface appears to your satisfaction we are ready to start writing some Swift code to add some logic to our controller.

16.4 Adding Actions and Outlets

When the user enters a temperature value into the text field and touches the convert button we need to trigger an action which will perform a calculation to convert the temperature. The result of that calculation will then be presented to the user via the label object. The *Action* will be in the form of a method which we will declare and implement in our View Controller class. Access to the text field and label objects from the view controller method will be implemented through the use of *Outlets*.

Before we begin, now is a good time to highlight an example of the use of subclassing as previously described in *The iOS 12 Application and Development Architecture*, the UIKit Framework contains a class called UIViewController which provides the basic foundation for adding view controllers to an application. In order to create a functional application, however, we inevitably need to add functionality specific to our application to this generic view controller class. This is achieved by subclassing the UIViewController class and extending it with the additional functionality we need.

When we created our new project, Xcode anticipated our needs and automatically created a subclass of UIViewController and named it ViewController. In so doing, Xcode also created a source code file named *ViewController.swift*.

Selecting the *ViewController.swift* file in the Xcode project navigator panel will display the contents of the file in the editing pane:

```
import UIKit

class ViewController: UIViewController {

    override func viewDidLoad() {
        super.viewDidLoad()
        // Do any additional setup after loading the view, typically from a
nib.
    }
}
```

As we can see from the above code, a new class called ViewController has been created that is a subclass of the UIViewController class belonging to the UIKit framework.

The next step is to extend the subclass to include the two outlets and our action method. This could be achieved by manually declaring the outlets and actions within the *ViewController.swift* file. A much easier approach is to use the Xcode Assistant Editor to do this for us.

With the *Main.storyboard* file selected, display the Assistant Editor by selecting the *View -> Assistant Editor -> Show Assistant Editor* menu option. Alternatively, it may also be displayed by selecting the center button (the one containing an image of interlocking circles) of the row of Editor toolbar buttons in the top right-hand corner of the main Xcode window as illustrated in the following figure:

Figure 16-7

In the event that multiple Assistant Editor panels are required, additional tiles may be added using the *View -> Assistant Editor -> Add Assistant Editor* menu option.

By default, the editor panel will appear to the right of the main editing panel in the Xcode window. For example, in Figure 16-8 the panel (marked A) to the immediate right of the Interface Builder panel is the Assistant Editor:

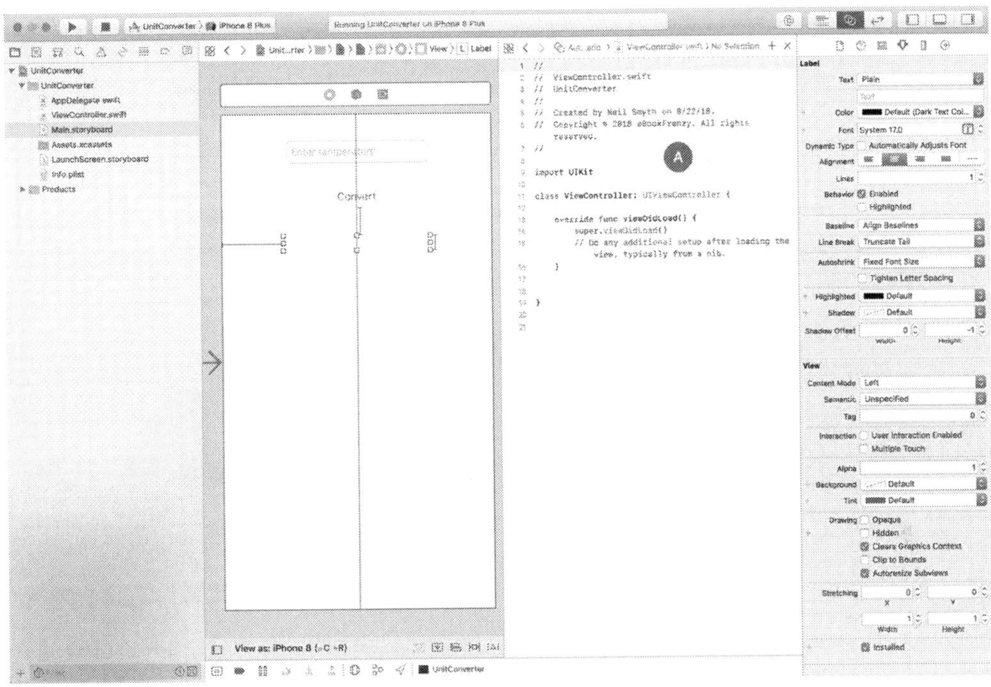

Figure 16-8

By default, the Assistant Editor will be in *Automatic* mode, whereby it automatically attempts to display the correct source file based on the currently selected item in Interface Builder. If the correct file is not displayed, use the toolbar along the top of the editor panel to select the correct file. The small instance of the Assistant Editor icon in this toolbar can be used to switch to *Manual* mode allowing the file to be selected from a pull-right menu containing all the source files in the project.

Make sure that the *ViewController.swift* file is displayed in the Assistant Editor and establish an outlet for the Text Field object by Ctrl-clicking on the Text Field object in the view and dragging the resulting line to the area immediately beneath the class declaration line in the Assistant Editor panel as illustrated in Figure 16-9:

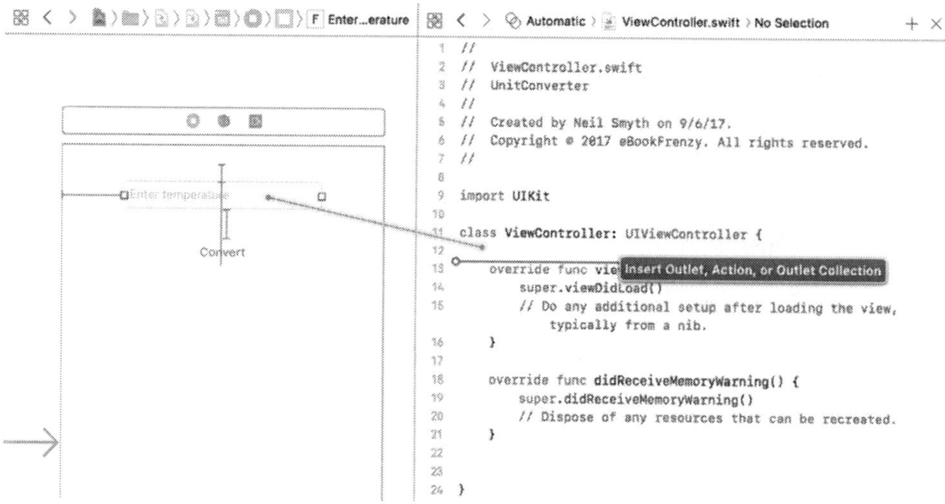

Figure 16-9

Upon releasing the line, the configuration panel illustrated in Figure 16-10 will appear requesting details about the outlet to be defined.

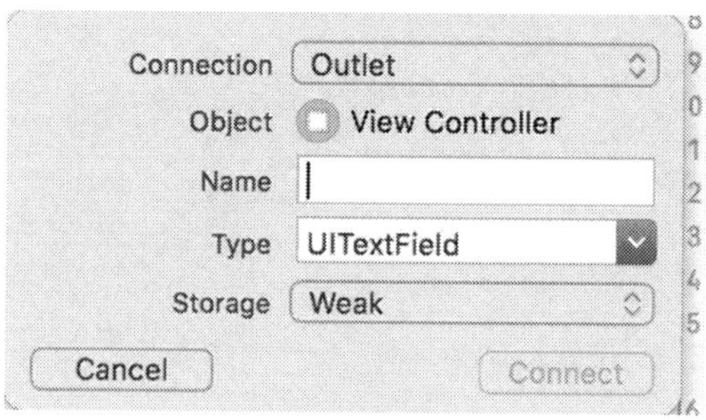

Figure 16-10

Since this is an outlet, the *Connection* menu should be left as *Outlet*. The type and storage values are also correct for this type of outlet. The only task that remains is to enter a name for the outlet, so in the *Name* field enter *tempText* before clicking on the *Connect* button.

Once the connection has been established, select the *ViewController.swift* file and note that the outlet property has been declared for us by the assistant:

```
import UIKit

class ViewController: UIViewController {

    @IBOutlet weak var tempText: UITextField!
.
.
.
}
```

Repeat the above steps to establish an outlet for the Label object named *resultLabel.*

Next we need to establish the action that will be called when the user touches the Convert button in our user interface. The steps to declare an action using the Assistant Editor are essentially the same as those for an outlet. Once again, select the *Main.storyboard* file, but this time Ctrl-click on the button object. Drag the resulting line to the area beneath the existing *viewDidLoad* method in the Assistant Editor panel before releasing it. The connection box will once again appear. Since we are creating an action rather than an outlet, change the *Connection* menu to *Action.* Name the action *convertTemp* and make sure the *Event* type is set to *Touch Up Inside*:

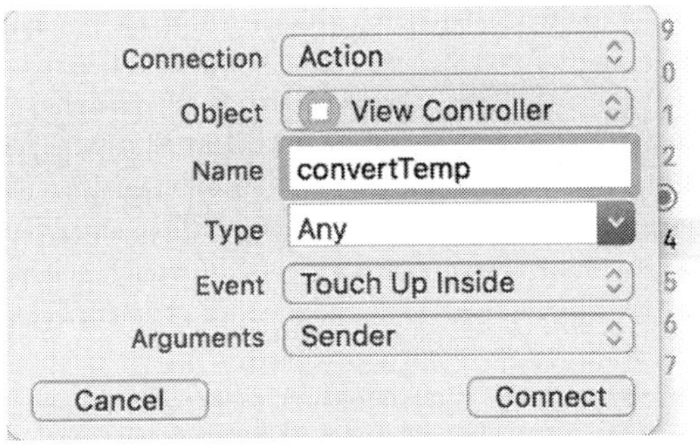

Figure 16-11

Click on the *Connect* button to create the action.

Close the Assistant Editor panel, select the *ViewController.swift* file and note that a stub method for the action has now been declared for us by the assistant:

```
@IBAction func convertTemp(_ sender: Any) {
}
```

All that remains is to write the Swift code in the action method to perform the conversion:

```
@IBAction func convertTemp(_ sender: Any) {

    guard let tempString = tempText.text else { return }

    if let fahrenheit = Double(tempString) {
        let celsius = (fahrenheit - 32)/1.8
        let resultText = "Celsius \(celsius)"
        resultLabel.text = resultText
    }
}
```

Before we proceed it is probably a good idea to pause and explain what is happening in the above code. Those already familiar with Swift, however, may skip the next few paragraphs.

In this file we are implementing the *convertTemp* method, a template for which was created for us by the Assistant Editor. This method takes as a single argument a reference to the *sender.* The sender is the object that triggered the call to the method (in this case our Button object). The sender is declared as being of type *Any* (different type options are available using the *Type* menu located in the connection dialog shown in Figure 16-11 above). This is a special type which can be used to represent any type of class. While we won't be using this object in the current example, this can be used to create a general purpose method in which the behavior of the method changes depending on how (i.e. via which object) it was called. We could, for example, create two buttons labeled *Convert to Fahrenheit* and *Convert to Celsius* respectively, each of which calls the same *convertTemp* method. The method would then access the *sender* object to identify which button triggered the event and perform the corresponding type of unit conversion.

Within the body of the method we use a guard statement to verify that the tempText view contains some text. If it does not, the method simply returns.

Next, dot notation is used to access the *text* property (which holds the text displayed in the text field) of the UITextField object to access the text in the field. This property is itself an object of type String. This string is converted to be of type Double and assigned to a new constant named *fahrenheit*. Since it is possible that the user has not entered a valid number into the field the use of optional binding is employed to prevent an attempt to perform the conversion on invalid data.

Having extracted the text entered by the user and converted it to a number, we then perform the conversion to Celsius and store the result in another constant named *celsius*. Next, we create a new string object and initialize it with text comprising the word Celsius and the result of our conversion. In doing so, we declare a constant named *resultText*.

Finally, we use dot notation to assign the new string to the text property of our UILabel object so that it is displayed to the user.

16.5 Building and Running the Finished Application

From within the Xcode project window click on the run button located in the Xcode toolbar (the triangular "play" style button) to compile the application and run it in the simulator or a connected iOS device. Once the application is running, click inside the text field and enter a Fahrenheit temperature. Next, click on the Convert button to display the equivalent temperature in Celsius. Assuming all went to plan your application should appear as outlined in the following figure:

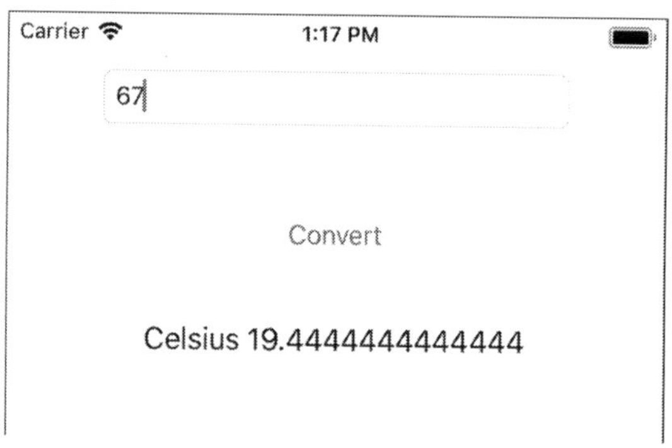

Figure 16-12

16.6 Hiding the Keyboard

The final step in the application implementation is to add a mechanism for hiding the keyboard. Ideally, the keyboard should withdraw from view when the user touches the background view or taps the return key on the keyboard (note when testing on the simulator that the keyboard may not appear unless the *Hardware -> Keyboard -> Toggle Software Keyboard* menu option is selected).

To achieve this, we will begin by implementing the *touchesBegan* event handler method on the view controller in the *ViewController.swift* file as follows:

```
override func touchesBegan(_ touches: Set<UITouch>, with event: UIEvent?) {
    tempText.endEditing(true)
}
```

When the background view is touched by the user, the keyboard will now be hidden.

The next step is to hide the keyboard when the return key is tapped. To do this, display the Assistant Editor and Ctrl-click and drag from the Text Field to a position beneath the *viewDidLoad* method within the *ViewController.swift* file. On releasing the line, change the settings in the connection dialog to establish an Action connection named *textFieldReturn* for the *Did End on Exit* event with the Type menu set to UITextField as shown in Figure 16-13 and click on the *Connect* button to establish the connection.

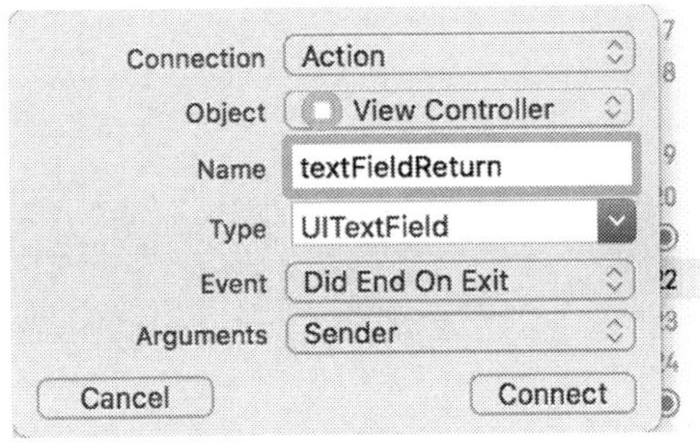

Figure 16-13

Select the *ViewController.swift* file in the project navigator, locate and edit the *textFieldReturn* stub method so that it now reads as follows:

```
@IBAction func textFieldReturn(_ sender: UITextField) {
    _ = sender.resignFirstResponder()
}
```

In the above method we are making a call to the *resignFirstResponder* method of the object that triggered the event. The *first responder* is the object with which the user is currently interacting (in this instance, the virtual keyboard displayed on the device screen). Note that the result of the method call is assigned to a value represented by the underscore character (_). The *resignFirstResponder()* method returns a Boolean value indicating whether or not the resign request was successful. Assigning the result in this way indicates to the Swift compiler that we are intentionally ignoring this value.

Save the code and then build and run the application. When the application starts up, select the text field so that the keyboard appears. Touching any area of the background or tapping the return key should cause the keyboard to disappear.

16.7 Summary

In this chapter we have put into practice some of the theory covered in previous chapters, in particular the separation of the view from the controller, the use of subclassing and the implementation of the Target-Action pattern through the use of actions and outlets.

This chapter also provided steps on how to hide the keyboard when either the keyboard Return key or the background view are touched by the user.

Chapter 17

17. Understanding iOS 12 Views, Windows and the View Hierarchy

In the preceding chapters we have created a number of user interfaces in the course of building our example iOS applications. In doing so, we have been using *views* and *windows* without actually providing much in the way of explanation. Before moving on to other topics, however, it is important to have a clear understanding of the concepts behind the way that iOS user interfaces are constructed and managed. In this chapter we will cover the concepts of *views, windows* and *view hierarchies.*

17.1 An Overview of Views and the UIKit Class Hierarchy

Views are visual objects that are assembled to create the user interface of an iOS application. They essentially define what happens within a specified rectangular area of the screen, both visually and in terms of user interaction. All views are subclasses of the UIView class which is part of the UIKit class hierarchy. Common types of view that subclass from UIView include items such as the label (UILabel) and image view (UIImageView) and controls such as the button (UIButton) and text field (UITextField).

Another type of view that is of considerable importance is the UIWindow class.

17.2 The UIWindow Class

If you have developed (or even used) applications for desktop systems such as Windows or macOS you will be familiar with the concept of windows. A typical desktop application will have multiple windows, each of which has a title bar of some sort containing controls that allow you to minimize, maximize or close the window. Windows in this context essentially provide a surface area on the screen onto which the application can present information and controls to the user.

The UIWindow class provides a similar function for iOS based applications in that it also provides the surface on which the view components are displayed. There are, however, some differences in that an iOS app typically only has one window which usually fills the entire screen (the exception being when the app is in multitasking mode as outlined in the chapter entitled *A Guide to Multitasking in iOS 12*) and it lacks the title bar we've come to expect on desktop applications.

As with the views described previously, UIWindow is also a subclass of the UIView class and sits at the root of the view hierarchy which we will discuss in the next section. The user does not see or interact directly with the UIWindow object. These windows may be created programmatically, but are typically created automatically by Interface Builder when you design your user interface.

17.3 The View Hierarchy

iOS user interfaces are constructed using a hierarchical approach whereby different views are related through a parent/child relationship. At the top of this hierarchy sits the UIWindow object. Other views are then added to the hierarchy. If we take the example from the chapter entitled *Creating an Interactive iOS 12 App* we have a design that consists of a window, a view, a text field, a button and a label. The view hierarchy for this user interface would be drawn as illustrated in Figure 17-1:

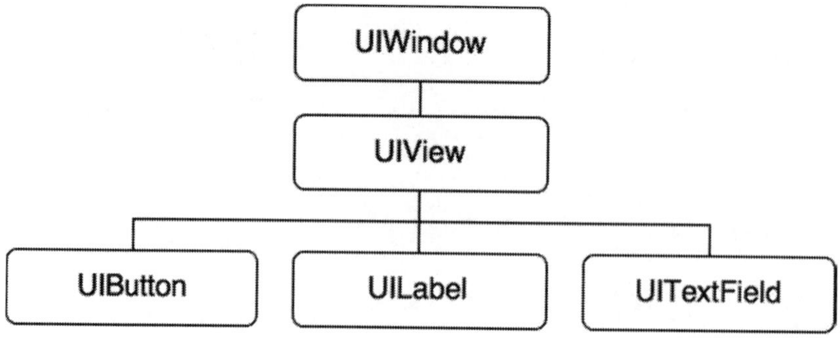

Figure 17-1

In this example, the UIWindow object is the parent or *superview* of the UIView instance and the UIView is the child, or *subview* of the UIWindow. Similarly, the text, label and button objects are all *subviews* of the UIView. A subview can only have one direct parent. As shown in the above example, however, a superview may have multiple subviews.

In addition, view hierarchies can be nested to any level of depth. Consider, for example, the following hierarchy diagram:

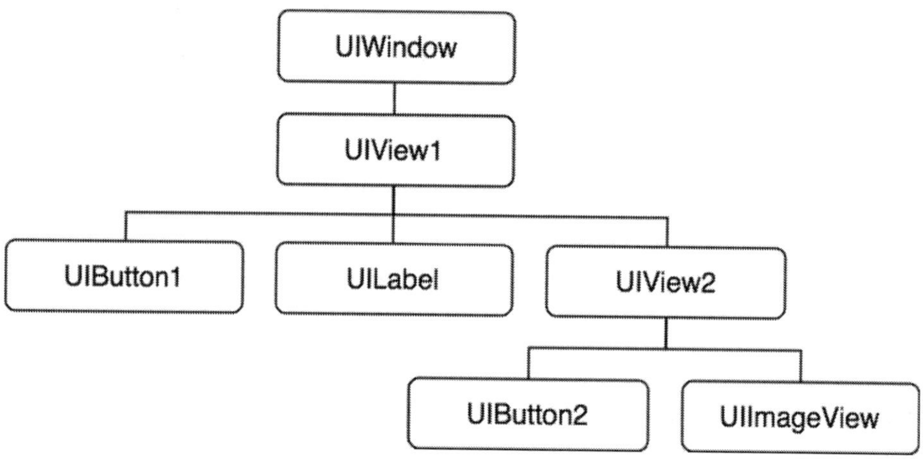

Figure 17-2

The hierarchical structure of a user interface has significant implications for how the views appear and behave. Visually, subviews always appear on top of and within the visual frame of their corresponding parent. The button in the above example, therefore, appears on top of the parent view in the running application. Furthermore, the resizing behavior of subviews (in other words the way in which the views change size when the device is rotated) is defined in relation to the parent view. Superviews also have the ability to modify the positioning and size of their subviews.

If we were to design the above nested view hierarchy in Interface Builder it might appear as illustrated in Figure 17-3.

In this example, the UIWindow instance is not visible because it is fully obscured by the UIView1 instance. Displayed on top of, and within the frame of UIView1, are the UIButton1, UILabel and UIView2 subviews. Displayed on top of, and within the frame of, UIView2 are its respective subviews, namely UIButton2 and UIImageView.

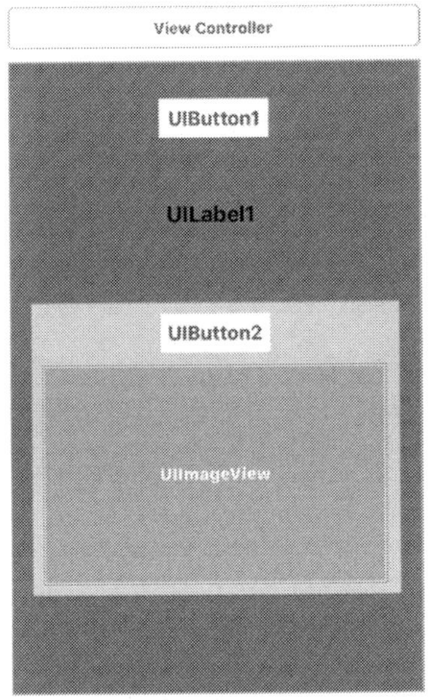

Figure 17-3

The view hierarchy also defines how events are handled when a user interacts with the interface, essentially defining something called the *responder chain.* If, for example, a subview receives an event that it cannot handle, that event is passed up to the immediate superview. If that superview is also unable to handle the event it is passed up to the next parent and so on until it reaches a level within the responder chain where it can be dealt with.

17.4 Viewing Hierarchy Ancestors in Interface Builder

A useful technique for displaying the hierarchical ancestors of a view object is to perform a Ctrl-Shift-Click operation (or a mouse pad force touch on newer MacBook devices) over the object in Interface Builder. Figure 17-4, for example, shows the results of this operation on the Convert button from the UnitConverter project storyboard scene:

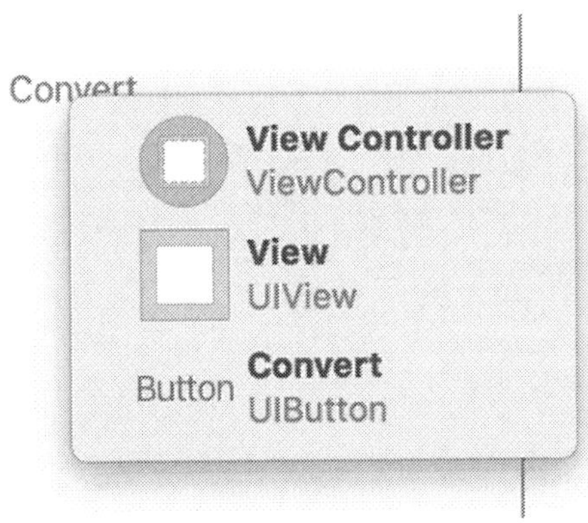

Figure 17-4

17.5 View Types

Apple groups the various views included in the UIKit Framework into a number of different categories:

17.5.1 The Window

The UIWindow is the root view of the view hierarchy and provides the surface on which all subviews draw their content.

17.5.2 Container Views

Container views enhance the functionality of other view objects. The UIScrollView class, for example, provides scrollbars and scrolling functionality for the UITableView and UITextView classes. Another example is the UIToolbar view which serves to group together multiple controls in a single view.

17.5.3 Controls

The controls category encompasses views that both present information and respond to user interaction. Control views inherit from the UIControl class (itself a subclass of UIView) and include items such as buttons, sliders and text fields.

17.5.4 Display Views

Display views are similar to *controls* in that they provide visual feedback to the user, the difference being that they do not respond to user interaction. Examples of views in this category include the UILabel and UIImageView classes.

17.5.5 Text and WebKit Views

The UITextView and WKWebView classes both fall into this category and are designed to provide a mechanism for displaying formatted text to the user. The WKWebView class, for example, is designed to display HTML content formatted so that it appears as it would if loaded into a web browser.

17.5.6 Navigation Views and Tab Bars

Navigation views and tab bars provide mechanisms for navigating through an application user interface. They work in conjunction with the view controller and are typically created from within Interface Builder.

17.5.7 Alert Views

Views in this category are designed specifically for prompting the user with urgent or important information together with optional buttons to call the user to action.

17.6 Summary

In this chapter we have explored the concepts of using views in terms of constructing an iOS application user interface and also how these views relate to each other within the context of a view hierarchy. We have also discussed how the view hierarchy dictates issues such as the positioning and resize behavior of subviews and defines the response chain for the user interface.

Chapter 18

18. An Introduction to Auto Layout in iOS 12

Arguably one of the most important parts of designing the user interface for an application involves getting the layout correct. In an ideal world, designing a layout would simply consist of dragging view objects to the desired location on the screen and fixing them at these positions using absolute X and Y screen coordinates. In reality, the world of iOS devices is more complex than that and a layout must be able to adapt to variables such as the device rotating between portrait and landscape modes, dynamic changes to content and differences in screen resolution and size.

Prior to the release of iOS 6, layout handling involved use of a concept referred to as *autosizing*. Autosizing involves the use of a series of "springs" and "struts" to define, on a view by view basis, how a subview will be resized and positioned relative to the superview in which it is contained. Limitations of autosizing, however, typically meant that considerable amounts of coding were required to augment the autosizing in response to orientation or other changes.

Perhaps one of the most significant features in iOS 6 was the introduction of Auto Layout, which has continued to evolve with the release of subsequent iOS versions. Auto Layout is an extremely large subject area allowing layouts of just about any level of flexibility and complexity to be created once the necessary skills have been learned.

The goal of this and subsequent chapters will be to introduce the basic concepts of Auto Layout, work through some demonstrative examples and provide a basis on which to continue learning about Auto Layout as your application design needs evolve. Auto Layout introduces a lot of new concepts and can, initially, seem a little overwhelming. By the end of this sequence of chapters, however, it should be clearer how the pieces fit together to provide a powerful and flexible layout management system for iOS based user interfaces.

18.1 An Overview of Auto Layout

The purpose of Auto Layout is to allow the developer to describe the behavior that is required from the views in a layout independent of the device screen size and orientation. This behavior is implemented through the creation of *constraints* on the views that comprise a user interface screen. A button view, for example, might have a constraint that tells the system that it is to be positioned in the horizontal center of its superview. A second constraint might also declare that the bottom edge of the button should be positioned a fixed distance from the bottom edge of the superview. Having set these constraints, no matter what happens to the superview, the button will always be centered horizontally and a fixed distance from the bottom edge.

Unlike autosizing, Auto Layout allows constraints to be declared not just between a subview and superview, but between subviews. Auto Layout, for example, would allow a constraint to be configured such that two button views are always positioned a specific distance apart from each other regardless of changes in size and orientation of the superview. Constraints can also be configured to cross superview boundaries to allow, for example, two views with different superviews (though in the same screen) to be aligned. This is a concept referred to as *cross-view hierarchy constraints*.

Constraints can also be explicit or variable (otherwise referred to in Auto Layout terminology as *equal* or *unequal*). Take for example, a width constraint on a label object. An explicit constraint could be declared to fix the width of the label at 70 points. This might be represented as a constraint equation that reads as follows:

```
myLabel.width = 70
```

This explicit width setting might, however, become problematic if the label is required to display dynamic content. An attempt to display text on the label that requires a greater width will result in the content being clipped.

Constraints can, however, also be declared using *less-than or equal to* or *greater than or equal to* controls. For example the width of a label could be constrained to any width as long as it is less than or equal to 800:

```
myLabel.width <= 800
```

The label is now permitted to grow in width up to the specified limit, allowing longer content to be displayed without clipping.

Auto Layout constraints are by nature interdependent and, as such, situations can arise where a constraint on one view competes with a constraint on another view to which it is connected. In such situations it may be necessary to make one constraint *stronger* and the other *weaker* in order to provide the system with a way of arriving at a layout solution. This is achieved by assigning *priorities* to constraints.

Priorities are assigned on a scale of 0 to 1000 with 1000 representing a *required constraint* and lower numbers equating to *optional constraints*. When faced with a decision between the needs of a required constraint and an optional constraint, the system will meet the needs of the required constraint exactly while attempting to get as close as possible to those of the optional constraint. In the case of two optional constraints, the needs of the constraint with the higher priority will be addressed before those of the lower.

18.2 Alignment Rects

When working with constraints it is important to be aware that constraints operate on the content of a view, not the frame in which a view is displayed. This content is referred to as the *alignment rect* of the view. Alignment constraints such as those that cause the center of one view to align with that of another will do so based on the alignment rects of the views, disregarding any padding that may have been configured for the frame of the view.

18.3 Intrinsic Content Size

Some views also have what is known as an *intrinsic content size*. This is the preferred size that a view itself believes it needs to be to display its content to the user. A Button view, for example, will have an intrinsic content size in terms of height and width that is based primarily on the text or image it is required to display and internal rules on the margins that should be placed around that content. When a view has an intrinsic content size, Auto Layout will automatically assign two constraints for each dimension for which the view has indicated an intrinsic content size preference (i.e. height and/or width). One constraint is intended to prevent the size of the view becoming larger than the size of the content (otherwise known as the *content hugging* constraint). The other constraint is intended to prevent the view from being sized smaller than the content (referred to as the *compression resistance* constraint).

18.4 Content Hugging and Compression Resistance Priorities

The resize behavior of a view with an intrinsic content size can be controlled by specifying compression resistance and content hugging priorities. A view with a high compression resistance priority and a low content hugging priority will be allowed to grow but will resist shrinking in the corresponding dimension.

Similarly, a high compression resistance priority in conjunction with a high content hugging priority will cause the view to resist any form of resizing, keeping the view as close as possible to its intrinsic content size.

18.5 Safe Area Layout Guide

In addition to the views that comprise the layout, a screen may also contain navigation and tab bars at the top and bottom of the screen. If the layout is designed to use the full screen height there is a risk that some views will be obscured by navigation and tab bars. To avoid this problem, UIView provides a *safe area layout guide* to which views may be constrained. Constraining views to the safe area instead of the outer edges of the parent UIView ensures that the views are not obscured by title and tab bars. The screen in Figure 18-1 includes both navigation and tab bars. The dotted line represents the safe area layout guide to which the top edge of the Button and bottom edge of the Label have been constrained:

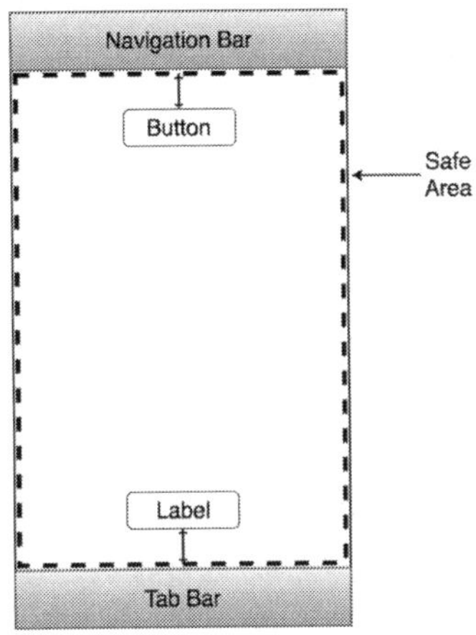

Figure 18-1

18.6 Three Ways to Create Constraints

There are three ways in which constraints in a user interface layout can be created:

- **Interface Builder** – Interface Builder has been modified extensively to provide support for the visual implementation of Auto Layout constraints in user interface designs. Examples of using this approach are covered in the *Working with iOS 12 Auto Layout Constraints in Interface Builder* and *An iOS 12 Auto Layout Example* chapters of this book.
- **Visual Format Language** – The visual format language defines a syntax that allows constraints to be declared using a sequence of ASCII characters that visually approximate the nature of the constraint being created with the objective of making constraints in code both easier to write and understand. Use of the visual format language is documented in the chapter entitled *Understanding the iOS 12 Auto Layout Visual Format Language*.
- **Writing API code** – This approach involves directly writing code to create constraints using the standard programming API calls, the topic of this is covered in *Implementing iOS 12 Auto Layout Constraints in Code*.

Wherever possible, Interface Builder is the recommended approach to creating constraints. When creating constraints in code, the visual format language is generally recommended over the API based approach.

18.7 Constraints in more Detail

A constraint is created as an instance of the NSLayoutConstraint class which, having been created, is then added to a view. The rules for a constraint can generally be represented as an equation, the most complex form of which can be described as follows:

```
view1.attribute = multiplier * view2.attribute2 + constant
```

In the above equation, a constraint relationship is being established between two views named view1 and view2 respectively. In each case an attribute is being targeted by the constraint. Attributes are represented by NSLayoutConstraint.Attribute.*<name>* constants where *<name>* is one of a number of options including left, right, top, bottom, leading, trailing, width, height, centerX, centerY and baseline (i.e. NSLayoutConstraint.Attribute.width). The multiplier and constant elements are floating point values used to modify the constraint.

A simple constraint that dictates that view1 and view2 should, for example, be the same width would be represented using the following equation:

```
view1.width = view2.width
```

Similarly, the equation for a constraint to align the horizontal center of view1 with the horizontal center of view2 would read as follows:

```
view1.centerX = view2.centerX
```

A slightly more complex constraint to position view1 so that its bottom edge is positioned a distance of 20 points above the bottom edge of view2 would be expressed as follows:

```
view1.bottom = view2.bottom - 20
```

The following constraint equation specifies that view1 is to be twice the width of view2 minus a width of 30 points:

```
view1.width = view2.width * 2 - 30
```

So far the examples have focused on equality. As previously discussed, constraints also support inequality in the form of <= and >= operators. For example:

```
view1.width >= 100
```

A constraint based on the above equation would limit the width of view1 to any value greater than or equal to 100.

The reason for representing constraints in the form of equations is less obvious when working with constraints within Interface Builder but will become invaluable when setting constraints in code either using the API or the visual format language.

18.8 Summary

Auto Layout involves the use of constraints to descriptively express the geometric properties, behavior and relationships of views in a user interface.

Constraints can be created using Interface Builder, or in code using either the visual format language or the standard SDK API calls of the NSLayoutConstraint class.

Constraints are typically expressed using a linear equation, an understanding of which will be particularly beneficial when working with constraints in code.

Having covered the basic concepts of Auto Layout, the next chapter will introduce the creation and management of constraints within Interface Builder.

Chapter 19

19. Working with iOS 12 Auto Layout Constraints in Interface Builder

By far the most productive and intuitive way to work with constraints is to do so using the Auto Layout features of Interface Builder. Not only does this avoid the necessity to write time consuming code (though for complex layout requirements some code will be inevitable) but it also provides instant visual feedback on constraints as they are configured.

Within this chapter, a simple example will be used to demonstrate the effectiveness of Auto Layout together with an in-depth look at the Auto Layout features of Interface Builder. The chapter will then move on to demonstrate the concepts of content hugging and constraint priorities.

19.1 A Simple Example of Auto Layout in Action

Before digging deeper into the Auto Layout features of Interface Builder, the first step in this chapter will be to quickly demonstrate the basic concept of Auto Layout. Begin, therefore, by creating a new Xcode project using the *Single View Application* template, entering *AutoLayoutExample* as the product name.

19.2 Working with Constraints

Although Auto Layout is enabled by default, the Interface Builder tool does not automatically apply any default constraints as views are added to the layout. Views are instead positioned using absolute x and y coordinates. To see this in action, drag a label view from the Library and position it towards the bottom of the view in the horizontal center of the view canvas so the vertical blue guideline appears indicating that it is centered before dropping the view into place. In actual fact, the location of the view has just been defined using hard coded absolute x and y coordinates on the screen. As far as the view is concerned, the label is positioned perfectly as long as the device remains in portrait orientation:

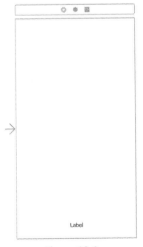

Figure 19-1

A problem arises, however, when the device rotates to landscape orientation. This can be demonstrated by compiling and running the application on a physical iPhone or iPad device or iOS Simulator in the usual way. Alternatively, the effect of an orientation change can be tested within the Interface Builder environment. To rotate to landscape mode, click on the *View as:* entry located in the status bar positioned along the bottom edge of the Interface Builder panel as highlighted in Figure 19-2 below:

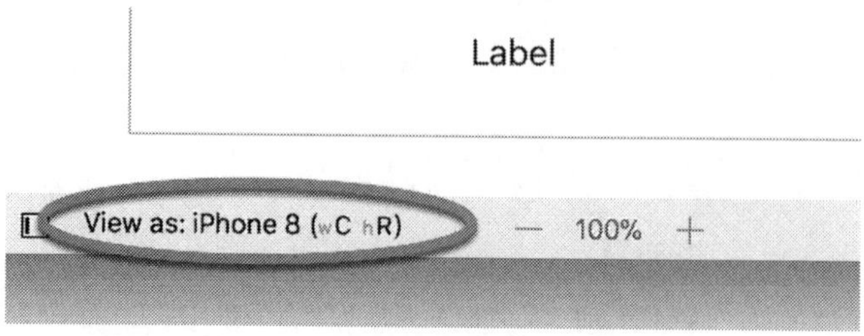

Figure 19-2

When the button is clicked, the device type and orientation selection panel will appear. Within this panel (Figure 19-3) click on the landscape orientation option:

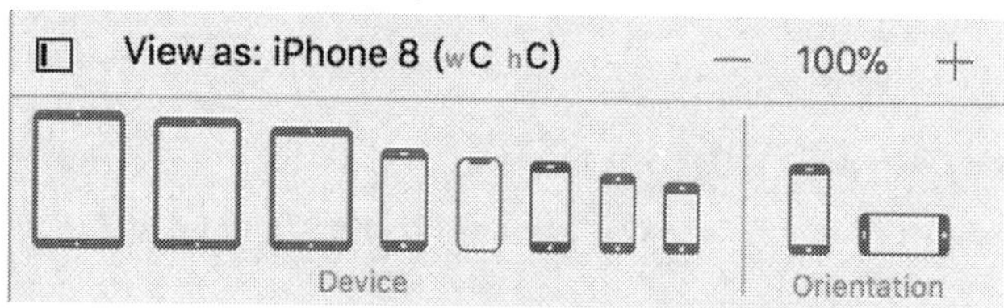

Figure 19-3

As illustrated in Figure 19-4, the label is no longer visible with the device in landscape orientation. This is because it remains positioned at the same geographical coordinates in relation to the parent view which, in landscape orientation, is outside the visible bounds of the parent view.

Figure 19-4

Similar problems can occur when the application runs on different sizes of iPhone device which can be tested by clicking on the *View as:* button and selecting different device types.

Note that on larger and smaller display form factors in portrait orientation, the label is once again positioned incorrectly. Clearly layout is important, not only for handling device orientation, but also to ensure correct user interface appearance on different device models.

Prior to the introduction of Auto Layout, options to address this would have either involved using springs and struts or writing code to detect the rotation of the device and to move the label to the new location on the screen. Now, however, the problem can be solved using Auto Layout.

Begin by returning the view to portrait orientation so that the label is once again visible and select the label within the view canvas. Xcode provides a number of different ways to add constraints to a layout. These options will be covered later in this chapter but by far the easiest is to use the Auto Layout toolbar. With the label selected, click on the *Add New Constraints* menu (Figure 19-5):

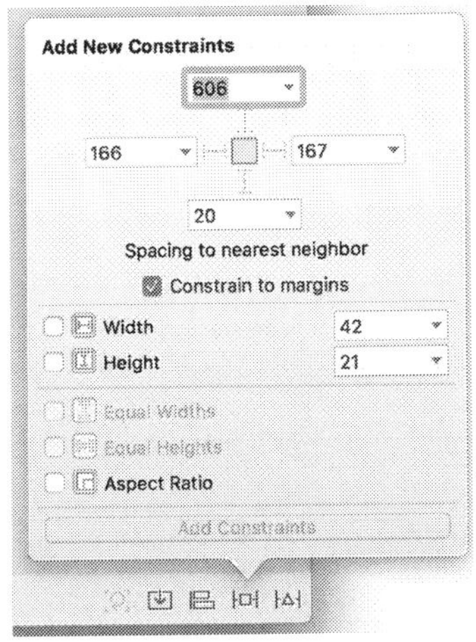

Figure 19-5

The goal for this example is to add a constraint to the label such that the bottom edge of the label is always positioned the same distance from the bottom of the containing superview and so that it remains centered horizontally. To do this we are first interested in the *Spacing to nearest neighbor* section of this panel. This provides a visual representation of the view in question (in this case the label) which is represented by the square in the middle. Extending from each side of the square are faded and dotted I-beam icons that connect with fields containing values. The fact that the I-beams are dotted and faded indicates that these are constraints that have not been set. The values indicate the current distances within the layout of the corresponding side to the nearest neighbor. The "nearest neighbor" will either be the nearest view to that side of the currently selected view, or the corresponding side of the superview.

Select the constraint I-beam icon located beneath the view so that it appears in solid red (as shown in Figure 19-6) to indicate that the constraint is now set before clicking on the *Add 1 Constraint* button to add the constraint to the view.

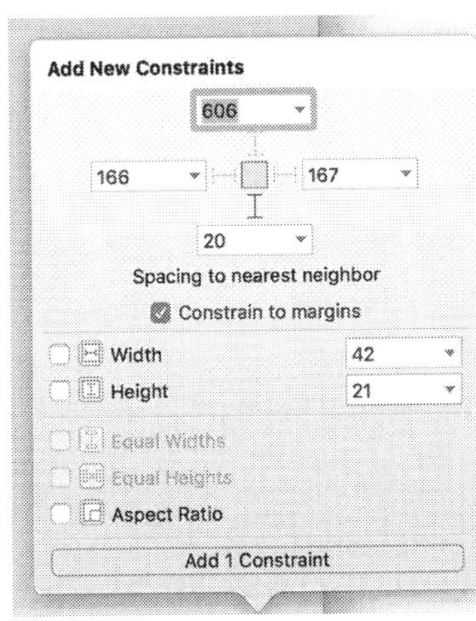

Figure 19-6

Having added a constraint, Auto Layout now knows that the bottom edge of the label must always be positioned a fixed distance from the bottom edge of the containing superview. The layout is still missing a constraint to designate the horizontal position of the label in the superview. One way to add this constraint is to make use of the *Align* menu. With the label still selected in the view canvas and the Align menu panel displayed, enable the checkbox next to the *Horizontally in Container* property (Figure 19-7). Since no offset from the center is required, leave the offset value at 0.

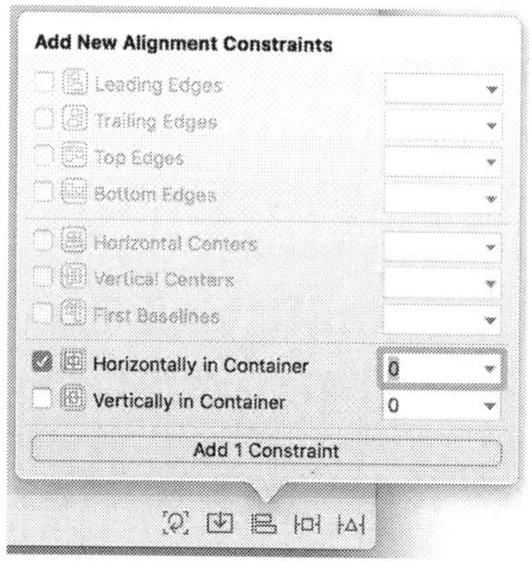

Figure 19-7

With the constraint appropriately configured, click on the *Add 1 Constraint* button to add the constraint to the view.

Having configured some constraints, rotate the orientation once again, noting this time that the label is visible and positioned sensibly. Testing different display form factors should also demonstrate that the constraints are working to keep the label correctly positioned for different devices.

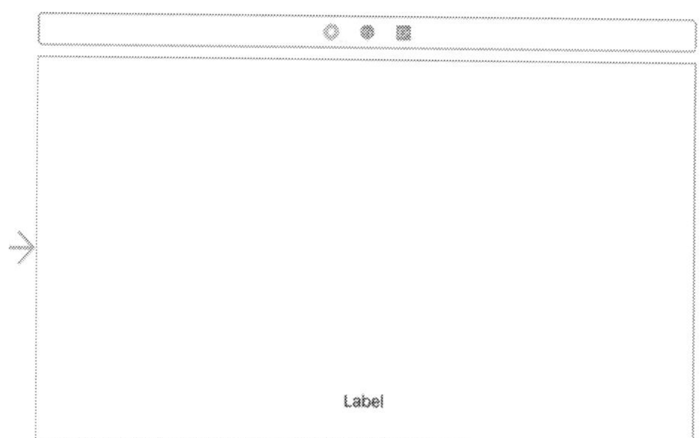

Figure 19-8

In this example so far only a small subset of the Auto Layout features provided by Xcode has been used. In actual fact, Xcode provides a wide range of options and visual cues that are designed to ease the task of creating Auto Layout constraints.

19.3 The Auto Layout Features of Interface Builder

A number of features are provided in Xcode in order to assist in the implementation of Auto Layout based constraints. This section will present a guided tour of many of these features.

19.3.1 Suggested Constraints

When objects are added to a layout canvas, Interface Builder does not implement any default constraints on those views leaving the developer to add constraints as needed. There is, however, the option to have Interface Builder apply suggested constraints. When this option is used, Interface Builder will apply what it believes to be the correct constraints for the layout based on the positioning of the views. Suggested constraints can be added either to the currently selected view objects, or to an entire scene layout.

In situations where constraints are missing from a layout resulting in warnings, Interface Builder also provides the option to automatically add the constraints that it believes are missing.

The options to perform these tasks are accessed via the *Resolve Auto Layout Issues* menu in the toolbar as illustrated in Figure 19-9.

The top section of the menu represents tasks that relate to the currently selected views in the canvas, while the options in the lower section apply to all views in the currently selected view controller scene.

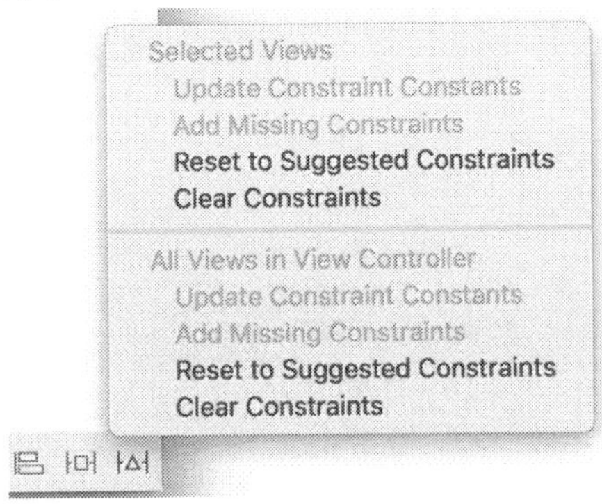

Figure 19-9

Most of the time, the suggested constraints will exactly match the required layout behavior and occasionally, the suggested constraints will be incorrect. Most of the time, however, the suggested constraints provide an excellent starting point for implementing Auto Layout. A typical process for designing a user interface might, therefore, involve positioning the views by dragging and dropping them into place, applying suggested constraints and then editing and fine tuning those constraints to perfect the layout.

To see suggested constraints in action, select the label view in the AutoLayoutExample project and select the *Clear Constraints* option from the *Resolve Auto Layout Issues* menu. At this point there are no constraints in the layout and the old positioning problem appears when the view is rotated. With the label still selected, choose the *Reset to Suggested Constraints* menu option listed under *Selected Views*. A review of the view canvas, and change of orientation should demonstrate that Interface Builder has suggested and applied the exact same constraints that we previously added manually.

19.3.2 Visual Cues

Interface Builder includes a number of visual cues in the layout canvas to highlight the constraints currently configured on a view and to draw attention to areas where problems exist. When a view is selected within the layout canvas, the constraints that reference that view will be represented visually. Consider, for example, the label view created in our *AutoLayoutExample* application. When selected in the canvas, a number of additional lines appear as shown in Figure 19-10:

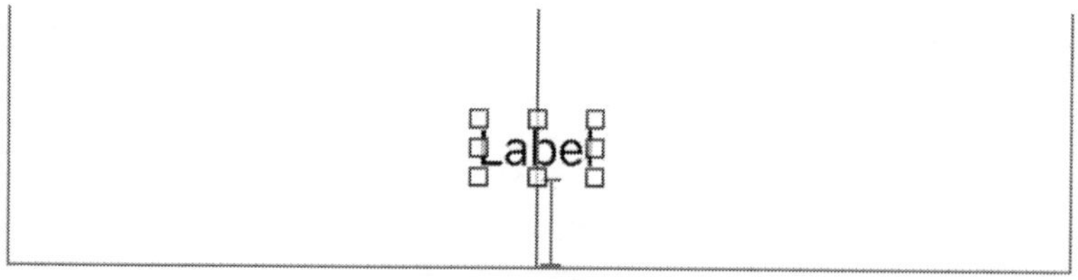

Figure 19-10

The vertical line that runs through the center of the label indicates the presence of a constraint that positions the label in the horizontal center of the parent view (analogous to the NSLayoutConstraint.Attribute.centerX attribute). If expressed as an equation, therefore, this would read as:

```
label.NSLayoutConstraint.Attribute.centerX =
                    superview.NSLayoutConstraint.Attribute.centerX
```

The I-beam line running from the bottom edge of the label view to the bottom edge of the parent view indicates that a vertical space constraint is in place between the label and safe area. The absence of any additional visual information on the line indicates that this is an *equality* constraint. Figure 19-11 shows an example of a "greater than or equal to" horizontal constraint between two button views:

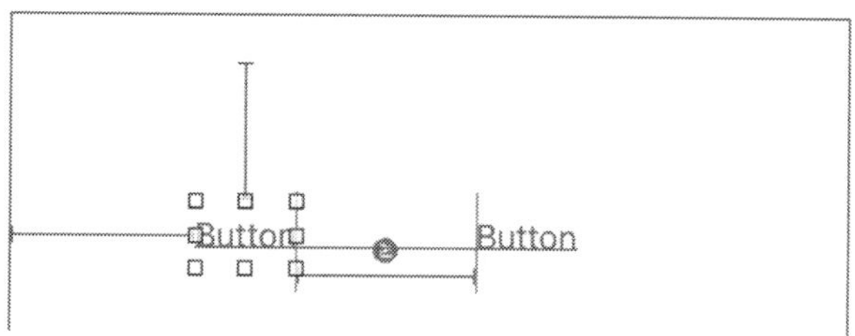

Figure 19-11

The horizontal line running beneath the Button label text indicates that constraints are in place to horizontally align the content baseline (represented by NSLayoutConstraint.Attribute.baseline) of the two buttons.

Width constraints are indicated by an I-beam line running parallel to the edge of the view in the corresponding dimension. The text view object in Figure 19-12, for example, has a "greater than or equal to" width constraint configured:

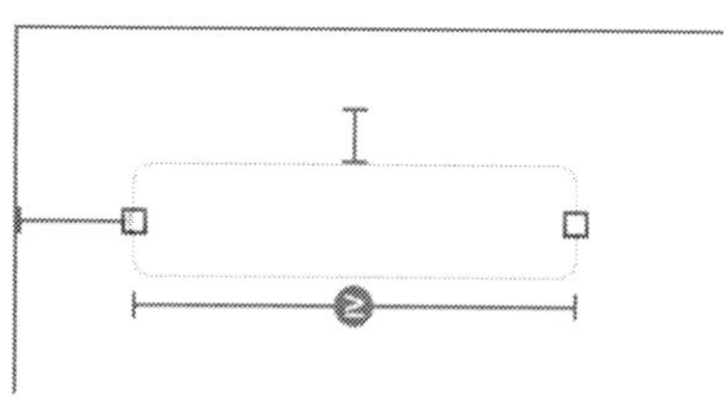

Figure 19-12

19.3.3 Highlighting Constraint Problems

Interface Builder also uses a range of visual cues and decorations to indicate that constraints are either missing, ambiguous or in conflict. Valid and complete Auto Layout configurations are drawn using blue lines. When part of a layout is ambiguous the constraint lines are orange.

Ambiguity typically occurs when a constraint is missing. Take for example the label view used earlier in the chapter. If only the horizontal center constraint is set, that constraint line will appear in orange because Auto Layout does not know where to position the view in the vertical plane. Once the second constraint is set between the bottom edge of the label and the bottom of the superview the constraint line will turn blue to indicate that the layout is no longer ambiguous.

Red constraint lines are used to indicate that constraints are in conflict. Consider, for example, a view object on which two width constraints have been configured, each for a different width value. The Auto Layout system categorizes such a situation as a constraint conflict and Interface Builder draws the offending constraint lines on the layout canvas in red. Figure 19-13, for example, illustrates a conflict where one constraint is attempting to set the width of a view to 110 points while a second constraint dictates that the width must be greater than or equal to 120 points:

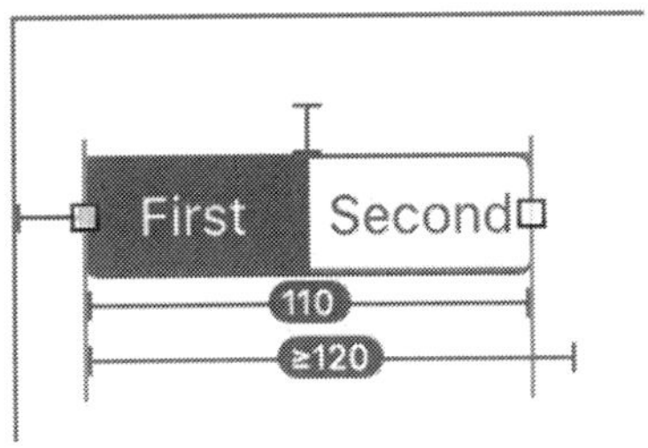

Figure 19-13

The layout canvas will dynamically update the positions and sizes of the views that make up a user interface as constraints are added. It is possible under certain circumstances, however, to have constraints configured that will result in layout behavior different to that currently displayed within the canvas. When such a situation arises, Interface Builder will draw a dotted orange outline indicating the actual size and location of the frame for the currently selected item. This is, perhaps, best demonstrated with an example. Within the *AutoLayoutExample* project, add a Text Field object to the layout so that it is positioned near to the top of the view and to the right of the horizontal center as shown in Figure 19-14:

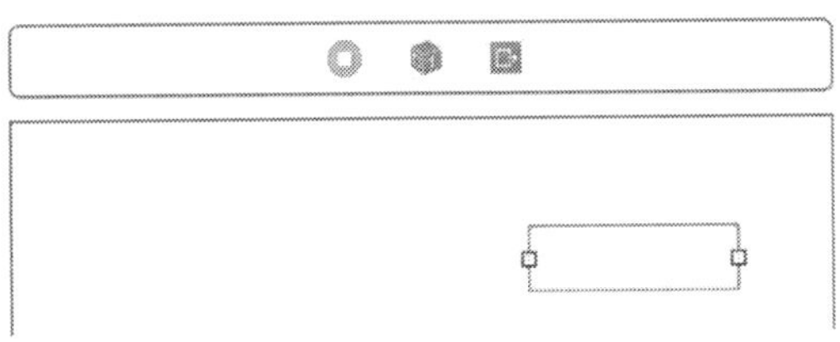

Figure 19-14

Select the new Text Field object and, using the *Add New Constraints* menu, establish a *Spacing to nearest neighbor* constraint from the top of the text view to the top of the safe area. Using the *Align* menu, add another constraint that aligns the view with the horizontal center in the container. Having established these constraints, review the layout within the view canvas and note that the Text View is positioned in compliance with the newly added constraints.

Click and drag the Text View so that it is no longer in the correct position. As outlined in Figure 19-15, the horizontal center constraint appears in orange with a number assigned to it. A dotted box also appears on this line, level with the Text View object. Interface Builder is attempting to warn us that the size and position of this view is going to resemble the dotted orange box at run time, and not the size and position currently shown for the view in the canvas. The number on the horizontal center constraint tells us that the horizontal position of the object is going to be a specific number of points to the left of the current position.

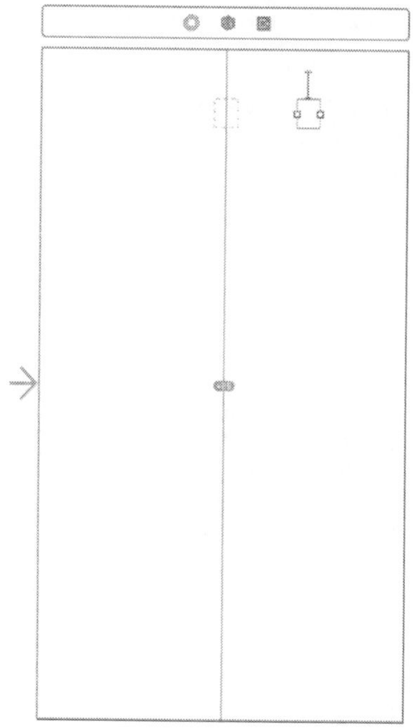

Figure 19-15

To reset the view to the size and position dictated by the constraints so that the canvas matches the runtime layout, simply select the Text View object and click on the *Update Frames* button located in the Interface Builder status bar as highlighted in Figure 19-16:

Figure 19-16

The canvas will subsequently update to reflect the correct layout appearance (Figure 19-17):

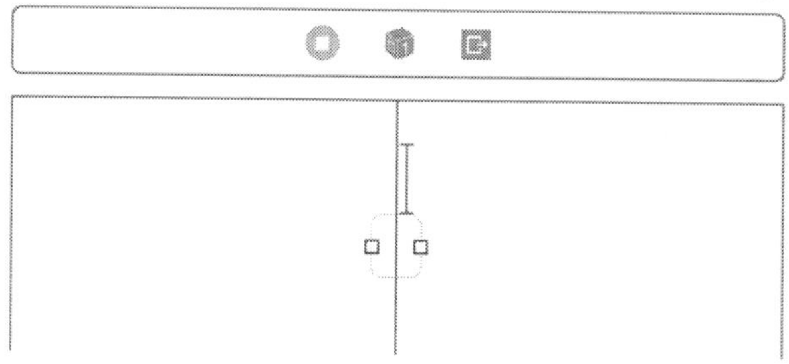

Figure 19-17

If, on the other hand, the text view had been positioned correctly (in other words the visual position was correct but the constraints were wrong), the current constraints could have been adjusted to match the actual position of the view using the *Update Constraint Constants* option of the *Resolve Auto Layout Issues* menu.

19.3.4 Viewing, Editing and Deleting Constraints

All of the constraints currently set on the views of a user interface may be viewed at any time from within the Document Outline panel that is positioned to the left of the Interface Builder canvas area. Hidden by default, this panel can be displayed by clicking on the button in the bottom left-hand corner of the storyboard canvas (marked by the arrow in Figure 19-18).

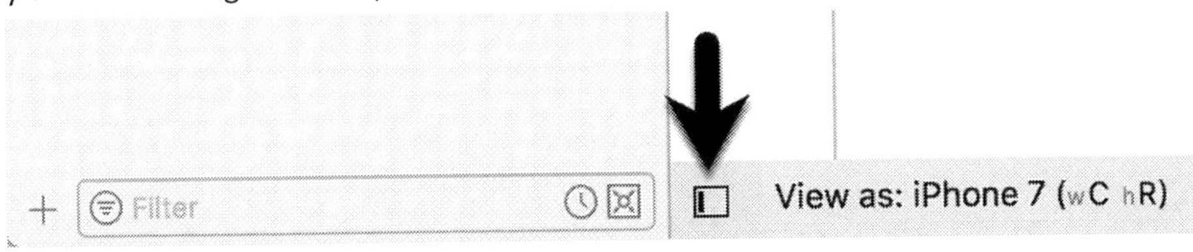

Figure 19-18

Within this outline, a category listed as *Constraints* will be present which, when unfolded, will list all of the constraints currently configured for the layout. Note that when more than one container view is present in the view hierarchy there will be a separate constraints list for each one. Figure 19-19, for example, lists the constraints for the user interface represented in Figure 19-10 above:

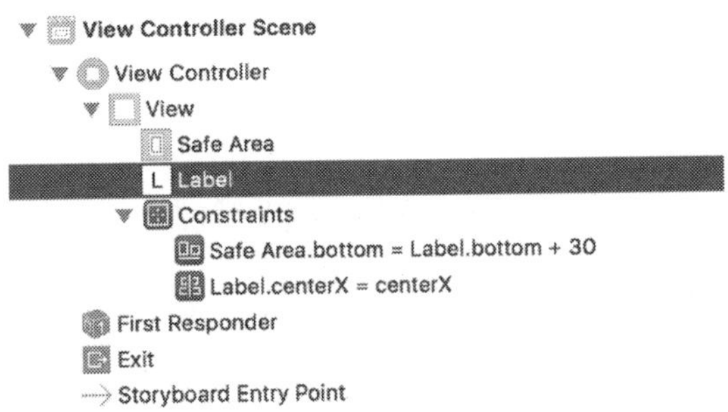

Figure 19-19

Also listed within the outline is the safe area belonging to the UIView component. As indicated, the bottom of the label is constrained to the bottom edge of the safe area.

As each constraint is selected from the outline list, the corresponding visual cue element will highlight within the layout canvas.

The details of a particular constraint may be viewed and edited at any time using a variety of methods. One method is simply to double-click on the constraint line in the canvas to display a constraint editing panel:

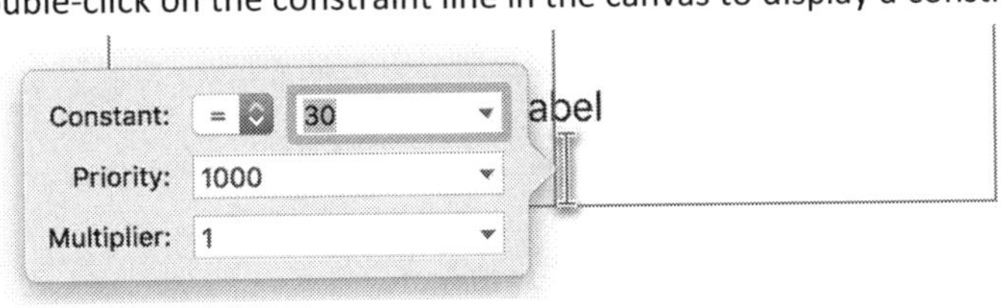

Figure 19-20

Another option is to select the constraint either from within the layout canvas or in the Document Outline panel. Once selected, display the Attributes Inspector in the Utilities panel (*View -> Utilities -> Show Attributes Inspector*) to view and edit the properties of the constraint. Figure 19-21 illustrates the settings for an equality spacing constraint.

Figure 19-21

A listing of the constraints associated with a specific view can be obtained by selecting that view in the layout canvas and displaying the Size Inspector in the Utilities panel. Figure 19-22, for example, lists two constraints that reference the currently selected view. Clicking on the edit button on any constraint will provide options to edit the constraint properties. In addition, constraints can be removed by selecting them in the layout canvas and pressing the keyboard Delete key.

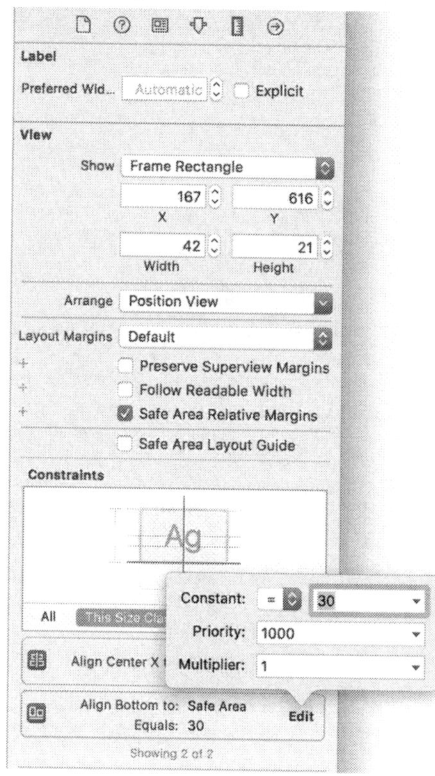

Figure 19-22

19.4 Creating New Constraints in Interface Builder

New user constraints can be created in Interface Builder using a variety of approaches, keeping in mind that constraints can relate to more than one view at a time. For example to configure an alignment constraint, all of the views which are to be included in the alignment operation must be selected before creating the constraints.

One of the easiest ways, as demonstrated earlier in this chapter, is to use the various options in the toolbar in the bottom right-hand corner of the storyboard canvas.

Another useful option is simply to Ctrl-click within a view and then drag the resulting line outside of the boundary of the view. On releasing the line, a context menu will appear providing constraint options. The menu options provided will depend on the direction in which the line was dragged. If the line is dragged downwards, for example, the menu will include options to add a constraint to the bottom of the view, or to center vertically within the container. Dragging horizontally, on the other hand, provides the option to attach to the corresponding edge of the safe area or to center horizontally. Dragging the line to another view in the canvas will provide options (Figure 19-23) to set up spacing, alignment and size equality constraints between those views.

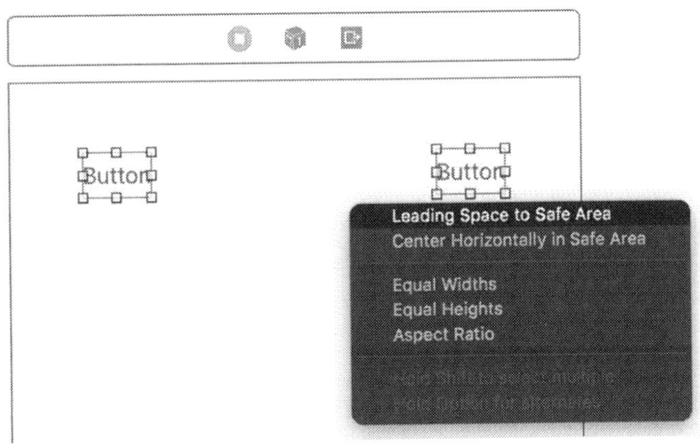

Figure 19-23

19.5 Adding Aspect Ratio Constraints

The height and width of a view can be constrained to retain aspect ratio by Ctrl-clicking in the view, dragging diagonally and then releasing. In the resulting menu, selecting *Aspect Ratio* ensures that regardless of whether the view shrinks or grows, the current aspect ratio will be preserved.

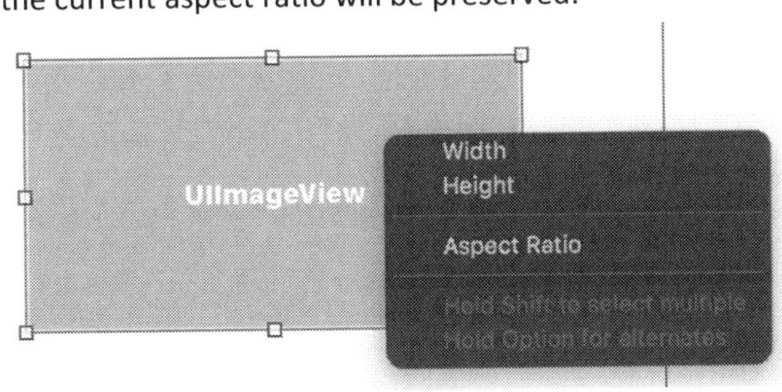

Figure 19-24

19.6 Resolving Auto Layout Problems

Another advantage of implementing Auto Layout constraints in Xcode is that a number of features are available in Xcode to assist in resolving problems.

In the first instance, descriptions of current issues can be obtained by clicking on the yellow warning triangle in the top right-hand corner of the canvas area:

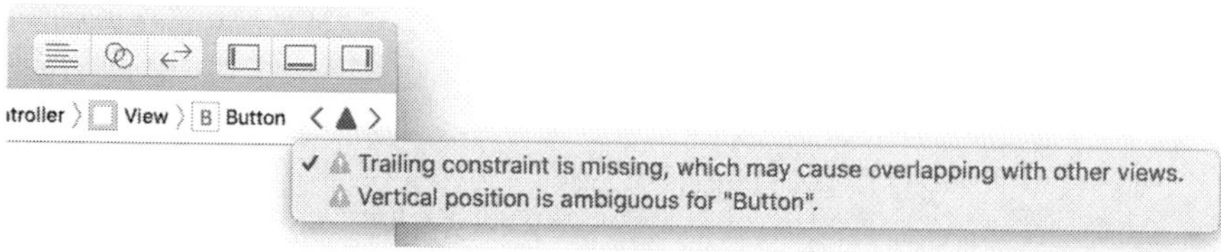

Figure 19-25

Solutions to some problems may be implemented by using the options in the *Resolve Auto Layout Issues* menu to perform tasks such as automatically adding missing constraints or resetting to suggested constraints.

More detailed resolution options are available from within the document outline panel. When issues need to be resolved, a red circle with a white arrow appears next to the corresponding view controller name in the outline panel as shown in Figure 19-26:

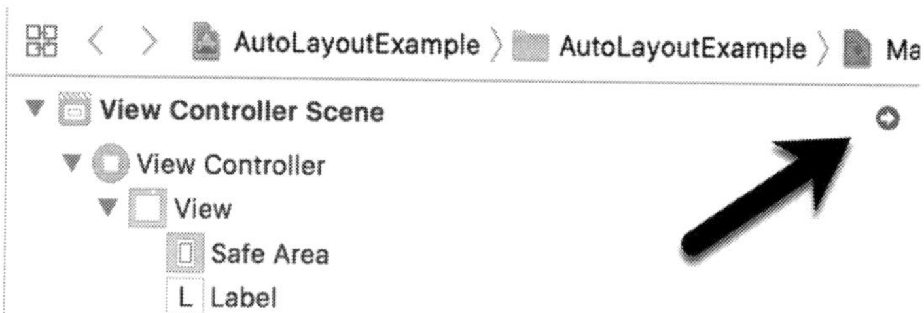

Figure 19-26

Clicking on the red circle displays all current layout issues listed by category:

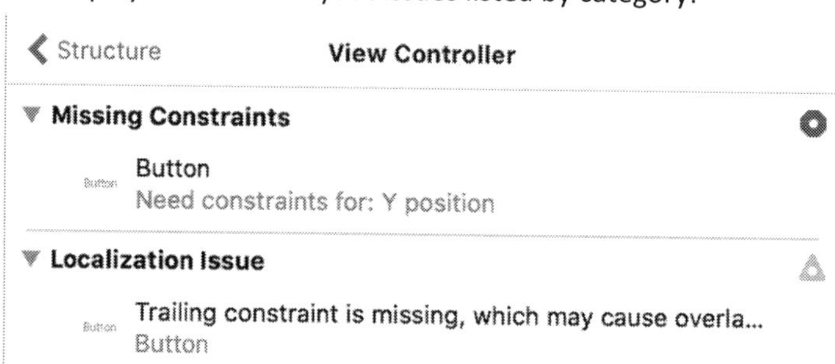

Figure 19-27

Hovering over a category title (for example Missing Constraints) will display an information symbol which, when clicked, will display a detailed description of the problem type.

Clicking on the error or warning symbol will display a panel providing one or more possible solutions together with a button to apply the selected change:

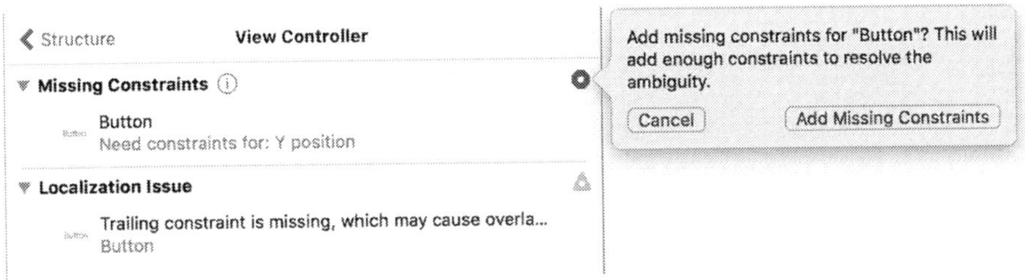

Figure 19-28

19.7 Summary

Within this chapter we have looked at a very simplistic example of the benefits of using Auto Layout in iOS user interface design. The remainder of the chapter has been dedicated to providing an overview of the Auto Layout features that are available in Interface Builder.

Chapter 20

20. An iOS 12 Auto Layout Example

Having covered the basics of Auto Layout and the Auto Layout features of Interface Builder in the preceding chapters, this chapter will work through an example user interface design intended to demonstrate the use of Interface Builder to create Auto Layout constraints. This example will also include a demonstration of constraint priorities.

20.1 Preparing the Project

Launch Xcode and load the *AutoLayoutExample* project created in the previous chapter. Once loaded, select the *Main.storyboard* file and remove the Label view and any other views added while working through the chapter.

20.2 Designing the User Interface

Initially, the user interface will simply require two Label views and a second View object. Begin, however, by selecting the *Main.storyboard* file and selecting the background view canvas. Display the Attributes Inspector in the Utilities panel and change the background color to a light shade of gray.

Drag a Label view from the Library and position it so that it is centered horizontally and on the top margin guideline as indicated in Figure 20-1. Drag a second Label view and position it to the left of the first label.

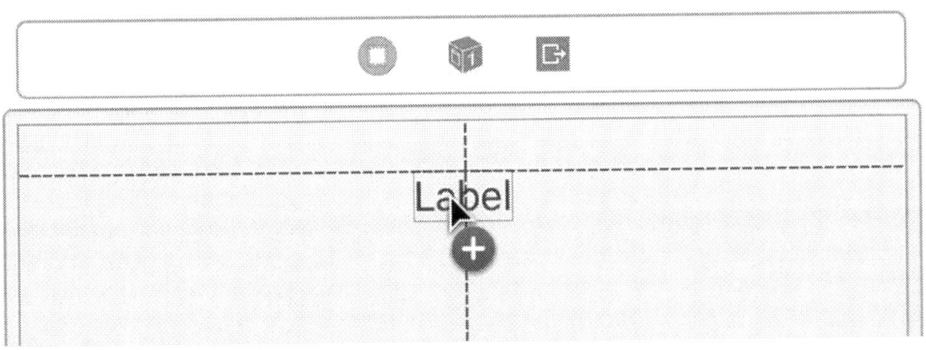

Figure 20-1

Display the Library panel again and, as a shortcut, type the word "UIView" into the search bar (Figure 20-2) to narrow the search criteria and then scroll to find the View object.

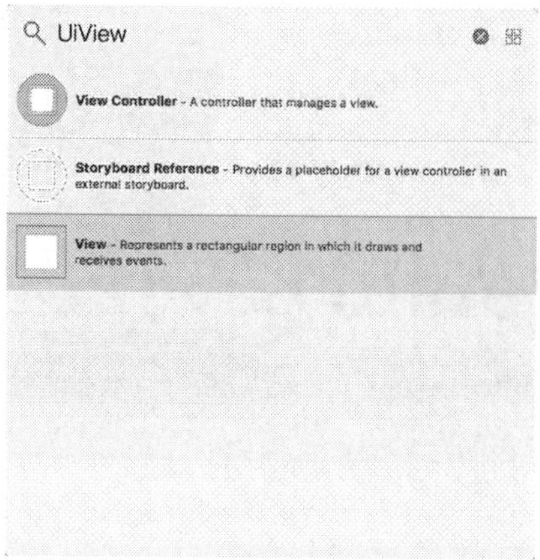

Figure 20-2

Drag and drop the View object onto the layout and resize it to fill the space below the two labels with appropriate margins from the outer edges of the screen. Cancel the Library search filter by clicking on the "x" at the right-hand edge of the search box.

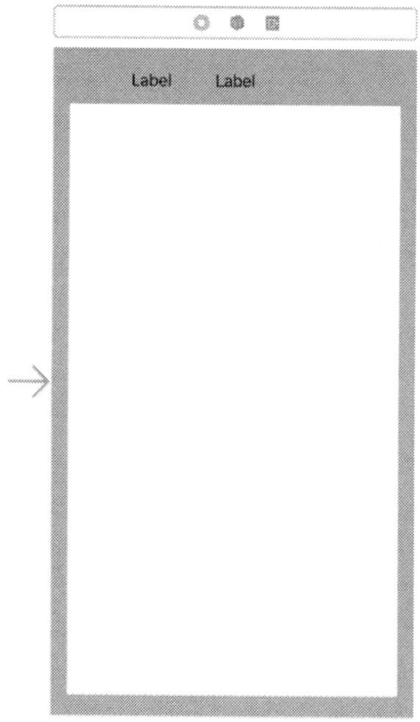

Figure 20-3

20.3 Adding Auto Layout Constraints

A number of constraints now need to be added to the layout so that it resizes and positions the views correctly when the device is rotated.

Select the View object in the layout and display the *Add New Constraints* menu from the toolbar in the bottom right-hand corner of the storyboard canvas. In the *Spacing to nearest neighbor* section of the panel enable constraints on each of the four sides of the view with the *Constrain to margins* option enabled as outlined in Figure 20-4:

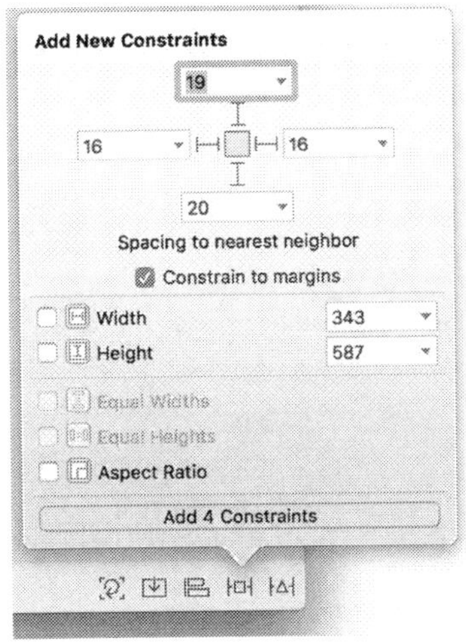

Figure 20-4

With the settings entered, click on the *Add 4 Constraints* button to implement the constraints.

Next, select the right most of the two labels, display the *Add New Constraints* menu and enable the *Spacing to nearest neighbor* constraint for the top edge of the view with the value set to 8 and click on the *Add 1 Constraint* button.

With the label still selected, use the *Align* menu to constrain the label to the horizontal center of the container.

All that now remains is to establish some constraints between the two labels. Ctrl-click on the left most label and drag the line to the right-hand label before releasing the line. From the resulting menu, hold down the Shift key on the keyboard and select the *First Baseline* and *Horizontal Spacing* options to align the content baselines of the two labels and to add a spacing constraint. With both options selected, hit the keyboard Return key to add the constraints.

Rotate the canvas display into landscape mode by clicking on the *View as:* button in the bottom status bar of the Interface Builder panel and selecting the landscape device orientation option. Note that the layout now re-organizes to accommodate the orientation change:

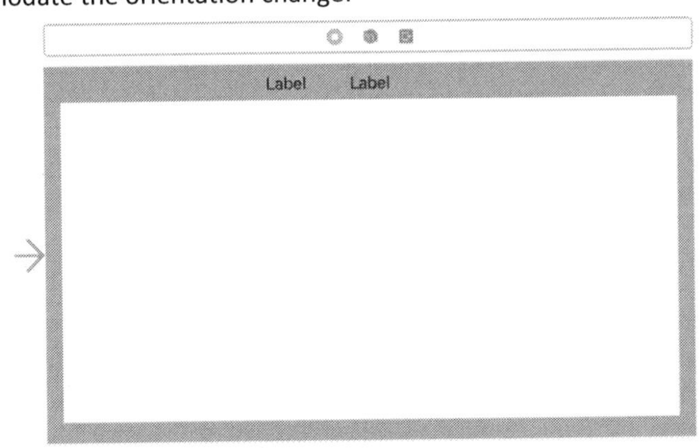

Figure 20-5

If the layout does not match that shown above, it may be necessary to update the frames to adopt the new constraint settings using the *Update Frames* button (Figure 19-16).

20.4 Adjusting Constraint Priorities

Up until this point, the layout is behaving correctly using basic constraints with default priorities. We are now going to introduce some problems that cannot be handled adequately by the constraints as they currently stand. With the view still in landscape mode, double-click on the left-hand label and change the text so that it reads *Customer Record:*. Using the Attributes Inspector, change the Alignment property so that the text is right aligned.

With the view in landscape mode the label appears correctly positioned. Rotate the view to portrait orientation, however, and the label is clearly being clipped by the left-hand edge of the parent view:

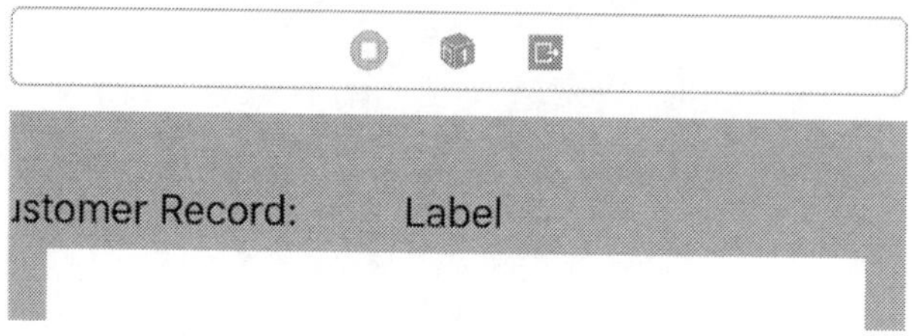

Figure 20-6

Clearly there is some work to be done to make the user interface appear correctly in both orientations. The first step is to consider the constraints that are currently set on the label views. The right-hand label has a constraint that forces it to be centered horizontally in the parent view. The left-hand label, on the other hand, has a constraint that connects its trailing edge to the leading edge of the second label. The absence of a constraint on the left-hand edge of the Customer Record label is resulting in the label being pushed off the screen in portrait mode.

One possible solution to this problem might be to create a new constraint on the Customer Record label that puts some space between the left-hand edge of the customer record label and the left-hand edge of the parent view's safe area. To add this constraint, rotate the view back to landscape so that the label is fully visible, select the Customer Record label, display the *Add New Constraints* menu, and establish a space constraint between the left-hand edge of the view and the nearest neighbor with the value set to 16.

Now rotate to Portrait mode and note that the label is, unfortunately, now clipped on the right-hand edge.

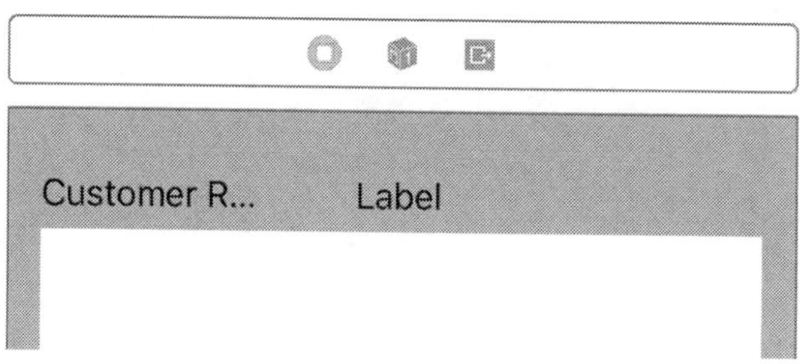

Figure 20-7

The reason for this problem is that the right-hand label contains a constraint which forces it to be centered horizontally within the super view with a priority of 1000. Similarly, the customer record label has constraints that dictate that the leading and trailing edges of the label must be the standard width from the superview and right-hand label respectively. Since these also have a priority of 1000, the system has no choice but to clip the label in order to satisfy the constraints. In order for the label to be fully visible, one of these priorities needs to be reduced.

We already know from experience that without the constraint on the leading edge of the customer record label, the left-hand edge will be clipped by the superview window when the device is in portrait orientation.

Another option is to lower the priority on the space constraint between the two labels. Unfortunately, this will just cause the left-hand label to overlap the right-hand label within the layout.

The only remaining constraint to experiment with is the horizontal center constraint on the right-hand label. Select this label so that the constraints for that view are drawn on the canvas and double-click on the horizontal center constraint (the vertical blue line) to display the constraint settings as shown in Figure 20-8. Using the drop down menu, reduce the priority by selecting the *Prevent "Customer Record:" From Clipping* menu option. When this option is selected, Xcode will calculate the optimal priority to ensure the label is not clipped.

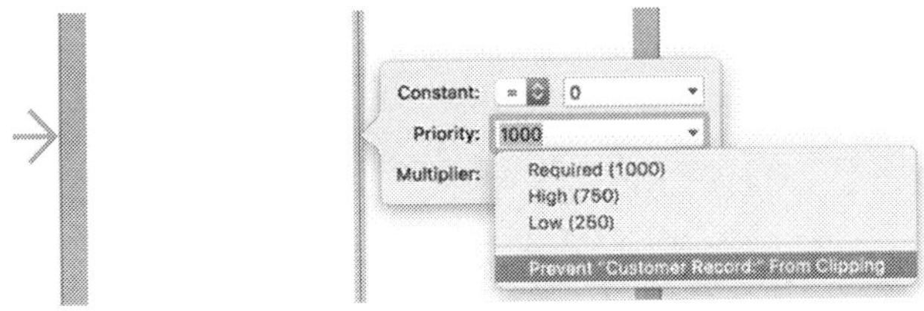

Figure 20-8

As a result of this setting, the label will only be centered when another constraint with a higher priority does not require that the label be moved. As such, the label will be centered when the device is in landscape mode but will be pushed off center when the space is needed by the Customer Record label in portrait orientation.

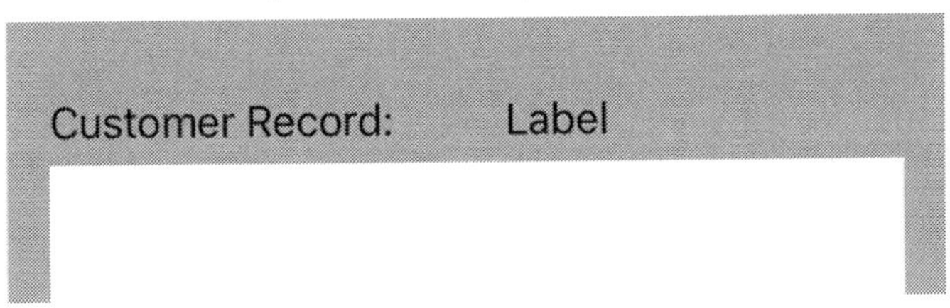

Figure 20-9

20.5 Testing the Application

Throughout this tutorial, the behavior of the user interface layout in response to orientation changes has been performed using simulated metrics within Xcode. As a full test of the layout, build and run the application either on a physical iPhone device or the iOS Simulator and check that the layout handles device rotation. This involves both a visual check that the views appear as intended and a review of the console to ensure no errors are reported with relation to the Auto Layout constraints.

20.6 Summary

Within this chapter, a sequence of steps have been outlined demonstrating the creation of an application that uses Auto Layout constraints to design a user interface that responds sensibly to orientation changes of the device. The example also introduced practical examples of the importance of constraint priorities.

Now that the implementation of Auto Layout constraints in Interface Builder has been covered, the next chapter will begin to explore the creation of constraints in code.

Chapter 21

21. Implementing iOS 12 Auto Layout Constraints in Code

In addition to using Interface Builder, it is also possible to create Auto Layout constraints directly within the code of an application. These approaches, however, are not necessarily mutually exclusive. There are, for example, situations where a layout will be constructed using a combination of Interface Builder and manual coding. Furthermore, some types of constraint cannot yet be implemented in Interface Builder, constraints that cross view hierarchies being a prime example. Interface Builder is also of limited use when user interfaces are created dynamically at run time.

Given these facts, an understanding of how to create Auto Layout constraints in code is an important skill, and is the focus of this chapter.

21.1 Creating Constraints in Code

Implementing constraints in code is a two-step process which involves first creating the constraint, and then adding the constraint to a view.

In order to create a constraint, an instance of the NSLayoutConstraint class must be created and initialized with the appropriate settings for the Auto Layout behavior it is to implement. This is achieved by initializing an NSLayoutConstraint instance, passing through a set of arguments for the constraint.

When considering this syntax, it is helpful to recall the way in which constraints can be represented using linear equations (as outlined in *An Introduction to Auto Layout in iOS 12*) because the elements of the equation match the arguments used to create an NSLayoutConstraint instance.

Consider, for example, the following constraint expressed as an equation:

```
view1.bottom = view2.bottom - 20
```

The objective of this constraint is to position view1 so that its bottom edge is positioned a distance of 20 points above the bottom edge of view2. This same equation can be represented in code as follows:

```
var myConstraint =
          NSLayoutConstraint(item: view1,
             attribute: NSLayoutConstraint.Attribute.bottom,
             relatedBy: NSLayoutRelation.equal,
             toItem: view2,
             attribute: NSLayoutConstraint.Attribute.bottom,
             multiplier: 1.0,
             constant: -20)
```

As we can see, the arguments to the method exactly match those of the equation (with the exception of the multiplier which is absent from the equation and therefore equates to 1 in the method call).

The following equation sets the width of a Button view named *myButton* to be 5 times the width of a Label view named *myLabel:*

```
var myConstraint =
          NSLayoutConstraint(item: myButton,
             attribute: NSLayoutConstraint.Attribute.width,
             relatedBy: NSLayoutRelation.equal,
             toItem: myLabel,
             attribute: NSLayoutConstraint.Attribute.width,
             multiplier: 5.0,
             constant: 0)
```

So far the examples shown in this chapter have been *equality* based constraints and, as such, the *relatedBy:* argument has been set to NSLayoutRelation.Equal. The following equation uses a greater than or equal to operator:

```
myButton.width >= 200
```

Translated into code, this reads as follows:

```
var myConstraint =
          NSLayoutConstraint(item: myButton,
             attribute: NSLayoutConstraint.Attribute.width,
             relatedBy: NSLayoutRelation.greaterThanOrEqual,
             toItem: nil,
             attribute: NSLayoutConstraint.Attribute.width,
             multiplier: 1.0,
             constant: 200)
```

Note that since this constraint is not related to another view, the *toItem:* argument is set to *nil.*

21.2 Adding a Constraint to a View

Once a constraint has been created, it needs to be assigned to a view in order to become active. This is achieved by passing it through as an argument to the *addConstraint* method of the view instance to which it is being added. In the case of multiple constraints, each is added by a separate call to the *addConstraint* method. This leads to the question of how to decide which view the constraint should be added to.

In the case of a constraint that references a single view, the constraint must be added to the immediate parent of the view. When a constraint references two views, the constraint must be applied to the closest ancestor of the two views. Consider, for the purposes of an example, the view hierarchy illustrated in Figure 21-1.

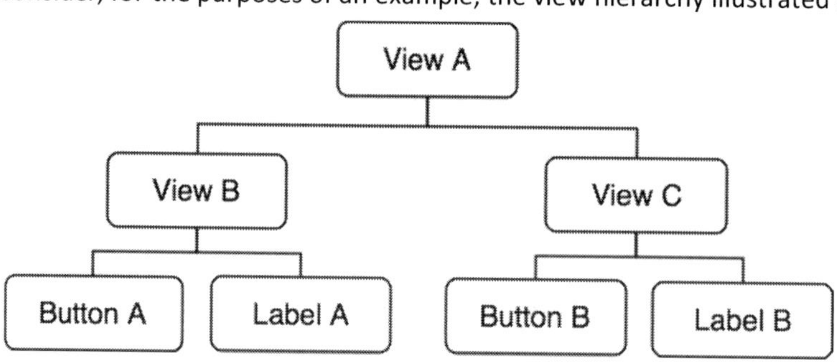

Figure 21-1

A constraint referencing only *Label A* should be added to the immediate parent, in this case *View B*. A constraint referencing *Button B* and *Label B*, on the other hand, must be added to the nearest common ancestor, which in this case is *View C*. A constraint referencing *Button A* and *Button B* must, once again, be added to the nearest common ancestor which equates to *View A*.

For the purposes of an example, the following code excerpt creates a new constraint and adds it to a view:

```
var myConstraint =
        NSLayoutConstraint(item: myButton,
            attribute: NSLayoutConstraint.Attribute.width,
            relatedBy: NSLayoutRelation.equal,
            toItem: myLabel,
            multiplier: 5.0,
            constant: 0)

self.view.addConstraint(myConstraint)
```

21.3 Turning off Auto Resizing Translation

When adding views to a layout in code the toolkit will, by default, attempt to convert the autosizing mask for that view to Auto Layout constraints. Unfortunately those auto-generated constraints will conflict with any constraints added within the application code. It is essential, therefore, that translation be turned off for views to which constraints are to be added in code. This is achieved by setting the *setTranslatesAutoresizingMaskIntoConstraints* property of the target view to *false*. For example, the following code creates a new Button view, turns off translation and then adds it to the parent view:

```
let myButton = UIButton()

myButton.setTitle("My Button", forState: UIControlState.normal)
myButton.translatesAutoresizingMaskIntoConstraints = false

self.view.addSubview(myButton)
```

21.4 An Example Application

Create a new Xcode project using the *Single View Application* template, select *Swift* from the language menu and enter *AutoLayoutCode* as the product name.

21.5 Creating the Views

For the purpose of this example, the code to create the views and constraints will be implemented in a new method named *createLayout* which will, in turn, be called from the *viewDidLoad* method of the *AutoLayoutCode* view controller. Select the *ViewController.swift* file and add this code to create a button and a label and add them to the main view:

```
override func viewDidLoad() {
    super.viewDidLoad()
    createLayout()
}

func createLayout() {
    let superview = self.view
```

```
    let myLabel = UILabel()
    myLabel.translatesAutoresizingMaskIntoConstraints = false
    myLabel.text = "My Label"

    let myButton = UIButton()

    myButton.setTitle("My Button", for: UIControl.State.normal)
    myButton.backgroundColor = UIColor.blue
    myButton.translatesAutoresizingMaskIntoConstraints = false

    superview?.addSubview(myLabel)
    superview?.addSubview(myButton)
}
```

21.6 Creating and Adding the Constraints

Constraints will be added to position the label in the horizontal and vertical center of the superview. The button will then be constrained to be positioned to the left of the label with the baselines of both views aligned. To achieve this layout, the *createLayout* method needs to be modified as follows:

```
func createLayout() {

    let superview = self.view

    let myLabel = UILabel()
    myLabel.translatesAutoresizingMaskIntoConstraints = false
    myLabel.text = "My Label"

    let myButton = UIButton()

    myButton.setTitle("My Button", for: UIControlState.normal)
    myButton.backgroundColor = UIColor.blue
    myButton.translatesAutoresizingMaskIntoConstraints = false

    superview?.addSubview(myLabel)
    superview?.addSubview(myButton)

    var myConstraint =
        NSLayoutConstraint(item: myLabel,
                attribute: NSLayoutConstraint.Attribute.centerY,
                relatedBy: NSLayoutConstraint.Relation.equal,
                toItem: superview,
                attribute: NSLayoutConstraint.Attribute.centerY,
                multiplier: 1.0,
                constant: 0)
```

```
    superview?.addConstraint(myConstraint)

    myConstraint =
        NSLayoutConstraint(item: myLabel,
                attribute: NSLayoutConstraint.Attribute.centerX,
                relatedBy: NSLayoutConstraint.Relation.equal,
                toItem: superview,
                attribute: NSLayoutConstraint.Attribute.centerX,
                multiplier: 1.0,
                constant: 0)

    superview?.addConstraint(myConstraint)

    myConstraint =
        NSLayoutConstraint(item: myButton,
                attribute: NSLayoutConstraint.Attribute.trailing,
                relatedBy: NSLayoutConstraint.Relation.equal,
                toItem: myLabel,
                attribute: NSLayoutConstraint.Attribute.leading,
                multiplier: 1.0,
                constant: -10)

    superview?.addConstraint(myConstraint)

    myConstraint =
        NSLayoutConstraint(item: myButton,
                attribute: NSLayoutConstraint.Attribute.lastBaseline,
                relatedBy: NSLayoutConstraint.Relation.equal,
                toItem: myLabel,
                attribute: NSLayoutConstraint.Attribute.lastBaseline,
                multiplier: 1.0,
                constant: 0)

    superview?.addConstraint(myConstraint)
}
```

When the application is compiled and run, the layout of the two views should match that illustrated in Figure 21-2.

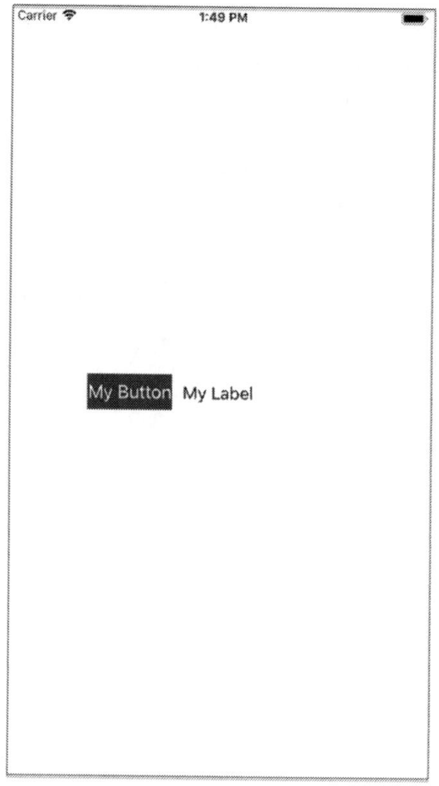

Figure 21-2

21.7 Removing Constraints

While it has not been necessary to do so in this example, it is important to be aware that it is also possible to remove constraints from a view. This can be achieved simply by calling the *removeConstraint* method of the view to which the constraint was added, passing through as an argument the NSLayoutConstraint object matching the constraint to be removed:

```
self.myview.removeConstraint(myconstraint)
```

It is also worth knowing that constraints initially created in Interface Builder can be connected to outlet properties, thereby allowing them to be referenced in code. The steps involved in creating an outlet for a constraint are covered in more detail in *Implementing Cross-Hierarchy Auto Layout Constraints in iOS 12*.

21.8 Summary

While Interface Builder is the recommended method for implementing Auto Layout constraints, there are still situations where it may be necessary to implement constraints in code. This is typically necessary when dynamically creating user interfaces, or in situations where specific layout behavior cannot be achieved using Interface Builder (a prime example of this being constraints that cross view hierarchies as outlined in the next chapter).

Constraints are created in code by instantiating instances of the NSLayoutConstraint class, configuring those instances with the appropriate constraint settings and then adding the constraints to the appropriate views in the user interface.

Chapter 22

22. Implementing Cross-Hierarchy Auto Layout Constraints in iOS 12

One of the few types of Auto Layout constraint that cannot be implemented within the Interface Builder environment is one that references views contained in different view hierarchies. Constraints of this type must, therefore, be implemented in code. Fortunately, however, the steps to achieve this are quite simple. The objective of this chapter is to work through an example that demonstrates the creation of a cross-view hierarchy Auto Layout constraint.

22.1 The Example Application

For the purposes of this example, a very simple user interface will be created consisting of two Views, a Button and a Label. In terms of the physical view hierarchy, the user interface will be constructed as outlined in Figure 22-1.

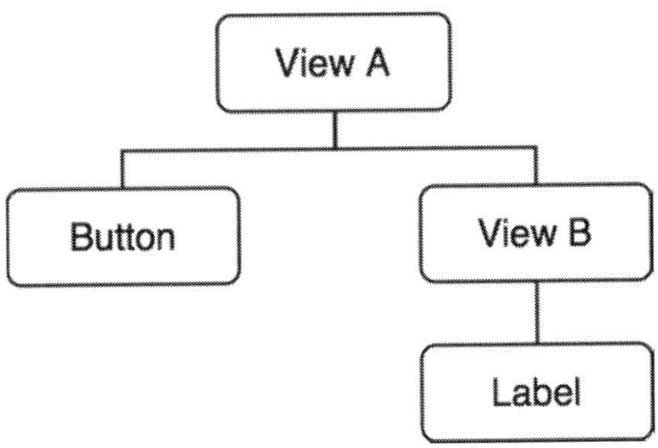

Figure 22-1

The goal will be to implement a constraint that aligns the centers of the Button and Label which are part of different view hierarchies - the button being part of the hierarchy contained by View A and the label being part of the View B sub-hierarchy.

In terms of visual layout, the user interface should appear as illustrated in Figure 22-2. Key points to note are that the label should have constraints associated with it which horizontally and vertically center it within View B and the button view should be positioned so that it is off center in the horizontal axis:

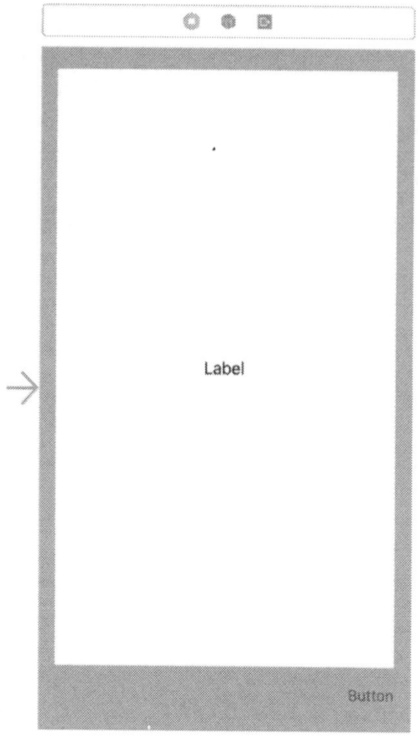

Figure 22-2

Begin by launching Xcode and selecting the options to create a new iOS application based on the *Single View Application* template. Enter *CrossView* as the product name and set the Language menu to *Swift*.

Select the *Main.storyboard* file from the project navigator panel, select the view and change the background color to a light shade of grey using the Attributes Inspector. Drag and drop UIView, Button and Label views onto the design canvas as illustrated in Figure 22-2, making sure to center the label object horizontally and vertically within the parent view.

Select the newly added View object, click on the *Resolve Auto Layout Issues* menu from the toolbar in the lower right-hand corner of the canvas and select the *Reset to Suggested Constraints* option listed under *All Views in View Controller*.

22.2 Establishing Outlets

In order to set a cross hierarchy constraint within code, it will be necessary to implement some outlets. Since the constraint will need to reference both the button and the label, outlets need to be configured for these views. Select the label object and display the Assistant Editor using the *View -> Assistant Editor -> Show Assistant Editor* menu option or by selecting the center button (the one containing an image of two interlocking circles) of the row of Editor toolbar buttons in the top right-hand corner of the main Xcode window.

Make sure that the Assistant Editor is showing the *ViewController.swift* file. Ctrl-click on the Label object in the view and drag the resulting line to the area immediately beneath the class declaration directive in the Assistant Editor panel. Upon releasing the line, the connection panel will appear. Configure the connection as an *Outlet* named *myLabel* and click on the *Connect* button. Repeat the above steps to add an outlet for the button object named *myButton*.

As currently constrained, the label object is centered horizontally within the view we are referring to as View B. In place of this constraint, we need the label to be aligned with the center of the button object. This will involve removing the CenterX constraint and replacing it with a new constraint referencing the button. This requires outlets for both the View B instance and the CenterX constraint.

Ctrl-click on the View B parent of the label object and drag the resulting line to the area immediately beneath the previously declared outlets in the Assistant Editor. Release the line and configure an outlet named *viewB*.

Next, select the label object so that the associated constraint lines appear. Click on the vertical line passing through the label view so that it highlights. Ctrl-click on the constraint line and drag to the Assistant Editor panel (Figure 22-3) and create a new outlet for this object named *centerConstraint*.

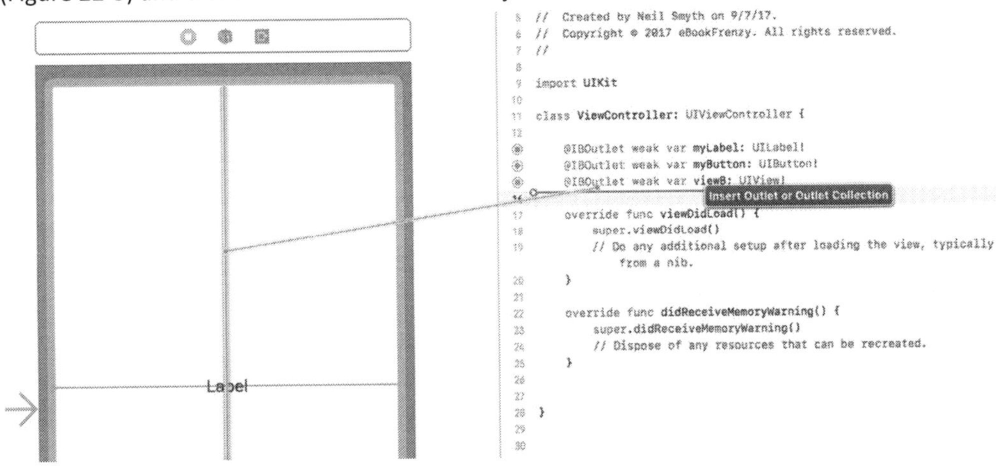

Figure 22-3

22.3 Writing the Code to Remove the Old Constraint

With the necessary outlets created, the next step is to write some code to remove the center constraint from the label object. For the purposes of this example, all code will be added to the *viewDidLoad* method of the view controller. Select the *ViewController.swift* file and locate and modify the method as follows:

```
override func viewDidLoad() {
    super.viewDidLoad()
    viewB.removeConstraint(centerConstraint)
}
```

All that the code is doing is calling the *removeConstraint* method of view B using the previously configured outlet, passing through a reference to the CenterX constraint, once again using the previously configured outlet to that object.

22.4 Adding the Cross Hierarchy Constraint

All that remains is to add the constraint to align the centers of the label and button. With the appropriate outlets already configured, this is simply a matter of creating the NSLayoutConstraint object with the appropriate values, and adding it to the closest common ancestor:

```
override func viewDidLoad() {
    super.viewDidLoad()

    viewB.removeConstraint(centerConstraint)
```

```
    let constraint =
        NSLayoutConstraint(item: myLabel,
                attribute: NSLayoutConstraint.Attribute.centerX,
                relatedBy: NSLayoutConstraint.Relation.equal,
                toItem: myButton,
                attribute: NSLayoutConstraint.Attribute.centerX,
                multiplier: 1.0,
                constant: 0.0)

    self.view.addConstraint(constraint)
}
```

22.5 Testing the Application

Compile and run the application either on a physical iOS device, or using the iOS Simulator. When the application is running, the label view should be aligned with the button and this alignment should be maintained when the device is rotated into landscape orientation.

22.6 Summary

The current version of Interface Builder does not provide a way to select two views that reside in different view-hierarchies and configure a constraint between them. The desired result can, as outlined in this chapter, be achieved in code. Of key importance in this process is the fact that constraints, just like any other view object in a user interface, may be connected to an outlet and accessed via code.

Chapter 23

23. Understanding the iOS 12 Auto Layout Visual Format Language

The third and final option for the creation of Auto Layout constraints involves a combination of code and the visual format language. The goal of this chapter is to provide an introduction to the visual format language and to work through some code samples that demonstrate the concept in action.

23.1 Introducing the Visual Format Language

The visual format language is not a new programming language in the way that C++, Java and Swift are all programming languages. Instead, the visual format language defines a syntax through which Auto Layout constraints may be created using sequences of ASCII characters. These visual format character sequences are then turned into constraints by passing them through to the *constraints(withVisualFormat:)* method of the NSLayoutConstraint class.

What makes the language particularly appealing and intuitive is that the syntax used to define a constraint involves characters sequences that, to a large extent, visually represent the constraint that is being created.

23.2 Visual Format Language Examples

By far the easiest way to understand the concepts behind the visual format language is to look at some examples of the syntax. Take for example, visual format language syntax to describe a view object:

```
[myButton]
```

As we can see, view objects are described in the visual format language by surrounding the view name with square brackets ([]).

Two views may be constrained to be positioned flush with each other by placing the views side by side in the visual format string:

```
[myButton1][myButton2]
```

Similarly, a horizontal spacer between two view objects is represented by a hyphen:

```
[myButton1]-[myButton2]
```

The above example instructs the Auto Layout system to create a constraint using the standard spacing for views. The following construct, on the other hand, specifies a spacing distance of 30 points between the two views:

```
[myButton1]-30-[myButton2]
```

By default, constraints of the type outlined above are assumed to be horizontal constraints. Vertical constraints are declared using a *V:* prefix. For example, the following syntax establishes a vertical spacing constraint between two views:

```
V:[myLabel]-50-[myButton]
```

For consistency and completeness, horizontal constraints may, optionally, be prefixed with *H:*.

The width of a view can be set specifically as follows:

```
[myButton(100)]
```

Alternatively, inequality can be used:

```
[myButton(<=100)]
```

Using similar syntax, the width of one view can be constrained to match that of a second view:

```
[myLabel(==myButton2)]
```

When using the visual format language, the superview of the view for which the constraint is being described is represented by the | character. For example, the following visual format language construct declares a constraint for the myButton1 view that attaches the leading and trailing edges of the view to the left and right edges of the containing superview with a spacing of 20 and 30 points respectively:

```
|-20-[myButton1]-30-|
```

The language also allows priorities to be declared. The following excerpt specifies that the width of myButton1 must be greater than, or equal to 70 points with a priority value of 500:

```
[myButton1(>=70@500)]
```

Of particular importance, however, is the fact that the language may be used to construct multiple constraints in a single sequence, for example:

```
V:|-20-[myButton1(>=70@500)]-[myButton2(==myButton1)]-30-[myButton3]-|
```

23.3 Using the constraints(withVisualFormat:) Method

As previously described, visual language format based constraints are created via a call to the *constraints(withVisualFormat:)* method of the NSLayoutConstraint class. There are, however a number of other arguments that the method is able to accept. The syntax for the method is as follows:

```
NSLayoutConstraint.constraints(withVisualFormat: <visual format string>,
        options: <options>,
        metrics: <metrics>,
        views: <views dictionary>)
```

The <visual format string> is, of course, the visual format language string that describes the constraints that are to be created. The <options> are required to be set when the constraint string references more than one view. The purpose of this is to indicate how the views are to be aligned and the value must be of type NSLayoutFormatOptions, for example .alignAllLeft, .alignAllRight, .alignAllTop, .alignAllLastBaselines etc.

The <metrics> argument is an optional Dictionary object containing the corresponding values for any constants referenced in the format string.

Finally, the <views dictionary> is a Dictionary object that contains the view objects that match the view names referenced in the format string.

When using a visual format string that will result in the creation of multiple constraints, the options should include an alignment directive such as NSLayoutFormatOptions.alignAllLastBaseLines.

Since the method is able to create multiple constraints based on the visual format string, it returns an array of NSLayoutConstraint objects, one for each constraint, which must then be added to the appropriate view object.

Some sample code to create views and then specify multiple constraints using a visual format language string, would, therefore, read as follows:

```
// Get a reference to the superview
let superview = self.view

//Create a label
let myLabel = UILabel()
myLabel.translatesAutoresizingMaskIntoConstraints = false
myLabel.text = "My Label"
//Create a button
let myButton = UIButton()
myButton.backgroundColor = UIColor.red
myButton.setTitle("My Button", for: UIControlState.normal)
myButton.translatesAutoresizingMaskIntoConstraints = false

// Add the button and label to the superview
superview?.addSubview(myLabel)
superview?.addSubview(myButton)

// Create the views dictionary
let viewsDictionary = ["myLabel": myLabel, "myButton": myButton]

// Create and add the vertical constraints
superview?.addConstraints(NSLayoutConstraint.constraints(
   withVisualFormat: "V:|-[myButton]-|",
       options: NSLayoutConstraint.FormatOptions.alignAllLastBaseline,
       metrics: nil,
       views: viewsDictionary))

// Create and add the horizontal constraints
superview?.addConstraints(NSLayoutConstraint.constraints(
    withVisualFormat: "|-[myButton]-[myLabel(==myButton)]-|",
      options: NSLayoutConstraint.FormatOptions.alignAllLastBaseline,
      metrics: nil,
      views: viewsDictionary))
```

23.4 Summary

The visual format language allows Auto Layout constraints to be created using sequences of characters that have been designed to visually represent the constraint that is being described. Visual format strings are converted into constraints via a call to the *constraints(withVisualFormat:)* method of the NSLayoutConstraints class which, in turn, returns an array containing an NSLayoutConstraint object for each new constraint created as a result of parsing the visual format string.

Chapter 24

24. Using Trait Variations to Design Adaptive iOS 12 User Interfaces

In 2007 developers only had to design user interfaces for a single screen size and resolution (that of the first generation iPhone). Taking into consideration the range of iOS devices, screen sizes and resolutions available today, the task of designing a single user interface layout to target the full range of device configurations now seems a much more daunting task.

Although eased to some degree by the introduction of Auto Layout, designing a user interface layout that would work on both iPhone and iPad device families (otherwise known as an *adaptive interface*) typically involved the creation and maintenance of two storyboard files, one for each device type.

iOS 9 and Xcode 7 introduced the concepts of *trait variations* and *size classes*, intended specifically to allow a user interface layout for multiple screen sizes and orientations to be designed within a single storyboard file. In this chapter of iOS 12 App Development Essentials, the concept of traits and size classes will be covered together with a sample application that demonstrates how to use them to create an adaptive user interface.

24.1 Understanding Traits and Size Classes

Traits define the features of the environment an app is likely to encounter when running on an iOS device. Traits can be defined both by the hardware of the device and the way in which the iOS environment has been configured by the user. Examples of hardware based traits include hardware features such as the range of colors supported by the device display (also referred to as the *display gamut*) and whether or not the device supports features such as 3D Touch. The traits of a device that are dictated by user configuration include the dynamic type size setting and whether the device is configured for left to right or right to left text direction.

Arguably the most powerful trait category, however, relates specifically to the size and orientation of the device screen. These trait values are referred to as *size classes*.

Size classes categorize the various screen areas that an application user interface is likely to encounter during execution. Rather than represent specific screen dimensions and orientations, size classes represent *width* (w) and *height* (h) in terms of being *compact* (C) or *regular* (R).

All iPhone models in portrait orientation are represented by the compact width and regular height size class (wC hR). When the iPhone 8 or iPhone XS is rotated to landscape orientation the device is considered to be of compact height and compact width (wC hC). The iPhone 8 Plus, iPhone XR or XS Max models in landscape orientation, on the other hand, are categorized as being of compact height and regular width (wR hC).

In terms of size class categorization, the iPad family of devices (including the iPad Pro) is considered to be of regular height and regular width (wR hR) in both portrait and landscape orientation. A range of different size class settings are used when apps are displayed on the iPad using multitasking, a topic covered in detail in the *A Guide to Multitasking in iOS 12* chapter of this book.

24.2 Size Classes in Interface Builder

Interface Builder in Xcode 10 allows different Auto Layout constraints to be configured for different size class settings within a single storyboard file. In other words, size classes allow a single user interface file to store multiple sets of layout data, with each data set targeting a particular size class. At runtime, the application will use the layout data set for the size class that matches the device and prevailing orientation on which it is executing, ensuring that the user interface appears correctly.

By default, any layout settings configured within the Interface Builder environment will apply to all size classes. Only when *trait variations* are specifically specified will the layout configuration settings differ between size classes.

Customizing a user interface for different size classes goes beyond the ability to configure different Auto Layout constraints for different size classes. Size classes may also be used to designate which views in a layout are visible within each class, and also which version of a particular image is displayed to the user. A smaller image may be used when an app is running on an iPhone SE, for example, or extra buttons might be made to appear to take advantage of the larger iPad screen.

24.3 Setting "Any" Defaults

When designing user interfaces using size classes, there will often be situations where particular Auto Layout constraints or view settings will be appropriate for all size classes. Rather than having to configure these same settings for each size class these can, instead, be configured within the *Any* category. Such settings will be picked up by default by all other size classes unless specifically overridden within those classes.

24.4 Working with Trait Variations in Interface Builder

A key part of working with trait variations involves the use of the device configuration bar. Located along the bottom edge of the Interface Builder storyboard canvas is an indicator showing the currently selected device and the corresponding size class as illustrated in Figure 24-1:

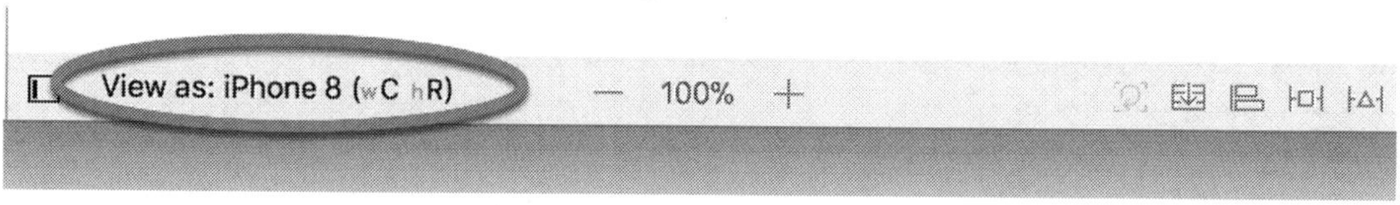

Figure 24-1

Clicking on the current setting in the status bar will display the device configuration bar shown in Figure 24-2. This panel displays all of the different iOS device types together with the option to select portrait or landscape orientation:

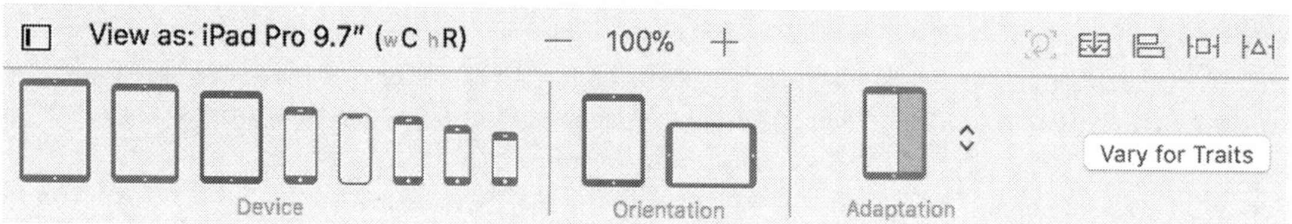

Figure 24-2

Note that when an iPad model is selected from the device options, in addition to orientation settings, adaptation options are also provided so that layout behavior can be tested for multitasking split-screen and slide over modes.

When device and orientation selections are made from the configuration bar, the scenes within the storyboard canvas will re-size to match exactly the screen size corresponding to the selected device and orientation. This provides a quick way to test the adaptivity of layouts within the storyboard without the need to compile and run the app on different devices or emulator sessions.

24.5 Attributes Inspector Trait Variations

Regardless of the current selection in the device configuration panel, any changes made to layouts or views within the current storyboard will, by default, apply to all devices and size classes (essentially the "Any" size class). Trait variations (in other words configuration settings that apply to specific size classes) may, however, be configured in two ways.

One option is to set size class specific properties within the Attributes Inspector panel. Consider, for example, a Label view contained within a storyboard scene. This label is required to display text at a 17pt font size for all size classes with the exception of regular width and height where a 30pt font is required. Reviewing the Attributes Inspector panel shows that the 17pt font setting is already configured as shown in Figure 24-3:

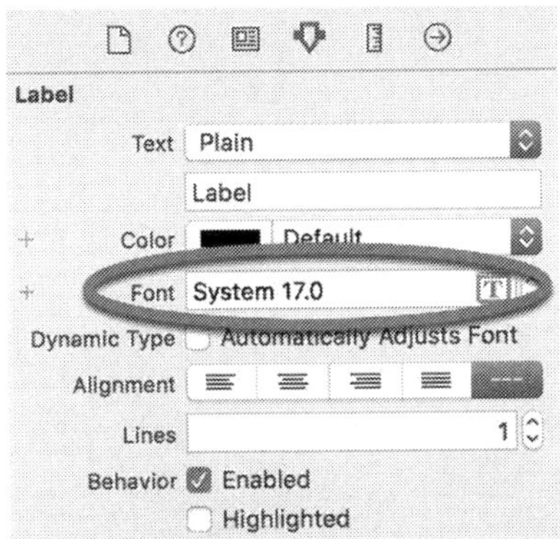

Figure 24-3

The absence of any size class information next to the attribute setting tells us that the font setting corresponds to the any width, any height, any gamut size class and will be used on all devices and orientations unless overridden. To the left of the attribute field is a + button as indicated in Figure 24-4:

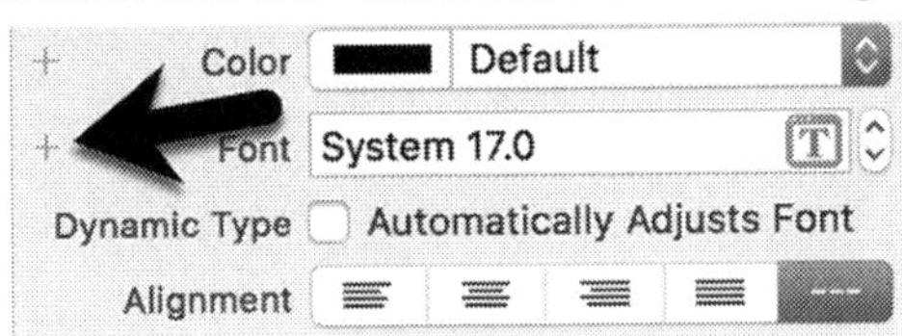

Figure 24-4

This is the *Add customization* button which, when selected, displays a panel of menus allowing size class selections to be made for a trait variation. To configure a different font size for any height, regular width and any gamut, for example, the menu selections shown in Figure 24-5 would need to be made:

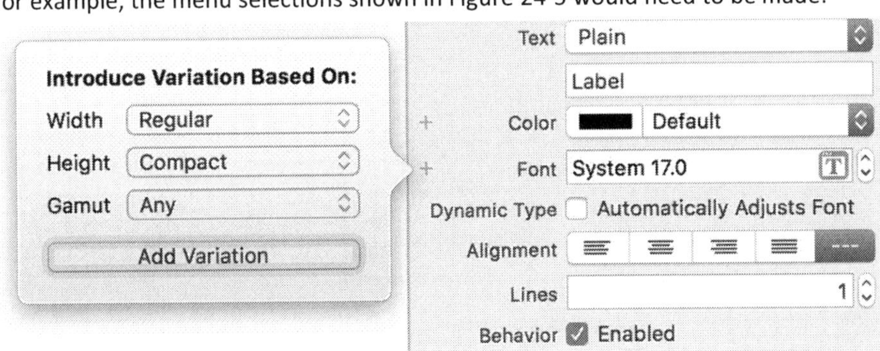

Figure 24-5

Once the trait configuration has been added, it appears within the Attributes Inspector panel labelled as wR and may be used to configure a larger font for any regular width size class regardless of height or gamut:

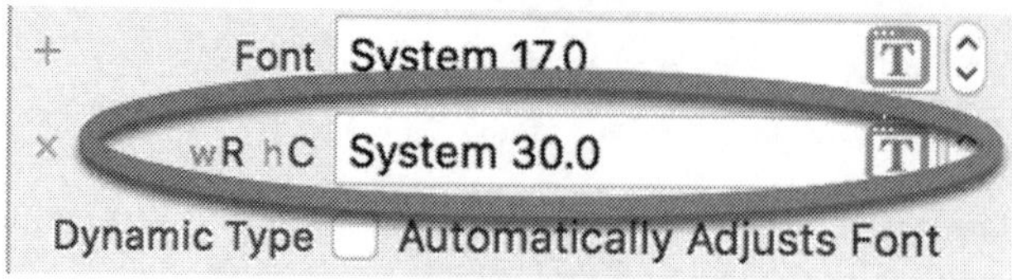

Figure 24-6

24.6 Using Vary for Traits Layout Variations

An alternative, and more wide ranging approach to implementing trait variations, and one that applies to layouts as opposed to individual attributes, is to use the *Vary for Traits* menu located on the right-hand side of the device configuration bar. Using this menu, trait variations may be enabled in width, height or both dimensions as shown in Figure 24-7:

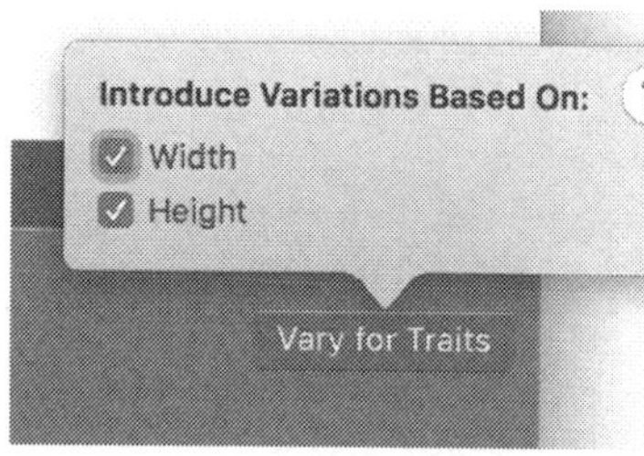

Figure 24-7

Once enabled, any subsequent layout changes made within the storyboard will apply only to the currently selected size class within the device configuration panel. Once this mode has been enabled, the device configuration bar turns blue as a reminder that future layout changes are size class specific.

As an example, assume that a layout contains a Button view that is to be centered horizontally and vertically within the scene when encountering regular width size class configurations. The first step in achieving this result using *Vary for Traits* mode is to display the device configuration bar and select a regular width device configuration:

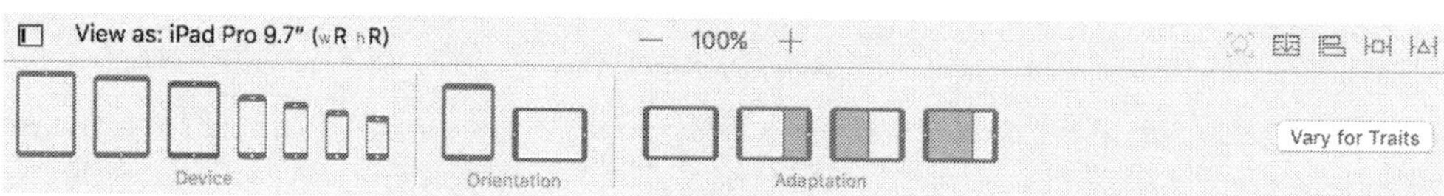

Figure 24-8

Next, click on the *Vary for Traits* button and enable only the width option (since the layout requirement applies only to regular width configurations). Having made this selection, the device configuration panel turns blue and now lists only the subset of configurations that conform to the regular width size class requirement:

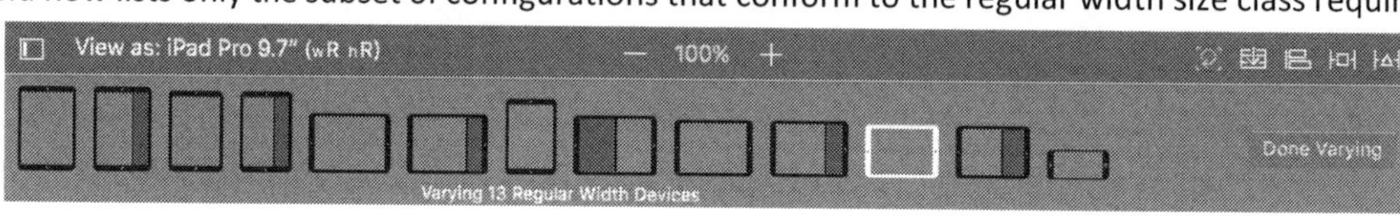

Figure 24-9

Finally, the Button is selected in the scene and the Auto Layout alignment menu used to center the view both horizontally and vertically.

As long as the vary for traits mode is enabled all layout configuration settings will apply only to the subset of regular width size class configurations shown in the device configuration panel. Once the changes are complete, click on the *Done Varying* button located on the right-hand side of the device configuration panel to turn off trait variations.

24.7 An Adaptive User Interface Tutorial

The remainder of this chapter will work through the creation of an adaptive user interface example.

Create a new Xcode Single View Application project named *AdaptiveDemo* with the language option set to Swift.

The goal of this tutorial is to create a very simple adaptive layout that demonstrates each of the key features of trait variations including setting individual attributes, using the vary for traits process and the implementation of image asset catalogs in the context of size classes.

24.8 Designing the Initial Layout

The iPhone 8 in portrait orientation will serve as the base layout configuration for the user interface, so begin by selecting the *Main.storyboard* file and making sure that the device configuration bar currently has the iPhone 8 (wC hR) device selected.

Drag and drop a Label view so that it is positioned in the horizontal center of the scene and slightly beneath the top edge of the safe area of the view controller scene. With the Label still selected, use the Auto Layout Align menu to add a constraint to center the view horizontally within the container. Using the *Add New Constraints* menu, set a *Spacing to nearest neighbor* constraint on the top edge of the Label using the current value and with the *Constrain to Margins* option enabled.

Double-click on the Label and change the text to read "A Sunset Photo". Next, drag and drop an Image View object from the Library panel so that it is positioned beneath the Label and centered horizontally within the scene. Resize the Image View so that the layout resembles that illustrated in Figure 24-10:

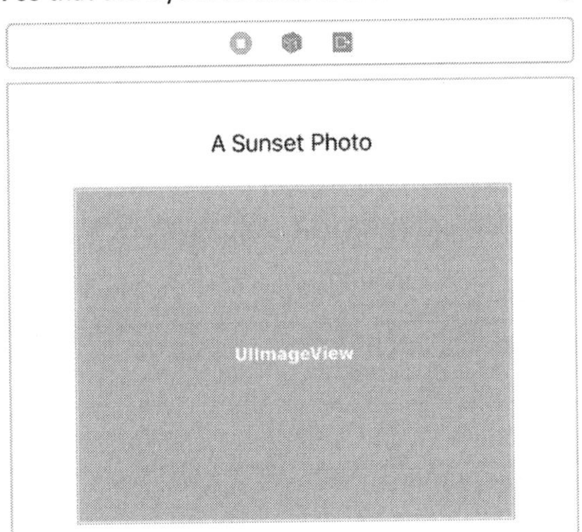

Figure 24-10

With the Image View selected, display the Align menu and enable the option to center the view horizontally within the container, then use the *Add New Constraints* menu to add a nearest neighbor constraint on the top edge of the Image View with the *Constrain to Margins* option disabled and to set a Width constraint of 320:

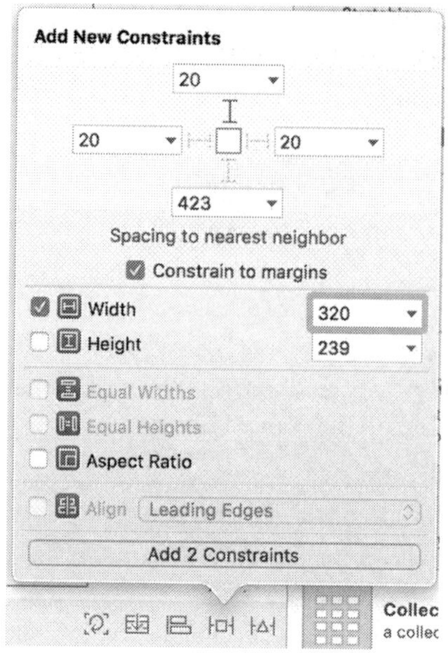

Figure 24-11

Ctrl-click and drag diagonally across the Image View as shown in Figure 24-12. On releasing the line, select *Aspect Ratio* from the resulting menu.

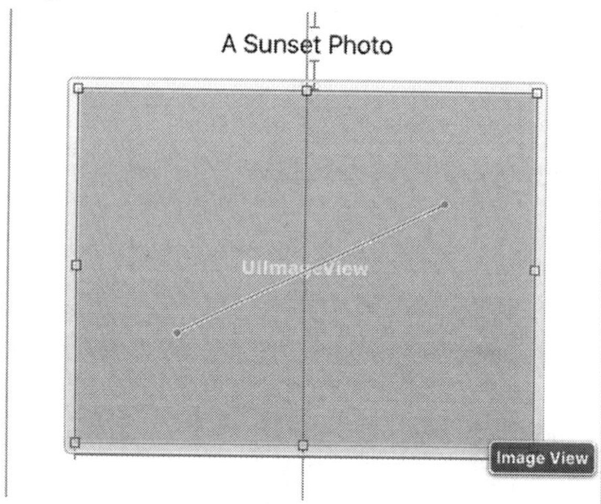

Figure 24-12

If necessary, click the Update Frames button in the status bar to reset the views to match the constraints.

24.9 Adding Universal Image Assets

The next step in the tutorial is to add some image assets to the project. The images can be found in the *adaptive_images* directory of the code samples download which can be obtained from:

https://www.ebookfrenzy.com/retail/ios12/

Within the project navigator panel, locate and click on the *Assets.xcassets* entry and, once loaded, select the *Editor -> Add Assets -> New Image Set* menu option. Double-click on the new image set which will have been named *Image* and rename it to *Sunset*.

Locate the *sunset_wAny_hAny@2x.jpg* file in a Finder window and drag and drop it onto the 2x image box as illustrated below:

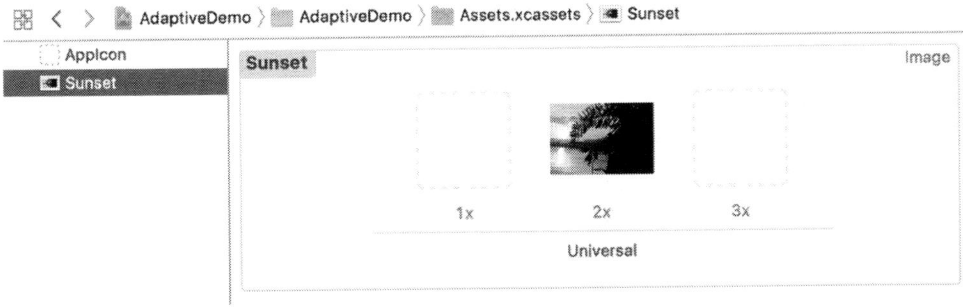

Figure 24-13

Return to the *Main.storyboard* file, select the Image View and display the Attributes Inspector panel. Click on the down arrow at the right of the Image field and select *Sunset* from the resulting menu. The Image View in the view controller canvas will update to display the sunset image from the asset catalog.

Switch between device types and note that the same image is used for all size classes. The next step is to add a different image to be displayed in regular width size class configurations.

Once again, select *Assets.xcassets* from the project navigator panel and, with the *Sunset* image set selected, display the Attributes Inspector and change the *Width Class* attribute to *Any & Compact*. Within the Sunset image set, an additional row of image options will appear. Once again, locate the images in the sample source code download, this time dragging and dropping the *sunset_wCompact_hRegular@2x.jpg* file onto the 2x image well in the compact row as shown in Figure 24-14:

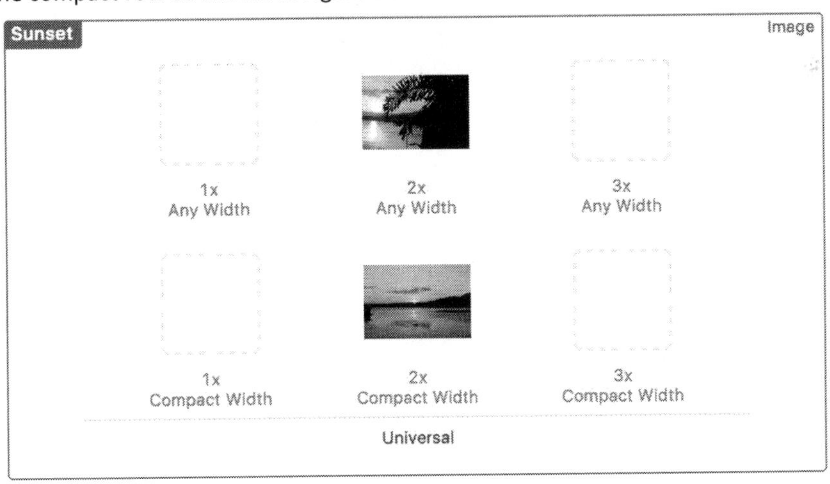

Figure 24-14

Return to the *Main.storyboard* file and verify that different sunset images appear when switching between compact and regular width size class configurations.

24.10 Increasing Font Size for iPad Devices

The next step in the tutorial is to add some trait variations that will apply when the app is running in regular width and regular height size class device configurations (in other words when running on an iPad). The first variation is to use a larger font on the Label object.

Begin by choosing an iPad device from the device configuration bar, then selecting the Label object in the scene. Display the Attributes Inspector panel and click on the + button next to the font property as illustrated in Figure 24-4 above. From the resulting menu, select the *Regular Width | Regular Height | Any Gamut* menu settings and click on the *Add Variation* button. Within the new wR hR font attribute field, increase the font size to 35pt.

Using the device configuration bar, test that the new font applies only to iPad device configurations.

24.11 **Using Vary for Traits**

The next step is to increase the size of the Image View when the app encounters an iPad device size class. Since the Image View has a constraint that preserves aspect ratio, only the width constraint needs to be modified to achieve this goal.

Select an iPad from the device configuration bar, click on the *Vary for Traits* button and enable variations for both height and width. Note that the bar changes to blue to warn us that any layout changes will apply only to wR hR size classes.

Click twice on the Image View object in the scene so that the width constraint marker line appears. Double-click on the width constraint line so that the configuration popup panel appears as shown in Figure 24-15:

Figure 24-15

Within the panel, increase the width constant property to 600 at which point the Image View should proportionally increase in size.

The final step is to add a button that will only be present on regular width, regular height size class configurations. Remaining in Vary for Traits mode, select a Button from the Library panel and place it so that it is centered horizontally beneath the Image View. Use the Align menu to position the Button horizontally within the container and the *Add New Constraints* menu to add a nearest neighbor constraint on the top edge using the current value with the *Constrain to Margins* option disabled.

Double-click on the Button object and change the text to read "Edit". With the variations completed, click on the *Done Varying* button to revert to the normal layout mode.

24.12 **Testing the Adaptivity**

Use the device configuration bar to test a range of size class permutations. Assuming that the adaptivity settings are working, a larger font together with a larger, different image and an extra button should appear when previewing iPad configurations. Note also that the image changes when displayed on an iPhone 8 Plus since the image change only required a regular width configuration, which is the case for the iPhone 8 Plus in landscape orientation (wR hC). Since the height in this configuration is compact, however, the additional Button and increased image size do not apply since these trait variations required both regular height and width.

24.13 Testing the Application

Use the iOS simulator to perform test runs of the application on different device families and note that, depending on the target device and orientation, the appropriate layout and image are adopted.

24.14 Summary

The range of iOS device screen sizes and resolutions is much more diverse than it was when the original iPhone was introduced in 2007. Today, developers need to be able to target an increasingly wide range of display sizes when designing user interface layouts for iOS applications. With size classes and trait variations, it is possible to target all screen sizes, resolutions and orientations from within a single storyboard. This chapter has outlined the basics of size classes and trait variations, and worked through a simple example user interface layout designed for both the iPad and iPhone device families.

Chapter 25

25. Using Storyboards in Xcode 10

Storyboarding is a feature built into Xcode that allows both the various screens that comprise an iOS application and the navigation path through those screens to be visually assembled. Using the Interface Builder component of Xcode, the developer simply drags and drops view and navigation controllers onto a canvas and designs the user interface of each view in the normal manner. The developer then drags lines to link individual trigger controls (such as a button) to the corresponding view controllers that are to be displayed when the control is selected by the user. Having designed both the screens (referred to in the context of storyboarding as *scenes*) and specified the transitions between scenes (referred to as *segues*) Xcode generates all the code necessary to implement the defined behavior in the completed application. The style of transition for each segue (page fold, cross dissolve etc) may also be defined within Interface Builder. Further, segues may also be triggered programmatically in situations where behavior cannot be defined graphically using Interface Builder.

The finished design is saved by Xcode to a *storyboard file*. Typically, an application will have a single storyboard file, though there is no restriction preventing the use of multiple storyboard files within a single application.

The remainder of this chapter will work through the creation of a simple application using storyboarding to implement multiple scenes with segues defined to allow user navigation.

25.1 Creating the Storyboard Example Project

Begin by launching Xcode and creating a new project named *Storyboard* using the *Single View Application* template with the language menu set to *Swift*. Save the project to a suitable location by clicking on the *Create* button.

25.2 Accessing the Storyboard

Upon creation of the new project, Xcode will have created what appears to be the usual collection of files for a single view application, including a storyboard file named *Main.storyboard.* Select this file in the project navigator panel to view the storyboard canvas as illustrated in Figure 25-1.

The view displayed on the canvas is the view for the *ViewController* class created for us by Xcode when we selected the *Single View Application* template. The arrow pointing inwards to the left side of the view indicates that this is the initial view controller and will be the first view displayed when the application launches. To change the initial view controller simply drag this arrow to any other scene in the storyboard and drop it in place.

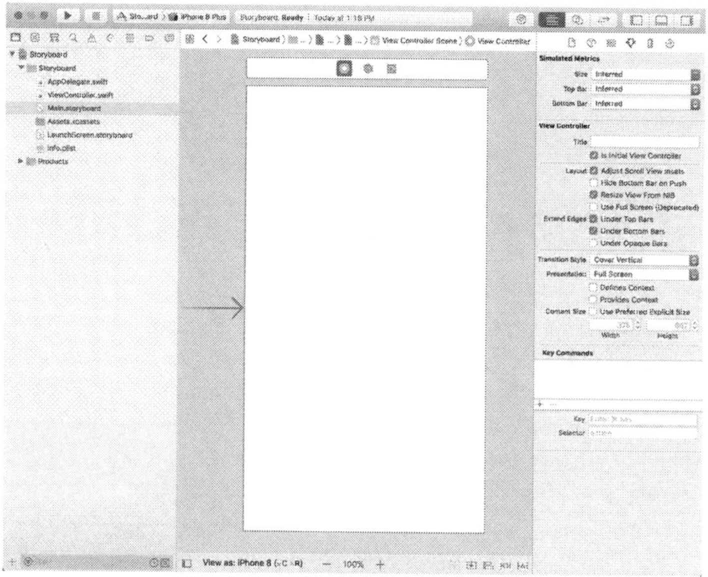

Figure 25-1

Objects may be added to the view in the usual manner by displaying the Library panel and dragging and dropping objects onto the view canvas. For the purposes of this example, drag a label and a button onto the view canvas. Using the properties panel, change the label text to *Scene 1* and the button text to *Go to Scene 2*.

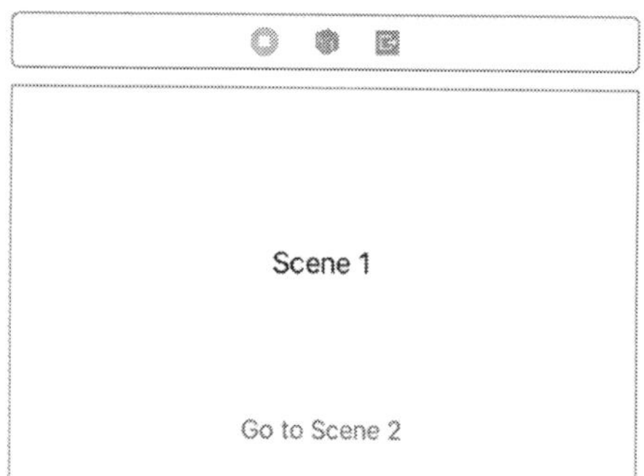

Figure 25-2

Using the *Resolve Auto Layout Issues* menu, select the *Reset to Suggested Constraints* option listed under *All Views in View Controller.*

In order to manipulate text displayed on the label object from within the application code it will be necessary to first establish an outlet. Select the label in the storyboard canvas and display the Assistant Editor (*View -> Assistant Editor -> Show Assistant Editor*). Check that the Assistant Editor is showing the content of the *ViewController.swift* file and then Ctrl-click on the label and drag the resulting line to just below the class declaration line in the Assistant Editor panel. In the resulting connection dialog, enter *scene1Label* as the outlet name and click on the *Connect* button. Upon completion of the connection, the top of the *ViewController.swift* file should read as follows:

```
import UIKit

class ViewController: UIViewController {
```

```
@IBOutlet weak var scene1Label: UILabel!
```

25.3 Adding Scenes to the Storyboard

To add a second scene to the storyboard, simply drag a View Controller object from the Library panel onto the canvas. Figure 25-3 shows a second scene added to a storyboard:

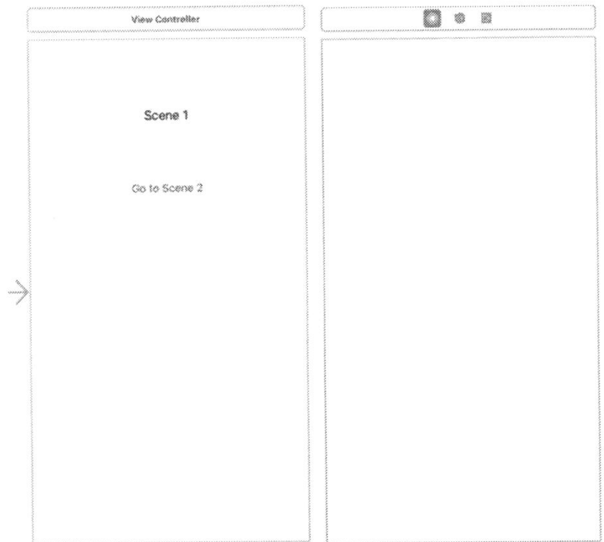

Figure 25-3

Drag and drop a label and a button into the second scene and configure the objects so that the view appears as shown in Figure 25-4. Repeat the steps performed for the first scene to configure the necessary Auto Layout constraints on the two views.

Figure 25-4

As many scenes as necessary may be added to the storyboard, but for the purposes of this exercise we will use just two scenes. Having implemented the scenes the next step is to configure segues between the scenes.

25.4 Configuring Storyboard Segues

As previously discussed, a segue is the transition from one scene to another within a storyboard. Within the example application, touching the *Go To Scene 2* button will segue to scene 2. Conversely, the button on scene 2 is intended to return the user to scene 1. To establish a segue, hold down the Ctrl key on the keyboard, click over a control (in this case the button on scene 1) and drag the resulting line to the scene 2 view. Upon releasing the mouse button a menu will appear. Select the *Present Modally* menu option to establish the segue.

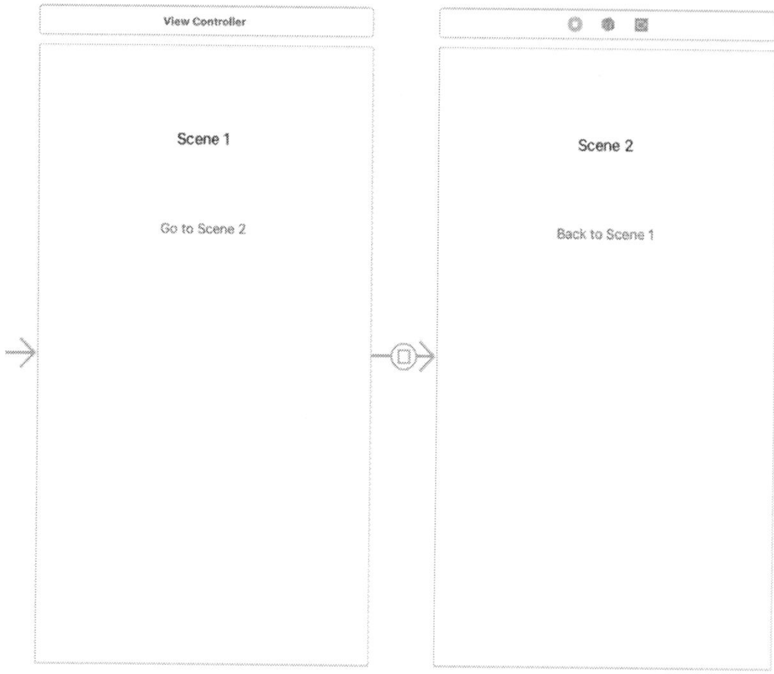

Figure 25-5

As more scenes are added to a storyboard, it becomes increasingly difficult to see more than a few scenes at one time on the canvas. To zoom out double-click on the canvas. To zoom back in again simply double-click once again on the canvas. The zoom level may also be changed using the plus and minus control buttons located in the status bar along the bottom edge of the storyboard canvas, or by Ctrl-clicking on the storyboard canvas background to access a menu containing a number of zoom level options.

25.5 Configuring Storyboard Transitions

Xcode provides the option to change the visual appearance of the transition that takes place during a segue. To change the transition, select the corresponding segue line, display the Attributes Inspector (*View -> Utilities -> Show Attributes Inspector*) and modify the *Transition* setting. In Figure 25-6 the transition has been changed to *Cross Dissolve:*

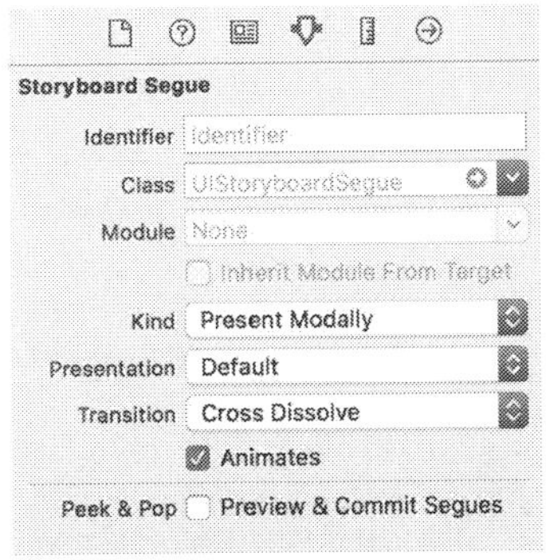

Figure 25-6

If animation is not required during the transition, turn off the *Animates* option. To delete a segue from a storyboard simply select the segue line in the storyboard canvas and press the keyboard delete key.

Compile and run the application. Note that touching the "Go to Scene 2" button causes Scene 2 to appear.

25.6 Associating a View Controller with a Scene

At this point in the example we have two scenes but only one view controller (the one created by Xcode when we selected *Single View Application*). Clearly in order to be able to add any functionality behind scene 2 it too will need a view controller. The first step, therefore, is to add the class source file for a view controller to the project. Ctrl-click on the *Storyboard* target at the top of the project navigator panel and select *New File…* from the resulting menu. In the new file panel, select *iOS* in the top bar followed by *Cocoa Touch Class* in the main panel and click *Next* to proceed. On the options screen ensure that the *Subclass of* menu is set to *UIViewController* and that the *Also create XIB file* option is deselected (since the view already exists in the storyboard there is no need for an XIB user interface file), name the class *Scene2ViewController* and proceed through the screens to create the new class file.

Select the *Main.storyboard* file in the project navigator panel and select the View Controller button located in the panel above the Scene 2 view as shown in Figure 25-7:

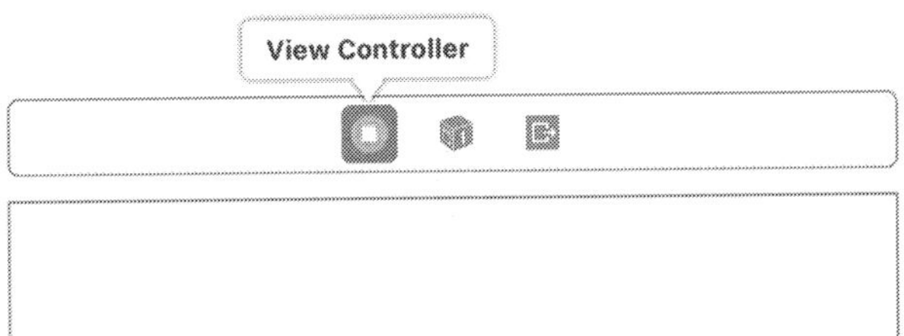

Figure 25-7

With the view controller for scene 2 selected within the storyboard canvas, display the Identity Inspector (*View -> Utilities -> Identity Inspector*) and change the *Class* from *UIViewController* to *Scene2ViewController:*

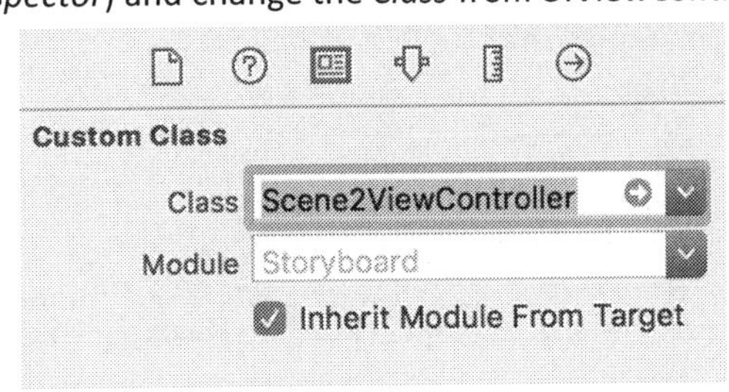

Figure 25-8

Scene 2 now has a view controller and corresponding Swift source file where code may be written to implement any required functionality.

Select the label object in scene 2 and display the Assistant Editor. Make sure that the *Scene2ViewController.swift* file is displayed in the editor and then establish an outlet for the label named *scene2Label.*

25.7 Passing Data Between Scenes

One of the most common requirements when working with storyboards involves the transfer of data from one scene to another during a segue transition. Before a segue is performed by the storyboard runtime environment, a call is made to the *prepare(for segue:)* method of the current view controller. If any tasks need to be performed prior to the segue taking place simply implement this method in the current view controller and add code to perform any necessary tasks. Passed as an argument to this method is a segue object from which a reference to the destination view controller may be obtained and subsequently used to transfer data.

To see this in action, begin by selecting *Scene2ViewController.swift* and adding a new variable property:

```
import UIKit

class Scene2ViewController: UIViewController {

    @IBOutlet weak var scene2Label: UILabel!

    var labelText: String?
.
.
.
```

This property will hold the text to be displayed on the label when the storyboard transitions to this scene. As such, some code needs to be added to the *viewDidLoad* method located in the *Scene2ViewController.swift* file:

```
override func viewDidLoad() {
    super.viewDidLoad()
    scene2Label.text = labelText
}
```

Finally, select the *ViewController.swift* file and implement the *prepare(for segue:)* method as follows:

```
override func prepare(for segue: UIStoryboardSegue, sender: Any?) {
    let destination = segue.destination
                                as! Scene2ViewController
    destination.labelText = "Arrived from Scene 1"
}
```

All this method does is obtain a reference to the destination view controller and then assigns a string to the *labelText* property of the object so that it appears on the label.

Compile and run the application once again and note that when scene 2 is displayed the new label text appears. We have, albeit using a very simple example, transferred data from one scene to the next.

25.8 Unwinding Storyboard Segues

The next step is to configure the button on scene 2 to return to scene 1. It might seem as though the obvious choice is to simply implement a segue from the button on scene 2 to scene 1. Instead of returning to the original instance of scene 1, however, this would create an entirely new instance of the ViewController class. If a user were to perform this transition repeatedly the application would continue to use more memory and would eventually be terminated by the operating system.

The application should instead make use of the Storyboard *unwind* feature. This involves implementing a method in the view controller of the scene to which the user is to be returned and then connecting a segue to that method from the source view controller. This enables an unwind action to be performed across multiple levels of scene.

To implement this in our example application, begin by selecting the *ViewController.swift* file and implementing a method to be called by the unwind segue named *returned:*

```
@IBAction func returned(segue: UIStoryboardSegue) {
    scene1Label.text = "Returned from Scene 2"
}
```

All that is required of this method for this example is that it set some new text on the label object of scene 1. Once the method has been added, it is important to save the *ViewController.swift* file before continuing.

The next step is to establish the unwind segue. To achieve this, locate scene 2 within the storyboard canvas and Ctrl-click and drag from the button view to the “exit” icon (the orange button with the white square and the right facing arrow pointing outward shown in Figure 25-9) in the panel located along the top edge of the scene view. Release the line and select the *returnedWithSegue* method from the resulting menu:

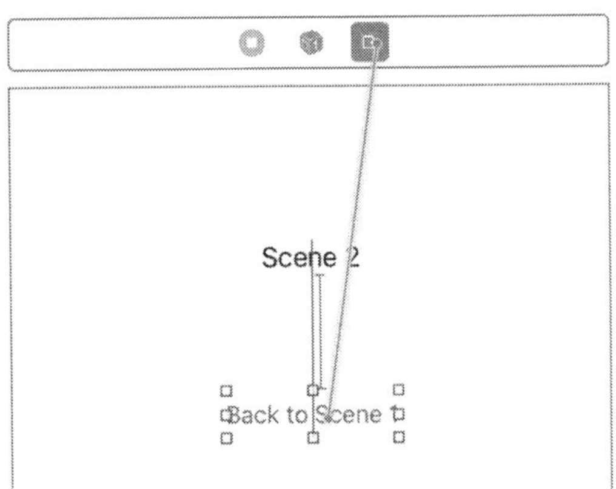

Figure 25-9

Once again, run the application and note that the button on scene 2 now returns to scene 1 and, in the process, calls the *returned* method resulting in the label on scene 1 changing.

25.9 Triggering a Storyboard Segue Programmatically

In addition to wiring up controls in scenes to trigger a segue, it is also possible to initiate a preconfigured segue from within the application code. This can be achieved by assigning an identifier to the segue and then making a call to the *performSegue(withIdentifier:)* method of the view controller from which the segue is to be triggered.

To set the identifier of a segue, select it in the storyboard canvas, display the Attributes Inspector (*View -> Utilities -> Show Attributes Inspector*) and set the value in the *Identifier* field.

Assuming a segue with the identifier of *SegueToScene1*, this could be triggered from within code as follows:

```
self.performSegue(withIdentifier: "SegueToScene1", sender: self)
```

25.10 Summary

The Storyboard feature of Xcode allows for the navigational flow between the various views in an iOS application to be visually constructed without the need to write code. In this chapter we have covered the basic concepts behind storyboarding and worked through the creation of an example iOS application using storyboards and, in doing so, also explored the storyboard unwind feature.

Chapter 26

26. Organizing Scenes over Multiple Storyboard Files

The storyboard created in the preceding chapter is a small example consisting of only two scenes. When developing complex applications, however, it is not unusual for a user interface to consist of many more scenes. Once a storyboard begins to grow in terms of the number of scenes it can become difficult to navigate and to locate specific scenes. This problem can be alleviated by organizing the scenes over multiple storyboards and then using *storyboard references* to reference a scene in one storyboard from within another storyboard.

Continuing to use the project created in the preceding chapter, this chapter will cover the steps involved in organizing scenes in separate storyboard files and the use of storyboard references to establish segues between scenes in different storyboard files.

26.1 Organizing Scenes into Multiple Storyboards

The storyboard created in this chapter is a small example consisting of only two scenes. When developing complex applications, however, it is not unusual for a user interface to consist of many more scenes. Existing scenes in a storyboard file can be exported to a second storyboard file using a simple menu selection. To see this in action, select the *Main.storyboard* file and drag and drop an additional view controller onto the storyboard canvas and add button and label views so that it appears as illustrated in Figure 26-1 using the same steps as those followed for the previous scenes:

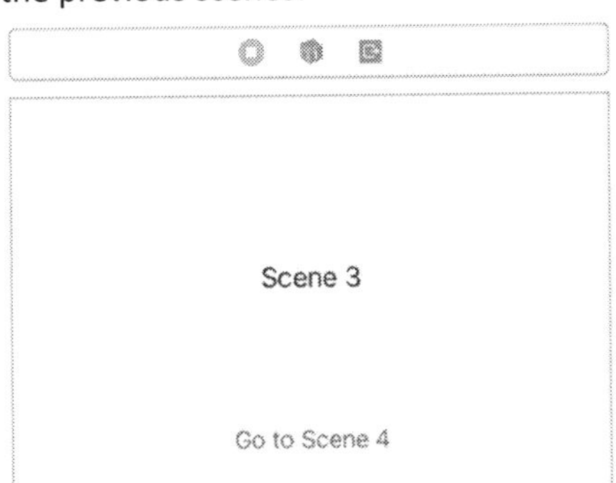

Figure 26-1

Before moving the new scene to a different storyboard file, first add a second button to Scene 2 labelled "Go to Scene 3" and establish a modal presentation segue to the newly added scene. As before, be sure to set the Auto Layout settings to suggested constraints.

To move this new scene to a second storyboard, select it in the storyboard and choose the *Editor -> Refactor to Storyboard...* menu option (note that although only a single scene is being exported in this case, multiple scenes can also be selected and moved in a single operation). Once the menu option is selected, a panel (Figure 26-2) will appear seeking the name to be given to the new storyboard. In the *Save As:* field, name the file *Second.storyboard*:

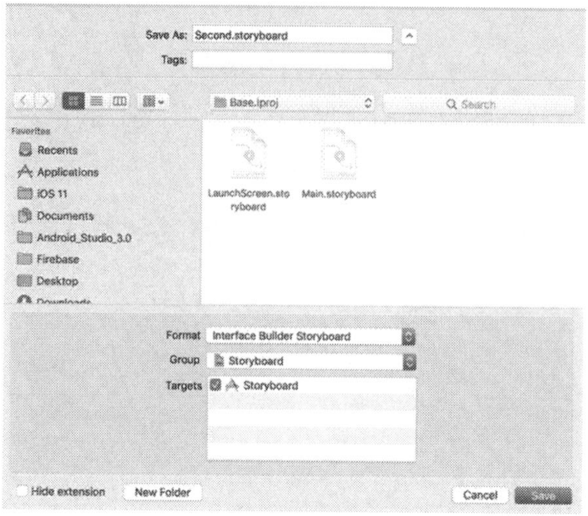

Figure 26-2

Click on the Save button to save the scene to the new storyboard. Once saved, two changes will have taken place. First, a review of the Project Navigator panel will reveal the presence of a new storyboard file named *Second.storyboard* which, when selected will reveal that it contains the third scene that was originally located in the *Main.storyboard* file.

Second, a review of the *Main.storyboard* file will show that the third scene has now been replaced by a storyboard reference as shown in Figure 26-3 and that the segue is still in place:

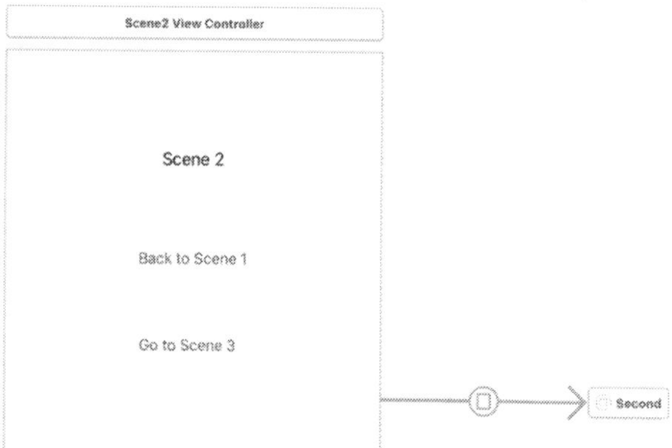

Figure 26-3

Select the *Second* storyboard reference and display the Attributes Inspector panel. Note that the Storyboard property is set to the Second storyboard file and that, by default, it is configured to display the *Initial View Controller* within that storyboard, which in this case is the only scene within the second storyboard:

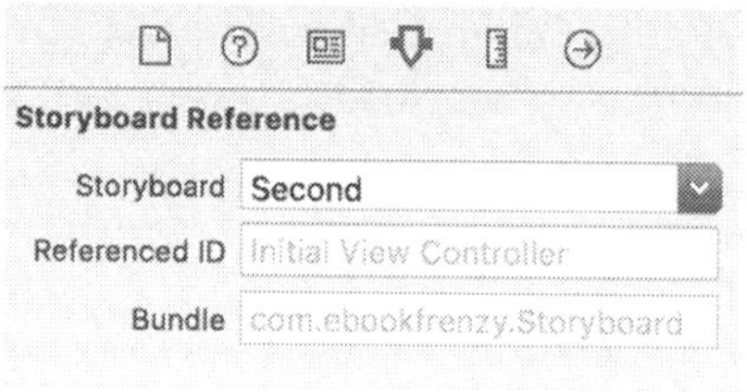

Figure 26-4

Compile and run the app and verify that the *Go to Scene 3* button does indeed segue to the third scene.

26.2 Establishing a Connection between Different Storyboards

The previous section explored the separation of existing scenes within a storyboard into separate storyboard files. Consider, however, a scenario where a segue needs to be established between two scenes in two different storyboards where no reference has yet been established. To see this in action, select the *File -> New File...* menu option and, in the resulting panel, locate the *User Interface* section and select the *Storyboard* option. Click *Next* and name the file *Third.storyboard* before clicking on *Create*.

Select the *Third.storyboard* file from the Project Navigator panel and drag and drop a View Controller instance from the Library panel onto the storyboard canvas. Add a label to the view and change the text to read *Scene 4* before setting appropriate Auto Layout constraints.

The objective is now to establish a segue from the "Go to Scene 4" button in the scene in the *Second.storyboard* file to the new scene in the *Third.storyboard* file.

The first step is to assign a storyboard ID to scene 4. Within the *Third.storyboard* file, select the View Controller so that it is highlighted in blue, display the Identity Inspector (*View -> Utilities -> Show Identity Inspector*) and change the Storyboard ID setting to *Scene4Controller*.

The next step is to add a reference to this scene from within the *Second.storyboard* file. Select this file and drag and drop a Storyboard Reference object from the Library onto the canvas. Select the reference object, display the Attributes Inspector, change the Storyboard menu to *Third* and enter *Scene4Controller* into the *Referenced ID* field as shown in Figure 26-5:

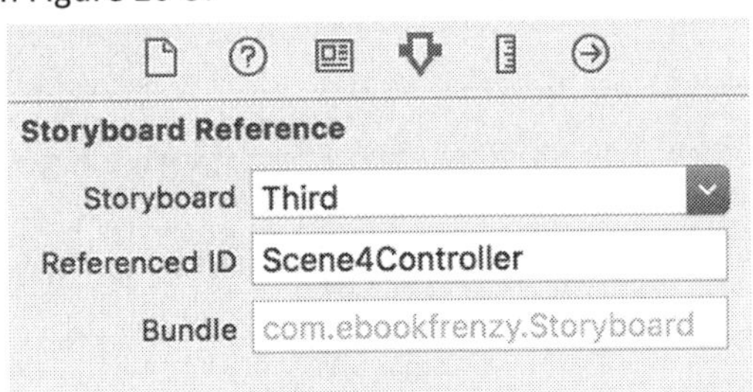

Figure 26-5

The storyboard reference is now configured to reference the scene 4 view controller in the Third storyboard file and can be used as the target for a segue. Remaining in the *Second.storyboard* file, Ctrl-click on the Go to Scene 4 button and drag the resulting line to the storyboard reference object. Release the line and select *Present Modally* from the popup menu.

Compile and run the application a final time and verify that the button initiates the segue to the fourth scene as configured.

26.3 Summary

This chapter has covered the steps involved in organizing scenes over multiple storyboard files. It has covered the exporting of scenes from an existing storyboard file to a new storyboard file and also outlined the steps required to manually establish storyboard references between scenes residing in different storyboard files.

Chapter 27

27. Using Xcode 10 Storyboards to Create an iOS 12 Tab Bar Application

Having worked through a simple Storyboard based application in the previous chapter, the goal of this chapter will be to create a slightly more complex storyboard example.

So far in this book we have worked primarily with applications that present a single view to the user. In practice, however, it is more likely that an application will need to display a variety of different content depending on the actions of the user. This is typically achieved by creating multiple views (often referred to as content views) and then providing a mechanism for the user to navigate from one view to another. One of a number of mechanisms for achieving this involves the use of either the UINavigationBar or UITabBar components. In this chapter we will begin by using the storyboard feature of Xcode to implement a multiview application using a Tab Bar.

27.1 An Overview of the Tab Bar

The UITabBar component is typically located at the bottom of the screen and presents an array of tabs containing text and an optional icon that may be selected by the user to display a different content view. Typical examples of the tab bar in action include the iPhone's built-in Music and Phone applications. The Music application, for example, presents a tab bar with options to display different music options. Depending on the selection made from the tab bar, a different content view is displayed to the user.

27.2 Understanding View Controllers in a Multiview Application

In preceding chapters we have talked about the model-view-controller concept in relation to each view having its own view controller (for additional information on this read the chapter entitled *The iOS 12 Application and Development Architecture*). In a multiview application, on the other hand, each content view will still have a view controller associated with it to handle user interaction and display updates. Multiview applications, however, also require an additional controller.

Multiview applications need a visual control that will be used by the user to switch from one content view to another, and this often takes the form of a tab or navigation bar. Both of these components are also *views* and as such also need to have a *view controller*. In the context of a multiview application, this is known as the *root controller* and is responsible for controlling which content view is currently displayed to the user. As an app developer you are free to create your own root controller by subclassing from the UIViewController class, but in practice it usually makes more sense to use an instance of either the UIKit UITabBarController or UINavigationController classes.

Regardless of the origins of your chosen root controller, it is the first controller that is loaded by the application when it launches. Once loaded, it is responsible for displaying the first content view to the user and then switching the various content views in and out as required based on the user's subsequent interaction with the application.

Since this chapter is dedicated to the creation of a tab bar based application we will be using an instance of the UITabBarController as our root controller.

27.3 Setting up the Tab Bar Example Application

The first step in creating our example application is to create a new Xcode project. To do so, launch Xcode and select the option to *Create a new Xcode project.*

Among the new project template options provided by Xcode is the *Tabbed Application* template. When selected, this template creates a pre-configured application consisting of a Tab Bar application with two content views. While we could have used this template in this chapter, to do so would fail to convey a number of skills that will be essential when developing more complicated applications using storyboards. Although it is useful, therefore, to be aware of this template option for future reference, in the interest of providing a sound knowledge foundation we will be using the *Single View Application* template in this example.

On the template selection screen, select *Single View Application* and click *Next* to proceed. On the next screen enter *TabBar* as the product name and make sure that *Swift* is selected as the language. Proceed to the final screen and browse to a suitable location for the project files before clicking on the *Create* button.

27.4 Reviewing the Project Files

Based on our selections during the project creation process, Xcode has pre-populated the project with a number of files. In addition to the standard application delegate files it has, for example, provided the file necessary for a single view controller based application named *ViewController.swift.* A *Main.storyboard* file has also been created.

To start with an entirely clean project, select the *ViewController.swift* file in the project navigator panel and press the keyboard Delete key to remove the file from the project, choosing the option to move the file to the trash when prompted to do so.

27.5 Adding the View Controllers for the Content Views

The ultimate goal of this chapter is to create a tab bar based application consisting of two tabs with corresponding views, each of these will require a view controller. The first step, therefore, is to add the view controller for the first view. To achieve this, select the *File -> New -> File...* menu option and, on the resulting panel, select the *iOS* option from the toolbar and *Cocoa Touch Class* from the list of templates. Click *Next* and on the next screen, name the new class *Tab1ViewController* and change the *Subclass of* menu to *UIViewController.* Ensure that the *Also create XIB file* option is switched off before clicking *Next.* Select the desired location for the creation of the class files before clicking on *Create.*

Repeat the above steps to add a second view controller class named *Tab2ViewController.*

The scene within the storyboard file now needs to be associated with one of these view controller classes. Open the *Main.storyboard* file and select the scene added by Xcode so that it is highlighted with a blue border before displaying the Identity Inspector panel (*View -> Utilities -> Show Identity Inspector*). Within the inspector panel change the *Class* setting from *UIViewController* to *Tab1ViewController.*

The second view controller may be added to the storyboard simply by dragging and dropping one from the Library panel (*View -> Utilities -> Show Library*) onto the storyboard canvas. Once it has been added, follow the same steps to change the view controller class within the Identity Inspector panel, this time selecting *Tab2ViewController* in the *Class* field.

27.6 Adding the Tab Bar Controller to the Storyboard

As previously explained, the navigation between view controllers in a Tab Bar based interface is handled by a Tab Bar Controller. It will be necessary, therefore, to add one of these to our storyboard. Begin by selecting the *Main.storyboard* file in the Xcode project navigator panel.

In order to add a Tab Bar Controller to the storyboard, select the Tab1ViewController in the storyboard design area followed by the *Editor -> Embed In -> Tab Bar Controller* menu option. The Tab Bar Controller will subsequently appear in the storyboard already connected to the Tab 1 View Controller as shown in Figure 27-1:

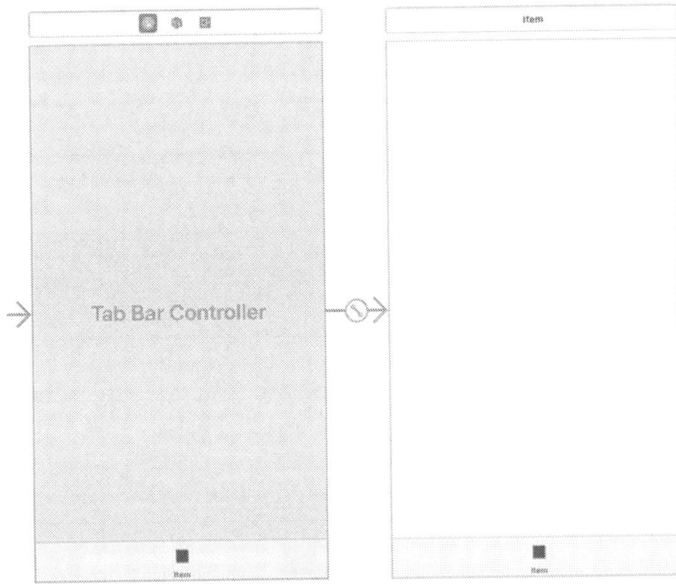

Figure 27-1

A relationship now needs to be established between the *Tab2ViewController* class and the Tab Bar Controller. To achieve this simply Ctrl-click on the Tab Bar Controller object in the storyboard canvas and drag the line to the *Tab2ViewController* scene. Upon releasing the line select the *view controllers* menu option listed under *Relationship Segue* as illustrated in Figure 27-2. This will add the *Tab2ViewController* to the *viewControllers* property of the Tab Bar Controller object so that it will be included in the tab navigation.

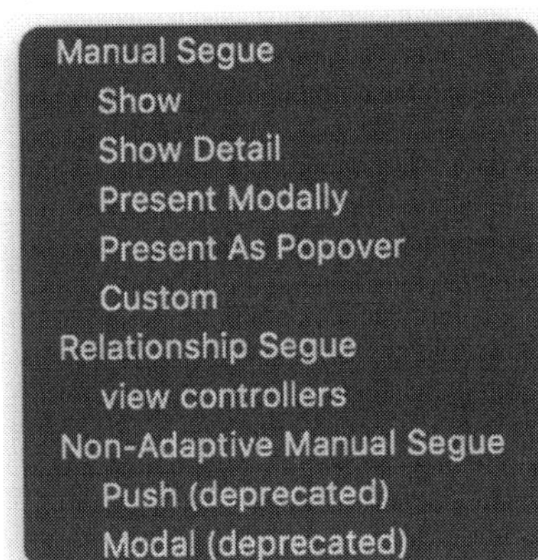

Figure 27-2

At this point in the design process the storyboard should now consist of one Tab Bar Controller with relationships established with both *Tab1ViewController* and *Tab2ViewController*. Allowing for differences in positioning of the storyboard elements, the canvas should now appear as shown in the following figure:

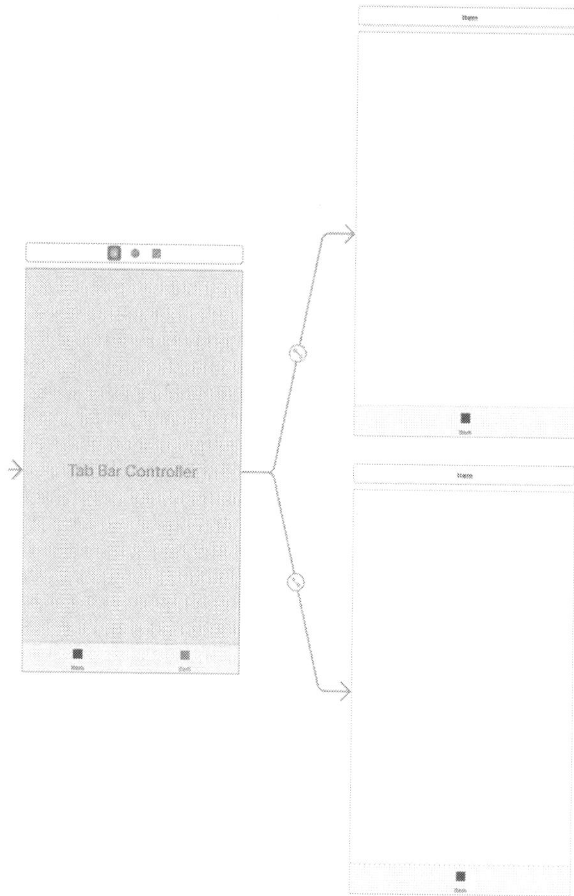

Figure 27-3

All that remains in order to complete the application is to configure the tab bar items and design rudimentary user interfaces for the two view controllers.

27.7 Designing the View Controller User interfaces

In order to visually differentiate the two view controllers we will add labels to the views and change the background colors. Begin by selecting the view of the Tab1ViewController scene. Within the Attributes Inspector panel (*View -> Utilities -> Show Attributes Inspector*) click on the white rectangle next to the *Background* label, select the *Custom...* menu option and choose a shade of red from the resulting Colors dialog. Next, drag and drop a Label object from the Library panel and position it in the center of the red view. Double-click on the label so that it becomes editable and change the text to *Screen One.* With the label still selected, use the Auto Layout Align menu to enable both the horizontal and vertical "in Container" constraint options.

Once completed, the Tab1ViewController storyboard scene should appear as shown in Figure 27-4. Repeat the above steps to change the background of the Tab2ViewController view to green and to add a label displaying text that reads *Screen Two.*

Figure 27-4

27.8 Configuring the Tab Bar Items

As is evident from the tab bars shown across the bottom of the two view controller elements, the tab items are currently configured to display text which reads "Item". The final task prior to compiling and running the application, therefore, is to rectify this issue. Begin by double-clicking on the word "Item" in the tab bar of Tab1ViewController so that the text highlights and enter *Screen One*. Repeat this step to change the text of the tab bar item for Tab2ViewController to *Screen Two.*

In the event that you already have some icons suitable to be displayed on the tab bar items feel free to use them for this project. Alternatively, example icons can be found in the *tabicons* folder of the sample code archive which can be downloaded from the following URL:

https://www.ebookfrenzy.com/retail/ios12/

The icon archive contains two PNG format icon images named *first.png* and *second.png*.

Select the *Assets.xcassets* entry in the Project Navigator panel, Ctrl-click in the left-hand panel of the asset catalog screen and select the *Import…* menu option. In the file selection dialog, navigate to and select the tabicons folder and click on the *Open* button to import the images into a new image set.

With the icons added to the project, click on the placeholder icon in the tab bar of the Tab1ViewController and in the Attributes Inspector panel use the *Image* drop down menu to select *first* as the image file:

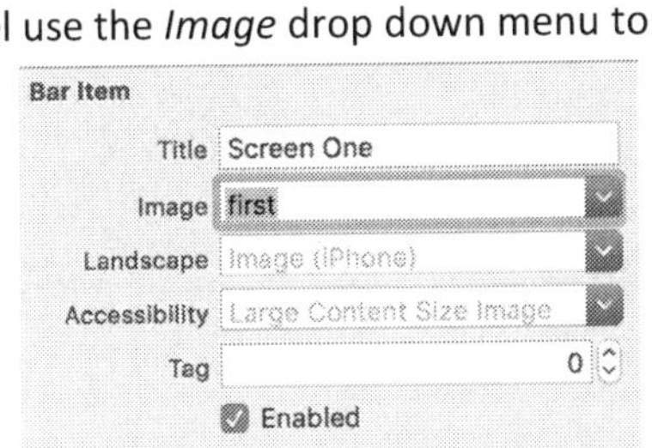

Figure 27-5

Note that it is also possible to select one of a number of built-in images using the *System Item* attribute menu, and to display a different image when a tab is selected by providing an image for the *Selected Image* setting. Perform the same steps to specify *second* as the image file for Tab2ViewController.

27.9 Building and Running the Application

The design and implementation of the example application is now complete and all that remains is to build and run it. Click on the run button located in the Xcode toolbar and wait for the code to compile and the application to launch within the iOS Simulator environment. The application should appear with the Tab1ViewController active and the two tab items in the tab bar visible across the bottom of the screen. Clicking on the Screen Two tab will navigate to the Tab2ViewController view:

Figure 27-6

27.10 Summary

The Storyboard feature of Xcode allows Tab Bar based navigation to be quickly and easily built into applications. Perhaps the most significant point to make is that the example project created in this chapter was implemented without the need to write a single line of Swift code.

Chapter 28

28. An Overview of iOS 12 Table Views and Xcode 10 Storyboards

If you have spent an appreciable amount of time using iOS the chances are good that you have interacted with a UIKit Table View object. Table Views are the cornerstone of the navigation system for many iOS applications. For example, both the iPhone *Mail* and *Settings* applications make extensive use of Table Views to present information to users in a list format and to enable users to drill down to more detailed information by selecting a particular list item.

Historically, table views have been one of the more complex areas of iOS user interface implementation. In recognition of this fact, Apple introduced ways to implement table views through the use of the Xcode Storyboard feature.

The goal of this chapter is to provide an overview of the concept of the UITableView class together with an introduction to the ways in which storyboards can be used to ease the table view implementation process. Once these basics have been covered a series of chapters, starting with *Using Xcode 10 Storyboards to Build Dynamic TableViews*, will work through the creation of example projects intended to demonstrate the use of storyboards in the context of table views.

28.1 An Overview of the Table View

Table Views present the user with data in a list format and are represented by the UITableView class of the UIKit framework. The data is presented in rows, whereby the content of each row is implemented in the form of a UITableViewCell object. By default, each table cell can display a text label (textLabel), a subtitle (detailedTextLabel) and an image (imageView). More complex cells can be created by either adding subviews to the cell, or subclassing UITableViewCell and adding your own custom functionality and appearance.

28.2 Static vs. Dynamic Table Views

When implementing table views using an Xcode storyboard it is important to understand the distinction between *static* and *dynamic* tables. Static tables are useful in situations when a fixed number of rows need to be displayed in a table. The settings page for an application, for example, would typically have a predetermined number of configuration options and would be an ideal candidate for a static table.

Dynamic tables (also known as *prototype-based* tables), on the other hand, are intended for use when a variable number of rows need to be displayed from a data source. Within the storyboard editor, Xcode allows you to visually design a prototype table cell which will then be replicated in the dynamic table view at runtime in order to display data to the user.

28.3 The Table View Delegate and dataSource

Each table view in an application needs to have a *delegate* and a *dataSource* associated with it (with the exception of static tables which do not have a data source). The dataSource implements the UITableViewDataSource protocol, which basically consists of a number of methods that define title information, how many rows of data are to be displayed, how the data is divided into different sections and, most importantly, supplies the table view with the cell objects to be displayed. The delegate implements the

UITableViewDelegate protocol and provides additional control over the appearance and functionality of the table view including detecting when a user touches a specific row, defining custom row heights and indentations and also implementation of row deletion and editing functions.

28.4 Table View Styles

Table views may be configured to use either *plain* or *grouped* style. In the grouped style, the rows are grouped together in sections separated by optional headers and footers. For example, Figure 28-1 shows a table view configured to use the grouped style:

Figure 28-1

In the case of the plain style, the items are listed without separation and using the full width of the display:

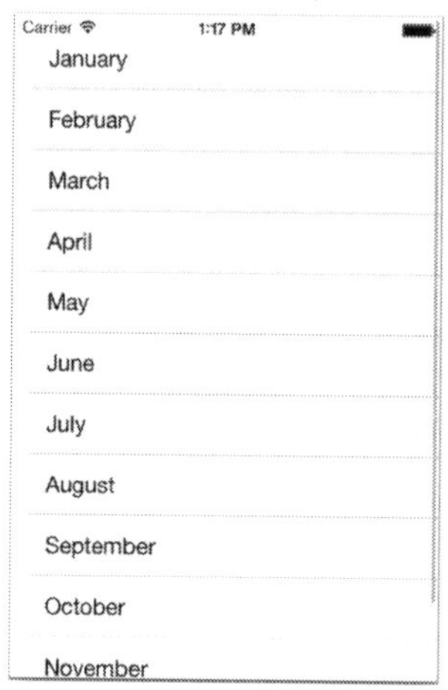

Figure 28-2

Table Views using plain style can also be *indexed*, whereby rows are organized into groups according to specified criteria, such as alphabetical or numerical sorting.

28.5 Self-Sizing Table Cells

With self-sizing cells, each row of a table is sized according to the content of the corresponding cell based on the Auto Layout constraints applied to the cell contents. Self-sizing will be demonstrated in the next chapter entitled *Using Xcode 10 Storyboards to Build Dynamic TableViews*, but is of particular importance when the labels in a cell are configured to use dynamic type.

28.6 Dynamic Type

iOS provides a way for the user to select a preferred text size which applications are expected to adopt when displaying text. The current text size can be configured on a device via the *Settings -> Display & Brightness -> Text Size* screen which provides a slider to adjust the font size as shown in Figure 28-3:

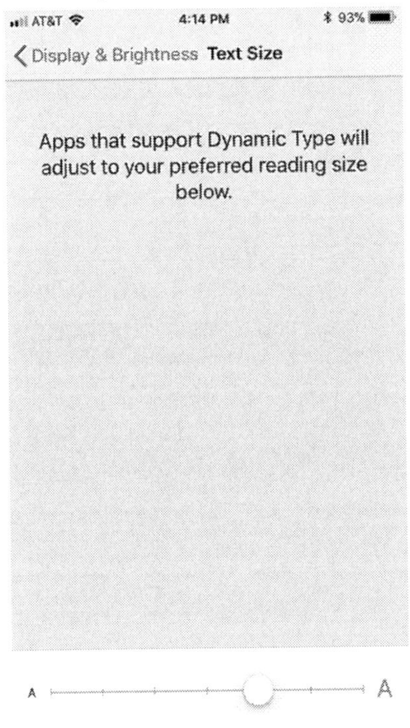

Figure 28-3

Almost without exception, the built-in iOS apps adopt the font size setting selected by the user when displaying text. Apple recommends that third-party apps also conform to the user's text size selection and since iOS 8, support for dynamic type has been extended to table views. This is achieved by specifying a preferred text style setting for the font of any custom labels in a cell. iOS specifies a variety of different preferred text styles for this purpose including headings, sub-headings, body, captions and footnotes. The text style used by a label can be configured using Interface Builder or in code. To configure the text style in Interface Builder, select the label, display the Attributes Inspector and click on the "T" button in the font setting field as demonstrated in Figure 28-4. From the drop-down menu click on the Font menu button and select an item from the options listed under the *Text Styles* heading:

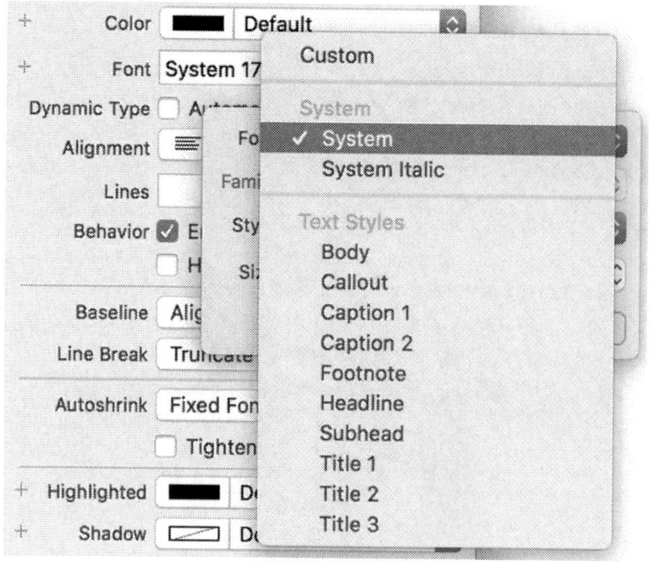

Figure 28-4

The preferred font is configured in code by setting the *preferredFont* property to one of the following pre-configured text style values:

- UIFontTextStyle.headline
- UIFontTextStyle.subheadline
- UIFontTextStyle.body
- UIFontTextStyle.callout
- UIFontTextStyle.footnote
- UIFontTextStyle.caption1
- UIFontTextStyle.caption2

The following code, for example, sets a dynamic type font on a label using the headline font style:

```
cell.myLabel.font =
        UIFont.preferredFont(forTextStyle: .headline)
```

Clearly, the text size selected by a user will dictate the size of any cells containing labels that use dynamic type, hence the importance of using self-sizing to ensure the table rows are displayed using an appropriate height.

28.7 Table View Cell Styles

In addition to the style of the Table View itself, different styles may also be specified for the individual table cells (unless custom table cells are being used). The iOS SDK currently supports four different cell styles:

- **UITableViewCellStyle.default** – only the labelText in black and left aligned.
- **UITableViewCellStyle.subtitle** – labelText in black and left aligned with the detailLabelText positioned beneath it in a smaller font using a gray foreground.
- **UITableViewCellStyle.value1** – labelText in black left aligned and the smaller detailLabelText in blue, on the same line and right aligned.

- **UITableViewCellStyle.value2** – labelText in blue on left side of cell, right aligned and detailedLabelText on right of cell, left aligned and black.

28.8 Table View Cell Reuse

A table view is, at the basic level, comprised of a UITableView object and a UITableViewCell for each row to be displayed. The code for a typical iOS application using a table view will not directly create instances of a cell. The reasoning behind this becomes evident when performance and memory requirements are taken into consideration. Consider, for example, a table view that is required to display 1000 photo images. It can be assumed with a reasonable degree of certainty that only a small percentage of cells will be visible to the user at any one time. If the application was permitted to create each of the 1000 cells in advance the device would very quickly run into memory and performance limitations.

Instead, the application begins by registering with the table view object the class to be used for cell objects, along with the *reuse identifier* previously assigned to that class. If the cell class was written in code, the registration is performed using the *register* method of UITableView object. For example:

```
self.tableView.register(AttractionTableViewCell.self,
                        forCellReuseIdentifier: "MyTableCell")
```

In the event that the cell is contained within an Interface Builder NIB file, the *registerNib* method is used instead.

Perhaps the most important point to remember from this chapter is that if the cell is created using prototypes within a storyboard it is not necessary to register the class and, in fact, doing so will prevent the cell or view from appearing when the application runs.

As the table view initializes, it calls the *tableView(_:cellForRowAt:)* method of the datasource class passing through the index path for which a cell object is required. This method will then call the *dequeueReusableCell* method of the table view object, passing through both the index path and the reuse ID assigned to the cell class when it was registered, to find out if there is a reusable cell object in the queue that can be used for this new cell. Since this is the initialization phase and no cells have been deemed eligible for reuse, the method will create a new cell and return it. Once all the visible cells have been created, the table view will stop asking for more cells. The code for *tableView(_:cellForRowAt:)* method will typically read as follows (the code to customize the cell before returning it will be implementation specific):

```
override func tableView(_ tableView: UITableView, cellForRowAt indexPath:
    IndexPath) -> UITableViewCell {

    let cell =
        self.tableView.dequeueReusableCell(withIdentifier:
            "MyTableCell", for: indexPath)
                as! MyTableViewCell

    // Configure the cell here
    return cell
}
```

As the user scrolls through the table view, some cells will move out of the visible frame. When this happens, the table view places them on the reuse queue. As cells are moving out of view, new ones are likely to be coming into view. For each cell moving into the view area, the table view will call *tableView(_:cellForRowAt:)*.

This time, however, when a call to the *dequeueReusableCell* method is made, it is most likely that an existing cell object will be returned from the reuse queue, thereby avoiding the necessity to create a new object.

28.9 Table View Swipe Actions

The TableView delegate protocol provides delegate methods that allow the app to respond to left and right swipes over table rows by displaying an action button. Figure 28-5, for example, shows a leading swipe action configured with an action titled "Share":

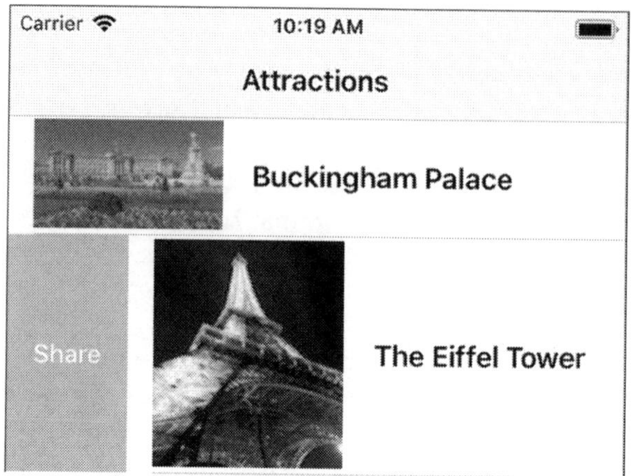

Figure 28-5

The two delegate methods are declared as follows:

```
override func tableView(_ tableView: UITableView,
  leadingSwipeActionsConfigurationForRowAt indexPath: IndexPath) ->
   UISwipeActionsConfiguration? {

}

override func tableView(_ tableView: UITableView,
 trailingSwipeActionsConfigurationForRowAt indexPath: IndexPath) ->
  UISwipeActionsConfiguration? {
}
```

The methods return a UISwipeActionsConfiguration object configured with the action that is to be performed. This consists of a UIContextualAction object configured with a style (either *destructive* or *normal),* the title to appear in the action and a completion handler to be called when the user taps the action button, for example:

```
override func tableView(_ tableView: UITableView,
 leadingSwipeActionsConfigurationForRowAt indexPath: IndexPath) ->
  UISwipeActionsConfiguration? {

    let configuration = UISwipeActionsConfiguration(actions: [
        UIContextualAction(style: .normal, title: "Share",
          handler: { (action, view, completionHandler) in

            // Code here will be executed when the user selects the action
```

```
                completionHandler(true)
            })
        ])
        return configuration
}
```

Destructive actions appear in red when displayed and remove the corresponding row from the table view when selected while normal actions appear in gray and do not remove the row.

28.10 Summary

While table views provide a popular mechanism for displaying data and implementing view navigation within applications, implementation has historically been a complex process. That changed with the introduction of storyboard support in Xcode. Xcode provides a mechanism for visually implementing a considerable amount of Table View functionality with minimal coding. Such table views can be implemented as either *static* or *dynamic* depending on the requirements of the table and the nature of the data being displayed.

The text within a table cell should be configured using text styles rather than with specific font settings. This allows the text to appear in accordance with the user's device-wide text preferences as defined in the Settings app.

iOS also supports swipe actions within TableViews, allowing options to be presented when the user swipes left or right on a table cell.

Chapter 29

29. Using Xcode 10 Storyboards to Build Dynamic TableViews

Arguably one of the most powerful features of Xcode storyboards involves the implementation of table views through the concept of prototype table cells. This allows the developer to visually design the user interface elements that will appear in a table cell (such as labels, images etc) and then replicate that prototype cell on demand within the table view of the running application. Prior to the introduction of Storyboards, this would have involved a considerable amount of coding work combined with trial and error.

The objective of this chapter is to work through a detailed example designed to demonstrate dynamic table view creation within a storyboard using table view prototype cells. Once this topic has been covered, the next chapter (entitled *Implementing iOS 12 TableView Navigation using Storyboards*) will explore the implementation of table view navigation and the passing of data between scenes using storyboards.

29.1 Creating the Example Project

Start Xcode and create a Single View Application project named *TableViewStory* with the Swift programming language option selected.

A review of the files in the project navigator panel will reveal that, as requested, Xcode has created a view controller subclass for us named ViewController. In addition, this view controller is represented within the Storyboard file, the content of which may be viewed by selecting the *Main.storyboard* file.

In order to fully understand the steps involved in creating a Storyboard based TableView application we will start with a clean slate by removing the view controller added for us by Xcode. Within the storyboard canvas, select the *View Controller* scene so that it is highlighted in blue and press the Delete key on the keyboard. Next, select and delete the corresponding *ViewController.swift* file from the project navigator panel. In the resulting panel select the option to move the file to trash.

At this point we have a template project consisting solely of a storyboard file and the standard app delegate code file and are ready to begin building a storyboard based application using the UITableView and UITableViewCell classes.

29.2 Adding the TableView Controller to the Storyboard

From the perspective of the user, the entry point into this application will be a table view containing a list of tourist attractions, with each table view cell containing the name of the attraction and corresponding image. As such, we will need to add a Table View Controller instance to the storyboard file. Select the *Main.storyboard* file so that the canvas appears in the center of the Xcode window. Display the Library panel, drag a *Table View Controller* object and drop it onto the storyboard canvas as illustrated in Figure 29-1:

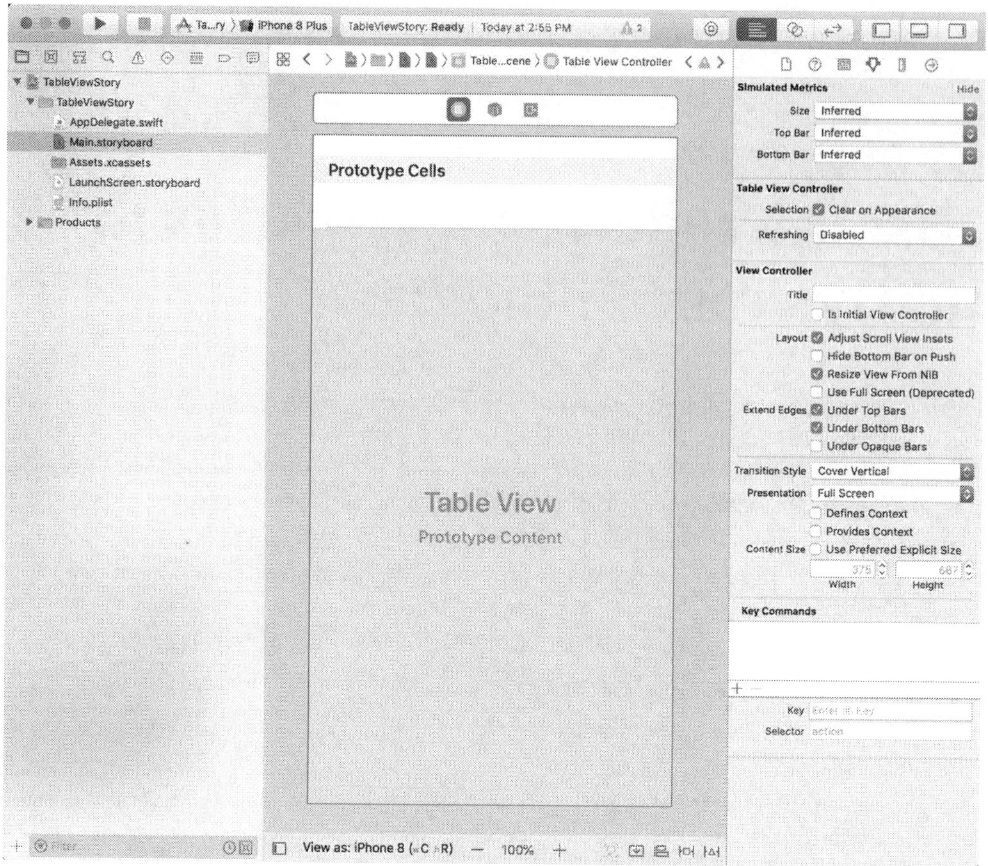

Figure 29-1

With the new view controller selected in the storyboard, display the Attributes Inspector and enable the *Is initial View Controller* attribute as shown in Figure 29-2. Without this setting, the system will not know which view controller to display when the application launches.

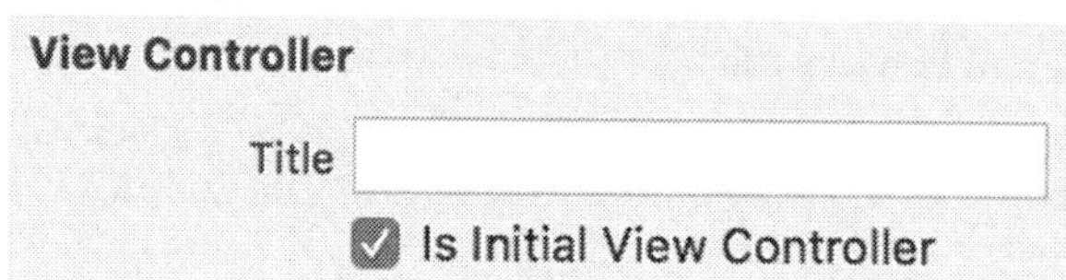

Figure 29-2

Within the storyboard we now have a table view controller instance. Within this instance is also a prototype table view cell that we will be able to configure to design the cells for our table. At the moment these are generic UITableViewCell and UITableViewController classes that do not give us much in the way of control within our application code. So that we can extend the functionality of these instances we need to declare them as being subclasses of UITableViewController and UITableViewCell respectively. Before doing so, however, we need to actually create those subclasses.

29.3 Creating the UITableViewController and UITableViewCell Subclasses

We will be declaring the Table View Controller instance within our storyboard as being a subclass of UITableViewController named AttractionTableViewController. At present, this subclass does not exist within our project so clearly we need to create it before proceeding. To achieve this, select the *File -> New -> File...*

menu option and in the resulting panel select the option to create a new iOS Source Cocoa Touch class. Click *Next* and on the subsequent screen, name the class AttractionTableViewController and change the *Subclass of* menu to *UITableViewController.* Make sure that the *Also create XIB file* option is turned off and click *Next.* Select a location into which to generate the new class files before clicking the *Create* button.

Within the Table View Controller added to the storyboard in the previous section, Xcode also added a prototype table cell. Later in this chapter we will add a label and an image view object to this cell. In order to extend this class it is necessary to, once again, create a subclass. Perform this step by selecting the *File -> New -> File...* menu option. Within the new file dialog select *Cocoa Touch Class* and click *Next.* On the following screen, name the new class *AttractionTableViewCell*, change the *Subclass of* menu to *UITableViewCell* and proceed with the class creation. Select a location into which to generate the new class files and click on *Create*.

Next, the items in the storyboard need to be configured to be instances of these subclasses. Begin by selecting the *Main.storyboard* file and select the Table View Controller scene so that it is highlighted in blue. Within the Identity Inspector panel (*View -> Utilities -> Show Identity Inspector*) use the *Class* drop down menu to change the class from *UITableViewController* to *AttractionTableViewController* as illustrated in Figure 29-3:

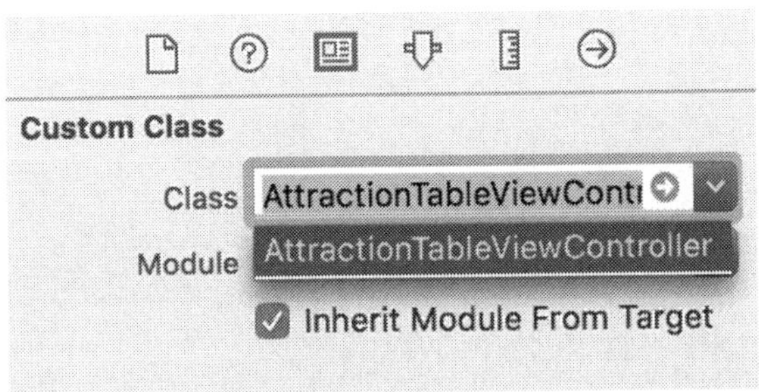

Figure 29-3

Similarly, select the prototype table cell within the table view controller storyboard scene and change the class from *UITableViewCell* to the new *AttractionTableViewCell* subclass.

With the appropriate subclasses created and associated with the objects in the storyboard, the next step is to design the prototype cell.

29.4 Declaring the Cell Reuse Identifier

Later in the chapter some code will be added to the project to replicate instances of the prototype table cell. This will require that the cell be assigned a reuse identifier. With the storyboard still visible in Xcode, select the prototype table cell and display the Attributes Inspector. Within the inspector, change the *Identifier* field to *AttractionTableCell*:

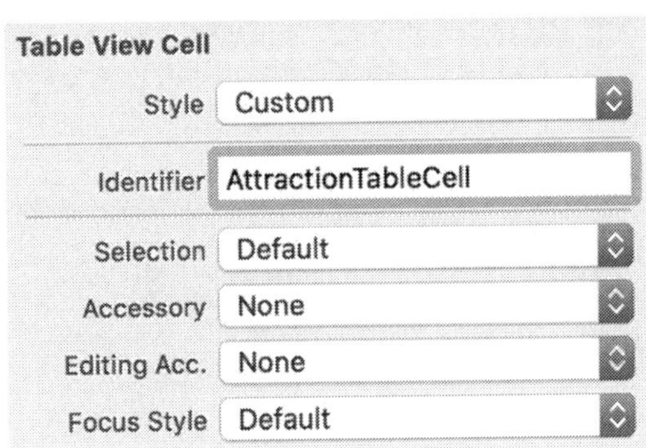

Figure 29-4

29.5 Designing a Storyboard UITableView Prototype Cell

Table Views are made up of multiple cells, each of which is actually either an instance of the UITableViewCell class or a subclass thereof. A useful feature of storyboarding allows the developer to visually construct the user interface elements that are to appear in the table cells and then replicate that cell at runtime. For the purposes of this example each table cell needs to display an image view and a label which, in turn, will be connected to outlets that we will later declare in the *AttractionTableViewCell* subclass. Much like any other Interface Builder layout, components may be dragged from the Library panel and dropped onto a scene within the storyboard. With this in mind, drag and drop a Label and an Image View object onto the prototype table cell. Resize and position the items so that the cell layout resembles that illustrated in Figure 29-5, making sure to stretch the label object so that it extends toward the right-hand edge of the cell.

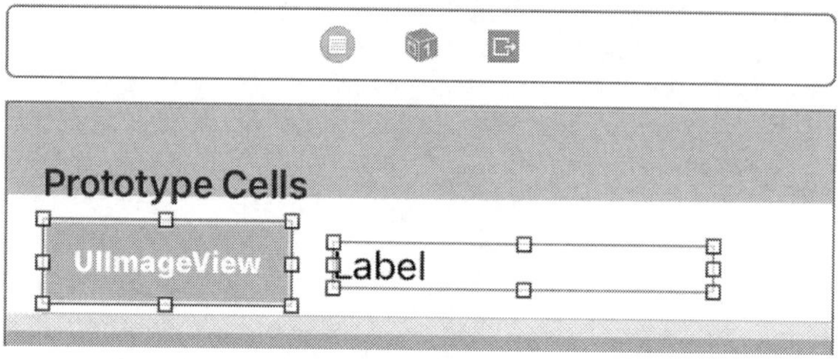

Figure 29-5

Select the Image View and, using the Auto Layout *Add New Constraints* menu, set *Spacing to nearest neighbor* constraints on the top, left and bottom edges of the view with the *Constrain to margins* option switched off. Before adding the constraints, also enable the *Width* constraint.

Select the Label view, display the Auto Layout Align menu and add a *Vertically in Container* constraint to the view. With the Label still selected, display the *Add New Constraints* menu and add a *Spacing to nearest neighbor* constraint on the left-hand edge of the view with the *Constrain to margins* option off.

Having configured the storyboard elements for the table view portion of the application it is time to begin modifying the table view and cell subclasses.

29.6 Modifying the AttractionTableViewCell Class

Within the storyboard file, a label and an image view were added to the prototype cell which, in turn, has been declared as an instance of our new AttractionTableViewCell class. In order to manipulate these user interface objects from within our code we need to establish two outlets connected to the objects in the storyboard scene. Begin, therefore, by selecting the image view object, displaying the Assistant Editor and making sure that it is displaying the content of the *AttractionTableViewCell.swift* file. If it is not, use the bar across the top of the Assistant Editor panel to select this file:

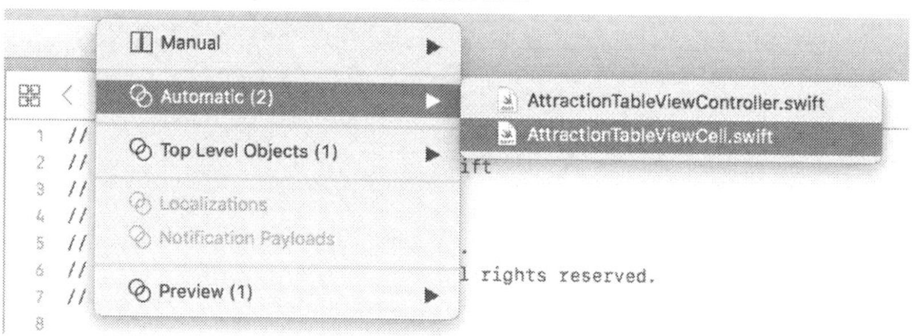

Figure 29-6

Ctrl-click on the image view object in the prototype table cell and drag the resulting line to a point just below the class declaration line in the Assistant Editor window. Release the line and use the connection panel to establish an outlet named *attractionImage*.

Repeat these steps to establish an outlet for the label named *attractionLabel*.

29.7 Creating the Table View Datasource

Dynamic Table Views require a *datasource* to provide the data that will be displayed to the user within the cells. By default, Xcode has designated the *AttractionTableViewController* class as the datasource for the table view controller in the storyboard. Consequently, it is within this class that we can build a very simple data model for our application consisting of a number of arrays. The first step is to declare these as properties in the *AttractionTableViewController.swift* file:

```
import UIKit

class AttractionTableViewController: UITableViewController {

    var attractionImages = [String]()
    var attractionNames = [String]()
    var webAddresses = [String]()
.
.
.
```

In addition, the arrays need to be initialized with some data when the application has loaded, making the *viewDidLoad* method an ideal location. Remaining within the *AttractionTableViewController.swift* file, add a method named *initialize* and call it from the *viewDidLoad* method as outlined in the following code fragment:

```
override func viewDidLoad() {
    super.viewDidLoad()
    initialize()
}

func initialize() {
    attractionNames = ["Buckingham Palace",
                       "The Eiffel Tower",
                       "The Grand Canyon",
                       "Windsor Castle",
                       "Empire State Building"]

    webAddresses = ["https://en.wikipedia.org/wiki/Buckingham_Palace",
                "https://en.wikipedia.org/wiki/Eiffel_Tower",
                "https://en.wikipedia.org/wiki/Grand_Canyon",
                "https://en.wikipedia.org/wiki/Windsor_Castle",
                "https://en.wikipedia.org/wiki/Empire_State_Building"]

    attractionImages = ["buckingham_palace.jpg",
                        "eiffel_tower.jpg",
```

```
                              "grand_canyon.jpg",
                              "windsor_castle.jpg",
                              "empire_state_building.jpg"]

    tableView.estimatedRowHeight = 50
}
```

In addition to initializing the arrays, the code also sets an estimated row height for the table view. This will prevent the row heights from collapsing when table view navigation is added later in the tutorial and also improves the performance of the table rendering.

For a class to act as the datasource for a table view controller a number of methods must be implemented. These methods will be called by the table view object in order to obtain both information about the table and also the table cell objects to display. When we created the AttractionTableViewController class we specified that it was to be a subclass of UITableViewController. As a result, Xcode created templates of these data source methods for us within the *AttractionTableViewController.swift* file. To locate these template datasource methods, scroll down the file until the *// MARK: – Table view data source* marker comes into view. The first template method, named *numberOfSections* needs to return the number of sections in the table. For the purposes of this example we only need one section so will simply return a value of 1 (note also that the #warning line needs to be removed):

```
override func numberOfSections(in tableView: UITableView) -> Int {
    return 1
}
```

The next method is required to return the number of rows to be displayed in the table. This is equivalent to the number of items in our attractionNames array so can be modified as follows:

```
override func tableView(tableView: UITableView,
                numberOfRowsInSection section: Int) -> Int {
    return attractionNames.count
}
```

The above code returns the *count* property of the *attractionNames* array object to obtain the number of items in the array and returns that value to the table view.

The final datasource method that needs to be modified is *tableView(_:cellForRowAt:)*. Each time the table view controller needs a new cell to display it will call this method and pass through an index value indicating the row for which a cell object is required. It is the responsibility of this method to return an instance of our *AttractionTableViewCell* class and extract the correct attraction name and image file name from the data arrays based on the index value passed through to the method. The code will then set those values on the appropriate outlets on the AttractionTableViewCell object. Begin by removing the comment markers (/* and */) from around the template of this method and then re-write the method so that it reads as follows:

```
override func tableView(_ tableView: UITableView,
            cellForRowAt indexPath: IndexPath) -> UITableViewCell {

    let cell =
        self.tableView.dequeueReusableCell(withIdentifier:
        "AttractionTableCell", for: indexPath)
                as! AttractionTableViewCell
```

```
    let row = indexPath.row
    cell.attractionLabel.font =
        UIFont.preferredFont(forTextStyle: UIFont.TextStyle.headline)
    cell.attractionLabel.text = attractionNames[row]
    cell.attractionImage.image = UIImage(named: attractionImages[row])
    return cell
}
```

Before proceeding with this tutorial we need to take some time to deconstruct this code to explain what is actually happening.

The code begins by calling the *dequeueReusableCell(withIdentifier:)* method of the table view object passing through the cell identifier assigned to the cell (AttractionTableCell) and index path as arguments. The system will find out if an AttractionTableViewCell cell object is available for reuse, or create a new one and return it to the method:

```
let cell =
    self.tableView.dequeueReusableCell(withIdentifier:
        "AttractionTableCell", for: indexPath)
            as! AttractionTableViewCell
```

Having either created a new cell, or obtained an existing reusable cell the code simply uses the outlets previously added to the AttractionTableViewCell class to set the label with the attraction name, using the row from the index path as an index into the data array. Because we want the text displayed on the label to reflect the preferred font size selected by the user within the Settings app, the font on the label is set to use the preferred font for headline text.

The code then creates a new UIImage object configured with the image of the current attraction and assigns it to the image view outlet. Finally, the method returns the modified cell object to the table view:

```
let row = indexPath.row
cell.attractionLabel.font =
        UIFont.preferredFont(forTextStyle: UIFont.TextStyle.headline)
cell.attractionLabel.text = attractionNames[row]
cell.attractionImage.image = UIImage(named: attractionImages[row])
return cell
```

29.8 Downloading and Adding the Image Files

Before a test run of the application can be performed the image files referenced in the code need to be added to the project. An archive containing the images may be found in the *attractionImages* folder of the code sample archive which can be downloaded from the following URL:

https://www.ebookfrenzy.com/retail/ios12/

Select the *Assets.xcassets* entry in the Project Navigator panel, Ctrl-click in the left-hand panel of the asset catalog screen and select the *Import...* menu option. In the file selection dialog, navigate to and select the *attractionImages* folder and click on the *Open* button to import the images into a new image set.

29.9 Compiling and Running the Application

Now that the storyboard work and code modifications are complete the next step in this chapter is to run the application by clicking on the run button located in the Xcode toolbar. Once the code has compiled the application will launch and execute within an iOS Simulator session as illustrated in Figure 29-7.

Clearly the table view has been populated with multiple instances of our prototype table view cell, each of which has been customized through outlets to display different text and images. Note that the self-sizing rows feature has caused the rows to automatically size to accommodate the attraction images.

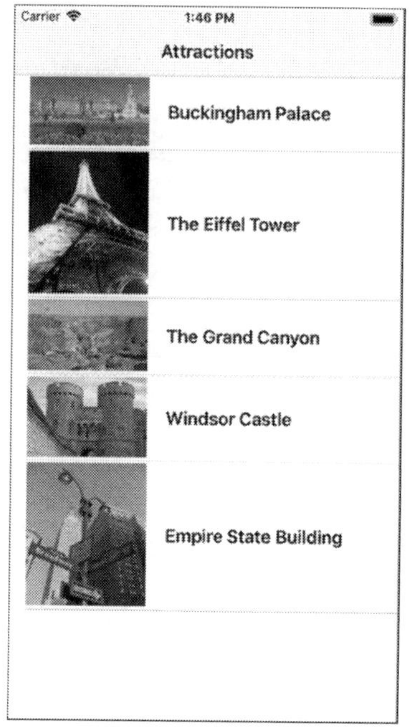

Figure 29-7

Verify that the preferred font size code is working by running the app on a physical iOS device, displaying *Settings -> Display & Brightness -> Text Size* and dragging the slider to change the font size. If using the Simulator, use the slider on the *Settings -> General -> Accessibility -> Larger Text Size* screen. Stop and restart the application and note that the attraction names are now displayed using the newly selected font size.

29.10 Handling TableView Swipe Gestures

The final task in this chapter is to enhance the app so that the user can swipe left on a table row to reveal a delete button which, when tapped, will remove that row from the table. This will involve the addition of a table view trailing swipe delegate method to the AttractionTableViewController class as follows:

```
override func tableView(_ tableView: UITableView,
  trailingSwipeActionsConfigurationForRowAt indexPath: IndexPath) ->
      UISwipeActionsConfiguration? {

    let configuration = UISwipeActionsConfiguration(actions: [
            UIContextualAction(style: .destructive, title: "Delete",
                  handler: { (action, view, completionHandler) in
```

```
                let row = indexPath.row
                self.attractionNames.remove(at: row)
                self.attractionImages.remove(at: row)
                self.webAddresses.remove(at: row)
                completionHandler(true)
                tableView.reloadData()
        })
    ])
    return configuration
}
```

The code within the method creates a new UISwipeActionsConfiguration instance configured with a destructive contextual action with the title set to "Delete". Declaring the action as destructive ensures that the table view will remove the entry from the table when the user taps the Delete button. Although this will have removed the visual representation of the row in the table view, the entry will still exist in the data model causing the row to reappear next time the table reloads. To address this, the method implements a completion handler to be called when the deletion occurs. This handler simply identifies the row that was swiped and removes the matching data model array entries.

Build and run the app one final time and swipe left on one of the rows to reveal the delete option (Figure 29-8). Tap the delete button to remove the item from the list.

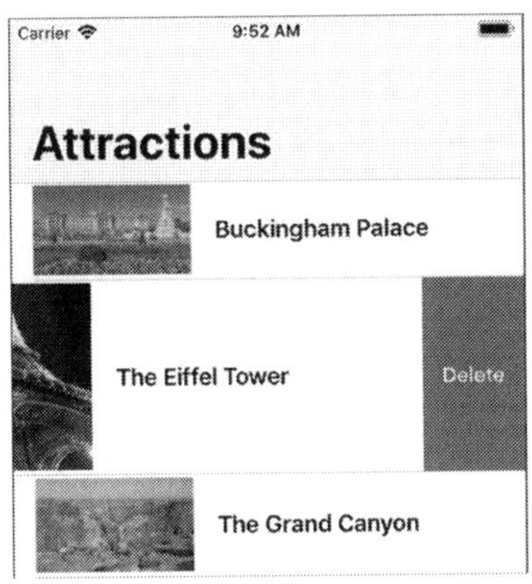

Figure 29-8

The next step, which will be outlined in the following chapter entitled *Implementing iOS 12 TableView Navigation using Storyboards* will be to use the storyboard to add navigation capabilities to the application so that selecting a row from the table results in a detail scene appearing to the user.

29.11 Summary

The storyboard feature of Xcode significantly eases the process of creating complex table view based interfaces within iOS applications. Arguably the most significant feature is the ability to visually design the appearance of a table view cell and then have that cell automatically replicated at run time to display information to the user in table form. iOS also includes support for automatic table cell sizing and the adoption of the user's preferred font setting within table views. iOS also includes support for swipe interactions within table views. This chapter demonstrated the implementation of a destructive trailing swipe handler designed to allow the user to delete rows from a table view.

Chapter 30

30. Implementing iOS 12 TableView Navigation using Storyboards

The objective of this chapter is to extend the application created in the previous chapter (entitled *Using Xcode 10 Storyboards to Build Dynamic TableViews*) and, in so doing, demonstrate the steps involved in implementing table view navigation within a storyboard. In other words, we will be modifying the attractions example from the previous chapter such that selecting a row from the table view displays a second scene in which a web page providing information about the chosen location will be displayed to the user. As part of this exercise we will also explore the transfer of data between different scenes in a storyboard.

30.1 Understanding the Navigation Controller

Navigation based applications present a hierarchical approach to displaying information to the user. Such applications typically take the form of a navigation bar (UINavigationBar) and a series of Table based views (UITableView). Selecting an item from the table list causes the view associated with that selection to be displayed. The navigation bar will display a title corresponding to the currently displayed view together with a button that returns the user to the previous view when selected. For an example of this concept in action, spend some time using the iPhone *Mail* or *Music* applications.

When developing a navigation-based application, the central component of the architecture is the *navigation controller*. In addition, each scene has a view and a corresponding view controller. The navigation controller maintains a stack of these view controllers. When a new view is displayed it is *pushed* onto the navigation controller's stack and becomes the currently active controller. The navigation controller automatically displays the navigation bar and the "back" button. When the user selects the button in the navigation bar to move back to the previous level, that view controller is *popped* off the stack and the view controller beneath it moved to the top becoming the currently active controller.

The view controller for the first table view that appears when the application is started is called the *root view controller*. The root view controller cannot be popped off the navigation controller stack.

30.2 Adding the New Scene to the Storyboard

For the purposes of this example we will be adding a new View Controller to our storyboard to act as the second scene. With this in mind, begin by loading the *TableViewStory* project created in the previous chapter into Xcode.

Once the project has loaded we will need to add a new UIViewController subclass to our project files so select the *File -> New -> File...* menu item and choose the *Cocoa Touch Class* option from the *iOS* category. On the options screen, make sure that the *Subclass of* menu is set to UIViewController, name the new class *AttractionDetailViewController* and make sure that the *Also create XIB file* option is switched off. Click *Next* before clicking on *Create*.

Next, select the *Main.storyboard* file from the project navigator so that the storyboard canvas is visible. From the Library, select a View Controller and drag and drop it to the right of the existing table view controller as outlined in Figure 30-1. With the new view controller added, select it and display the identity inspector (*View*

-> *Utilities -> Show Identity Inspector*) and change the class setting from UIViewController to AttractionDetailViewController.

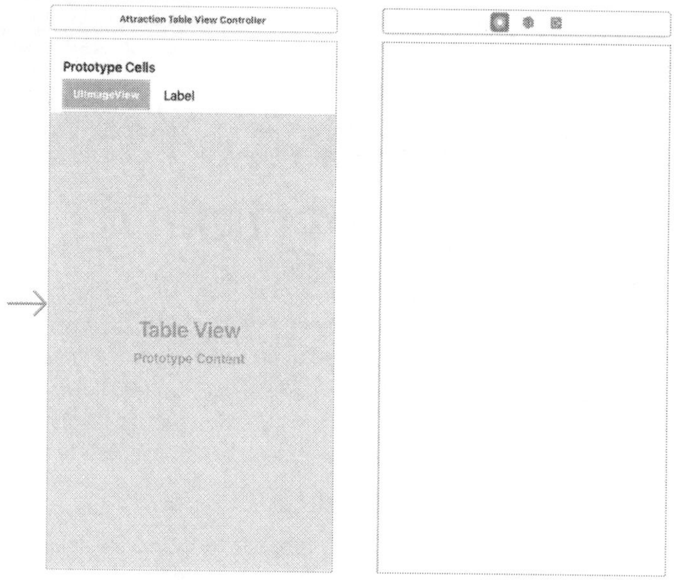

Figure 30-1

The detail scene has now been added and assigned to the newly created subclass where code can be added to bring the scene to life.

30.3 Adding a Navigation Controller

Once the application is completed, selecting a row from the Table View will trigger a segue to display the detail view controller. The detail view will contain a button which, when selected by the user, will navigate back to the table view. This functionality will be made possible by the addition of a Navigation Controller to the storyboard. This can be added by selecting the Attraction Table View Controller scene in the storyboard so that it highlights in blue, and then selecting the Xcode *Editor -> Embed In -> Navigation Controller* menu option. Once performed, the storyboard will appear as outlined in Figure 30-2:

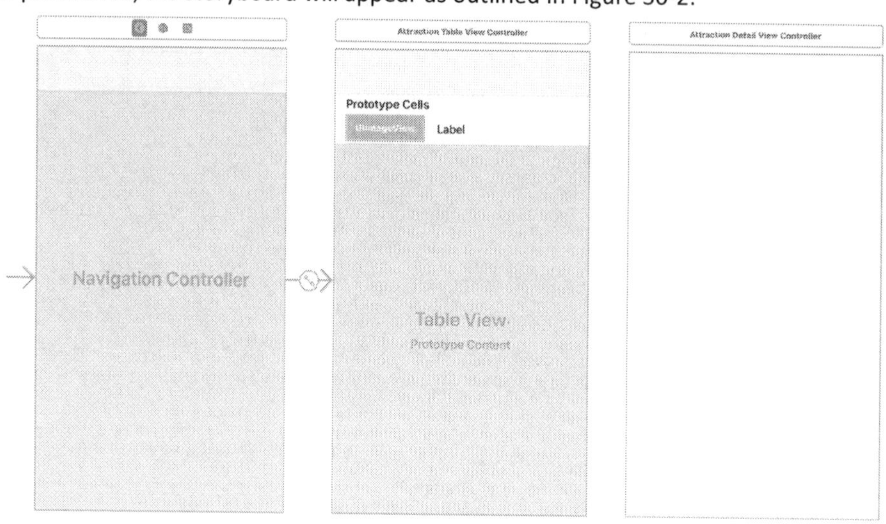

Figure 30-2

30.4 Establishing the Storyboard Segue

When the user selects a row within the table view, a segue needs to be triggered to display the attraction detail view controller. In order to establish this segue, Ctrl-click on the *prototype cell* located in the Attraction Table View Controller scene and drag the resulting line to the Attraction Detail View Controller scene. Upon releasing the line, select the *Show* option from the *Selection Segue* section of the resulting menu. The storyboard will update to display a segue connection between the table view cell and the view controller. In code that will be implemented later in this chapter it will be necessary to reference this specific segue. In order to do so it must, therefore, be given an identifier. Click on the segue connection between Attraction Table View Controller and Attraction Detail View Controller, display the Attributes Inspector (*View -> Utilities -> Show Attributes Inspector*) and change the Identifier value to *ShowAttractionDetails*.

In addition, a toolbar should have appeared in both scenes. Click in the Attraction Table View Controller toolbar area to select the Navigation Item component, display the Attributes inspector panel and change the title property to "Attractions". Next, drag a Navigation Item view from the Library and drop it onto the toolbar of the Attraction Detail View Controller. Select the new item and change the title property in the Attributes inspector to "Attraction Details":

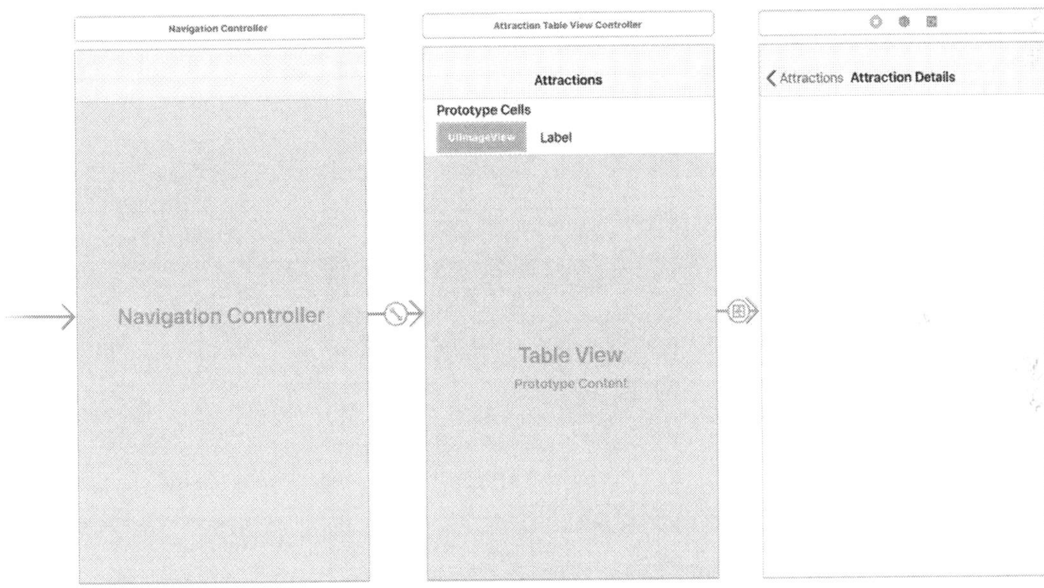

Figure 30-3

Build and run the application and note that selecting a row in the table view now displays the second view controller which, in turn, contains a button in the toolbar to return to the "Attractions" table view. Clearly, we now need to do some work on the AttractionDetailViewController class so that information about the selected tourist location is displayed in the view.

30.5 Modifying the AttractionDetailViewController Class

For the purposes of this example application, the attraction detail view is going to display a WebKit View loaded with a web page relating to the selected tourist attraction. In order to achieve this, the class is going to need a WKWebView object which will later be added to the view.

In addition to the WebKit View, the class is also going to need an internal data model that contains the URL of the web page to be displayed. It will be the job of the table view controller to update this variable prior to the segue occurring so that it reflects the selected attraction. For the sake of simplicity, the data model will take the form of a String object. Select the *AttractionDetailViewController.swift* file and modify it as follows to declare this variable and also to import the WebKit framework which will be used in the next step:

```
import UIKit
import WebKit

class AttractionDetailViewController: UIViewController {

    var webSite: String?
.
.
.
```

The next step is to add the WebKit View to the view controller. Select the storyboard file in the Project Navigator, and drag and drop a WebKit View from the Library panel onto the Attraction Detail scene. Resize the view so that it fills the entire scene area as illustrated in Figure 30-4:

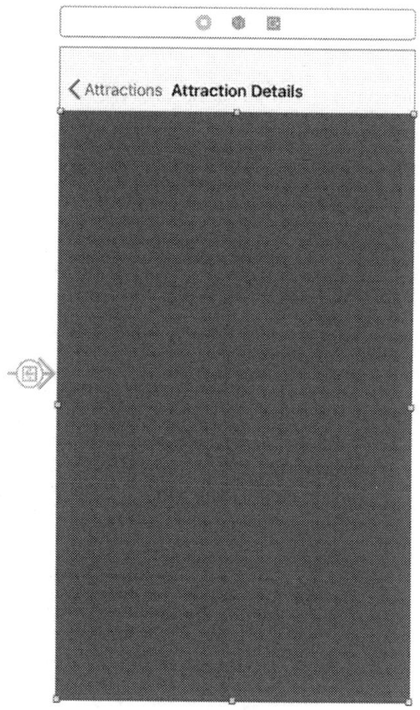

Figure 30-4

With the WebKit View selected in the storyboard canvas, display the Auto Layout *Add New Constraints* menu and add *Spacing to nearest neighbor* constraints on all four sides of the view with the *Constrain to margins* option disabled.

Display the Assistant Editor panel and verify that the editor is displaying the contents of the *AttractionDetailViewController.swift* file. Ctrl-click on the WebKit View and drag to a position just below the class declaration line in the Assistant Editor. Release the line and in the resulting connection dialog establish an outlet connection named *webView*.

When the detail view appears, the WebKit View will need to load the web page referenced by the *webSite* string variable. This can be achieved by adding code to the *viewDidLoad* method of the *AttractionDetailViewController.swift* file as follows:

```
override func viewDidLoad() {
    super.viewDidLoad()

    if let address = webSite,
        let webURL = URL(string: address) {
        let urlRequest = URLRequest(url: webURL)
        webView.load(urlRequest)
    }
}
```

30.6 Using prepare(for segue:) to Pass Data between Storyboard Scenes

The last step in the implementation of this project is to add code so that the data model contained within the AttractionDetailViewController class is updated with the URL of the selected attraction when a table view row is touched by the user. As previously outlined in *Using Xcode 10 Storyboards to Build Dynamic TableViews*, the *prepare(for segue:)* method on an originating scene is called prior to a segue being performed. This is the ideal place to add code to pass data between source and destination scenes. The *prepare(for segue:)* method needs to be added to the *AttractionTableViewController.swift* file as outlined in the following code fragment:

```
override func prepare(for segue: UIStoryboardSegue, sender: Any?) {
    if segue.identifier == "ShowAttractionDetails" {

        let detailViewController = segue.destination
            as! AttractionDetailViewController

        let myIndexPath = self.tableView.indexPathForSelectedRow!
        let row = myIndexPath.row
        detailViewController.webSite = webAddresses[row]
    }
}
```

The first task performed by this method is to check that the triggering segue is the *ShowAttractionDetails* segue we added to the storyboard. Having verified that to be the case the code then obtains a reference to the view controller of the destination scene (in this case an instance of our AttractionDetailViewController class). The table view object is then interrogated to find out the index of the selected row which, in turn, is used to prime the URL string variable in the AttractionDetailViewController instance.

30.7 Testing the Application

Compile and run the application, click on the run button located in the Xcode toolbar and wait for the application to launch. Select an entry from the table and watch as the second view controller appears and loads the appropriate web page:

Figure 30-5

30.8 Customizing the Navigation Title Size

The inclusion of a navigation controller in this example caused a navigation bar to appear on each scene within the app. By default this includes a title navigation item and, when necessary, a "back" button to return to the previous view controller. Many of the built-in apps provided with iOS now use a larger text size for these titles. The size of the title text within the navigation bar can be increased to conform with the general look and feel of the standard iOS apps by setting the *prefersLargeTitles* property on the navigation bar to *true*. To see this in action, modify the *initialize* method within the *AttractionTableViewController.swift* file to set this property:

```
func initialize() {
.
.
    navigationController?.navigationBar.prefersLargeTitles = true
}
```

Run the app again and note that the title now appears in larger text:

Figure 30-6

By default, this change will propagate down to any other view controllers displayed by the navigation controller. Selecting an entry from the table, for example, will show that the DetailViewController navigation bar has inherited the larger title property:

Figure 30-7

To prevent the setting from applying to this view controller, a property is available on the navigation bar's navigation item which specifies the display mode for the title. Modify the *viewDidLoad* method of the *AttractionDetailViewController.swift* file to set this property so that the larger title is not used on this screen:

```
override func viewDidLoad() {
    super.viewDidLoad()

    navigationItem.largeTitleDisplayMode = .never
    if let address = webSite {
        let webURL = URL(string: address)
        let urlRequest = URLRequest(url: webURL!)
        webView.load(urlRequest)
    }

}
```

The full range of settings for this property are as follows:

- **automatic** – The default behavior. Causes the navigation item to inherit the size setting from the previous navigation bar item.
- **always** – The navigation item title always uses large text.
- **never** – The title always uses smaller text.

30.9 Summary

A key component of implementing table view navigation using storyboards involves the use of segues and the transfer of data between scenes. In this chapter we have used a segue to display a second scene based on table view row selections. The use of the *prepare(for segue:)* method as a mechanism for passing data during a segue has also been explored and demonstrated.

When a navigation controller is embedded into a storyboard, a navigation bar appears at the top of each view controller scene. The size of the title displayed in this navigation bar can be increased by setting a property on the navigation bar. To prevent this larger title from being inherited by other scenes in the navigation stack, simply change the display mode on the corresponding navigation item.

Chapter 31

31. Integrating Search using the iOS UISearchController

The previous chapters have covered the creation of a table view using prototype cells and the introduction of table view navigation using a navigation controller. This, the final chapter dedicated to table views and table view navigation, will cover the integration of a search bar into the navigation bar of the TableViewStory app created in the earlier chapters.

31.1 Introducing the UISearchController Class

The UISearchController class is designed to be used alongside existing view controllers to provide a way to integrate search features into apps. The UISearchController class includes a search bar (UISearchBar) into which the user enters the search text.

The search controller is assigned a *results updater* delegate which must conform to the UISearchResultsUpdating protocol. The *updateSearchResults(for searchController:)* method of this delegate is called repeatedly as the user enters text into the search bar and is responsible for filtering the results. The results updater object is assigned to the search controller via the controller's *searchResultsUpdater* property.

In addition to the results updater, the search controller also needs a view controller to display the search results. The results updater object can also serve as the results view controller, or a separate view controller can be designated for the task via the search controller's *searchViewController* property.

A wide range of notifications relating to the user's interaction with the search bar can be intercepted by the app by assigning classes that conform to the UISearchControllerDelegate and UISearchBarDelegate protocols.

In terms of integrating the search controller into a navigation bar, this is achieved by assigning the search controller instance to the *searchController* property of the navigation bar's navigation item.

Once all of the configuration criteria have been met, the search bar will appear within the navigation bar when the user scrolls down within the view controller as shown in Figure 31-1:

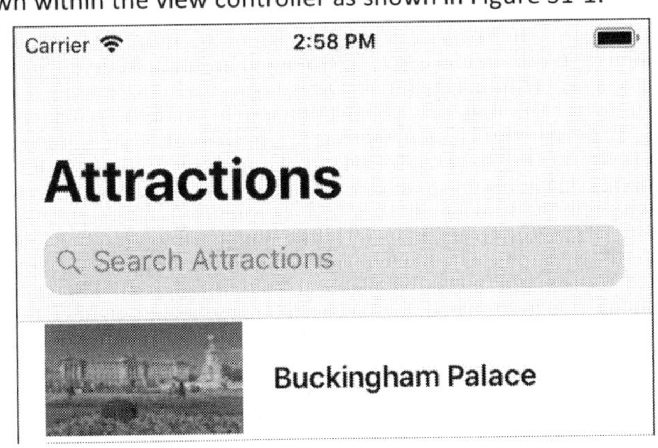

Figure 31-1

31.2 Adding a Search Controller to the TableViewStory Project

To add search to the TableViewStory app, begin by editing the *AttractionTableViewController.swift* file and adding search related delegate declarations, a UISearchController instance and a new array into which any matching search results will be stored. Also add a Boolean variable that will be used to track whether or not the user is currently performing a search:

```
class AttractionTableViewController: UITableViewController,
        UISearchResultsUpdating, UISearchBarDelegate {

    var attractionImages = [String]()
    var attractionNames = [String]()
    var webAddresses = [String]()

    var searching = false
    var matches = [Int]()
    let searchController = UISearchController(searchResultsController: nil)
.
.
```

Next, modify the *initialize* method to designate the table view controller instance as both the search bar and results updater delegates for the search controller. The code also sets properties to display some placeholder text in the search text field and to prevent the search from obscuring the search results view controller:

```
func initialize() {
.
.
    navigationController?.navigationBar.prefersLargeTitles = true

    searchController.searchBar.delegate = self
    searchController.searchResultsUpdater = self
    searchController.obscuresBackgroundDuringPresentation = false
    searchController.searchBar.placeholder = "Search Attractions"
}
```

With the search controller configured, it can now be added to the navigation item, the code for which can be added at the end of the *initialize* method as follows:

```
func initialize() {
.
.
    navigationItem.searchController = searchController
    definesPresentationContext = true
}
```

The *definesPresentationContext* setting is a property of the view controller and ensures that any view controllers displayed from the current controller will be able to navigate back to the current view controller.

31.3 Implementing the updateSearchResults Method

With AttractionTableViewController designated as the results updater delegate, the next step is to implement the *updateSearchResults(for searchController:)* method within this class file as follows:

```
func updateSearchResults(for searchController: UISearchController) {
    if let searchText = searchController.searchBar.text,
                              !searchText.isEmpty {
        matches.removeAll()

        for index in 0..<attractionNames.count {
            if attractionNames[index].lowercased().contains(
                                   searchText.lowercased()) {
                matches.append(index)
            }
        }
        searching = true
    } else {
        searching = false
    }
    tableView.reloadData()
}
```

The method is passed a reference to the search controller object which contains the text entered into the search bar. The code accesses this text property and verifies that it contains text. If no text has been entered, the method sets the *searching* variable to false before returning. This variable will be used later to identify if the table view is currently displaying search results or the full list of attractions.

If search text has been entered, any existing entries in the *matches* array are removed and a *for* loop used to iterate through each entry within the *attractionNames* array, checking to see if each name contains the search text. If a match is found, the index value of the matching array item is stored into the *matches* array.

Finally, the *searching* variable is set to true and the table view data reloaded.

31.4 Reporting the Number of Table Rows

Since the AttractionTableViewController is being used to display both the full list of attractions and the search results, the number of rows displayed will clearly depend on whether or not the controller is in search mode. In search mode, for example, the number of rows will be dictated by the number of items in the *matches* array. Locate the *tableView(_:numberOfRowsInSection:)* table view data source delegate method and modify it as follows:

```
override func tableView(_ tableView: UITableView,
              numberOfRowsInSection section: Int) -> Int {
    return searching ? matches.count : attractionNames.count
}
```

The method now uses a ternary statement to return either the total number of attractions or the number of matches based on the current value of the *searching* variable.

31.5 Modifying the cellForRowAt Method

The next step is to ensure that the *tableView(_:cellForRowAt:)* method returns the appropriate cells when the view controller is displaying search results. Specifically, if the user is currently performing a search, the index into the attraction arrays must be taken from the array of index values in the *matches* array. Modify the method so that it reads as follows:

```
override func tableView(_ tableView: UITableView, cellForRowAt indexPath:
                IndexPath) -> UITableViewCell {

    let cell =
        self.tableView.dequeueReusableCell(withIdentifier:
            "AttractionTableCell", for: indexPath)
            as! AttractionTableViewCell

    let row = indexPath.row
    cell.attractionLabel.font =
        UIFont.preferredFont(forTextStyle: UIFont.TextStyle.headline)

    cell.attractionLabel.text =
        searching ? attractionNames[matches[row]] : attractionNames[row]
    let imageName =
        searching ? attractionImages[matches[row]] : attractionImages[row]

    cell.attractionImage.image = UIImage(named: imageName)

    return cell
}
```

Once again ternary statements are being used to control which row index is used based on the prevailing setting of the *searching* variable.

31.6 Modifying the Trailing Swipe Delegate Method

The previous chapter added a trailing swipe delegate method to the table view class to allow the user to delete rows from the table. This method also needs to be updated to allow items to be removed during a search operation. Locate this method in the *AttractionTableViewController.swift* file and modify it as follows:

```
override func tableView(_ tableView: UITableView,
   trailingSwipeActionsConfigurationForRowAt indexPath: IndexPath) ->
      UISwipeActionsConfiguration? {

    let configuration = UISwipeActionsConfiguration(actions: [
            UIContextualAction(style: .destructive, title: "Delete",
handler: { (action, view, completionHandler) in

                let row = indexPath.row
```

```
                if self.searching {
                    self.attractionNames.remove(at: self.matches[row])
                    self.attractionImages.remove(at: self.matches[row])
                    self.webAddresses.remove(at: self.matches[row])
                    self.matches.remove(at: indexPath.row)
                    self.updateSearchResults(for: self.searchController)
                } else {
                    self.attractionNames.remove(at: row)
                    self.attractionImages.remove(at: row)
                    self.webAddresses.remove(at: row)
                }
                completionHandler(true)
                tableView.reloadData()
        })
    ])
    return configuration
}
```

31.7 Modifying the Detail Segue

When search results are displayed in the table view, the user will still be able to select an attraction and segue to the details view. When the segue is performed, the URL of the selected attraction is assigned to the *webSite* property of the DetailViewController class so that the correct page is loaded into the WebKit View. The *prepare(forSegue:)* method now needs to be modified to handle the possibility that the user triggered the segue from a list of search results. Locate this method in the AttractionTableViewController class and modify it as follows:

```
override func prepare(for segue: UIStoryboardSegue, sender: Any?) {
    if segue.identifier == "ShowAttractionDetails" {

        let detailViewController = segue.destination
            as! AttractionDetailViewController

        let myIndexPath = self.tableView.indexPathForSelectedRow!
        let row = myIndexPath.row
        detailViewController.webSite =
                searching ? webAddresses[matches[row]] : webAddresses[row]
    }
}
```

31.8 Handling the Search Cancel Button

The final task is to make sure when the user clicks the Cancel button in the search bar that the view controller switches out of search mode and displays the full list of attractions. Since the AttractionTableViewController class has already been declared as implementing the UISearchBarDelegate protocol, all that remains is to add the *searchBarCancelButtonClicked* delegate method in the *AttractionTableViewController.swift* file. All this method needs to do is set the *searching* variable to false and instruct the table view to reload data:

```
func searchBarCancelButtonClicked(_ searchBar: UISearchBar) {
    searching = false
    tableView.reloadData()
}
```

31.9 Testing the Search Controller

Build and run the app and drag the table view down to display the search bar. Begin entering text into the search bar and confirm that the list of results narrows with each key stroke to display only matching attractions:

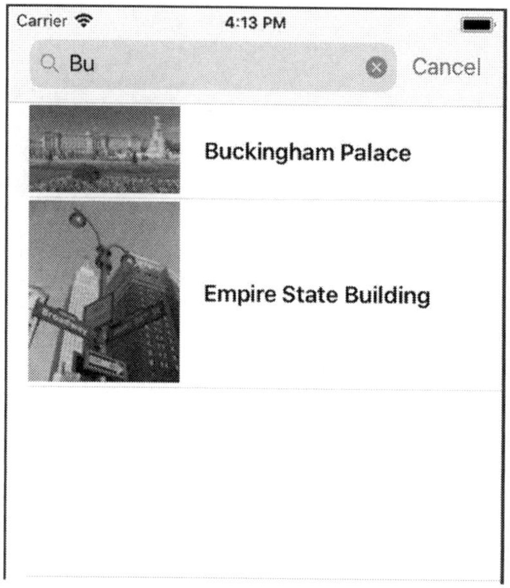

Figure 31-2

Verify that the correct images are displayed for the attraction results and that selecting an attraction from the list presents the correct web page in the detail view controller. Return to the search results screen and tap the Cancel button to return to the full list of attractions. Also confirm that deleting a row from the search results also removes the item from the full attraction list.

31.10 Summary

The UISearchController class provides an easy way to integrate a search bar into iOS apps. When assigned to a navigation item, the search bar appears within the navigation bar of view controllers with an embedded navigation controller. At a minimum, a search controller needs delegates to filter the search and display those results. This chapter has worked through an example search controller implementation in the context of a table view and navigation controller configuration.

32. Working with the iOS 12 Stack View Class

With hindsight it seems hard to believe, but until the introduction of iOS 9 there was no easy way to build stack based user interface layouts that would adapt automatically to different screen sizes and changes in device orientation. While such results could eventually be achieved with careful use of size classes and Auto Layout this was far from a simple task. That changed with the introduction of the UIStackView class in the iOS 9 SDK.

32.1 Introducing the UIStackView Class

The UIStackView class is a user interface element that allows subviews to be arranged linearly in either a column or row orientation. The class makes extensive use of Auto Layout and automatically sets up many of the Auto Layout constraints needed to provide the required layout behavior. The class goes beyond simple stacking of views, allowing additional Auto Layout constraints to be added to subviews, and providing a range of properties that enable the layout behavior of those subviews to be modified to meet different requirements.

The UIStackView object is available for inclusion within Storyboard scenes simply by dragging and dropping either the *Horizontal Stack View* or *Vertical Stack View* from the Library panel onto the scene canvas. Once added to a scene, subviews are added simply by dragging and dropping the required views onto the stack view.

Existing views in a storyboard scene may be wrapped in a stack view simply by Shift-clicking on the views so that they are all selected before clicking on the Stack button located in the bottom of the Interface Builder panel as highlighted in Figure 32-1. Interface Builder will decide whether to encapsulate the selected views into a horizontal or vertical stack depending on the layout positions of the views:

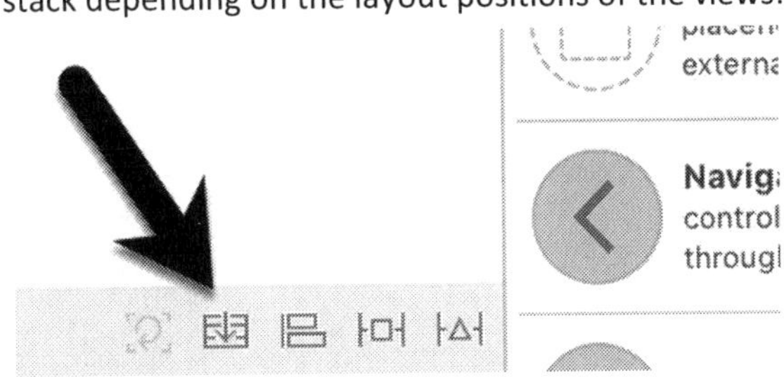

Figure 32-1

By default the stack view will resize to accommodate the subviews as they are added. As with any other view type, however, Auto Layout constraints may be used to constrain and influence the resize behavior of the stack view in relation to the containing view and any the other views in the scene layout.

Once added to a storyboard scene, a range of properties are available within the Attributes Inspector to customize the layout behavior of the object.

Stack views may be used to create simple column or row based layouts, or nested within each other to create more complex layouts. Figure 32-2, for example, shows an example layout consisting of a vertical stack view containing 3 horizontal stack views each containing a variety of subviews:

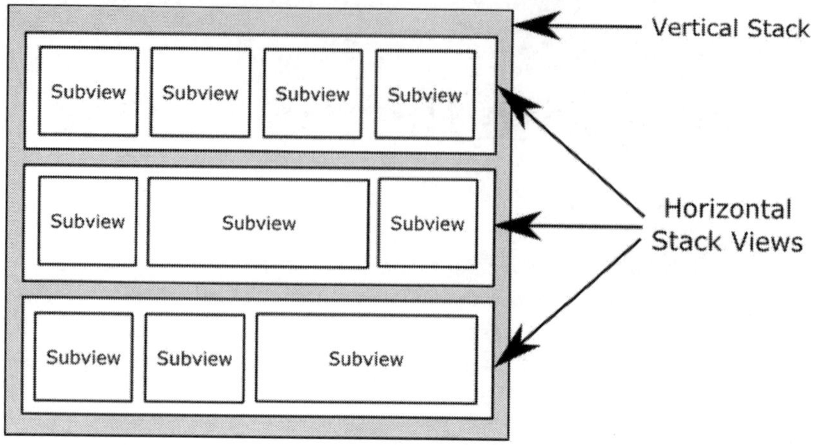

Figure 32-2

UIStackView class instances may also be created and managed from within the code of an iOS app. Stack view instances can be created in code and initialized with an array of subviews. Views may also be inserted and removed dynamically from within code and the attributes of the stack view changed via a range of properties. The subviews of a stack view object are held in an array which can be accessed via the *arrangedSubviews* property of the stack view instance.

32.2 Understanding Subviews and Arranged Subviews

The UIStackView class contains a property named *subviews*. This is an array containing each of the child views of the stack view object. Figure 32-3, for example shows the view hierarchy for a stack view with four subviews:

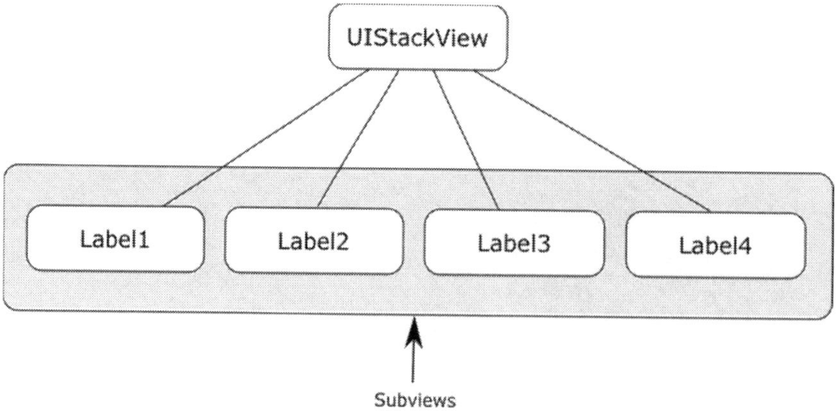

Figure 32-3

At any particular time, however, the stack view will not necessarily be responsible for arranging the layout and positions of all of the subviews it contains. The stack view might, for example, only be configured to arrange the Label3 and Label4 views in the above hierarchy. This essentially means that Label1 and Label2 may still be visible within the user interface but will not be positioned within the stack view. Subviews that are being arranged by the stack view are contained within a second array which is accessible via the *arrangedSubviews* property. Figure 32-4 shows both the subviews and the subset of the subviews which are currently being arranged by the stack view.

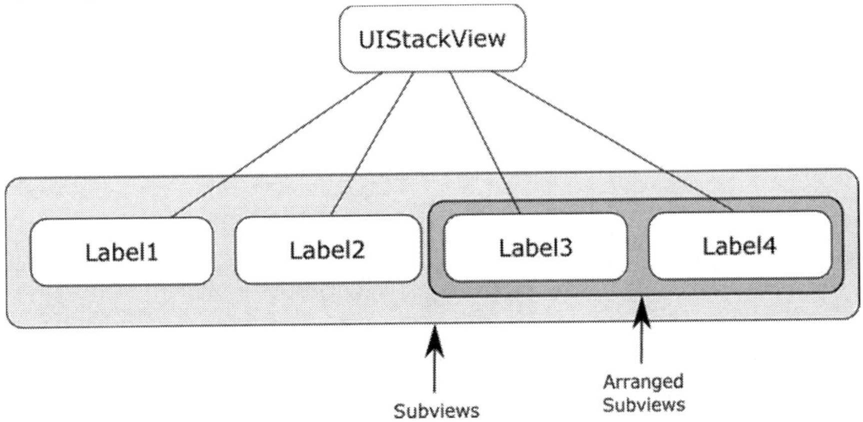

Figure 32-4

As will be outlined later in this chapter, the distinction between subview and arranged subviews is of particular importance when removing arranged subviews from a stack view.

32.3 StackView Configuration Options

A range of options are available to customize the way in which the stack view arranges its subviews. These properties are available both from within the Interface Builder Attributes Inspector panel at design time and also to be set dynamically from within the code of the app:

32.3.1 axis

The axis property controls the orientation of the stack in terms of whether the subviews are arranged in a vertical column layout or a horizontal row. When setting this property in code the axis should be set to UILayoutConstraintAxis.vertical or UILayoutConstraintAxis.horizontal.

32.3.2 Distribution

The distribution property dictates the way in which the subviews of the stack view are sized. Options available are as follows:

- **Fill** – The subviews are resized so as to fill the entire space available along the axis of the stack view. In other words the height of the subviews will be modified to fill the full height of the stack view in vertical orientation while the widths will be changed for a stack view in horizontal orientation. The amount by which each subview is resized relative to the other views can be controlled via the compression resistance and hugging priorities of the views (details of which were covered in the chapter entitled *An Introduction to Auto Layout in iOS 12*) and the position of the views in the stack view's arrangedSubviews array.

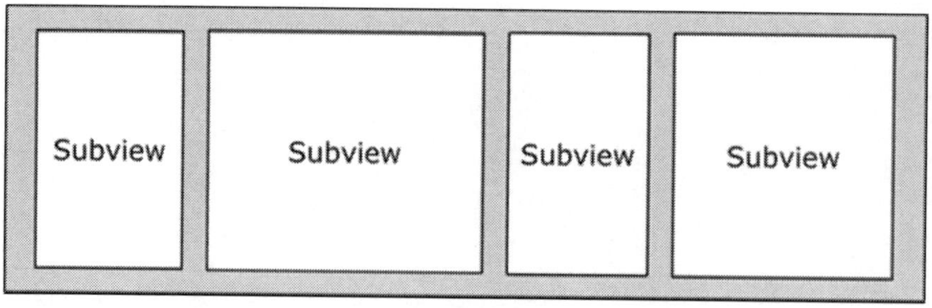

Figure 32-5

- **FillEqually** – The subviews are resized equally to fill the stack view along the view's axis. In a vertical stack, therefore, all of the subviews will be of equal height while in a horizontal axis orientation the subviews will be of equal width.

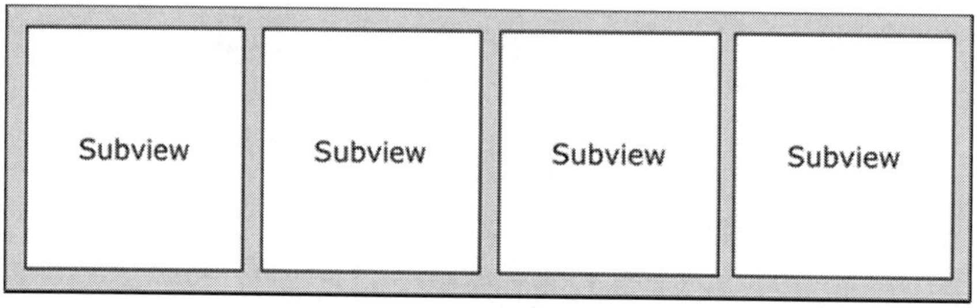

Figure 32-6

- **FillProportionally** – In this mode, the subviews are resized proportionally to their intrinsic content size along the axis of the stack view to fill the width or height of the view.
- **EqualSpacing** – Padding is used to space the subviews equally to fill the stack view along the axis. The size of the subviews will be reduced if necessary in order to fit within the available space based on the compression resistance priority setting and the position within the arrangedSubviews array.

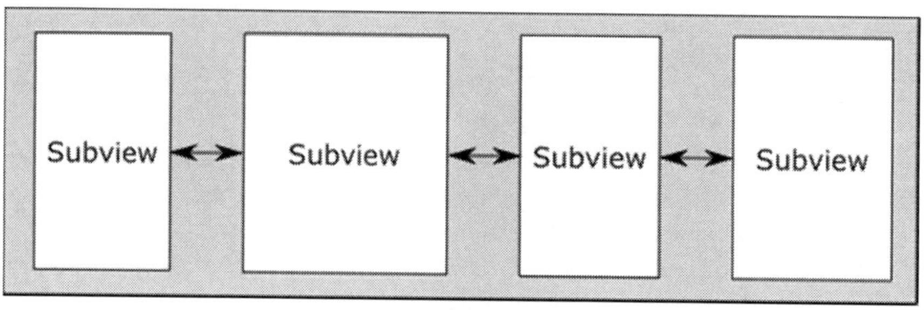

Figure 32-7

- **EqualCentering** – This mode tries to position the subviews along the stack view's axis such that the views have equal center to center spacing. The spacing used in this mode is influenced by the *spacing* property (outlined below). Where possible the stack view will honor the prevailing spacing property value, but will reduce this value if necessary. If the views still do not fit, the size of the subviews will be reduced if necessary in order to fit within the available space based on the compression resistance priority setting and the position within the arrangedSubviews array.

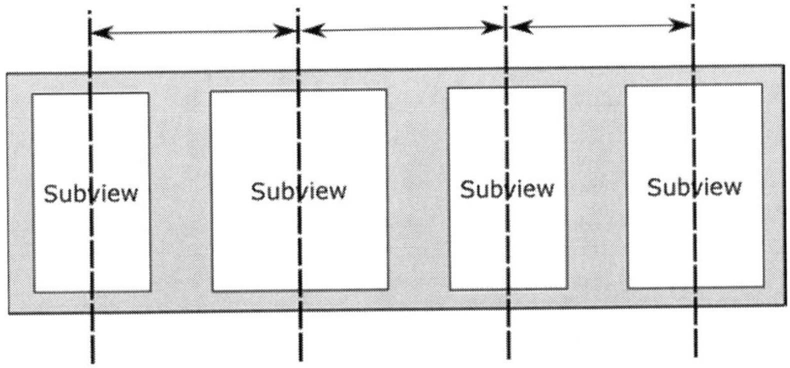

Figure 32-8

32.3.3 spacing

The spacing property specifies the distance (in points) between the edges of adjacent subviews within a stack view. When the stack view distribution property is set to *FillProportionally* the spacing value dictates the spacing between the subviews. In *EqualSpacing* and *EqualCentering* modes, the spacing value indicates the minimum allowed spacing between the adjacent edges of the subviews. A negative spacing value causes subviews to overlap.

32.3.4 alignment

The alignment property controls the positioning of the subviews perpendicularly to the axis of the stack view. Available alignment options are as follows:

- **Fill** – In fill mode, the subviews are resized to fill the space perpendicularly to the stack view's axis. In other words, the width of the subviews in a vertical stack view are resized to fill the full width of the stack view.

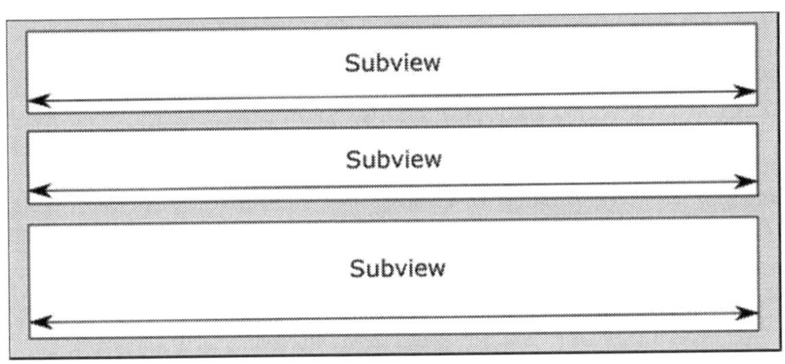

Figure 32-9

- **Leading** – In a vertically oriented stack view, the leading edges of the subviews are aligned with the leading edge of the stack view.

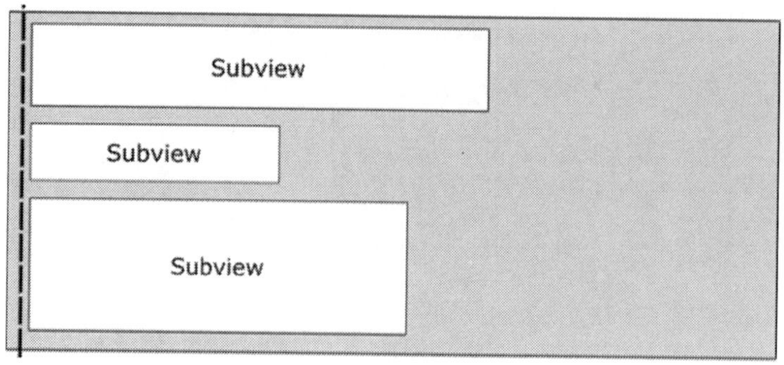

Figure 32-10

- **Trailing** - In a vertically oriented stack view, the trailing edges of the subviews are aligned with the trailing edge of the stack view.

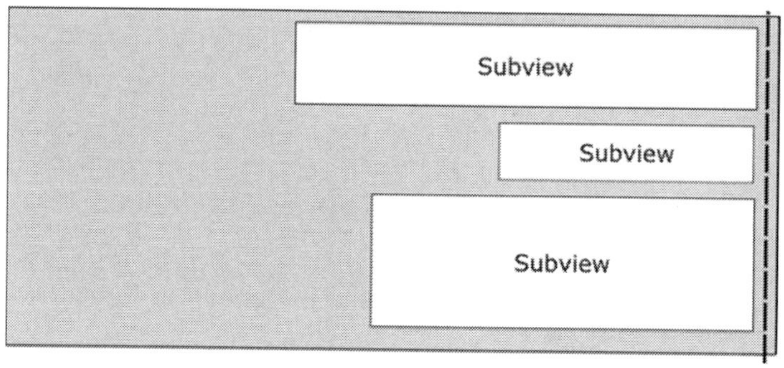

Figure 32-11

- **Top** – In a horizontally oriented stack view, the top edges of the subviews are aligned with the top edge of the stack view.

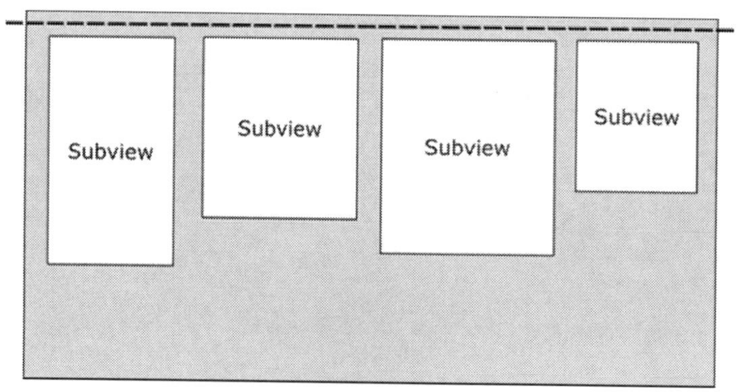

Figure 32-12

- **Bottom** - In a horizontally oriented stack view, the bottom edges of the subviews are aligned with the bottom edge of the stack view.

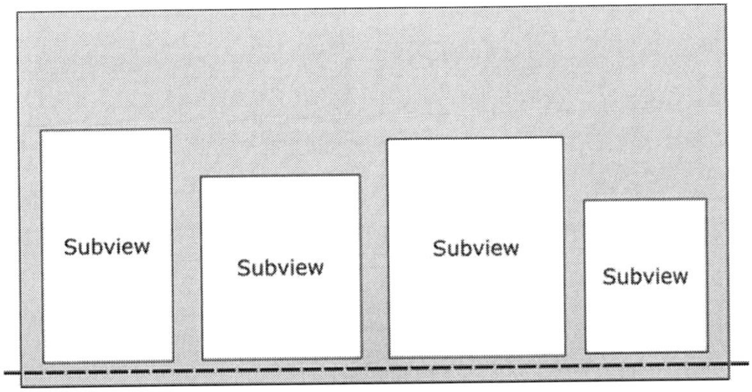

Figure 32-13

- **Center** – The centers of the subviews are aligned with the center axis of the stack view.

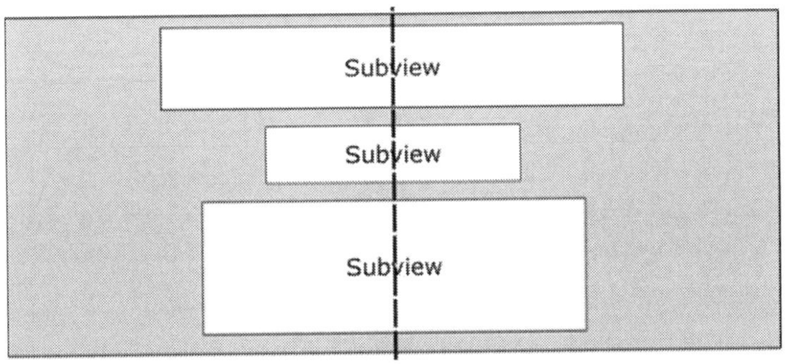

Figure 32-14

- **FirstBaseline** – Used only with horizontal stack views, this mode aligns all of the subviews with their first baseline. An array of subviews displaying text content, for example, would all be aligned based on the vertical position of the first line of text.

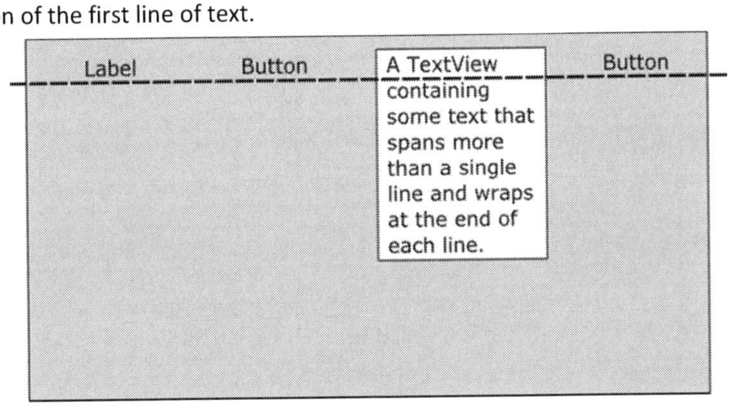

Figure 32-15

- **LastBaseline** – Similar to FirstBaseline, this mode aligns all of the subviews with their last baseline. For example, an array of subviews displaying text content would all be aligned based on the vertical position of the last line of text.

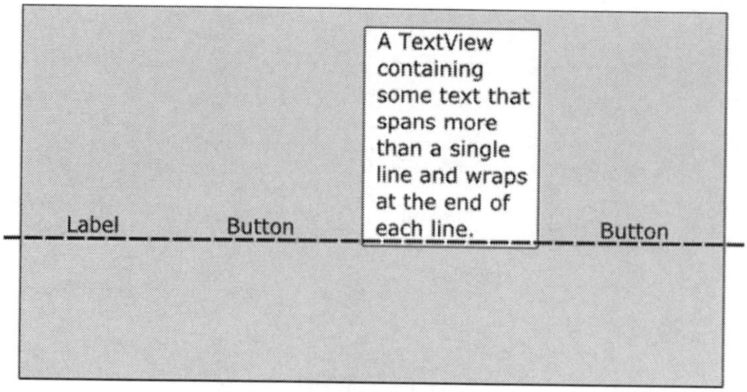

Figure 32-16

32.3.5 baseLineRelativeArrangement

Used only for vertical stack views, this property is a Boolean value that controls whether or not the vertical spacing between subviews is arranged relative to the baseline of the text contained within the views.

32.3.6 layoutMarginsRelativeArrangement

A Boolean value which, if set to true, causes subviews to be arranged relative to the layout margins of the containing stack view. If set to false, the subviews are arranged relative to the edges of the stack view.

32.4 Creating a Stack View in Code

UIStackView instances can be created in code by passing through an array object containing the subviews to be arranged by the stack. Once created, all of the previously outlined properties may also be set dynamically from within the code. The following Swift code, for example, creates a new stack view object, configures it for horizontal axis orientation with *FillEqually* distribution and assigns two Label objects as subviews:

```
let labelOne = UILabel(frame: CGRect(x: 0, y: 0, width: 200, height: 21))
labelOne.text = "Hello"
labelOne.backgroundColor = UIColor.red

let labelTwo = UILabel(frame: CGRect(x: 0, y: 0, width: 200, height: 21))
labelTwo.text = "There"
labelTwo.backgroundColor = UIColor.blue

let myStack = UIStackView(arrangedSubviews: [labelOne, labelTwo])

myStack.distribution = .fillEqually
myStack.axis = .horizontal
```

32.5 Adding Subviews to an Existing Stack View

Additional subviews may be appended to the end of a stack view's arrangedSubviews array using the *addArrangedSubview* method as follows:

```
myStack.addArrangedSubview(labelThree)
```

Alternatively, a subview may be inserted into a specific index position within the array of arranged subviews via a call to the *insertArrangedSubview:atIndex* method. The following line of code, for example, inserts an additional label at index position 0 within the arrangedSubviews array of a stack view:

```
myStack.insertArrangedSubview(labelZero, atIndex: 0)
```

32.6 Hiding and Removing Subviews

To remove an arranged subview from a stack view, call the *removeArrangedSubview* method of the stack view object, passing through the view object to be removed.

```
myStack.removeArrangedSubview(labelOne)
```

It is important to be aware that the *removeArrangedSubview* method only removes the specified view from the *arrangedSubviews* array of the stack view. The view still exists in the subviews array and will probably still be visible within the user interface layout after removal (typically in the top left-hand corner of the stack view).

An alternative to removing the subview is to simply hide it. This has the advantage of making it easy to display the subview later within the app code. A useful way to hide a subview is to obtain a reference to the subview to be hidden from within the arrangedSubviews array. The following code identifies and then hides the subview located at index position 1 in the array of arranged subviews:

```
let subview = myStack.arrangedSubviews[1]
subview.hidden = true
```

If the subview will not be needed again, however, it can be removed entirely by calling the *removeFromSuperview* method of the subview after it has been removed from the *arrangedSubviews* array as follows:

```
myStack.removeArrangedSubview(labelOne)
labelOne.removeFromSuperview()
```

This approach will remove the view entirely from the view hierarchy.

32.7 Summary

The UIStackView class allows user interface views to be arranged either in rows or columns. A wide range of configuration options combined with the ability to create and manage stack views dynamically from within code make this a powerful and flexible user interface layout solution.

With the basics of the UIStackView class covered in this chapter, the next chapter will create an example iOS app that makes use of this class.

Chapter 33

33. An iOS 12 Stack View Tutorial

The previous chapter covered a considerable amount of detail relating to the UIStackView class. This chapter will create an iOS app project that makes use of a wide range of features of both the UIStackView class and the Interface Builder tool. At the end of this tutorial, topics such as stack view nesting, adding and removing subviews both within Interface Builder and in code and the use of Auto Layout constraints to influence stack view layout behavior will have been covered.

33.1 About the Stack View Example App

The app created in this chapter is intended as an example of many of the ways in which the UIStackView class can be used to design a user interface. The example is going to consist of a single scene (Figure 33-1) containing multiple stack view instances that combine to create the screen for a coffee ordering app.

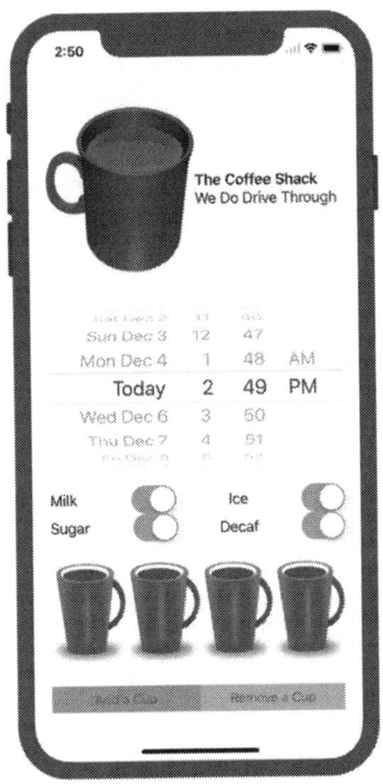

Figure 33-1

33.2 Creating the First Stack View

Create a new Xcode iOS project based on the Single View Application template and named *StackViewDemo*.

The first stack view to create within the user interface layout is a vertical stack view containing two labels. Select the *Main.storyboard* file from the Project Navigator panel and click on the current *View as:* device setting in the bottom left-hand corner of the canvas to display the device configuration bar. Select an iPad configuration from the bar (the layout will still work on iPhone size screens but the iPad setting provides more room in the scene when designing the layout). Drag and drop two Labels from the Library panel onto the storyboard canvas and edit the text on each label so that the layout resembles that shown in Figure 33-2:

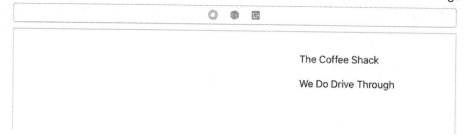

Figure 33-2

Select the uppermost label, display the Attributes Inspector panel and click on the T icon in the Font field to display the font selection menu. From within this menu, set the font for this label to Headline:

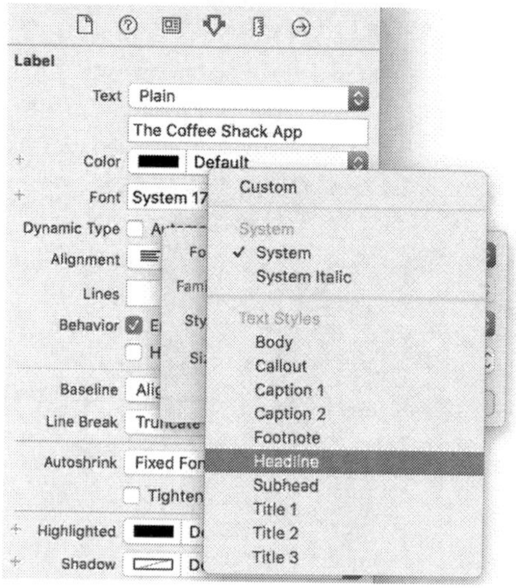

Figure 33-3

Finally, Shift-click on both of the labels and add them to a vertical stack view using the Embed In button located in the lower right-hand corner of the storyboard canvas as highlighted in Figure 33-4. From the resulting menu, select the *Stack View* option.

Figure 33-4

Once the button has been clicked, the two labels will be contained within a vertical stack view. Display the Document Outline panel, locate the newly inserted stack view from the hierarchy and select it, click on it a second time to enter editing mode and change the name to "Title Stack View". Naming stack views in this way makes it easier to understand the layout of the user interface as additional stack views are added to the design:

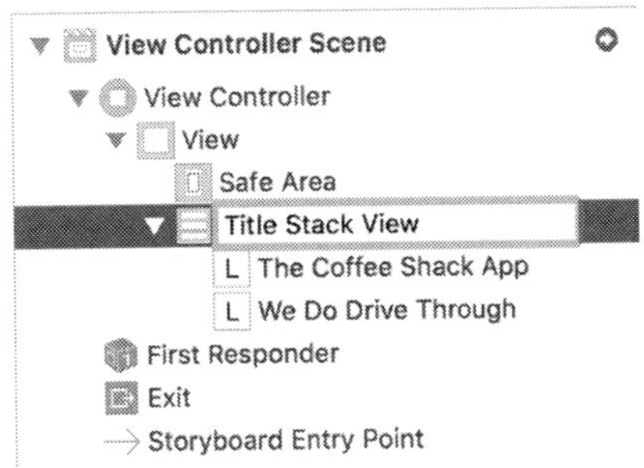

Figure 33-5

33.3 Creating the Banner Stack View

The top section of the storyboard scene is going to consist of a banner containing an image of a coffee cup and the Title Stack View created above. Begin by dragging and dropping an Image View object onto the scene and positioning and resizing it so that it resembles the layout in Figure 33-6:

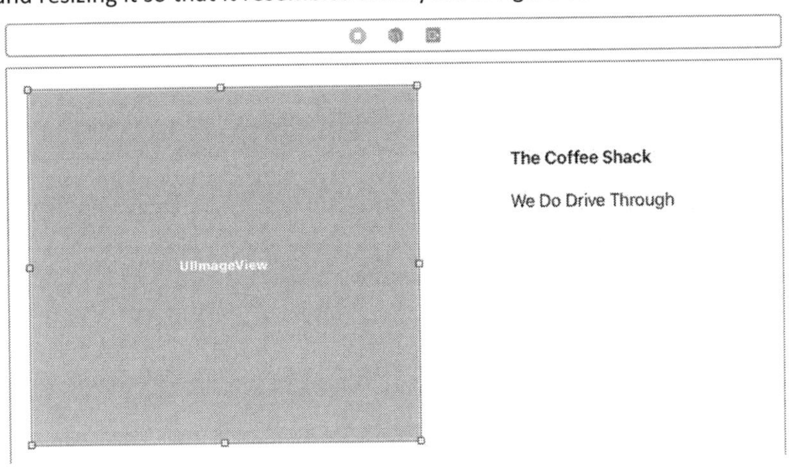

Figure 33-6

With the Image View object selected, display the Attributes Inspector panel and change the *Content Mode* setting to *Aspect Fit* so that the aspect ratio of the image is retained when it is added to the view. From the source code download archive for the book and, using a Finder window, locate both the *BlueCoffeeCup.png* and *RedCoffeeCup.png* files located in the *stackview_images* folder. Select the *Assets.xcassets* entry in the Project Navigator panel and drag and drop the two image files beneath the AppIcon entry:

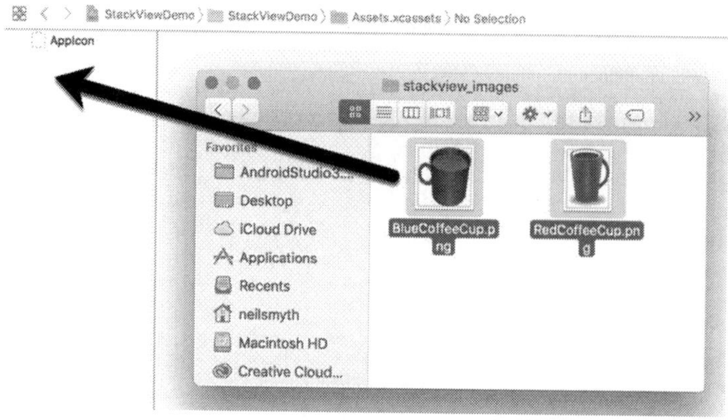

Figure 33-7

Display the *Main.storyboard* file once again, select the image view and use the *Image* property menu to select the *BlueCoffeeCup* image. Once selected the image should appear within the storyboard scene.

Shift-click on both the Image View object and the Title Stack View objects in the scene so that both are selected and click the Embed In button once again to add both to a new horizontal stack view instance. Locate the new stack view in the Document Outline panel, select it and click on it a second time. Once in editing mode, change the name to Banner Stack View.

With the Banner Stack View entry still selected in the Document Outline panel, display the Attributes Inspector panel and change the Alignment property to *Center* and the Distribution property to *Fill Equally*. This will ensure that the content is centered vertically within the stack view.

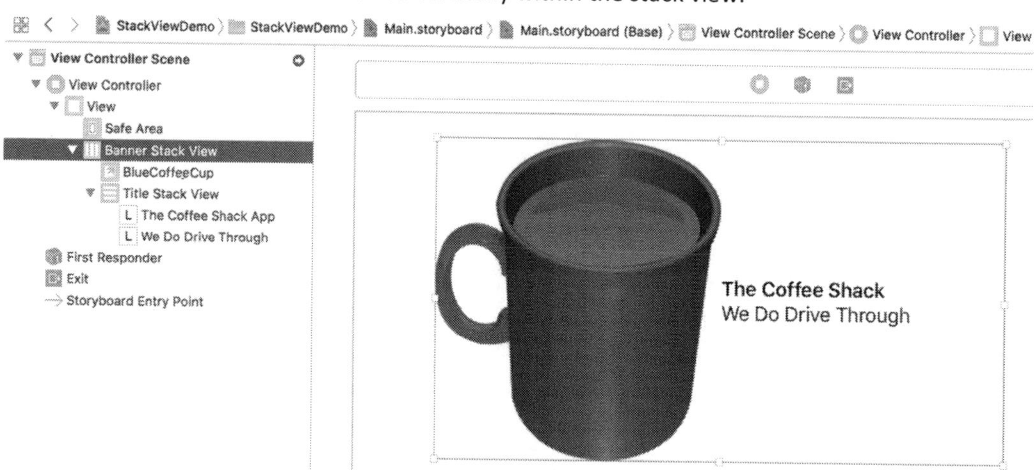

Figure 33-8

33.4 Adding the Switch Stack Views

The next stack views to create are those containing the two rows of Switch and Label objects. From the Library panel, drag and drop four Label and four Switch objects onto the scene canvas so that they are positioned beneath the Banner Stack View. Edit the text on the labels so that the views match those contained in Figure 33-9:

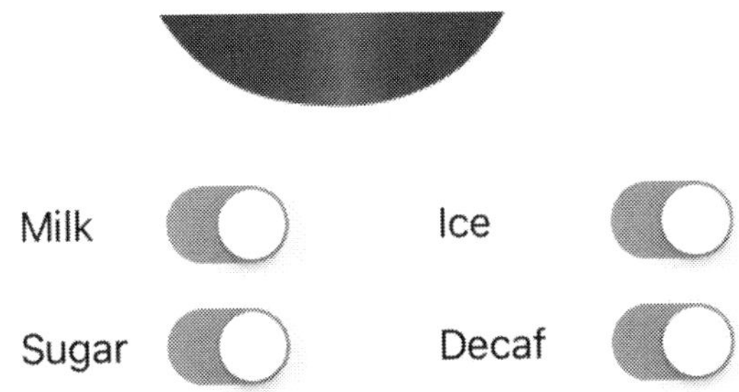

Figure 33-9

Use click and drag to select the first row of labels and switches so that all four views are selected. Using the Embed In button at the bottom of the storyboard, add these views to a new horizontal stack view. Referring to the Document Outline panel, change the name of this stack view to "Switches 1 Stack View". Repeat these steps to add the second row to a stack view, this time named "Switches 2 Stack View".

Select the Switches 1 Stack View in the Document Outline panel and, using the Attributes Inspector panel, change Alignment to *Fill* and Distribution to *Equal Spacing*. Repeat this step for the Switches 2 Stack View entry.

33.5 Creating the Top Level Stack View

The next step is to add the existing stack views to a new vertical stack view. To achieve this, select all three of the stack views in the storyboard scene and click on the Embed In button. Within the Document Outline panel locate this new parent stack view and change the name to "Top Level Stack View". At this point verify that the view outline matches that of Figure 33-10:

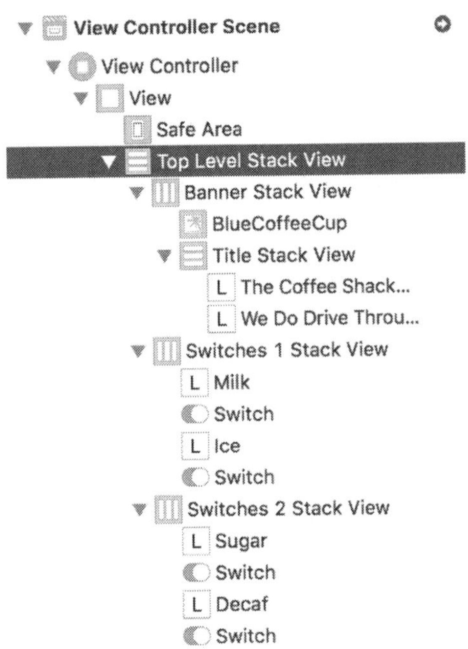

Figure 33-10

With the Top Level Stack View object selected, change both the Alignment and Distribution settings to *Fill.*

With these changes made, the storyboard scene should appear as shown in Figure 33-11:

Figure 33-11

33.6 Adding the Button Stack View

Two Button objects now need to be added to the Top Level Stack View but instead of using the Embed In button, this time the stack view and buttons will be added directly to the top level stack. With the *Main.storyboard* file selected, locate the Horizontal Stack View in the Library panel and drag it to the bottom edge of the Top Level Stack View in the storyboard scene so that a bold blue line appears together with a tag that reads "Top Level Stack View":

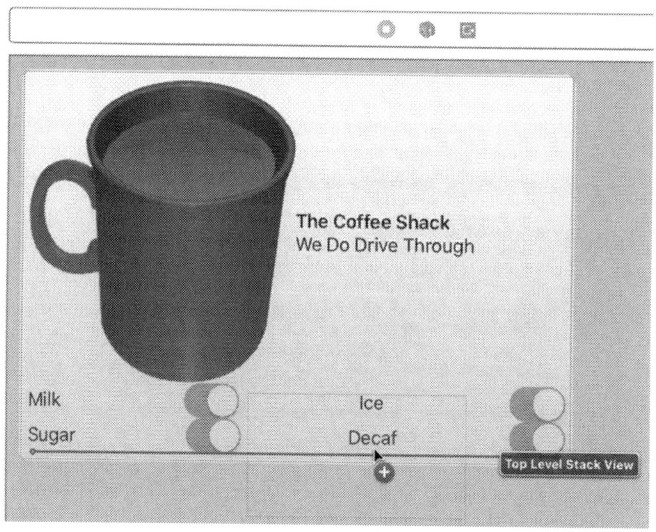

Figure 33-12

Release the stack view to add it as a subview of the top level stack then use the Document Outline panel to name the stack "Button Stack View". Drag and drop two Button views from the Library onto the new stack view. Select the Button Stack View entry in the Document Outline and change the Distribution property to *Fill Equally.* The buttons should now be spread equally over the width of the top level stack view.

With the left button selected, change the text to read "Add a Cup" and the background color property in the View section of the Attributes Inspector panel to green. Repeat these steps for the right-hand button, this time setting the text to "Remove a Cup" and the background color to cyan.

Display the Assistant Editor panel and establish action connections from the left and right buttons to methods named *addCup* and *removeCup* respectively.

33.7 Adding the Final Subviews to the Top Level Stack View

Two final subviews now need to be added to the top level stack view to complete the layout. From the Library panel, drag a Date Picker object and drop it immediately above the Switches 1 Stack View in the Document Outline panel. Be sure to move the object toward the left so that the blue insertion line extends to the left-hand edge of the Switches 1 Stack View entry (highlighted in Figure 33-13) before dropping the view to ensure that it is added as a subview of the Top Level Stack View and not the banner or title stack views:

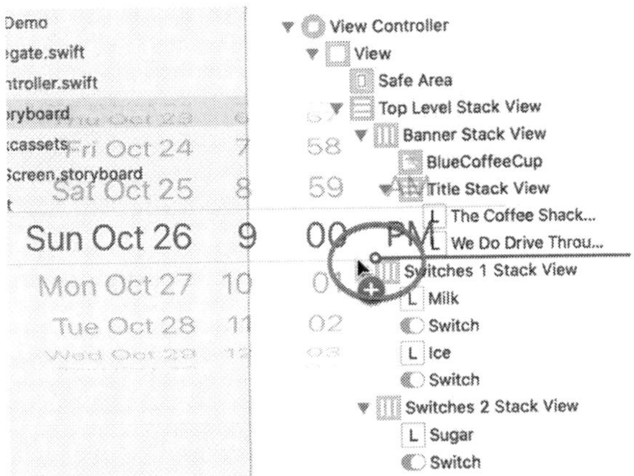

Figure 33-13

Repeat the above step to insert a Horizontal Stack View immediately above the Button Stack View, once again pulling the dragged view to the left before dropping to add the view to the Top Level Stack View. Once added, name the stack view "Cup Stack View".

With the Cup Stack View entry selected in the Outline Panel, display the Attributes Inspector panel and set the Alignment and Distribution properties to *Center* and *Fill Equally* respectively.

Select the Top Level Stack View entry in the Document Outline panel and use the Auto Layout *Add New Constraints* menu to set *Spacing to nearest neighbor* constraints of 20 on all four edges of the view before clicking the *Add 4 Constraints* button:

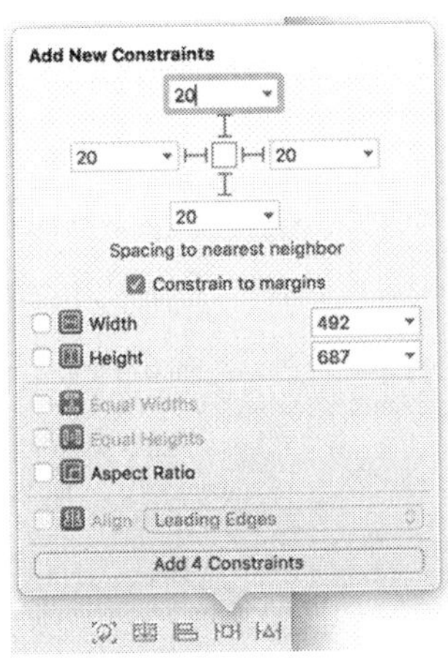

Figure 33-14

At this point in the project, the layout of the storyboard scene should appear as illustrated in Figure 33-15:

Figure 33-15

Compile and run the app on a physical device or Simulator session and verify that the layout appears correctly.

33.8 Dynamically Adding and Removing Subviews

The final step is to add the code to the two action methods to add and remove the subviews within the Cups Stack View. Select this view in the storyboard scene, display the Assistant Editor and establish an outlet connection named *cupStackView*.

Within the *ViewController.swift* file, implement the code within the *addCup* method as follows:

```
@IBAction func addCup(_ sender: Any) {

    let cupImage = UIImageView(image: UIImage(named: "RedCoffeeCup"))
    cupImage.contentMode = .scaleAspectFit

    UIView.animate(withDuration: 0.75, animations: {
        self.cupStackView.addArrangedSubview(cupImage)
        self.cupStackView.layoutIfNeeded()
    })
}
```

The code begins by creating a new UIImageView object initialized with the red coffee cup image previously added to the asset catalog. This image view is then set to aspect fit mode so that the image will retain the original aspect ratio when displayed. An animation block is then used to animate the addition of the subview to the Cup Stack View instance.

The final step in this example is to add the code to remove the last coffee cup subview added to the stack within the *removeCup* method:

```
@IBAction func removeCup(_ sender: Any) {

    let lastAddedCup = self.cupStackView.arrangedSubviews.last

    if let cup = lastAddedCup
    {
        UIView.animate(withDuration: 0.25, animations: {
            self.cupStackView.removeArrangedSubview(cup)
            cup.removeFromSuperview()
            self.cupStackView.layoutIfNeeded()
        })
    }
}
```

This method accesses the arrangedSubviews array of the stack view to obtain the last added subview. This subview is then removed both from the arrangedSubviews array and the subviews of the parent view, all from within an animation block.

Compile and run the app and test that the buttons now add and remove coffee cup subviews and that the changes are animated.

33.9 Summary

This chapter has worked through the creation of an example application that makes use of the UIStackView class. The tutorial demonstrated the use of horizontal and vertical stack views, stack view nesting, the addition of subviews to a stack in Interface Builder both manually and using the Stack button and the dynamic addition and removal of subviews from within code. The example also demonstrated the use of compression priority settings to fine tune the layout behavior of a stack view.

Chapter 34

34. An iOS 12 Split View Master-Detail Example

While it is possible to use the UITableView class as both an information display and application navigation tool on iPhone applications, it is extremely inefficient in terms of the use of screen space when used on an iPad or iPhone Plus or Max device. In recognition of this fact, Apple introduced the Split View and Popover concepts for use when developing iOS applications specifically for the iPad and carried this functionality to the iPhone Plus and Max range of devices.

The purpose of this chapter is to provide an overview of Split Views and Popovers followed by a tutorial that implements these concepts in a simple example iPad application.

34.1 An Overview of Split View and Popovers

When an iPad or iPhone Plus/Max device is in landscape mode, the UISplitViewController class divides the screen into two side-by-side panels which implement a *master-detail* model. Within this model, the left-hand panel is the *master* panel and presents a list of items to the user. The right-hand panel is the *detail* panel and displays information relating to the currently selected item in the *master* panel.

A prime example of this concept in action can be seen with the iPad Mail app which lists messages in the master panel and displays the content of the currently selected message in the detail panel.

When an iPad or iPhone Plus/Max device is in portrait mode, however, the Split View Controller hides the master panel so that the detail panel is able to utilize the entire screen. In this instance, the master panel is provided in the form of a full screen table view which segues to the detail view when items are selected from the list. When the device is rotated back to landscape orientation, the master and detail panels appear side by side once again. When in this "split view" mode, a button is provided to hide the master panel, leaving the full screen available for use by the detail panel.

When a split view user interface is run on a smaller iPhone screen, it behaves in the same way as when running on an iPad or iPhone Plus/Max device in portrait mode.

The UISplitterViewController is essentially a container to which two child view controllers are added to act as the master (also referred to as the *root view controller*) and detail views.

In the remainder of this chapter we will work through a tutorial that involves the creation of a simple iOS application that demonstrates the use of a split view configuration.

34.2 About the Example Split View Project

The goal of this tutorial is to create an application containing a split view user interface. The master panel will contain a table view listing a number of web site addresses. When a web site URL is selected from the list, the detail panel will load the corresponding web site and display it using a WKWebView component.

34.3 Creating the Project

Begin by launching Xcode and creating a new application using the *Master-Detail App* template. Enter *SplitView* as the product name and select *Swift* from the language menu.

By using this template we save a lot of extra coding effort in the implementation of the split view behavior. Much of the code generated for us is standard boilerplate code that does not change from one split view implementation to another. In fact, much of this template can be copied even if you plan to hand code split view behavior in future applications. That said, there are some unusual aspects to the template which will need to be modified during the course of this tutorial.

34.4 Reviewing the Project

The Split View template has created a number of project files for us. The most significant of these are the files relating to the Master View Controller and Detail View Controller classes. These classes correspond to the master and detail views and are named MasterViewController and DetailViewController respectively.

Xcode has also created a custom *didFinishLaunchingWithOptions* method located within the *AppDelegate* class. While the custom *didFinishLaunchingWithOptions* method fits perfectly with our requirements, the template actually creates a simple application in which the date and time may be added to the master view and then displayed in the detail view when selected. Since this is not quite the behavior we need for our example it will be necessary to delete some of this template code as our project progresses.

Finally, a *Main.storyboard* file has been created configured with the following elements:

- A UISplitViewController
- A View Controller named DetailViewController for the detail pane
- A Table View Controller named MasterViewController for the master pane
- Two navigation controllers

This represents the standard storyboard configuration for a typical split view implementation. The only changes to this storyboard that will be necessary for this example will be to change the user interface of the detail view pane and to modify the title of the master pane. The rest of the storyboard will remain unchanged. To change the title of the master pane, locate it within the storyboard canvas, double-click on the title text which currently reads “Master” and enter “Favorite Web Sites” as the new title as outlined in Figure 34-1:

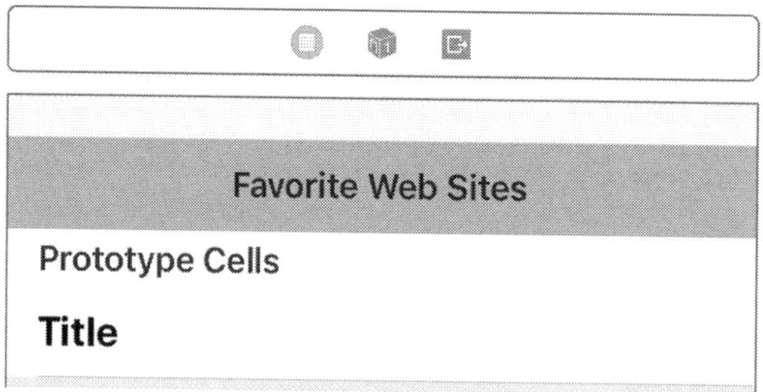

Figure 34-1

34.5 Configuring Master View Items

The master view controller created for us by Xcode is actually a subclass of UITableViewController. The next step, therefore, is to configure the table view to display the list of web sites. For this purpose we will need to configure two array objects to store the web site names and corresponding URL addresses. Select the *MasterViewController.swift* file and modify it as follows to declare these two arrays:

```
import UIKit

class MasterViewController: UITableViewController {

    var siteNames: [String]?
    var siteAddresses: [String]?
    var detailViewController: DetailViewController? = nil
    var objects = [AnyObject]()
.
.
.
```

Having declared the arrays, modify the *MasterViewController.swift* file further to initialize the arrays in the *viewDidLoad* method. Note that Xcode has already added some code to the *viewDidLoad* method for the template example so be sure to remove this before adding the new code below:

```
override func viewDidLoad() {
    super.viewDidLoad()

    siteNames = ["Yahoo", "Google", "Apple", "Bing"]
    siteAddresses = ["https://www.yahoo.com",
                     "https://www.google.com",
                     "https://www.apple.com",
                     "https://www.bing.com"]

    if let split = splitViewController {
        let controllers = split.viewControllers
        self.detailViewController = (controllers[controllers.count-1] as!
            UINavigationController).topViewController
                as? DetailViewController
    }
}
```

There are a number of methods that must be implemented in order for the items to appear within the table view object. Fortunately, Xcode has already placed template methods for us to use in the *MasterViewController.swift* file. First, modify the *numberOfSections(in tableView:)* method to notify the table view of the number of items to be displayed (in this case, a value equal to the number of items in our siteNames array). Since there is only one section in the table also modify the *numberOfRowsInSection* method accordingly. Note that Xcode has, once again, added some code for the template example so be sure to remove this code where necessary:

```
override func numberOfSections(in tableView: UITableView) -> Int {
    return 1
}
```

```
override func tableView(_ tableView: UITableView, numberOfRowsInSection
section: Int) -> Int {
    return siteNames!.count
}
```

Next, modify the *tableView(_:cellForRowAt:)* method to return the item to be displayed, using the row number argument as an index into the siteNames array:

```
override func tableView(_ tableView: UITableView, cellForRowAt
      indexPath: IndexPath) -> UITableViewCell {

    let cell = tableView.dequeueReusableCell(withIdentifier: "Cell",
                                              for: indexPath)

    cell.textLabel!.text = siteNames![indexPath.row]
    return cell
}
```

Click on the run button located in the Xcode toolbar to test the current state of the application, using a physical iPad or iPhone Plus/Max device, or a corresponding simulator as the target. Once the application loads, rotate the device into landscape mode (using the *Hardware -> Rotate Left* menu if running on a simulator):

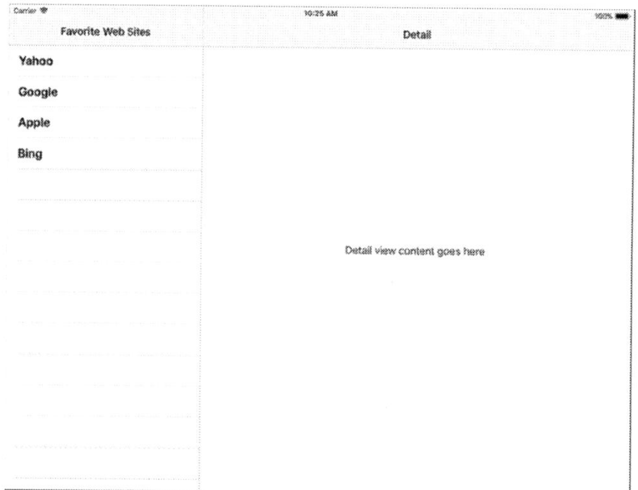

Figure 34-2

At this point the detail panel still displays the place holder label provided by Xcode when the project was first created. The next step is to change this behavior and add the WebKit View to the detail view controller.

34.6 Configuring the Detail View Controller

When a user selects a web site item from the master panel, the detail panel will load the selected web site into a WebKit View object.

Begin by selecting the *Main.storyboard* file, locate the DetailViewController scene, click on the placeholder label that reads "Detail view content goes here" and press the Delete key. Drag and drop a WebKit View object from the Library panel onto the view and resize it so that it fills the entire safe view area. With the WebKit

View instance selected in the storyboard, use the Auto Layout *Add New Constraints* menu to set *Spacing to nearest neighbor* constraints on all four sides of the view with the *Constrain to margins* option disabled.

Select the WebKit View object, display the Assistant Editor panel and verify that the editor is displaying the contents of the *DetailViewController.swift* file. Ctrl-click on the WebKit View again and drag to a position just below the class declaration line in the Assistant Editor. Release the line and in the resulting connection dialog establish an outlet connection named *webView.*

Remaining in the *DetailViewController.swift* file, add an import statement for the WebKit framework:

```
import UIKit
import WebKit

class DetailViewController: UIViewController {
.
.
```

34.7 Connecting Master Selections to the Detail View

The next task is to configure the detail panel to update based on selections made in the master panel. When a user makes an item selection from the table view the *prepare(for segue:)* method in the master view controller is triggered. This template method needs to be modified to assign the selected URL to the *detailItem* property of the DetailViewController class. Select the *MasterViewController.swift* file and locate the method. Once again, Xcode has added code to the template example so remove the current code and modify the method as follows:

```
override func prepare(for segue: UIStoryboardSegue, sender: Any?) {
    if let indexPath = self.tableView.indexPathForSelectedRow {
        let urlString = siteAddresses?[indexPath.row]

        let controller = (segue.destination
                as! UINavigationController).topViewController
        as! DetailViewController

        controller.detailItem = urlString
        controller.navigationItem.leftBarButtonItem =
                        splitViewController?.displayModeButtonItem
        controller.navigationItem.leftItemsSupplementBackButton
                                                        = true
    }
}
```

The method begins by verifying that this is the segue associated with the transition to the detail view before identifying the URL of the selected web site by using the selected row as an index into the siteAddresses array. A reference to the destination view controller is then obtained and the *detailItem* property of that instance set to the URL of the web page to be displayed. Finally, a bar button item is added to the detail navigation bar. The button added is the UISplitViewController's "display mode" button. This button provides the user with the option to expand the detail view to fill the entire display, causing the master panel to be hidden from view.

34.8 Modifying the DetailViewController Class

The DetailViewController class created by Xcode is designed to display some text on a Label view. Given that the Label view has now been replaced by a WebKit View, some changes to the class will inevitably need to be made. Locate the *DetailViewController.swift* file in the project navigator panel and locate and modify the *configureView* method so that it now reads as follows:

```
func configureView() {
    // Update the user interface for the detail item.
    if let detail = self.detailItem {
        if let myWebview = webView {
            let url = NSURL(string: detail)
            let request = NSURLRequest(url: url! as URL)
            myWebview.load(request as URLRequest)
        }
    }
}
```

The code checks to make sure that the detailItem variable has a value assigned to it, verifies that the webView view has been created and then performs a number of steps to load the designated URL into the view. Note that in order to make the web page scale to fit the detail view area the scalePagesToFit property of the WKWebView object is set to true.

The final step before testing the app is to modify the detailItem variable declaration within the DetailViewController class to be a String type. Locate this declaration in the code and modify it so that it reads as follows:

```
var detailItem: String? {
    didSet {
        // Update the view.
        self.configureView()
    }
}
```

34.9 Testing the Application

All that remains is to test the application so select a suitable iPad or iPhone Plus/Max device or simulator as the target, click on the Xcode run button and wait for the application to load. In portrait mode only the master panel should be visible. Selecting an item from the master list should trigger the segue to the detail panel within which the selected web page should load into the WebKit View instance.

Tapping the "Favorite Web Sites" button in the detail panel should return back to the master panel.

Select the *Hardware -> Rotate Left* menu option to switch the device into landscape mode and note that both the master and detail panels are now visible:

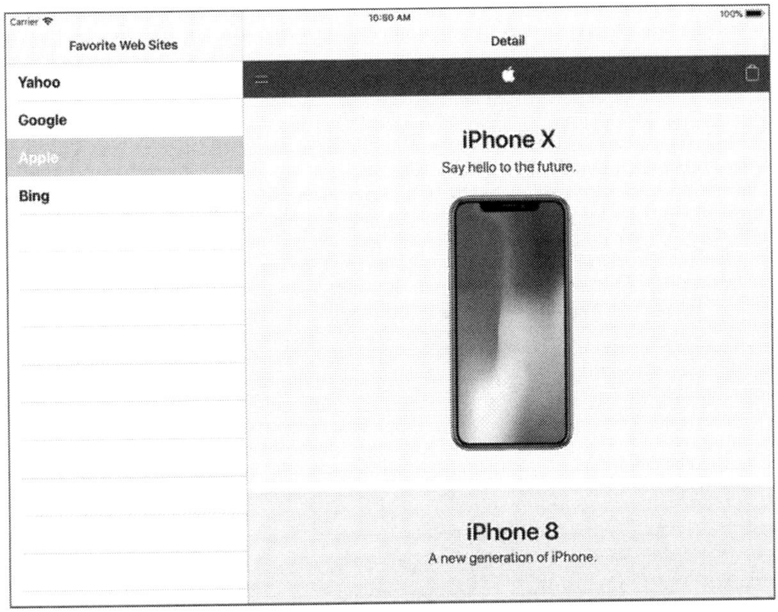

Figure 34-3

34.10 Summary

Split views provide iOS applications with a master-detail interface paradigm designed to make better use of the larger screen space of the device. Wherever possible, this approach should be taken in favor of the table view based navigation common in iPhone based applications. In this chapter we have explored split views in general and worked through the implementation of an example application.

Chapter 35

35. A Guide to Multitasking in iOS 12

Since the introduction of iOS 9 it is possible for users to display and interact with two apps side by side on the iPad screen, a concept referred to as *multitasking*. Although inclusion of support for multitasking within an iOS iPad app is optional, enabling support where appropriate is recommended to provide the user with the best possible experience when using the app.

This chapter will provide an introduction to multitasking in terms of what it means to the user and the steps that can be taken to effectively adopt and support multitasking within an iOS app running on an iPad device. Once these areas have been covered, the next chapter (*An iOS 12 Multitasking Example*) will create an example project designed to support multitasking.

Before reading this chapter, it is important to understand that multitasking support makes extensive use of both the Size Classes and Auto Layout features of iOS, topics which were covered in the *An Introduction to Auto Layout in iOS 12* and *Using Trait Variations to Design Adaptive iOS 12 User Interfaces* chapters of this book.

35.1 Using iPad Multitasking

Before implementing multitasking support for an iPad app it is first important to understand multitasking from the perspective of the user. Traditionally, when an app was launched from the iPad screen it would fill the entire display and continue to do so until placed into the background by the user. Since the introduction of iOS 9, two apps are now able to share the iPad display.

Multitasking mode is initiated using the iPad dock panel. The dock is always visible when no apps are currently in the foreground and appears (as shown in Figure 35-1) when an upward swiping motion is made starting at the bottom of the device screen while an app is currently visible:

Figure 35-1

To place an app into multitasking mode, simply select the icon for that app from the dock and drag it upwards as shown in Figure 35-2:

Figure 35-2

If the app icon is dragged to the far right or left of the screen before being released, the app will be displayed alongside the currently running app in *Split View mode*:

Figure 35-3

When multitasking is in effect, the original app (i.e. the Photos app in the above figure) is referred to as the *primary app* and the new app the *secondary app*.

Once the display is in Split View mode, touching and dragging the narrow white button located in the divider between the two panels allows the position of the division between the primary and secondary apps to be adjusted. In the above example, dragging partially to the left will cause the two apps to share the screen width equally while dragging all the way to the right will remove the secondary app from the screen leaving the primary app to fill the entire display. Dragging all the way to the left will cause the secondary app to fill the entire screen, thereby making it the primary app.

If, on the other hand, the dock app icon is dropped away from the sides of the screen, the app will appear in a floating window (referred to as *Slide Over* mode) as is the case in Figure 35-4 below:

Figure 35-4

The narrow shaded bar at the top of the secondary app can be used to move the slide over window to the left or right side of the screen by touching and dragging. An upward drag will switch the app into Split View mode. Conversely, a downward drag on this bar when the app is in Split View mode will switch back to Slide Over mode. To hide a Slide Over view app, simply drag it sideways off the right side of the screen. To restore the app, swipe left from the right-hand screen edge.

35.2 Picture-In-Picture Multitasking

In addition to Split View and Slide Over modes, multitasking also supports the presentation of a moveable and resizable video playback window over the top of the primary app window. This is a topic which will be covered in the chapter entitled *An iOS 12 Multitasking Example*.

35.3 iPad Devices with Multitasking Support

It is important to be aware that not all iPad models support all forms of multitasking. In fact, at the time of writing only the iPad Air 2 and subsequent models support Slide Over, Split View and Picture in Picture multitasking.

The iPad Mini 2 and 3 models and the original iPad Air support both Slide Over and Picture in Picture but not Split View multitasking. Earlier iPad models do not support multitasking of any type.

35.4 Multitasking and Size Classes

Clearly, a key part of supporting multitasking involves making sure that the storyboard scenes within an app are able to adapt to a variety of different window sizes. In actual fact, each of the different window sizes an app is likely to encounter in a multitasking mode corresponds to one of the existing size classes as outlined in the chapter entitled *Using Trait Variations to Design Adaptive iOS 12 User Interfaces*. As outlined in that chapter, the height and width available to an app is classed as being either *compact* or *regular*. An app running in portrait mode on an iPhone 8, for example, would use the compact width and regular height size class while the same app running in portrait orientation would use the regular width and compact height size class.

When running in a multitasking environment the primary and secondary apps will pass through a range of compact and regular widths depending on the prevailing multitasking configuration. The diagrams in Figure 35-5 illustrate the way in which the different multitasking modes translate to equivalent regular and compact size classes.

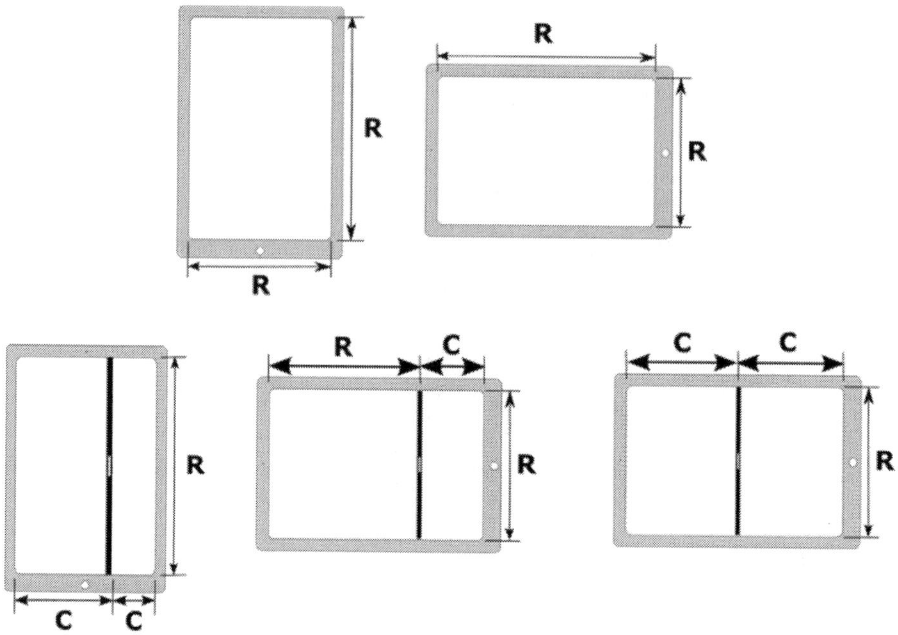

Figure 35-5

The above rules change slightly when the app is running in Split View mode on an iPad Pro. Due to the larger screen size of the iPad Pro, both apps are presented in Split View mode using the regular width as illustrated in Figure 35-6:

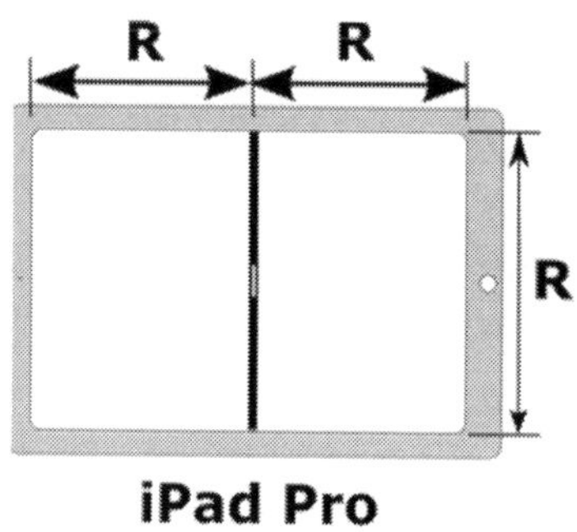

Figure 35-6

Implementing multitasking support within an iOS app is essentially a matter of designing layouts that adapt appropriately to the different size classes outlined in the above diagram.

35.5 Multitasking and the Master-Detail Split View

The previous chapter introduced the master-detail split view interface. In this configuration both a master panel and a detail panel are displayed at the same time whereby selecting an item from the master panel influences what is displayed in the detail panel. While this "split view" approach should not be confused with the multitasking Split View mode, it is useful to know that a master-detail user interface will automatically work within multitasking. Consider, for the purpose of an example, the *SplitView* app created in the previous chapter. When selected as a secondary app, the master panel will appear within a Split View or Slide Over panel as shown in Figure 35-7:

Figure 35-7

When an item is selected from the master panel, the detail panel is then displayed in place of the master panel together with a toolbar button to return to the master panel as shown in Figure 35-7 where the detail panel is displayed in Slide Over mode alongside the Photos app:

Figure 35-8

35.6 Handling Multitasking in Code

Much can be achieved in terms of using Auto Layout and Size Classes to adapt to the size changes associated with multitasking. There will, however, inevitably be instances where some code needs to be executed when a scene transitions from one size class to another (for example when an app transitions from Slide Over to Split View). Fortunately, UIKit will call three delegate methods on the container instance (typically a view controller) of the current scene during the transition to notify it of the transition where code can be added to perform app specific tasks at different points in the transition. These delegate methods are outlined below in the order in which they are called during the transition:

35.6.1 willTransition(to newcollection: with coordinator:)

This method is called immediately before the traits for the currently displayed view controller view are to change. A *trait* is represented by the UITraitCollection class, instances of which contain a collection of values consisting of size class settings, the display density of the screen and the user interface idiom (which is simply a value indicating whether the device on which the app is running is an iPhone or iPad).

When called, this method is passed a UITraitCollection object containing the new trait collection from which information can be accessed and used to decide how to respond to the transition. The following code, for example, checks that the app is running on an iPad before identifying whether the horizontal size class is transitioning to a regular or compact size class:

```
override func willTransition(to newCollection: UITraitCollection, with
        coordinator: UIViewControllerTransitionCoordinator) {

    super.willTransition(to: newCollection,
                with: coordinator)

    if newCollection.userInterfaceIdiom == .pad {

        if newCollection.horizontalSizeClass == .regular {

                // Transitioning to Regular Width Size Class

        } else if newCollection.horizontalSizeClass == .compact {

                // Transitioning to Compact Width Size Class

        }
    }
}
```

The second argument passed through to the method is a UIViewControllerTransitionCoordinator object. This is the coordinator object that is handling the transition and can be used to add additional animations to those being performed by UIKit during the transition.

35.6.2 viewWillTransition(to size: with coordinator:)

This method is also called before the size change is implemented and is passed a CGSize value and a coordinator object. The size object can be used to obtain the new height and width to which the view is transitioning. The following sample code simply outputs the new height and width values to the console:

```
override func viewWillTransition(to size: CGSize,
                        with coordinator:
    UIViewControllerTransitionCoordinator) {

    super.viewWillTransition(to: size,
                        with: coordinator)

    print("Height = \(size.height), Width = \(size.width)")
}
```

35.6.3 traitCollectionDidChange(_:)

This method is called once the transition from one trait collection to another is complete and is passed the UITraitCollection object for the previous trait. In the following example implementation, the method simply checks to find out whether the previous horizontal size class was regular or compact:

```
override func traitCollectionDidChange(_ previousTraitCollection:
                UITraitCollection?) {

    super.traitCollectionDidChange(previousTraitCollection)

    if previousTraitCollection?.horizontalSizeClass == .regular {
        // The previous horizontal size class was regular
    }

    if previousTraitCollection?.horizontalSizeClass == .compact {
        // The previous horizontal size class was compact
    }
}
```

35.7 Lifecycle Method Calls

In addition to the transition delegate methods outlined above, a number of lifecycle methods are called on the application delegate of the app during a multitasking transition. When the user moves the divider the *applicationWillResignActive* method is called at the point that the divider position changes. When the user slides the divider all the way to the edge of the screen so that the app is no longer visible, the *applicationDidEnterBackground* delegate method is called.

These method calls are of particular significance when taking into consideration what is taking place behind the scenes when the divider is moved by the user. As the divider is moving, the system repeatedly resizes the app off screen and takes snapshots at various sizes as the slider moves. These snapshots are used to make the sliding transition appear to take place smoothly. The *applicationWillResignActive* method may need to be used to preserve the state of the user interface so that when the user releases the divider the same data and navigation position within the user interface is presented as before the slider change.

35.8 Opting Out of Multitasking

To disable multitasking support for an app, simply add the UIRequiresFullScreen key to the project's *Info.plist* file with the value set to true. This can be set manually within the *Info.plist* file itself, or within the *Deployment Info* section of the *General* settings panel for the project target:

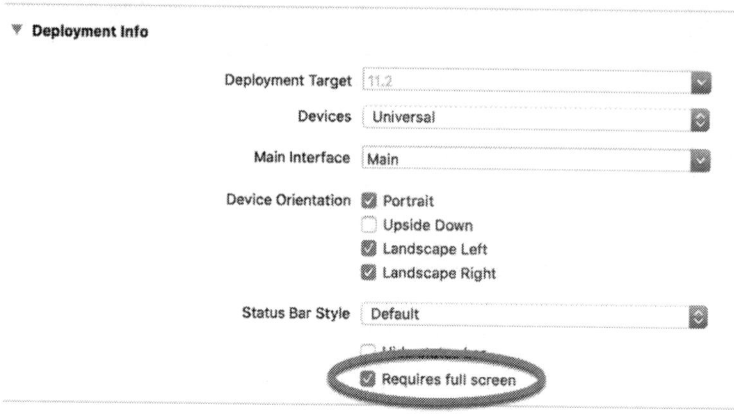

Figure 35-9

35.9 Summary

Multitasking provides the user with the ability to display and interact with two apps concurrently when running on recent models of iPad device. Multitasking apps are categorized as primary and secondary and can be displayed in either Slide Over or Split View configurations. Multitasking also supports a "Picture-in-Picture" option whereby video playback is displayed in a floating, resizable window over the top of the existing app.

Supporting multitasking within an iOS app primarily involves designing the user interface such that it supports both regular and compact size classes. A range of delegate methods also allow view controllers to receive notification of size changes and to respond accordingly.

Projects created in Xcode 10 are configured to support multitasking by default. It is also possible to opt out of multitasking with a change to the project *Info.plist* file.

Chapter 36

36. An iOS 12 Multitasking Example

With the basics of multitasking in iOS covered in the previous chapter, this chapter will involve the creation of a simple example application that makes use of multitasking within an app when running on an iPad device. In addition to the use of size classes, the example will also demonstrate how the UIStackView class can be of particular use when implementing multitasking user interface adaptability.

36.1 Creating the Multitasking Example Project

Start the Xcode environment, selecting the option to create a new project. Select the *Single View Application* template, *Swift* as the language and name the product *MultitaskingDemo*.

36.2 Adding the Image Files

The completed app will include the use of two images which will need to be added to the asset catalog of the project. Both image files are contained within the *multitasking_images* folder of the sample code download.

Within Xcode, locate and select the *Assets.xcassets* entry within the Project Navigator panel to load the asset catalog into the main panel. In the left-hand panel, Ctrl-click immediately beneath the existing *AppIcon* entry and select *New Image Set* from the resulting menu. Double-click on the new image set entry (which will default to the name *image*) and change the name to *Waterfalls*.

Open a Finder window, locate the *multitasking_images* folder from the code sample download and drag and drop the *waterfall_landscape@2x.jpg* file onto the 2x placeholder within the image asset catalog. This portrait image will be displayed within the app when it is displayed using a regular width size class.

Remaining within the asset catalog and with the Waterfalls image set still selected, display the Attributes Inspector panel and change the *Width Class* property from *Any* to *Any & Compact*. A second row of image placeholders will now appear within the image set. Drag and drop the *waterfall_portrait@2x.jpg* image file from the Finder window onto the 2x Compact Width placeholder within the image set. On completion of these steps the image set within the asset catalog should match that shown in Figure 36-1:

Figure 36-1

36.3 Designing the Regular Width Size Class Layout

The baseline user interface layout will be the one used for the regular width size class. In the next section, trait variations will be made to the layout for the compact width size class. Begin, therefore, by selecting the *Main.storyboard* file, displaying the device configuration bar (Figure 36-2) and selecting an iPad configuration:

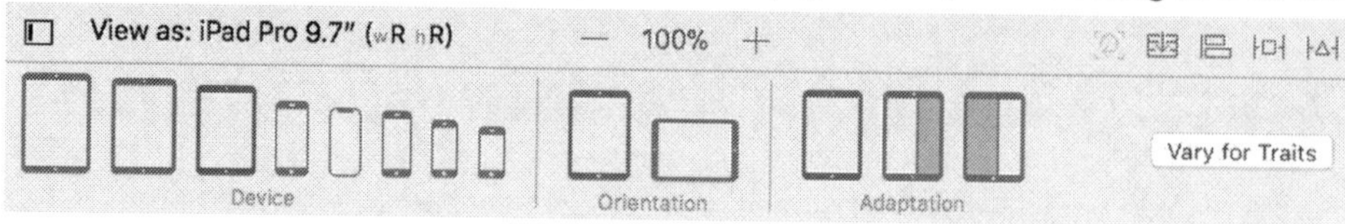

Figure 36-2

For the purposes of this example, the layout will be controlled by a UIStackView instance so drag and drop a Horizontal Stack View from the Library panel onto the scene canvas. With the Stack View selected, display the Auto Layout *Add New Constraints* menu and set *Spacing to nearest neighbor* constraints on all four sides of the view with the spacing set to 0 and the *Constrain to margins* option enabled as illustrated in Figure 36-3:

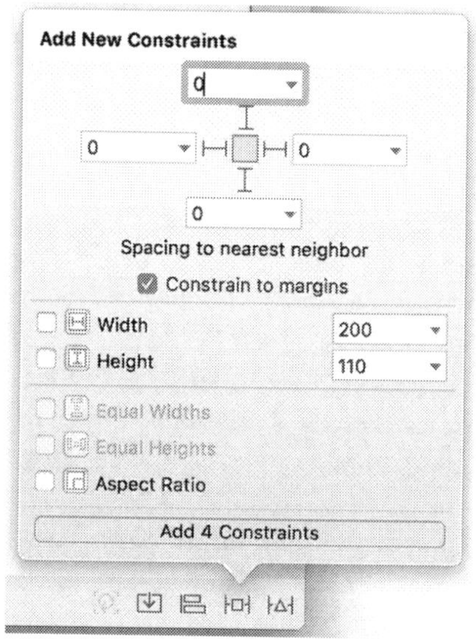

Figure 36-3

Display the Document Outline panel and select the Stack View entry. Using the Attributes Inspector panel, set the Alignment to *Center* and the Distribution property to *Fill Equally.*

Drag an Image object and drop it onto the stack view instance in the storyboard scene canvas. Locate the Text View object within the Library panel and drag it to the right-hand edge of the Image view within the scene canvas. When a bold blue vertical line appears (referenced by the arrow in Figure 36-4) indicating that the Text View will be placed to the right of the Image view in the stack, drop the Text View to add it to the scene.

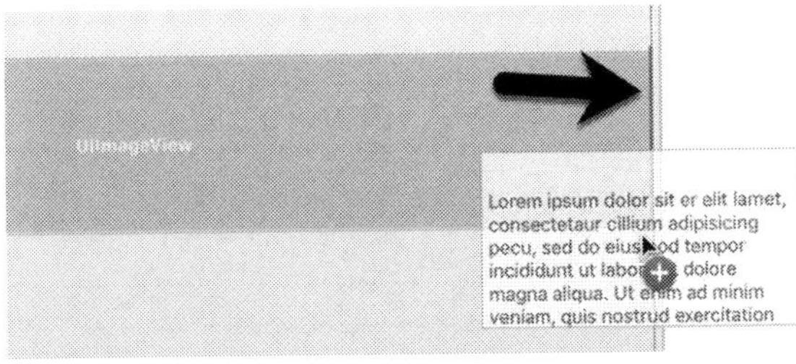

Figure 36-4

With the Image View selected, use the Attributes Inspector panel to set the Content Mode attribute to *Aspect Fit* and the Image menu to *Waterfalls*. Select the Text View object and stretch it vertically so that all of the Latin text is visible. With the Text View object still selected, display the Auto Layout *Add New Constraints* menu and enable the *Height* constraint option based on the current value before clicking on the *Add 1 Constraint* button. At this point the user interface layout should resemble Figure 36-5:

Figure 36-5

36.4 Designing the Compact Width Size Class

When the app is displayed in Slide Over and certain Split View configurations, the compact size class will be used to arrange the scene layout. To ensure that the scene appears correctly in these situations, this size class now needs to be designed within the project. With the *Main.storyboard* file still loaded into Interface Builder, select the iPhone 8 device from the device configuration bar.

With Interface Builder now displaying the compact width, regular height size class, the stack view needs to be configured to use vertical orientation to accommodate the narrower width available for the subviews.

Select the Stack View object within the Document Outline panel and display the Attributes Inspector panel. When the app is displayed in compact width, the axis orientation of the stack view object needs to change from horizontal to vertical. To configure this, click on the + button located to the left of the Axis setting in the Attributes Inspector and, from the resulting panel, set the Width option to *Compact* and Height option to *Regular*, leaving the Gamut set to *Any*. Once the options have been selected, click on the *Add Variation* button:

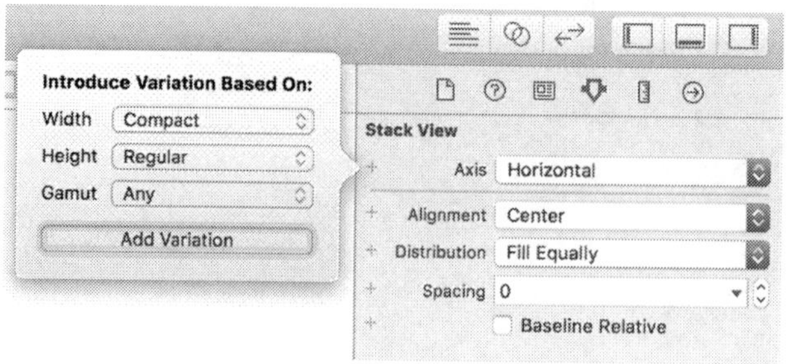

Figure 36-6

Once selected, a new Axis property setting will be added to the attributes list for the current size class labeled *wC hR* as highlighted in Figure 36-7. Change the setting for this property to *Vertical* and note that the orientation of the scene has changed in the storyboard canvas.

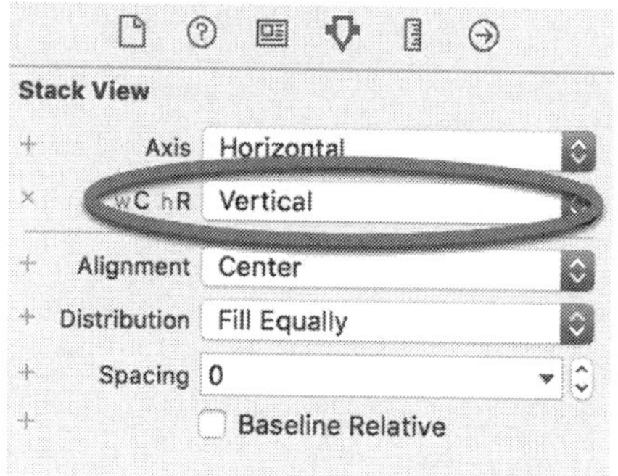

Figure 36-7

Repeat these steps to add an Alignment setting for the compact width and regular height size class set to *Fill*:

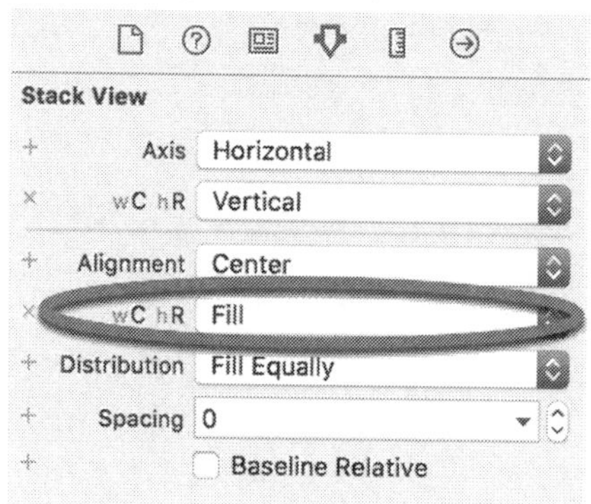

Figure 36-8

This setting will ensure that the Text View object expands to fill the width of the display in compact width mode.

Finally, the Height constraint added to the Text View needs to be removed for the current size class. In the Document Outline panel, locate and select the *height* constraint for the Text View as shown in Figure 36-9:

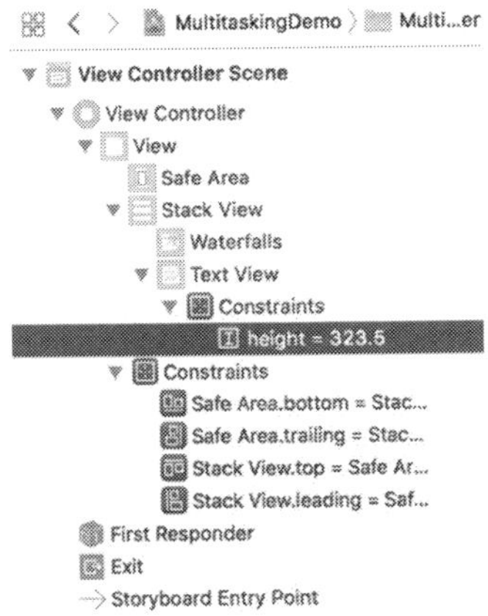

Figure 36-9

Once selected, display the Attributes Inspector panel, click on the + button to the left of the *Installed* property and select the *Compact Width | Regular Height* size class configuration before clicking on the *Add Variation* button. Turn off the check box next to the *wC hR Installed* option as illustrated in Figure 36-10:

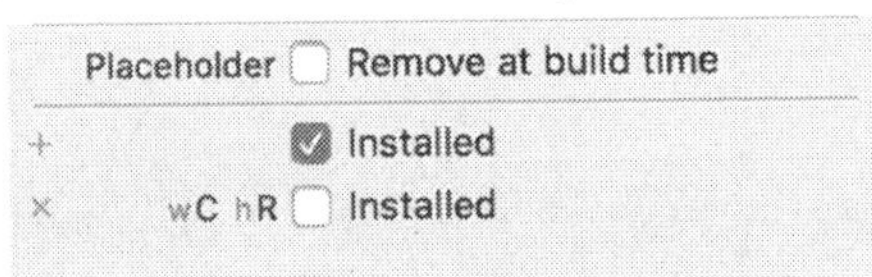

Figure 36-10

36.5 Testing the Project in a Multitasking Environment

With the project completed, it is time to test that the layouts associated with the size classes work within the various multitasking modes. Compile and run the app on an iPad model which supports multitasking or a suitable iOS simulator session. Once the app is running place it into the background and launch another app (for example the Photos or Calendar app).

Swipe up from the bottom of the screen, then select and drag the icon for the MultitaskingDemo app up onto the center of the display so that it appears in a Slide Over window as shown in Figure 36-11. Note that the app is displayed using the compact width layout configuration:

Figure 36-11

Touch the narrow gray horizontal bar at the top of the Slider Over view and drag upwards until the view switches to Split View mode. Since the view is only occupying 25% of the width of the display, the compact layout is still being used. Drag the divider to the left until the Split View window is occupying 75% of the display width. On releasing the divider, the layout should have switched to the regular width configuration (Figure 36-12):

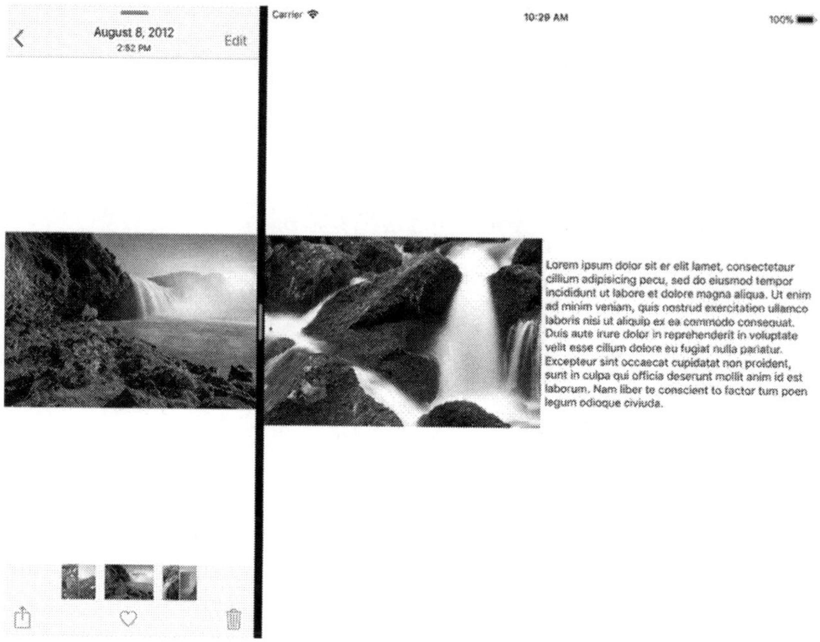

Figure 36-12

36.6 Summary

In this chapter we have created an example iOS project which makes use of size classes to display a user interface scene appropriately configured for both compact and regular width categories of size class. Once implemented, the app was able to adopt different layouts when running in various multitasking modes on an iPad.

Chapter 37

37. Working with Directories in Swift on iOS 12

It is sometimes easy to forget that iOS is an operating system much like that running on many other computers today. Given this fact, it should come as no surprise that iOS has a file system much like any other operating system allowing applications to store persistent data on behalf of the user. Much like other platforms, the iOS file system provides a directory based structure into which files can be created and organized.

Since the introduction of iOS 5 the iOS app developer has had two options in terms of storing data. Files and data may now be stored on the file system of the local device or remotely using Apple's iCloud service. In practice, however, it is most likely that an application will utilize iCloud storage to augment, rather than replace, the use of the local file system so familiarity with both concepts is still a necessity.

The topic of iCloud-based storage will be covered in detail beginning with the chapter entitled *Preparing an iOS 12 App to use iCloud Storage.* The goal of this chapter, however, is to provide an overview of how to work with local file system directories from within an iOS application. Topics covered include identifying the application's document and temporary directories, finding the current working directory, creating, removing and renaming directories and obtaining listings of a directory's content. Once the topic of directory management has been covered, we will move on to handling files in *Working with Files in Swift on iOS 12*.

37.1 The Application Documents Directory

An iPhone or iPad user can install multiple applications on a single device. The iOS platform is responsible for ensuring that these applications cannot interfere with each other, both in terms of memory usage and data storage. As such, each application is restricted in terms of where it can store data on the file system of the device. iOS achieves this by allowing applications to read and write only to their own *Documents* and *tmp* directories. Within these two directories the corresponding application can create files and also sub-directories to any required level of depth. This area constitutes the application's *sandbox* and the application cannot usually create or modify files or directories outside of these directories unless using the UIDocumentPickerViewController class.

37.2 The FileManager, FileHandle and Data Classes

The Foundation Framework provides three classes that are indispensable when it comes to working with files and directories:

- **FileManager** - The *FileManager* class can be used to perform basic file and directory operations such as creating, moving, reading and writing files and reading and setting file attributes. In addition, this class provides methods for, amongst other tasks, identifying the current working directory, changing to a new directory, creating directories and listing the contents of a directory.
- **FileHandle** - The *FileHandle* class is provided for performing lower level operations on files, such as seeking to a specific position in a file and reading and writing a file's contents by a specified number of

byte chunks and appending data to an existing file. This class will be used extensively in the chapter entitled *Working with Files in Swift on iOS 12*.

- **Data** - The *Data* class provides a useful storage buffer into which the contents of a file may be read, or from which dynamically stored data may be written to a file.

37.3 Understanding Pathnames in Swift

As with macOS, iOS defines pathnames using the standard UNIX convention. As such each component of a path is separated by a forward slash (/). When an application starts, the current working directory is the file system's *root directory* represented by a single /. From this location, the application must navigate to its own *Documents* and *tmp* directories in order to be able to write files to the file system. Path names that begin with a / are said to be *absolute path names* in that they specify a file system location relative to the root directory. For example, */var/mobile* is an absolute path name.

Paths that do not begin with a slash are interpreted to be *relative* to a current working directory. For example, if the current working directory is */User/demo* and the path name is *mapdata/local.xml* then the file is considered to have an equivalent full, absolute pathname of */User/demo/mapdata/local.xml*.

37.4 Obtaining a Reference to the Default FileManager Object

The FileManager class contains a property named *default* that is used to obtain a reference to the application's default file manager instance:

```
let filemgr = FileManager.default
```

Having obtained the object reference we can begin to use it to work with files and directories.

37.5 Identifying the Current Working Directory

As previously mentioned, when an application first loads, its current working directory is the application's root directory, represented by a / character. The current working directory may be identified at any time by accessing the *currentDirectoryPath* property of the file manager object. For example, the following code fragment identifies the current working directory:

```
let currentPath = filemgr.currentDirectoryPath
```

37.6 Identifying the Documents Directory

Each iOS application on a device has its own private *Documents* and *tmp* directories into which it is permitted to read and write data. Because the location of these directories is different for each application the only way to find the correct path is to ask iOS. In fact, the exact location will also differ depending on whether the application is running on a physical iPhone or iPad device or in the iOS Simulator. The *Documents* directory for an application may be identified by making a call to a file manager method named *urls(for:)*, passing through an argument (in this case *.documentDirectory*) indicating that we require the path to the Documents directory. The *.userDomainMask* argument indicates to the *urls(for:)* method that we are looking for the Documents directory located in the application's home directory. The method returns an object in the form of an array containing the results of the request. We can, therefore, obtain the path to the current application's Documents directory as follows:

```
let filemgr = FileManager.default

let dirPaths = filemgr.urls(for: .documentDirectory, in: .userDomainMask)

let docsDir = dirPaths[0].path
```

In order to access the path string contained within the URL, we simply access the *path* property of the URL at index position 0 in the array and assign it to the *docsDir* constant as outlined above.

When executed within the iOS Simulator environment, the path returned will take the form of:

```
/Users/<user name>/Library/Developer/CoreSimulator/Devices/<device
id>/data/Containers/Data/Application/<app id>/Documents
```

Where *<user name>* is the name of the user currently logged into the macOS system on which the simulator is running, *<device id>* is the unique ID of the device on which the app is running and *<app id>* is the unique ID of the app, for example:

```
06A3AEBA-8C34-476E-937F-A27BDD2E450A
```

Clearly this references a path on your macOS system so feel free to open up a Finder window and explore the file system sandbox areas for your iOS applications.

When executed on a physical iOS device, however, the path returned by the function call will take the following form:

```
/var/mobile/Containers/Data/Application/<app id>/Documents
```

37.7 Identifying the Temporary Directory

In addition to the *Documents* directory, iOS applications are also provided with a *tmp* directory for the storage of temporary files. The path to the current application's temporary directory may be ascertained with a call to the *NSTemporaryDirectory* C function as follows:

```
let tmpDir = NSTemporaryDirectory()
```

Once executed, the string object referenced by tmpDir will contain the path to the temporary directory for the application.

37.8 Changing Directory

Having identified the path to the application's document or temporary directory the chances are good that you will need to make that directory the current working directory. The current working directory of a running iOS application can be changed with a call to the *changeCurrentDirectoryPath* method of a FileManager instance. The destination directory path is passed as an argument to the instance method in the form of a String object. Note that this method returns a Boolean *true* or *false* result to indicate if the requested directory change was successful or not. A failure result typically indicates either that the specified directory does not exist, or that the application lacks the appropriate access permissions:

```
let filemgr = FileManager.default

let dirPaths = filemgr.urls(for: .documentDirectory, in: .userDomainMask)

let docsDir = dirPaths[0].path

if filemgr.changeCurrentDirectoryPath(docsDir) {
    // Success
} else {
    // Failure
}
```

In the above example, the path to the *Documents* directory is identified and then used as an argument to the *changeCurrentDirectoryPath* method of the file manager object to change the current working directory to that location.

37.9 Creating a New Directory

A new directory on an iOS device is created using the *createDirectory(atPath:)* instance method of the FileManager class, once again passing through the pathname of the new directory as an argument and returning a Boolean success or failure result. The second argument to this method defines whether any intermediate directory levels should be created automatically. For example, if we wanted to create a directory with the path */var/mobile/Containers/Data/Application/<app id>/Documents/mydata/maps* and the *mydata* subdirectory does not yet exist, setting the *withIntermediateDirectories* argument to *true* will cause this directory to be created automatically before then creating the *maps* sub-directory within it. If this argument is set to *false*, then the attempt to create the directory will fail because *mydata* does not already exist and we have not given permission for it to be created on our behalf.

This method also takes additional arguments in the form of a set of attributes for the new directory. Specifying *nil* will use the default attributes.

The following code fragment identifies the documents directory and creates a new sub-directory named *data* in that directory:

```
let filemgr = FileManager.default

let dirPaths = filemgr.urls(for: .documentDirectory, in: .userDomainMask)

let docsURL = dirPaths[0]

let newDir = docsURL.appendingPathComponent("data").path

do {
    try filemgr.createDirectory(atPath: newDir,
                withIntermediateDirectories: true, attributes: nil)
    } catch let error as NSError {
            print("Error: \(error.localizedDescription)")
}
```

37.10 Deleting a Directory

An existing directory may be removed from the file system using the *removeItem(atPath:)* method, passing through the path of the directory to be removed as an argument. For example, to remove the data directory created in the preceding example we might write the following code:

```
do {
    try filemgr.removeItem(atPath: newDir)
} catch let error {
    print("Error: \(error.localizedDescription)")
}
```

37.11 Listing the Contents of a Directory

A listing of the files contained within a specified directory can be obtained using the *contentsOfDirectory(atPath:)* method. This method takes the directory pathname as an argument and returns an array object containing the names of the files and sub-directories in that directory. The following example obtains a listing of the contents of the root directory (/) and displays each item in the Xcode console panel during execution:

```
do {
    let filelist = try filemgr.contentsOfDirectory(atPath: "/")

    for filename in filelist {
        print(filename)
    }
} catch let error {
    print("Error: \(error.localizedDescription)")
}
```

37.12 Getting the Attributes of a File or Directory

The attributes of a file or directory may be obtained using the *attributesOfItem(atPath:)* method. This takes as arguments the path of the directory and an optional Error object into which information about any errors will be placed (may be specified as *nil* if this information is not required). The results are returned in the form of an NSDictionary dictionary object. The keys for this dictionary are as follows:

```
NSFileType
NSFileTypeDirectory
NSFileTypeRegular
NSFileTypeSymbolicLink
NSFileTypeSocket
NSFileTypeCharacterSpecial
NSFileTypeBlockSpecial
NSFileTypeUnknown
NSFileSize
NSFileModificationDate
NSFileReferenceCount
NSFileDeviceIdentifier
NSFileOwnerAccountName
NSFileGroupOwnerAccountName
NSFilePosixPermissions
NSFileSystemNumber
```

```
NSFileSystemFileNumber

NSFileExtensionHidden

NSFileHFSCreatorCode

NSFileHFSTypeCode

NSFileImmutable

NSFileAppendOnly

NSFileCreationDate

NSFileOwnerAccountID

NSFileGroupOwnerAccountID
```

For example, we can extract the file type for the */Applications* directory using the following code excerpt:

```
let filemgr = FileManager.default

do {
    let attribs: NSDictionary =
          try filemgr.attributesOfItem(atPath: "/Applications") as
NSDictionary
    let type = attribs["NSFileType"] as! String
    print("File type \(type)")
} catch let error {
    print("Error: \(error.localizedDescription)")
}
```

When executed, results similar to the following output will appear in the Xcode console:

```
File type NSFileTypeDirectory
```

37.13 Summary

iOS provides options for both local and cloud-based file storage. In common with most other operating systems, iOS includes support for storing and managing files on local devices using a file and directory based filesystem structure. Each iOS app installed on a device is provided with a filesystem area within which files and directories may be stored and retrieved. This chapter has explored the ways in which directories are created, deleted and navigated from within Swift code. The next chapter will continue this theme by covering device-based file handing within iOS.

Chapter 38

38. Working with Files in Swift on iOS 12

In the chapter entitled *Working with Directories in Swift on iOS 12* we looked at the FileManager, FileHandle and Data Foundation Framework classes and discussed how the FileManager class in particular enables us to work with directories when developing iOS based applications. We also spent some time covering the file system structure used by iOS and, in particular, looked at the temporary and *Documents* directories assigned to each application and how the location of those directories can be identified from within the application code.

In this chapter we move on from working with directories to covering the details of working with files within the iOS SDK. Once we have covered file handling topics in this chapter, the next chapter will work through an application example that puts theory into practice.

38.1 Obtaining a FileManager Instance Reference

Before proceeding, first we need to recap the steps necessary to obtain a reference to the application's FileManager instance. As discussed in the previous chapter, the FileManager class contains a property named *default* that is used to obtain a reference. For example:

```
let filemgr = FileManager.default
```

Once a reference to the file manager object has been obtained it can be used to perform some basic file handling tasks.

38.2 Checking for the Existence of a File

The FileManager class contains an instance method named *fileExists(atPath:)* which checks whether a specified file already exists. The method takes as an argument an NSString object containing the path to the file in question and returns a Boolean value indicating the presence or otherwise of the specified file:

```
let filemgr = FileManager.default

if filemgr.fileExists(atPath: "/Applications") {
    print("File exists")
} else {
    print("File not found")
}
```

38.3 Comparing the Contents of Two Files

The contents of two files may be compared for equality using the *contentsEqual(atPath:)* method. This method takes as arguments the paths to the two files to be compared and returns a Boolean result to indicate whether the file contents match:

```
let filePath1 = docsDir + "/myfile1.txt"
```

```
let filePath2 = docsDir + "/myfile2.txt"

if filemgr.contentsEqual(atPath: filePath1, andPath: filePath2) {
    print("File contents match")
} else {
    print("File contents do not match")
}
```

38.4 Checking if a File is Readable/Writable/Executable/Deletable

Most operating systems provide some level of file access control. These typically take the form of attributes designed to control the level of access to a file for each user or user group. As such, it is not a certainty that your program will have read or write access to a particular file, or the appropriate permissions to delete or rename it. The quickest way to find out if your program has a particular access permission is to use the *isReadableFile(atPath:)*, *isWritableFile(atPath:)*, *isExecutableFile(atPath:)* and *isDeletableFile(atPath:)* methods. Each method takes a single argument in the form of the path to the file to be checked and returns a Boolean result. For example, the following code excerpt checks to find out if a file is writable:

```
if filemgr.isWritableFile(atPath: filePath1) {
    print("File is writable")
} else {
    print("File is read-only")
}
```

To check for other access permissions simply substitute the corresponding method name in place of *isWritableFile(atPath:)* in the above example.

38.5 Moving/Renaming a File

A file may be renamed (assuming adequate permissions) using the *moveItem(atPath:)* method. This method takes as arguments the pathname for the file to be moved and the destination path. Note that if the destination file path already exists this operation will fail.

```
do {
    try filemgr.moveItem(atPath: filePath1, toPath: filePath2)
    print("Move successful")
} catch let error {
    print("Error: \(error.localizedDescription)")
}
```

38.6 Copying a File

File copying can be achieved using the *copyItem(atPath:)* method. As with the *move* method, this takes as arguments the source and destination pathnames:

```
do {
    try filemgr.copyItem(atPath: filePath1, toPath: filePath2)
    print("Copy successful")
} catch let error {
    print("Error: \(error.localizedDescription)")
}
```

38.7 Removing a File

The *removeItem(atPath:)* method removes the specified file from the file system. The method takes as an argument the pathname of the file to be removed:

```
do {
    try filemgr.removeItem(atPath: filePath2)
    print("Removal successful")
} catch let error {
    print("Error: \(error.localizedDescription)")
}
```

38.8 Creating a Symbolic Link

A symbolic link to a particular file may be created using the *createSymbolicLink(atPath:)* method. This takes as arguments the path of the symbolic link and the path to the file to which the link is to refer:

```
do {
    try filemgr.createSymbolicLink(atPath: filePath2,
            withDestinationPath: filePath1)
    print("Link successful")
} catch let error {
    print("Error: \(error.localizedDescription)")
}
```

38.9 Reading and Writing Files with FileManager

The FileManager class includes some basic file reading and writing capabilities. These capabilities are somewhat limited when compared to the options provided by the FileHandle class, but can be useful nonetheless.

First, the contents of a file may be read and stored in a Data object through the use of the *contents(atPath:)* method:

```
let databuffer = filemgr.contents(atPath: filePath1)
```

Having stored the contents of a file in a Data object that data may subsequently be written out to a new file using the *createFile(atPath:)* method:

```
filemgr.createFile(atPath: filePath2, contents: databuffer,
                                     attributes: nil)
```

In the above example we have essentially copied the contents from an existing file to a new file. This, however, gives us no control over how much data is to be read or written and does not allow us to append data to the end of an existing file. If the file in the above example had already existed it, and any data it contained, would have been overwritten by the contents of the source file. Clearly some more flexible mechanism is required. This is provided by the Foundation Framework in the form of the FileHandle class.

38.10 Working with Files using the FileHandle Class

The FileHandle class provides a range of methods designed to provide a more advanced mechanism for working with files. In addition to files, this class can also be used for working with devices and network sockets. In the following sections we will look at some of the more common uses for this class.

38.11 Creating a FileHandle Object

A FileHandle object can be created when opening a file for reading, writing or updating (in other words both reading and writing). Having opened a file, it must subsequently be closed when we have finished working with it using the *closeFile* method. If an attempt to open a file fails, for example because an attempt is made to open a non-existent file for reading, these methods return *nil*.

For example, the following code excerpt opens a file for reading and then closes it without actually doing anything to the file:

```
let file: FileHandle? = FileHandle(forReadingAtPath: filePath1)

    if file == nil {
        print("File open failed")
    } else {
        file?.closeFile()
}
```

38.12 FileHandle File Offsets and Seeking

FileHandle objects maintain a pointer to the current position in a file. This is referred to as the *offset*. When a file is first opened the offset is set to 0 (the beginning of the file). This means that any read or write operations performed using the FileHandle instance methods will take place at offset 0 in the file. To perform operations at different locations in a file (for example to append data to the end of the file) it is first necessary to *seek* to the required offset. For example to move the current offset to the end of the file, use the *seekToEndOfFile* method.

Alternatively, *seek(toFileOffset:)* allows you to specify the precise location in the file to which the offset is to be positioned. Finally, the current offset may be identified using the *offsetInFile* method. In order to accommodate large files, the offset is stored in the form of an unsigned 64-bit integer.

The following example opens a file for reading and then performs a number of method calls to move the offset to different positions, outputting the current offset after each move:

```
let file: FileHandle? = FileHandle(forReadingAtPath: filePath1)

if file == nil {
    print("File open failed")
} else {
    print("Offset = \(file?.offsetInFile ?? 0)")
    file?.seekToEndOfFile()
    print("Offset = \(file?.offsetInFile ?? 0)")
    file?.seek(toFileOffset: 30)
    print("Offset = \(file?.offsetInFile ?? 0)")
    file?.closeFile()
}
```

File offsets are a key aspect of working with files using the FileHandle class so it is worth taking extra time to make sure you understand the concept. Without knowing where the current offset is in a file it is impossible to know the location in the file where data will be read or written.

38.13 Reading Data from a File

Once a file has been opened and assigned a file handle, the contents of that file may be read from the current offset position. The *readData(ofLength:)* method reads a specified number of bytes of data from the file starting at the current offset. For example, the following code reads 5 bytes of data from offset 10 in a file. The data read is returned encapsulated in a Data object:

```
let file: FileHandle? = FileHandle(forReadingAtPath: filepath1)

if file == nil {
    print("File open failed")
} else {
    file?.seek(toFileOffset: 10)
    let databuffer = file?.readData(ofLength: 5)
    file?.closeFile()
}
```

Alternatively, the *readDataToEndOfFile* method will read all the data in the file starting at the current offset and ending at the end of the file.

38.14 Writing Data to a File

The *write* method writes the data contained in a Data object to the file starting at the location of the offset. Note that this does not insert data but rather overwrites any existing data in the file at the corresponding location.

To see this in action, let's assume the existence of a file named *quickfox.txt* containing the following text:

```
The quick brown fox jumped over the lazy dog
```

Next, we will write code that opens the file for updating, seeks to position 10 and then writes some data at that location:

```
let file: FileHandle? = FileHandle(forUpdatingAtPath: filePath1)

if file == nil {
    print("File open failed")
} else {
    if let data = ("black cat" as
        NSString).data(using: String.Encoding.utf8.rawValue) {
        file?.seek(toFileOffset: 10)
        file?.write(data)
        file?.closeFile()
    }
}
```

When the above program is compiled and executed the contents of the *quickfox.txt* file will have changed to:

```
The quick black cat jumped over the lazy dog
```

38.15 Truncating a File

A file may be truncated at the specified offset using the *truncateFile(atOffset:)* method. To delete the entire contents of a file, specify an offset of 0 when calling this method:

```
let file: FileHandle? = FileHandle(forUpdatingAtPath: filePath1)

if file == nil {
    print("File open failed")
} else {
    file?.truncateFile(atOffset: 0)
    file?.closeFile()
}
```

38.16 Summary

Much like other operating systems, iOS provides a file system for the purposes of locally storing user and application files and data. In this and the preceding chapter, details of file and directory handling have been covered in some detail. The next chapter, entitled *iOS 12 Directory Handling and File I/O in Swift – A Worked Example* will work through the creation of an example designed specifically to demonstrate iOS file and directory handling.

Chapter 39

39. iOS 12 Directory Handling and File I/O in Swift – A Worked Example

In the *Working with Directories in Swift on iOS 12* and *Working with Files in Swift on iOS 12* chapters of this book we discussed in some detail the steps involved in working with the iOS file system in terms of both file and directory handling from within iOS applications. The goal of this chapter is to put theory into practice by working through the creation of a simple application that demonstrates some of the key concepts outlined in the preceding chapters.

39.1 The Example Application

The steps in this chapter walk through the creation of an iOS application consisting of a text field and a button. When the user touches the button after entering text into the text field, that text is saved to a file. The next time the application is launched the content of the file is read by the application and pre-loaded into the text field.

39.2 Setting up the Application Project

The first step in creating the application is to set up a new project. To do so, start the Xcode environment and select the option to create a new project (or select the *File -> New -> Project* menu option if Xcode is already running or the welcome screen does not appear by default).

Select the *Single View Application* template, *Swift* as the language and name the product *FileExample.*

39.3 Designing the User Interface

The example application is going to consist of a button and a text field. To begin the user interface design process, select the *Main.storyboard* file to load it into the Interface Builder environment. Drag a Button and then a Text Field from the Library panel (*View -> Libraries -> Show Library*) onto the view. Double-click on the button and change the text to *Save.* Position the components and resize the width of the text field so that the layout appears as illustrated in Figure 39-1:

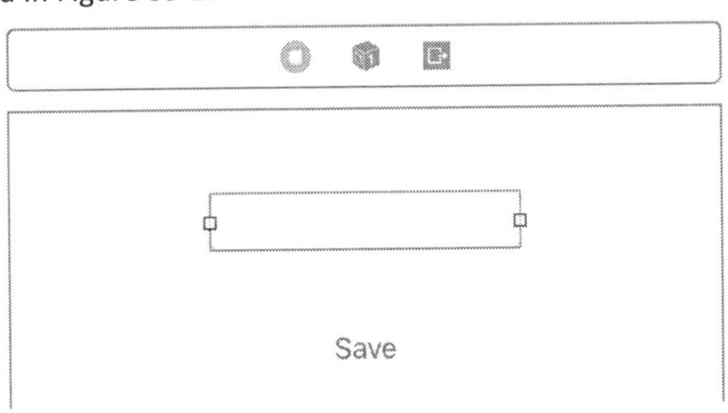

Figure 39-1

Using the *Resolve Auto Layout Issues* menu, select the *Reset to Suggested Constraints* option listed under All Views in View Controller.

Select the Text Field object in the view canvas, display the Assistant Editor panel and verify that the editor is displaying the contents of the *ViewController.swift* file. Ctrl-click on the text field object and drag to a position just below the class declaration line in the Assistant Editor. Release the line and in the resulting connection dialog establish an outlet connection named *textBox*.

Ctrl-click on the button object and drag the line to the area immediately beneath the *viewDidLoad* method in the Assistant Editor panel. Release the line and, within the resulting connection dialog, establish an Action method on the *Touch Up Inside* event configured to call a method named *saveText*.

39.4 Checking the Data File on Application Startup

Each time the application is launched by the user it will need to check to see if the data file already exists (if the user has not previously saved any text, the file will not have been created). If the file does exist, the contents need to be read by the application and displayed within the text field. A good place to put initialization code of this nature is in a method to be called from the *viewDidLoad* method of the view controller. With this in mind, select the *ViewController.swift* file, declare some variables that will be needed in the code and scroll down to the *viewDidLoad* method and edit the file as follows:

```
import UIKit

class ViewController: UIViewController {

    @IBOutlet weak var textBox: UITextField!

    var fileMgr: FileManager = FileManager.default
    var docsDir: String?
    var dataFile: String = ""

    override func viewDidLoad() {
        super.viewDidLoad()
        checkFile()
    }

    func checkFile() {

        let dirPaths = fileMgr.urls(for: .documentDirectory,
                                    in: .userDomainMask)

        dataFile =
            dirPaths[0].appendingPathComponent("datafile.dat").path

        if fileMgr.fileExists(atPath: dataFile) {

            if let databuffer = fileMgr.contents(atPath: dataFile) {
                let datastring = NSString(data: databuffer,
                                   encoding: String.Encoding.utf8.rawValue)
                textBox.text = datastring as String?
            }
```

```
        }
    }
.
.
.
```

Before proceeding we need to take some time to talk about what the above code is doing. First, we declare some variables that will be used in the method and create an instance of the FileManager class. Because each iOS application on a device has its own *Documents* directory, we next make the appropriate calls to identify the path to that directory. Once we know where the documents directory is located we construct the full path to our file (which is named *datafile.dat*) before checking whether the file already exists. If it exists, we read the contents of the file and assign it to the *text* property of our text field object so that it is visible to the user.

Now that we have the initialization code implemented, we need to write the code for our action method.

39.5 Implementing the Action Method

When the user enters text into our text field component and touches the save button, the text needs to be saved to the *datafile.dat* file located in the application's *Documents* directory. In order to make this happen we need, therefore, to implement the code in our *saveText* action method. Select the *ViewController.swift* file if it is not already open and modify the template *saveText* method we created previously so that it reads as follows:

```
@IBAction func saveText(_ sender: Any) {

    if let text = textBox?.text {

        let dataBuffer = text.data(using: String.Encoding.utf8)

        fileMgr.createFile(atPath: dataFile, contents: dataBuffer,
                               attributes: nil)
    }
}
```

This code converts the text contained in the text field object and assigns it to a Data object, the contents of which are written to the data file by calling the *createFile(atPath:)* method of the file manager object.

39.6 Building and Running the Example

Once the appropriate code changes have been made, test the application by clicking on the run button located in the toolbar of the main Xcode project window.

When the application has loaded, enter some text into the text field and click on the *Save* button. Next, stop the app by clicking on the stop button in the Xcode toolbar and then restart the app by clicking the run button again. On loading for a second time the text field will be primed with the text saved during the previous session:

Figure 39-2

39.7 Summary

This chapter has demonstrated the use of the iOS FileManager class to read and write data to the file system of the local device. Now that the basics of working with local files have been covered, the following chapters will introduce the use of cloud-based storage.

Chapter 40

40. Preparing an iOS 12 App to use iCloud Storage

From the perspective of the average iPhone or iPad owner, iCloud represents a vast remote storage service onto which device based data may be backed up and music stored for subsequent streaming to multiple iCloud supported platforms and devices.

From the perspective of the iOS application developer, on the other hand, iCloud represents a set of programming interfaces and SDK classes that facilitate the storage of files and data on iCloud servers hosted at Apple's data centers from within an iOS application.

This chapter is intended to provide an overview of iCloud and to walk through the steps involved in preparing an iOS application to utilize the services of iCloud.

40.1 iCloud Data Storage Services

The current version of the iOS SDK provides support for four types of iCloud-based storage, namely *iCloud Document Storage*, *iCloud Key-Value Data Storage*, *iCloud Drive Storage* and *CloudKit Data Storage*.

iCloud document storage allows an app to store data files and documents on iCloud in a special area reserved for that app. Once stored, these files may be subsequently retrieved from iCloud storage by the same app at any time as long as it is running on a device with the user's iCloud credentials configured.

The iCloud key-value storage service allows small amounts of data packaged in key/value format to be stored in the cloud. This service is intended to provide a way for the same application to synchronize user settings and status when installed on multiple devices. A user might, for example, have the same game application installed on both an iPhone and an iPad. The game application would use iCloud key-value storage to synchronize the player's current position in the game and the prevailing score, thereby allowing the user to switch between devices and resume the game from the same state.

Every Apple user account has associated with it an iCloud Drive storage area into which files may be stored and accessed from different devices and apps. Unlike files stored using the iCloud Storage option (which are generally only accessible to the app that saved the file), however, files stored on iCloud Drive can also be accessed via the built-in *Files* app on iOS, other apps, the Finder on macOS, the iCloud Drive application on Windows and even via the iCloud.com web portal. Saving files to iCloud Drive will be outlined in the chapter entitled*Using iCloud Drive Storage in an iOS 12 App* .

CloudKit data storage provides applications with access to the iCloud servers hosted by Apple and provides an easy to use way to store, manage and retrieve data and other asset types (such as large binary files, videos and images) in a structured way. This provides a way for users to store private data and access it from multiple devices, and also for the developer to provide data that is publicly available to all the users of an application. CloudKit data storage is covered in detail beginning with the chapter entitled *An Introduction to CloudKit Data Storage on iOS 12*.

40.2 Preparing an Application to Use iCloud Storage

In order for an application to be able to use iCloud services it must be code signed with an App ID with iCloud support enabled. In addition to enabling iCloud support within the App ID, the application itself must also be configured with specific entitlements to enable one or more of the iCloud storage services outlined in the preceding section of this chapter.

Fortunately, both of these tasks can be performed within the *Capabilities* screen within Xcode 10.

Clearly, iOS developers who are not yet members of the iOS Developer Program will need to enroll before implementing any iCloud functionality. Details on enrolling in this program were outlined in the *Joining the Apple Developer Program* chapter of this book.

40.3 Enabling iCloud Support for an iOS 12 Application

In order to enable iCloud support for an application, load the project into Xcode and select the application name target from the top of the project navigator panel. From the resulting project settings panel, select the *Capabilities* tab and locate and switch on *iCloud* support as outlined in Figure 40-1, selecting a Development Team to use for the provisioning profile if prompted to do so:

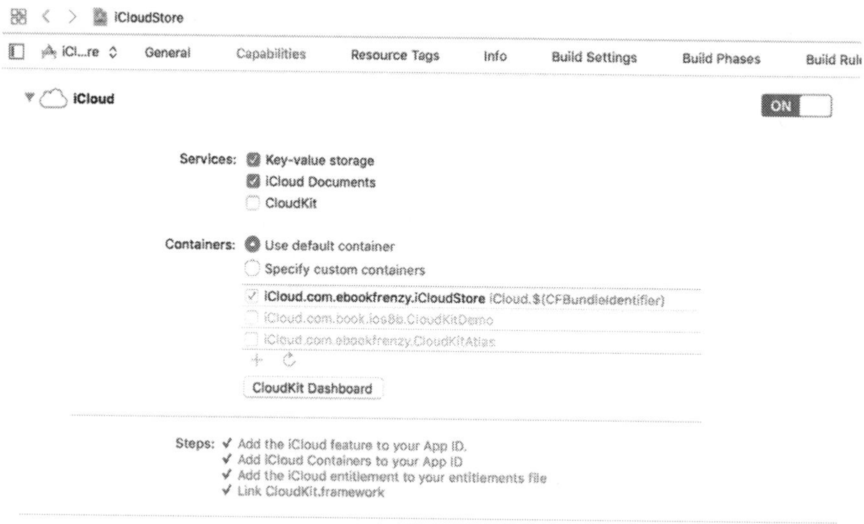

Figure 40-1

The iCloud capabilities section provides options to enable key-value storage, iCloud Documents (which enables both the iCloud Storage and iCloud Drive capabilities) and CloudKit services.

Enabling iCloud support will have automatically added the iCloud entitlement to the application's App ID, and also created an entitlements file to the project containing the application's iCloud container identifiers.

40.4 Reviewing the iCloud Entitlements File

Once iCloud capabilities have been enabled for an application within Xcode, a new file will appear in the project named *<product name>*.entitlements. Any applications that intend to use iCloud storage in any way must obtain entitlements appropriate to the iCloud features to be used. These entitlements are placed into this *entitlements file* and built into the application at compile time.

If the application is intended to make use of iCloud document storage then the entitlements file must include a request for the *com.apple.developer.icloud-container-identifiers* entitlement. Similarly, if the key-value store is to be used then the *com.apple.developer.ubiquity-kvstore-identifier* entitlement must be included. Applications that require both forms of iCloud storage must include both entitlements.

The entitlements file is an XML file in which the requests are stored in a key-value format. The keys are the entitlement identifiers outlined above and the values are represented by one or more *container identifiers* comprised of the developer's ID and a custom string that uniquely identifies the application (the corresponding application's App ID is generally recommended, though not mandatory, for this value).

The entitlements file may be created either manually or, as outlined above, automatically from within the Xcode environment. When using the *Capabilities* settings, the entitlements file will appear in the project navigator panel.

A single iCloud container is added to the entitlements file by default when using the *Capabilities* panel. Additional containers may be added by selecting the *Specify custom containers* option and clicking on the '+' button located beneath the *Containers* list.

40.5 Accessing Multiple Ubiquity Containers

The *ubiquity-container-identifiers* value is an array that may reference multiple iCloud containers. If an application requires access to more than one ubiquity container it will need to specifically reference the identifier of the required container. This is achieved by specifying the container identifier when constructing URL paths to documents within the iCloud storage. For example, the following code fragment defines a container identifier constant and then uses it to obtain the URL of the container in storage:

```
let UBIQUITY_CONTAINER_URL = "ABCDEF12345.com.yourdomain.icloudapp"

let ubiquityURL = FileManager.default.url(forUbiquityContainerIdentifier:
            UBIQUITY_CONTAINER_URL)?.appendingPathComponent("Documents")
```

If *nil* is passed through as an argument in place of the container identifier the method will simply return the URL of the first container in the *ubiquity-container-identifiers* array of the entitlements file:

```
let ubiquityURL = FileManager.default.url(
   forUbiquityContainerIdentifier: nil)?.appendingPathComponent("Documents")
```

40.6 Ubiquity Container URLs

When documents are saved to the cloud they will be placed in subfolders of a folder on iCloud using the following path:

```
/private/var/mobile/Library/Mobile Documents/
<ubiquity container id>/Documents
```

40.7 Summary

iCloud brings cloud-based storage and application data synchronization to iOS 12 based applications. Before an application can take advantage of iCloud it must first be provisioned with an iCloud enabled profile and built against an appropriately configured entitlements file.

Chapter 41

41. Managing Files using the iOS 12 UIDocument Class

Use of iCloud to store files requires a basic understanding of the UIDocument class. Introduced as part of the iOS 5 SDK, the UIDocument class is the recommended mechanism for working with iCloud-based file and document storage.

The objective of this chapter is to provide a brief overview of the UIDocument class before working through a simple example demonstrating the use of UIDocument to create and perform read and write operations on a document on the local device file system. Once these basics have been covered the next chapter will extend the example to store the document using the iCloud document storage service.

41.1 An Overview of the UIDocument Class

The iOS UIDocument class is designed to provide an easy to use interface for the creation and management of documents and content. While primarily intended to ease the process of storing files using iCloud, UIDocument also provides additional benefits in terms of file handling on the local file system such as reading and writing data asynchronously on a background queue, handling of version conflicts on a file (a more likely possibility when using iCloud) and automatic document saving.

41.2 Subclassing the UIDocument Class

UIDocument is an *abstract class*, in that it cannot be directly instantiated from within code. Instead applications must create a subclass of UIDocument and, at a minimum, override two methods:

- **contents(forType:)** - This method is called by the UIDocument subclass instance when data is to be written to the file or document. The method is responsible for gathering the data to be written and returning it in the form of a Data or FileWrapper object.
- **load(fromContents:)** - Called by the subclass instance when data is being read from the file or document. The method is passed the content that has been read from the file by the UIDocument subclass and is responsible for loading that data into the application's internal data model.

41.3 Conflict Resolution and Document States

Storage of documents using iCloud means that multiple instances of an application can potentially access the same stored document consecutively. This considerably increases the risk of a conflict occurring when application instances simultaneously make different changes to the same document. One option is to simply let the most recent save operation overwrite any changes made by the other application instances. A more user friendly alternative, however, is to implement conflict detection code in the application and present the user with the option to resolve the conflict. Such resolution options will be application specific but might include presenting the file differences and letting the user choose which one to save, or allowing the user to merge the conflicting file versions.

The current state of a UIDocument subclass object may be identified by accessing the object's *documentState* property. At any given time this property will be set to one of the following constants:

- **UIDocumentState.normal** – The document is open and enabled for user editing.
- **UIDocumentState.closed** – The document is currently closed. This state can also indicate an error in reading a document.
- **UIDocumentState.inConflict** – Conflicts have been detected for the document.
- **UIDocumentState.savingError** – An error occurred when an attempt was made to save the document.
- **UIDocumentState.editingDisabled** – The document is busy and is not currently safe for editing.
- **UIDocumentState.progressAvailable** – The current progress of the document download is available via the *progress* property of the document object.

Clearly one option for detecting conflicts is to periodically check the *documentState* property for a UIDocumentState.inConflict value. That said, it only really makes sense to check for this state when changes have actually been made to the document. This can be achieved by registering an observer on the *UIDocumentStateChangedNotification* notification. When the notification is received that the document state has changed, the code will need to check the *documentState* property for the presence of a conflict and act accordingly.

41.4 The UIDocument Example Application

The remainder of this chapter will focus on the creation of an application designed to demonstrate the use of the UIDocument class to read and write a document locally on an iOS 12 based device or simulator.

To create the project, begin by launching Xcode and creating a new product named *iCloudStore* using the *Single View Application* template and the Swift programming language.

41.5 Creating a UIDocument Subclass

As previously discussed, UIDocument is an abstract class that cannot be directly instantiated. It is necessary, therefore, to create a subclass and to implement some methods in that subclass before using the features that UIDocument provides. The first step in this project is to create the source file for the subclass so select the Xcode *File -> New -> File...* menu option and in the resulting panel select *iOS* in the tab bar and the *Cocoa Touch Class* template before clicking on *Next.* On the options panel, set the *Subclass of* menu to *UIDocument,* name the class *MyDocument* and click *Next* to create the new class.

With the basic outline of the subclass created the next step is to begin implementing the user interface and the corresponding outlets and actions.

41.6 Designing the User Interface

The finished application is going to consist of a user interface comprising a UITextView and UIButton. The user will enter text into the text view and initiate the saving of that text to a file by touching the button.

Select the *Main.storyboard* file and display the Interface Builder Library panel. Drag and drop the Text View and Button objects into the view canvas, resizing the text view so that it occupies only the upper area of the view. Double-click on the button object and change the title text to "Save":

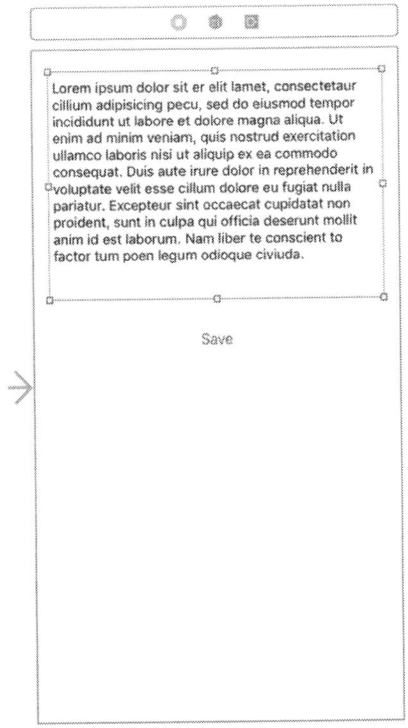

Figure 41-1

Click on the Text View so that it is selected and use the Auto Layout *Add New Constraints* menu to add *Spacing to nearest neighbor* constraints on the top, left and right-hand edges of the view with the *Constrain to margins* option switched on. Before adding the nearest neighbor constraints, also enable the *Height* constraint so that the height of the view is preserved at runtime.

Having configured the constraints for the Text View, select the Button view and use the Auto Layout Align menu to configure a *Horizontal Center in Container* constraint. With the Button view still selected, display the *Add New Constraints* menu and add a *Spacing to nearest neighbor* constraint on the top edge of the view using the current value and with the *Constrain to margins* option switched off.

Remove the example Latin text from the text view object by selecting it in the view canvas and deleting the value from the *Text* property in the Attributes Inspector panel.

With the user interface designed it is now time to connect the action and outlet. Select the Text View object in the view canvas, display the Assistant Editor panel and verify that the editor is displaying the contents of the *ViewController.swift* file. Ctrl-click on the Text View object and drag to a position just below the "class ViewController" declaration line in the Assistant Editor. Release the line and in the resulting connection dialog establish an outlet connection named *textView*.

Finally, Ctrl-click on the button object and drag the line to the area immediately beneath the *viewDidLoad* method declaration in the Assistant Editor panel. Release the line and, within the resulting connection dialog, establish an Action method on the *Touch Up Inside* event configured to call a method named *saveDocument*.

41.7 Implementing the Application Data Structure

So far we have created and partially implemented a UIDocument subclass named *MyDocument* and designed the user interface of the application together with corresponding actions and outlets. As previously discussed, the *MyDocument* class will require two methods that are responsible for interfacing between the

MyDocument object instances and the application's data structures. Before we can implement these methods, however, we first need to implement the application data structure. In the context of this application the data simply consists of the string entered by the user into the text view object. Given the simplicity of this example we will declare the data structure, such as it is, within the *MyDocument* class where it can be easily accessed by the *contents(forType:)* and *load(fromContents:)* methods. To implement the data structure, albeit a single data value, select the *MyDocument.swift* file and add a declaration for a String object:

```
import UIKit

class MyDocument: UIDocument {

    var userText: String? = "Some Sample Text"
}
```

Now that the data model is defined it is time to complete the *MyDocument* class implementation.

41.8 Implementing the contents(forType:) Method

The *MyDocument* class is a subclass of UIDocument. When an instance of MyDocument is created and the appropriate method is called on that instance to save the application's data to a file, the class makes a call to its *contents(forType:)* instance method. It is the job of this method to collect the data to be stored in the document and to pass it back to the MyDocument object instance in the form of a Data object. The content of the Data object will then be written to the document. While this may sound complicated most of the work is done for us by the parent UIDocument class. All the method needs to do, in fact, is get the current value of the *userText* String object, put it into a Data object and return it.

Select the *MyDocument.swift* file and add the *contents(forType:)* method as follows:

```
override func contents(forType typeName: String) throws -> Any {
    if let content = userText {

        let length =
          content.lengthOfBytes(using: String.Encoding.utf8)
        return NSData(bytes:content, length: length)
    } else {
        return Data()
    }
}
```

41.9 Implementing the load(fromContents:) Method

The *load(fromContents:)* instance method is called by an instance of MyDocument when the object is instructed to read the contents of a file. This method is passed a Data object containing the content of the document and is responsible for updating the application's internal data structure accordingly. All this method needs to do, therefore, is convert the Data object contents to a string and assign it to the *userText* object:

```
override func load(fromContents contents: Any, ofType typeName: String?)
 throws {
    if let userContent = contents as? Data {
        userText = NSString(bytes: (contents as AnyObject).bytes,
                    length: userContent.count,
```

```
                    encoding: String.Encoding.utf8.rawValue) as String?
    }
}
```

The implementation of the MyDocument class is now complete and it is time to begin implementing the application functionality.

41.10 Loading the Document at App Launch

The ultimate goal of the application is to save any text in the text view to a document on the local file system of the device. When the application is launched it needs to check if the document exists and, if so, load the contents into the text view object. If, on the other hand, the document does not yet exist it will need to be created. As is usually the case, the best place to perform these tasks is the *viewDidLoad* method of the view controller.

Before implementing the code for the *viewDidLoad* method we first need to perform some preparatory work. First, both the *viewDidLoad* and *saveDocument* methods will need access to a URL object containing a reference to the document and also an instance of the *MyDocument* class, so these need to be declared in the view controller implementation file. With the *ViewController.swift* file selected in the project navigator, modify the file as follows:

```
import UIKit

class ViewController: UIViewController {

    @IBOutlet weak var textView: UITextView!

    var document: MyDocument?
    var documentURL: URL?
.
.
.
}
```

The first task for the *viewDidLoad* method is to identify the path to the application's *Documents* directory (a task outlined in *Working with Directories in Swift on iOS 12*) and construct a full path to the document which will be named *savefile.txt*. The method will then need to use the document URL to create an instance of the *MyDocument* class. The code to perform these tasks can be implemented as outlined in the following code fragment:

```
let filemgr = FileManager.default

let dirPaths = filemgr.urls(for: .documentDirectory,
                            in: .userDomainMask)

documentURL = dirPaths[0].appendingPathComponent("savefile.txt")
if let url = documentURL {
    document = MyDocument(fileURL: url)
    document?.userText = ""
```

The next task for the method is to identify whether the save file exists. In the event that it does, the *open(completionHandler:)* method of the *MyDocument* instance object is called to open the document and load the contents (thereby automatically triggering a call to the *load(fromContents:)* method created earlier in the chapter).

The *open(completionHandler:)* method allows for a code block to be written to which is passed a Boolean value indicating the success or otherwise of the file opening and reading process. On a successful read operation this handler code simply needs to assign the value of the *userText* property of the *MyDocument* instance (which has been updated with the document contents by the *load(fromContents:)* method) to the text property of the *textView* object, thereby making it visible to the user.

In the event that the document does not yet exist, the *save(to:)* method of the *MyDocument* class will be called using the argument to create a new file:

```
if filemgr.fileExists(atPath: (url.path)!) {

    document?.open(completionHandler: {(success: Bool) -> Void in
        if success {
            print("File open OK")
            self.textView.text = self.document?.userText
        } else {
            print("Failed to open file")
        }
    })
} else {
    document?.save(to: url, for: .forCreating,
             completionHandler: {(success: Bool) -> Void in
        if success {
            print("File created OK")
        } else {
            print("Failed to create file ")
        }
    })
}
```

Note that for the purposes of debugging, print calls have been made at key points in the process. These can be removed once the application is verified to be working correctly.

Bringing the above code fragments together results in the following, fully implemented *loadFile* method which will need to be called from the *viewDidLoad* method:

```
override func viewDidLoad() {
    super.viewDidLoad()
    loadFile()
}
.
.
func loadFile() {
    let filemgr = FileManager.default
```

```
    let dirPaths = filemgr.urls(for: .documentDirectory,
                                in: .userDomainMask)

    documentURL = dirPaths[0].appendingPathComponent("savefile.txt")

    if let url = documentURL {
        document = MyDocument(fileURL: url)
        document?.userText = ""

        if filemgr.fileExists(atPath: (url.path)) {

            document?.open(completionHandler: {(success: Bool) -> Void in
                if success {
                    print("File open OK")
                    self.textView.text = self.document?.userText
                } else {
                    print("Failed to open file")
                }
            })
        } else {
            document?.save(to: url, for: .forCreating,
               completionHandler: {(success: Bool) -> Void in
                if success {
                    print("File created OK")
                } else {
                    print("Failed to create file ")
                }
            })
        }
    }
}
```

41.11 Saving Content to the Document

When the user touches the application's save button the content of the text view object needs to be saved to the document. An action method has already been connected to the user interface object for this purpose and it is now time to write the code for this method.

Since the *viewDidLoad* method has already identified the path to the document and initialized the *document* object, all that needs to be done is to call that object's *save(to:)* method using the *.saveForOverwriting* option. The *save(to:)* method will automatically call the *contents(forType:)* method implemented previously in this chapter. Prior to calling the method, therefore, it is important that the *userText* property of the *document* object be set to the current text of the *textView* object.

Bringing this all together results in the following implementation of the *saveDocument* method:

```
@IBAction func saveDocument(_ sender: Any) {
```

```
    document?.userText = textView.text

    if let url = documentURL {
        document?.save(to: url,
                for: .forOverwriting,
                completionHandler: {(success: Bool) -> Void in
                 if success {
                     print("File overwrite OK")
                 } else {
                     print("File overwrite failed")
                 }
        })
    }
}
```

41.12 Testing the Application

All that remains is to test that the application works by clicking on the Xcode run button. Upon execution, any text entered into the text view object should be saved to the *savefile.txt* file when the Save button is touched. Once some text has been saved, click on the stop button located in the Xcode toolbar. On subsequently restarting the application the text view should be populated with the previously saved text.

41.13 Summary

While the UIDocument class is the cornerstone of document storage using the iCloud service it is also of considerable use and advantage in terms of using the local file system storage of an iOS device. As an abstract class, UIDocument must be subclassed and two mandatory methods implemented within the subclass in order to operate. This chapter worked through an example of using UIDocument to save and load content using a locally stored document. The next chapter will look at using UIDocument to perform cloud-based document storage and retrieval.

Chapter 42

42. Using iCloud Storage in an iOS 12 Application

The two preceding chapters of this book were intended to convey the knowledge necessary to begin implementing iCloud based document storage in iOS applications. Having outlined the steps necessary to enable iCloud access in the chapter entitled *Preparing an iOS 12 App to use iCloud Storage*, and provided an overview of the UIDocument class in *Managing Files using the iOS 12 UIDocument Class*, the next step is to actually begin to store documents using the iCloud service.

Within this chapter the *iCloudStore* application created in the previous chapter will be re-purposed to store a document using iCloud storage instead of the local device-based file system. The assumption is also made that the project has been enabled for iCloud document storage following the steps outlined in *Preparing an iOS 12 App to use iCloud Storage*.

Before starting on this project it is important to note that membership to the Apple Developer Program will be required as outlined in *Joining the Apple Developer Program*.

42.1 iCloud Usage Guidelines

Before implementing iCloud storage in an application there are a few rules that must first be understood. Some of these are mandatory rules and some are simply recommendations made by Apple:

- Applications must be associated with a provisioning profile enabled for iCloud storage.
- The application projects must include a suitably configured entitlements file for iCloud storage.
- Applications should not make unnecessary use of iCloud storage. Once a user's initial free iCloud storage space is consumed by stored data the user will either need to delete files or purchase more space.
- Applications should, ideally, provide the user with the option to select which documents are to be stored in the cloud and which are to be stored locally.
- When opening a *previously created* iCloud-based document the application should never use an absolute path to the document. The application should instead search for the document by name in the application's iCloud storage area and then access it using the result of the search.
- Documents stored using iCloud should be placed in the application's *Documents* directory. This gives the user the ability to delete individual documents from the storage. Documents saved outside the *Documents* folder can only be deleted in bulk.

42.2 Preparing the iCloudStore Application for iCloud Access

Much of the work performed in creating the local storage version of the *iCloudStore* application in the previous chapter will be reused in this example. The user interface, for example, remains unchanged and the implementation of the UIDocument subclass will not need to be modified. In fact, the only methods that need to be rewritten are the *saveDocument* and *viewDidLoad* methods of the view controller.

Load the *iCloudStore* project into Xcode and select the *ViewController.swift* file. Locate the *saveDocument* method and remove the current code from within the method so that it reads as follows:

```
@IBAction func saveDocument(_ sender: Any) {
```

```
}
```

Next, locate the *loadFile* method and modify it accordingly to match the following fragment:

```
func loadFile() {
}
```

42.3 Configuring the View Controller

Before writing any code there are a number of variables that need to be defined within the view controller's *ViewController.swift* file in addition to those implemented in the previous chapter.

It will also now be necessary to create a URL to the document location in the iCloud storage. When a document is stored on iCloud it is said to be *ubiquitous* since the document is accessible to the application regardless of the device on which it is running. The object used to store this URL will, therefore, be named *ubiquityURL.*

As previously stated, when opening a stored document, an application should search for the document rather than directly access it using a stored path. An iCloud document search is performed using an *NSMetaDataQuery* object which needs to be declared in the view controller class, in this instance using the name *metaDataQuery.* Note that declaring the object locally to the method in which it is used will result in the object being released by the automatic reference counting system (ARC) before it has completed the search.

To implement these requirements, select the *ViewController.swift* file in the Xcode project navigator panel and modify the file as follows:

```
import UIKit

class ViewController: UIViewController {

    @IBOutlet weak var textView: UITextView!

    var document: MyDocument?
    var documentURL: URL?
    var ubiquityURL: URL?
    var metaDataQuery: NSMetadataQuery?
.
.
.
}
```

42.4 Implementing the loadFile Method

The purpose of the code in the view controller *loadFile* method is to identify the URL for the ubiquitous version of the file to be stored using iCloud (assigned to *ubiquityURL*). The ubiquitous URL is constructed by calling the *url(forUbiquityContainerIdentifier:)* method of the FileManager passing through *nil* as an argument to default to the first container listed in the entitlements file.

```
ubiquityURL = filemgr.url(forUbiquityContainerIdentifier: nil)
```

The app will only be able to obtain the ubiquityURL if the user has configured a valid Apple ID within the iCloud page of the iOS Settings app. Some defensive code needs to be added, therefore, to notify the user and return from the method if a valid ubiquityURL could not be obtained. For the purposes of testing in this example we will simply output a message to the console before returning:

```
guard ubiquityURL != nil else {
    print("Unable to access iCloud Account")
    print("Open the Settings app and enter your Apple ID into iCloud
settings")
    return
}
```

Since it is recommended that documents be stored in the *Documents* sub-directory, this needs to be appended to the URL path along with the file name:

```
ubiquityURL =
        ubiquityURL?.appendingPathComponent("Documents/savefile.txt")
```

The final task for the *loadFile* method is to initiate a search in the application's iCloud storage area to find out if the *savefile.txt* file already exists and to act accordingly subject to the result of the search. The search is performed by calling the methods on an instance of the *NSMetaDataQuery* object. This involves creating the object, setting a predicate to indicate the files to search for and defining a ubiquitous search scope (in other words instructing the object to search within the Documents directory of the app's iCloud storage area). Once initiated, the search is performed on a separate thread and issues a notification when completed. For this reason, it is also necessary to configure an observer to be notified when the search is finished. The code to perform these tasks reads as follows:

```
metaDataQuery = NSMetadataQuery()

metaDataQuery?.predicate =
    NSPredicate(format: "%K like 'savefile.txt'",
        NSMetadataItemFSNameKey)
metaDataQuery?.searchScopes = [NSMetadataQueryUbiquitousDocumentsScope]

NotificationCenter.default.addObserver(self,
    selector: #selector(
          ViewController.metadataQueryDidFinishGathering),
    name: NSNotification.Name.NSMetadataQueryDidFinishGathering,
    object: metaDataQuery!)

metaDataQuery?.start()
```

Once the *start* method is called, the search will run and call the *metadataQueryDidFinishGathering* method when the search is complete. The next step, therefore, is to implement the *metadataQueryDidFinishGathering* method. Before doing so, however, note that the *loadFile* method is now complete and the full implementation should read as follows:

```
func loadFile() {

    let filemgr = FileManager.default
```

```
    ubiquityURL = filemgr.url(forUbiquityContainerIdentifier: nil)

    guard ubiquityURL != nil else {
        print("Unable to access iCloud Account")
        print("Open the Settings app and enter your Apple ID into iCloud 
settings")
        return
    }

    ubiquityURL = ubiquityURL?.appendingPathComponent(
                                        "Documents/savefile.txt")

    metaDataQuery = NSMetadataQuery()

    metaDataQuery?.predicate =
        NSPredicate(format: "%K like 'savefile.txt'",
            NSMetadataItemFSNameKey)
    metaDataQuery?.searchScopes =
                [NSMetadataQueryUbiquitousDocumentsScope]

    NotificationCenter.default.addObserver(self,
        selector: #selector(
                ViewController.metadataQueryDidFinishGathering),
        name: NSNotification.Name.NSMetadataQueryDidFinishGathering,
        object: metaDataQuery!)

    metaDataQuery?.start()
}
```

42.5 Implementing the metadataQueryDidFinishGathering Method

When the meta data query was triggered in the *loadFile* method to search for documents in the Documents directory of the application's iCloud storage area, an observer was configured to call a method named *metadataQueryDidFinishGathering* when the initial search completed. The next logical step is to implement this method. The first task of the method is to identify the query object that caused this method to be called. This object must then be used to disable any further query updates (at this stage the document either exists or doesn't exist so there is nothing to be gained by receiving additional updates) and stop the search. It is also necessary to remove the observer that triggered the method call. Combined, these requirements result in the following code:

```
let query: NSMetadataQuery = notification.object as! NSMetadataQuery

query.disableUpdates()

NotificationCenter.default.removeObserver(self,
        name: NSNotification.Name.NSMetadataQueryDidFinishGathering,
```

```
        object: query)

query.stop()
```

The next step is to make sure at least one match was found and to extract the URL of the first document located during the search:

```
if query.resultCount == 1 {
        let resultURL = query.value(ofAttribute: NSMetadataItemURLKey,
                                forResultAt: 0) as! URL
```

A more complex application would, in all likelihood, need to implement a *for* loop to iterate through more than one document in the array. Given that the iCloudStore application searched for only one specific file name we can simply check the array element count and assume that if the count is 1 then the document already exists. In this case, the ubiquitous URL of the document from the query object needs to be assigned to our *ubiquityURL* member property and used to create an instance of our MyDocument class called *document*. The *open(completionHandler:)* method of the *document* object is then called to open the document in the cloud and read the contents. This will trigger a call to the *load(fromContents:)* method of the *document* object which, in turn, will assign the contents of the document to the *userText* property. Assuming the document read is successful the value of *userText* needs to be assigned to the *text* property of the text view object to make it visible to the user. Bringing this together results in the following code fragment:

```
    document = MyDocument(fileURL: resultURL as URL)

    document?.open(completionHandler: {(success: Bool) -> Void in
        if success {
            print("iCloud file open OK")
            self.textView.text = self.document?.userText
            self.ubiquityURL = resultURL as URL
        } else {
            print("iCloud file open failed")
        }
    })
} else {
}
```

In the event that the document does not yet exist in iCloud storage the code needs to create the document using the *save(to:)* method of the *document* object passing through the value of *ubiquityURL* as the destination path on iCloud:

```
.
.
} else {
    if let url = ubiquityURL {
        document = MyDocument(fileURL: url)

        document?.save(to: url,
                       for: .forCreating,
```

```
                                completionHandler: {(success: Bool) -> Void in
                                 if success {
                                     print("iCloud create OK")
                                 } else {
                                     print("iCloud create failed")
                                 }
        })
    }
}
```

The individual code fragments outlined above combine to implement the following *metadataQueryDidFinishGathering* method which should be added to the *ViewController.swift* file:

```
@objc func metadataQueryDidFinishGathering(notification: NSNotification)
     -> Void
{
    let query: NSMetadataQuery = notification.object as! NSMetadataQuery

    query.disableUpdates()

    NotificationCenter.default.removeObserver(self,
            name: NSNotification.Name.NSMetadataQueryDidFinishGathering,
            object: query)

    query.stop()

    if query.resultCount == 1 {
        let resultURL = query.value(ofAttribute: NSMetadataItemURLKey,
                                        forResultAt: 0) as! URL

        document = MyDocument(fileURL: resultURL as URL)

        document?.open(completionHandler: {(success: Bool) -> Void in
            if success {
                print("iCloud file open OK")
                self.textView.text = self.document?.userText
                self.ubiquityURL = resultURL as URL
            } else {
                print("iCloud file open failed")
            }
        })
    } else {
        if let url = ubiquityURL {
            document = MyDocument(fileURL: url)
```

```
            document?.save(to: url,
                          for: .forCreating,
                          completionHandler: {(success: Bool) -> Void in
                           if success {
                               print("iCloud create OK")
                           } else {
                               print("iCloud create failed")
                           }
            })
        }
    }
}
```

42.6 Implementing the saveDocument Method

The final task before building and running the application is to implement the *saveDocument* method. This method simply needs to update the *userText* property of the *document* object with the text entered into the text view and then call the *saveToURL* method of the *document* object, passing through the *ubiquityURL* as the destination URL using the *.forOverwriting* option:

```
@IBAction func saveDocument(_ sender: Any) {
    document?.userText = textView.text

    if let url = ubiquityURL {
        document?.save(to: url,
                 for: .forOverwriting,
                 completionHandler: {(success: Bool) -> Void in
                  if success {
                      print("Save overwrite OK")
                  } else {
                      print("Save overwrite failed")
                  }
        })
    }
}
```

All that remains now is to build and run the iCloudStore application on an iOS device, but first some settings need to be checked.

42.7 Enabling iCloud Document and Data Storage

When testing iCloud on an iOS Simulator session, it is important to make sure that the simulator is configured with a valid Apple ID within the Settings app. To configure this, launch the simulator, load the Settings app and click on the iCloud option. If no account information is configured on this page, enter a valid Apple ID and corresponding password before proceeding with the testing.

Whether or not applications are permitted to use iCloud storage on an iOS device or Simulator is controlled by the iCloud settings. To review these settings, open the Settings application on the device or simulator, select your account at the top of the settings list and, on the resulting screen, select the *iCloud* category. Scroll down the list of various iCloud related options and verify that the *iCloud Drive* option is set to *On*:

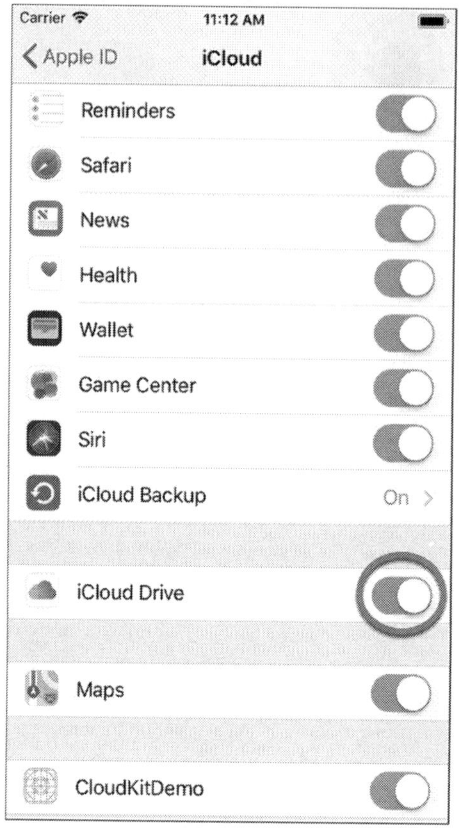

Figure 42-1

42.8 Running the iCloud Application

Once you have logged in to an iCloud account on the device or simulator, test the iCloudStore app by clicking on the run button. Once running, edit the text in the text view and touch the *Save* button. In the Xcode toolbar click on the stop button to exit the application followed by the run button to re-launch the application. On the second launch the previously entered text will be read from the document in the cloud and displayed in the text view object.

42.9 Reviewing and Deleting iCloud-based Documents

The files currently stored in a user's iCloud account may be reviewed or deleted from the iOS Settings app running on a physical device. To review the currently stored documents select the *iCloud* option from the main screen of the *Settings* app. On the *iCloud* screen select the *Storage* option and, on the resulting screen, select *Manage Storage* followed by the name of the application for which stored documents are to be listed. A list of documents stored using iCloud for the selected application will then appear including the current file size:

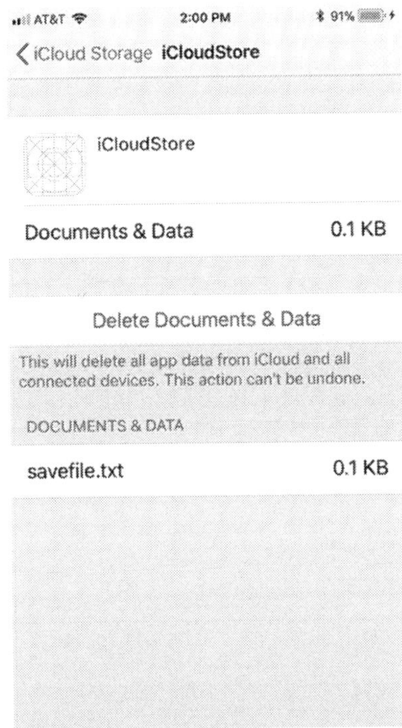

Figure 42-2

To delete the document, select the *Edit* button located in the toolbar. All listed documents may be deleted using the *Delete All* button, or deleted individually.

42.10 Making a Local File Ubiquitous

In addition to writing a file directly to iCloud storage as illustrated in this example application, it is also possible to transfer a pre-existing local file to iCloud storage, thereby making it ubiquitous. This can be achieved using the *setUbiquitous* method of the FileManager class. Assuming that *documentURL* references the path to the local copy of the file, and *ubiquityURL* the iCloud destination, a local file can be made ubiquitous using the following code:

```
do {
    try filemgr.setUbiquitous(true, itemAt: documentUrl,
                destinationURL: ubiquityURL)
} catch let error {
    print("setUbiquitous failed: \(error.localizedDescription)")
}
```

42.11 Summary

The objective of this chapter was to work through the process of developing an application that stores a document using the iCloud service. Both techniques of directly creating a file in iCloud storage, and making an existing locally created file ubiquitous were covered. In addition, some important guidelines that should be observed when using iCloud were outlined.

Chapter 43

43. Using iCloud Drive Storage in an iOS 12 App

The previous chapter designed an app which made use of iCloud Storage to remotely store a text file. While the presence of the stored file could be confirmed by accessing the iCloud Storage section of the iOS Settings app, the file and its content were only accessible to the iCloudStore example app. In this chapter, a simple app will be created that uses iCloud Drive to store a sample text file and show how the file can be accessed in a variety of ways from outside of the app.

43.1 Preparing an App to use iCloud Drive Storage

As with other forms of iCloud storage, a number of steps must be taken in order to add support for iCloud Drive to an Xcode app project. The first step is to enable the iCloud Documents capability as outlined in the chapter entitled *Preparing an iOS 12 App to use iCloud Storage*.

When an app stores files on iCloud Drive it places them within the Documents folder of an iCloud ubiquitous container. Any files stored at this location will appear within iCloud Drive within a Folder with the name assigned to the container (by default this is simply the app name).

The ubiquitous container is configured for the project via a NSUbiquitousContainers key entry which needs to be added to the project's *Info.plist* file which takes the following form:

```
<key>NSUbiquitousContainers</key>
<dict>
    <key>iCloud.$(PRODUCT_BUNDLE_IDENTIFIER)</key>
    <dict>
        <key>NSUbiquitousContainerIsDocumentScopePublic</key>
        <true/>
        <key>NSUbiquitousContainerName</key>
        <string>MyAppName</string>
        <key>NSUbiquitousContainerSupportedFolderLevels</key>
        <string>None</string>
    </dict>
</dict>
```

The first entry in the dictionary consists of the app's bundle identifier pre-fixed with "iCloud." (for example iCloud.com.ebookfrenzy.MyApp). This entry must exactly match the app's bundle identifier otherwise the stored files will not appear in iCloud Drive. Since the bundle ID has already been declared by Xcode in the *Info.plist* file via the PRODUCT_BUNDLE_IDENTIFIER key, the safest option is to simply reference this key as follows:

```
<key>iCloud.$(PRODUCT_BUNDLE_IDENTIFIER)</key>
```

Next, the *access scope* of the container is declared. If set to false, the contents of the container will be accessible to the app but will not otherwise be visible within iCloud Drive (in other words it will not show up in the iOS Files app or macOS Finder).

The *container name* entry defines the name of the container and represents the folder name under which the files will be listed in iCloud Drive.

Finally, the number of directory levels within the container to which the user will have access via iCloud Drive is declared. If this is set to *None*, iCloud Drive only has access to the container's Documents directory and sub-directories cannot be created using apps such as Files or Finder. A setting of *One* allows iCloud Drive to access and create sub-folders up to one level beyond the Documents folder. Finally, a setting of *Any* allows sub-directories of any level to be accessed and created via iCloud Drive.

Once these preparations have been made, working with iCloud Drive from within an iOS app is simply a matter of obtaining the URL of the ubiquitous container and using it to perform the necessary file operations.

43.2 Making Changes to the NSUbiquitousContainers Key

When making modifications to the iCloud Drive container settings in the *Info.plist* file it is important to be aware that once the app has been run once, subsequent changes to these settings may not be registered with iCloud unless the CFBundleVersion number value in the *Info.plist* file is incremented, for example:

```
.
.
    <key>CFBundleVersion</key>
            <string>2</string>
.
.
```

43.3 Creating the iCloud Drive Example Project

Start the Xcode environment, selecting the option to create a new project. Select the *Single View Application* template, *Swift* as the language and name the product *TestDrive*. Select the TestDrive target at the top of the project navigator panel, select the *Capabilities* tab in the main panel, locate and switch on *iCloud* support and enable the iCloud Documents option.

43.4 Modifying the Info.plist File

Locate the *Info.plist* file in the project navigator panel, right-click on it and select the *Open As -> Source Code* menu option. With the file open in the editor, add the NSUbiquitousContainers entry as follows:

```
.
.
                <string>UIInterfaceOrientationLandscapeLeft</string>
                <string>UIInterfaceOrientationLandscapeRight</string>
        </array>
    <key>NSUbiquitousContainers</key>
    <dict>
        <key>iCloud.$(PRODUCT_BUNDLE_IDENTIFIER)</key>
        <dict>
            <key>NSUbiquitousContainerIsDocumentScopePublic</key>
            <true/>
            <key>NSUbiquitousContainerName</key>
```

```
            <string>TestDrive</string>
            <key>NSUbiquitousContainerSupportedFolderLevels</key>
            <string>None</string>
        </dict>
    </dict>
</dict>
</plist>
```

43.5 Designing the User Interface

The user interface will, once again, consist of a UITextView and UIButton. The user will enter text into the text view and save that text to a file on iCloud Drive by clicking on the button.

Select the *Main.storyboard* file and display the Interface Builder Library panel. Drag and drop the Text View and Button objects into the view canvas, resizing the text view so that it occupies only the upper area of the view. Double-click on the button object and change the title text to "Save to iCloud Drive":

Figure 43-1

Display the *Resolve Auto Layout Issues* menu and select the *Reset to Suggested Constraints* menu option.

Remove the example Latin text from the text view object by selecting it in the view canvas and deleting the value from the *Text* property in the Attributes Inspector panel.

Select the Text View object in the view canvas, display the Assistant Editor panel and verify that the editor is displaying the contents of the *ViewController.swift* file. Ctrl-click on the Text View object and drag to a position just below the "class ViewController" declaration line in the Assistant Editor. Release the line and in the resulting connection dialog establish an outlet connection named *textView*.

Finally, Ctrl-click on the button object and drag the line to the area immediately beneath the *viewDidLoad* method declaration in the Assistant Editor panel. Release the line and, within the resulting connection dialog, establish an Action method on the *Touch Up Inside* event configured to call a method named *saveToDrive*.

43.6 Accessing the Ubiquitous Container

Each time the TestDrive app launches, it will need to obtain the URL of the container, check whether the text file already exists and, if so, read the file content and display it within the Text View object. Edit the *ViewController.swift* file and modify it to read as follows:

```
import UIKit

class ViewController: UIViewController {

    @IBOutlet weak var textView: UITextView!

    let containerURL =
        FileManager.default.url(forUbiquityContainerIdentifier: nil)
    var documentURL: URL?

    override func viewDidLoad() {
        super.viewDidLoad()

        documentURL = containerURL?.appendingPathComponent(
                                "Documents/MyTextFile.txt")

        if let documentPath = documentURL?.path {
            if (FileManager.default.fileExists(atPath: documentPath,
                                 isDirectory: nil)) {

                if let databuffer = FileManager.default.contents(
                                 atPath: documentPath) {
                    let datastring = NSString(data: databuffer,
                            encoding: String.Encoding.utf8.rawValue)
                    textView.text = datastring as String?
                }
            }
        }
    }
.
.
```

The code changes begin by declaring a constant named *containerURL* and assigning to it the URL of the default ubiquity container and a variable into which the full URL of the text file will be stored:

```
let containerURL =
```

```
        FileManager.default.url(forUbiquityContainerIdentifier: nil)
var documentURL: URL?
```

The text file will be named MyTextFile.txt and must be stored in the container's Documents folder. This URL is constructed by appending to the end of the containerURL as follows:

```
documentURL = containerURL?.appendingPathComponent(
                                        "Documents/MyTextFile.txt"
```

Finally, the FileManager class is used to check if the text file already exists. If it exists the contents are read and displayed to the user.

```
if (FileManager.default.fileExists(atPath: documentPath, isDirectory: nil)) {
    if let databuffer = FileManager.default.contents(atPath: documentPath) {
        let datastring = NSString(data: databuffer,
                                  encoding: String.Encoding.utf8.rawValue)
        textView.text = datastring as String?
    }
}
```

43.7 Saving the File to iCloud Drive

The final task before testing the app is to implement the code in the *saveToDrive()* method to write the file to iCloud Drive. Within the *ViewController.swift* file, locate the stub method and implement the code as follows:

```
@IBAction func saveToDrive(_ sender: Any) {

    if let url = documentURL {
        do {
            try textView.text.write(to: url, atomically:true,
                encoding:String.Encoding.utf8)
        } catch let error {
            print(error.localizedDescription)
        }
    }
}
```

Using the previously initialized *documentURL* constant, the method simply writes the contents of the Text View to the text file stored on iCloud Drive, reporting an error in the event that the write operation fails.

43.8 Testing the App

Build and run the app on a device or emulator on which the user's iCloud credentials have been configured, enter some text and click the button to save the file to iCloud Drive. Stop the app, relaunch it and make sure that the text entered previously is restored.

Place the app into the background, launch the iOS Files app and select the iCloud Drive option from the Locations section of the main screen. Among the folders already stored on iCloud Drive will be a folder named TestDrive within which will reside the *MyTextFile.txt* file:

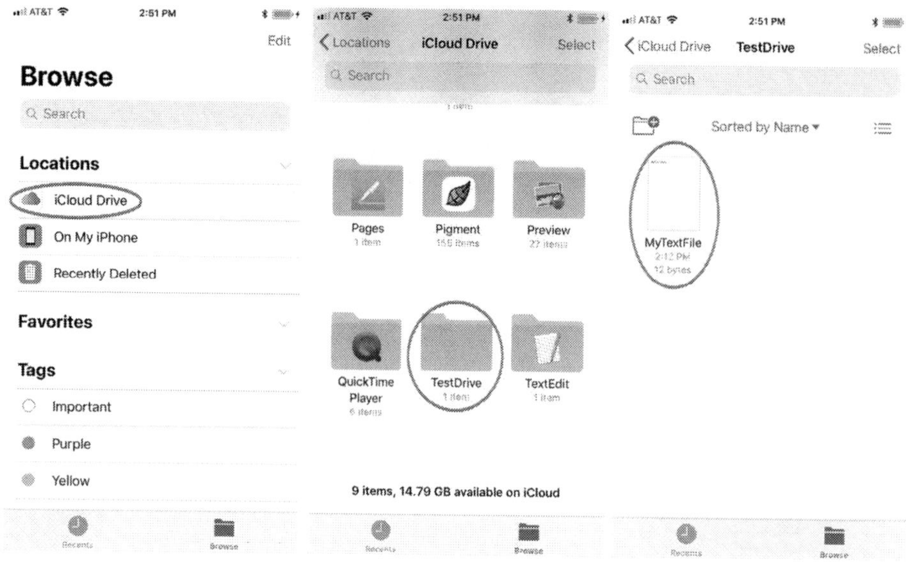

Figure 43-2

When selected, the file should open and display the text entered within the TestDrive app.

On a macOS system configured with the same iCloud user account, open the Finder window and navigate to *iCloud Drive -> TestDrive -> MyTextFile.txt* where the preview panel should display the text saved to the file from within the TestDrive app:

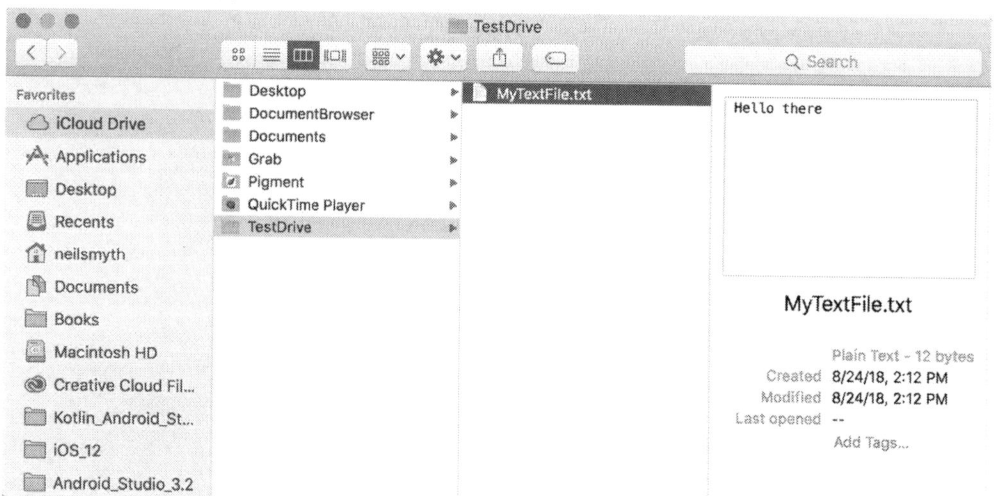

Figure 43-3

43.9 Summary

The iCloud Drive support built into the iOS SDK allows apps to store and retrieve iCloud Drive-based files. This requires that the appropriate iCloud capabilities be enabled for the project within Xcode together with the addition of ubiquitous container settings within the project's *Info.plist* file. Once these steps have been taken, a reference to the URL of the container is obtained and used to read, write, delete and copy files on iCloud Drive. This chapter outlined these steps before creating an example app that makes use of iCloud Drive to store and access a simple text file.

Chapter 43

44. An Overview of the iOS 12 Document Browser View Controller

The previous chapters have introduced ways to integrate file handling into an iOS application in terms of local and iCloud-based storage. In these chapters, the assumption has been made that all of the user interface aspects of the file handling and file system navigation will be provided in some way by the app itself. An alternative to integrating file handling in this way is to make use of the iOS document browser view controller.

This chapter provides a basic overview of this class in preparation for a tutorial in the next chapter.

44.1 An Overview of the Document Browser View Controller

The document browser view controller is implemented using the UIDocumentBrowserViewController class and provides a visual environment in which users can navigate file systems and select and manage files from within an iOS app. The document browser provides the user with access to both the local device file system and iCloud storage in addition to third-party providers such as Google Drive.

To see the browser in action, take some time to explore the Files app included as standard with iOS 12. Figure 44-1, for example, shows the Files app being used to browse a user's iCloud Drive files and folders:

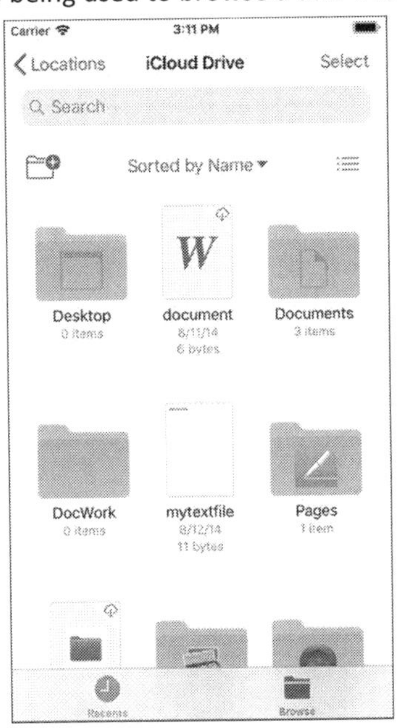

Figure 44-1

When integrated into an app, the document browser provides the same functionality as the Files app in addition to the ability to create new files.

As with the Files app, when the browser is integrated into an app, performing a deep press over the app's launcher icon will display a popup containing the most recently accessed files:

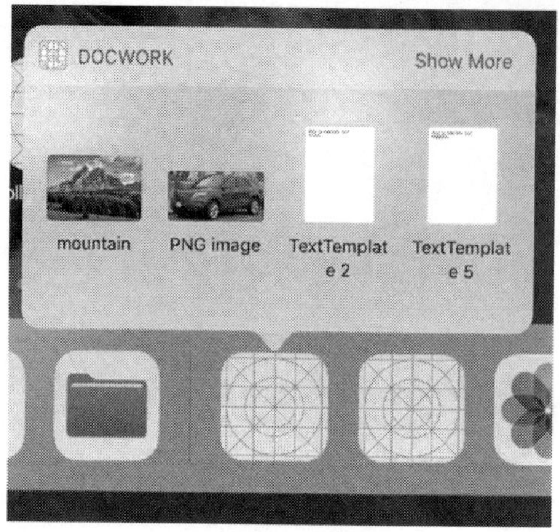

Figure 44-2

44.2 The Anatomy of a Document Based App

The key elements that interact to provide the document browser functionality within an iOS app are a UIDocumentBrowserViewController instance, access to one or more file providers (for example the local file system, iCloud Drive, Google Drive etc.) and at least one additional view controller in which to present any selected file content to the user. When working with files in conjunction with the document browser, the use of the UIDocument class for the lower level file handling tasks is still recommended, so a subclass of UIDocument will also typically be included (the UIDocument class was covered in the chapter entitled *Managing Files using the iOS 12 UIDocument Class*).

Adding document browser support to an app is a multistep process that begins with the creation of a UIDocumentBrowserViewController instance. When doing this it is essential that the browser is the *root view controller* of the app. By far the easiest way to start the development process is to use the Xcode Document Based App template when creating a new project as shown in Figure 44-3:

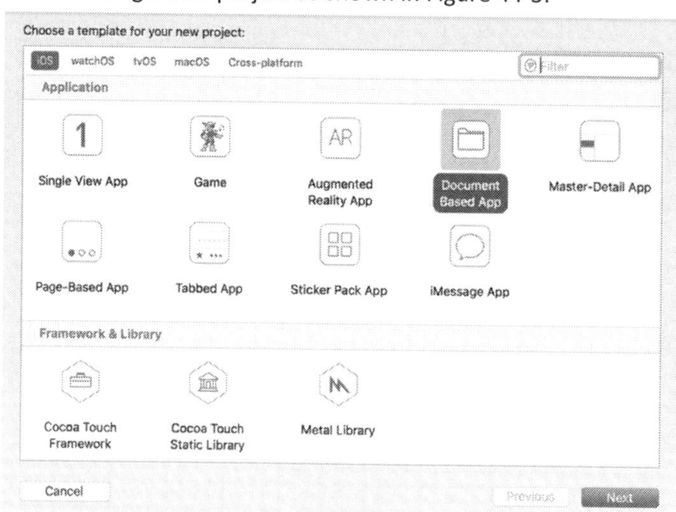

Figure 44-3

A project created using the Document Based App template will contain the following files by default:

- **DocumentBrowserViewController.swift** - The root view controller for the app derived from the UIDocumentBrowserViewController class. This file contains stub delegate methods ready to be completed to implement app specific document browser behavior.
- **Document.swift** – A subclass of the UIDocument class containing stub methods.
- **DocumentViewController.swift** – A template view controller intended to present the selected files to the user. This template implementation simply displays the file name and a "Done" button to return to the document browser.

44.3 Document Browser Project Settings

A number of *Info.plist* settings need to be configured to enable document browser support within an app project. The first is the *Supports Document Browser* (UISupportsDocumentBrowser) key which must to set to *YES*.

Next, the app needs to declare the *document types* it is capable of handling and the action the app is able to perform on those types (i.e. viewing only or viewing and editing). These settings dictate the types of file that will be selectable within the document browser.

Each supported type must, at a minimum, include the following key-value information:

- **CFBundleTypeName** - A string value that uniquely identifies the type within the context of the app.
- **CFBundleTypeRole** – A string value indicating the action that the app will perform on the file (i.e. *Editor* or *Viewer*)
- **LSHandlerRank** – A string value that declares to the system how the app relates to the file type. If the app uses its own custom file type, this should be set to *Owner.* If the app is to be opened as the default app for files of this type, the value should be set to *Default.* If, on the other hand, the app can handle files of this type but is not intended to be the default handler a value of *Alternate* should be used. Finally, *None*, should be used if the app is not to be associated with the file type.
- **LSItemContentTypes** – An array of Universal Type Identifiers (UTI) indicating the file types supported by the app. These can be custom file types unique to the app or, more commonly, standard identifiers provided by Apple such as *public.image*, *public.text*, *public.plain-text* and *public.rtf*.

As will be outlined in the next chapter, the easiest way to configure these keys is within the *Info* panel of the Xcode project target screen.

44.4 The Document Browser Delegate Methods

When the user selects a file from within the document browser of an app, a number of delegate methods implemented within the document browser view controller will be called. These methods can be summarized as follows:

44.4.1 didRequestDocumentCreationWithHandler

This method is called when the user requests the creation of a new file from within the document browser. It is the responsibility of this method to provide a template file and to pass the URL for that file to the *importHandler* method. The template file can either be a file that is already bundled with the app, or a file that is created on demand within the delegate method. This method also provides the app with the opportunity to display a selection screen to choose the template type if the app supports more than one file type or template option.

The *importHandler* method interacts with the appropriate file provider to create the file in the designated location. If, for example, the user was browsing an iCloud Drive location when making the file creation request, the *importHandler* method will work with the iCloud Drive file provider to create the new file in that location.

In addition to providing the URL of the template file, the *importHandler* method also needs to be passed a value indicating whether the template file should be moved (*.move)* or copied *(.copy*) to the location on the file provider. If the delegate method created a temporary file to act as the template a move operation is more likely. For a template file bundled with the app it will make more sense to copy the file since it will need to be available for future creation operations.

If the user cancels the creation process the *importHandler* method must be called with a nil file URL and a none (*.none*) value. The following code shows an example method implementation which uses a bundled file named *template.txt* as the template:

```
func documentBrowser(_ controller: UIDocumentBrowserViewController,
  didRequestDocumentCreationWithHandler importHandler: @escaping (URL?,
   UIDocumentBrowserViewController.ImportMode) -> Void) {

    let newDocumentURL: URL? = Bundle.main.url(forResource: "template",
                                        withExtension: "txt")

    if newDocumentURL != nil {
        importHandler(newDocumentURL, .copy)
    } else {
        importHandler(nil, .none)
    }
}
```

44.4.2 didImportDocumentAt

This method is called when a new document has been successfully created by the file provider (in other words, the *importHandler* method call was successful). When called, this method is passed both the source URL of the local template file and the destination URL of the file now residing on the file provider. This method will typically display the view controller that is responsible for presenting the file content to the user:

```
func documentBrowser(_ controller: UIDocumentBrowserViewController,
  didImportDocumentAt sourceURL: URL, toDestinationURL destinationURL: URL) {

    presentDocument(at: destinationURL)
}
```

The *presentDocument* method called in the above example is a useful utility method included as part of the Document Based App project template for the document browser view controller class.

44.4.3 didPickDocumentURLs

This method is called when the user requests the opening of one or more existing files within the document browser. The URLs for the selected files are passed to the method in the form of an array and it is the responsibility of this method to pass these URLs to, and present, the document view controller. The default implementation for this method simply passes the first URL in the array to the *presentDocument* method:

```
func documentBrowser(_ controller: UIDocumentBrowserViewController,
  didPickDocumentURLs documentURLs: [URL]) {
```

```
        guard let sourceURL = documentURLs.first else { return }

    presentDocument(at: sourceURL)
}
```

44.4.4 failedToImportDocumentAt

Called when the document import request fails, this method should notify the user of the failure, details of which can be extracted from the error object:

```
func documentBrowser(_ controller: UIDocumentBrowserViewController,
  failedToImportDocumentAt documentURL: URL, error: Error?) {

        notifyUser(error?.localizedDescription
}
```

44.5 Customizing the Document Browser

A number of properties are available for customizing the document browser. The *allowsPickingMultipleItems* property controls whether the user is able to select multiple files:

```
allowsPickingMultipleItems = false
```

The *allowsDocumentCreation* property defines whether the user can create new files (essentially defining whether or not the create file buttons appear in the browser):

```
allowsDocumentCreation = true
```

The visual appearance of the browser can be changed by setting the *browserUserInterfaceStyle* property to dark, light or white:

```
browserUserInterfaceStyle = .dark
```

Finally the tint color used by the browser (primarily the color used for text foreground and icons) can be changed via the *tintColor* property:

```
view.tintColor = .yellow
```

44.6 Adding Browser Actions

Performing a long press on a file within the document browser displays the edit menu (Figure 44-4) containing a range of built-in options including copy, delete, rename and share.

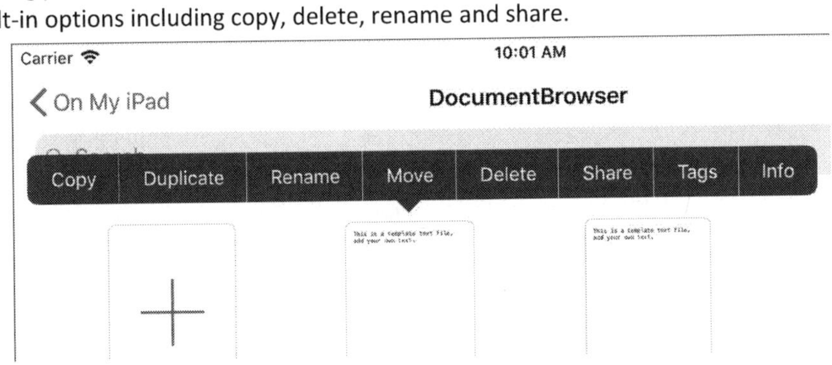

Figure 44-4

These options also appear in the navigation bar at the bottom of the screen when the user enters select mode by tapping the *Select* button in the top right hand corner of the browser window.

Custom actions may be added to these menus by assigning an array of UIDocumentBrowserActions objects to the *customActions* property of the document browser view controller instance. A UIDocumentBrowserActions object consists of a unique identifier, a string to appear on the button, an array of locations where the action is to be available (options are menu and navigation bar) and a completion handler to be called when the action is selected. The completion handler is provided with an array of URLs representing the files selected at the time the action was triggered.

The action object also needs to be configured with the file types for which it is to appear and a property setting indicating whether the action can work with multiple file selections. The following example creates and assigns a browser action for text and plain text file types that works only with single file selections and displays "Convert" as the action title:

```
let action = UIDocumentBrowserAction(identifier:
   "com.ebookfrenzy.docdemo.convert", localizedTitle: "Convert",
        availability: [.menu, .navigationBar], handler: { urls in

        // Code to be executed when action is selected

})

action.supportedContentTypes = ["public.text", "public.plain-text"]
action.supportsMultipleItems = false
customActions = [action]
```

44.7 Summary

The UIDocumentBrowserViewController class provides an easy way to build document browsing into iOS apps. Designed to integrate with the local filesystem, iCloud Drive and other third-party file providers such as Google Drive and DropBox, the document browser can be integrated with minimal programming effort. Integration primarily consists of adding a UIDocumentBrowserViewController as the root view controller, setting some *Info.plist* properties and writing some delegate methods. Much of the preparatory work is performed automatically when a new Xcode project is created using the Document Based App template.

Chapter 45

45. An iOS 12 Document Browser Tutorial

The objective of this chapter is to work through the creation of an iOS app that makes use of the UIDocumentBrowserViewController class to integrate document browsing support. The app will demonstrate using the Document Based App template to create an app that can navigate all available file providers in addition to creating, opening and editing text based documents.

45.1 Creating the DocumentBrowser Project

Launch Xcode and create a new iOS project named *DocumentBrowser* based on the Document Based App template with Swift selected as the programming language.

Once the project has loaded, select the *File -> New -> File...* menu option, scroll down the list of file types until the *Empty* option appears listed under *Other* as shown in Figure 45-1:

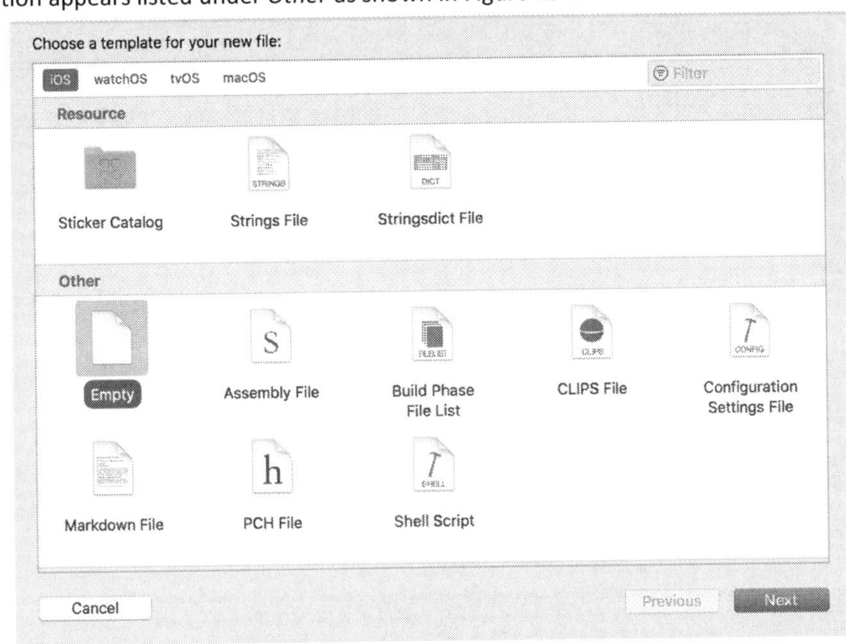

Figure 45-1

Click *Next* and name the file *template.txt* before clicking on the *Create* button. This file will serve as the template when the user creates new documents. Select the file in the project navigator and add a line of text which reads as follows:

```
This is a template text file, add your own text.
```

45.2 Declaring the Supported File Types

The app will be configured to support text files (both plain text and text files containing markup such as HTML). Within Xcode, select the DocumentBrowser target at the top of the project navigator panel and, within the settings screen, select the *Info* tab highlighted in Figure 45-2:

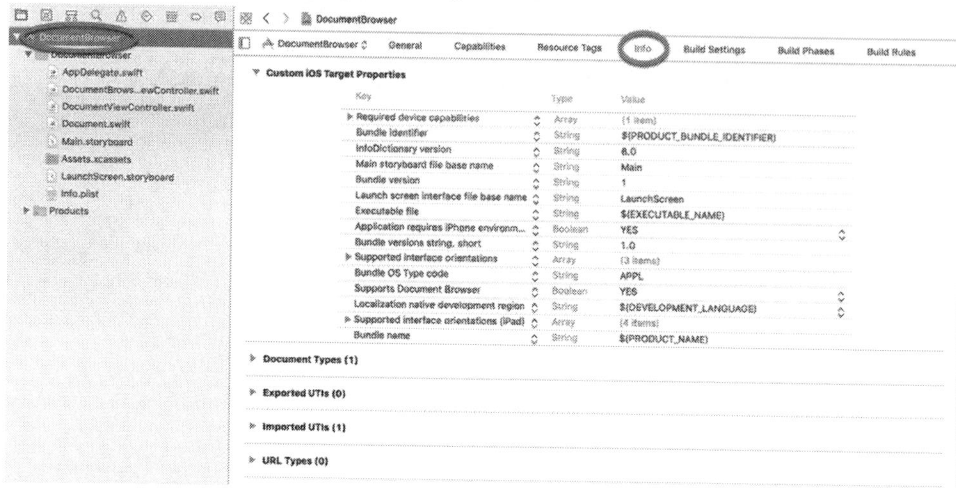

Figure 45-2

Check that the *Supports Document Browser* key value is set to *YES*, then click on the disclosure arrow next to the *Document Types* heading to unfold the list of types currently supported, followed by the arrow next to the *Additional document type properties* section:

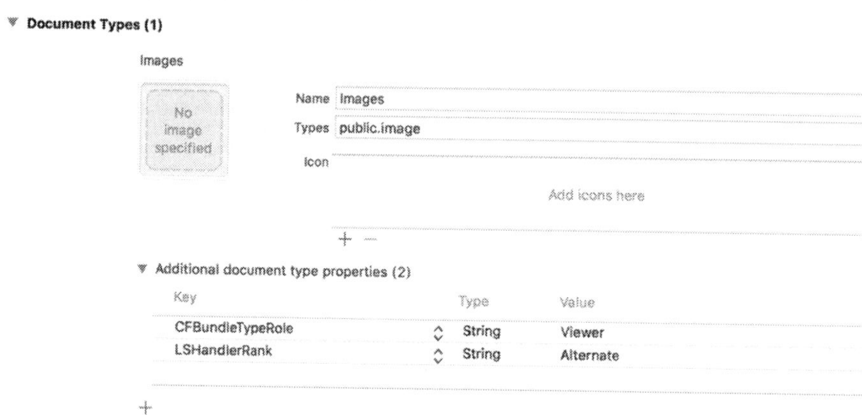

Figure 45-3

Clearly the project template has already been configured to support the viewing of images. Since this app is intended to edit text files, modify this entry as follows:

- **Name** – Text
- **Types** – public.text
- **CFBundleTypeRole** – Editor
- **LSHandlerRank** – Alternate

Next, add another document type by clicking on the + button located beneath the *Additional document type properties* section. Fill in the information for this entry as follows:

- **Name** – Plain Text
- **Types** – public.plain-text
- **CFBundleTypeRole** – Editor
- **LSHandlerRank** – Alternate

Build and run the app and make sure that the document browser appears and that it is possible to navigate around the local device or iCloud Drive for your account. Local files can be found by selecting the *On My iPad/iPhone* location option. If this option is not listed it usually means that no local files have been saved yet or that this option has not yet been enabled on the device. To check this, tap the Edit button located in the *Browse* navigation panel and check the switch settings:

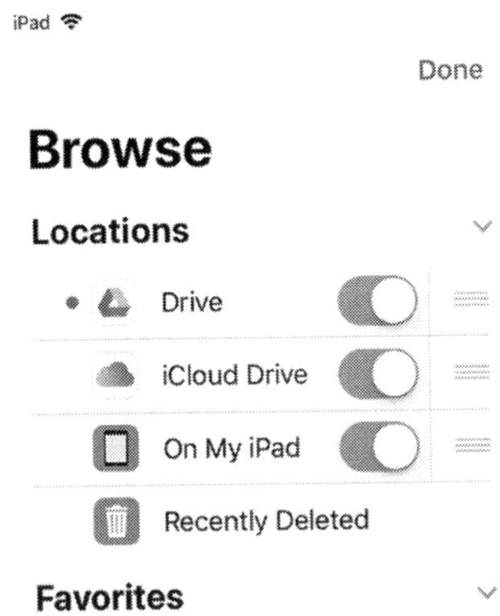

Figure 45-4

If the option is not listed, open the Photos app, select a photo and display the action menu (indicated by the arrow in Figure 45-5):

Figure 45-5

From the list of action options, select the *Save to Files* option and choose a location on your device before tapping the *Add* button. On returning to the DocumentBrowser app edit the settings once again at which point the *On My iPad/iPhone* switch should be visible.

45.3 Completing the didRequestDocumentCreationWithHandler Method

Edit the *DocumentBrowserViewController.swift* file and add code to create a temporary template file and to pass the URL for that file to the *importHandler* method. Note that since the template file is bundled with the app, the file is copied to the file provider rather than moved. This ensures the template is still available for future creation requests:

```
func documentBrowser(_ controller: UIDocumentBrowserViewController,
```

```
    didRequestDocumentCreationWithHandler importHandler: @escaping (URL?,
      UIDocumentBrowserViewController.ImportMode) -> Void) {

    let newDocumentURL: URL? = Bundle.main.url(forResource:
                                  "template", withExtension: "txt")

    if newDocumentURL != nil {
        importHandler(newDocumentURL, .copy)
    } else {
        importHandler(nil, .none)
    }
}
```

Run the app, select the *Browse* item in the navigation bar at the bottom of the screen and verify that the browser has defaulted to the *DocumentBrowser* folder on iCloud Drive as shown in Figure 45-6. If the browser is displaying a different location, navigate to the iCloud Drive *DocumentBrowser* folder before continuing.

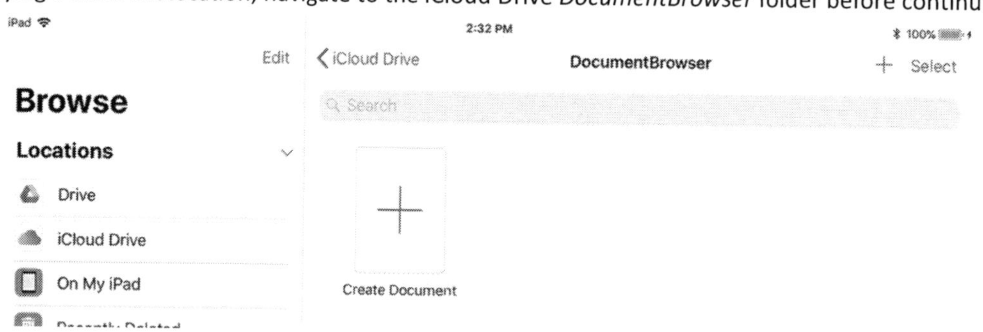

Figure 45-6

Click on the *Create Document* option, at which point the new document should be created and the document view controller displayed containing the name of the file and a Done button. Tap the Done button to return to the browser where the new file will be listed:

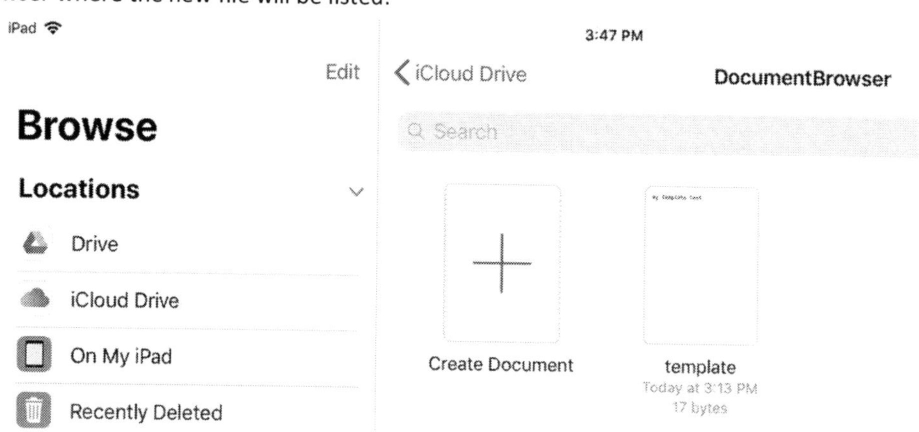

Figure 45-7

Before moving to the next step, scroll to the top of the *DocumentBrowserViewController.swift* class file and verify that the *allowsDocumentCreation* and *allowsPickingMultipleItems* properties are set to *true* and *false* respectively within the *viewDidLoad()* method:

```
allowsDocumentCreation = true
allowsPickingMultipleItems = false
```

45.4 Finishing the UIDocument Subclass

Xcode has provided a template UIDocument subclass in the *Document.swift* file. This class now needs to be completed so that it will read and write file content. The code for this is identical to that used in the chapter entitled *Managing Files using the iOS 12 UIDocument Class*. Edit the *Document.swift* file and modify it to reads as follows:

```
import UIKit

class Document: UIDocument {

    var userText: String? = ""

    override func contents(forType typeName: String) throws -> Any {

        if let content = userText {

            let length =
                content.lengthOfBytes(using: String.Encoding.utf8)
            return NSData(bytes:content, length: length)
        } else {
            return Data()
        }
    }

    override func load(fromContents contents: Any, ofType
                 typeName: String?) throws {

        if let userContent = contents as? Data {
            userText = NSString(bytes: (contents as AnyObject).bytes,
                       length: userContent.count,
                       encoding: String.Encoding.utf8.rawValue) as String?
        }
    }
}
```

45.5 Modifying the Document View Controller

The final task is to modify the document view controller so that it displays the content of the text file and allows that content to be edited and saved. Begin by loading the *Main.storyboard* file into Interface Builder and locating the *Document View Controller* Scene. Drag and drop a TextView and a Button view onto the scene. Change the text on the Button to "Save" and, using the Attributes inspector panel, change the *Font* setting to *Title 2* so that it matches the existing Done button. Position the new views so that the layout matches Figure 45-8 and set appropriate layout constraints:

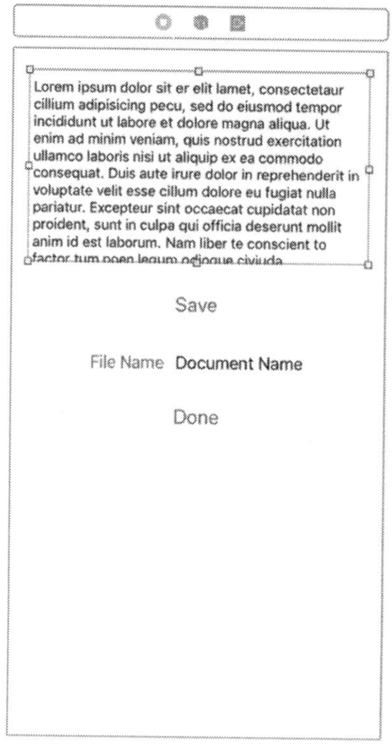

Figure 45-8

Double-click on the Latin text in the TextView and press the keyboard Delete key to remove it. Display the Assistant Editor, confirm that it is displaying the *DocumentViewController.swift* file and establish an outlet from the TextView to a variable named *documentText* and an action connection from the Save button to a method named *saveFile*.

Edit the *DocumentViewController.swift* file and modify the *document* variable and the template *viewWillLoad* method as follows:

```
.
.
var document: UIDocument?
var document: Document?

override func viewWillAppear(_ animated: Bool) {
    super.viewWillAppear(animated)

    document?.open(completionHandler: { (success) in
        if success {
            self.documentNameLabel.text =
                self.document?.fileURL.lastPathComponent
            self.documentText.text = self.document?.userText
```

```
        } else {
        }
    })
}
.
.
```

Finally, add code to the *saveFile* method to write the content of the TextView to the document:

```
@IBAction func save(_ sender: Any) {

    document?.userText = documentText.text

    if let url = document?.fileURL {
        document?.save(to: url,
                       for: .forOverwriting,
                       completionHandler: {(success: Bool) -> Void in
                        if success {
                            print("File overwrite OK")
                        } else {
                            print("File overwrite failed")
                        }
        })
    }
}
```

45.6 Testing the Document Browser App

Run the app and select the *template.txt* file added earlier in the chapter. When the document view controller appears, enter new text into the TextView before clicking on Save followed by Done to return to the document browser. The icon for the file should now reflect the extra text added to the file and, when selected, the document view controller should also load the new file content.

Place the app in the background and perform a long press on the app icon. When the pop up appears it should contain the recently created text file.

45.7 Summary

This chapter has provided a tutorial covering the steps involved in implementing a document browser using the Xcode Document Based App template. Topics covered included declaration of supported document types, creation of a template document file, implementation of the *didRequestDocumentCreationWithHandler* method, use of the UIDocument class and the customization of the document view controller.

Chapter 46

46. Synchronizing iOS 12 Key-Value Data using iCloud

When considering the use of iCloud in an application it is important to note that the Apple ecosystem is not limited to the iOS platform. In fact, it also encompasses a range of macOS based laptop and desktop computer systems, all of which have access to iCloud services. This increases the chance that a user will have the same app in one form or another on a number of different devices and platforms. Take, for the sake of an example, a hypothetical news magazine application. A user may have an instance of this application installed on both an iPhone and an iPad. If the user begins reading an article on the iPhone instance of the application and then switches to the same app on the iPad at a later time, the iPad application should take the user to the position reached in the article on the iPhone so that the user can resume reading.

This kind of synchronization between applications is provided by the Key-Value data storage feature of iCloud. The goal of this chapter is to provide an overview of this service and work through a very simple example of the feature in action in an iOS application.

46.1 An Overview of iCloud Key-Value Data Storage

The primary purpose of iCloud Key-Value data storage is to allow small amounts of data to be shared between instances of applications running on different devices, or even different applications on the same device. The data may be synchronized as long as it is encapsulated in either an array, dictionary, String, Date, Data, Boolean or Number object.

iCloud data synchronization is achieved using the NSUbiquitousKeyValueStore class introduced as part of the iOS 5 SDK. Values are saved with a corresponding key using the *set(forKey:)* method. For example, the following code fragment creates an instance of an NSUbiquitousKeyValueStore object and then saves a string value using the key "MyString":

```
var keyStore = NSUbiquitousKeyValueStore()
keyStore.set("Saved String", forKey: "MyString")
```

Once key-value pairs have been saved locally they will not be synchronized with iCloud storage until a call is made to the *synchronize* method of the NSUbiquitousKeyValueStore instance:

```
keyStore.synchronize()
```

It is important to note that a call to the synchronize method does not result in an immediate synchronization of the locally saved data with the iCloud store. iOS will, instead, perform the synchronization at what the Apple documentation refers to as "an appropriate later time".

A stored value may be retrieved by a call to the appropriate method corresponding to the data type to be retrieved (the format of which is *<datatype>*(forKey:)) and passing through the key as an argument. For example, the stored string in the above example may be retrieved as follows:

```
let storedString = keyStore.string(forKey: "MyString")
```

46.2 Sharing Data Between Applications

As with iCloud document storage, key-value data storage requires the implementation of appropriate iCloud entitlements. In this case the application must have the *com.apple.developer.ubiquity-kvstore-identifier* entitlement key configured in the project's entitlements file. The value assigned to this key is used to identify which applications are able to share access to the same iCloud stored key-value data.

If, for example, the *ubiquity-kvstore-identifier* entitlement key for an application named *MyApp* is assigned a value of *ABCDE12345.com.mycompany.MyApp* (where ABCDEF12345 is the developer's unique team or individual ID) then any other applications using the same entitlement value will also be able to access the same stored key-value data. This, by definition, will be any instance of the *MyApp* running on multiple devices, but applies equally to entirely different applications (for example *MyOtherApp*) if they also use the same entitlement value.

46.3 Data Storage Restrictions

iCloud key-value data storage is provided to meet the narrow requirement of performing essential synchronization between application instances, and the data storage limitations imposed by Apple clearly reflect this.

The amount of data that can be stored per key-value pair is 1MB. The per-application key-value storage limit is 1024 individual keys which, combined, must also not exceed 1MB in total.

46.4 Conflict Resolution

In the event that two application instances make changes to the same key-value pair, the most recent change is given precedence.

46.5 Receiving Notification of Key-Value Changes

An application may register to be notified when stored values are changed by another application instance. This is achieved by setting up an observer on the *NSUbiquitousKeyValueStoreDidChangeExternallyNotification* notification. This notification is triggered when a change is made to any key-value pair in a specified key value store and is passed an array of strings containing the keys that were changed together with an NSNumber indicating the reason for the change. In the event that the available space for the key-value storage has been exceeded this number will match the *NSUbiquitousKeyValueStoreQuotaViolationChange* constant value.

46.6 An iCloud Key-Value Data Storage Example

The remainder of this chapter is devoted to the creation of an application that uses iCloud key-value storage to store a key with a string value using iCloud. In addition to storing a key-value pair, the application will also configure an observer to receive notification when the value is changed by another application instance.

Before starting on this project it is important to note that membership to the Apple Developer Program will be required as outlined in *Joining the Apple Developer Program.*

Begin the application creation process by launching Xcode and creating a new *Single View Application* project named *iCloudKeys* with *Swift* selected as the programming language.

46.7 Enabling the Application for iCloud Key Value Data Storage

A mandatory step in the development of the application is to configure the appropriate iCloud entitlement. This is achieved by selecting the application target at the top of the Xcode project navigator panel and selecting the *Capabilities* tab in the main project settings panel. Switch on iCloud support and enable the *Key-value storage* option:

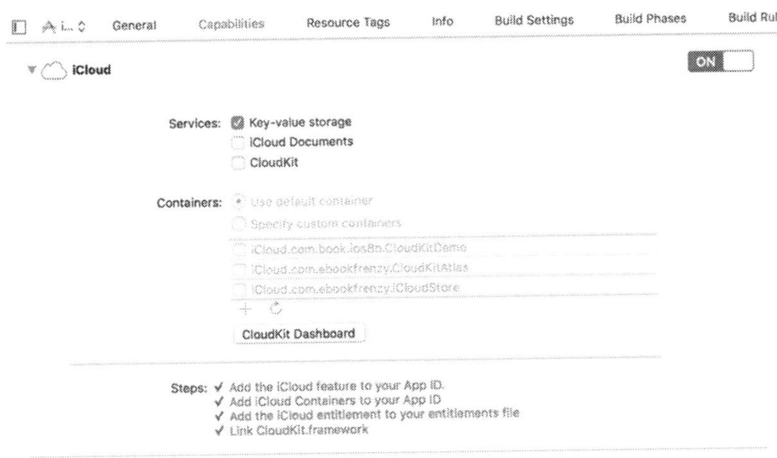

Figure 46-1

Once selected, Xcode will create an entitlements file for the project named *iCloudKeys.entitlements* containing the appropriate iCloud entitlements key-value pairs. Select the entitlements file from the project navigator and note the value assigned to the *iCloud Key-Value Store* key. By default this is typically comprised of your team or individual developer ID combined with the application's Bundle identifier. Any other applications that use the same value for the entitlement key will share access to the same iCloud-based key-value data stored by this application.

46.8 Designing the User Interface

The application is going to consist of a text field into which a string may be entered by the user and a button which, when selected, will save the string to the application's iCloud key-value data store. Select the *Main.storyboard* file, display the Library panel (*View -> Utilities -> Show Library*) and drag and drop the two objects onto the view canvas. Double-click on the button object and change the text to *Store Key*. The completed view should resemble Figure 46-2:

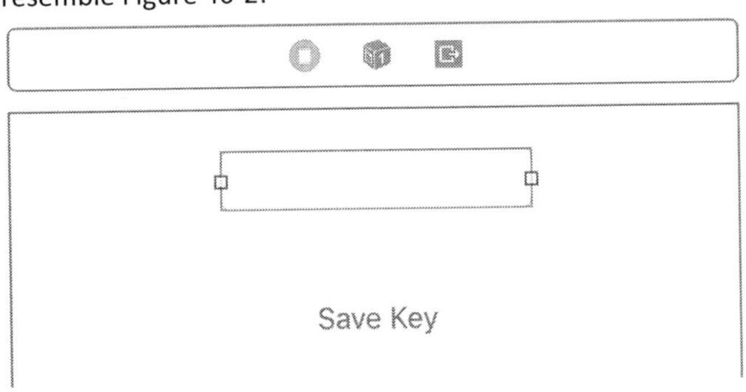

Figure 46-2

Click on the background View component in the layout, display the *Resolve Auto Layout Issues* menu and select the *Reset to Suggested Constraints* option listed under *All Views in the View Controller*.

Select the text field object in the view canvas, display the Assistant Editor panel and verify that the editor is displaying the contents of the *ViewController.swift* file. Ctrl-click on the text field object and drag to a position just below the class declaration line in the Assistant Editor. Release the line and in the resulting connection dialog establish an outlet connection named *textField*.

Finally, Ctrl-click on the button object and drag the line to the area immediately beneath the newly created outlet in the Assistant Editor panel. Release the line and, within the resulting connection dialog, establish an Action method on the *Touch Up Inside* event configured to call a method named *saveKey*.

46.9 Implementing the View Controller

In addition to the action and outlet references created above, an instance of the NSUbiquitousKeyStore class will be needed. Choose the *ViewController.swift* file, therefore, and modify it as follows:

```
class ViewController: UIViewController {

    var keyStore: NSUbiquitousKeyValueStore?

    @IBOutlet weak var textField: UITextField!
.
.
.
```

46.10 Modifying the viewDidLoad Method

The next step is to add a method to perform the initialization and call it from the *viewDidLoad* method of the view controller. Remaining within the *ViewController.swift* file modify the code so that it reads as follows:

```
override func viewDidLoad() {
    super.viewDidLoad()

    initCloud()
}

func initCloud() {

    keyStore = NSUbiquitousKeyValueStore()

    let storedString = keyStore?.string(forKey: "MyString")

    if let stringValue = storedString {
        textField.text = stringValue
    }

    NotificationCenter.default.addObserver(self,
        selector: #selector(
        ViewController.ubiquitousKeyValueStoreDidChange),
        name: NSUbiquitousKeyValueStore.didChangeExternallyNotification,
        object: keyStore)
}
```

The method begins by allocating and initializing an instance of the NSUbiquitousKeyValueStore class and assigning it to the keyStore variable. Next, the *string(forKey:)* method of the keyStore object is called to check if the *MyString* key is already in the key-value store. If the key exists, the string value is assigned to the *text* property of the text field object via the textField outlet.

Finally, the method sets up an observer to call the *ubiquitousKeyValueStoreDidChange* method when the stored key value is changed by another application instance.

Having implemented the code in the *initCloud* method the next step is to write the *ubiquitousKeyValueStoreDidChange* method.

46.11 Implementing the Notification Method

Within the context of this example application the *ubiquitousKeyValueStoreDidChange* method, which is triggered when another application instance modifies an iCloud stored key-value pair, is provided to notify the user of the change via an alert message and to update the text in the text field with the new string value. The code for this method, which needs to be added to the *ViewController.swift* file is as follows:

```
@objc func ubiquitousKeyValueStoreDidChange(notification: NSNotification) {

    let alert = UIAlertController(title: "Change detected",
            message: "iCloud key-value-store change detected",
        preferredStyle: UIAlertController.Style.alert)

    let cancelAction = UIAlertAction(title: "OK",
            style: .cancel, handler: nil)

    alert.addAction(cancelAction)
    self.present(alert, animated: true,
                completion: nil)
    textField.text = keyStore?.string(forKey: "MyString")
}
```

46.12 Implementing the saveData Method

The final coding task involves implementation of the *saveData* action method. This method will be called when the user touches the button in the user interface and needs to be implemented in the *ViewController.swift* file:

```
@IBAction func saveKey(_ sender: Any) {
    keyStore?.set(textField.text, forKey: "MyString")
    keyStore?.synchronize()
}
```

The code for this method is quite simple. The *set(forKey:)* method of the keyStore object is called, assigning the current text property of the user interface textField object to the “MyString” key. The synchronize method of the keyStore object is then called to ensure that the key-value pair is synchronized with the iCloud store.

46.13 Testing the Application

Click on the run button in the Xcode toolbar and, once the application is installed and running on the device or iOS Simulator, enter some text into the text field and touch the *Save Key* button. Stop the application from running by clicking on the stop button in the Xcode toolbar then re-launch by clicking the run button. When the application reloads, the text field should be primed with the saved value string.

In order to test the change notification functionality, install the application on both a device and the iOS simulator. With the application running on both, change the text on the iOS Simulator instance and save the key. After a short delay the device based instance of the app will detect the change, display the alert and update the text field to the new value:

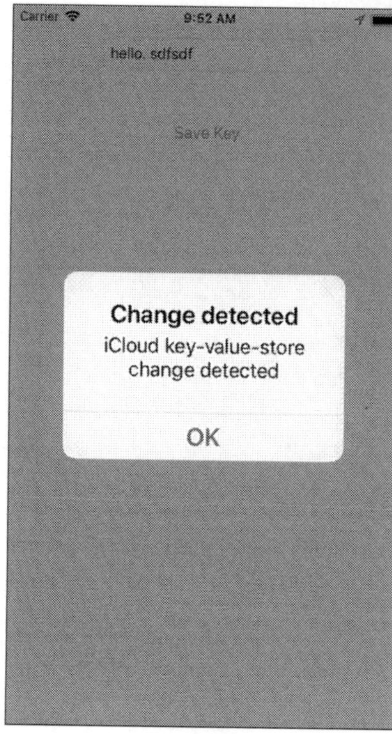

Figure 46-3

46.14 Summary

iOS key-value data storage allows small amounts of data in the form of array, dictionary, String, Date, Data, Boolean or Number objects to be shared between instances of applications running on different devices running iOS and macOS. This chapter has outlined the steps involved in enabling and implementing this data sharing including enabling key-value storage support and configuring a listener to detect data changes.

Chapter 47

47. iOS 12 Database Implementation using SQLite

Whilst the preceding chapters of this book have looked at data storage within the context of iOS based applications, this coverage has been limited to using basic file and directory handling. In many instances, by far the most effective data storage and retrieval strategy requires the use of some form of database management system.

In order to address this need, the iOS SDK includes everything necessary to integrate SQLite based databases into iOS applications. The goal of this chapter, therefore, is to provide an overview of how to use SQLite to perform basic database operations within your iOS application. Once the basics have been covered, the next chapter (*An Example SQLite based iOS 12 Application using Swift and FMDB*) will work through the creation of an actual application that uses a SQLite database to store and retrieve data.

47.1 What is SQLite?

SQLite is an embedded, relational database management system (RDBMS). Most relational databases (Oracle and MySQL being prime examples) are standalone server processes that run independently, and in cooperation with, applications that require database access. SQLite is referred to as *embedded* because it is provided in the form of a library that is linked into applications. As such, there is no standalone database server running in the background. All database operations are handled internally within the application through calls to functions contained in the SQLite library.

The developers of SQLite have placed the technology into the public domain with the result that it is now a widely deployed database solution.

SQLite is written in the C programming language and therefore using SQLite from within Swift code either requires some complex handling of C function calls, data types and pointers, or the easier approach of using an existing SQLite wrapper as a layer between SQLite and Swift. In this chapter we will look at one such wrapper in the form of FMDB.

For additional information about SQLite refer to *https://www.sqlite.org*.

47.2 Structured Query Language (SQL)

Data is accessed in SQLite databases using a high level language known as Structured Query Language. This is usually abbreviated to SQL and pronounced *sequel*. SQL is a standard language used by most relational database management systems. SQLite conforms mostly to the SQL-92 standard.

While some basic SQL statements will be used within this chapter, a detailed overview of SQL is beyond the scope of this book. There are, however, many other resources that provide a far better overview of SQL than we could ever hope to provide in a single chapter here.

47.3 Trying SQLite on macOS

For readers unfamiliar with databases in general and SQLite in particular, diving right into creating an iOS application that uses SQLite may seem a little intimidating. Fortunately, macOS is shipped with SQLite preinstalled, including an interactive environment for issuing SQL commands from within a Terminal window. This is both a useful way to learn about SQLite and SQL, and also an invaluable tool for identifying problems with databases created by applications in the iOS simulator.

To launch an interactive SQLite session, open a Terminal window on your macOS system, change directory to a suitable location and run the following command:

```
sqlite3 ./mydatabase.db

SQLite version 3.6.12
Enter ".help" for instructions
Enter SQL statements terminated with a ";"
sqlite>
```

At the *sqlite>* prompt, commands may be entered to perform tasks such as creating tables and inserting and retrieving data. For example, to create a new table in our database with fields to hold ID, name, address and phone number fields the following statement is required:

```
create table contacts (id integer primary key autoincrement, name text,
address text, phone text);
```

Note that each row in a table must have a *primary key* that is unique to that row. In the above example we have designated the ID field as the primary key, declared it as being of type *integer* and asked SQLite to automatically increment the number each time a row is added. This is a common way to make sure that each row has a unique primary key. The remaining fields are each declared as being of type *text.*

To list the tables in the currently selected database use the *.tables* statement:

```
sqlite> .tables
contacts
```

To insert records into the table:

```
sqlite> insert into contacts (name, address, phone) values ("Bill Smith",
"123 Main Street, California", "123-555-2323");
sqlite> insert into contacts (name, address, phone) values ("Mike Parks", "10
Upping Street, Idaho", "444-444-1212");
```

To retrieve all rows from a table:

```
sqlite> select * from contacts;
1|Bill Smith|123 Main Street, California|123-555-2323
2|Mike Parks|10 Upping Street, Idaho|444-444-1212
```

To extract a row that meets specific criteria:

```
sqlite> select * from contacts where name="Mike Parks";
2|Mike Parks|10 Upping Street, Idaho|444-444-1212
```

To exit from the sqlite3 interactive environment:

```
sqlite> .exit
```

When running an iOS application in the iOS Simulator environment, any database files will be created on the file system of the computer on which the simulator is running. This has the advantage that you can navigate to the location of the database file, load it into the sqlite3 interactive tool and perform tasks on the data to identify possible problems occurring in the application code. If, for example, an application creates a database file named *contacts.db* in its documents directory, the file will be located on the host system in the following folder:

```
/Users/<user>/Library/Developer/CoreSimulator/Devices/<simulator id>/data/Containers/Data/Application/<id>/Documents
```

Where *<user>* is the login name of the user logged into the macOS system, *<simulator id>* is the id of the simulator session and *<id>* is the unique ID of the application.

47.4 Preparing an iOS Application Project for SQLite Integration

By default, the Xcode environment does not assume that you will be including SQLite in your application. When developing SQLite based applications a few additional steps are required to ensure the code will compile when the application is built. First, the project needs to be configured to include the *libsqlite3.tbd* dynamic library during the link phase of the build process. To achieve this select the target entry in the Xcode project navigator (the top entry with the product name) to display the summary information. Select the *Build Phases* tab to display the build information.

The *Link Binary with Libraries* section lists the libraries and frameworks already included in the project. To add another library or framework click on the '+' button to display the full list. From this list, select the required item (in this case *libsqlite3.tbd*) and click *Add.*

47.5 SQLite, Swift and Wrappers

As previously discussed, SQLite is written in the C programming language. While it was still possible to use the C-based SQLite API from within Objective-C code with relative ease, this is not the case when programming in Swift without dealing with complex issues when bridging the gap between C and Swift. A common solution to this dilemma involves the use of a SQLite "wrapper". A number of wrappers are now available for this purpose many of which show considerable potential. For the purposes of this book, however, we will be working with the FMDB wrapper. Although this is essentially an Objective-C wrapper, it can be used easily from within Swift code. FMDB has been chosen for the examples in this book because it has been available for some time, is considered to be stable and feature rich and will be familiar to the many developers who have previously used it with Objective-C. FMDB is an open-source project released under the terms of the MIT license.

Details on how to obtain FMDB and incorporate it into an iOS Xcode project are covered in detail in the next chapter (*An Example SQLite based iOS 12 Application using Swift and FMDB*).

47.6 Key FMDB Classes

When implementing a database using SQLite with FMDB it will be necessary to utilize a number of FMDB classes contained within the wrapper. A summary of the most commonly used classes is as follows:

- **FMDatabase** – Used to represent a single SQLite database. The object on which SQL statements are executed from within code.
- **FMResultSet** – Used to hold the results of a SQL query operation on an FMDatabase instance.
- **FMDatabaseQueue** – A version of FMDatabase designed to allow database queries to be performed from multiple threads.

For more detailed information, the FMDB Class Reference documentation is available online at:

http://ccgus.github.io/fmdb/html/Classes/FMDatabase.html

47.7 Creating and Opening a Database

Before work can commence on a database it must first be created and opened. The following code opens the database file at the path specified by *<database file path>*. If the database file does not already exist it will be created when the FMDatabase instance is initialized:

```
let myDatabase = FMDatabase(path: <database file path>)

if (myDatabase.open()) {
    // Database is ready
} else {
    print("Error: \(myDatabase.lastErrorMessage())")
}
```

47.8 Creating a Database Table

Database data is organized into *tables.* Before data can be stored into a database, therefore, a table must first be created. This is achieved using the SQL CREATE TABLE statement. The following code example illustrates the creation of a table named *contacts* using FMDB:

```
let sql_stmt = "CREATE TABLE IF NOT EXISTS CONTACTS (ID INTEGER PRIMARY KEY
AUTOINCREMENT, NAME TEXT, ADDRESS TEXT, PHONE TEXT)"

if !myDatabase.executeStatements(sql_stmt) {
     // Table creation failed
}
```

47.9 Extracting Data from a Database Table

Those familiar with SQL will be aware that data is retrieved from databases using the SELECT statement. Depending on the criteria defined in the statement, it is typical for more than one data row to be returned. It is important, therefore, to learn how to retrieve data from a database using the SQLite FMDB wrapper.

In the following code excerpt, a SQL SELECT statement is used to extract the address and phone fields from all the rows of a database table named *contacts* via a call to the *executeQuery* method of the FMDatabase instance:

```
let querySQL = "SELECT address, phone FROM CONTACTS WHERE name =
          '\(name.text!)'"

do {
    let results:FMResultSet? = try myDatabase.executeQuery(querySQL,
                                                   values: nil)
} catch {
    print("Error: \(error.localizedDescription)")
}
```

On completion of the query execution, the FMResults object returned from the method call contains the results of the query. Regardless of whether one or more results are expected, the *next* method of the returned FMResultSet object must be called. A *false* return value from the *next* method call indicates either that no results were returned, or that the end of the result set has been reached.

In the event that results were returned, the data can be accessed using the column name as a key. The following code, for example, outputs the "address" and "phone" values for all of the matching records returned as the result of the above query operation:

```
while results?.next() == true {
    print(results?.stringForColumn("address"))
    print(results?.stringForColumn("phone"))
}
```

47.10 Closing a SQLite Database

When an application has finished working on a database it is important that the database be closed. This is achieved with a call to the *close* method of the FMDatabase instance:

```
myDatabase.close()
```

47.11 Summary

In this chapter we have looked at the basics of implementing a database within an iOS application using the embedded SQLite relational database management system together with the FMDB wrapper to make access to the database possible from within Swift code. In the next chapter we will put this theory into practice and work through an example that creates a functional iOS application that is designed to store data in a database.

Chapter 48

48. An Example SQLite based iOS 12 Application using Swift and FMDB

In the chapter entitled *iOS 12 Database Implementation using SQLite* the basic concepts of integrating a SQLite based database into iOS applications were discussed. In this chapter we will put this knowledge to use by creating a simple example application that demonstrates SQLite-based database implementation and management on iOS using Swift and the FMDB wrapper.

48.1 About the Example SQLite Application

The focus of this chapter is the creation of a somewhat rudimentary iOS application that is designed to store contact information (names, addresses and telephone numbers) in a SQLite database. In addition to data storage, a feature will also be implemented to allow the user to search the database for the address and phone number of a specified contact name. Some knowledge of SQL and SQLite is assumed throughout the course of this tutorial. Those readers unfamiliar with these technologies in the context of iOS application development are encouraged to first read the *previous chapter* before proceeding.

48.2 Creating and Preparing the SQLite Application Project

Begin by launching the Xcode environment and creating a new iOS *Single View Application* project named *Database* configured for the Swift programming language.

Once the project has been created, the next step is to configure the project to include the SQLite dynamic library *(libsqlite3.tbd)* during the link phase of the build process. Failure to include this library will result in build errors.

To add this library, select the target entry in the Xcode project navigator (the top entry with the product name) to display the *General* information panel. Select the *Build Phases* tab to display the build information. The *Link Binary with Libraries* section lists the libraries and frameworks already included in the project. To add another library or framework click on the '+' button to display the full list. From this list search for, and then select *libsqlite3.tbd* and click *Add.*

48.3 Checking Out the FMDB Source Code

In order to use FMDB, the source files for the wrapper will need to be added to the project. The source code for FMDB is stored on the GitHub source code repository and can be downloaded directly onto your development system from within Xcode. Begin by selecting the Xcode *Source Control -> Clone...* menu option to display the Clone dialog:

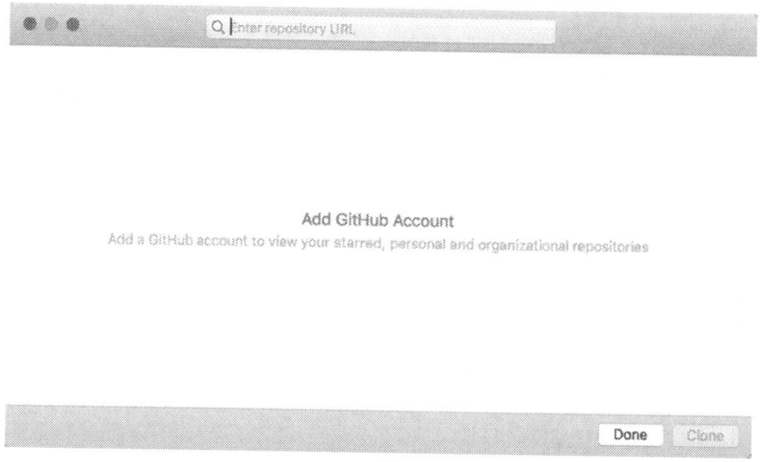

Figure 48-1

In the dialog, enter the following GitHub URL into the repository URL field and click on *Clone*:

https://github.com/ccgus/fmdb.git

Choose a location on your local file system into which the files are to be checked out before clicking on the *Clone* button. Xcode will check out the files and save them at the designated location. A new Xcode project window will also open containing the FMDB source files. Within the project navigator panel, unfold the *fmdb -> Source -> fmdb* folder to list the source code files (highlighted in Figure 48-2) for the FMDB wrapper.

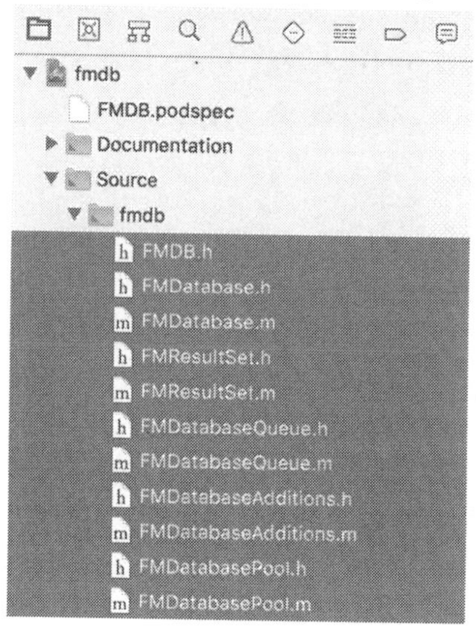

Figure 48-2

Shift-click on the first and last of the files in the *fmdb* folder to select all of the .h and .m files in the navigator panel and drag and drop them onto the Database project folder in the Xcode window containing the Database project. On the options panel click on the *Finish* button. Since these files are written in Objective-C rather than Swift, Xcode will offer to configure and add an *Objective-C bridging header* file as shown in Figure 48-3:

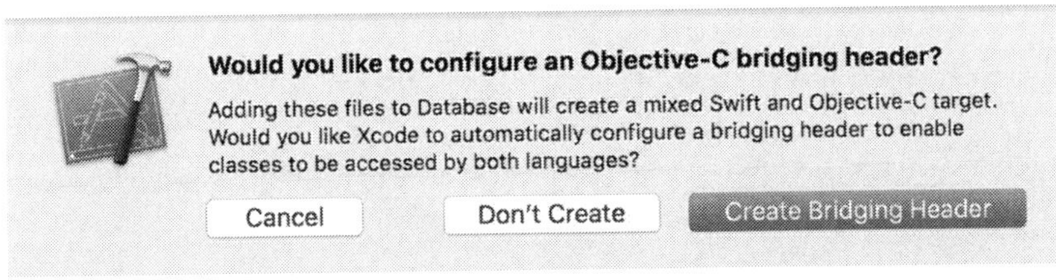

Would you like to configure an Objective-C bridging header?
Adding these files to Database will create a mixed Swift and Objective-C target. Would you like Xcode to automatically configure a bridging header to enable classes to be accessed by both languages?
Cancel
Don't Create
Create Bridging Header

Figure 48-3

Click on the option to add the bridging file. Once added, it will appear in the project navigator panel with the name *Database-Bridging-Header.h*. Select this file and edit it to add a single line to import the FMDB.h file:

```
#import "FMDB.h"
```

With the project fully configured to support SQLite from within Swift application projects, the remainder of the project may now be completed.

48.4 Designing the User Interface

The next step in developing our example SQLite iOS application involves the design of the user interface. Begin by selecting the *Main.storyboard* file to edit the user interface and drag and drop components from the Library panel onto the view canvas and edit properties so that the layout appears as illustrated in Figure 48-4:

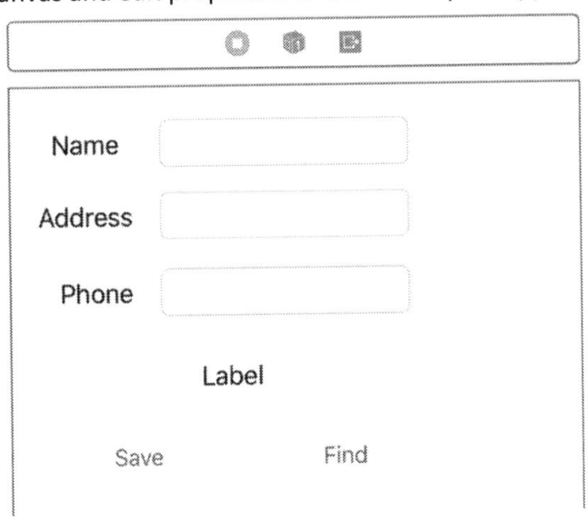

Figure 48-4

Before proceeding, stretch the status label (located above the two buttons) so that it is the same width as the combined labels and text field views and change the text alignment in the Attributes Inspector so that it is centered. Finally, edit the label and remove the word "Label" so that it is blank, display the *Resolve Auto Layout Issues* menu and select the *Reset to Suggested Constraints* option listed under *All Views in View Controller*.

Select the top-most text field object in the view canvas, display the Assistant Editor panel and verify that the editor is displaying the contents of the *ViewController.swift* file. Ctrl-click on the text field object again and drag to a position just below the class declaration line in the Assistant Editor. Release the line and in the resulting connection dialog establish an outlet connection named *name*.

Repeat the above steps to establish outlet connections for the remaining text fields and the label object to properties named *address*, *phone* and *status* respectively.

Ctrl-click on the *Save* button object and drag the line to the area immediately beneath the existing *viewDidLoad* method in the Assistant Editor panel. Release the line and, within the resulting connection dialog, establish an Action method on the *Touch Up Inside* event configured to call a method named *saveContact.* Repeat this step to create an action connection from the *Find* button to a method named *findContact.*

Close the Assistant Editor panel, select the *ViewController.swift* file and add a variable to store a reference to the database path:

```
class ViewController: UIViewController {

    @IBOutlet weak var name: UITextField!
    @IBOutlet weak var address: UITextField!
    @IBOutlet weak var phone: UITextField!
    @IBOutlet weak var status: UILabel!

    var databasePath = String()

    override func viewDidLoad() {
        super.viewDidLoad()

    }

    @IBAction func saveContact(_ sender: Any) {
    }

    @IBAction func findContact(_ sender: Any) {
    }
.
.
}
```

48.5 Creating the Database and Table

When the application is launched it will need to check whether the database file already exists and, if not, create both the database file and a table within the database in which to store the contact information entered by the user. The code to perform this task will be placed in a method named *initDB* which will be called from the *viewDidLoad* method of our view controller class. Select the *ViewController.swift* file and modify it as follows:

```
override func viewDidLoad() {
    super.viewDidLoad()
    initDB()
}

func initDB() {
    let filemgr = FileManager.default
    let dirPaths = filemgr.urls(for: .documentDirectory,
                                in: .userDomainMask)
```

```
    databasePath = dirPaths[0].appendingPathComponent("contacts.db").path

    if !filemgr.fileExists(atPath: databasePath) {

        let contactDB = FMDatabase(path: databasePath)

        if (contactDB.open()) {
            let sql_stmt = "CREATE TABLE IF NOT EXISTS CONTACTS (ID INTEGER
PRIMARY KEY AUTOINCREMENT, NAME TEXT, ADDRESS TEXT, PHONE TEXT)"
            if !(contactDB.executeStatements(sql_stmt)) {
                print("Error: \(contactDB.lastErrorMessage())")
            }
            contactDB.close()
        } else {
            print("Error: \(contactDB.lastErrorMessage())")
        }
    }
}
```

The code in the above method performs the following tasks:

- Identifies the application's Documents directory and constructs a path to the *contacts.db* database file.
- Checks if the database file already exists.
- If the file does not yet exist the code creates the database by creating an FMDatabase instance initialized with the database file path. If the database creation is successful it is then opened via a call to the *open* method of the new database instance.
- Prepares a SQL statement to create the *contacts* table in the database and executes it via a call to the FMDB *executeStatements* method of the database instance.
- Closes the database

48.6 Implementing the Code to Save Data to the SQLite Database

The saving of contact data to the database is the responsibility of the *saveContact* action method. This method will need to open the database file, extract the text from the three text fields and construct and execute a SQL INSERT statement to add this data as a record to the database. Having done this, the method will then need to close the database.

In addition, the code will need to clear the text fields ready for the next contact to be entered, and update the status label to reflect the success or failure of the operation.

In order to implement this behavior, therefore, we need to modify the template method created previously as follows:

```
@IBAction func saveContact(_ sender: Any) {
    let contactDB = FMDatabase(path: databasePath)

    if (contactDB.open()) {

        let insertSQL = "INSERT INTO CONTACTS (name, address, phone) VALUES
('\(name.text ?? "")', '\(address.text ?? "")', '\(phone.text ?? "")')"
```

```
        do {
            try contactDB.executeUpdate(insertSQL, values: nil)
        } catch {
            status.text = "Failed to add contact"
            print("Error: \(error.localizedDescription)")
        }

        status.text = "Contact Added"
        name.text = ""
        address.text = ""
        phone.text = ""

    } else {
        print("Error: \(contactDB.lastErrorMessage())")
    }
}
```

The next step in our application development process is to implement the action for the find button.

48.7 Implementing Code to Extract Data from the SQLite Database

As previously indicated, the user will be able to extract the address and phone number for a contact by entering the name and touching the find button. To this end, the *Touch Up Inside* event of the find button has been connected to the *findContact* method, the code for which is outlined below:

```
@IBAction func findContact(_ sender: Any) {
    let contactDB = FMDatabase(path: databasePath)

    if (contactDB.open()) {
        let querySQL =
         "SELECT address, phone FROM CONTACTS WHERE name = '\(name.text!)'"

        do {
            let results:FMResultSet? = try contactDB.executeQuery(querySQL,
                                                          values: nil)

            if results?.next() == true {
                address.text = results?.string(forColumn: "address")
                phone.text = results?.string(forColumn: "phone")
                status.text = "Record Found"
            } else {
                status.text = "Record not found"
                address.text = ""
                phone.text = ""
            }
        } catch {
```

```
            print("Error: \(error.localizedDescription)")
        }
        contactDB.close()

    } else {
        print("Error: \(contactDB.lastErrorMessage())")
    }
}
```

This code opens the database and constructs a SQL SELECT statement to extract any records in the database that match the name entered by the user into the name text field. The SQL statement is then executed via a call to the *executeQuery* method of the FMDatabase instance. The search results are returned in the form of an FMResultSet object.

The *next* method of the FMResultSet object is called to find out if at least one match was found. In the event that a match was found, the values corresponding to the address and phone columns are extracted and assigned to the text fields in the user interface.

48.8 Building and Running the Application

The final step is to build and run the application. Click on the run button located in the toolbar of the main Xcode project window. Once running, enter details for a few contacts, pressing the *Save* button after each entry. Be sure to check the status label to ensure the data is being saved successfully. Finally, enter the name of one of your contacts and click on the *Find* button. Assuming the name matches a previously entered record, the address and phone number for that contact should be displayed and the status label updated with the message "Record Found":

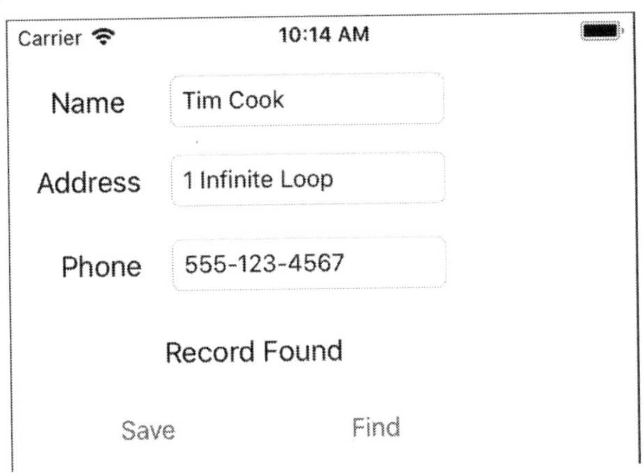

Figure 48-5

48.9 Summary

In this chapter we have looked at the basics of storing data on iOS using the SQLite database environment using the FMDB wrapper approach to using SQLite from within Swift code. For developers unfamiliar with SQL and reluctant to learn it, an alternative method for storing data in a database involves the use of the Core Data framework. This topic will be covered in detail in the next chapter entitled *Working with iOS 12 Databases using Core Data*.

Chapter 49

49. Working with iOS 12 Databases using Core Data

The preceding chapters covered the concepts of database storage using the SQLite database. In these chapters the assumption was made that the iOS application code would directly manipulate the database using SQLite API calls to construct and execute SQL statements. While this is a perfectly good approach for working with SQLite in many cases, it does require knowledge of SQL and can lead to some complexity in terms of writing code and maintaining the database structure. This complexity is further compounded by the non-object oriented nature of the SQLite API functions. In recognition of these shortcomings, Apple introduced the *Core Data Framework*. Core Data is essentially a framework that places a wrapper around the SQLite database (and other storage environments) enabling the developer to work with data in terms of Swift objects without requiring any knowledge of the underlying database technology.

We will begin this chapter by defining some of the concepts that comprise the Core Data model before providing an overview of the steps involved in working with this framework. Once these topics have been covered, the next chapter will work through *An iOS 12 Core Data Tutorial*.

49.1 The Core Data Stack

Core Data consists of a number of framework objects that integrate to provide the data storage functionality. This stack can be visually represented as illustrated in Figure 49-1.

As we can see from Figure 49-1, the iOS based application sits on top of the stack and interacts with the managed data objects handled by the managed object context. Of particular significance in this diagram is the fact that although the lower levels in the stack perform a considerable amount of the work involved in providing Core Data functionality, the application code does not interact with them directly.

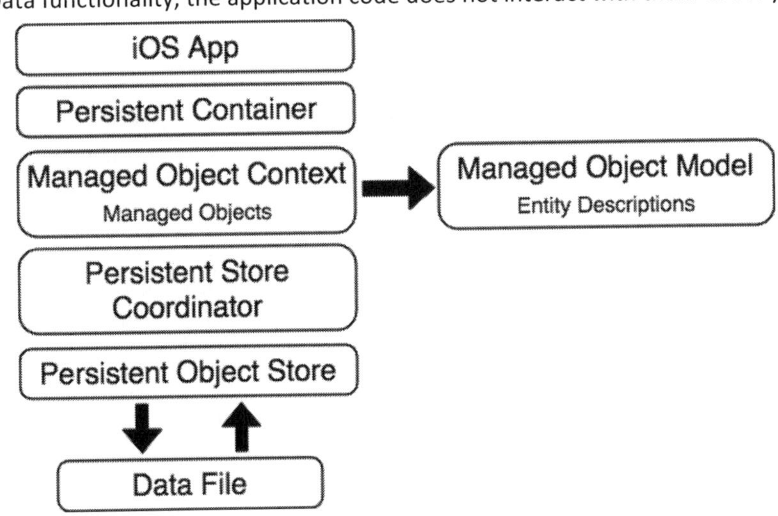

Figure 49-1

Before moving on to the more practical areas of working with Core Data it is important to spend some time explaining the elements that comprise the Core Data stack in a little more detail.

49.2 Persistent Container

The *persistent container* handles the creation of the Core Data stack and is designed to be easily subclassed to add additional application specific methods to the base Core Data functionality. Once initialized, the persistent container instance provides access to the *managed object context.*

49.3 Managed Objects

Managed objects are the objects that are created by your application code to store data. A managed object may be thought of as a row or a record in a relational database table. For each new record to be added, a new managed object must be created to store the data. Similarly, retrieved data will be returned in the form of managed objects, one for each record matching the defined retrieval criteria. Managed objects are actually instances of the NSManagedObject class, or a subclass thereof. These objects are contained and maintained by the *managed object context*.

49.4 Managed Object Context

Core Data based applications never interact directly with the persistent store. Instead, the application code interacts with the managed objects contained in the managed object context layer of the Core Data stack. The context maintains the status of the objects in relation to the underlying data store and manages the relationships between managed objects defined by the *managed object model*. All interactions with the underlying database are held temporarily within the context until the context is instructed to save the changes, at which point the changes are passed down through the Core Data stack and written to the persistent store.

49.5 Managed Object Model

So far we have focused on the management of data objects but have not yet looked at how the data models are defined. This is the task of the *Managed Object Model* which defines a concept referred to as *entities*.

Much as a class description defines a blueprint for an object instance, entities define the data model for managed objects. In essence, an entity is analogous to the schema that defines a table in a relational database. As such, each entity has a set of attributes associated with it that define the data to be stored in managed objects derived from that entity. For example, a *Contacts* entity might contain *name, address* and *phone number* attributes.

In addition to attributes, entities can also contain *relationships, fetched properties* and *fetch requests*:

- **Relationships** – In the context of Core Data, relationships are the same as those in other relational database systems in that they refer to how one data object relates to another. Core Data relationships can be *one-to-one, one-to-many* or *many-to-many.*
- **Fetched property** – This provides an alternative to defining relationships. Fetched properties allow properties of one data object to be accessed from another data object as though a relationship had been defined between those entities. Fetched properties lack the flexibility of relationships and are referred to by Apple's Core Data documentation as "weak, one way relationships" best suited to "loosely coupled relationships".
- **Fetch request** – A predefined query that can be referenced to retrieve data objects based on defined predicates. For example, a fetch request can be configured into an entity to retrieve all contact objects where the name field matches "John Smith".

49.6 Persistent Store Coordinator

The *persistent store coordinator* is responsible for coordinating access to multiple *persistent object stores*. As an iOS developer you will never directly interact with the persistence store coordinator and, in fact, will very rarely need to develop an application that requires more than one persistent object store. When multiple stores are required, the coordinator presents these stores to the upper layers of the Core Data stack as a single store.

49.7 Persistent Object Store

The term *persistent object store* refers to the underlying storage environment in which data are stored when using Core Data. Core Data supports three disk-based and one memory-based persistent store. Disk based options consist of SQLite, XML and binary. By default, the iOS SDK will use SQLite as the persistent store. In practice, the type of store being used is transparent to you as the developer. Regardless of your choice of persistent store, your code will make the same calls to the same Core Data APIs to manage the data objects required by your application.

49.8 Defining an Entity Description

Entity descriptions may be defined from within the Xcode environment. When a new project is created with the option to include Core Data, a template file will be created named *<projectname>*.xcdatamodeld. Selecting this file in the Xcode project navigator panel will load the model into the entity editing environment as illustrated in Figure 49-2:

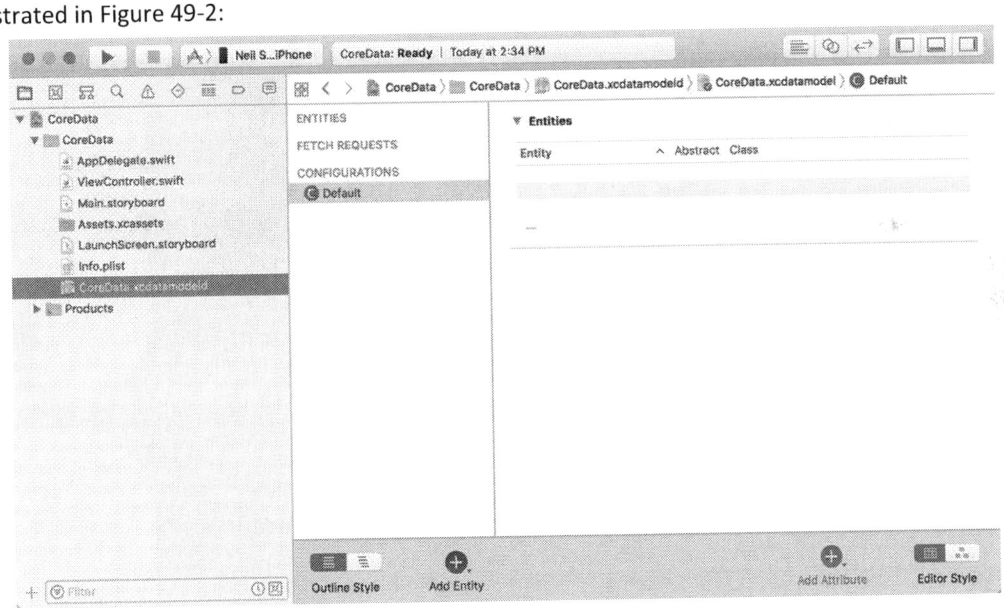

Figure 49-2

Create a new entity by clicking on the *Add Entity* button located in the bottom panel. The new entity will appear as a text box in the *Entities* list. By default this will be named *Entity*. Double-click on this name to change it.

To add attributes to the entity, click on the *Add Attribute* button located in the bottom panel, or use the + button located beneath the *Attributes* section. In the *Attributes* panel, name the attribute and specify the type and any other options that are required.

Repeat the above steps to add more attributes and additional entities.

The Xcode entity environment also allows relationships to be established between entities. Assume, for example, two entities named *Contacts* and *Sales*. In order to establish a relationship between the two tables select the *Contacts* entity and click on the + button beneath the *Relationships* panel. In the detail panel, name the relationship, specify the destination as the *Sales* entity and any other options that are required for the relationship. Once the relationship has been established it is, perhaps, best viewed graphically by selecting the *Table, Graph* option in the *Editor Style* control located in the bottom panel:

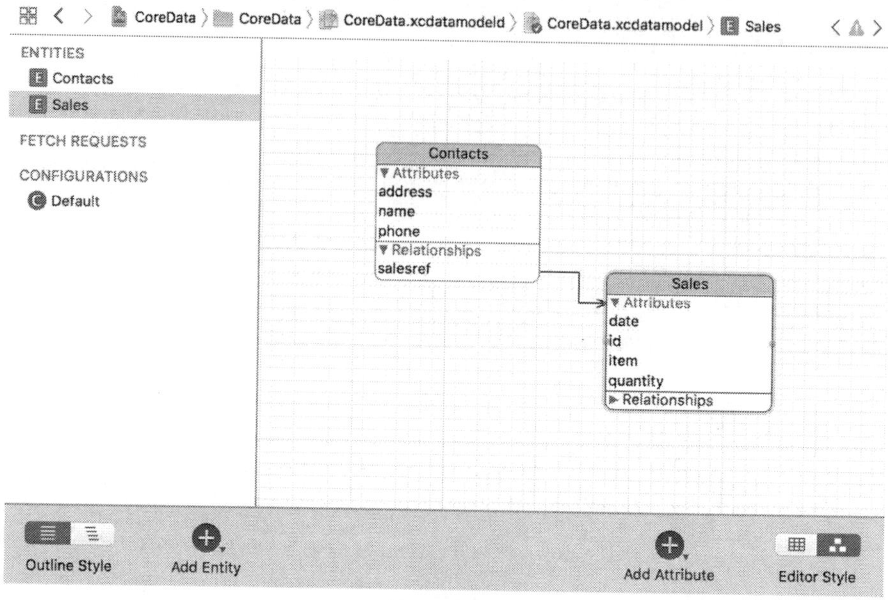

Figure 49-3

As demonstrated, Xcode makes the process of entity description creation fairly straightforward. While a detailed overview of the process is beyond the scope of this book there are many other resources available that are dedicated to the subject.

49.9 Initializing the Persistent Container

The persistent container is initialized by creating a new NSPersistentContainer instance, passing through the name of the model to be used and then making a call to the *loadPersistentStores* method of that object as follows:

```
let container = NSPersistentContainer(name: "CoreDataDemo")
    container.loadPersistentStores(completionHandler: {
                                (description, error) in
        if let error = error {
            fatalError("Unable to load persistent stores: \(error)")
        }
    })
```

49.10 Obtaining the Managed Object Context

Since many of the Core Data methods require the managed object context as an argument, the next step after defining entity descriptions often involves obtaining a reference to the context. This can be achieved by accessing the viewContext property of the persistent container instance:

```
let managedObjectContext = persistentContainer.viewContext
```

49.11 Getting an Entity Description

Before managed objects can be created and manipulated in code, the corresponding entity description must first be loaded. This is achieved by calling the *entity(forName:in:)* method of the NSEntityDescription class, passing through the name of the required entity and the context as arguments. The following code fragment obtains the description for an entity with the name *Contacts:*

```
let entity = NSEntityDescription.entity(
                forName: "Contacts", in: context)
```

49.12 Setting the Attributes of a Managed Object

As previously discussed, entities and the managed objects from which they are instantiated contain data in the form of attributes. Once a managed object instance has been created as outlined above, those attribute values can be used to store the data before the object is saved. Assuming a managed object named *contact* with attributes named *name, address* and *phone* respectively, the values of these attributes may be set as follows prior to the object being saved to storage:

```
contact.name = "John Smith"
contact.address = "1 Infinite Loop"
contact.phone = "555-564-0980"
```

49.13 Saving a Managed Object

Once a managed object instance has been created and configured with the data to be stored it can be saved to storage using the *save* method of the managed object context as follows:

```
do {
    try context.save()
} catch let error {
    // Handle error
}
```

49.14 Fetching Managed Objects

Once managed objects are saved into the persistent object store it is highly likely that those objects and the data they contain will need to be retrieved. Objects are retrieved by executing a fetch request and are returned in the form of an array. The following code assumes that both the context and entity description have been obtained prior to making the fetch request:

```
let request: NSFetchRequest<Contacts> = Contacts.fetchRequest()
request.entity = entity

do {
    let results = try context.fetch(request as!
                        NSFetchRequest<NSFetchRequestResult>)
} catch let error {
    // Handle error
}
```

Upon execution, the *results* array will contain all the managed objects retrieved by the request.

49.15 Retrieving Managed Objects based on Criteria

The preceding example retrieved all of the managed objects from the persistent object store for a specified entity. More often than not only managed objects that match specified criteria are required during a retrieval operation. This is performed by defining a *predicate* that dictates criteria that a managed object must meet in order to be eligible for retrieval. For example, the following code implements a predicate in order to extract only those managed objects where the *name* attribute matches "John Smith":

```
let request: NSFetchRequest<Contacts> = Contacts.fetchRequest()
request.entity = entity

let pred = NSPredicate(format: "(name = %@)", "John Smith")
request.predicate = pred

do {
        let results = try context.fetch(request as!
                        NSFetchRequest<NSFetchRequestResult>)
} catch let error {
    // Handle error
}
```

49.16 Accessing the Data in a Retrieved Managed Object

Once results have been returned from a fetch request, the data within the returned objects may be accessed using *keys* to reference the stored values. The following code, for example, accesses the first result from a fetch operation results array and extracts the values for the *name*, *address* and *phone* keys from that managed object:

```
let match = results[0] as! NSManagedObject

let nameString = match.value(forKey: "name") as! String
let addressString = match.value(forKey: "address") as! String
let phoneString = match.value(forKey: "phone") as! String
```

49.17 Summary

The Core Data Framework stack provides a flexible alternative to directly managing data using SQLite or other data storage mechanisms. By providing an object-oriented abstraction layer on top of the data the task of managing data storage is made significantly easier for the iOS application developer. Now that the basics of Core Data have been covered the next chapter entitled *An iOS 12 Core Data Tutorial* will work through the creation of an example application.

50. An iOS 12 Core Data Tutorial

In the previous chapter, entitled *Working with iOS 12 Databases using Core Data*, an overview of the Core Data stack was provided, together with details of how to write code to implement data persistence using this infrastructure. In this chapter we will continue to look at Core Data in the form of a step by step tutorial that implements data persistence using Core Data in an iOS 12 application.

50.1 The Core Data Example Application

The application developed in this chapter will take the form of the same contact database application used in previous chapters, the objective being to allow the user to enter name, address and phone number information into a database and then search for specific contacts based on the contact's name.

50.2 Creating a Core Data based Application

As is often the case, we can rely on Xcode to do much of the preparatory work for us when developing an iOS application that will use Core Data. To create the example application project, launch Xcode and select the option to create a new project. In the new project window, select the *Single View Application* option. In the next screen make sure that the language is set to *Swift*. Enter *CoreDataDemo* into the *Product Name* field, enable the *Use Core Data* checkbox and click *Next* to select a location to store the project files.

Xcode will create the new project and display the main project window. In addition to the usual files that are present when creating a new project, this time an additional file named *CoreDataDemo.xcdatamodeld* is also created. This is the file where the entity descriptions for our data model are going to be stored.

50.3 Creating the Entity Description

The entity description defines the model for our data, much in the way a schema defines the model of a database table. To create the entity for the Core Data application, select the *CoreDataDemo.xcdatamodeld* file to load the entity editor:

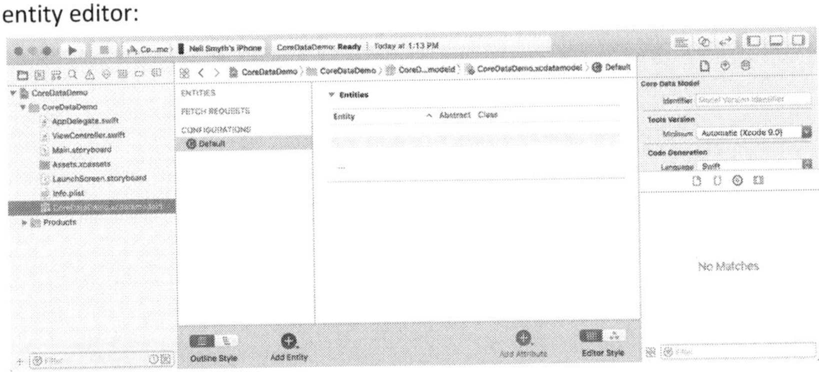

Figure 50-1

To create a new entity, click on the *Add Entity* button located in the bottom panel. Double-click on the new *Entity* item that appears beneath the *Entities* heading and change the entity name to *Contacts*. With the entity created, the next step is to add some attributes that represent the data that is to be stored. To do so, click on the *Add Attribute* button. In the *Attribute* pane, name the attribute *name* and set the Type to *String*. Repeat these steps to add two other String attributes named *address* and *phone* respectively:

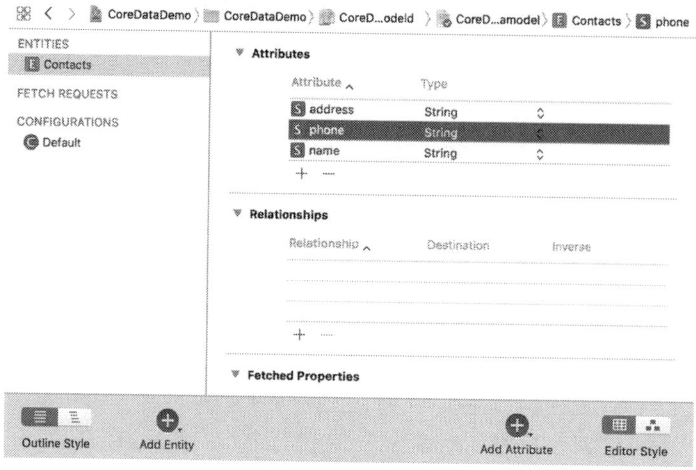

Figure 50-2

50.4 Designing the User Interface

With the entity defined, now is a good time to design the user interface and establish the outlet and action connections. Select the *Main.storyboard* file to begin the design work. The user interface and corresponding connections used in this tutorial are the same as those in previous data persistence chapters. The completed view should, once again, appear as outlined in Figure 50-3 (note that objects may be cut and pasted from the previous *Database* project to save time in designing the user interface layout):

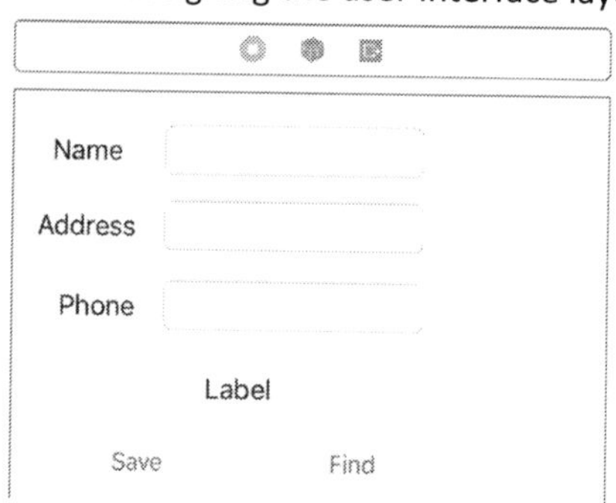

Figure 50-3

Before proceeding, stretch the status label (located above the two buttons) so that it covers most of the width of the view and configure the alignment attribute so that the text is centered. Finally, edit the label and remove the word "Label" so that it is blank.

Select the top most text field object in the view canvas, display the Assistant Editor panel and verify that the editor is displaying the contents of the *ViewController.swift* file. Ctrl-click on the text field object again and drag to a position just below the class declaration line in the Assistant Editor. Release the line and in the resulting connection dialog establish an outlet connection named *name*.

Repeat the above steps to establish outlet connections for the remaining text fields and the label object to properties named *address, phone* and *status* respectively.

Ctrl-click on the *Save* button object and drag the line to the area immediately beneath the *viewDidLoad* method in the Assistant Editor panel. Release the line and, within the resulting connection dialog, establish an Action method on the *Touch Up Inside* event configured to call a method named *saveContact*. Repeat this step to create an action connection from the *Find* button to a method named *findContact*.

50.5 Initializing the Persistent Container

The next step in this project is to initialize the Core Data stack and obtain a reference to the managed object context. Begin by editing the *ViewController.swift* file to import the Core Data framework and to declare a variable in which to store a reference to the managed object context object:

```
import UIKit
import CoreData

class ViewController: UIViewController {

    var managedObjectContext: NSManagedObjectContext?
.
.
```

Next, implement a method named *initCoreStack* to initialize the persistent container and access the managed object context. Also modify the *viewDidLoad* method so that this new method is called when the View Controller starts:

```
override func viewDidLoad() {
    super.viewDidLoad()

    initCoreStack()
}

func initCoreStack() {
    let container = NSPersistentContainer(name: "CoreDataDemo")
    container.loadPersistentStores(completionHandler: {
                                (description, error) in
        if let error = error {
            fatalError("Unable to load persistent stores: \(error)")
        } else {
            self.managedObjectContext = container.viewContext
        }
    })
}
.
.
```

50.6 Saving Data to the Persistent Store using Core Data

When the user touches the Save button the *saveContact* method is called. It is within this method, therefore, that we must implement the code to create and store managed objects containing the data entered by the user. Select the *ViewController.swift* file, scroll down to the template *saveContact* method and implement the code as follows:

```
@IBAction func saveContact(_ sender: Any) {
```

```
    if let context = managedObjectContext, let entityDescription =
        NSEntityDescription.entity(forEntityName: "Contacts",
                                   in: context) {

        let contact = Contacts(entity: entityDescription,
                               insertInto: managedObjectContext)

        contact.name = name.text
        contact.address = address.text
        contact.phone = phone.text

        do {
            try managedObjectContext?.save()
            name.text = ""
            address.text = ""
            phone.text = ""
            status.text = "Contact Saved"
        } catch let error {
            status.text = error.localizedDescription
        }
    }
}
```

The above code uses the managed object context to obtain the Contacts entity description and then uses it to create a new instance of the Contacts managed object subclass. The name, address and phone attribute values of this managed object are then set to the current text field values. Finally, the context is instructed to save the changes to the persistent store with a call to the context's *save* method. The success or otherwise of the operation is reported on the status label and, in the case of a successful outcome, the text fields are cleared ready for the next contact to be entered.

50.7 Retrieving Data from the Persistent Store using Core Data

In order to allow the user to search for a contact it is now necessary to implement the *findContact* action method. As with the save method, this method will need to identify the entity description for the Contacts entity and then create a predicate to ensure that only objects with the name specified by the user are retrieved from the store. Matching objects are placed in an array from which the attributes for the first match are retrieved using the *value(forKey:)* method and displayed to the user. A full count of the matches is displayed in the status field.

The code to perform these tasks is as follows:

```
@IBAction func findContact(_ sender: Any) {
    if let context = managedObjectContext {
        let entityDescription =
            NSEntityDescription.entity(forEntityName: "Contacts",
                                       in: context)
```

```
        let request: NSFetchRequest<Contacts> = Contacts.fetchRequest()
        request.entity = entityDescription

        if let name = name.text {
            let pred = NSPredicate(format: "(name = %@)", name)
            request.predicate = pred
        }

        do {
            var results =
                try context.fetch(request as!
                    NSFetchRequest<NSFetchRequestResult>)

            if results.count > 0 {
                let match = results[0] as! NSManagedObject

                name.text = match.value(forKey: "name") as? String
                address.text = match.value(forKey: "address") as? String
                phone.text = match.value(forKey: "phone") as? String
                status.text = "Matches found: \(results.count)"
            } else {
                status.text = "No Match"
            }

        } catch let error {
            status.text = error.localizedDescription
        }
    }
}
```

50.8 Building and Running the Example Application

The final step is to build and run the application. Click on the run button located in the toolbar of the main Xcode project window. If errors are reported check the syntax of the code you have written, using the error messages provided by Xcode as guidance. Once the application compiles it will launch and load into the device or iOS Simulator. Enter some test contacts (some with the same name). Having entered some test data, enter the name of the contact for which you created duplicate records and tap the Find button. The address and phone number of the first matching record should appear together with an indication in the status field of the total number of matching objects that were retrieved.

50.9 Summary

The Core Data Framework provides an abstract, object-oriented interface to database storage within iOS applications. As demonstrated in the example application created in this chapter, Core Data does not require any knowledge of the underlying database system and, combined with the visual entity creation features of Xcode, allows database storage to be implemented with relative ease.

Chapter 51

51. An Introduction to CloudKit Data Storage on iOS 12

The CloudKit Framework is one of the more remarkable developer features available in the iOS SDK solely because of the ease with which it allows for the structured storage and retrieval of data on Apple's iCloud database servers.

It is not an exaggeration to state that CloudKit allows developers to work with cloud-based data and media storage without any prior database experience and with a minimal amount of coding effort.

This chapter will provide a high level introduction to the various elements that make up CloudKit, build a foundation for the CloudKit tutorials presented in the next two chapters and provide a basis from which to explore other capabilities of CloudKit.

51.1 An Overview of CloudKit

The CloudKit Framework provides applications with access to the iCloud servers hosted by Apple and provides an easy to use way to store, manage and retrieve data and other asset types (such as large binary files, videos and images) in a structured way. This provides a platform for users to store private data and access it from multiple devices, and also for the developer to provide data that is publicly available to all the users of an application.

The first step in learning to use CloudKit is to gain an understanding of the key components that constitute the CloudKit framework.

51.2 CloudKit Containers

Each CloudKit enabled application has at least one container on iCloud. The container for an application is represented in the CloudKit Framework by the CKContainer class and it is within these containers that the databases reside. Containers may also be shared between multiple applications.

A reference to an application's default cloud container can be obtained via the *default* property of the CKContainer class:

```
let container = CKContainer.default
```

51.3 CloudKit Public Database

Each cloud container contains a single public database. This is the database into which is stored data that is needed by all users of an application. A map application, for example, might have a set of data about locations and routes that are applicable to all users of the application. This data would be stored within the public database of the application's cloud container.

CloudKit databases are represented within the CloudKit Framework by the CKDatabase class. A reference to the public cloud database for a container can be obtained via the *publicCloudDatabase* property of a container instance:

```
let publicDatabase = container.publicCloudDatabase
```

51.4 CloudKit Private Databases

Private cloud databases are used to store data that is private to each specific user. Each cloud container, therefore, will contain one private database for each user of the application. A reference to the private cloud database can be obtained via the *privateCloudDatabase* property of the container object:

```
let privateDatabase = container.privateCloudDatabase
```

51.5 Data Storage and Transfer Quotas

Data and assets stored in the public cloud database of an application count against the storage quota of the application. Anything stored in a private database, on the other hand, is counted against the iCloud quota of the corresponding user. Applications should, therefore, try to minimize the amount of data stored in private databases to avoid users having to unnecessarily purchase additional iCloud storage space.

At the time of writing, each application begins with 50MB of public database storage space and 5GB of space for assets free of charge. In addition, each application starts with an initial 25MB per day of free data transfer for assets and 250Kb for database data.

For each additional application user, the free storage quotas increase by 100MB and 1MB for assets and database data respectively. Data transfer quotas also increase by 0.5MB per day and 5KB per day for assets and data for each additional user. As long as these quota limits are not exceeded, the resources remain free up to a limit of 1PB for assets and 10TB for databases. Maximum data transfer quotas are 5TB per day for assets and 50GB per day for databases.

The latest quota limits can be reviewed online at:

https://developer.apple.com/icloud/documentation/cloudkit-storage/

51.6 CloudKit Records

Data is stored in both the public and private databases in the form of records. Records are represented by the CKRecord class and are essentially dictionaries of key-value pairs where keys are used to reference the data values stored in the record. A wide range of data types can be stored in a record including strings, numbers, dates, arrays, locations, data objects and references to other records. New key-value fields may be added to a record at any time without the need to perform any database restructuring.

Records in a database are categorized by a *record type* which must be declared when the record is created and takes the form of a string value. In practice this should be set to a meaningful value that assists in identifying the purpose of the record type. Records in a cloud database can be added, updated, queried and deleted using a range of methods provided by the CKDatabase class.

The following code demonstrates the creation of a CKRecord instance initialized with a record type of "Schools" together with three key-value pair fields:

```
let myRecord = CKRecord(recordType: "Schools")

myRecord.setObject("Silver Oak Elementary" as CKRecordValue?,
                                    forKey: "schoolname")
myRecord.setObject("100 Oak Street" as CKRecordValue?,
                                    forKey: "address")
myRecord.setObject(150 as CKRecordValue?, forKey: "studentcount")
```

Once created and initialized, the above record could be saved via a call to the *save* method of a database instance as follows:

```
publicDatabase.save(myRecord, completionHandler:
    ({returnRecord, error in

            if let err = error {
                // save operation failed
            } else {
                // save operation succeeded
            }
    }))
```

The method call passes through the record to be saved and specifies a completion handler in the form of a closure expression to be called when the operation returns.

Alternatively, a group of record operations may be performed in a single transaction using the CKModifyRecordsOperation class. This class also allows timeout durations to be specified for the transaction, together with completion handlers to be called at various stages during the process. The following code, for example, uses the CKModifyRecordsOperation class to add three new records and delete two existing records in a single operation. The code also establishes timeout parameters and implements all three completion handlers. Once the modify operation object has been created and configured, it is added to the database for execution:

```
let modifyRecordsOperation = CKModifyRecordsOperation(
            recordsToSave: [myRecord1, myRecord2, myRecord3],
            recordIDsToDelete: [myRecord4, myRecord5])

let configuration = CKOperation.Configuration()

configuration.timeoutIntervalForRequest =  10
configuration.timeoutIntervalForResource = 10

modifyRecordsOperation.configuration = configuration

modifyRecordsOperation.perRecordCompletionBlock = { record, error in
    // Called after each individual record operation completes
}

modifyRecordsOperation.perRecordProgressBlock = { record, progress in
    // Called to update the status of an individual operation
    // progress is a Double value indicating progress so far
}

modifyRecordsOperation.modifyRecordsCompletionBlock = {
            records, recordIDs, error in
    // Called after all of the record operations are complete
}
```

```
privateDatabase?.add(modifyRecordsOperation)
```

It is important to understand that CloudKit operations are predominantly asynchronous, enabling the calling application to continue to function while the CloudKit Framework works in the background to handle the transfer of data to and from the iCloud servers. In most cases, therefore, a call to CloudKit API methods will require that a completion handler be provided. This handler code will then be executed when the corresponding operation completes and passed results data where appropriate, or an error object in the event of a failure. Given the asynchronous nature of CloudKit operations, it is important to implement robust error handling within the completion handler.

The steps involved in creating, updating, querying and deleting records will be covered in greater detail in the next chapter entitled *An iOS 12 CloudKit Example*.

The overall concept of an application cloud container, private and public databases and records can be visualized as illustrated in Figure 51-1:

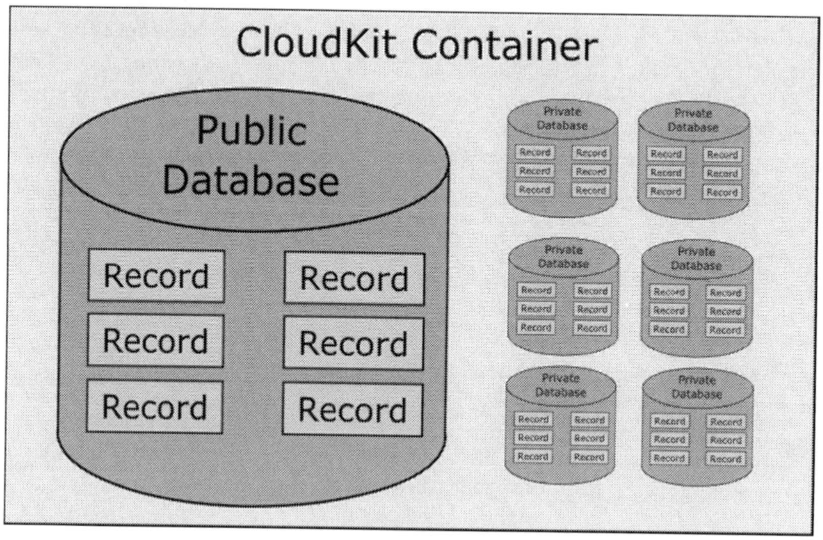

Figure 51-1

51.7 CloudKit Record IDs

Each CloudKit record has associated with it a unique record ID represented by the CKRecordID class. If a record ID is not specified when a record is first created, one is provided for it automatically by the CloudKit framework.

51.8 CloudKit References

CloudKit references are implemented using the CKReference class and provide a way to establish relationships between different records in a database. A reference is established by creating a CKReference instance for an originating record and assigning to it the record to which the relationship is to be targeted. The CKReference object is then stored in the originating record as a key-value pair field. A single record can contain multiple references to other records.

Once a record is configured with a reference pointing to a target record, that record is said to be *owned* by the target record. When the owner record is deleted, all records that refer to it are also deleted and so on down the chain of references (a concept referred to as *cascading deletes*).

51.9 CloudKit Assets

In addition to data, CloudKit may also be used to store larger assets such as audio or video files, large documents, binary data files or images. These assets are stored within CKAsset instances. Assets can only be stored as part of a record and it is not possible to directly store an asset in a cloud database. Once created, an asset is added to a record as just another key-value field pair. The following code, for example, demonstrates the addition of an image asset to a record:

```
let imageAsset = CKAsset(fileURL: imageURL)

let myRecord = CKRecord(recordType: "Vacations")

myRecord.setObject("London" as CKRecordValue?, forKey: "city")
myRecord.setObject(imageAsset as CKRecordValue?, forKey: "photo")
```

At the time of writing, individual CloudKit assets are limited in size to 250Mb.

51.10 Record Zones

CloudKit record zones (CKRecordZone) provide a mechanism for relating groups of records within a private database. Unless a record zone is specified when a record is saved to the cloud it is placed in the *default zone* of the target database. Custom zones can be added to private databases and used to organize related records and perform tasks such as writing to multiple records simultaneously in a single transaction. Each record zone has associated with it a unique record zone ID (CKRecordZoneID) which must be referenced when adding new records to a zone.

Adding a record zone to a private database involves the creation of a CKRecordZone instance initialized with the name to be assigned to the zone:

```
let myRecordZone = CKRecordZone(zoneName: "MyRecordZone")
```

The zone is then saved to the database via a call to the *save* method of a CKDatabase instance, passing through the CKRecordZone instance together with a completion handler to be called upon completion of the operation:

```
privateDatabase.save(myRecordZone, completionHandler:
        ({returnRecord, error in
            if let err = error {
               // Zone creation failed
            } else {
                // Zone creation succeeded
            }
        }))
```

Once the record zone has been established on the cloud database, records may be added to that zone by including the record type and a record ID when creating CKRecord instances:

```
let myRecord = CKRecord(recordType: "Addresses",
                        recordID: CKRecord.ID(zoneID: zoneId))
```

In the above code the zone ID is passed through to the CKRecord.ID initializer to obtain an ID containing a unique CloudKit generated record name. The following is a typical example of a CloudKit generated record name:

```
88F54808-2606-4176-A004-7E8AEC210B04
```

To manually specify the record name used within the record ID, modify the code to read as follows:

```
let myRecord = CKRecord(recordType: "Houses",
    recordID: CKRecord.ID(recordName: "MyRecordName", zoneID: zoneId))
```

Care should be taken, however, when manually specifying a record name to ensure that each record has a unique record name.

When the record is subsequently saved to the database it will be associated with the designated record zone.

51.11 CloudKit Sharing

Clearly, a CloudKit record contained within the public database of an app is accessible to all users of that app. Situations might arise, however, where a user wants to share with others specific records contained within a private database. This was made possible with the introduction of *CloudKit sharing* in iOS 10, a topic that is covered in detail in the chapters entitled *An Introduction to CloudKit Sharing* and *An iOS 12 CloudKit Sharing Example*.

51.12 CloudKit Subscriptions

CloudKit subscriptions allow users to be notified when a change occurs within the cloud databases belonging to an installed app. Subscriptions use the standard iOS push notifications infrastructure and can be triggered based on a variety of criteria such as when records are added, updated or deleted. Notifications can also be further refined using predicates so that notifications are based on data in a record matching certain criteria. When a notification arrives, it is presented to the user in the same way as other notifications through an alert or a notification entry on the lock screen.

CloudKit subscriptions are configured using the CKSubscription class and are covered in detail in the chapter entitled *An iOS 12 CloudKit Subscription Example*.

51.13 Obtaining iCloud User Information

Within the scope of an application's cloud container, each user has a unique, application specific iCloud user ID and a user info record where the user ID is used as the record ID for the user's info record.

The record ID of the current user's info record can be obtained via a call to the *fetchUserRecordID(completionHandler:)* method of the container instance. Once the record ID has been obtained, this can be used to fetch the user's record from the cloud database:

```
container.fetchUserRecordID(completionHandler: {recordID,
        error in
            if let err = error {
                // Failed to get record ID
            } else {
                    // Success - fetch the user's record here
              }
```

The record is of type CKRecordTypeUserRecord and is initially empty. Once fetched, it can be used to store data in the same way as any other CloudKit record.

CloudKit can also be used to perform user discovery. This allows the application to obtain an array of the users in the current user's address book who have also used the app. In order for the user's information to be provided, the user must have run the app and opted in to provide the information. User discovery is performed via a call to the *discoverAllIdentities(completionHandler:)* method of the container instance.

The discovered data is provided in the form of an array of CKApplicationUserInfo objects which contain the user's iCloud ID, first name and last name. The following code fragment, for example, performs a user discovery operation and outputs to the console the first and last names of any users that meet the requirements for discoverability:

```
container.discoverAllIdentities(completionHandler: (
    {users, error in

        if let err = error {
            print("discovery failed %@",
                  err.localizedDescription)
        } else {

            for userInfo in user {
                let userRecordID = userInfo.userRecordID
                print("First Name = %@", userInfo.firstName)
                print("Last Name = %@", userInfo.lastName)
            }
        }
    })
```

51.14 CloudKit Dashboard

The CloudKit Dashboard is a web based portal that provides an interface for managing the CloudKit options and storage for applications. The dashboard can be accessed via the *https://icloud.developer.apple.com/dashboard/* URL or using the *CloudKit Dashboard* button located in the iCloud section of the Xcode Capabilities panel for a project as shown in Figure 51-2:

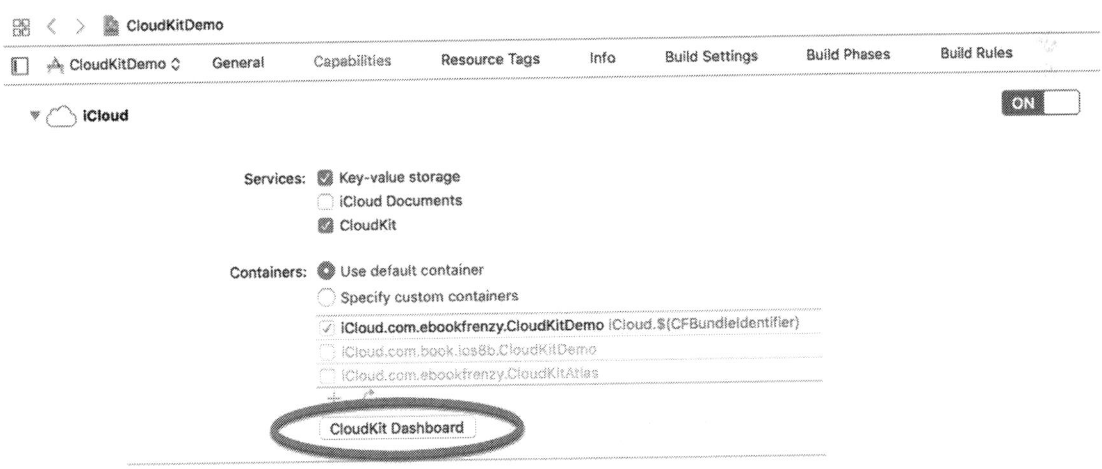

Figure 51-2

Access to the dashboard requires a valid Apple developer login and password and, once loaded into a browser window, will appear listing all of the CloudKit containers associated with your team account. If you have yet to create a CloudKit container the screen illustrated in Figure 51-3 will appear:

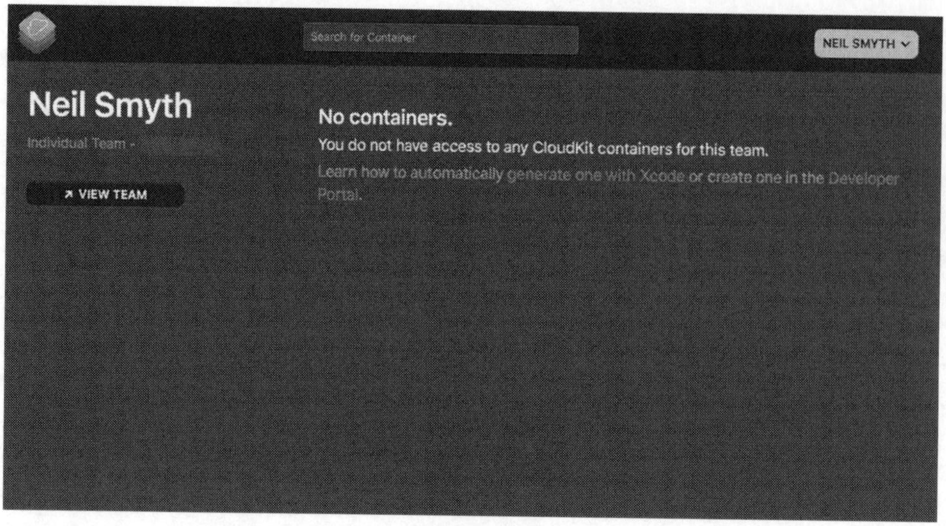

Figure 51-3

Once one or more containers have been created, the dashboard provides the ability to view data, add, update, query and delete records, modify database schema, view subscriptions and configure new security roles. It also provides an interface for migrating data from a development environment over to a production environment in preparation for an application to go live in the Apple App Store:

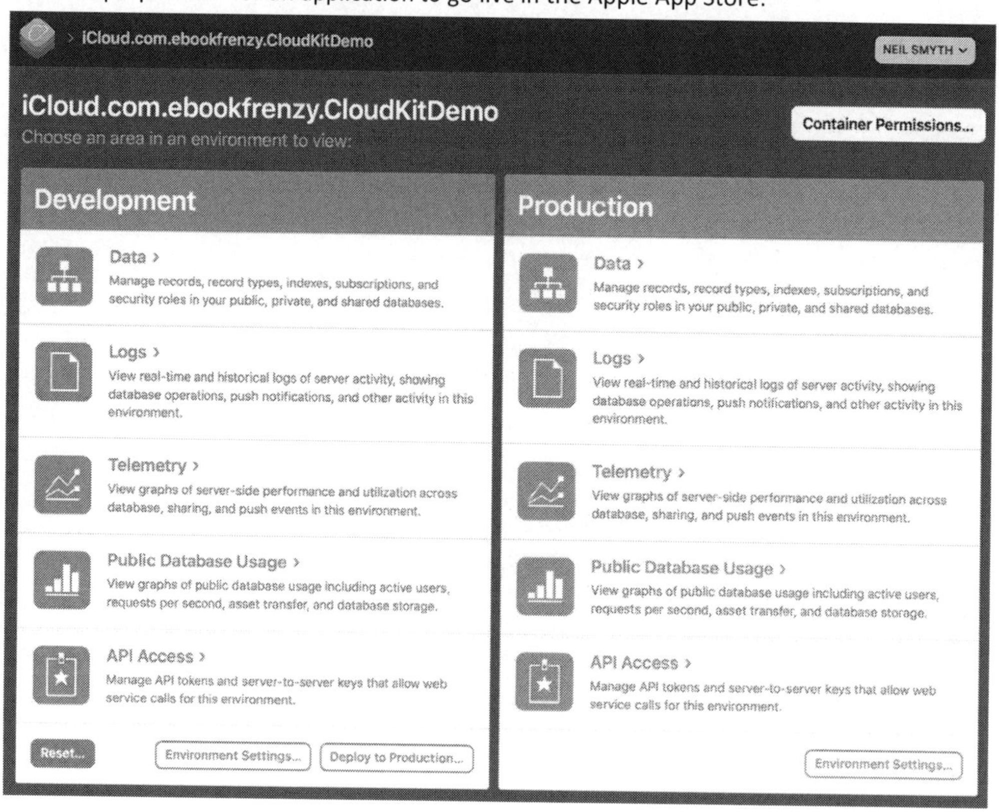

Figure 51-4

The Logs and Telemetry options provide an overview of CloudKit usage by the currently selected container, including operations performed per second, average data request size and error frequency and log details of each individual transaction:

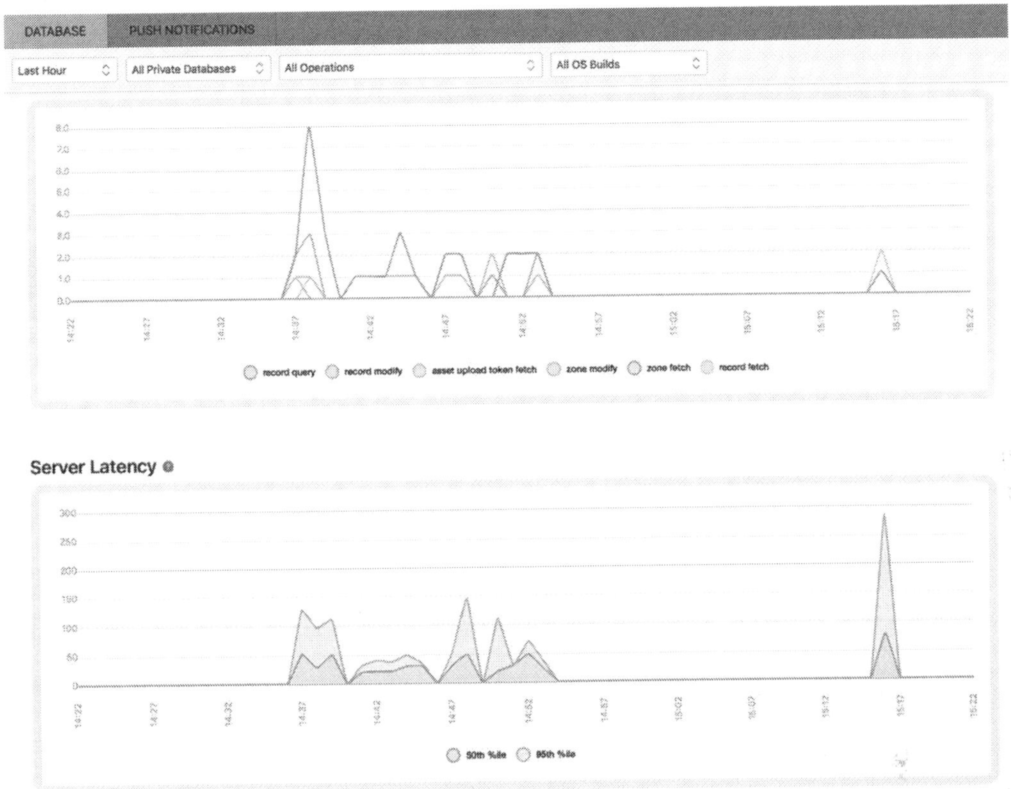

Figure 51-5

In the case of data access through the CloudKit Dashboard, it is important to be aware that private user data cannot be accessed using the dashboard interface. Only data stored in the public database and the private databases belonging to the developer account used to log into the dashboard can be viewed and modified.

51.15 Summary

This chapter has covered a number of the key classes and elements that make up the data storage features of the CloudKit framework. Each application has its own cloud container which, in turn, contains a single public cloud database in addition to one private database for each application user. Data is stored in databases in the form of records using key-value pair fields. Larger data such as videos and photos are stored as assets which, in turn, are stored as fields in records. Records stored in private databases can be grouped together into record zones and records may be associated with each other through the creation of relationships. Each application user has an iCloud user id and a corresponding user record both of which can be obtained using the CloudKit framework. In addition, CloudKit user discovery can be used to obtain, subject to permission having been given, a list of IDs for those users in the current user's address book who have also installed and run the app.

Finally, the CloudKit Dashboard is a web based portal that provides an interface for managing the CloudKit options and storage for applications.

Chapter 52

52. An Introduction to CloudKit Sharing

Prior to the release of iOS 10, the only way to share CloudKit records between users was to store those records in a public database. With the introduction of CloudKit sharing it is now possible for individual app users to share private database records with other users.

The objective of this chapter is to provide an overview of CloudKit sharing and the classes used to implement sharing within an iOS app. The techniques outlined in this chapter will be put to practical use in the chapter entitled *An iOS 12 CloudKit Sharing Example*.

52.1 Understanding CloudKit Sharing

CloudKit sharing provides a way for records contained within a private database to be shared with other app users, entirely at the discretion of the owner of that database. When a user decides to share CloudKit data, a *share link* in the form of a URL is sent to the person with whom the data is to be shared. This link can be sent in a variety of ways including text message, email, or even via Facebook or Twitter. When the recipient taps on the share link, the app (if installed) will be launched and provided with the shared record information ready to be displayed.

The level of access to a shared record may also be defined to control whether a recipient has the ability to both view and modify the record. It is important to be aware that when a share recipient accepts a share they are actually receiving a reference to the original record in the owner's private database. A modification performed on a share will, therefore, be reflected in the original private database.

52.2 Preparing for CloudKit Sharing

Before an app can take advantage of CloudKit sharing, the CKSharingSupported key needs to be added to the project *Info.plist* file with a Boolean value of true. Also, a CloudKit record may only be shared if it is stored in a private database and is a member of a record zone other than the default zone.

52.3 The CKShare Class

CloudKit sharing is made possible primarily by the CKShare class. This class is initialized with the root CKRecord instance that is to be shared with other users together with the permission setting. The CKShare object may also be configured with title and icon information to be included in the share link message. Both the CKShare and associated CKRecord object are then saved to the private database. The following code, for example, creates a CKShare object containing the record to be shared and configured for read-only access:

```
let share = CKShare(rootRecord: myRecord)
share[CKShare.SystemFieldKey.title] = "My First Share" as CKRecordValue
share.publicPermission = .readOnly
```

Once the share has been created, it is saved to the private database using a CKModifyRecordsOperation object. Note the *recordsToSave:* argument is declared as an array containing both the share and record objects:

```
let modifyRecordsOperation = CKModifyRecordsOperation(
                recordsToSave: [myRecord, share],
```

```
                recordIDsToDelete: nil)

modifyRecordsOperation.modifyRecordsCompletionBlock =
        { records, recordIDs, error in

    if error != nil {
        print(error?.localizedDescription)
    }
}
self.privateDatabase?.add(modifyRecordsOperation)
```

52.4 The UICloudSharingController Class

In order to send a share link to another user, CloudKit needs to know both the identity of the recipient and the method by which the share link is to be transmitted. One option is to manually create CKShareParticipant objects for each participant and add them to the CKShare object. Alternatively, the CloudKit framework includes a view controller intended specifically for this purpose. When presented to the user (Figure 52-1), the UICloudSharingController class provides the user with a variety of options for sending the share link to another user:

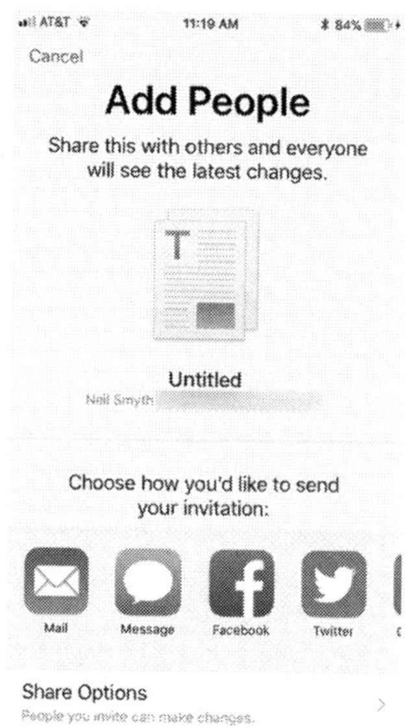

Figure 52-1

The app is responsible for creating and presenting the controller to the user, template code for which is outlined below:

```
let controller = UICloudSharingController {
        controller, preparationCompletionHandler in

        // Code here to create the CKShare and save it to the database
}

controller.availablePermissions =
```

```
        [.allowPublic, .allowReadOnly, .allowReadWrite, .allowPrivate]
controller.popoverPresentationController?.barButtonItem =
                        shareButton as? UIBarButtonItem

present(controller, animated: true)
```

Note that the above code fragment also specifies the range of permissions that are to be provided as options within the controller user interface. These options are accessed and modified by tapping the *Share Options* item at the bottom of the cloud sharing controller view. Figure 52-2 shows an example share options settings screen:

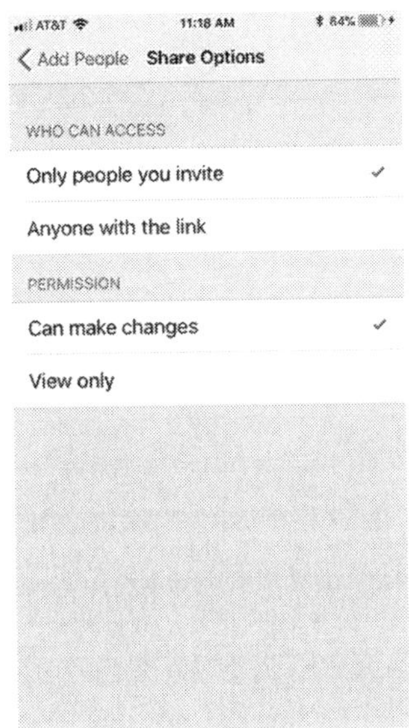

Figure 52-2

Once a method of communication has been selected by the user from the cloud sharing controller, the completion handler assigned to the controller will be called. Within this handler, the CKShare object must be created and saved as outlined in the previous section. After the share has been saved to the database, the cloud sharing controller needs to be notified that the share is ready to be sent. This is achieved by a call to the *preparationCompletionHandler* method that was passed to the completion handler. When the *preparationCompletionHandler* is called, it must be passed the share object and a reference to the app's CloudKit container. Bringing these requirements together gives us the following code:

```
let controller = UICloudSharingController { controller,
               preparationCompletionHandler in

        let share = CKShare(rootRecord: myRecord!)
        share[CKShare.SystemFieldKey.title] =
                        "My First Share" as CKRecordValue
        share.publicPermission = .readOnly

        let modifyRecordsOperation = CKModifyRecordsOperation(
                        recordsToSave: [self.currentRecord!, share],
```

```
                        recordIDsToDelete: nil)

        modifyRecordsOperation.timeoutIntervalForRequest = 10
        modifyRecordsOperation.timeoutIntervalForResource = 10

        modifyRecordsOperation.modifyRecordsCompletionBlock = { records,
                        recordIDs, error in
            if error != nil {
                print(error?.localizedDescription)
            }
            preparationCompletionHandler(share,
                            CKContainer.default(), error)
        }
        self.privateDatabase?.add(modifyRecordsOperation)
    }

controller.availablePermissions = [.allowPublic, .allowReadOnly]
controller.popoverPresentationController?.barButtonItem =
                shareButton as? UIBarButtonItem

present(controller, animated: true))
```

Once the *preparationCompletionHandler* method has been called, the app for the chosen form of communication (Messages, Mail etc) will launch preloaded with the share link. All the user needs to do at this point is enter the contact details for the intended share recipient and send the message. Figure 52-3, for example, shows a share link loaded into the Mail app ready to be sent:

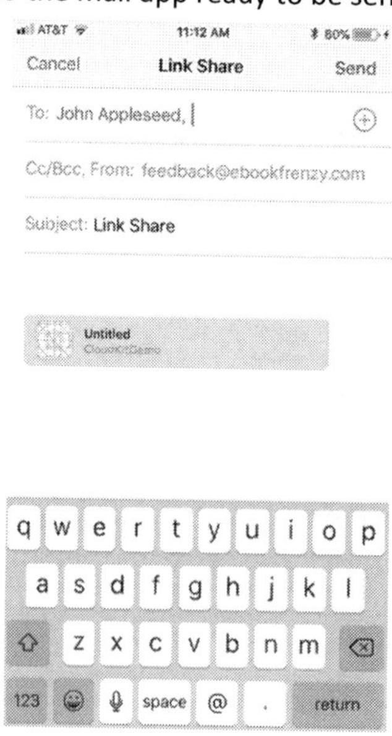

Figure 52-3

52.5 Accepting a CloudKit Share

When a user receives a share link and selects it, a dialog will appear providing the option to accept the share and open it in the corresponding app. When the app opens, the *userDidAcceptCloudKitShareWith* method is called on the app delegate class:

```
func application(_ application: UIApplication, userDidAcceptCloudKitShareWith
   cloudKitShareMetadata: CKShare.Metadata) {
}
```

When this method is called it is passed a CKShare.Metadata object containing information about the share. Although the user has accepted the share, the application must also accept the share using the CKAcceptSharesOperation class as follows:

```
func application(_ application: UIApplication, userDidAcceptCloudKitShareWith
   cloudKitShareMetadata: CKShare.Metadata) {

    let acceptSharesOperation = CKAcceptSharesOperation(
                        shareMetadatas: [cloudKitShareMetadata])

    acceptSharesOperation.perShareCompletionBlock = {
                metadata, share, error in
        if error != nil {
            print(error?.localizedDescription)
        }
        // Add code here to fetch shared record and display to user
    }

    CKContainer(identifier: cloudKitShareMetadata.containerIdentifier)
                                    .add(acceptSharesOperation)
}
```

52.6 Fetching a Shared Record

Once a share has been accepted by both the user and the app, the shared record needs to be fetched and presented to the user. This involves the creation of a CKFetchRecordsOperation object using the record ID contained within the CKShare.Metadata object. It is important to be aware that this fetch operation must be executed on the *shared cloud database* instance of the app instead of the recipient's private database. The following code, for example, fetches the record associated with a CloudKit share:

```
let operation = CKFetchRecordsOperation(
                        recordIDs: [cloudKitShareMetadata.rootRecordID])

operation.perRecordCompletionBlock = { record, _, error in

    if error != nil {
        print(error?.localizedDescription)
    }
```

```
    if let shareRecord = record {
        DispatchQueue.main.async() {
            // Shared record successfully fetched. Update user
            // interface here to present to user.
        }
    }
}

operation.fetchRecordsCompletionBlock = { _, error in
    if error != nil {
        print(error?.localizedDescription)
    }
}

CKContainer.default().sharedCloudDatabase.add(operation)
```

Once the record has been fetched it can be presented to the user, taking necessary steps as above to perform any user interface updates asynchronously on the main thread.

52.7 Summary

CloudKit sharing allows records stored within a private CloudKit database to be shared with other app users at the discretion of the record owner. A user of an app could, for example, make one or more records accessible to other users so that they can view and, optionally, modify the record. When a record is shared, a share link is sent to the recipient user in the form of a URL. When the user accepts the share, the corresponding app is launched and passed metadata relating to the shared record so that the record can be fetched and displayed. CloudKit sharing involves the creation of CKShare objects initialized with the record to be shared. The UICloudSharingController class provides a pre-built view controller which handles much of the work involved in gathering the necessary information to send a share link to another user. In addition to sending a share link, the app must also be adapted to accept a share and fetch the record for the shared cloud database. This chapter has covered the basics of CloudKit sharing, a topic which will be covered further in a later chapter entitled *An iOS 12 CloudKit Sharing Example*.

53. An iOS 12 CloudKit Example

With the basics of the CloudKit Framework covered in the previous chapters, many of the concepts covered in those chapters will now be explored in greater detail through the implementation of an example iOS project. The app created in this chapter will demonstrate the use of the CloudKit Framework to create, update, query and delete records in a private CloudKit database. In the next chapter, the project will be extended further to demonstrate the use of CloudKit subscriptions to notify users when new records are added to the application's database. Later, the project will be further modified to implement CloudKit Sharing.

53.1 About the Example CloudKit Project

The steps outlined in this chapter are intended to make use of a number of key features of the CloudKit framework. The example will take the form of the prototype for an application designed to appeal to users while looking for a new home. The app allows the users to store the addresses, take photos and enter notes about properties visited. This information will be stored on iCloud using the CloudKit Framework and will include the ability to save, delete, update and search for records.

Before starting on this project keep in mind that membership to the Apple Developer Program will be required as outlined in *Joining the Apple Developer Program*.

53.2 Creating the CloudKit Example Project

Launch Xcode and create a new Single View Application project named CloudKitDemo, with the programming language set to Swift.

Once the project has been created, the first step is to enable CloudKit entitlements for the application. Select the CloudKitDemo entry listed at the top of the project navigator panel and, in the main panel, click on the *Capabilities* tab. Within the resulting list of entitlements, make sure that the iCloud option is switched to the *On* position, that the *CloudKit* services option is enabled and the Containers section is configured to use the default container:

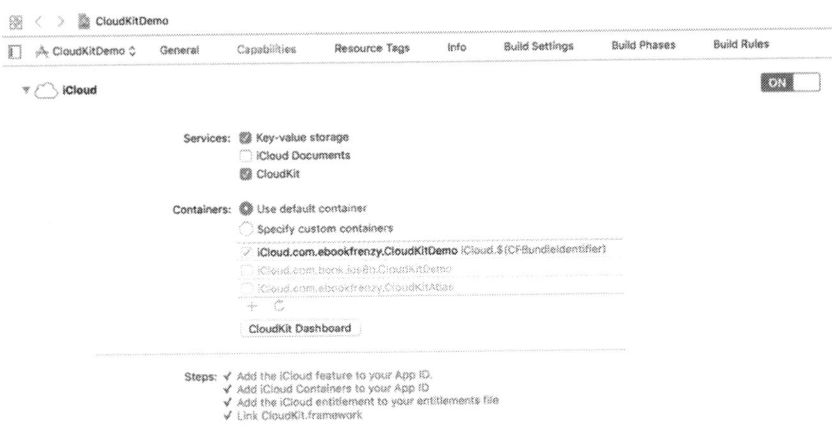

Figure 53-1

Note that if you are using the pre-created version of the project from the book sample download, it will be necessary to assign your own Apple Developer ID to the project. To achieve this, switch to the *General* view and use the *Team* menu in the Identity section to select or add your Apple Developer ID to the project.

53.3 Designing the User Interface

The user interface layout for this project will consist of an Image View, Text Field, Text View and a Toolbar containing five Bar Button Items. Begin the design process by selecting the *Main.storyboard* file in the project navigator panel so that the storyboard loads into the Interface Builder environment.

Drag and drop views from the Library panel onto the storyboard canvas and resize, position and configure the views so that the layout resembles that outlined in Figure 53-2, making sure to stretch the views horizontally so that they align with the margins of the containing view (represented by the dotted blue lines that appear when resizing a view). After adding the Text View and before adding the Image View, select the Text View object, display the Auto Layout *Add New Constraints* menu and add a *Height* constraint.

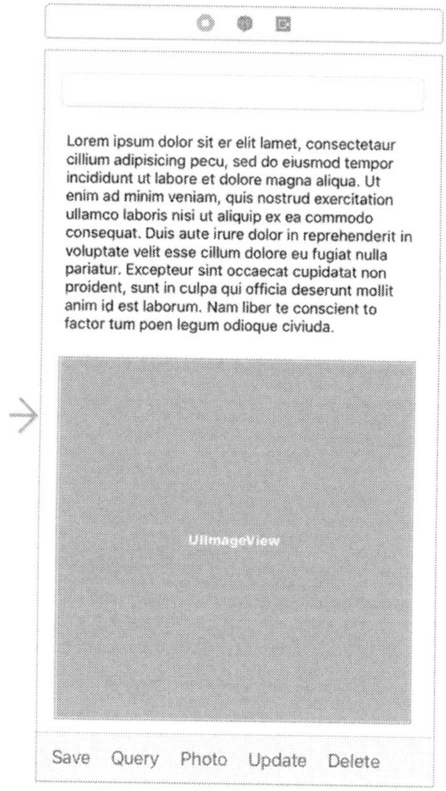

Figure 53-2

Select the Text Field view, display the Attributes Inspector and enter *Address* into the *Placeholder* attribute field. Select the Image View and change the Content Mode attribute to *Aspect Fit.*

Click on the white background of the view controller layout so that none of the views in the layout are currently selected. Using the *Resolve Auto Layout Issues* menu located in the lower right-hand corner of the Interface Builder panel, select the *Add Missing Constraints* menu option.

With the Text View selected in the storyboard, display the Attributes Inspector in the Utilities panel and delete the example Latin text.

53.4 Establishing Outlets and Actions

Display the Assistant Editor, select the Text Field view in the storyboard and Ctrl-click and drag from the view to a position beneath the "class ViewController" declaration and release the line. In the resulting connection panel, establish an outlet connection named *addressField*. Repeat these steps for the Text View and Image View, establishing Outlets named *commentsField* and *imageView* respectively.

Using the same technique establish *Action* connections from the five Bar Button Items to action methods named *saveRecord*, *queryRecord*, *selectPhoto*, *updateRecord* and *deleteRecord* respectively. Once the connections have been established, the *ViewController.swift* file should read as follows:

```
import UIKit

class ViewController: UIViewController {

    @IBOutlet weak var addressField: UITextField!
    @IBOutlet weak var commentsField: UITextView!
    @IBOutlet weak var imageView: UIImageView!

    override func viewDidLoad() {
        super.viewDidLoad()
    }

    @IBAction func saveRecord(_ sender: Any) {
    }

    @IBAction func queryRecord(_ sender: Any) {
    }

    @IBAction func selectPhoto(_ sender: Any) {
    }

    @IBAction func updateRecord(_ sender: Any) {
    }

    @IBAction func deleteRecord(_ sender: Any) {
    }

    override func didReceiveMemoryWarning() {
        super.didReceiveMemoryWarning()
    }
}
```

53.5 Implementing the notifyUser Method

The *notifyUser* method will be used to display messages to the user and takes as parameters two string values representing a title and message. These strings are then used in the construction of an Alert View. Implement this method as follows:

```
func notifyUser(_ title: String, message: String) -> Void
{
    let alert = UIAlertController(title: title,
                                  message: message,
                                  preferredStyle: .alert)

    let cancelAction = UIAlertAction(title: "OK",
                                     style: .cancel, handler: nil)

    alert.addAction(cancelAction)
    self.present(alert, animated: true,
                 completion: nil)
}
```

53.6 Accessing the Private Database

Since the information entered into the app is only relevant to the current user, the data entered into the application will be stored on iCloud using the application's private cloud database. Obtaining a reference to the private cloud database first involves gaining a reference to the application's container. Within the *ViewController.swift* file make the following additions, noting the inclusion of import statements for frameworks that will be needed later in the tutorial, together with variables to store the current database record, record zone and photo image URL:

```
import UIKit
import CloudKit
import MobileCoreServices

class ViewController: UIViewController {

    @IBOutlet weak var addressField: UITextField!
    @IBOutlet weak var commentsField: UITextView!
    @IBOutlet weak var imageView: UIImageView!

    let container = CKContainer.default
    var privateDatabase: CKDatabase?
    var currentRecord: CKRecord?
    var photoURL: URL?
    var recordZone: CKRecordZone?

    override func viewDidLoad() {
        super.viewDidLoad()
        performSetup()
    }

    func performSetup() {
        privateDatabase = container().privateCloudDatabase
```

```
        recordZone = CKRecordZone(zoneName: "HouseZone")

        if let zone = recordZone {
            privateDatabase?.save(zone,
                   completionHandler: {(recordzone, error) in
                     if (error != nil) {
                         self.notifyUser("Record Zone Error",
                           message: "Failed to create custom record zone.")
                     } else {
                         print("Saved record zone")
                     }
            })
        }
    }
.
.
}
```

Note that the code added to the *performSetup* method also initializes the recordZone variable with a CKRecordZone object configured with the name "HouseZone" and saves it to the private database.

53.7 Hiding the Keyboard

It is important to include code to ensure that the user has a way to hide the keyboard after entering text into the two text areas in the user interface. Within the *ViewController.swift* file, override the *touchesBegan* method to hide the keyboard when the user taps the background view of the user interface:

```
override func touchesBegan(_ touches: Set<UITouch>,
                        with event: UIEvent?) {
    addressField.endEditing(true)
    commentsField.endEditing(true)
}
```

53.8 Implementing the selectPhoto method

The purpose of the Photo button in the toolbar is to allow the user to include a photo in the database record. Begin by declaring that the View Controller class implements the UIImagePickerControllerDelegate and UINavigationControllerDelegate protocols, then locate the template *selectPhoto* action method within the *ViewController.swift* file and implement the code as follows:

```
class ViewController: UIViewController, UIImagePickerControllerDelegate,
        UINavigationControllerDelegate {
.
.
@IBAction func selectPhoto(_ sender: Any) {

    let imagePicker = UIImagePickerController()
```

```
        imagePicker.delegate = self
        imagePicker.sourceType =
                UIImagePickerController.SourceType.photoLibrary
        imagePicker.mediaTypes = [kUTTypeImage as String]

        self.present(imagePicker, animated: true,
                        completion:nil)
    }
.
.
}
```

When executed, the code will cause the image picker view controller to be displayed from which the user can select a photo from the photo library on the device to be stored along with the current record in the application's private cloud database. The final step in the photo selection process is to implement the delegate methods which will be called when the user has either made a photo selection or cancels the selection process:

```
func imagePickerController(_ picker: UIImagePickerController,
didFinishPickingMediaWithInfo info: [UIImagePickerController.InfoKey : Any])
{
    self.dismiss(animated: true, completion: nil)
    let image =
        info[UIImagePickerController.InfoKey.originalImage] as! UIImage
    imageView.image = image
    photoURL = saveImageToFile(image)
}

func imagePickerControllerDidCancel(_ picker: UIImagePickerController) {
    self.dismiss(animated: true, completion: nil)
}
```

In both cases the image picker view controller is dismissed from view. In the case of a photo being selected, the image is displayed within the application via the Image View instance before being written to the file system of the device and the corresponding URL stored in the *photoURL* variable for later reference. Clearly the code expects the image file writing to be performed by a method named *saveImageToFile* which must now be implemented:

```
func saveImageToFile(_ image: UIImage) -> URL
{
    let filemgr = FileManager.default

    let dirPaths = filemgr.urls(for: .documentDirectory,
                                in: .userDomainMask)

    let fileURL = dirPaths[0].appendingPathComponent("currentImage.jpg")
```

```
    if let renderedJPEGData =
        image.jpegData(compressionQuality: 0.5) {
        try! renderedJPEGData.write(to: fileURL)
    }

    return fileURL
}
```

The method obtains a reference to the application's Documents directory and constructs a path to an image file named *currentImage.jpg*. The image is then written to the file in JPEG format using a compression rate of 0.5 in order to reduce the amount of storage used from the application's iCloud allowance. The resulting file URL is then returned to the calling method.

53.9 Saving a Record to the Cloud Database

When the user has entered an address and comments and selected a photo, the data is ready to be saved to the cloud database. This will require that code be added to the *saveRecord* method as follows:

```
@IBAction func saveRecord(_ sender: Any) {

    var asset: CKAsset?

    if (photoURL == nil) {
        notifyUser("No Photo",
          message: "Use the Photo option to choose a photo for the record")
        return
    } else {
        asset = CKAsset(fileURL: photoURL!)
    }

    if let zoneId = recordZone?.zoneID {

        let myRecord = CKRecord(recordType: "Houses",
                              recordID: CKRecord.ID(zoneID: zoneId))

        myRecord.setObject(addressField.text as CKRecordValue?,
                         forKey: "address")

        myRecord.setObject(commentsField.text as CKRecordValue?,
                         forKey: "comment")

        myRecord.setObject(asset, forKey: "photo")

        let modifyRecordsOperation = CKModifyRecordsOperation(
            recordsToSave: [myRecord],
            recordIDsToDelete: nil)
```

```
        let configuration = CKOperation.Configuration()

        configuration.timeoutIntervalForRequest =  10
        configuration.timeoutIntervalForResource = 10

        modifyRecordsOperation.configuration = configuration

        modifyRecordsOperation.modifyRecordsCompletionBlock =
            { records, recordIDs, error in
                if let err = error {
                    self.notifyUser("Save Error", message:
                        err.localizedDescription)
                } else {
                    DispatchQueue.main.async {
                        self.notifyUser("Success",
                                        message: "Record saved successfully")
                    }
                    self.currentRecord = myRecord
                }
        }
        privateDatabase?.add(modifyRecordsOperation)
    }
}
```

The method begins by verifying that the user has selected a photo to include in the database record. If one has not yet been selected the user is notified that a photo is required (the *notifyUser* method will be implemented in the next section).

Next a new CKAsset object is created and initialized with the URL to the photo image previously selected by the user. A new CKRecord instance is then created and assigned a record type of "Houses". The record is then initialized with the content of the Text Field and Text View, the CKAsset object containing the photo image and ID of the zone with which the record is to be associated.

Once the record is ready to be saved, a CKModifyRecordsOperation object is initialized with the record object and then executed against the user's private database. A completion handler is used to report the success or otherwise of the save operation. Since this involves working with the user interface, it is dispatched to the main thread to prevent the application from locking up. The new record is then saved to the *currentRecord* variable where it can be referenced should the user subsequently decide to update or delete the record.

53.10 Testing the Record Saving Method

Compile and run the application on a device or simulator on which you are signed into iCloud using the Apple ID associated with your Apple Developer account. Enter text into the address and comments fields and select an image from the photo library (images can be added to the photo library of a simulator instance by dragging images from a Finder window and dropping them onto the simulator window).

Tap the Save button to save the record and wait for the alert to appear indicating that the record has been saved successfully. Note that CloudKit operations are performed asynchronously so the amount of time for a successful save to be reported will vary depending on the size of the record being saved, network speed and responsiveness of the iCloud servers.

Once the record has been saved, return to the Capabilities screen for the application (Figure 53-1) and click on the *CloudKit Dashboard* button. This will launch the default web browser on the system and load the CloudKit Dashboard portal. Enter your Apple developer login and password and, once the dashboard has loaded, select the CloudKitDemo container from the Dashboard home screen. The subsequent screen (Figure 53-3) will provide a range of options for both Development and Production modes.

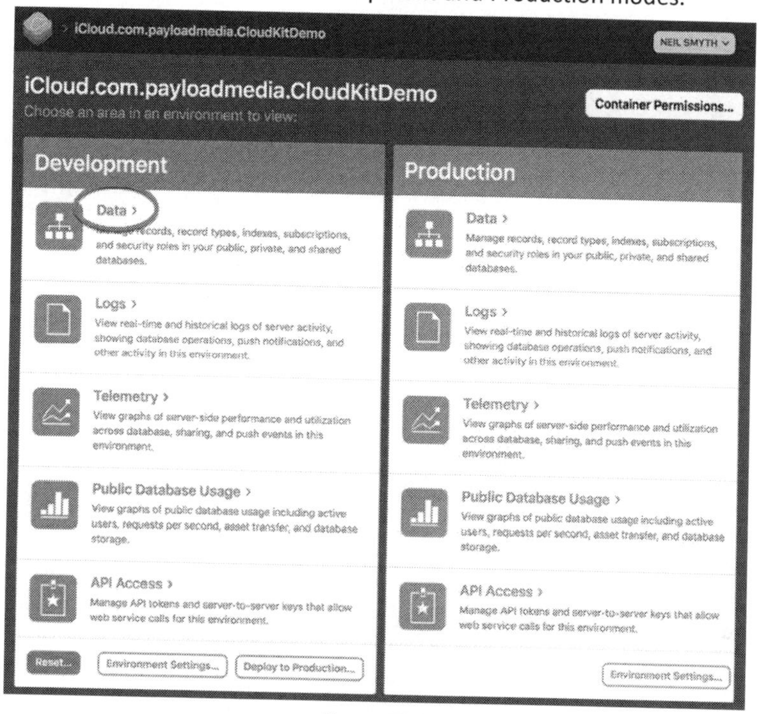

Figure 53-3

Since this app is not yet in production and available within the App Store, click on the *Data* option listed under the *Development* heading as highlighted in the above figure.

When the development data screen appears, select the Zones tab (marked A in Figure 53-4) followed by *Private Database* load option (B). To list the currently configured zones within the container, click on the *List Zones* button (C). Assuming that the app was successful in creating a zone, *HouseZone* should appear in the list (D) together with the default zone:

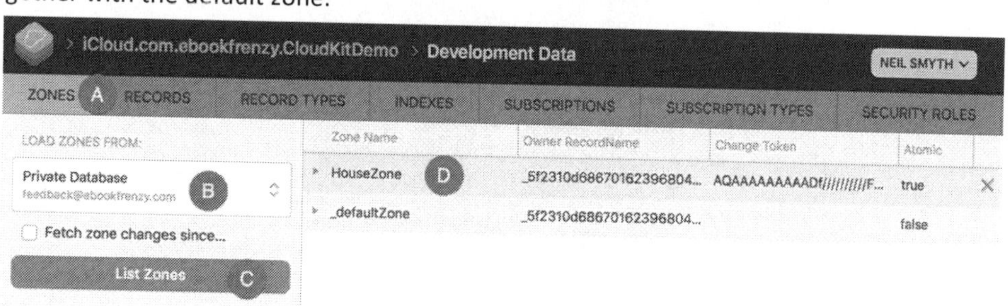

Figure 53-4

If HouseZone is not listed, make sure that the device or simulator on which the app is running is signed in using the same Apple ID as that used to log into the CloudKit Dashboard.

From the tab bar, select the Records tab (marked A in Figure 53-5), make sure that both the *Private Database* and *HouseZone* are selected (B) and that the query is configured for records of type *Houses* (C) before clicking on the *Query Records* button (D). The record added from within the CloudKitDemo app should appear in the records list (E):

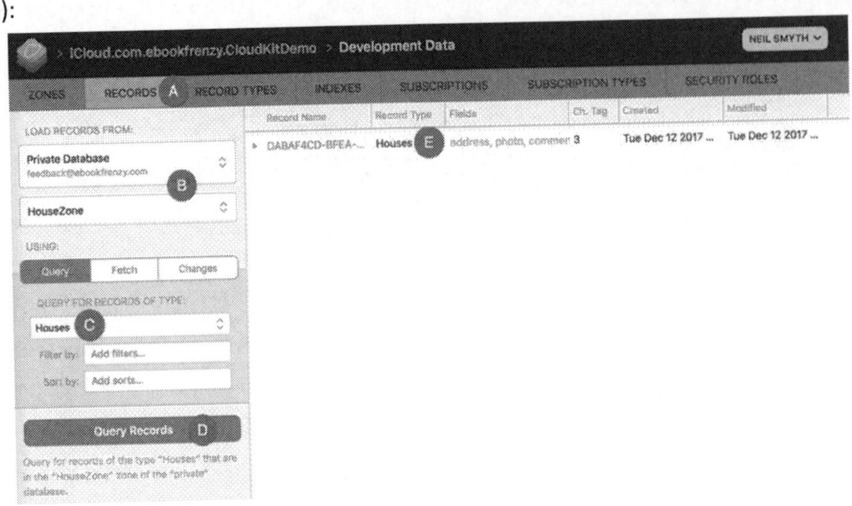

Figure 53-5

Within the records list, click on the record name to display the data and assets contained within that record. The information displayed in the *Editing Record* panel (Figure 53-6) should match that entered within the CloudKitDemo app:

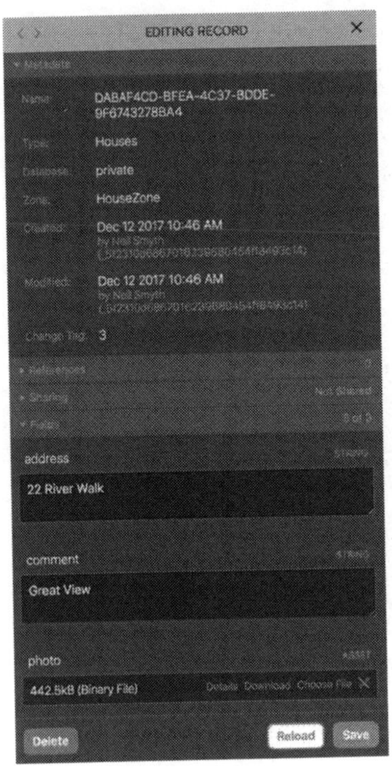

Figure 53-6

Having verified that the record was saved, the next task is to implement the remaining action methods.

53.11 Searching for Cloud Database Records

The Query feature of the application allows a record matching a specified address to be retrieved and displayed to the user. Locate the template *queryRecord* method in the *ViewController.swift* file and implement the body of the method to perform the query operation:

```
@IBAction func queryRecord(_ sender: Any) {

    if let text = addressField.text {

        let predicate = NSPredicate(format: "address = %@", text)

        let query = CKQuery(recordType: "Houses", predicate: predicate)

        privateDatabase?.perform(query, inZoneWith: recordZone?.zoneID,
                completionHandler: ({results, error in

            if let err = error {
                DispatchQueue.main.async() {
                    self.notifyUser("Cloud Access Error",
                                message: err.localizedDescription)
                }
            } else {
                if let resultsArray = results, resultsArray.count > 0 {

                    let record = resultsArray[0]
                    self.currentRecord = record

                    DispatchQueue.main.async() {

                        self.commentsField.text =
                            record.object(forKey: "comment")
                                              as? String

                        let photo =
                            record.object(forKey: "photo")
                                              as! CKAsset

                        let image = UIImage(contentsOfFile:
                                         photo.fileURL.path)

                        if let img = image {
                            self.imageView.image = img
                            self.photoURL = self.saveImageToFile(img)
```

```
                        }
                    }
                } else {
                    DispatchQueue.main.async() {
                        self.notifyUser("No Match Found", message:
                            "No record matching the address was found")
                    }
                }
            }
        }))
    }
}
```

Despite the seeming complexity of this method it actually performs some very simple tasks. First a new predicate instance is configured to indicate that the query is to search for records where the address field matches the content of the address entered by the user into the application user interface. This predicate is then used to create a new CKQuery object together with the record type for which the search is to be performed.

The *perform(query:)* method of the private cloud database object is then called, passing through the query object together with the record zone ID and a completion handler to be executed when the query returns (as with all CloudKit operations, queries are performed asynchronously).

In the event of an error or a failure to find a match, the user is notified via an alert. In the event that one or more matches are found, the first matching record is extracted from the results array and the data and image contained therein displayed to the user via the user interface outlet connections.

Compile and run the application, enter the address used when the record was saved in the previous section and tap the Query button. After a short delay, the display should update with the content of the record.

53.12 Updating Cloud Database Records

When updating existing records in a cloud database, the ID of the record to be updated must be referenced since this is the only way to uniquely identify one record from another. In the case of the CloudKitDemo application, this means that the record must already have been loaded into the application and assigned to the currentRecord variable, thereby allowing the recordID to be obtained and used for the update operation. With these requirements in mind, implement the code in the stub *updateRecord* method as follows:

```
@IBAction func updateRecord(_ sender: Any) {

    if let record = currentRecord, let url = photoURL {

        let asset = CKAsset(fileURL: url)

        record.setObject(addressField.text as CKRecordValue?,
                         forKey: "address")
        record.setObject(commentsField.text as CKRecordValue?,
                         forKey: "comment")
        record.setObject(asset, forKey: "photo")
```

```
        privateDatabase?.save(record, completionHandler:
            ({returnRecord, error in
                if let err = error {
                    DispatchQueue.main.async() {
                        self.notifyUser("Update Error",
                                        message: err.localizedDescription)
                    }
                } else {
                    DispatchQueue.main.async() {
                        self.notifyUser("Success", message:
                            "Record updated successfully")
                    }
                }
            }))
    } else {
        notifyUser("No Record Selected", message:
            "Use Query to select a record to update")
    }
}
```

This method performs similar tasks to the *saveRecord* method. This time, however, instead of creating a new CKRecord instance, the existing record assigned to the *currentRecord* variable is updated with the latest text and photo content entered by the user. When the save operation is performed, CloudKit will identify that the record has an ID that matches an existing record in the database and update that matching record with the latest data provided by the user.

53.13 Deleting a Cloud Record

CloudKit record deletions can be achieved by calling the *deleteRecordWithID* method of the CKDatabase instance, passing through as arguments the ID of the record to be deleted and a completion handler to be executed when the deletion operation returns. As with the *updateRecord* method, a deletion can only be performed when the record to be deleted has already been selected within the application and assigned to the *currentRecord* variable:

```
@IBAction func deleteRecord(_ sender: Any) {
    if let record = currentRecord {

        privateDatabase?.delete(withRecordID: record.recordID,
                completionHandler: ({returnRecord, error in
            if let err = error {
                DispatchQueue.main.async() {
                    self.notifyUser("Delete Error", message:
                                    err.localizedDescription)
                }
            } else {
                DispatchQueue.main.async() {
                    self.notifyUser("Success", message:
```

```
                                "Record deleted successfully")
                }
            }
        }))
    } else {
        notifyUser("No Record Selected", message:
                             "Use Query to select a record to delete")
    }
}
```

53.14 Testing the Application

With the basic functionality of the application implemented, compile and run it on a device or simulator instance and add, query, update and delete records to verify that the application functions as intended.

53.15 Summary

CloudKit provides an easy way to implement the storage and retrieval of iCloud-based database records from within iOS applications. The objective of this chapter has been to demonstrate in practical terms the techniques available to save, search, update and delete database records stored in an iCloud database using the CloudKit convenience API.

One area of CloudKit that was not addressed in this chapter involves the use of CloudKit subscriptions to notify the user when changes have been made to a cloud database. In the next chapter, entitled *An iOS 12 CloudKit Subscription Example* the CloudKitDemo application will be extended to add this functionality.

Chapter 54

54. An iOS 12 CloudKit Subscription Example

In the previous chapter, entitled *An iOS 12 CloudKit Example*, an example application was created that demonstrated the use of the iOS CloudKit Framework to save, query, update and delete cloud database records. In this chapter, the CloudKitDemo application created in the previous chapter will be extended so that users of the application receive push notifications when a new record is added to the application's private database by other instances of the app.

54.1 Push Notifications and CloudKit Subscriptions

A push notification occurs when a remote server associated with an app installed on an iOS device sends a notification of importance to the user. On receipt of the notification the user will be notified either via an alert on the lock screen, or by an alert panel appearing at the top of the screen accompanied by an optional sound. Generally, selecting the notification alert will launch the associated app in a context that is relevant to the nature of the notification. When enabled, a red *badge* will also appear in the corner of the application's launch icon containing a number representing the amount of outstanding notifications received for the application since it was last launched.

Consider, for example, a news based application that is configured to receive push notifications from a remote server when a breaking news headline is available. Once the push notification is received, brief details of the news item will be displayed to the user and, in the event that the user selected the notification alert, the news app will launch and display the news article corresponding to the notification.

CloudKit subscriptions use the iOS push notifications infrastructure to enable users to receive notifications when changes occur to the data stored in a cloud database. Specifically, CloudKit subscriptions can be used to notify the user when CloudKit based records of a specific record type are created, updated or deleted. As with other push notifications, the user can select the notification and launch the corresponding application. Making the application appear in the appropriate context (for example with a newly created record loaded), however, requires some work. The remainder of this chapter will outline the steps to implement this behavior.

54.2 Configuring the Project for Remote Notifications

Before adding any code to the project, a couple of configuration changes need to be made to the project to add support for notifications. First, the *Info.plist* file needs to be updated to indicate that the app supports remote notifications when in the background. To add these settings, select the CloudKitDemo target located at the top of the project navigator panel, select the *Capabilities* tab in the main panel and scroll down to the *Background Modes* section. Enable the background modes option if it is not already switched on and enable both the *Background Fetch* and *Remote Notifications* options as shown in Figure 54-1:

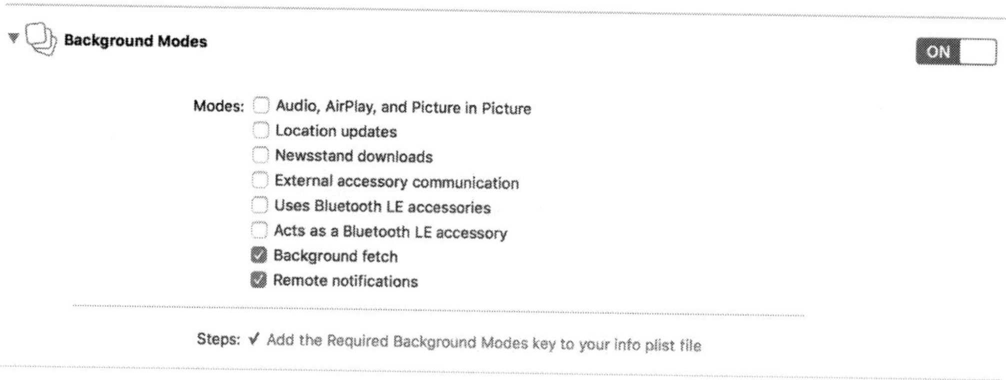

Figure 54-1

54.3 Registering an App to Receive Push Notifications

By default, applications installed on a user's device will not be allowed to receive push notifications until the user specifically grants permission. An application seeks this permission by registering for remote notifications. The first time this registration request occurs the user will be prompted to grant permission. Once permission has been granted, the application will be able to receive remote notifications until the user changes the notifications setting for the application in the Settings app.

To register for remote notifications for the CloudKitDemo project, locate and select the *AppDelegate.swift* file in the project navigator panel and modify the *didFinishLaunchingWithOptions* method to add the appropriate registration code. Now is also an opportune time to import the CloudKit and UserNotifications Frameworks into the class:

```
import UIKit
import CloudKit
import UserNotifications

@UIApplicationMain
class AppDelegate: UIResponder, UIApplicationDelegate {

    var window: UIWindow?

    func application(_ application: UIApplication,
didFinishLaunchingWithOptions launchOptions: [UIApplicationLaunchOptionsKey:
Any]?) -> Bool {

        UNUserNotificationCenter.current().requestAuthorization(options:
            [[.alert, .sound, .badge]],
                completionHandler: { (granted, error) in
                    // Handle Error
            })
        application.registerForRemoteNotifications()

        return true
    }
```

```
.
.
}
```

The code in the method configures the notification settings such that the system will display an alert to the user when a notification is received, display a badge on the application's launch icon and also, if configured, play a sound to get the user's attention. Although sound is enabled for this example, only the alert and badge settings will be used.

Having made these code changes, run the application and, when prompted, allow the application to receive notifications.

54.4 Configuring a CloudKit Subscription

A CloudKit subscription is configured using an instance of the CKQuerySubscription class. When the CKQuerySubscription instance is created it is passed the record type, a predicate and an option indicating whether the notifications are to be triggered when records of the specified type are created, deleted or updated. The predicate allows additional rules to be declared which the subscription must meet before the notification can be triggered. For example, a user might only be interested in notifications when records are added for houses on a particular street.

An instance of the CKNotification class is also assigned to the CKQuerySubscription object and is used to define the information that is to be delivered to the application with the notification such as the message to be displayed in the notification alert, a sound to be played and whether or not a badge should be displayed on the application's launch icon.

Once the CKQuerySubscription is fully configured, it is committed to the cloud database using the *save* method of the cloud database object. For the purposes of this example, the code to implement the subscription should be implemented in the *performSetup* method located in the *ViewController.swift* file:

```
func performSetup() {
    super.viewDidLoad()
    privateDatabase = container().privateCloudDatabase
    recordZone = CKRecordZone(zoneName: "HouseZone")

    privateDatabase?.save(recordZone!,
                completionHandler: {(recordzone, error) in
        if (error != nil) {
            self.notifyUser("Record Zone Error", message: "Failed to create
custom record zone.")
        } else {
            print("Saved record zone")
        }
    })

    let predicate = NSPredicate(format: "TRUEPREDICATE")

    let subscription = CKQuerySubscription(recordType: "Houses",
                        predicate: predicate,
                        options: .firesOnRecordCreation)
```

```
        let notificationInfo = CKSubscription.NotificationInfo()

        notificationInfo.alertBody = "A new House was added"
        notificationInfo.shouldBadge = true

        subscription.notificationInfo = notificationInfo

        privateDatabase?.save(subscription,
                  completionHandler: ({returnRecord, error in
            if let err = error {
                print("subscription failed %@",
                            err.localizedDescription)
            } else {
                DispatchQueue.main.async() {
                    self.notifyUser("Success",
                        message: "Subscription set up successfully")
                }
            }
        }))
}
```

Note that the NSPredicate object was created using "TRUEPREDICATE". This is a special value that configures the predicate to always return a true value and is the equivalent of indicating that all records of the specified type match the predicate.

The *.firesOnRecordCreation* option indicates that the user is to be notified whenever a new record of type "Houses" is added to the database. Other options available are *.firesOnRecordUpdate*, *.firesOnRecordDelete* and *.firesOnce*. The *.firesOnce* option causes the subscription to be deleted from the server after it has fired for the first time.

Compile and run the application on a device or simulator and click on the *Allow* button when the dialog appears asking permission for CloudKitDemo to send notifications:

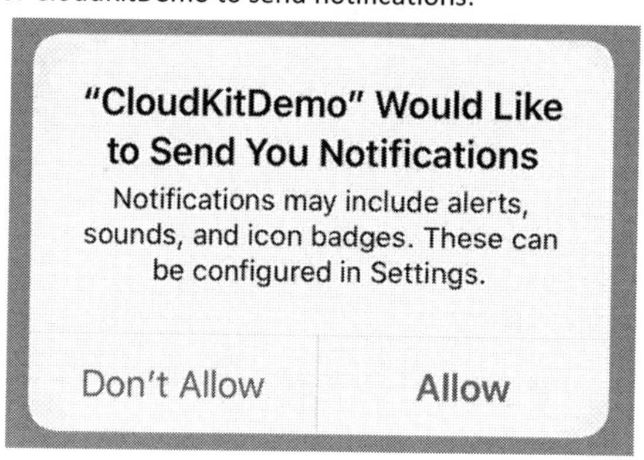

Figure 54-2

Log into the iCloud Dashboard and select the CloudKitDemo container. When the main menu screen appears, select the *Data* option listed under *Development*. On the data screen, select the *Subscription Types* tab. If the subscription was successfully configured it should be listed as shown in Figure 54-3:

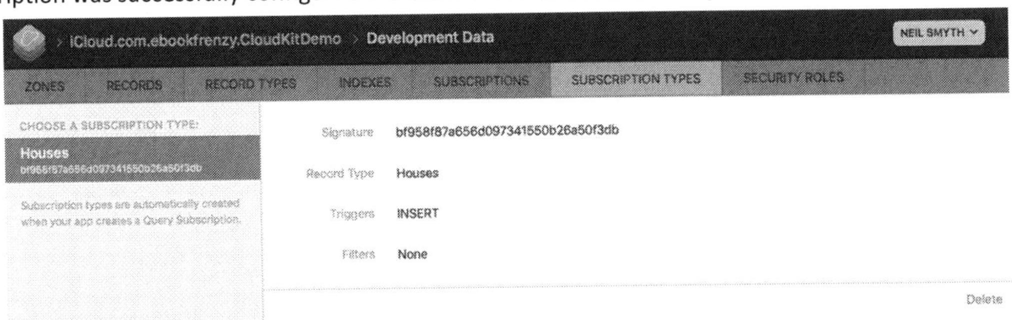

Figure 54-3

54.5 Handling Remote Notifications

When the user selects a notification alert on an iOS device, the CloudKitDemo application will be launched by the operating system. At the point that the user selects the notification, the application will currently be in one of three possible states – foreground, background or not currently running.

If the application is in the background when the alert is selected, it is simply brought to the foreground. If it was not currently running, the application is launched by the operating system and brought to the foreground.

When the application is already in foreground or background state when a CloudKit notification alert is selected, the *didReceiveRemoteNotification* method of the application delegate class is called and passed as an argument an NSDictionary instance containing a CKNotification object which contains, among other information, the ID of the cloud database record that triggered the notification.

If the application was not already in the foreground or background when the alert is selected, the *didReceiveRemoteNotification* method is not called. Instead, information about the database change is passed as an argument to the *didFinishLaunchingWithOptions* method of the application delegate.

54.6 Implementing the didReceiveRemoteNotification Method

The *didReceiveRemoteNotification* method will be called when the user selects an alert and the CloudKitDemo application is either already in the foreground or currently in the background. The method will need to be implemented in the *AppDelegate.swift* file so locate this file in the project navigator panel and modify it to add this method:

```
func application(_ application: UIApplication, didReceiveRemoteNotification
userInfo: [AnyHashable : Any], fetchCompletionHandler completionHandler:
@escaping (UIBackgroundFetchResult) -> Void) {

    let viewController: ViewController =
       self.window?.rootViewController as! ViewController

    let notification: CKNotification =
        CKNotification(fromRemoteNotificationDictionary:
            userInfo as! [String : NSObject])

    if (notification.notificationType ==
```

```
                    CKNotification.NotificationType.query) {

            let queryNotification =
                notification as! CKQueryNotification

            if let recordID = queryNotification.recordID {
                viewController.fetchRecord(recordID: recordID)
            }
        }
}
```

The method begins by obtaining a reference to the root view controller of the application. The code then extracts the CKNotification object from the NSDictionary that was passed to the method by the operating system. The *notificationType* property of the CKNotification object is then checked to make sure it matches CKNotificationType.query (which indicates that the notification was triggered as a result of a subscription).

The record ID is then obtained and passed to the *fetchRecord* method on the view controller. The next step is to implement the *fetchRecord* method.

54.7 Fetching a Record From a Cloud Database

Records can be fetched by record ID from a cloud database using the *fetch(withRecordID:)* method of the cloud database object. Within the *ViewController.swift* file, implement the *fetchRecord* method as follows:

```
func fetchRecord(recordID: CKRecord.ID) -> Void
{
    privateDatabase?.fetch(withRecordID: recordID,
        completionHandler: ({record, error in
         if let err = error {
             DispatchQueue.main.async() {
                 self.notifyUser("Fetch Error", message:
                     err.localizedDescription)
             }
         } else {
             DispatchQueue.main.async() {

                 if let newRecord = record {
                         self.currentRecord = newRecord
                         self.addressField.text =
                             newRecord.object(forKey: "address") as? String
                         self.commentsField.text =
                             newRecord.object(forKey: "comment") as? String
                         let photo =
                             newRecord.object(forKey: "photo") as! CKAsset

                         if let image = UIImage(contentsOfFile:
                             photo.fileURL.path) {
                         self.imageView.image = image
```

```
                    self.photoURL = self.saveImageToFile(image)
                }
            }
        }
    }
  }))
}
```

The code obtains a reference to the private cloud database (keep in mind that this code will be executed before the *performSetup* method where this has previously been obtained) and then fetches the record from the cloud database based on the record ID passed through as a parameter. If the fetch operation is successful, the data and photo are extracted from the record and displayed to the user. Since the fetched record is also now the current record, it is stored in the *currentRecord* variable.

54.8 Completing the didFinishLaunchingWithOptions Method

As previously outlined, the *didReceiveRemoteNotification* method is only called when the user selected an alert notification and the application is already running either in the foreground or background. When the application was not already running, the *didFinishLaunchingWithOptions* method is called and passed information about the notification. In this scenario, it will be the responsibility of this method to ensure that the newly added record is displayed to the user when the application loads. Within the *AppDelegate.swift* file, locate the *didFinishLaunchingWithOptions* method and modify it as follows:

```
func application(application: UIApplication!, didFinishLaunchingWithOptions
   launchOptions: NSDictionary!) -> Bool {

    UNUserNotificationCenter.current().requestAuthorization(options:
            [[.alert, .sound, .badge]],
                        completionHandler: { (granted, error) in
                            // Handle Error
        })

    applicationregisterForRemoteNotifications()

    if let options: NSDictionary = launchOptions as NSDictionary? {
        let remoteNotification =
                options[UIApplication.LaunchOptionsKey.remoteNotification]


        if let notification = remoteNotification {

            self.application(application, didReceiveRemoteNotification:
                        notification as! [AnyHashable : Any],
                         fetchCompletionHandler:  { (result) in
            })

        }
```

```
    }
    return true
}
```

The added source code begins by verifying that data has been passed to the method via the *launchOptions* parameter. The remote notification key is then used to obtain the NSDictionary object containing the notification data. If the key returns a value, it is passed to the *didReceiveRemoteNotification* method so that the record can be fetched and displayed to the user.

54.9 Testing the Application

Install and run the application on two devices or simulators (or a mixture thereof) remembering to log into iCloud on both instances with the same Apple ID via the *iCloud* screen of the *Settings* app. From one instance of the application add a new record to the database. When the notification alert appears on the other device or simulator (Figure 54-4), select it to launch the CloudKitDemo application which should, after a short delay, load and display the newly added record.

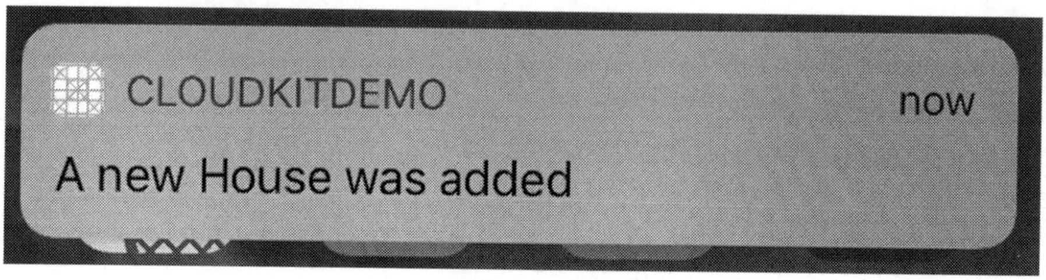

Figure 54-4

Repeat these steps both when the application on the second device is in the background and not currently running. In each case the behavior should be the same.

54.10 Summary

The iOS Push Notification system is used to notify users of events relating to applications installed on a device. This infrastructure has been integrated into CloudKit allowing applications to notify users about changes to the data stored on iCloud using CloudKit.

Chapter 55

55. An iOS 12 CloudKit Sharing Example

The chapter entitled *An Introduction to CloudKit Sharing* provided an overview of the way in which CloudKit sharing works and the steps involved in integrating sharing into an iOS app. The intervening chapters have focused on the creation of a project that demonstrates the integration of CloudKit data storage into iOS apps, together with the use of CloudKit subscriptions to notify users of changes to stored data records.

This chapter will extend the project created in the previous chapters to add CloudKit sharing to the CloudKitDemo app.

55.1 Preparing the Project for CloudKit Sharing

Launch Xcode and open the CloudKitDemo project created in the chapter entitled *An iOS 12 CloudKit Example* and subsequently updated in the *An iOS 12 CloudKit Subscription Example* chapter of this book. In you have not completed the tasks in the previous chapters and are only interested in learning about CloudKit sharing, a snapshot of the project is included as part of the sample code archive for this book at the following web page:

https://www.ebookfrenzy.com/retail/ios12/

Once the project has been loaded into Xcode, the CKSharingSupported key needs to be added to the project *Info.plist* file with a Boolean value of true. Select the *Info.plist* file in the Project Navigator panel so that it loads into the property editor. Add a new entry to the file with the key field set to CKSharingSupported, the type to Boolean and the value to YES as illustrated in Figure 55-1:

Figure 55-1

55.2 Adding the Share Button

The user interface for the app now needs to be modified to add a share button to the toolbar. Select the *Main.storyboard* file, locate the Bar Button Item in the Library panel and drag and drop an instance onto the toolbar so that it is position to the right of the existing Delete button. Once added, double-click on the button and change the text to read "Share":

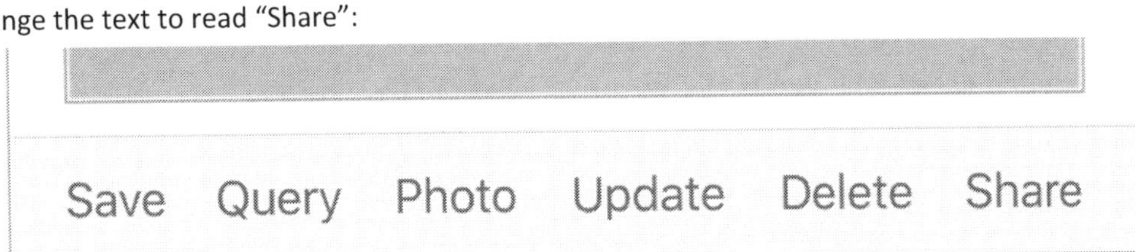

Figure 55-2

With the Share button still selected, display the Assistant Editor panel and establish an Action connection to a method named *shareRecord*.

55.3 Creating the CloudKit Share

The next step is to add some code to the *shareRecord* action method to initialize and display the UICloudSharingController and to create and save the CKShare object. Select the *ViewController.swift* file, locate the stub *shareRecord* method and modify it so that it reads as follows:

```
@IBAction func shareRecord(_ sender: Any) {

    let controller = UICloudSharingController { controller,
        preparationCompletionHandler in

        if let thisRecord = self.currentRecord {
            let share = CKShare(rootRecord: thisRecord)

            share[CKShare.SystemFieldKey.title]
                    = "An Amazing House" as CKRecordValue
            share.publicPermission = .readOnly

            let modifyRecordsOperation = CKModifyRecordsOperation(
                recordsToSave: [thisRecord, share],
                recordIDsToDelete: nil)

            let configuration = CKOperation.Configuration()

            configuration.timeoutIntervalForResource = 10
            configuration.timeoutIntervalForRequest = 10

            modifyRecordsOperation.modifyRecordsCompletionBlock = {
                records, recordIDs, error in
                if let err = error {
                    print(err.localizedDescription)
                }
                preparationCompletionHandler(share,
                                            CKContainer.default(), error)
            }
            self.privateDatabase?.add(modifyRecordsOperation)
        } else {
            print("User error: No record selected")
        }
    }

    controller.availablePermissions = [.allowPublic, .allowReadOnly,
                         .allowReadWrite, .allowPrivate]
    controller.popoverPresentationController?.barButtonItem =
        sender as? UIBarButtonItem
```

```
    present(controller, animated: true)
}
```

The code added to this method follows the steps outlined in the chapter entitled *An Introduction to CloudKit Sharing* to display the CloudKit sharing view controller, create a share object initialized with the currently selected record and save it to the user's private database.

55.4 Accepting a CloudKit Share

Now that the user has the ability to create a CloudKit share, the app also needs to be modified to accept a share and display the shared record to the user. The first step in this process is to implement the *userDidAcceptCloudKitShareWith* method within the project app delegate class. Edit the *AppDelegate.swift* file and implement this method as follows:

```
func application(_ application: UIApplication, userDidAcceptCloudKitShareWith
  cloudKitShareMetadata: CKShare.Metadata) {

    let acceptSharesOperation =
        CKAcceptSharesOperation(shareMetadatas: [cloudKitShareMetadata])
    acceptSharesOperation.perShareCompletionBlock = {
        metadata, share, error in
        if let err = error {
            print(err.localizedDescription)
        } else {
            let viewController: ViewController =
                self.window?.rootViewController as! ViewController
            viewController.fetchShare(cloudKitShareMetadata)

        }
    }
    CKContainer(identifier:
        cloudKitShareMetadata.containerIdentifier).add(
            acceptSharesOperation)
}
```

As outlined previously, this delegate method creates a CKAcceptSharesOperation using the share metadata object passed in to the method. This operation is then performed on the CloudKit container referenced in the share metadata. The share operation has assigned to it a completion handler which, in this instance, is configured to call a method on the view controller named *fetchShare*. The next task is to implement this method.

55.5 Fetching the Shared Record

At this point the share has been accepted and a CKShare.Metadata object provided from which information about the shared record may be extracted. All that remains before the app can be tested is to implement the *fetchShare* method within the *ViewController.swift* file:

```
func fetchShare(_ metadata: CKShare.Metadata) {

    let operation = CKFetchRecordsOperation(
```

```
            recordIDs: [metadata.rootRecordID])

    operation.perRecordCompletionBlock = { record, _, error in

        if let err = error {
            print(err.localizedDescription)
        }

        if record != nil {
            DispatchQueue.main.async() {
                self.currentRecord = record
                self.addressField.text =
                    record?.object(forKey: "address") as? String
                self.commentsField.text =
                    record?.object(forKey: "comment") as? String
                let photo =
                    record?.object(forKey: "photo") as! CKAsset
                let image = UIImage(contentsOfFile:
                    photo.fileURL.path)
                self.imageView.image = image
                self.photoURL = self.saveImageToFile(image!)
            }
        }
    }

    operation.fetchRecordsCompletionBlock = { _, error in
        if let err = error {
            print(err.localizedDescription)
        }
    }

    CKContainer.default().sharedCloudDatabase.add(operation)
}
```

The method prepares a standard CloudKit fetch operation based on the record ID contained within the share metadata object and performs the fetch using the *sharedCloudDatabase* instance. On a successful fetch, the completion handler is used to extract the data from the shared record and display it to the user.

55.6 Testing the CloudKit Share Example

To fully test CloudKit sharing, two devices with different Apple IDs need to be used. If you have access to two devices, create a second Apple ID for testing purposes and sign in using that ID on one of the devices. Once logged in, make sure that the devices are able to send and receive iMessage or email messages between each other and install and run the CloudKitDemo on both devices. Once the testing environment is set up, launch the CloudKitDemo app on one of the devices and add a record to the private database. Once added, tap the

Share button and use the share view controller interface to send a share link to the Apple ID associated with the second device. When the message arrives on the second device, tap the share link and accept the share when prompted to do so. Once the share has been accepted, the CloudKitDemo app should launch and display the shared record.

55.7 Summary

This chapter put the theory of CloudKit sharing outlined in the chapter entitled *An Introduction to CloudKit Sharing* into practice by enhancing the CloudKitDemo project to include the ability to share CloudKit-based records with other app users. This involved the creation and saving of a CKShare object, use of the UICloudSharingController class and the addition of code to handle the acceptance and fetching of a shared CloudKit database record.

Chapter 56

56. An Overview of iOS 12 Multitouch, Taps and Gestures

In terms of physical points of interaction between the device and the user, the iPhone and iPad provide four buttons (three in the case of the iPhone X), a switch and a touch screen. Without question, the user will spend far more time using the touch screen than any other aspect of the device. It is essential, therefore, that any application be able to handle gestures (touches, multitouches, taps, swipes and pinches etc) performed by the user's fingers on the touch screen.

Before writing code to handle these gestures, this chapter will spend some time talking about the responder chain in relation to touch screen events before delving a little deeper into the types of gestures an iOS application is likely to encounter.

56.1 The Responder Chain

In the chapter entitled *Understanding iOS 12 Views, Windows and the View Hierarchy* we spent some time talking about the view hierarchy of an application's user interface and how that hierarchy also defined part of the application's *responder chain*. In order to fully understand the concepts behind the handling of touch screen gestures it is first necessary to spend a little more time learning about the responder chain.

When the user interacts with the touch screen of an iPhone or iPad the hardware detects the physical contact and notifies the operating system. The operating system subsequently creates an *event* associated with the interaction and passes it into the currently active application's *event queue* where it is then picked up by the *event loop* and passed to the current *first responder* object; the first responder being the object with which the user was interacting when this event was triggered (for example a UIButton or UIView object). If the first responder has been programmed to handle the type of event received it does so (for example a button may have an action defined to call a particular method when it receives a touch event). Having handled the event, the responder then has the option of discarding that event, or passing it up to the *next responder* in the *response chain* (defined by the object's *next* property) for further processing, and so on up the chain. If the first responder is not able to handle the event it will also pass it to the next responder in the chain and so on until it either reaches a responder that handles the event or it reaches the end of the chain (the UIApplication object) where it will either be handled or discarded.

Take, for example, a UIView with a UIButton subview. If the user touches the screen over the button then the button, as first responder, will receive the event. If the button is unable to handle the event it will need to be passed up to the view object. If the view is also unable to handle the event it would then be passed to the view controller and so on.

When working with the responder chain, it is important to note that the passing of an event from one responder to the next responder in the chain does not happen automatically. If an event needs to be passed to the next responder, code must be written to make it happen.

56.2 Forwarding an Event to the Next Responder

To pass an event to the next responder in the chain, a reference to the next responder object must first be obtained. This can be achieved by accessing the *next* property of the current responder. Once the next responder has been identified, the method that triggered the event is called on that object and passed any relevant event data.

Take, for example, a situation where the current responder object is unable to handle a *touchesBegan* event. In order to pass this to the next responder, the *touchesBegan* method of the current responder will need to make a call as follows:

```
override func touchesBegan(_ touches: Set<UITouch>, with event: UIEvent?) {
        self.next?.touchesBegan(touches, with: event)
}
```

In this case, the *touchesBegan* method is called on the next responder and passed the original touches and event parameters.

56.3 Gestures

Gesture is an umbrella term used to encapsulate any single interaction between the touch screen and the user, starting at the point that the screen is touched (by one or more fingers) and the time that the last finger leaves the surface of the screen. *Swipes, pinches, stretches* and *flicks* are all forms of gesture.

56.4 Taps

A *tap*, as the name suggests, occurs when the user touches the screen with a single finger and then immediately lifts it from the screen. Taps can be single-taps or multiple-taps and the event will contain information about the number of times a user tapped on the screen.

56.5 Touches

A *touch* occurs when a finger establishes contact with the screen. When more than one finger touches the screen each finger registers as a touch up to a maximum of five fingers.

56.6 Touch Notification Methods

Touch screen events cause one of four methods on the first responder object to be called. The method that gets called for a specific event will depend on the nature of the interaction. In order to handle events, therefore, it is important to ensure that the appropriate methods from those outlined below are implemented within your responder chain. These methods will be used in the worked example contained in the *An Example iOS 12 Touch, Multitouch and Tap Application* and *Detecting iOS 12 Touch Screen Gesture Motions* chapters of this book.

56.6.1 touchesBegan method

The *touchesBegan* method is called when the user first touches the screen. Passed to this method are an argument called *touches* of type NSSet and the corresponding UIEvent object. The touches object contains a UITouch event for each finger in contact with the screen. The *tapCount* method of any of the UITouch events within the *touches* set can be called to identify the number of taps, if any, performed by the user. Similarly, the coordinates of an individual touch can be identified from the UITouch event either relative to the entire screen or within the local view itself.

56.6.2 touchesMoved method

The *touchesMoved* method is called when one or more fingers move across the screen. As fingers move across the screen this method gets called multiple times allowing the application to track the new coordinates and touch count at regular intervals. As with the *touchesBegan* method, this method is provided with an event object and an NSSet object containing UITouch events for each finger on the screen.

56.6.3 touchesEnded method

This method is called when the user lifts one or more fingers from the screen. As with the previous methods, *touchesEnded* is provided with the event and NSSet objects.

56.6.4 touchesCancelled method

When a gesture is interrupted due to a high level interrupt, such as the phone detecting an incoming call, the *touchesCancelled* method is called.

56.7 Touch Prediction

A feature introduced as part of the iOS 9 SDK is touch prediction. Each time the system updates the current coordinates of a touch on the screen, a set of algorithms attempt to predict the coordinates of the next location. A finger sweeping across the screen, for example, will trigger multiple calls to the *touchesMoved* method passing through the current touch coordinates. Also passed through to the method is a UIEvent object on which a method named *predictedTouchesForTouch* may be called, passing through the touch object representing the current location. In return, the method will provide an array of UITouch objects that predict the next few locations of the touch motion. This information can then be used to improve the performance and responsiveness of the app to the touch behavior of the user.

56.8 Touch Coalescing

iOS devices are categorized by two metrics known as the *touch sample rate* and *touch delivery rate*. The touch sample rate is the frequency with which the screen scans for the current position of touches on the screen. The touch delivery rate, on the other hand, is the frequency with which that information is passed to the currently running app.

On most devices (including all recent iPhone models except the iPhone X), both the sample and delivery rates run at 60 Hz (in other words 60 times a second). On other device models, however, the sample and delivery frequencies do not match. The iPhone X, for example, samples at 120 Hz but delivers at a slower 60 Hz, while an iPad Pro with an Apple Pencil samples at an impressive 240 Hz while delivering at only 120 Hz.

To avoid the loss of touch information caused by the gap in sampling and delivery frequencies, UIKit uses a system referred to as *touch coalescing* to deliver the additional touch data generated by the higher sampling frequencies.

With touch coalescing, the same touch notification methods are called and passed the same UITouch objects which are referred to as the *main touches.* Also passed through to each method is a UIEvent object on which the *coalescedTouchesForTouch* method may be called, passing through as an argument the current main touch object. When called within an app running on a device where the sampling rate exceeds the delivery rate, the method will return an array of touch objects consisting of both a copy of the current main touch together with the intermediate touch activity between the current main touch and the previous main touch. These intermediate touch objects are referred to as *coalesced touches*. On iOS devices with matching rates, no coalesced touch objects will be returned by this method call.

56.9 3D Touch

3D Touch is a hardware feature introduced with the iPhone 6s family of devices. 3D Touch uses a capacitive layer behind the device screen to gauge the amount of pressure that is being applied to the device display during a touch. The presence or otherwise of support for 3D Touch on an iOS device can be identified by checking the *forceTouchCapability* property of the trait collection on a view controller. The following code, for example, checks for 3D Touch support:

```
if traitCollection.forceTouchCapability == .available {
    // 3D Touch is available on device
} else {
    // 3D Touch is not available on device
}
```

When handling touches on a 3D Touch capable device, the *force* property of the UITouch events passed to the touch notification methods described above will contain a value representing the force currently being applied to the display by a touch. This topic is covered in detail in the chapter entitled *A 3D Touch Force Handling Tutorial*.

3D Touch also allows two additional features, referred to as *Home Screen Quick Actions* and *Peek and Pop*, to be built into iOS apps, details of which are covered in the chapters entitled *A 3D Touch Force Handling Tutorial* and *An iOS 12 3D Touch Peek and Pop Tutorial*.

56.10 Summary

In order to fully appreciate the mechanisms for handling touch screen events within an iOS application, it is first important to understand both the responder chain and the methods that are called on a responder depending on the type of interaction. We have covered these basics in this chapter. In the next chapter, entitled *An Example iOS 12 Touch, Multitouch and Tap Application* we will use these concepts to create an example application that demonstrates touch screen event handling.

Chapter 57

57. An Example iOS 12 Touch, Multitouch and Tap Application

Having covered the basic concepts behind the handling of iOS user interaction with an iPhone or iPad touch screen in the previous chapter, this chapter will work through a tutorial designed to highlight the handling of taps and touches. Topics covered in this chapter include the detection of single and multiple taps and touches, identifying whether a user single or double tapped the device display and extracting information about a touch or tap from the corresponding event object.

57.1 The Example iOS Tap and Touch Application

The example application created in the course of this tutorial will consist of a view and some labels. The view object's view controller will implement a number of the touch screen event methods outlined in *An Overview of iOS 12 Multitouch, Taps and Gestures* and update the status labels to reflect the detected activity. The application will, for example, report the number of fingers touching the screen, the number of taps performed and the most recent touch event that was triggered. In the next chapter, entitled *Detecting iOS 12 Touch Screen Gesture Motions* we will look more closely at detecting the motion of touches.

57.2 Creating the Example iOS Touch Project

Begin by launching the Xcode development environment and selecting the option to create a new project. Select the iOS *Single View Application* template and set the language menu to *Swift*. Name the project *Touch* and, when the main Xcode project screen appears, we are ready to start writing the code and designing our application.

57.3 Designing the User Interface

Load the storyboard by selecting the *Main.storyboard* file. Using Interface Builder, modify the user interface by adding label components from the Library (*View -> Utilities -> Show Library*) and modifying properties until the view appears as outlined in Figure 57-1.

When adding the rightmost labels, be sure to stretch them so that the right-hand edges reach approximately three quarters across the overall layout width.

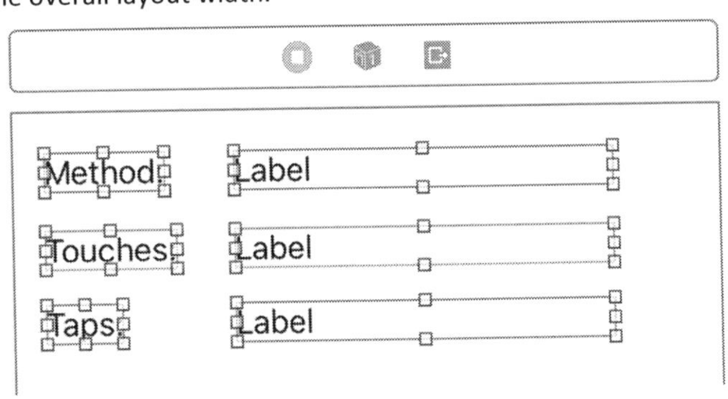

Figure 57-1

Display the *Resolve Auto Layout Issues* menu and select the *Reset to suggested constraints* option listed under *All Views in View Controller*.

Select the label to the right of the "Method:" label, display the Assistant Editor panel and verify that the editor is displaying the contents of the *ViewController.swift* file. Ctrl-click on the same label object and drag to a position just below the class declaration line in the Assistant Editor. Release the line and in the resulting connection dialog establish an outlet connection named *methodStatus*.

Repeat the above steps to establish outlet connections for the remaining label objects to properties named *touchStatus* and *tapStatus*.

57.4 Enabling Multitouch on the View

By default, views are configured to respond to only single touches (in other words a single finger touching or tapping the screen at any one time). For the purposes of this example we plan to detect multiple touches. In order to enable this support it is necessary to change an attribute of the view object. To achieve this, click on the background of the *View* window, display the Attributes Inspector (*View -> Utilities -> Show Attributes Inspector*) and make sure that the *Multiple Touch* option is selected in the *Interaction* section:

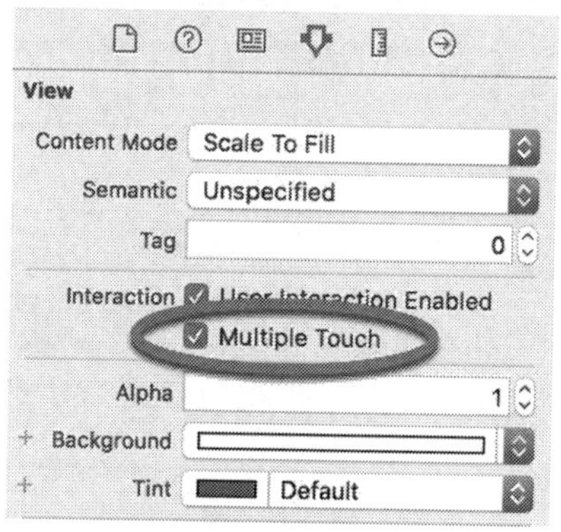

Figure 57-2

57.5 Implementing the touchesBegan Method

When the user touches the screen, the *touchesBegan* method of the first responder is called. In order to capture these event types, we need to implement this method in our view controller. In the Xcode project navigator, select the *ViewController.swift* file and add the *touchesBegan* method as follows:

```
override func touchesBegan(_ touches: Set<UITouch>, with event: UIEvent?) {
    let touchCount = touches.count
    if let touch = touches.first {
        let tapCount = touch.tapCount

        methodStatus.text = "touchesBegan"
        touchStatus.text = "\(touchCount) touches"
        tapStatus.text = "\(tapCount) taps"
    }
}
```

This method obtains a count of the number of touch objects contained in the *touches* set (essentially the number of fingers touching the screen) and assigns it to a variable. It then gets the tap count from one of the touch objects. The code then updates the *methodStatus* label to indicate that the *touchesBegan* method has been triggered, constructs a string indicating the number of touches and taps detected and displays the information on the *touchStatus* and *tapStatus* labels accordingly.

57.6 Implementing the touchesMoved Method

When the user moves one or more fingers currently in contact with the surface of the touch screen, the *touchesMoved* method is called repeatedly until the movement ceases. In order to capture these events it is necessary to implement the touchesMoved method in our view controller class:

```
override func touchesMoved(_ touches: Set<UITouch>, with event: UIEvent?) {
    let touchCount = touches.count
    if let touch = touches.first {
        let tapCount = touch.tapCount

        methodStatus.text = "touchesMoved";
        touchStatus.text = "\(touchCount) touches"
        tapStatus.text = "\(tapCount) taps"
    }
}
```

Once again we report the number of touches and taps detected and indicate to the user that this time the *touchesMoved* method is being triggered.

57.7 Implementing the touchesEnded Method

When the user removes a finger from the screen the *touchesEnded* method is called. We can, therefore, implement this method as follows:

```
override func touchesEnded(_ touches: Set<UITouch>, with event: UIEvent?) {
    let touchCount = touches.count
    if let touch = touches.first {
        let tapCount = touch.tapCount

        methodStatus.text = "touchesEnded";
        touchStatus.text = "\(touchCount) touches"
        tapStatus.text = "\(tapCount) taps"
    }
}
```

57.8 Getting the Coordinates of a Touch

Although not part of this particular example, it is worth knowing that the coordinates of the location on the screen where a touch has been detected may be obtained in the form of a CGPoint structure by calling the *location(in:)* method of the touch object. For example:

```
let touch = touches.first
let point = touch.location(in: self.view)
```

The X and Y coordinates may subsequently be extracted from the CGPoint structure by accessing the corresponding elements:

```
let pointX = point.x
let pointY = point.y
```

57.9 Building and Running the Touch Example Application

Build and run the application on a physical iOS device by clicking on the run button located in the toolbar of the main Xcode project window. With each tap and touch on the device screen, the status labels should update to reflect the interaction:

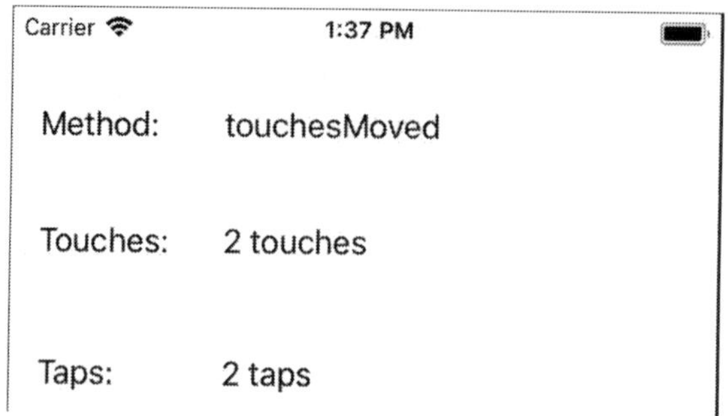

Figure 57-3

Note that when running within the iOS Simulator, multiple touches may be simulated by holding down the Option key while clicking in the simulator window.

57.10 Checking for Touch Predictions

Having implemented code to detect touches and touch motion on the screen, code will now be added to output to the console any touch predictions available within the UIEvent object passed to the *touchesMoved* method. Locate this method within the *ViewController.swift* file and modify it so that it now reads as follows:

```
override func touchesMoved(_ touches: Set<UITouch>, with event: UIEvent?) {
    let touchCount = touches.count
    if let touch = touches.first {
        let tapCount = touch.tapCount

        methodStatus.text = "touchesMoved";
        touchStatus.text = "\(touchCount) touches"
        tapStatus.text = "\(tapCount) taps"

        if let eventObj = event,
           let predictedTouches = eventObj.predictedTouches(for: touch) {
            for predictedTouch in predictedTouches {
                let point = predictedTouch.location(in: self.view)
                print("Predicted location X = \(point.x), Y = \(point.y)")
            }
            print("============")
        }
    }
}
```

The added code begins by checking that an event object was passed to the method before calling the *predictedTouches(for:)* method of that object. For each touch object within the returned array, the X and Y coordinates of the predicted touch location are output to the console.

Compile and run the application once again and monitor the console as a touch moves around the display. When it is able to do so, UIKit will provide predictions on future touch locations. Note that at time of writing this feature would only work on a physical iOS device.

57.11 Accessing Coalesced Touches

The final task in this tutorial is to display any coalesced touch information that might be available. Once again, modify the *touchesMoved* method, this time implementing code to display the location information for any coalesced touches:

```
override func touchesMoved(_ touches: Set<UITouch>, with event: UIEvent?) {
    let touchCount = touches.count
    if let touch = touches.first {
        let tapCount = touch.tapCount

        methodStatus.text = "touchesMoved";
        touchStatus.text = "\(touchCount) touches"
        tapStatus.text = "\(tapCount) taps"

        if let eventObj = event,
            let coalescedTocuhes = eventObj.coalescedTouches(for: touch) {
             for coalescedTouch in coalescedTocuhes {
                 let point = coalescedTouch.location(in: self.view)
                 print("Coalesced location X = \(point.x), Y = \(point.y)")
             }
             print("============")
        }
    }
}
```

To test this functionality it will be necessary to run the app on a physical iPad Air 2 (or newer) device. When run on such a device, moving a touch around the screen will cause the coordinates of the coalesced touches to be displayed to the Xcode console.

57.12 Summary

This chapter has created a simple example project designed to demonstrate the use of the *touchesBegan*, *touchesMoved* and *touchesEnded* methods to obtain information about the touches occurring on the display of an iOS device. Using these methods it is possible to detect when the screen is touched and released, the number of points of contact with the screen and the amount of taps being performed. Code was also added to detect and output information relating to touch predictions and coalesced touches.

Chapter 58

58. Detecting iOS 12 Touch Screen Gesture Motions

The next area of iOS touch screen event handling that we will look at in this book involves the detection of gestures involving movement. As covered in a previous chapter, a *gesture* refers to the activity that takes place in the time between a finger touching the screen and the finger then being lifted from the screen. In the chapter entitled *An Example iOS 12 Touch, Multitouch and Tap Application* we dealt with touches that did not involve any movement across the screen surface. We will now create an example that tracks the coordinates of a finger as it moves across the screen.

Note that the assumption is made throughout this chapter that the reader has already reviewed the *An Overview of iOS 12 Multitouch, Taps and Gestures* chapter of this book.

58.1 The Example iOS 12 Gesture Application

This example application will detect when a single touch is made on the screen of the iPhone or iPad and then report the coordinates of that finger as it is moved across the screen surface.

58.2 Creating the Example Project

Start the Xcode environment and select the option to create a new project using the *Single View Application* template. Name the project *TouchMotion*, and choose *Swift* as the programming language.

58.3 Designing the Application User Interface

The application will display the X and Y coordinates of the touch and update these values in real-time as the finger moves across the screen. When the finger is lifted from the screen, the start and end coordinates of the gesture will then be displayed on two label objects in the user interface. Select the *Main.storyboard* file and, using Interface Builder, create a user interface such that it resembles the layout in Figure 58-1.

Be sure to stretch the labels so that they both extend to cover a little over half of the width of the view layout.

Select the top label object in the view canvas, display the Assistant Editor panel and verify that the editor is displaying the contents of the *ViewController.swift* file. Ctrl-click on the same label object and drag to a position just below the class declaration line in the Assistant Editor. Release the line and in the resulting connection dialog establish an outlet connection named *xCoord*. Repeat this step to establish an outlet connection to the second label object named *yCoord*.

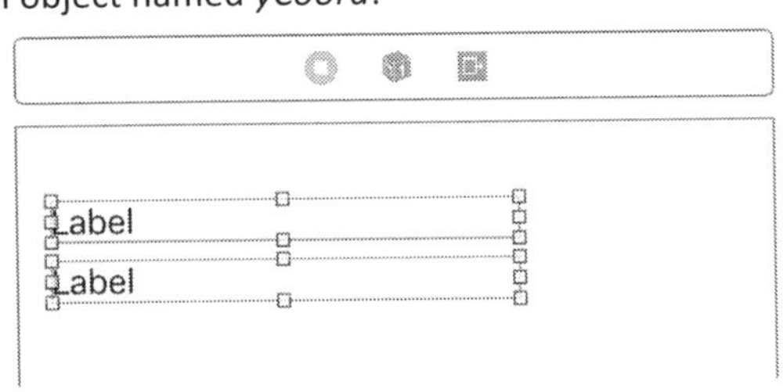

Figure 58-1

Next, review the *ViewController.swift* file to verify that the outlets are correct, then declare a property in which to store coordinates of the start location on the screen:

```
import UIKit

class ViewController: UIViewController {

    @IBOutlet weak var xCoord: UILabel!
    @IBOutlet weak var yCoord: UILabel!

    var startPoint: CGPoint!
.
.
.
}
```

58.4 Implementing the touchesBegan Method

When the user first touches the screen the location coordinates need to be saved in the *startPoint* instance variable and those coordinates reported to the user. This can be achieved by implementing the *touchesBegan* method in the *ViewController.swift* file as follows:

```
override func touchesBegan(_ touches: Set<UITouch>, with event: UIEvent?) {
    if let theTouch = touches.first {
        startPoint = theTouch.location(in: self.view)

        if let x = startPoint?.x, let y = startPoint?.y {

            xCoord.text = ("x = \(x)")
            yCoord.text = ("y = \(y)")
        }
    }
}
```

58.5 Implementing the touchesMoved Method

When the user's finger moves across the screen the *touchesMoved* event will be called repeatedly until the motion stops. By implementing the *touchesMoved* method in our view controller, therefore, we can detect the motion and display the revised coordinates to the user:

```
override func touchesMoved(_ touches: Set<UITouch>, with event: UIEvent?) {
    if let theTouch = touches.first {

        let touchLocation = theTouch.location(in: self.view)
        let x = touchLocation.x
        let y = touchLocation.y

        xCoord.text = ("x = \(x)")
        yCoord.text = ("y = \(y)")
```

```
    }
}
```

58.6 Implementing the touchesEnded Method

When the user's finger lifts from the screen the *touchesEnded* method of the first responder is called. The final task, therefore, is to implement this method in our view controller such that it displays the end point of the gesture:

```
override func touchesEnded(_ touches: Set<UITouch>, with event: UIEvent?) {
    if let theTouch = touches.first {

        let endPoint = theTouch.location(in: self.view)
        let x = endPoint.x
        let y = endPoint.y

        xCoord.text = ("x = \(x)")
        yCoord.text = ("y = \(y)")
    }
}
```

58.7 Building and Running the Gesture Example

Build and run the application using the run button located in the toolbar of the main Xcode project window. When the application starts (either in the iOS Simulator or on a physical device) touch the screen and drag to a new location before lifting your finger from the screen (or mouse button in the case of the iOS Simulator). During the motion the current coordinates will update in real time. Once the gesture is complete the end location of the movement will be displayed.

58.8 Summary

Simply by implementing the standard touch event methods the motion of a gesture can easily be tracked by an iOS application. Much of a user's interaction with applications, however, involves some very specific gesture types such as swipes and pinches. To write code to correlate finger movement on the screen with a specific gesture type would be extremely complex. Fortunately, iOS makes this task easy through the use of *gesture recognizers.* In the next chapter, entitled *Identifying Gestures using iOS 12 Gesture Recognizers* we will look at this concept in more detail.

Chapter 59

59. Identifying Gestures using iOS 12 Gesture Recognizers

In the chapter entitled *Detecting iOS 12 Touch Screen Gesture Motions* we looked at how to track the motion of contact with the touch screen of an iOS device. In practice, an application will need to respond to specific motions that take place during the course of a gesture. The swiping of a finger across the screen might, for example, be required to slide a new view onto the display. Similarly, a pinching motion is typically used in iOS applications to enlarge or reduce an image or view.

Prior to iOS 4, the identification of a gesture was the responsibility of the application developer and typically involved the creation of complex mathematical algorithms. In recognition of this complexity, and given the importance of gestures to user interaction with the iOS device, Apple introduced the UIGestureRecognizer class in iOS 4 thereby making the task of identifying the types of gestures a much easier task for the application developer.

The goal of this chapter, therefore, is to provide an overview of gesture recognition within the context of iOS 12. The next chapter will work through *An iOS 12 Gesture Recognition Tutorial*.

59.1 The UIGestureRecognizer Class

The UIGestureRecognizer class is used as the basis for a collection of subclasses, each designed to detect a specific type of gesture. These subclasses are as follows:

- **UITapGestureRecognizer** – This class is designed to detect when a user taps on the screen of the device. Both single and multiple taps may be detected based on the configuration of the class instance.
- **UIPinchGestureRecognizer** – Detects when a pinching motion is made by the user on the screen. This motion is typically used to zoom in or out of a view or to change the size of a visual component.
- **UIPanGestureRecognizer** – Detects when a dragging or panning gesture is made by the user.
- **UIScreenEdgePanGestureRecognizer** – Detects when a dragging or panning gesture is performed starting near the edge of the display screen.
- **UISwipeGestureRecognizer** – Used to detect when the user makes a swiping gesture across the screen. Instances of this class may be configured to detect motion only in specific directions (left, right, up or down).
- **UIRotationGestureRecognizer** – Identifies when the user makes a rotation gesture (essentially two fingers in contact with the screen located opposite each other and moving in a circular motion).
- **UILongPressGestureRecognizer** – Used to identify when the user touches the screen with one or more fingers for a specified period of time (also referred to as "touch and hold").

These gesture recognizers must be attached to the view on which the gesture will be performed via a call to the view object's *addGestureRecognizer* method. Recognizers must also be assigned an action method that is to be called when the specified gesture is detected. Gesture recognizers may subsequently be removed from a view via a call to the view's *removeGestureRecognizer* method, passing through as an argument the recognizer to be removed.

59.2 Recognizer Action Messages

The iOS gesture recognizers use the target-action model to notify the application of the detection of a specific gesture. When an instance of a gesture recognizer is created it is provided with the reference to the method to be called in the event that the corresponding gesture is detected.

59.3 Discrete and Continuous Gestures

Gestures fall into two distinct categories – *discrete* and *continuous.* A discrete gesture results in only a single call being made to the corresponding action method. Tap gestures (including multiple taps) are considered to be discrete because they only trigger the action method once. Gestures such as swipes, pans, rotations and pinches are deemed to be continuous in that they trigger a constant stream of calls to the corresponding action methods until the gesture ends.

59.4 Obtaining Data from a Gesture

Each gesture action method is passed as an argument a UIGestureRecognizer sender object which may be used to extract information about the gesture. For example, information about the scale factor and speed of a pinch gesture may be obtained by the action method. Similarly, the action method assigned to a rotation gesture recognizer may ascertain the amount of rotation performed by the user and the corresponding velocity.

59.5 Recognizing Tap Gestures

Tap gestures are detected using the UITapGestureRecognizer class. This must be allocated and initialized with an action selector referencing the method to be called when the gesture is detected. The number of taps that must be performed to constitute the full gesture may be defined by setting the *numberOfTapsRequired* property of the recognizer instance. The following code, for example, will result in a call to the *tapsDetected* method when two consecutive taps are detected on the corresponding view:

```
let doubleTap = UITapGestureRecognizer(target: self,
            action: #selector(tapDetected))
doubleTap.numberOfTapsRequired = 2

self.view.addGestureRecognizer(doubleTap)
```

A template method for the action method for this and other gesture recognizers is as follows:

```
@objc func tapDetected() {
        // Code to respond to gesture here
}
```

59.6 Recognizing Pinch Gestures

Pinch gestures are detected using the UIPinchGestureRecognizer class. For example:

```
let pinchRecognizer = UIPinchGestureRecognizer(target: self,
            action: #selector(pinchDetected))
self.view.addGestureRecognizer(pinchRecognizer)
```

59.7 Detecting Rotation Gestures

Rotation gestures are recognized by the UIRotationGestureRecognizer, the sample code for which is as follows:

```
let rotationRecognizer = UIRotationGestureRecognizer(target: self,
```

```
            action: #selector(rotationDetected))
self.view.addGestureRecognizer(rotationRecognizer)
```

59.8 Recognizing Pan and Dragging Gestures

Pan and dragging gestures are detected using the UIPanGestureRecognizer class. Pan gestures are essentially any *continuous* gesture. For example, the random meandering of a finger across the screen will generally be considered by the recognizer as a pan or drag operation:

```
let panRecognizer = UIPanGestureRecognizer(target: self,
            action: #selector(panDetected))
self.view.addGestureRecognizer(panRecognizer)
```

If both swipe and pan recognizers are attached to the same view it is likely that most swipes will be recognized as pans. Caution should be taken, therefore, when mixing these two gesture recognizers on the same view.

59.9 Recognizing Swipe Gestures

Swipe gestures are detected using the UISwipeGestureRecognizer class. All swipes, or just those in a specific direction, may be detected by assigning one of the following constants to the *direction* property of the class:

- UISwipeGestureRecognizerDirection.right
- UISwipeGestureRecognizerDirection.left
- UISwipeGestureRecognizerDirection.up
- UISwipeGestureRecognizerDirection.down

Note that when programming in Swift, the above constants may be abbreviated to *.right*, *.left*, *.up*, and *.down*.

If no direction is specified the default is to detect rightward swipes. The following code configures a UISwipeGestureRecognizer instance to detect upward swipes:

```
let swipeRecognizer = UISwipeGestureRecognizer(target: self,
          action: #selector(swipeDetected))
swipeRecognizer.direction = .up
self.view.addGestureRecognizer(swipeRecognizer)
```

59.10 Recognizing Long Touch (Touch and Hold) Gestures

Long touches are detected using the UILongPressGestureRecognizer class. The requirements for the gesture may be specified in terms of touch duration, number of touches, number of taps and allowable movement during the touch. These requirements are specified by the *minimumPressDuration*, *numberOfTouchesRequired*, *numberOfTapsRequired* and *allowableMovement* properties of the class respectively. The following code fragment configures the recognizer to detect long presses of 3 seconds or more involving one finger. The default allowable movement is not set and therefore defaults to 10 pixels:

```
let longPressRecognizer = UILongPressGestureRecognizer(target: self,
        action: #selector(longPressDetected))
longPressRecognizer.minimumPressDuration = 3
longPressRecognizer.numberOfTouchesRequired = 1
self.view.addGestureRecognizer(longPressRecognizer)
```

59.11 Summary

In this chapter we have provided an overview of gesture recognizers and outlined some examples of how to detect the various types of gesture typically used by iOS device users. In the next chapter we will work step-by-step through a tutorial designed to show these theories in practice.

Chapter 60

60. An iOS 12 Gesture Recognition Tutorial

Having covered the theory of gesture recognition on iOS in the chapter entitled *Identifying Gestures using iOS 12 Gesture Recognizers*, this chapter will work through an example application intended to demonstrate the use of the various UIGestureRecognizer subclasses.

The application created in this chapter will configure recognizers to detect a number of different gestures on the iPhone or iPad display and update a status label with information about each recognized gesture.

60.1 Creating the Gesture Recognition Project

Begin by invoking Xcode and creating a new iOS *Single View Application* project named *Recognizer* using Swift as the programming language.

60.2 Designing the User Interface

The only visual component that will be present on our UIView object will be the label used to notify the user of the type of gesture detected. Since the text displayed on this label will need to be updated from within the application code it will need to be connected to an outlet. In addition, the view controller will also contain five gesture recognizer objects to detect pinches, taps, rotations, swipes and long presses. When triggered, these objects will need to call action methods in order to update the label with a notification to the user that the corresponding gesture has been detected.

Select the *Main.storyboard* file and drag a Label object from the Library panel to the center of the view. Once positioned, display the Auto Layout *Resolve Auto Layout Issues* menu and select the *Reset to Suggested Constraints* menu option listed in the *All Views in View Controller* section of the menu.

Select the label object in the view canvas, display the Assistant Editor panel and verify that the editor is displaying the contents of the *ViewController.swift* file. Ctrl-click on the same label object and drag to a position just below the class declaration line in the Assistant Editor. Release the line and, in the resulting connection dialog, establish an outlet connection named *statusLabel*.

Next, the non-visual gesture recognizer objects need to be added to the design. Scroll down the list of objects in the Library panel until the *Tap Gesture Recognizer* object comes into view. Drag and drop the object onto the View in the design area (if the object is dropped outside the view, the connection between the recognizer and the view on which the gestures are going to be performed will not be established). Repeat these steps to add Pinch, Rotation, Swipe and Long Press Gesture Recognizer objects to the design. Note that the document outline panel (which can be displayed by clicking on the panel button in the lower left-hand corner of the storyboard panel) has updated to reflect the presence of the gesture recognizer objects as illustrated in Figure 60-1. An icon for each recognizer added to the view also appears within the toolbar across the top of the storyboard scene.

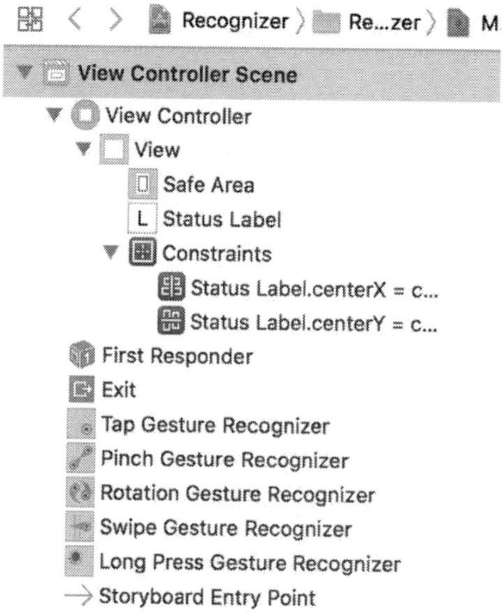

Figure 60-1

Within the document outline panel, select the Tap Gesture Recognizer instance and display the Attributes Inspector (*View -> Utilities -> Show Attributes Inspector*). Within the attributes panel, change the *Taps* value to 2 so that only double taps are detected.

Similarly, select the Long Press Recognizer object and change the *Min Duration* attribute to 3 seconds.

Having added and configured the gesture recognizers, the next step is to connect each recognizer to its corresponding action method.

Display the Assistant Editor and verify that it is displaying the content of *ViewController.swift*. Ctrl-click on the *Tap Gesture Recognizer* object either in the document outline panel or in the scene toolbar and drag the line to the area immediately beneath the *viewDidLoad* method in the Assistant Editor panel. Release the line and, within the resulting connection dialog, establish an Action method configured to call a method named *tapDetected* with the *Type* value set to *UITapGestureRecognizer* as illustrated in Figure 60-2:

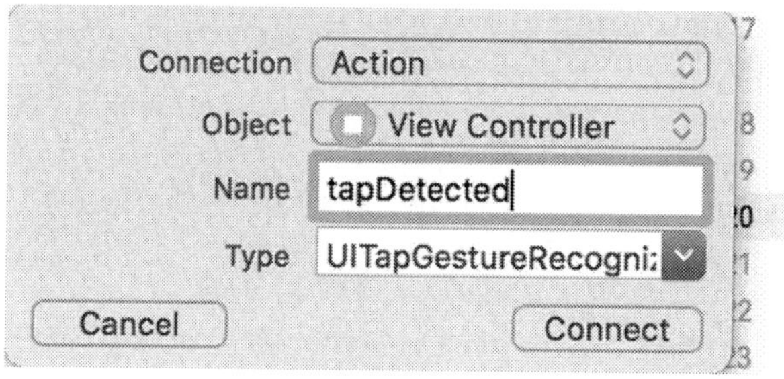

Figure 60-2

Repeat these steps to establish action connections for the pinch, rotation, swipe and long press gesture recognizers to methods named *pinchDetected*, *rotationDetected*, *swipeDetected* and *longPressDetected* respectively, taking care to select the corresponding type value for each action.

60.3 Implementing the Action Methods

Having configured the gesture recognizers, the next step is to add code to the action methods that will be called by each recognizer when the corresponding gesture is detected. The methods stubs created by Xcode reside in the *ViewController.swift* file and will update the status label with information about the detected gesture:

```
@IBAction func tapDetected(_ sender: UITapGestureRecognizer) {
    statusLabel.text = "Double Tap"
}

@IBAction func pinchDetected(_ sender: UIPinchGestureRecognizer) {
    let scale = sender.scale
    let velocity = sender.velocity
    let resultString =
        "Pinch - scale = \(scale), velocity = \(velocity)"

    statusLabel.text = resultString
}

@IBAction func rotationDetected(_ sender: UIRotationGestureRecognizer) {
    let radians = sender.rotation
    let velocity = sender.velocity
    let resultString =
        "Rotation - Radians = \(radians), velocity = \(velocity)"

    statusLabel.text = resultString
}

@IBAction func swipeDetected(_ sender: UISwipeGestureRecognizer) {
    statusLabel.text = "Right swipe"
}

@IBAction func longPressDetected(_ sender: UILongPressGestureRecognizer) {
    statusLabel.text = "Long Press"
}
```

60.4 Testing the Gesture Recognition Application

The final step is to build and run the application. Once the application loads on the device, perform the appropriate gestures on the display and watch the status label update accordingly. If using a simulator session, hold down the Option key while clicking with the mouse to simulate two touches for the pinch and rotation tests. Note that when testing on an iPhone it will be necessary to rotate the device into landscape orientation in order to be able to see the full text displayed on the label.

60.5 Summary

The iOS SDK includes a set of gesture recognizer classes designed to detect swipe, tap, long press, pan, pinch and rotation gestures. This chapter has worked through the creation of an example application that demonstrates how to implement gesture detection using these classes within the Interface Builder environment.

Chapter 61

61. Implementing Touch ID and Face ID Authentication in iOS 12 Apps

In the world of computer security, user authentication falls into the three categories of something you know, something you have and something you are. The "something you know" category typically involves a memorized password or PIN number and is considered the least secure option. A more secure option is the "something you have" approach which usually takes the form of a small authentication token or device which generates one-time access codes on request.

The final category, "something you are", refers to a physical attribute that is unique to the user. This, of course, involves biometrics in the form of a retina scan, facial or voice recognition or fingerprint.

With the iPhone 5s, Apple introduced a built-in fingerprint scanner which enabled users to access the device and make purchases in the iTunes, App and iBooks stores using fingerprint authentication. Since the introduction of iOS 8, this biometric authentication capability can now be built into your own applications. With the introduction of the iPhone X and iOS 11, biometric authentication using facial recognition can also be built into your iOS apps.

61.1 The Local Authentication Framework

Biometric authentication for iOS applications is implemented using the Local Authentication Framework. The key class within this framework is the LAContext class which, among other tasks, is used to evaluate the authentication abilities of the device on which the application is running and perform the authentication.

61.2 Checking for Biometric Authentication Availability

Not all iOS devices offer the fingerprint scanner or facial recognition support and, even on devices with the necessary hardware support, not all users will have activated these authentication features. The first step in using biometric authentication, therefore, is to check that biometric authentication is a viable option on the device:

```
let context = LAContext()

var error: NSError?

if context.canEvaluatePolicy(
        LAPolicy.DeviceOwnerAuthenticationWithBiometrics,
                error: &error) {
        // Biometry is available on the device
} else {
        // Biometry is not available on the device
        // No hardware support or user has not set up biometric auth
}
```

If biometric authentication is not available, the reason can be identified by accessing the errorCode property of the error parameter and will fall into one of the following categories:

- **LAError.biometryNotEnrolled** – The user has not enrolled in biometric authentication on the device.
- **LAError.passcodeNotSet** – The user has not yet configured a passcode on the device.
- **LAError.biometryNotAvailable** – The device does not have the required biometric hardware support.

61.3 Identifying Authentication Options

In the event that the device on which the app is running contains the necessary biometric hardware, it can be useful to identify the type of authentication that is supported. This can be achieved by evaluating the *biometryType* property of the LAContext instance as follows:

```
let context = LAContext()

var error: NSError?

if context.canEvaluatePolicy(
    LAPolicy.deviceOwnerAuthenticationWithBiometrics,
          error: &error) {

    if (context.biometryType == LABiometryType.faceID) {
        // Device support Face ID
    } else if context.biometryType == LABiometryType.touchID {
        // Device supports Touch ID
    } else {
        // Device has no biometric support
    }
```

61.4 Evaluating Biometric Policy

In the event that biometric authentication is available, the next step is to evaluate the policy. This task is performed by calling the *evaluatePolicy* method of the LAContext instance, passing through the authentication policy type and a message to be displayed to the user. The task is performed asynchronously and a *reply* closure expression called once the user has provided input:

```
context.evaluatePolicy(
        LAPolicy.deviceOwnerAuthenticationWithBiometrics,
        localizedReason: "Authentication is required for access",
        reply: {(success, error) in
                // Code to handle reply here
  })
```

The reply closure expression is passed a Boolean value indicating the success or otherwise of the authentication and an NSError object from which the nature of any failure can be identified via the corresponding error code. Failure to authenticate will fall into one of the following three categories:

- **LAError.systemCancel** – The authentication process was cancelled by the operating system. This error typically occurs when the application is placed in the background.
- **LAError.userCancel** - The authentication process was cancelled by the user.

- **LAError.userFallback** – The user opted to authenticate using a password instead of using Touch or Face ID.

In the event of the user fallback, it is the responsibility of the application to prompt for and verify a password before providing access.

If the authentication process is successful, however, the application should provide the user with access to whatever screens, data or functionality were being protected.

61.5 A Biometric Authentication Example Project

Launch Xcode and create a new iOS Single View Application project named *BiometricID* using Swift as the programming language.

Select the *Main.storyboard* file and drag and drop a Button view so that it is positioned in the center of the storyboard scene. Change the text on the button so that it reads *Authenticate*.

With the button selected, display the Auto Layout Align menu and configure both horizontal and vertical center in container constraints.

Display the Assistant Editor, Ctrl-click on the button view and drag the resulting line to a point beneath the ViewController class declaration line. On releasing the line, establish a connection to an outlet named *authButton*.

Finally, Ctrl-click and drag from the button view to a position just beneath the *viewDidLoad* method in the *ViewController.swift* file. Release the line and, in the connection dialog, establish an Action connection to a method named *authenticateUser*.

On completion of the user interface design the layout should resemble Figure 61-1:

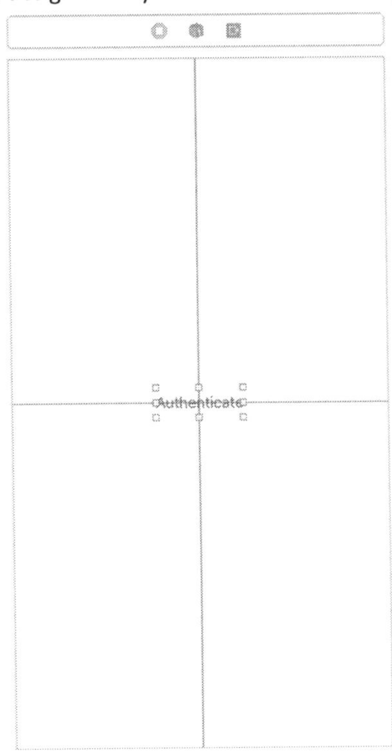

Figure 61-1

61.6 Checking for Biometric Availability

With the user interface designed, the next step is to add some code to the *authenticateUser* method to verify that the device can handle biometric authentication. Select the *ViewController.swift* file, import the LocalAuthentication Framework and add code to the *authenticateUser* method as follows:

```
import UIKit
import LocalAuthentication

class ViewController: UIViewController {

    override func viewDidLoad() {
        super.viewDidLoad()
        // Do any additional setup after loading the view, typically from a
nib.
    }

    @IBAction func authenticateUser(_ sender: Any) {

        let context = LAContext()

        var error: NSError?

        if context.canEvaluatePolicy(
            LAPolicy.deviceOwnerAuthenticationWithBiometrics,
            error: &error) {

            // Device can use biometric authentication

        } else {
            // Device cannot use biometric authentication
            if let err = error {
                switch err.code{

                case LAError.Code.biometryNotEnrolled.rawValue:
                    notifyUser("User is not enrolled",
                            err: err.localizedDescription)

                case LAError.Code.passcodeNotSet.rawValue:
                    notifyUser("A passcode has not been set",
                            err: err.localizedDescription)


                case LAError.Code.biometryNotAvailable.rawValue:
                    notifyUser("Biometric authentication not available",
```

```
                    err: err.localizedDescription)
            default:
                notifyUser("Unknown error",
                    err: err.localizedDescription)
        }
    }
  }
}
```

In addition to evaluating authentication policy, the above code also identifies whether the device supports Face ID or Touch ID authentication and updates the text displayed on the authButton instance accordingly.

Before proceeding, implement the *notifyUser* method as follows:

```
func notifyUser(_ msg: String, err: String?) {
    let alert = UIAlertController(title: msg,
                message: err,
                preferredStyle: .alert)

    let cancelAction = UIAlertAction(title: "OK",
                style: .cancel, handler: nil)

    alert.addAction(cancelAction)

    self.present(alert, animated: true,
                completion: nil)
}
```

61.7 Seeking Biometric Authentication

The next task is to attempt to obtain authentication from the user. This involves a call to the *evaluatePolicy* method of the local authentication context:

```
@IBAction func authenticateUser(_ sender: Any) {

    let context = LAContext()

    var error: NSError?

    if context.canEvaluatePolicy(
        LAPolicy.deviceOwnerAuthenticationWithBiometrics,
        error: &error) {

        // Device can use biometric authentication
        context.evaluatePolicy(
            LAPolicy.deviceOwnerAuthenticationWithBiometrics,
            localizedReason: "Access requires authentication",
            reply: {(success, error) in
```

```
                DispatchQueue.main.async {

                    if let err = error {

                        switch err._code {

                        case LAError.Code.systemCancel.rawValue:
                            self.notifyUser("Session cancelled",
                                            err: err.localizedDescription)

                        case LAError.Code.userCancel.rawValue:
                            self.notifyUser("Please try again",
                                            err: err.localizedDescription)

                        case LAError.Code.userFallback.rawValue:
                            self.notifyUser("Authentication",
                                            err: "Password option selected")
                            // Custom code to obtain password here

                        default:
                            self.notifyUser("Authentication failed",
                                            err: err.localizedDescription)
                        }

                    } else {
                        self.notifyUser("Authentication Successful",
                                        err: "You now have full access")
                    }
                }
        })

    } else {
        // Device cannot use biometric authentication
        if let err = error {
            switch err.code {

            case LAError.Code.biometryNotEnrolled.rawValue:
                notifyUser("User is not enrolled",
                           err: err.localizedDescription)

            case LAError.Code.passcodeNotSet.rawValue:
                notifyUser("A passcode has not been set",
                           err: err.localizedDescription)
```

```
            case LAError.Code.biometryNotAvailable.rawValue:
                notifyUser("Biometric authentication not available",
                           err: err.localizedDescription)
            default:
                notifyUser("Unknown error",
                           err: err.localizedDescription)
            }
        }
    }
}
```

The code added to the method initiates the authentication process and displays a message confirming a successful authentication. In the event of an authentication failure, a message is displayed to the user indicating the reason for the failure. Selection of the password option simply confirms that the option was selected. The actual action taken in this situation will be application specific but will likely involve prompting for a password and verifying it against a database of valid passwords.

61.8 Adding the Face ID Privacy Statement

The final step before testing is to configure the Face ID privacy statement within the project's *Info.plist* file. This is the statement that is displayed to the user when the app seeks permission to use Face ID authentication. To add this entry, select the *Info.plist* file in the project navigator panel and click on the + button located in the bottom entry of the list. From the resulting menu, select the *Privacy – Face ID Usage Description* option and enter a description into the value field:

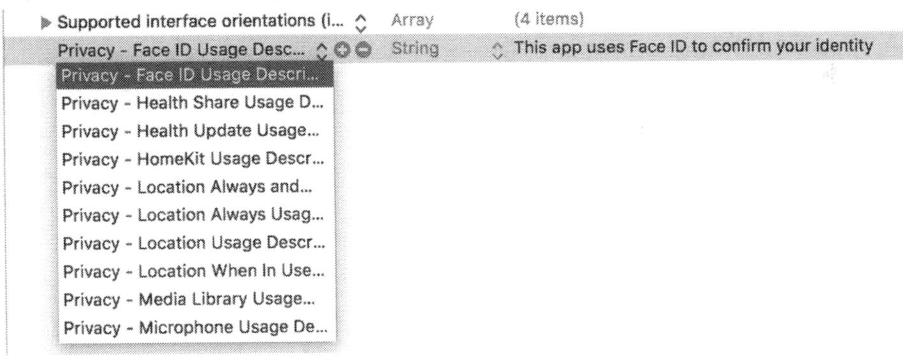

Figure 61-2

61.9 Testing the Application

Biometric authentication can be tested either on physical iOS devices that include biometric support, or using the simulator environment.

When testing Face ID support on a simulator, compile and run the app on an iPhone X series simulator. Once the app has launched, select the simulator's *Hardware -> Face ID* menu and make sure the *Enrolled* option is enabled (as highlighted in Figure 61-3) before tapping the *Authenticate* button within the app.

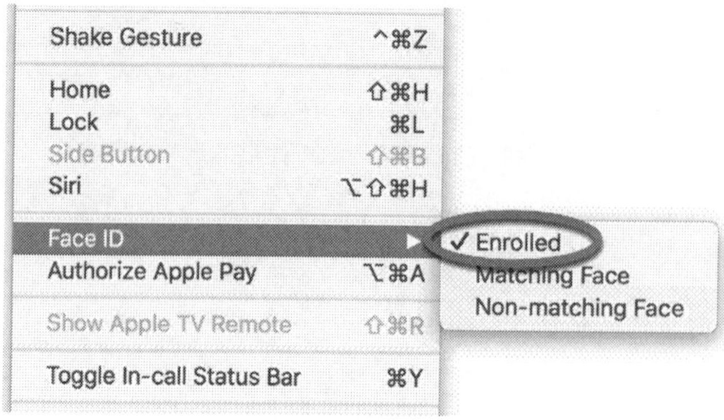

Figure 61-3

At this point, the Face ID permission request dialog will appear displaying the privacy statement that was previously entered into the *Info.plist* file as shown in Figure 61-4:

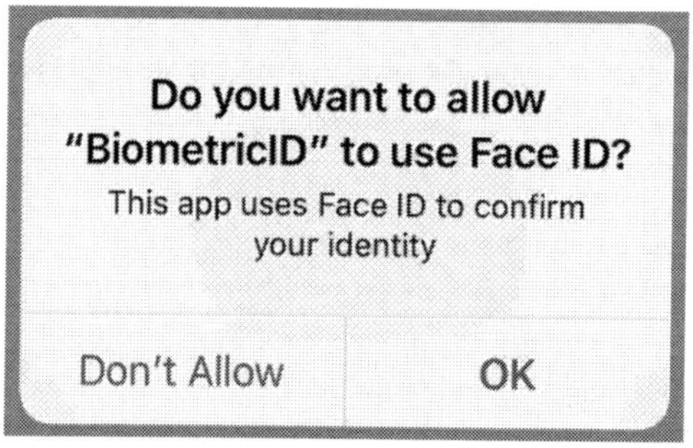

Figure 61-4

After granting permission by clicking on the OK button, the gray simulated Face ID panel (Figure 61-5) should appear:

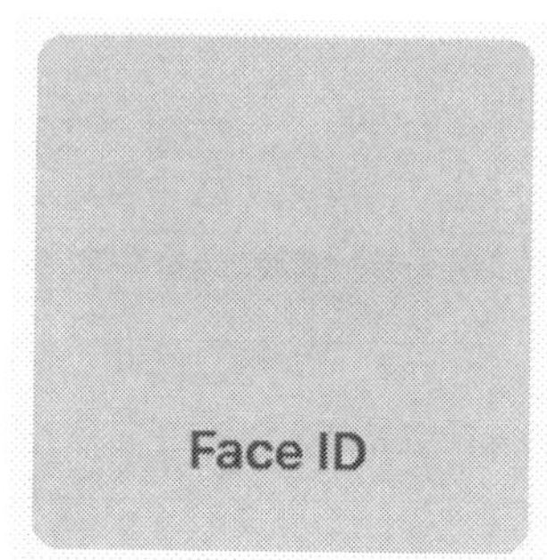

Figure 61-5

To simulate a matching face, select the *Hardware -> Face ID -> Matching Face* menu option after which the app should display the dialog shown in Figure 61-6 indicating that the authentication was successful:

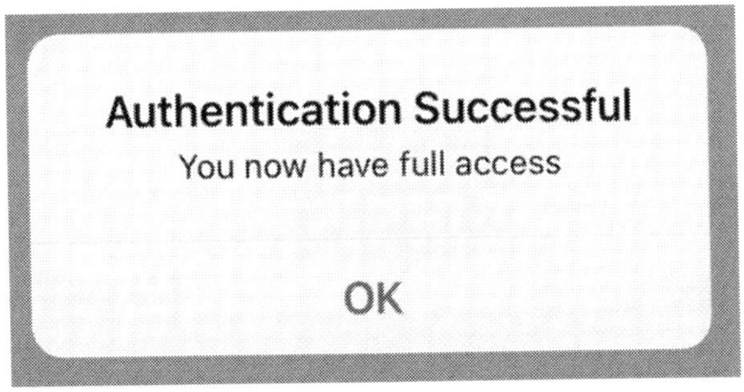
Authentication Successful
You now have full access
OK

Figure 61-6

Repeat the authentication process, this time selecting the Non-matching menu option and verify that the authentication fails.

Launch the app on a physical device with Touch ID support, or use a suitable simulator instance (for example an iPhone 8) to test Touch ID authentication. If using a simulator, make sure that the *Hardware -> Touch ID -> Enrolled* option is enabled before clicking the *Authenticate* button. When instructed to touch the home button, select the *Hardware -> Touch ID -> Matching Touch* menu option to test the authentication. After a successful authentication, try again using the *Non-matching Touch* option.

61.10 Summary

Introduced with iOS 7 and the iPhone 5s device, Touch ID has been provided to iOS users as a way to gain access to devices and to make Apple related purchases. Since the introduction of iOS 8, fingerprint authentication using the Touch ID system has been available to application developers. With the introduction of iOS 11 running on the iPhone X, authentication support has been extended to include facial recognition. This chapter has outlined the steps involved in using the Local Authentication Framework to implement biometric authentication using both the Touch ID and Face ID systems.

Chapter 62

62. Drawing iOS 12 2D Graphics with Core Graphics

The ability to draw two dimensional graphics on the iPhone and iPad is provided as part of the Core Graphics Framework in the form of the Quartz 2D API. The iOS implementation of Quartz on iOS is the same implementation as that provided with macOS and provides a graphics context object together with a set of methods designed to enable the drawing of 2D graphics in the form of images, lines, fill patterns and gradients.

In this chapter we will provide an overview of Quartz 2D. A later chapter, entitled *An iOS 12 Graphics Tutorial using Core Graphics and Core Image*, provides a step-by-step tutorial designed to teach the basics of two dimensional drawing on iOS.

62.1 Introducing Core Graphics and Quartz 2D

Quartz 2D is a two dimensional graphics drawing engine that makes up the bulk of the UIKit Core Graphics Framework. Quartz 2D drawing typically takes place on a UIView object (or, more precisely a subclass thereof). Drawings are defined in terms of the paths that a line must follow and rectangular areas into which shapes (rectangles, ellipses etc) must fit.

62.2 The draw Method

The first time a view is displayed, and each time part of that view needs to be redrawn as a result of another event, the *draw* method of the view is called. Drawing is achieved, therefore, by subclassing the UIView class, implementing the *draw* method and placing within that method the Quartz 2D API calls to draw the graphics.

In instances where the *draw* method is not automatically called, a redraw may be forced via a call to the *setNeedsDisplay* or *setNeedsDisplayInRect* methods.

62.3 Points, Coordinates and Pixels

The Quartz 2D API functions work on the basis of *points*. These are essentially the x and y coordinates of a two dimensional coordinate system on the device screen with 0, 0 representing the top left-hand corner of the display. These coordinates are stored in the form of CGFloat variables.

An additional C structure named CGPoint is used to contain both the x and y coordinates to specify a point on the display. Similarly, the CGSize structure stores two CGFloat values designating the width and height of an element on the screen.

Further, the position and dimension of a rectangle can be defined using the CGRect structure which contains a CGPoint (the location) and CGSize (the dimension) of a rectangular area.

Of key importance when working with points and dimensions is that these values do not correspond directly to screen pixels. In other words there is not a one to one correlation between pixels and points. Instead the underlying framework decides, based on a *scale factor*, where a point should appear and at what size, relative to the resolution of the display on which the drawing is taking place. This enables the same code to work on both higher and lower resolution screens (for example an iPhone 3GS screen and an iPhone 8 retina display) without the programmer having to worry about it.

For more precise drawing requirements, iOS version 4 and later allows the *scale factor* for the current screen to be obtained from UIScreen, UIView, UIImage, and CALayer classes allowing the correlation between pixels and points to be calculated for greater drawing precision. For iOS 3 or older the scale factor is always returned as 1.0.

62.4 The Graphics Context

Almost without exception, all Quartz API method calls are made on the *graphics context* object. Each view has its own context which is responsible for performing the requested drawing tasks and subsequently rendering those drawings onto the corresponding view. The graphics context can be obtained with a call to the *UIGraphicsGetCurrentContext()* function which returns a result of type *CGContextRef*:

```
let context = UIGraphicsGetCurrentContext()
```

62.5 Working with Colors in Quartz 2D

The Core Graphics CGColorRef data type is used to store colors when drawing with Quartz. This data type holds information about the *colorspace* of the color (RGBA, CMYK or gray scale) together with a set of component values that specify both the color and the transparency of that color. For example, the color red with no transparency would be defined with the RGBA components 1.0, 0.0, 0.0, 1.0.

A *colorspace* can be created via a Quartz API function call. For example, to create an RGB colorspace:

```
let colorSpace = CGColorSpaceCreateDeviceRGB()
```

If the function fails to create a colorspace, it will return a nil value.

Gray scale and CMYK color spaces may similarly be created using the *CGColorSpaceCreateDeviceGray()* and *CGColorSpaceCreateDeviceCMYK()* functions respectively.

Once the colorspace has been created, the next task is to define the components. The following declaration defines a set of RGBA components for a semi-transparent blue color:

```
let components: [CGFloat] = [0.0, 0.0, 1.0, 0.5]
```

With both the colorspace and the components defined, the CGColorRef structure can be created:

```
let color = CGColor(colorSpace: colorSpace, components: components)
```

The color may then be used to draw using the graphics context drawing API methods.

Another useful method for creating colors involves the UIKit UIColor class. While this class cannot be used directly within Quartz API calls since it is a Swift class, it is possible to extract a color in CGColorRef format from the UIColor class by referencing the cgColor property.

The advantage offered by UIColor, in addition to being object-oriented, is that it includes a range of convenience methods that can be used to create colors. For example, the following code uses the UIColor class to create the color red, and then accesses the cgColor property for use as an argument to the *setStrokeColor* context method:

```
context?.setStrokeColor(UIColor.red.cgColor)
```

The color selection and transparency can be further refined using this technique simply by specifying additional components. For example:

```
let color = UIColor(red:1.0 green:0.3 blue:0.8 alpha:0.5)
```

As we can see, the use of UIColor avoids the necessity to create colorspaces and components when working with colors. Refer to the Apple documentation for more details of the range of methods provided by the UIColor class.

62.6 Summary

This chapter has covered some of the basic principles behind the drawing of two dimensional graphics on iOS using the Quartz 2D API. Topics covered included obtaining the graphics context, implementing the *draw* method and the handling of colors and transparency. In *An iOS 12 Graphics Tutorial using Core Graphics and Core Image* this theory will be put into practice with examples of how to draw a variety of shapes and images on an iOS device screen. Before moving on to the drawing tutorial, however, the next chapter will begin by exploring the Live Views feature of Interface Builder. Live Views are particularly useful when writing dynamic user interface code such as drawing graphics.

Chapter 63

63. Interface Builder Live Views and iOS 12 Embedded Frameworks

Two related areas of iOS development will be covered in this chapter in the form of Live Views in Interface Builder and Embedded Frameworks, both of which are designed to make the tasks of sharing common code between projects and designing dynamic user interfaces easier.

63.1 Embedded Frameworks

A framework is defined by Apple as "a collection of code and resources to encapsulate functionality that is valuable across multiple projects". A typical iOS application project will use a multitude of Frameworks from the iOS SDK. All applications, for example, make use of the Foundation Framework while a game might also make use of the SpriteKit Framework.

Embedded Frameworks allow developers to create their own frameworks. Embedded frameworks are easy to create and provide a number of advantages, the most obvious of which is the ability to share common code between multiple application projects.

Embedded Frameworks are particularly useful when working with extensions. By nature, an extension will inevitably need to share code that already exists within the containing app. Rather than duplicate code between the app and the extension, a better solution is to place common code into an embedded framework.

Another benefit of embedded frameworks is the ability to publish code in the form of 3rd party frameworks that can be downloaded for use by other developers in their own projects.

One of the more intriguing features of embedded frameworks, however, is that they facilitate a powerful feature of Interface Builder known as Live Views.

63.2 Interface Builder Live Views

Traditionally, designing a user interface layout using Interface Builder has involved placing static representations of view components onto a canvas. The application logic behind these views to implement dynamic behavior is then implemented within the view controller and the application compiled and run on a device or simulator in order to see the live user interface in action.

Live views allow the dynamic code behind the views to be executed from within the Interface Builder storyboard file as the user interface is being designed without the necessity to compile and run the application.

Live views also allow variables within the code behind a view to be exposed in such a way that they can be accessed and modified in the Interface Builder Attributes Inspector panel, with the changes reflected in real-time within the live view.

The reason that embedded frameworks and live views are both covered in this chapter is that a prerequisite for live views is for the underlying code for a live view to be contained within an embedded framework.

The best way to gain a better understanding of both embedded frameworks and live views is to see them in action in an example project.

63.3 Creating the Example Project

Launch Xcode and create a new Single View Application project named LiveViewDemo using Swift as the programming language.

When the project has been created, select the *Main.storyboard* file and drag and drop a View object from the Library panel onto the view controller canvas. Resize the view, stretching it in each dimension until the blue dotted line appears indicating the recommended margin. Display the Auto Layout *Add New Constraints* menu and enable "spacing to nearest neighbor" constraints on all four sides of the view with the *Constrain to margins* option enabled as shown in Figure 63-1 before clicking on the *Add 4 Constraints* button:

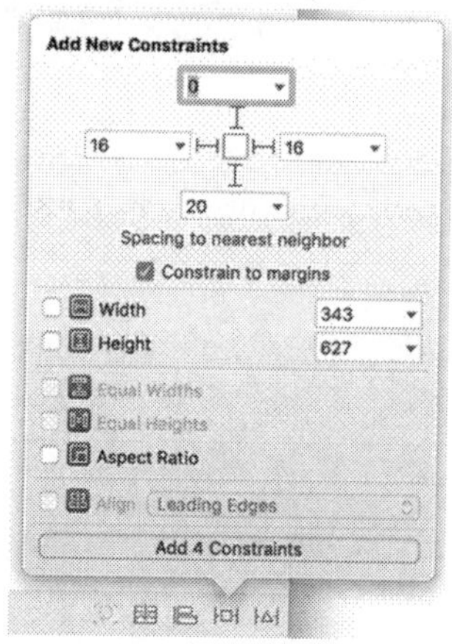

Figure 63-1

Once the above steps are complete, the layout should resemble that illustrated in Figure 63-2 below:

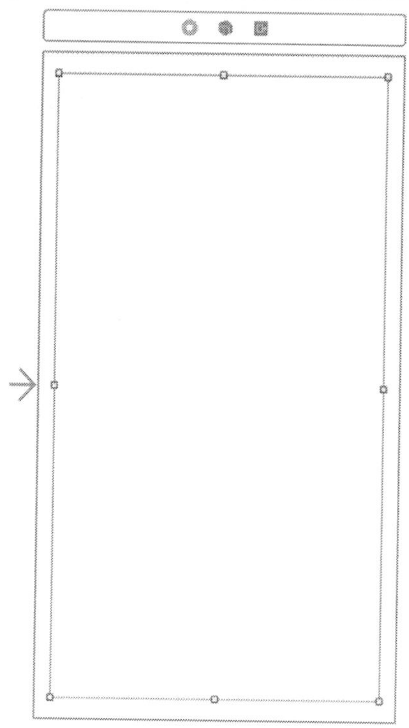

Figure 63-2

With the user interface designed, the next step is to add a framework to the project.

63.4 Adding an Embedded Framework

The framework to be added to the project will contain a UIView subclass containing some graphics drawing code.

Within Xcode, select the *File -> New -> Target...* menu option and, in the template selection panel, scroll to and select the *Cocoa Touch Framework* template (Figure 63-3):

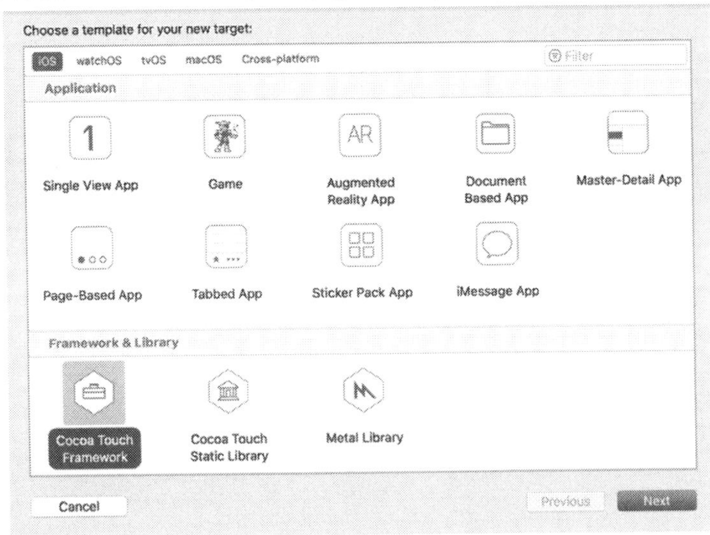

Figure 63-3

Click on the *Next* button and, on the subsequent screen, enter *MyDrawKit* into the product name field before clicking on the *Finish* button.

Within the project navigator panel, a new folder will have been added named *MyDrawKit* into which will be stored the files that make up the new framework. Ctrl-click on this entry and select the *New File...* menu option. In the template chooser panel, select *Cocoa Touch Class* before clicking on *Next*.

On the next screen, name the class *MyDrawView* and configure it as a subclass of UIView. Click the *Next* button and save the new class file into the *MyDrawKit* subfolder of the project directory.

Select the *Main.storyboard* file in the project navigator panel and click on the View object that was added in the previous section. Display the Identity Inspector in the utilities panel and change the Class setting from *UIView* to *MyDrawView*:

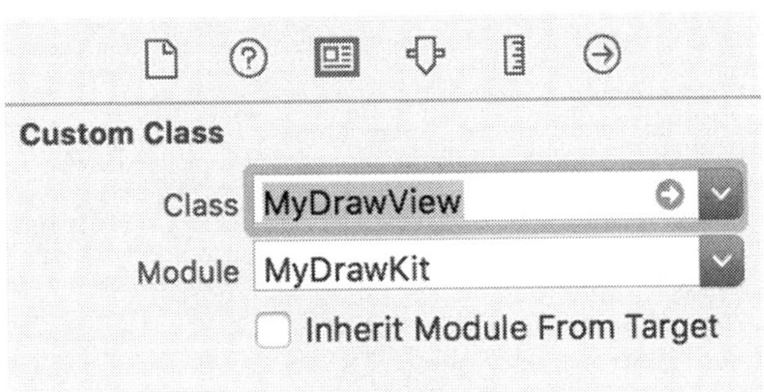

Figure 63-4

63.5 Implementing the Drawing Code in the Framework

The code to perform the graphics drawing on the View will reside in the *MyDrawView.swift* file which is located in the *MyDrawKit* folder. Locate this file in the project navigator panel and double-click on it to load it into a separate editing window (thereby allowing the *Main.storyboard* file to remain visible in Interface Builder).

Remove the comment markers (/* and */) from around the template *draw* method and implement the code for this method so that it reads as follows:

```
import UIKit
import QuartzCore

class MyDrawView: UIView {

    var startColor: UIColor = UIColor.white
    var endColor: UIColor = UIColor.blue
    var endRadius: CGFloat = 100

    override func draw(_ rect: CGRect) {
        let context = UIGraphicsGetCurrentContext()

        let colorspace = CGColorSpaceCreateDeviceRGB()
        let locations: [CGFloat] = [ 0.0, 1.0]

        if let gradient = CGGradient(colorsSpace: colorspace,
                       colors: [startColor.cgColor, endColor.cgColor]
                                         as CFArray,
                       locations: locations) {

            var startPoint = CGPoint()
            var endPoint = CGPoint()

            let startRadius: CGFloat = 0

            startPoint.x = 130
            startPoint.y = 100
            endPoint.x = 130
            endPoint.y = 120

            context?.drawRadialGradient(gradient,
                   startCenter: startPoint, startRadius: startRadius,
                   endCenter: endPoint, endRadius: endRadius,
                   options: .drawsBeforeStartLocation)
        }
    }
```

```
}
```

63.6 Making the View Designable

At this point the code has been added and running the application on a device or simulator will show the view with the graphics drawn on it. The object of this chapter, however, is to avoid the need to compile and run the application to see the results of the code. In order to make the view "live" within Interface Builder, the class needs to be declared as being "Interface Builder designable". This is achieved by adding an *@IBDesignable* directive immediately before the class declaration in the *MyDrawView.swift* file:

```
import UIKit
import QuartzCore

@IBDesignable
class MyDrawView: UIView {

    var startColor: UIColor = UIColor.white
    var endColor: UIColor = UIColor.blue
    var endRadius: CGFloat = 100
.
.
.
}
```

As soon as the directive is added to the file, Xcode will compile the class and render it within the Interface Builder storyboard canvas (Figure 63-5):

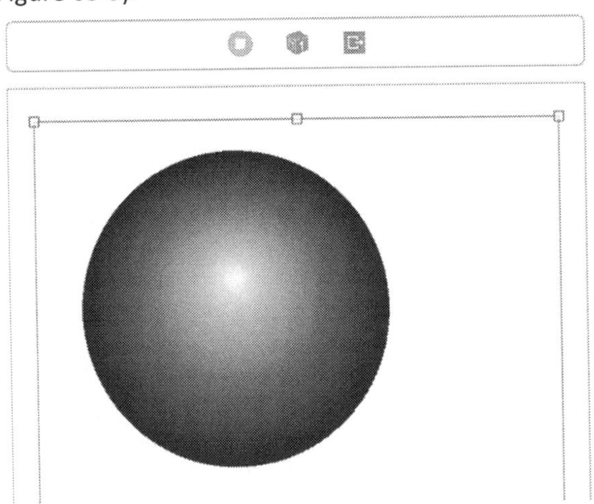

Figure 63-5

From now on, any changes made to the MyDrawView code will be reflected in the Interface Builder live view. To see this in action, change the endColor variable declaration so that it is assigned a different color and observe the color change take effect in the Interface Builder live view:

```
var endColor: UIColor = UIColor.red
```

63.7 Making Variables Inspectable

Although it is possible to modify variables by editing the code in the framework class, it would be easier if they could be changed just like any other property using the Attributes Inspector panel. In fact, this can be achieved simply by prefixing the variable declarations with the *@IBInspectable* directive as follows:

```
@IBDesignable
class MyDrawView: UIView {

    @IBInspectable var startColor: UIColor = UIColor.white
    @IBInspectable var endColor: UIColor = UIColor.red
    @IBInspectable var endRadius: CGFloat = 100
.
.
.
}
```

With the changes made to the code, select the View in the storyboard file and display the Attributes Inspector panel. The properties should now be listed for the view (Figure 63-6) and can be modified. Any changes to these variables made through the Attributes Inspector will take effect in real-time without the need for Xcode to recompile the framework code. These settings will also be generated into the application when it is compiled and run on a device or simulator.

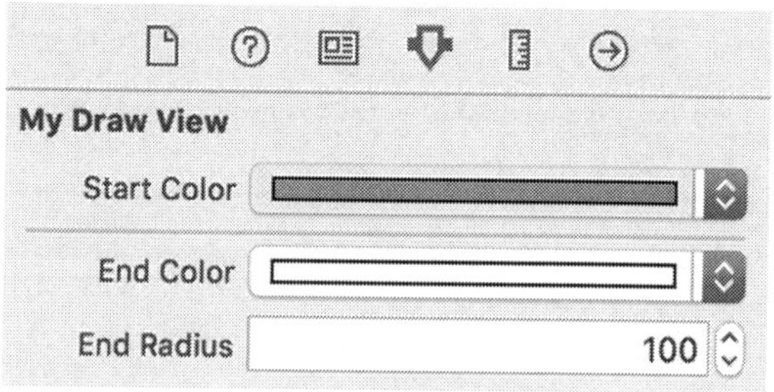

Figure 63-6

63.8 Summary

This chapter has introduced two concepts in the form of embedded frameworks and Interface Builder live views. Embedded frameworks allow developers to place source code into frameworks which can then be shared between multiple application projects. Embedded frameworks also provide the basis for the live views feature of Interface Builder. Prior to the introduction of live views, it was necessary to compile and run an application in order to be able to see dynamic user interface behavior in action. With live views, the dynamic behavior of a view can now be seen within Interface Builder, with code changes reflected in real-time.

Chapter 64

64. An iOS 12 Graphics Tutorial using Core Graphics and Core Image

As previously discussed in *Drawing iOS 12 2D Graphics with Core Graphics* the Quartz 2D API is the primary mechanism by which 2D drawing operations are performed within iOS applications. Having provided an overview of Quartz 2D as it pertains to iOS development in that chapter, the focus of this chapter is to provide a tutorial that provides examples of how 2D drawing is performed. If you are new to Quartz 2D and have not yet read *Drawing iOS 12 2D Graphics with Core Graphics* it is recommended that you do so now before embarking on this tutorial.

64.1 The iOS Drawing Example Application

If you are reading this book sequentially and have created the *LiveViewDemo* project as outlined in the chapter entitled *Interface Builder Live Views and iOS 12 Embedded Frameworks*, then the code in this chapter may simply be placed in the *draw* method contained within the *MyDrawView.swift* file and the results viewed dynamically within the live view in the *Main.storyboard* file. If you have not yet completed the tutorial in *Interface Builder Live Views and iOS 12 Embedded Frameworks*, follow the steps in the next three sections to create a new project, add a UIView subclass and locate the *draw* method.

64.2 Creating the New Project

The application created in this tutorial will contain a subclassed UIView component within which the *draw* method will be overridden and used to perform a variety of 2D drawing operations. Create the new project by launching the Xcode development environment and selecting the option to create a new project. When prompted to select a template for the application, choose the *Single View Application* option and name the project *Draw2D* with Swift selected as the programming language.

64.3 Creating the UIView Subclass

In order to draw graphics on the view it is necessary to create a subclass of the UIView object and override the *draw* method. In the project navigator panel located on the left-hand side of the main Xcode window Ctrl-click on the *Draw2D* folder entry and select *New File…* from the resulting menu. In the *New File* window, select the iOS source *Cocoa Touch Class* icon and click *Next.* On the subsequent options screen, change the *Subclass of* menu to *UIView* and the class name to *Draw2D.* Click *Next* and on the final screen click on the *Create* button.

Select the *Main.storyboard* file followed by the UIView component in either the view controller canvas or the document outline panel. Display the Identity Inspector (*View -> Utilities -> Show Identity Inspector*) and change the *Class* setting from *UIView* to our new class named *Draw2D:*

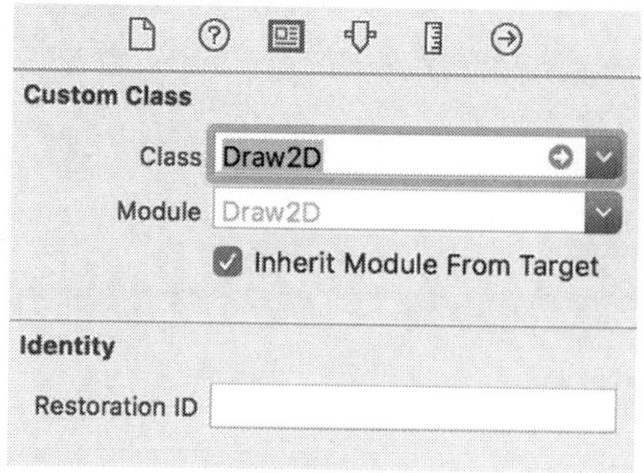

Figure 64-1

64.4 Locating the draw Method in the UIView Subclass

Now that we have subclassed our application's UIView the next step is to implement the *draw* method in this subclass. Fortunately Xcode has already created a template of this method for us. To locate this method, select the *Draw2D.swift* file in the project navigator panel. Having located the method in the file, remove the comment markers (/* and */) within which it is currently encapsulated:

```
import UIKit

class Draw2D: UIView {

    override func draw(_ rect: CGRect) {
        // Drawing code
    }
}
```

In the remainder of this tutorial we will modify the code in the *draw* method to perform a variety of different drawing operations.

64.5 Drawing a Line

In order to draw a line on a device screen using Quartz 2D we first need to obtain the graphics context for the view:

```
let context = UIGraphicsGetCurrentContext()
```

Once the context has been obtained, the width of the line we plan to draw needs to be specified:

```
context?.setLineWidth(2.0)
```

Next, we need to create a color reference. We can do this by specifying the RGBA components of the required color (in this case opaque blue):

```
let colorSpace = CGColorSpaceCreateDeviceRGB()
let components: [CGFloat] = [0.0, 0.0, 1.0, 1.0]
let color = CGColor(colorSpace: colorSpace, components: components)
```

Using the color reference and the context we can now specify that the color is to be used when drawing the line:

```
context?.setStrokeColor(color!)
```

The next step is to move to the start point of the line that is going to be drawn:

```
context?.move(to: CGPoint(x: 30, y: 30))
```

The above line of code indicates that the start point for the line is the top left-hand corner of the device display. We now need to specify the end point of the line, in this case 300, 400:

```
context?.addLine(to: CGPoint(x: 300, y: 400))
```

Having defined the line width, color and path, we are ready to draw the line:

```
context?.strokePath()
```

Bringing this all together gives us a *draw* method that reads as follows:

```
override func draw(_ rect: CGRect)
{
    let context = UIGraphicsGetCurrentContext()
    context?.setLineWidth(2.0)
    let colorSpace = CGColorSpaceCreateDeviceRGB()
    let components: [CGFloat] = [0.0, 0.0, 1.0, 1.0]
    let color = CGColor(colorSpace: colorSpace, components: components)
    context?.setStrokeColor(color!)
    context?.move(to: CGPoint(x: 30, y: 30))
    context?.addLine(to: CGPoint(x: 300, y: 400))
    context?.strokePath()
}
```

When compiled and run, the application should display as illustrated in Figure 64-2:

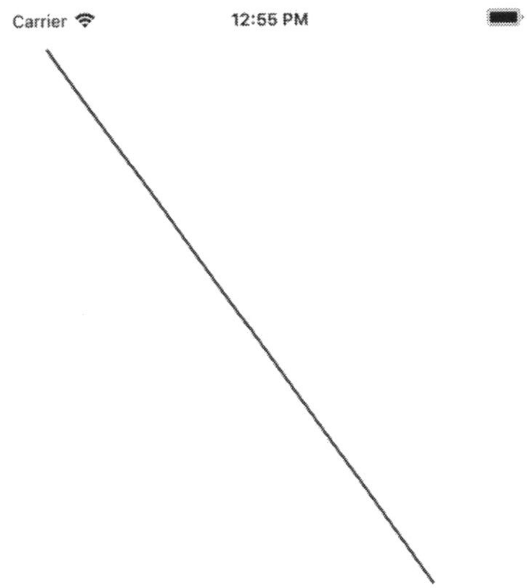

Figure 64-2

Note that in the above example we manually created the colorspace and color reference. As described in *Drawing iOS 12 2D Graphics with Core Graphics*, colors can also be created using the UIColor class. For example, the same result as outlined above can be achieved with fewer lines of code as follows:

```
override func draw(_ rect: CGRect) {
    let context = UIGraphicsGetCurrentContext()
    context?.setLineWidth(2.0)
    context?.setStrokeColor(UIColor.blue.cgColor)
    context?.move(to: CGPoint(x: 30, y: 30))
    context?.addLine(to: CGPoint(x: 300, y: 400))
    context?.strokePath()
}
```

64.6 Drawing Paths

As you may have noticed, in the above example we draw a single line by essentially defining the path between two points. Defining a path that comprises multiple points allows us to draw using a sequence of straight lines all connected to each other using repeated calls to the *addLine(to:)* method of the context. Non-straight lines may also be added to a shape using calls to, for example, the *addArc* method.

The following code, for example, draws a diamond shape:

```
override func draw(_ rect: CGRect)
{
    let context = UIGraphicsGetCurrentContext()
    context?.setLineWidth(2.0)
    context?.setStrokeColor(UIColor.blue.cgColor)
    context?.move(to: CGPoint(x:100, y: 100))
    context?.addLine(to: CGPoint(x: 150, y: 150))
    context?.addLine(to: CGPoint(x: 100, y: 200))
    context?.addLine(to: CGPoint(x: 50, y: 150))
    context?.addLine(to: CGPoint(x: 100, y: 100))
    context?.strokePath()
}
```

When executed, the above code should produce output that appears as shown in Figure 64-3:

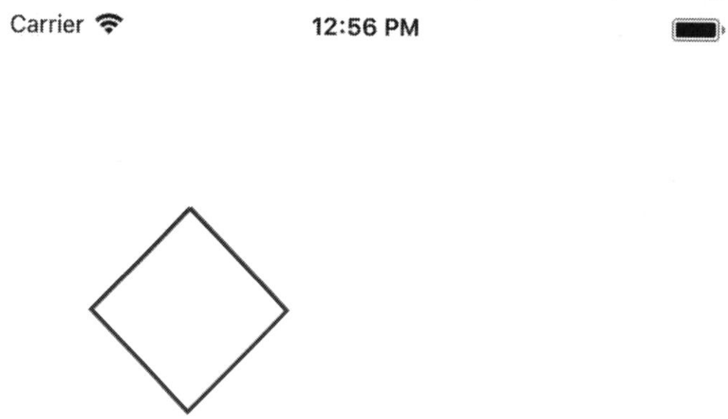

Figure 64-3

64.7 Drawing a Rectangle

Rectangles are drawn in much the same way as any other path is drawn, with the exception that the path is defined by specifying the x and y co-ordinates of the top left-hand corner of the rectangle together with the rectangle's height and width. These dimensions are stored in a CGRect structure and passed through as an argument to the *addRect* method:

```
override func draw(_ rect: CGRect)
{
    let context = UIGraphicsGetCurrentContext()
    context?.setLineWidth(4.0)
    context?.setStrokeColor(UIColor.blue.cgColor)
    let rectangle = CGRect(x: 90,y: 100,width: 200,height: 80)
    context?.addRect(rectangle)
    context?.strokePath()
}
```

The above code will result in the following display when compiled and executed:

Figure 64-4

64.8 Drawing an Ellipse or Circle

Circles and ellipses are drawn by defining the rectangular area into which the shape must fit and then calling the *addEllipse(in:)* context method:

```
override func draw(_ rect: CGRect)
{
    let context = UIGraphicsGetCurrentContext()
    context?.setLineWidth(4.0)
    context?.setStrokeColor(UIColor.blue.cgColor)
    let rectangle = CGRect(x: 85,y: 100,width: 200,height: 80)
    context?.addEllipse(in: rectangle)
    context?.strokePath()
}
```

When compiled, the above code will produce the following graphics:

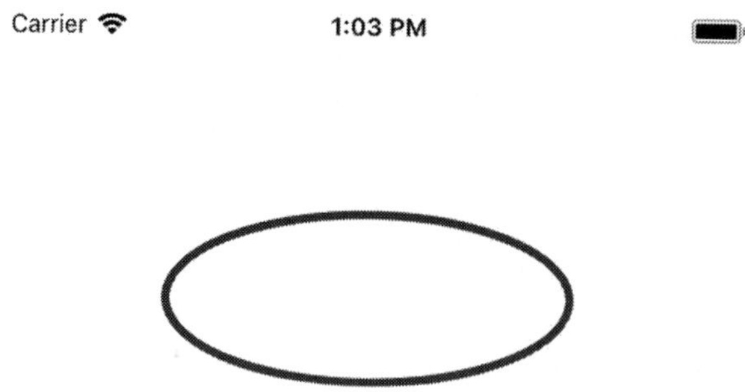

Figure 64-5

In order to draw a circle simply define a rectangle with equal length sides (a square in other words).

64.9 Filling a Path with a Color

A path may be filled with a color using a variety of Quartz 2D API functions. Rectangular and elliptical paths may be filled using the *fill(rect:)* and *fillEllipse(in:)* context methods respectively. Similarly, a path may be filled using the *fillPath* method. Prior to executing a fill operation, the fill color must be specified using the *setFillColor* method.

The following example defines a path and then fills it with the color red:

```
override func draw(_ rect: CGRect)
{
    let context = UIGraphicsGetCurrentContext()
    context?.move(to: CGPoint(x: 100, y: 100))
    context?.addLine(to: CGPoint(x: 150, y: 150))
    context?.addLine(to: CGPoint(x: 100, y: 200))
    context?.addLine(to: CGPoint(x: 50, y: 150))
    context?.addLine(to: CGPoint(x: 100, y: 100))
    context?.setFillColor(UIColor.red.cgColor)
    context?.fillPath()
}
```

The above code produces the following graphics on the device or simulator display when executed:

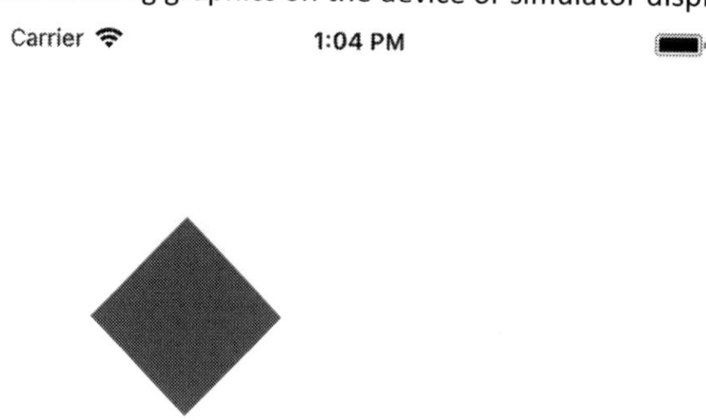

Figure 64-6

The following code draws a rectangle with a blue border and then once again fills the rectangular space with red:

```
override func draw(_ rect: CGRect)
{
    let context = UIGraphicsGetCurrentContext()
    context?.setLineWidth(4.0)
    context?.setStrokeColor(UIColor.blue.cgColor)
    let rectangle = CGRect(x: 85,y: 100,width: 200,height: 80)
    context?.addRect(rectangle)
    context?.strokePath()
    context?.setFillColor(UIColor.red.cgColor)
    context?.fill(rectangle)
}
```

When added to the example application, the resulting display should appear as follows:

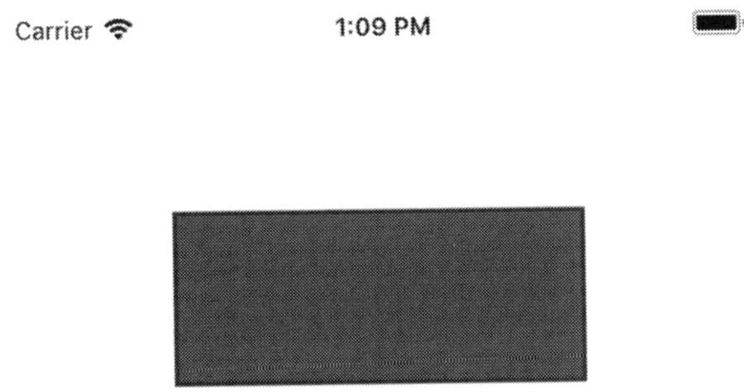

Figure 64-7

64.10 Drawing an Arc

An arc may be drawn by specifying two tangent points and a radius using the *addArc* context method, for example:

```
override func draw(_ rect: CGRect)
{
    let context = UIGraphicsGetCurrentContext()
    context?.setLineWidth(4.0)
    context?.setStrokeColor(UIColor.blue.cgColor)
    context?.move(to: CGPoint(x: 100, y: 100))
    context?.addArc(tangent1End: CGPoint(x: 100, y: 200),
               tangent2End: CGPoint(x: 300, y: 200), radius: 100)
    context?.strokePath()
}
```

The above code will result in the following graphics output:

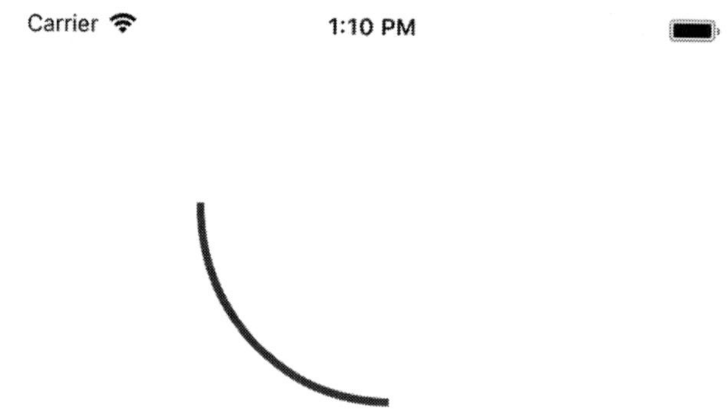

Figure 64-8

64.11 Drawing a Cubic Bézier Curve

A cubic Bézier curve may be drawn by moving to a start point and then passing two control points and an end point through to the *addCurve(to:)* method:

```
override func draw(_ rect: CGRect)
{
        let context = UIGraphicsGetCurrentContext()
        context?.setLineWidth(4.0)
        context?.setStrokeColor(UIColor.blue.cgColor)
        context?.move(to: CGPoint(x: 30, y: 30))
        context?.addCurve(to: CGPoint(x: 20, y: 50),
                    control1: CGPoint(x: 300, y: 250),
                    control2: CGPoint(x: 300, y: 70))
        context?.strokePath()
}
```

The above code will cause the curve illustrated in Figure 64-9 to be drawn when compiled and executed in our example application:

Figure 64-9

64.12 Drawing a Quadratic Bézier Curve

A quadratic Bézier curve is drawn using the *addQuadCurve(to:)* method, providing a control and end point as arguments having first moved to the start point:

```
override func draw(_ rect: CGRect)
{
    let context = UIGraphicsGetCurrentContext()
    context?.setLineWidth(4.0)
    context?.setStrokeColor(UIColor.blue.cgColor)
    context?.move(to: CGPoint(x: 10, y: 200))
    context?.addQuadCurve(to: CGPoint(x: 300, y: 200),
                control: CGPoint(x: 150, y: 10))
    context?.strokePath()
}
```

The above code, when executed, will display a curve that appears as illustrated in the following figure:

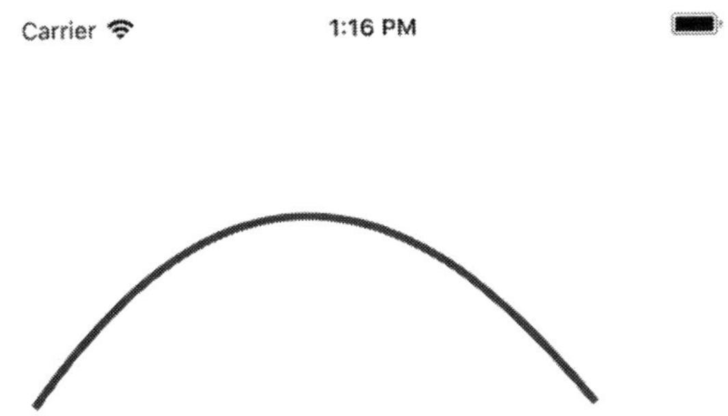

Figure 64-10

64.13 Dashed Line Drawing

So far in this chapter we have performed all our drawing with a solid line. Quartz also provides support for drawing dashed lines. This is achieved via the Quartz *setLineDash* method which takes as its arguments the following:

- **context** – The graphics context of the view on which the drawing is to take place
- **phase** - A floating point value that specifies how far into the dash pattern the line starts
- **lengths** – An array containing values for the lengths of the painted and unpainted sections of the line. For example an array containing 5 and 6 would cycle through 5 painted unit spaces followed by 6 unpainted unit spaces.
- **count** – A count of the number of items in the lengths array

For example, a [2,6,4,2] lengths array applied to a curve drawing of line thickness 5.0 will appear as follows:

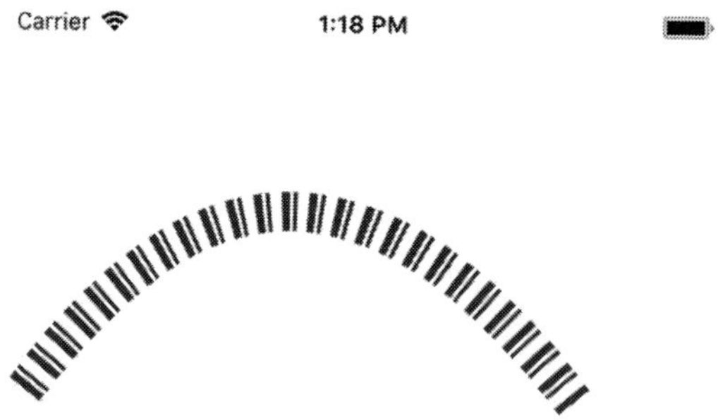

Figure 64-11

The corresponding *draw* method code that drew the above line reads as follows:

```
override func draw(_ rect: CGRect)
{
    let context = UIGraphicsGetCurrentContext()
    context?.setLineWidth(20.0)
    context?.setStrokeColor(UIColor.blue.cgColor)
    let dashArray:[CGFloat] = [2,6,4,2]
    context?.setLineDash(phase: 3, lengths: dashArray)
    context?.move(to: CGPoint(x: 10, y: 200))
    context?.addQuadCurve(to: CGPoint(x: 300, y: 200),
              control: CGPoint(x: 150, y: 10))
    context?.strokePath()
}
```

64.14 Drawing Shadows

In addition to drawing shapes, Core Graphics can also be used to create shadow effects. This is achieved using the *setShadow* method, passing through a graphics context, offset values for the position of the shadow relative to the shape for which the shadow is being drawn and a value specifying the degree of blurring required for the shadow effect.

The following code, for example, draws an ellipse with a shadow:

```
override func draw(_ rect: CGRect)
{
    let context = UIGraphicsGetCurrentContext()
    let myShadowOffset = CGSize (width: -10,  height: 15)

    context?.saveGState()
    context?.setShadow(offset: myShadowOffset, blur: 5)
    context?.setLineWidth(4.0)
    context?.setStrokeColor(UIColor.blue.cgColor)
    let rectangle = CGRect(x: 60,y: 170,width: 200,height: 80)
    context?.addEllipse(in: rectangle)
    context?.strokePath()
    context?.restoreGState()
```

```
}
```

When executed, the above code will produce the effect illustrated in Figure 64-12:

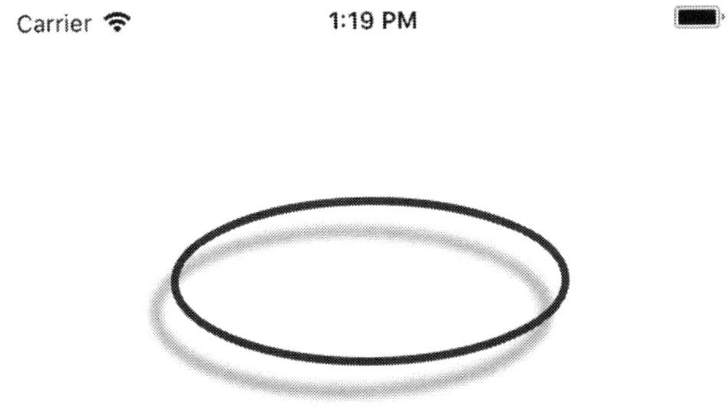

Figure 64-12

64.15 Drawing Gradients

Gradients are implemented using the Core Graphics CGGradient class which provides support for linear, radial and axial gradients. Use of the CGGradient class essentially involves the specification of two or more colors together with a set of location values. The location values are used to indicate the points at which the gradient should switch from one color to another as the gradient is drawn along an axis line where 0.0 represents the start of the axis and 1.0 the end point. Assume, for the purposes of an example, that you wish to create a gradient that transitions through three different colors along the gradient axis with each color being given an equal amount of space within the gradient. In this situation, three locations would be specified. The first would be 0.0 to represent the start of the gradient. Two more locations would then need to be specified for the transition points to the remaining colors. In order to equally divide the axis amongst the colors these would need to be set to 0.3333 and 0.6666 respectively.

Having configured a CGGradient instance, a linear gradient is then drawn via a call to the *drawLinearGradient* method of the context object, passing through the colors, locations and start and end points as arguments.

The following code, for example, draws a linear gradient using four colors with four equally spaced locations:

```
override func draw(_ rect: CGRect)
{
    let context = UIGraphicsGetCurrentContext()

    let locations: [CGFloat] = [ 0.0, 0.25, 0.5, 0.75 ]

    let colors = [UIColor.red.cgColor,
                  UIColor.green.cgColor,
                  UIColor.blue.cgColor,
                  UIColor.yellow.cgColor]

    let colorspace = CGColorSpaceCreateDeviceRGB()

    let gradient = CGGradient(colorsSpace: colorspace,
                  colors: colors as CFArray, locations: locations)
```

```
    var startPoint = CGPoint()
    var endPoint =  CGPoint()

    startPoint.x = 0.0
    startPoint.y = 0.0
    endPoint.x = 600
    endPoint.y = 600

    if let gradient = gradient {
        context?.drawLinearGradient(gradient,
                                    start: startPoint, end: endPoint,
                                    options: .drawsBeforeStartLocation)
    }
}
```

When executed, the above code will generate the gradient shown in Figure 64-13:

Figure 64-13

Radial gradients involve drawing a gradient between two circles. When the circles are positioned apart from each other and given different sizes a conical effect is achieved as shown in Figure 64-14:

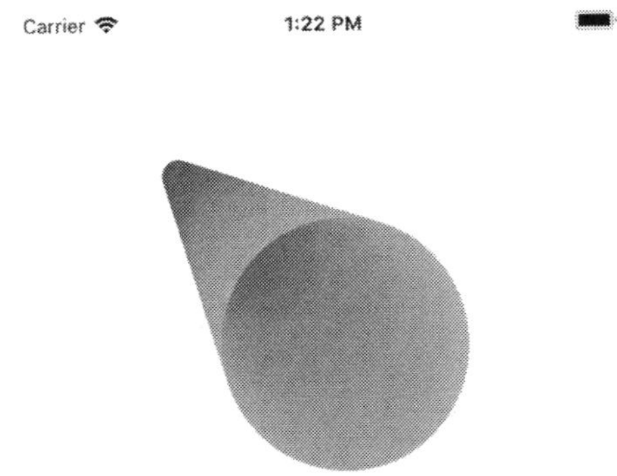

Figure 64-14

The code to draw the above radial gradient sets up the colors and locations for the gradient before declaring the center points and radius values for two circles. The gradient is then drawn via a call to the *drawRadialGradient* method:

```
override func draw(_ rect: CGRect)
{
    let context = UIGraphicsGetCurrentContext()

    let locations: [CGFloat] = [0.0, 0.5, 1.0]

    let colors = [UIColor.red.cgColor,
                  UIColor.green.cgColor,
                  UIColor.cyan.cgColor]

    let colorspace = CGColorSpaceCreateDeviceRGB()

    let gradient = CGGradient(colorsSpace: colorspace,
                    colors: colors as CFArray, locations: locations)

    var startPoint =  CGPoint()
    var endPoint   = CGPoint()

    startPoint.x = 100
    startPoint.y = 100
    endPoint.x = 200
    endPoint.y = 200
    let startRadius: CGFloat = 10
    let endRadius: CGFloat = 75

    if let gradient = gradient {
        context?.drawRadialGradient(gradient, startCenter: startPoint,
                                    startRadius: startRadius,
                                    endCenter: endPoint,
```

```
                                    endRadius: endRadius, options: [])
    }
}
```

Interesting effects may also be created by assigning a radius of 0 to the starting point circle and positioning it within the circumference of the end point circle:

```
override func draw(_ rect: CGRect)
{
    let context = UIGraphicsGetCurrentContext()
    let locations: [CGFloat] = [0.0, 1.0]

    let colors = [UIColor.white.cgColor,
                      UIColor.blue.cgColor]

    let colorspace = CGColorSpaceCreateDeviceRGB()

    let gradient = CGGradient(colorsSpace: colorspace,
                    colors: colors as CFArray, locations: locations)

    var startPoint = CGPoint()
    var endPoint = CGPoint()
    startPoint.x = 180
    startPoint.y = 180
    endPoint.x = 200
    endPoint.y = 200
    let startRadius: CGFloat = 0
    let endRadius: CGFloat = 75

    if let gradient = gradient {
        context?.drawRadialGradient (gradient, startCenter: startPoint,
                                    startRadius: startRadius,
                                    endCenter: endPoint,
                                    endRadius: endRadius,
                                    options: .drawsBeforeStartLocation)
    }
}
```

When executed, the above code creates the appearance of light reflecting on the surface of a shiny blue sphere:

Figure 64-15

64.16 Drawing an Image into a Graphics Context

An image may be drawn into a graphics context either by specifying the coordinates of the top left-hand corner of the image (in which case the image will appear full size) or resized so that it fits into a specified rectangular area. Before we can display an image in our example application, however, that image must first be added to the project resources.

Begin by locating the desired image using the Finder and then drag and drop that image onto the project navigator panel of the Xcode main project window.

The following example *draw* method code displays the image in a file named *cat.png* full size located at 0, 0:

```
override func draw(_ rect: CGRect)
{
    let myImage = UIImage(named: "cat.png")
    let imagePoint = CGPoint(x: 0, y: 0)
    myImage?.draw(at: imagePoint)
}
```

As is evident when the application is run, the size of the image far exceeds the available screen size:

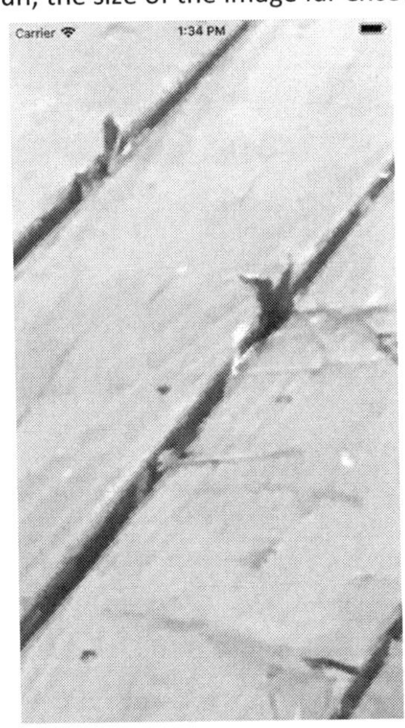

Figure 64-16

Using the *draw* method of the UIImage object, however, we can scale the image to fit better on the screen. In this instance it is useful to identify the screen size since this changes depending on the device on which the application is running. This can be achieved using the *mainScreen* and *bounds* methods of the UIScreen class. The *mainScreen* method returns another UIScreen object representing the device display. Calling the *bounds* method of that object returns the dimensions of the display in the form of a CGRect object:

```
override func draw(_ rect: CGRect)
{
    let myImage = UIImage(named: "cat.png")
    let imageRect = UIScreen.main.bounds
    myImage?.draw(in: imageRect)
}
```

This time, the entire image fits comfortably on the screen:

Figure 64-17

64.17 Image Filtering with the Core Image Framework

Having covered the concept of displaying images within an iOS application, now is a good time to provide a basic overview of the Core Image Framework.

Core Image was introduced with iOS 5 and provides a mechanism for filtering and manipulating still images and videos. Included with Core Image is a wide range of different filters together with the ability to build custom filters to meet specific requirements. Examples of filters that may be applied include cropping, color effects, blurring, warping, transformations and gradients. A full listing of filters is available in Apple's *Core Image Filter Reference* document which is located in the Apple Developer portal.

A CIImage object is typically initialized with a reference to the image to be manipulated. A CIFilter object is then created and configured with the type of filtering to be performed, together with any input parameters required by that filter. The CIFilter object is then instructed to perform the operation and the modified image is subsequently returned in the form of a CIImage object. The application's CIContext reference may then be used to render the image for display to the user.

By way of an example of Core Image in action we will modify the *draw* method of our Draw2D example application to render the previously displayed image in a sepia tone using the CISepiaTone filter. The first step, however, is to add the CoreImage Framework to the project. This is achieved by selecting the *Draw2D* target at the top of the project navigator and then selecting the *Build Phases* tab in the main panel. Unfold the *Link Binary with Libraries* section of the panel, click on the + button and locate and add the *CoreImage.framework* library from the resulting list.

Having added the framework, select the *Draw2D.swift* file and modify the *draw* method as follows:

```
override func draw(_ rect: CGRect) {

    if let myimage = UIImage(named: "cat.png"),
       let sepiaFilter = CIFilter(name: "CISepiaTone") {

        let cimage = CIImage(image: myimage)

        sepiaFilter.setDefaults()
        sepiaFilter.setValue(cimage, forKey: "inputImage")
        sepiaFilter.setValue(NSNumber(value: 0.8 as Float),
                             forKey: "inputIntensity")

        let image = sepiaFilter.outputImage

        let context = CIContext(options: nil)

        let cgImage = context.createCGImage(image!,
                                            from: image!.extent)

        let resultImage = UIImage(cgImage: cgImage!)
        let imageRect = UIScreen.main.bounds
        resultImage.draw(in: imageRect)
    }
}
```

The method begins by loading the image file used in the previous section of this chapter. Since Core Image works on CIImage objects it is then necessary to convert the UIImage to a CIImage. Next a new CIFilter object is created and initialized with the CISepiaTone filter. The filter is then set to the default settings before being configured with the input image (in this case our *cimage* object) and the value of intensity of the filter (0.8).

With the filter object configured, its *outputImage* method is called to perform the manipulation and the resulting modified image assigned to a new CImage object. The CIContext reference for the application is then obtained and used to convert the CImage object to a CGImageRef object. This, in turn, is converted to a UIImage object which is then displayed to the user using the object's *draw* method. When compiled and run, the image will appear in a sepia tone.

64.18 Summary

By subclassing the UIView class and overriding the *draw* method a variety of 2D graphics drawing operations may be performed on the view canvas. In this chapter we have explored some of the graphics drawing capabilities of Quartz 2D to draw a variety of line types and paths and to present images on the iOS device screen.

Introduced in iOS 5, the Core Image Framework is designed specifically for the filtering and manipulation of images and video. In this chapter we have provided a brief overview of Core Image and worked through a simple example that applied a sepia tone filter to an image.

65. iOS 12 Animation using UIViewPropertyAnimator

The majority of the visual effects used throughout the iOS user interface are performed using *UIKit animation*. UIKit provides a simple mechanism for implementing basic animation within an iOS application. If you need a user interface element to gently fade in or out of view, slide smoothly across the screen or gracefully resize or rotate before the user's eyes, these effects can be achieved using UIKit animation in just a few lines of code.

In this chapter we will provide an overview of the basics of the UIKit animation and work through a simple example. While much can be achieved with UIKit animation, however, it should be noted that if you plan to develop a graphics intensive 3D style application then it is more likely that OpenGL ES or SceneKit will need to be used, a subject area to which numerous books are dedicated.

65.1 The Basics of UIKit Animation

The cornerstone of animation in UIKit is the UIViewPropertyAnimator class. This class allows the changes made to the properties of a view object to be animated using a range of options.

As an example, consider a UIView object that contains a UIButton connected to an outlet named *theButton*. The application requires that the button gradually fade from view over a period of 3 seconds. This can be achieved by making the button transparent through the use of the *alpha* property:

```
theButton.alpha = 0
```

Simply setting the alpha property to 0, however, causes the button to immediately become transparent. In order to make it fade out of sight gradually we need to create a UIViewPropertyAnimator instance configured with the duration of the animation. This class also needs to know the *animation curve* of the animation. This curve is used to control the speed of the animation as it is running. An animation might start out slow, speed up and then slow down again before completion. The timing curve of an animation is controlled by the UICubicTimingParameters and UISpringTimingParameters classes. The following code configures a UIViewPropertyAnimator instance using the standard "ease in" animation curve dispersed over a 2 second duration:

```
let timing = UICubicTimingParameters(animationCurve: .easeIn)
let animator = UIViewPropertyAnimator(duration: 2.0,
                                timingParameters:timing)
```

Once the UIViewPropertyAnimator class has been initialized, the animation sequence to be performed needs to be added, followed by a call to the object's *startAnimation* method:

```
animator.addAnimations {
    self.theButton.alpha = 0
}
animator.startAnimation()
```

A range of other options are available for use when working with a UIViewPropertyAnimator instance. Animation may be paused or stopped at any time via calls to the *pauseAnimation* and *stopAnimation* methods respectively. To configure the animator to call a completion handler when the animation finishes, simply assign the handler to the object's *completion* property. The animation may also be reversed by assigning a true value to the *isReversed* property. The start of the animation may be delayed by passing through a delay duration when initializing the UIViewPropertyAnimator class as follows:

```
animator.startAnimation(afterDelay: 4.0)
```

65.2 Understanding Animation Curves

As previously mentioned, in addition to specifying the duration of an animation sequence, the linearity of the animation timeline may also be defined by specifying an *animation curve*. This setting controls whether the animation is performed at a constant speed, whether it starts out slow and speeds up and also provides options for adding spring-like behavior to an animation.

The UICubicTimingParameters class is used to configure time based animation curves. As demonstrated in the previous section, one option when using this class is to use one of the following four standard animation curves provided by UIKit:

- **.curveLinear** – The animation is performed at constant speed for the specified duration and is the option declared in the above code example.
- **.curveEaseOut** – The animation starts out fast and slows as the end of the sequence approaches.
- **.curveEaseIn** – The animation sequence starts out slow and speeds up as the end approaches.
- **.curveEaseInOut** – The animation starts slow, speeds up and then slows down again.

If the standard options do not meet your animation needs, a custom cubic curve may be created and used as the animation curve simply by specifying control points:

```
let timing = UICubicTimingParameters(
                controlPoint1: CGPoint(x:0.0, y:1.0),
               controlPoint2: CGPoint(x:1.0,y:0.0))
```

Alternatively, property changes to a view may be animated using a spring effect via the UISpringTimingParameters class. Instances of this class can be configured using mass, spring "stiffness", damping and velocity values as follows:

```
let timing = UISpringTimingParameters(mass: 0.5, stiffness: 0.5,
       damping: 0.3, initialVelocity: CGVector(dx:1.0, dy: 0.0))
```

Alternatively, the spring effect may be configured using just the damping ratio and velocity:

```
let timing = UISpringTimingParameters(dampingRatio: 0.4,
               initialVelocity: CGVector(dx:1.0, dy: 0.0))
```

65.3 Performing Affine Transformations

Transformations allow changes to be made to the coordinate system of a screen area. This essentially allows the programmer to rotate, resize and translate a UIView object. A call is made to one of a number of transformation functions and the result assigned to the *transform* property of the UIView object.

For example, to change the scale of a UIView object named *myView* by a factor of 2 in both height and width:

```
myView.transform = CGAffineTransform(scaleX: 2, y: 2)
```

Similarly, the UIView object may be rotated using the *CGAffineTransform(rotationAngle:)* function which takes as an argument the angle (in radians) by which the view is to be rotated. The following code, for example, rotates a view by 90 degrees:

```
let angle = CGFloat(90 * .pi / 180)
myView.transform = CGAffineTransform(rotationAngle: angle)
```

The key point to keep in mind with transformations is that they become animated effects when performed within an animation sequence. The transformations evolve over the duration of the animation and follow the specified animation curve in terms of timing.

65.4 Combining Transformations

Two transformations may be combined to create a single transformation effect via a call to the *concatenating* method of the first transformation instance, passing through the second transformation object as an argument. This function takes as arguments the two transformation objects that are to be combined. The result may then be assigned to the transform property of the UIView object to be transformed. The following code fragment, for example, creates a transformation combining both scale and rotatation:

```
let scaleTrans = CGAffineTransform(scaleX: 2, 2)

let angle = CGFloat(90 * .pi / 180)
let rotateTrans = CGAffineTransform(rotationAngle: angle)

scaleTrans.concatenating(rotateTrans)
```

Affine transformations offer an extremely powerful and flexible mechanism for creating animations and it is just not possible to do justice to these capabilities in a single chapter. In order to learn more about affine transformations, a good starting place is the *Transforms* chapter of Apple's *Quartz 2D Programming Guide*.

65.5 Creating the Animation Example Application

The remainder of this chapter is dedicated to the creation of an iOS application intended to demonstrate the use of UIKit animation. The end result is a simple application on which a blue square appears. When the user touches a location on the screen the box moves to that location using a spring-based animation curve. Through the use of affine transformations, the box will rotate 180 degrees as it moves to the new location while also changing in size and color. Finally, a completion handler will change the color a second time once the animation has finished.

Begin by launching Xcode and creating a new Single View Application project named *Animate* using Swift as the programming language.

65.6 Implementing the Variables

For the purposes of this application we will need a UIView to represent the blue square and variables to contain the rotation angle and scale factor by which the square will be transformed. These need to be declared in the *ViewController.swift* file as follows:

```
import UIKit

class ViewController: UIViewController {

    var scaleFactor: CGFloat = 2
    var angle: Double = 180
```

```
    var boxView: UIView?
.
.
.
```

65.7 Drawing in the UIView

Having declared the UIView reference, we now need to initialize an instance object and draw a blue square located at a specific location on the screen. We also need to add *boxView* as a subview of the application's main view object. These tasks only need to be performed once when the application first starts up so a good option is within a new method to be called from the *viewDidLoad* method of the *ViewController.swift* file:

```
override func viewDidLoad() {
    super.viewDidLoad()

    initView()
}

func initView() {
    let frameRect = CGRect(x: 20, y: 20, width: 45, height: 45)
    boxView = UIView(frame: frameRect)

    if let view = boxView {
        view.backgroundColor = UIColor.blue
        self.view.addSubview(view)
    }
}
```

65.8 Detecting Screen Touches and Performing the Animation

When the user touches the screen the blue box needs to move from its current location to the location of the touch. During this motion, the box will rotate 180 degrees and change in size. The detection of screen touches was covered in detail in *An Overview of iOS 12 Multitouch, Taps and Gestures*. For the purposes of this example we want to initiate the animation at the point that the user's finger is lifted from the screen so we need to implement the *touchesEnded* method in the *ViewController.swift* file:

```
override func touchesEnded(_ touches: Set<UITouch>, with event: UIEvent?) {

    if let touch = touches.first {
        let location = touch.location(in: self.view)
        let timing = UICubicTimingParameters(
                                    animationCurve: .easeInOut)
        let animator = UIViewPropertyAnimator(duration: 2.0,
                                    timingParameters:timing)

        animator.addAnimations {
            let scaleTrans =
                CGAffineTransform(scaleX: self.scaleFactor,
```

```
                                     y: self.scaleFactor)
            let rotateTrans = CGAffineTransform(
                rotationAngle: CGFloat(self.angle * .pi / 180))

            self.boxView!.transform =
                scaleTrans.concatenating(rotateTrans)

            self.angle = (self.angle == 180 ? 360 : 180)
            self.scaleFactor = (self.scaleFactor == 2 ? 1 : 2)
            self.boxView?.backgroundColor = UIColor.purple
            self.boxView?.center = location
        }

        animator.addCompletion {_ in
            self.boxView?.backgroundColor = UIColor.green
        }
        animator.startAnimation()
    }
}
```

Before compiling and running the application we need to take some time to describe the actions performed in the above method. First, the method gets the UITouch object from the *touches* argument and the *location(in:)* method of this object is called to identify the location on the screen where the touch took place:

```
if let touch = touches.first {
    let location = touch.location(in: self.view))
```

An instance of the UICubicTimingParameters class is then created and configured with the standard ease in, ease out animation curve:

```
let timing = UICubicTimingParameters(animationCurve: .easeInOut)
```

The animation object is then created and initialized with the timing object and a duration value of 2 seconds:

```
let animator = UIViewPropertyAnimator(duration: 2.0,
                                  timingParameters:timing)
```

The animation closure is then added to the animation object. This begins the creation of two transformations for the view, one to scale the size of the view and one to rotate it 180 degrees. These transformations are then combined into a single transformation and applied to the UIView object:

```
let scaleTrans =
            CGAffineTransform(scaleX: self.scaleFactor,
                                     y: self.scaleFactor)
let rotateTrans = CGAffineTransform(
                rotationAngle: CGFloat(self.angle * .pi / 180))

self.boxView?.transform = scaleTrans.concatenating(rotateTrans)
```

Ternary operators are then used to switch the scale and rotation angle variables ready for the next touch. In other words, after rotating 180 degrees on the first touch the view will need to be rotated to 360 degrees on the next animation. Similarly, once the box has been scaled by a factor of 2 it needs to scale back to its original size on the next animation:

```
self.angle = (self.angle == 180 ? 360 : 180)
self.scaleFactor = (self.scaleFactor == 2 ? 1 : 2)
```

Finally, the location of the view is moved to the point on the screen where the touch occurred and the color of the box changed to purple:

```
self.boxView?.backgroundColor = UIColor.purple
self.boxView?.center = location
```

Next, a completion handler is assigned to the animation and implemented such that it changes the color of the box view to green:

```
animator.addCompletion {_ in
    self.boxView?.backgroundColor = UIColor.green
}
```

After the animations have been added to the animation object, the animation sequence is started:

```
animator.startAnimation()
```

Once the *touchesEnded* method has been implemented it is time to try out the application.

65.9 Building and Running the Animation Application

Once all the code changes have been made and saved, click on the run button in the Xcode toolbar. Once the application has compiled it will load into the iOS Simulator or connected iOS device.

When the application loads the blue square should appear near the top left-hand corner of the screen. Click (or touch if running on a device) the screen and watch the box glide and rotate to the new location, the size and color of the box changing as it moves:

Figure 65-1

65.10 Implementing Spring Timing

The final task in this tutorial is to try out the UISpringTimingParameters class to implement a spring effect at the end of the animation. Edit the *ViewController.swift* file and change the timing constant so that it reads as follows:

```
.
.
let timing = UICubicTimingParameters(animationCurve: .easeInOut)

let timing = UISpringTimingParameters(mass: 0.5, stiffness: 0.5,
           damping: 0.3, initialVelocity: CGVector(dx:1.0, dy: 0.0))
.
.
```

Run the app once more, tap the screen and note the spring effect on the box when it reaches the end location in the animation sequence.

65.11 Summary

UIKit animation provides an easy to implement interface to animation within iOS applications. From the simplest of tasks such as gracefully fading out a user interface element to basic animation and transformations, UIKit animation provides a variety of techniques for enhancing user interfaces. This chapter covered the basics of UIKit animation, including the UIViewPropertyAnimator, UISpringTimingParameters and UICubicTimingParameters classes before working step-by-step through an example to demonstrate the implementation of motion, rotation and scaling animation.

Chapter 66

66. iOS 12 UIKit Dynamics – An Overview

UIKit Dynamics provides a powerful and flexible mechanism for combining user interaction and animation into iOS user interfaces. What distinguishes UIKit Dynamics from other approaches to animation is the ability to declare animation behavior in terms of real-world physics.

Before moving on to a detailed tutorial in the next chapter, this chapter will provide an overview of the concepts and methodology behind UIKit Dynamics in iOS.

66.1 Understanding UIKit Dynamics

UIKit Dynamics allows for the animation of user interface elements (typically view items) to be implemented within a user interface, often in response to user interaction. In order to fully understand the concepts behind UIKit Dynamics, it helps to visualize how real world objects behave.

Holding an object in the air and then releasing it, for example, will cause it to fall to the ground. This behavior is, of course, the result of gravity. Whether or not, and by how much, an object bounces upon impact with a solid surface is dependent upon that object's elasticity and its velocity at the point of impact.

Similarly, pushing an object positioned on a flat surface will cause that object to travel a certain distance depending on the magnitude and angle of the pushing force combined with the level of friction at the point of contact between the two surfaces.

An object tethered to a moving point will react in a variety of ways such as following the anchor point, swinging in a pendulum motion or even bouncing and spinning on the tether in response to more aggressive motions. An object similarly attached using a spring, however, will behave entirely differently in response to the movement of the point of attachment.

Having considered how objects behave in the real world, imagine the ability to selectively apply these same physics related behaviors to view objects in a user interface and you will begin to understand the basic concepts behind UIKit Dynamics. Not only does UIKit Dynamics allow user interface interaction and animation to be declared using concepts with which we are all already familiar, but in most cases it allows this to be achieved with just a few simple lines of code.

66.2 The UIKit Dynamics Architecture

Before looking at the details of how UIKit Dynamics are implemented in application code, it helps to first gain an understanding of the different elements that comprise the dynamics architecture.

The UIKit Dynamics implementation comprises four key elements consisting of a *dynamic animator*, a set of one or more *dynamic behaviors*, one or more *dynamic items* and a *reference view*.

66.2.1 Dynamic Items

The dynamic items are the view elements within the user interface that are to be animated in response to specified dynamic behaviors. A dynamic item is any view object that implements the *UIDynamicItem* protocol which includes the UIView and UICollectionView classes and any subclasses thereof (such as UIButton and

UILabel). Any custom view item can be made to work with UIKit Dynamics by making it conform to the UIDynamicItem protocol.

66.2.2 Dynamic Behaviors

Dynamic behaviors are used to configure the behavior which is to be applied to one or more dynamic items. A range of predefined dynamic behavior classes is available, including *UIAttachmentBehavior*, *UICollisionBehavior*, *UIGravityBehavior*, *UIDynamicItemBehavior*, *UIPushBehavior* and *UISnapBehavior.* Each of these is a subclass of the *UIDynamicBehavior* class which will be covered in detail later in this chapter.

In general, an instance of the class corresponding to the desired behavior (UIGravityBehavior for gravity, for example) will be created and the dynamic items for which the behavior is to be applied added to that instance. Dynamic items can be assigned to multiple dynamic behavior instances at the same time and may be added to, or removed from a dynamic behavior instance during runtime.

Once created and configured, behavior objects are then added to the *dynamic animator* instance. Once added to a dynamic animator, the behavior may be removed at any time.

66.2.3 The Reference View

The reference view dictates the area of the screen within which the UIKit Dynamics animation and interaction are to take place. This is typically the parent superclass view or collection view of which the dynamic item views are children.

66.2.4 The Dynamic Animator

The dynamic animator is responsible for coordinating the dynamic behaviors and items, and working with the underlying physics engine to perform the animation. The dynamic animator is represented by an instance of the *UIDynamicAnimator* class, and is initialized with the corresponding reference view at creation time. Once created, suitably configured dynamic behavior instances can be added and removed as required to implement the desired user interface behavior.

The overall architecture for an example UIKit Dynamics implementation can be represented visually using the diagram outlined in Figure 66-1:

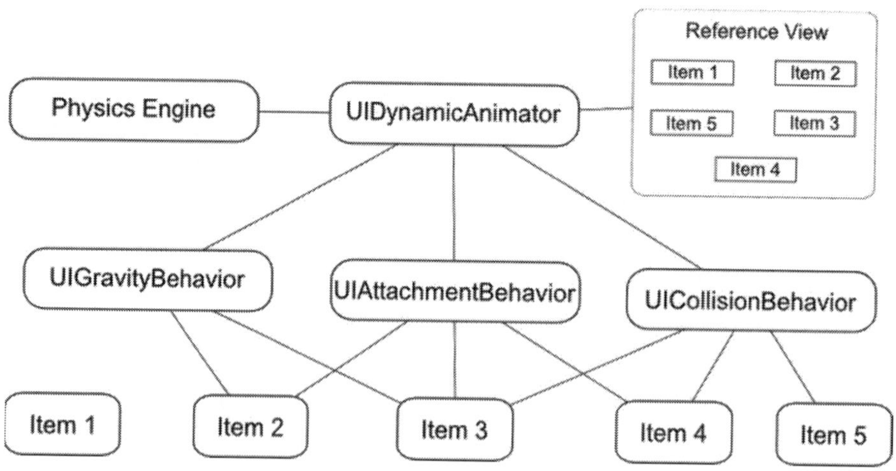

Figure 66-1

In the above example three dynamic behaviors have been added to the dynamic animator instance. The reference view contains 5 dynamic items, all but one of which have been added to at least one dynamic behavior instance.

66.3 Implementing UIKit Dynamics in an iOS Application

The implementation of UIKit Dynamics in an application requires three very simple steps:

1. Create an instance of the *UIDynamicAnimator* class to act as the dynamic animator and initialize it with a reference to the reference view.

2. Create and configure a dynamic behavior instance and assign to it the dynamic items on which the specified behavior is to be imposed.

3. Add the dynamic behavior instance to the dynamic animator.

4. Repeat from step 2 to create and add additional behaviors.

66.4 Dynamic Animator Initialization

The first step in implementing UIKit Dynamics is to create and initialize an instance of the UIDynamicAnimator class. The first step is to declare an instance variable for the reference:

```
var animator: UIDynamicAnimator?
```

Next, the dynamic animator instance can be created. The following code, for example, creates and initializes the animator instance within the *viewDidLoad* method of a view controller, using the view controller's parent view as the reference view:

```
override func viewDidLoad() {
    super.viewDidLoad()
    animator = UIDynamicAnimator(referenceView: self.view)
}
```

With the dynamic animator created and initialized, the next step is to begin to configure behaviors, the details for which differ slightly depending on the nature of the behavior.

66.5 Configuring Gravity Behavior

Gravity behavior is implemented using the UIGravityBehavior class, the purpose of which is to cause view items to want to "fall" within the reference view as though influenced by gravity. UIKit Dynamics gravity is slightly different from real world gravity in that it is possible to define a vector for the direction of the gravitational force using x and y components (x, y) contained within a CGVector instance. The default vector for this class is (0.0, 1.0) which corresponds to downwards acceleration at a speed of 1000 points per second^2. A negative x or y value will reverse the direction of gravity.

A UIGravityBehavior instance can be initialized as follows, passing through an array of dynamic items on which the behavior is to be imposed (in this case two views named view1 and view2):

```
let gravity = UIGravityBehavior(items: [view1, view2])
```

Once created, the default vector can be changed if required at any time:

```
let vector = CGVectorMake(0.0, 0.5)
gravity.gravityDirection = vector
```

Finally, the behavior needs to be added to the dynamic animator instance:

```
animator?.addBehavior(gravity)
```

At any point during the application lifecycle, dynamic items may be added to, or removed from, the behavior:

```
gravity.addItem(view3)
gravity.removeItem(view)
```

Similarly, the entire behavior may be removed from the dynamic animator:

```
animator?.removeBehavior(gravity)
```

When gravity behavior is applied to a view, and in the absence of opposing behaviors, the view will immediately move in the direction of the specified gravity vector. In fact, as currently defined, the view will fall out of the bounds of the reference view and disappear. This can be prevented by setting up a collision behavior.

66.6 Configuring Collision Behavior

UIKit Dynamics is all about making items move on the device display. When an item moves there is a high chance it will collide either with another item or with the boundaries of the encapsulating reference view. As previously discussed, in the absence of any form of collision behavior, a moving item can move out of the visible area of the reference view. Such a configuration will also cause a moving item to simply pass over the top of any other items that happen to be in its path. Collision behavior (defined using the UICollisionBehavior class) allows for such collisions to behave in ways more representative of the real world.

Collision behavior can be implemented between dynamic items (such that certain items can collide with others) or within boundaries (allowing collisions to occur when a designated boundary is reached by an item). Boundaries can be defined such that they correspond to the boundaries of the reference view, or entirely new boundaries can be defined using lines and Bezier paths.

As with gravity behavior, a collision is generally created and initialized with an array object containing the items to which the behavior is to be applied. For example:

```
let collision = UICollisionBehavior(items: [view1, view2])
animator?.addBehavior(collision)
```

As configured, view1 and view2 will now collide when coming into contact with each other. What then happens will be decided by the physics engine depending on the elasticity of the items, and the angle and speed of the collision. In other words, the engine will animate the items so that they behave as if they were physical objects subject to the laws of physics.

By default, an item under the influence of a collision behavior will collide both with other items in the same collision behavior set, and also with any boundaries set up. To declare the reference view as a boundary, simply set the *translatesReferenceBoundsIntoBoundary* property of the behavior instance to *true*:

```
collision.translatesReferenceBoundsIntoBoundary = true
```

A boundary inset from the edges of the reference view may be defined using the *setsTranslateReferenceBoundsIntoBoundaryWithInsets* method, passing through the required insets as an argument in the form of a *UIEdgeInsets* object.

The *collisionMode* property may be used to change default collision behavior by assigning one of the following constants:

- **UICollisionBehaviorMode.items** – Specifies that collisions only occur between items added to the collision behavior instance. Boundary collisions are ignored.
- **UICollisionBehaviorMode.boundaries** – Configures the behavior to ignore item collisions, recognizing only collisions with boundaries.
- **UICollisionBehaviorMode.everything** – Specifies that collisions occur between items added to the behavior and all boundaries. This is the default behavior.

The following code, for example, enables collisions only for items:

```
collision.collisionMode = UICollisionBehaviorMode.items
```

In the event that an application needs to react to a collision, simply declare a class instance that conforms to the UICollisionBehaviorDelegate class by implementing the following methods and assign it as the delegate for the UICollisionBehavior object instance.

- collisionBehavior(_:beganContactForItem:withBoundaryIdentifier:atPoint:)
- collisionBehavior(_:beganContactForItem:withItem:atPoint:)
- collisionBehavior(_:endedContactForItem:withBoundaryIdentifier:)
- collisionBehavior(_:endedContactForItem:withItem:)

When implemented, the application will be notified when collisions begin and end. Note that in most cases the delegate methods will be passed information about the collision such as the location and the items or boundaries involved.

In addition, aspects of the collision behavior such as friction and the elasticity of the colliding items (such that they bounce on contact) may be configured using the UIDynamicBehavior class. This class will be covered in detail later in this chapter.

66.7 Configuring Attachment Behavior

As the name suggests, the UIAttachmentBehavior class allows dynamic items to be configured such that they behave as if attached. These attachments can take the form of two items attached to each other or an item attached to an anchor point at specific coordinates within the reference view. The attachment can take the form of an imaginary piece of cord that does not stretch, or a spring attachment with configurable damping and frequency properties that control how "bouncy" the attached item is in response to motion.

By default, the attachment point within the item itself is positioned at the center of the view. This can, however, be changed to a different position causing the real world behavior outlined in Figure 66-2 to occur:

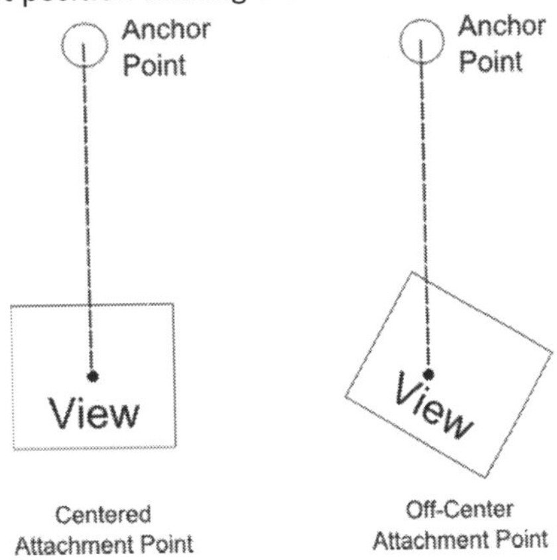

Figure 66-2

In general, the physics engine will simulate animation to match what would typically happen in the real world. As illustrated above, the item will tilt when not attached in the center. In the event that the anchor point moves, the attached view will also move. Depending on the motion, the item will swing in a pendulum motion and, assuming appropriate collision behavior configuration, bounce off any boundaries it collides with as it swings.

As with all UIKit Dynamics behavior, all the work to achieve this is performed for us by the physics engine. The only effort required by the developer is to write a few lines of code to set up the behavior before adding it to the dynamic animator instance. The following code, for example, sets up an attachment between two dynamic items:

```
let attachment = UIAttachmentBehavior(item: view1,
```

```
                                        attachedToItem: view2)
animator?.addBehavior(attachment)
```

The following code, on the other hand, specifies an attachment between view1 and an anchor point with the frequency and damping values set to configure a spring effect:

```
let anchorpoint = CGPoint(x: 100, y: 100)
let attachment = UIAttachmentBehavior(item: view1,
                        attachedToAnchor: anchorPoint)
attachment.frequency = 4.0
attachment.damping = 0.0
```

The above examples attach to the center point of the view. The following code fragment sets the same attachment as above, but with an attachment point offset 20, 20 points relative to the center of the view:

```
let anchorpoint = CGPoint(x: 100, y: 100)
let offset = UIOffset(horizontal: 20, vertical: 20)

let attachment = UIAttachmentBehavior(item: view1,
                              offsetFromCenter: offset,
                              attachedToAnchor: anchorPoint)
```

66.8 Configuring Snap Behavior

The UISnapBehavior class allows a dynamic item to be "snapped" to a specific location within the reference view. When implemented, the item will move toward the snap location as though pulled by a spring and, depending on the damping property specified, will oscillate a number of times before finally snapping into place. Until the behavior is removed from the dynamic animator, the item will continue to snap to the location when subsequently moved to another position.

The damping property can be set to any value between 0.0 and 1.0 with 1.0 specifying maximum oscillation. The default value for damping is 0.5.

The following code configures snap behavior for dynamic item view1 with damping set to 1.0:

```
let point = CGPoint(x: 100, y: 100)
let snap = UISnapBehavior(item: view1, snapToPoint: point)
snap.damping = 1.0

animator?.addBehavior(snap)
```

66.9 Configuring Push Behavior

Push behavior, defined using the UIPushBehavior class, simulates the effect of pushing one or more dynamic items in a specific direction with a specified force. The force can be specified as continuous or instantaneous. In the case of a continuous push, the force is continually applied causing the item to accelerate over time. The instantaneous push is more like a "shove" than a push in that the force is applied for a short pulse causing the item to quickly gain velocity, but gradually lose momentum and eventually stop. Once an instantaneous push event has completed, the behavior is disabled (though it can subsequently be re-enabled).

The direction of the push can be defined in radians or using x and y components. By default, the pushing force is applied to the center of the dynamic item, though as with attachments, this can be changed to an offset relative to the center of the view.

A force of magnitude 1.0 is defined as being a force of one UIKit Newton which equates to a view sized at 100 x 100 points with a density of value 1.0 accelerating at a rate of 100 points per second^2. The density of a view can, as will be explained in the next section, be configured using the UIDynamicItemBehavior class.

The following code pushes an item with instantaneous force at a magnitude of 0.2 applied on both the x and y axes, causing the view to move diagonally down and to the right.

```
let push = UIPushBehavior(items: [view1],
                    mode: UIPushBehaviorMode.instantaneous)
let vector = CGVector(dx: 0.2, dy: 0.2)
push.pushDirection = vector
```

Continuous push behavior can be achieved by changing the *mode* in the above code property to *UIPushBehaviorMode.continuous.*

To change the point where force is applied, configure the behavior using the *setTargetOffsetFromCenter(_:for:)* method of the behavior object, specifying an offset relative to the center of the view. For example:

```
let offset = UIOffset(horizontal: 20, vertical: 20)
push.setTargetOffsetFromCenter(offset, for:view1)
```

In most cases, an off-center target for the pushing force will cause the item to rotate as it moves as indicated in Figure 66-3:

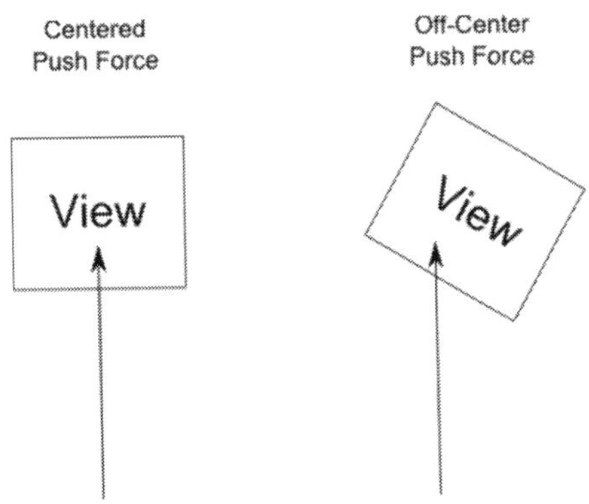

Figure 66-3

66.10 The UIDynamicItemBehavior Class

The UIDynamicItemBehavior class allows additional behavior characteristics to be defined that complement a number of the above primitive behaviors. This class can, for example, be used to define the density, resistance and elasticity of dynamic items so that they do not move as far when subjected to an instantaneous push, or bounce to a greater extent when involved in a collision. Dynamic items also have the ability to rotate by default. In the event that rotation is not required for an item, this behavior can be turned off using a UIDynamicItemBehavior instance.

Behavioral properties of dynamic items that can be governed by the UIDynamicItemBehavior class are as follows:

- **allowsRotation** – Controls whether or not the item is permitted to rotate during animation.
- **angularResistence** – The amount by which the item resists rotation. The higher the value, the faster the item will stop rotating.
- **density** – The mass of the item.

- **elasticity** – The amount of elasticity an item will exhibit when involved in a collision. The greater the elasticity the more the item will bounce.
- **friction** – The resistance exhibited by an item when it slides against another item.
- **resistence** – The overall resistance that the item exhibits in response to behavioral influences. The greater the value the sooner the item will come to a complete stop during animation.

In addition, the class includes the following methods that may be used to increase or decrease the angular or linear velocity of a specified dynamic item:

- **angularVelocity(for:)** – Increases or decreases the angular velocity of the specified item. Velocity is specified in radians per second where a negative value reduces the angular velocity.
- **linearVelocity(for:)** – Increases or decreases the linear velocity of the specified item. Velocity is specified in points per second where a negative value reduces the velocity.

The following code example creates a new UIDynamicItemBehavior instance and uses it to set resistance and elasticity for two views before adding the behavior to the dynamic animator instance:

```
let behavior = UIDynamicItemBehavior(items: [view1, view2])
behavior.elasticity = 0.2
behavior.resistance = 0.5
animator?.addBehavior(behavior)
```

66.11 Combining Behaviors to Create a Custom Behavior

Multiple behaviors may be combined to create a single custom behavior using an instance of the UIDynamicBehavior class. The first step is to create and initialize each of the behavior objects. An instance of the UIDynamicBehavior class is then created and each behavior added to it via calls to the *addChildBehavior* method. Once created, only the UIDynamicBehavior instance needs to be added to the dynamic animator. For example:

```
// Create multiple behavior objects here

let customBehavior = UIDynamicBehavior()

customBehavior.addChildBehavior(behavior)
customBehavior.addChildBehavior(attachment)
customBehavior.addChildBehavior(gravity)
customBehavior.addChildBehavior(push)

animator?.addBehavior(customBehavior)
```

66.12 Summary

UIKit Dynamics provide a new way to bridge the gap between user interaction with an iOS device and corresponding animation within an application user interface. UIKit Dynamics takes a novel approach to animation by allowing view items to be configured such that they behave in much the same way as physical objects in the real world. This chapter has covered an overview of the basic concepts behind UIKit Dynamics and provided some details on how such behavior is implemented in terms of coding. The next chapter will work through a tutorial that demonstrates many of these concepts in action.

Chapter 67

67. An iOS 12 UIKit Dynamics Tutorial

With the basics of UIKit Dynamics covered in the previous chapter, this chapter will take this knowledge and apply it to the creation of an example application designed to show UIKit Dynamics in action. The example application created in this chapter will make use of the gravity, collision, elasticity and attachment features in conjunction with touch handling to demonstrate how these key features are implemented.

67.1 Creating the UIKit Dynamics Example Project

Begin by launching Xcode and selecting the option to create a new project from the welcome screen (or select the *File -> New -> Project...* menu option if the welcome screen is not visible). From the resulting template selection screen, choose the *Single View Application* option before clicking *Next* to proceed. Enter *UIKitDynamics* into the Product Name field and select *Swift* from the language menu. Click on *Next* once again and, in the file selection screen, navigate to a suitable location for the project files before clicking on *Create*.

67.2 Adding the Dynamic Items

The user interface for the application is going to consist of two view objects which will be drawn in the form of squares colored blue and red respectively. The first step in the tutorial, therefore, is to implement the code to create and draw these views. Within the project navigator panel, locate and select the *ViewController.swift* file and add variables for these two views so that the file reads as follows:

```
import UIKit

class ViewController: UIViewController {

    var blueBoxView: UIView?
    var redBoxView: UIView?
```

With the references declared, select the *ViewController.swift* file, add a new method (and call it from the *viewDidLoad* method) to draw the views, color them appropriately and then add them to the parent view so that they appear within the user interface:

```
override func viewDidLoad() {
    super.viewDidLoad()
    initViews()
}

func initViews() {

    var frameRect = CGRect(x: 10, y: 20, width: 80, height: 80)
    blueBoxView = UIView(frame: frameRect)
    blueBoxView?.backgroundColor = UIColor.blue
```

```
        frameRect = CGRect(x: 150, y: 20, width: 60, height: 60)
        redBoxView = UIView(frame: frameRect)
        redBoxView?.backgroundColor = UIColor.red

        if let blueBox = blueBoxView, let redBox = redBoxView {
            self.view.addSubview(blueBox)
            self.view.addSubview(redBox)
        }
}
```

Perform a test run of the application on either a simulator or physical iOS device and verify that the new views appear as expected within the user interface (Figure 67-1):

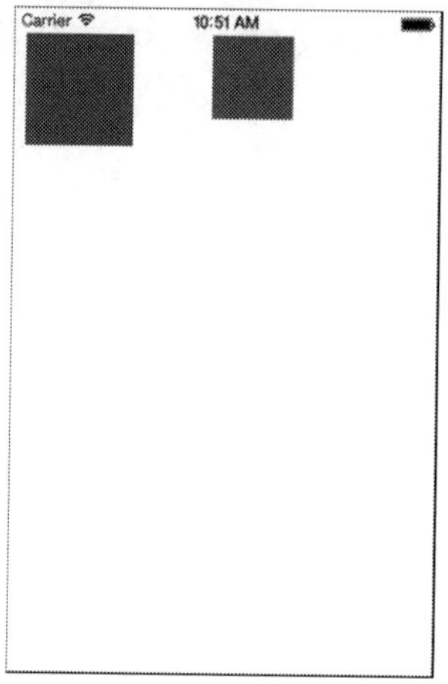

Figure 67-1

67.3 Creating the Dynamic Animator Instance

As outlined in the previous chapter, a key element in implementing UIKit Dynamics is an instance of the UIDynamicAnimator class. Select the *ViewController.swift* file and add an instance variable for a UIDynamicAnimator object within the application code:

```
import UIKit

class ViewController: UIViewController {

    var blueBoxView: UIView?
    var redBoxView: UIView?
    var animator: UIDynamicAnimator?
```

Next, modify the *initViews* method within the *ViewController.swift* file once again to add code to create and initialize the instance, noting that the top level view of the view controller is passed through as the reference view:

```
func initViews() {

    var frameRect = CGRect(x: 10, y: 20, width: 80, height: 80)
```

```
    blueBoxView = UIView(frame: frameRect)
    blueBoxView?.backgroundColor = UIColor.blue

    frameRect = CGRect(x: 150, y: 20, width: 60, height: 60)
    redBoxView = UIView(frame: frameRect)
    redBoxView?.backgroundColor = UIColor.red

    if let blueBox = blueBoxView, let redBox = redBoxView {
        self.view.addSubview(blueBox)
        self.view.addSubview(redBox)

        animator = UIDynamicAnimator(referenceView: self.view)
    }
}
```

With the dynamic items added to the user interface and an instance of the dynamic animator created and initialized, it is now time to begin creating dynamic behavior instances.

67.4 Adding Gravity to the Views

The first behavior to be added to the example application is going to be gravity. For the purposes of this tutorial, gravity will be added to both views such that a force of gravity of 1.0 UIKit Newton is applied directly downwards along the y axis of the parent view. To achieve this, the *initViews* method needs to be further modified to create a suitably configured instance of the UIGravityBehavior class and to add that instance to the dynamic animator:

```
func initViews() {

    var frameRect = CGRect(x: 10, y: 20, width: 80, height: 80)
    blueBoxView = UIView(frame: frameRect)
    blueBoxView?.backgroundColor = UIColor.blue

    frameRect = CGRect(x: 150, y: 20, width: 60, height: 60)
    redBoxView = UIView(frame: frameRect)
    redBoxView?.backgroundColor = UIColor.red

    if let blueBox = blueBoxView, let redBox = redBoxView {
        self.view.addSubview(blueBox)
        self.view.addSubview(redBox)

        animator = UIDynamicAnimator(referenceView: self.view)

        let gravity = UIGravityBehavior(items: [blueBox,
                                                redBox])
        let vector = CGVector(dx: 0.0, dy: 1.0)
        gravity.gravityDirection = vector
```

```
            animator?.addBehavior(gravity)
        }
}
```

Compile and run the application once again. Note that after launching, the gravity behavior causes the views to fall from the top of the reference view and out of view at the bottom of the device display. In order to keep the views within the bounds of the reference view, it is necessary to set up a collision behavior.

67.5 Implementing Collision Behavior

In terms of collision behavior, the example requires that collisions occur both when the views impact each other and when making contact with the boundaries of the reference view. With these requirements in mind, the collision behavior needs to be implemented as follows:

```
func initViews() {

    var frameRect = CGRect(x: 10, y: 20, width: 80, height: 80)
    blueBoxView = UIView(frame: frameRect)
    blueBoxView?.backgroundColor = UIColor.blue

    frameRect = CGRect(x: 150, y: 20, width: 60, height: 60)
    redBoxView = UIView(frame: frameRect)
    redBoxView?.backgroundColor = UIColor.red

    if let blueBox = blueBoxView, let redBox = redBoxView {
        self.view.addSubview(blueBox)
        self.view.addSubview(redBox)

        animator = UIDynamicAnimator(referenceView: self.view)

        let gravity = UIGravityBehavior(items: [blueBox,
                                                redBox])
        let vector = CGVector(dx: 0.0, dy: 1.0)
        gravity.gravityDirection = vector

        let collision = UICollisionBehavior(items: [blueBox,
                                                    redBox])

        collision.translatesReferenceBoundsIntoBoundary = true

        animator?.addBehavior(collision)
        animator?.addBehavior(gravity)
    }
}
```

Running the application should now cause the views to stop at the bottom edge of the reference view and bounce slightly after impact. The amount by which the views bounce in the event of a collision can be changed by creating a UIDynamicBehavior class instance and changing the elasticity property. The following code, for example, changes the elasticity of the blue box view so that it bounces to a higher degree than the red box:

```
func initViews() {
.
.
.
        collision.translatesReferenceBoundsIntoBoundary = true

        let behavior = UIDynamicItemBehavior(items: [blueBox])
        behavior.elasticity = 0.5

        animator?.addBehavior(behavior)
        animator?.addBehavior(collision)
        animator?.addBehavior(gravity)
    }
}
```

67.6 Attaching a View to an Anchor Point

So far in this tutorial we have added some behavior to the application but have not yet implemented any functionality that connects UIKit Dynamics to user interaction. In this section, however, the example will be modified such that an attachment is created between the blue box view and the point of contact of a touch on the screen. This anchor point will be continually updated as the user's touch moves across the screen, thereby causing the blue box to follow the anchor point. The first step in this process is to declare within the *ViewController.swift* file some instance variables within which to store both the current location of the anchor point and a reference to a UIAttachmentBehavior instance:

```
import UIKit

class ViewController: UIViewController {

    var blueBoxView: UIView?
    var redBoxView: UIView?
    var animator: UIDynamicAnimator?
    var currentLocation: CGPoint?
    var attachment: UIAttachmentBehavior?
```

As outlined in the chapter entitled *An Overview of iOS 12 Multitouch, Taps and Gestures*, touches can be detected by overriding the *touchesBegan*, *touchesMoved* and *touchesEnded* methods. The *touchesBegan* method in the *ViewController.swift* file now needs to be implemented to obtain the coordinates of the touch and to add an attachment behavior between that location and the blue box view to the animator instance:

```
override func touchesBegan(_ touches: Set<UITouch>, with event: UIEvent?) {

    if let theTouch = touches.first, let blueBox = blueBoxView {

        currentLocation = theTouch.location(in: self.view) as CGPoint?
```

```
        if let location = currentLocation {
            attachment = UIAttachmentBehavior(item: blueBox,
                                      attachedToAnchor: location)
        }

        if let attach = attachment {
            animator?.addBehavior(attach)
        }
    }
}
```

As the touch moves around within the reference view, the anchorPoint property of the attachment behavior needs to be modified to track the motion. This involves overriding the *touchesMoved* method as follows:

```
override func touchesMoved(_ touches: Set<UITouch>, with event: UIEvent?) {
    if let theTouch = touches.first {

        currentLocation = theTouch.location(in: self.view)

        if let location = currentLocation {
            attachment?.anchorPoint = location
        }
    }
}
```

Finally, when the touch ends, the attachment needs to be removed so that the view will be pulled down to the bottom of the reference view by the previously defined gravity behavior. Remaining within the *ViewController.swift* file, implement the *touchesEnded* method as follows:

```
override func touchesEnded(_ touches: Set<UITouch>, with event: UIEvent?) {

    if let attach = attachment {
        animator?.removeBehavior(attach)
    }
}
```

Compile and run the application and touch the display. As the touch is moved, note that the blue box view moves as though tethered to the touch point. Move the touch such that the blue and red boxes collide and observe that the red box will move in response to the collision while the blue box will rotate on the attachment point as illustrated in Figure 67-2:

Figure 67-2

Release the touch and note that gravity causes the blue box to fall once again and settle at the bottom edge of the reference view.

The code that creates the attachment currently attaches to the center point of the blue box view. Modify the *touchesBegan* method to adjust the attachment point so that it is off center:

```
override func touchesBegan(_ touches: Set<UITouch>, with event: UIEvent?) {

    if let theTouch = touches.first, let blueBox = blueBoxView {

        currentLocation = theTouch.location(in: self.view) as CGPoint?

        if let location = currentLocation {
            let offset = UIOffset(horizontal: 20, vertical: 20)
            attachment = UIAttachmentBehavior(item: blueBox,
                                        offsetFromCenter: offset,
                                         attachedToAnchor: location)
        }

        if let attach = attachment {
            animator?.addBehavior(attach)
        }
    }
}
```

When the blue box view is now suspended by the anchor point attachment, it will tilt in accordance with the offset attachment point.

67.7 Implementing a Spring Attachment Between two Views

The final step in this tutorial is to attach the two views together using a spring-style attachment. All that this involves is a few lines of code within the *viewDidLoad* method to create the attachment behavior, set the frequency and damping values to create the springing effect and then add the behavior to the animator instance:

```
func initViews() {
.
.
        let behavior = UIDynamicItemBehavior(items: [blueBox])
        behavior.elasticity = 0.5

        let boxAttachment = UIAttachmentBehavior(item: blueBox,
                                                attachedTo: redBox)
        boxAttachment.frequency = 4.0
        boxAttachment.damping = 0.0

        animator?.addBehavior(boxAttachment)

        animator?.addBehavior(behavior)
        animator?.addBehavior(collision)
        animator?.addBehavior(gravity)
    }
}
```

When the application is now run, the red box will move in relation to the blue box as though connected by a spring (Figure 67-3). The views will even spring apart when pushed together before the touch is released.

Figure 67-3

67.8 Summary

The example created in this chapter has demonstrated the steps involved in implementing UIKit Dynamics within an iOS application in the form of gravity, collision and attachment behaviors. Perhaps the most remarkable fact about the animation functionality implemented in this tutorial is that it was achieved in approximately 40 lines of UIKit Dynamics code, a fraction of the amount of code that would have been required to implement such behavior in the absence of UIKit Dynamics.

Chapter 68

68. An Overview of iOS Collection View and Flow Layout

The Collection View and Flow Layout combine to provide a flexible way to present content to the user. This is essentially achieved by providing a mechanism by which data driven content can be displayed in cells and the arrangement, appearance and behavior of those cells configured to meet a variety of different layout and organizational needs.

Before the introduction of Collection Views and Flow Layout, the closest iOS came to providing organized data presentation involved the use of the Table View. Whilst still a powerful user interface design option, the Table View was intended to fill a very specific need and, as such, has some limitations in terms of flexibility. Table View, for example, displays data in cells arranged in a single column layout. Collection views, on the other hand, provide a high degree of flexibility, allowing cells to be organized in just about any configuration imaginable, including grids, stacks, tiles and circular arrangements.

The goal of this chapter is to present an overview of the key elements that make up collection views prior to working through a step by step tutorial in the next chapter, entitled *An iOS 12 Storyboard-based Collection View Tutorial*.

68.1 An Overview of Collection Views

In the chapter entitled *Using Xcode 10 Storyboards to Build Dynamic TableViews* a Table View layout was used to display a list of tourist destinations and corresponding images. The fact is that while this presented the necessary information, the Table View provided very little in the way of customization options. Had the user interface been designed using a collection view, a much more visually appealing user interface could have been implemented. Figure 68-1, for example, illustrates how some images of cars could be organized using a collection view configuration.

Figure 68-1

Although not entirely obvious from the previous screenshot, the collection view is actually scrollable, allowing the user to swipe left or right to view other car images. It is also important to note that this example is just the default behavior of a collection view with a flow layout. Customization options far beyond this are possible using collection views.

At an abstract level, a collection view consists of four key elements consisting of *cells*, *supplementary views*, *decoration views* and a *layout object*. A cell is a representation of an item of data to be displayed (for example an image or a set of text based data).

As with the Table View, a collection view may be divided into multiple sections. Supplementary views are objects that provide additional information about a section in a collection view. These are somewhat similar to section headers and footers in table views but are more general purpose and provide a greater level of flexibility in terms of positioning and content.

Decoration views can be used to provide a decorative background for the collection view which scrolls along with the content. The classic example of a decoration view in Apple's own demonstrations involves constructing the image of a bookshelf behind a collection view containing photo images. It is important to note that the standard Flow Layout class does not support decoration views.

In practical terms, a collection view consists of multiple class instances, each of which will be described in more detail in the remainder of this chapter.

68.2 The UICollectionView Class

The UICollectionView class is responsible for managing the data items that are to be displayed to the user. The collection view instance needs a data source object from which to obtain the data items to be displayed, together with a delegate object to handle user interaction with the collection. These objects must implement the UICollectionViewDataSource and UICollectionViewDelegate protocols respectively.

Perhaps the most important requirement for the UICollectionView class is a layout object to control the layout and organization of the cells. By default, the UICollectionViewFlowLayout class is used by instances of the UICollectionView class. In the event that the flow layout does not provide the necessary behavior, this class may also be subclassed and extended to provide additional functionality. Perhaps the most impressive fact, however, is that an entirely new layout class may be created by subclassing UICollectionViewLayout and implementing application specific layout capabilities within that class. The custom layout is then essentially "plugged in" to the UICollectionView instance where it will dictate the layout of the data cells as it has been designed to do.

The UICollectionView class also includes a wide range of methods that can be used to perform such tasks as to add, remove, move, modify and select items.

68.3 The UICollectionViewCell Class

As the name suggests, the UICollectionViewCell class is responsible for displaying whatever data is provided to the UICollectionView instance by the data source with one cell corresponding to one data item. In terms of architecture, this class consists of two background views and one content view. The two background views may be used to provide a visual cue to the user when the corresponding cell is selected or highlighted. The content view contains the objects necessary to display the data to the user and can consist of any combination of valid UIKit classes. When adding subviews to a cell it is imperative that those objects be added to the *contentView* and not the background views, otherwise the objects will not be visible to the user.

There is a clear separation between layout and the contents of a cell. The cell only knows what to display, the sizing and positioning of the cell within the wider context of the collection view is controlled by the layout object assigned to the collection view.

Instances of UICollectionViewCell class are not typically instantiated directly in code. Instead, the class is registered as the cell class for a collection view and is then created internally as needed. Collection views are scrollable and, consequently, at any one time only a subset of the cells in a collection are visible. This enables the system to reuse cell objects that are currently scrolled outside of the viewable area of the screen and only create new ones when necessary. This is achieved using a queuing mechanism and results in improved performance, particularly when dealing with larger data sets.

68.4 The UICollectionReusableView Class

The base class from which the UICellCollectionView class is derived, this class is most typically subclassed in application code to create supplementary views.

68.5 The UICollectionViewFlowLayout Class

The UICollectionViewFlowLayout class is the default layout class for collection views and is designed to layout cells in a grid-like manner.

This class requires a delegate object that conforms to the UICollectionViewDelegateFlowLayout protocol which is typically the collection view's UICollectionViewDelegate object.

By default, flow is implemented in a manner similar to that of "line wrapping" in a text editor. When one row of cells is full, the cells flow onto the next row and so on until all cells capable of fitting into the currently visible display region are visible. The flow layout class supports both horizontal and vertical scrolling configurable via the *scrollDirection* property. In addition, properties such as the spacing between lines of cells in the grid and cells in a row may be configured, together with default sizes for cells and supplementary views (unless overridden via methods implemented in the delegate object).

68.6 The UICollectionViewLayoutAttributes Class

Each item in a collection view, be it a cell or a supplementary view, has associated with it a set of attributes. The UICollectionViewLayoutAttributes class serves as an object into which these attributes can be stored and transferred between objects. A Flow Layout object will, for example, be asked by the collection view object to return the attributes for a cell at a given index in a collection view via a call to the *collectionView(_:layoutAttributesForItemAt: indexPath)* method. This method, in turn, returns those attributes encapsulated in a UICollectionViewLayoutAttributes object. Similarly, such object instances can be used to apply new attributes to a collection view element. The attributes stored by the UICollectionViewLayoutAttributes class are as follows (keeping in mind that this class may be subclassed and extended to allow the storage of other values):

- **alpha** – The transparency of the item.
- **center** – The location of the center of the item.
- **frame** – The CGRect frame in which the item is displayed.
- **hidden** – Whether or not the item is currently visible.
- **indexPath** – The index path location of the item in the collection view.
- **representedElementCategory** – The type of item for which the attributes apply (i.e. for a cell, supplementary or decoration view).
- **size** – The size of the item.
- **transform3D** – The current transform of the item. This attribute can be used to perform tasks such as rotating or scaling the item.
- **zIndex** – Controls the position of the item in the z axis (in other words whether or not it is on top of or below other overlapping items).

68.7 The UICollectionViewDataSource Protocol

The UICollectionViewDataSource protocol needs to be implemented by the class responsible for supplying the collection view with the pre-configured cells and supplementary views to be displayed to the user. This basically consists of a number of methods that define information such as how many items of data are to be displayed, how the data is divided into different sections and, most importantly, supplies the collection view with the cell objects to be displayed.

Mandatory methods in the protocol are as follows:

- **collectionView(_:numberOfItemsInSection:)** - Returns the number of items to be displayed in the specified section of the collection view.
- **collectionView(_:cellForItemAt indexPath:)** - This method is called by the collection view when it is ready to display a cell at the specified index path location in the collection view. It is required to return a cell object configured appropriately for the referenced index.

Optional methods in the protocol are as follows:

- **numberOfSectionsInCollectionView(_:)** - Indicates to the collection view the number of sections into which the collection view is to be divided.
- **collectionView(_:viewForSupplementaryElementOfKind: at:)** - Called by the collection view to request a supplementary view of the specified kind. Returns an appropriately configured object to be displayed. In terms of the UICollectionViewFlowLayout class, the layout will request a supplementary view for either a header (UICollectionView.elementKindSectionHeader) or footer (UICollectionView.elementKindSectionFooter).

68.8 The UICollectionViewDelegate Protocol

The UICollectionViewDelegate protocol defines a set of optional methods which, if implemented, will be called when certain events take place within the corresponding collection. These methods relate primarily to handling user interaction with the collection view elements (such as selecting a specific cell). Some of the key methods in this protocol include:

- **collectionView(_:shouldSelectItemAt indexPath:)** - Returns a boolean value indicating whether the specified item is selectable by the user.
- **collectionView(_:didSelectItemAt indexPath:)** - Called by the collection view when the specified item has been selected by the user.
- **collectionView(_:shouldDeselectItemAt indexPath:)** - Returns a boolean value to indicate whether the specified item may be deselected by the user.
- **collectionView(_:didDeselectItemAt indexPath:)** - Called by the collection view when the specified item has been selected by the user.
- **collectionView(_:shouldHighlightItemAt indexPath:)** - Returns a boolean value indicating whether the specified item should be highlighted as a pre-cursor to possible selection by the user.
- **collectionView(_:didHighlightItemAt indexPath:)** - Called by the collection view when the specified item has been highlighted.

- **collectionView(_:didUnhighlightItemAt indexPath:)** - Called by the collection view when the specified item has been un-highlighted.
- **collectionView(_:didEndDisplayingCell:forItemAt indexPath:)** - Called by the collection view when the specified cell has been removed from the collection view.
- **collectionView(_:didEndDisplayingSupplementaryView:forElementOfKind:at:)** - Called by the collection view when the specified supplementary view has been removed from the collection view.

68.9 The UICollectionViewDelegateFlowLayout Protocol

The UICollectionViewFlowLayout class has a number of properties that can be set to globally set default characteristics for items within a collection view (for example section inset, item spacing, line spacing, inter-cell spacing, supplementary view header and footer sizing etc). Alternatively, these values may be overridden on a per-cell and per-section basis by implementing the following delegate methods in a class which conforms to the UICollectionViewDelegateFlowLayout protocol. In most cases, this will be the same class as that implementing the UICollectionViewDelegate protocol. Note that in each case, the method is passed a reference either to the cell or section for which information is required:

- **collectionView(_:layout:sizeForItemAt indexPath:)** - Required to return to the flow layout object the size attributes for the item at the specified index path.
- **collectionView(_:layout:insetForSectionAt index:)** - Required to return the inset value for the specified collection view section.
- **collectionView(_:layout:minimumLineSpacingForSectionAt:)** - Required to return the inset value for the specified collection view section.
- **collectionView(_:layout:minimumInteritemSpacingForSectionAt:)** - Required to return the interim spacing between cells in a row for the specified collection view section.
- **collectionView(_:layout:referenceSizeForHeaderInSection:)** - Required to return the size for the header supplementary view for the specified collection view section. Note that if a size is not specified, the view will not appear.
- **collectionView(_:layout:referenceSizeForFooterInSection:)** - Required to return the size for the footer supplementary view for the specified collection view section. Note that if a size is not specified, the view will not appear.

68.10 Cell and View Reuse

As previously discussed, the code for a typical application using a collection view will not directly create instances of either the cell or supplementary view classes. The reasoning behind this becomes evident when performance and memory requirements are taken into consideration. Consider, for example, a collection view that is required to display 1000 photo images. It can be assumed with a reasonable degree of certainty that only a small percentage of cells will be visible to the user at any one time. If the application were permitted to create each of the 1000 cells in advance the device would very quickly run into memory limitations.

Instead, the application begins by registering with the collection view the class to be used for cell objects, along with a *reuse identifier*. If the cell class was written in code, the registration is performed using the *registerClass* method of UICollectionView. For example:

```
self.collectionView?.registerClass(UICollectionViewCell.self,
            forCellWithReuseIdentifier: "MyCell")
```

In the event that the cell is contained within an Interface Builder NIB file, the *registerNib* method is used instead.

The same concept applies to supplementary views which must also be registered with the collection view using either the *registerClass:forSupplementaryViewOfKind:* and *registerNib:forSupplementaryViewOfKind* methods.

Perhaps the most important point to remember from this chapter is that if the cell or supplementary views are created using prototypes within a storyboard it is not necessary to register the class in code and, in fact, doing so will prevent the cell or view from appearing when the application runs and may cause the application to crash.

As the collection view initializes, it calls the *cellForItemAt* method of the datasource delegate passing through the index path for which a cell object is required. This method will then call the *dequeueReusableCell(withReuseIdentifier:)* method of the collection view, passing through both the index path and the reuse ID assigned to the cell class when it was registered, to find out if there is a reusable cell object in the queue that can be used for this new cell. Since this is the initialization phase and no cells have been deemed eligible for reuse, the method will create a new cell and return it. Once all the visible cells have been created the collection view will stop asking for more cells. The code for *collectionView(_:cellForItemAt: indexPath)* will typically read as follows (though the code to customize the cell before returning it will be implementation specific):

```
override func collectionView(_ collectionView: UICollectionView,
     cellForItemAt indexPath: IndexPath) -> UICollectionViewCell {

    let cell = collectionView.dequeueReusableCellWithReuseIdentifier(
         reuseIdentifier,
         forIndexPath: indexPath)

    // Configure the cell
    let image = UIImage(named: myImages[indexPath.row])
    cell.cellImage.image = image

    return cell
}
```

As the user scrolls through the collection view, some cells will move out of the visible frame. When this happens, the collection view places them on the reuse queue. As cells are moving out of view, new ones are likely to be coming into view. For each cell moving into the view area, the collection view will call *cellForItemAt*. This time, however, when a call to *dequeueReusableCell(withReuseIdentifier:)* is made, it is most likely that an existing cell object will be returned from the reuse queue, thereby avoiding the necessity to create a new object.

These same reuse concepts apply equally to supplementary views, with the exception that the collection view will call the *viewForSupplementaryElementOfKind* method of the data source when seeking a view object which must, in turn, call *dequeueReusableSupplementaryViewOfKind*.

68.11 Summary

Collection view and the flow layout were introduced into iOS to provide a flexible approach to displaying data items to the user. The key objectives of collection views are flexibility and performance.

This chapter has outlined the overall concepts behind collection views and flow layout before looking in some detail at the different classes that can be brought together to implement collection views in iOS applications. Finally, the chapter provided an explanation of cell and supplementary view object reuse.

The next chapter will work through the creation of an example application that utilizes collection views to present a gallery of images to the user.

Chapter 69

69. An iOS 12 Storyboard-based Collection View Tutorial

The primary goal of this chapter is to demonstrate, in a tutorial format, the steps involved in implementing a collection view based application user interface and, in doing so, serve to re-enforce the collection view concepts outlined in the previous chapter. By far the most productive way to implement collection views (and the approach used in this tutorial) is to take advantage of the Storyboard feature of Xcode and, in particular, the collection view cell and supplementary view prototyping options of Interface Builder.

69.1 Creating the Collection View Example Project

Launch Xcode and create a new project by selecting the options to create a new iOS application based on the *Single View Application* template. Enter *CollectionDemo* as the product name and choose Swift as the programming language.

69.2 Removing the Template View Controller

Based on the template selection made when the project was set up, Xcode has created a generic UIViewController based subclass for the application. For the purposes of this tutorial, however, this needs to be replaced with a UICollectionViewController subclass. Begin, therefore, by selecting the *ViewController.swift* file in the project navigator and pressing the keyboard delete key. When prompted, click the button to move the file to trash.

Next, select the *Main.storyboard* file and, in the storyboard canvas, select the view controller so that it is outlined in blue (the view controller is selected by clicking on the toolbar area at the top of the layout view) and tap the keyboard delete key to remove the controller and leave a blank storyboard.

69.3 Adding a Collection View Controller to the Storyboard

The first element that needs to be added to the project is a UICollectionViewController subclass. To add this, select the Xcode *File -> New -> File...* menu option. In the resulting panel, select *Source* listed under *iOS* in the left hand panel, followed by *Cocoa Touch Class* in the main panel before clicking *Next.*

On the subsequent screen, name the new class *MyCollectionViewController* and, from the *Subclass of* drop down menu, choose *UICollectionViewController*. Verify that the option to create an XIB file is switched off before clicking *Next*. Choose a location for the files and then click *Create*.

The project now has a new file named *MyCollectionViewController.swift* which represents a new class named *MyCollectionViewController* which is itself a subclass of *UICollectionViewController*.

The next step is to add a UICollectionViewController instance to the storyboard and then associate it with the newly created class. Select the *Main.storyboard* file and drag and drop a Collection View Controller object from the Library panel onto the storyboard canvas as illustrated in Figure 69-1.

Note that the UICollectionViewController added to the storyboard has also brought with it a UICollectionView instance (indicated by the white background) and a prototype cell (represented by the gray square outline located in the top left-hand corner of the collection view).

Figure 69-1

With the new view controller selected in the storyboard, display the Identity Inspector either by selecting the toolbar item in the Utilities panel or via the *View -> Utilities -> Show Identity Inspector* menu option and change the Class setting (Figure 69-2) from the generic UICollectionViewController class to the newly added *MyCollectionViewController* class.

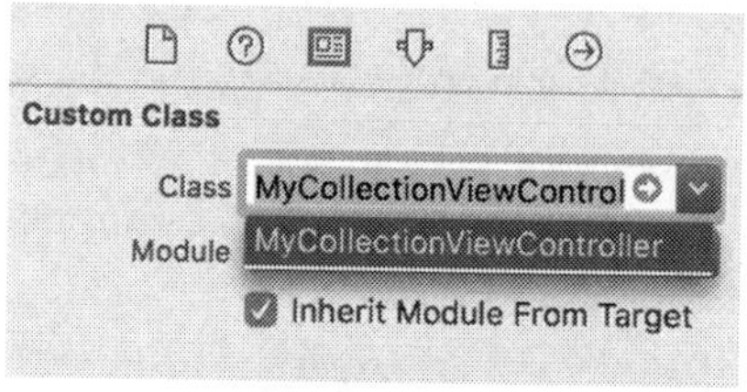

Figure 69-2

With the view controller scene still selected, display the Attributes Inspector and enable the *Is Initial View Controller* option so that the view controller is loaded when the app starts.

69.4 Adding the Collection View Cell Class to the Project

With a subclass of UICollectionViewController added to the project, a new class must now be added which subclasses UICollectionViewCell.

Once again, select the Xcode *File -> New -> File...* menu option. In the resulting panel, select the iOS *Source* option from the left hand panel, followed by *Cocoa Touch Class* in the main panel before clicking *Next.*

On the subsequent screen, name the new class *MyCollectionViewCell* and from the *Subclass of* drop down menu choose *UICollectionViewCell*. Click *Next*, choose a location for the files and then click *Create*.

Return to the *Main.storyboard* file and select the white square in the collection view. This is the prototype cell for the collection view and needs to be assigned a reuse identifier and associated with the new class. With the cell selected, open the Identity Inspector panel and change the Class to *MyCollectionViewCell.* Remaining in the Utilities panel, display the Attributes Inspector (Figure 69-3) and enter *MyCell* as the reuse identifier.

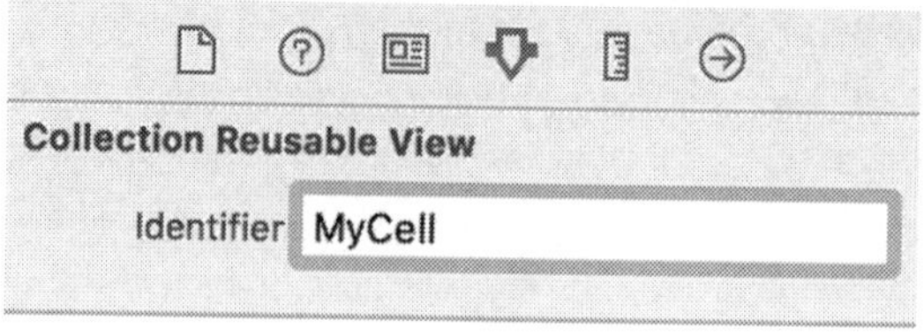

Figure 69-3

69.5 Designing the Cell Prototype

With the basic collection view classes implemented and associated with the storyboard objects, it is now time to design the cell. This is, quite simply, a matter of dragging and dropping items from the Library panel onto the prototype cell in the storyboard view. Additionally the size of the cell may be modified by selecting it and using the resulting resize handles. The exact design of the cell is entirely dependent on what is to be displayed. For the purposes of this example, however, each cell is simply going to display an image.

Begin by resizing the cell to a slightly larger size, locating the Image View object in the Library panel and dragging and dropping it into the prototype cell as shown in Figure 69-4.

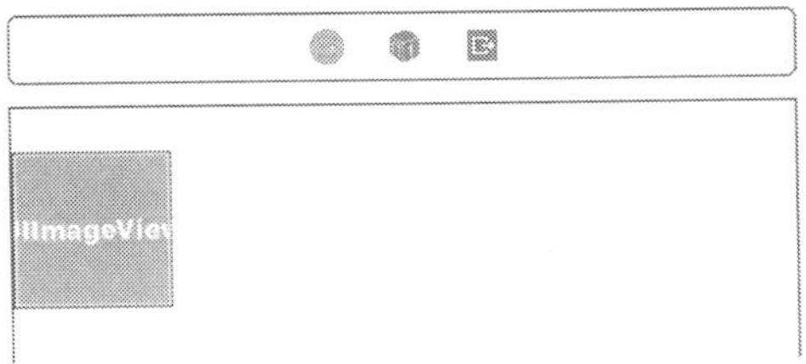

Figure 69-4

With the Image View object selected in the storyboard scene, select the *Add New Constraints* menu from the toolbar located in the lower right hand corner of the storyboard panel and set up *Spacing to nearest neighbor* constraints on all four sides of the view with the *Constrain to margins* option turned off. Once configured, click on the *Add 4 Constraints* button to establish the constraints.

Since it will be necessary to assign an image when a cell is configured, an outlet to the Image View will be needed. Display the Assistant Editor, make sure it is listing the code for the *MyCollectionViewCell.swift* file then Ctrl-click and drag from the Image View object to a position immediately beneath the class declaration line. Release the line and, in the resulting connection panel, establish an outlet connection named *imageView*. On completion of the connection, select *MyCollectionViewCell.swift* in the project navigator and verify that it reads as follows:

```
import UIKit

class MyCollectionViewCell: UICollectionViewCell {

    @IBOutlet weak var imageView: UIImageView!
}
```

With the connection established, the prototype cell implementation is complete.

69.6 Implementing the Data Model

The data model for this example application is going to consist of a set of images, each of which will be displayed in a cell within the collection view. The first step in creating this model is to load the images into the project. These images can be found in the *carImagesSmall* folder of the sample code archive which is downloadable from the following URL:

https://www.ebookfrenzy.com/retail/ios12/

Once downloaded, unzip the archive and drag and drop the image files onto the Xcode project navigator panel.

Next, select the *MyCollectionViewController.swift* file and declare the arrays into which will be stored the image file names and corresponding images. Also change the *reuseIdentifier* constant to match the identifier assigned to the cell in Interface Builder:

```
import UIKit

let reuseIdentifier = "MyCell"

class MyCollectionViewController: UICollectionViewController {

    var imageFiles = [String]()
    var images = [UIImage]()
.
.
.
}
```

Finally, edit the *MyCollectionViewController.swift* file and modify the *viewDidLoad* method to call a method named *initialize* which will, in turn, initialize the array with the names of the car image files and then use those files to initialize the images array. Also comment out or delete the following line so that it is no longer executed when the application runs. As outlined in the previous chapter, it is not necessary to register cell classes when using Storyboard prototypes:

```
self.collectionView?.registerClass(UICollectionViewCell.self,
            forCellWithReuseIdentifier: reuseIdentifier)
```

The completed *viewDidLoad* and *initialize* methods should read as follows:

```
override func viewDidLoad() {
    super.viewDidLoad()

    initialize()

    // Register cell classes
    self.collectionView?.registerClass(UICollectionViewCell.self,
                forCellWithReuseIdentifier: reuseIdentifier)
}

func initialize() {

    imageFiles = ["chevy_small.jpg",
                "mini_small.jpg",
                "rover_small.jpg",
                "smart_small.jpg",
                "highlander_small.jpg",
                "venza_small.jpg",
                "volvo_small.jpg",
                "vw_small.jpg",
```

```
                    "ford_small.jpg",
                    "nissan_small.jpg",
                    "honda_small.jpg",
                    "jeep_small.jpg"]

    for fileName in imageFiles {

        if let image = UIImage(named: fileName) {
            images.append(image)
        }
    }
}
```

The *initialize* method begins by populating the *imageFiles* array with the file names of the images to be displayed in the collection view. A *for-in* loop is then used to create a UIImage object for each image file and append the images to the *images* array.

69.7 Implementing the Data Source

As outlined in the chapter entitled *An Overview of iOS Collection View and Flow Layout*, a collection view needs a data source and a delegate in order to provide all the functionality it is capable of providing. By default, Xcode has designated the *MyCollectionViewController* class as both the delegate and data source for the UICollectionView in the user interface. To verify this, select the black background of the collection view controller in the storyboard to select the UICollectionView subclass instance and display the Connections Inspector (select the far right item at the top of the Utilities panel or use the *View -> Utilities -> Show Connection Inspector* menu option). Assuming that the connections have been made, the *Outlets* section of the panel will be configured as shown in Figure 69-5.

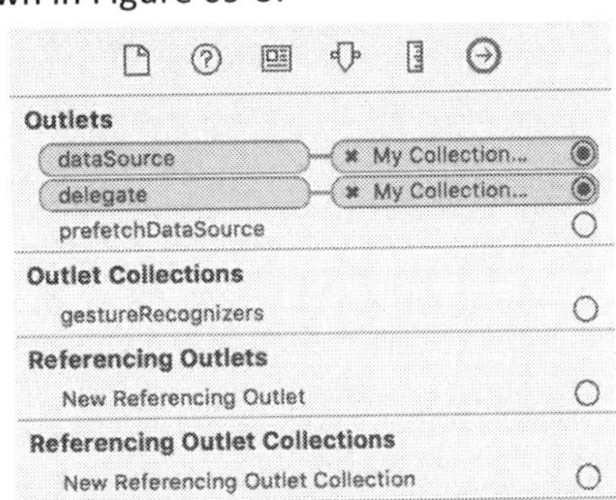

Figure 69-5

Next, the MyCollectionViewController class needs to be declared as implementing the flow layout delegate protocol as follows:

```
class MyCollectionViewController: UICollectionViewController,
  UICollectionViewDelegateFlowLayout {
```

A number of data source methods will now need to be modified to conform with the UICollectionViewDataSource protocol. The first lets the collection view know how many sections are to be displayed. For the purposes of this example there is only going to be one section, so locate the *numberOfSections* method generated by Xcode and modify it to return a value of 1.

```
override func numberOfSections(in collectionView: UICollectionView) -> Int {
    return 1
}
```

The next method is called by the collection view to identify the number of items that are to be displayed in each section. In this case, the sole collection view section will be required to display a cell for each element in the *imageFiles* array. Locate the template method and modify it as follows:

```
override func collectionView(_ collectionView: UICollectionView,
  numberOfItemsInSection section: Int) -> Int {

    return images.count
}
```

The *cellForItemAt* method will be called by the collection view in order to obtain cells configured based on the indexPath value passed to the method. This method will request a cell object from the reuse queue and then set the image on the Image View object which was configured in the cell prototype earlier in this chapter, using the index path row as the index into the *images* array:

```
override func collectionView(_ collectionView: UICollectionView,
  cellForItemAt indexPath: IndexPath) -> UICollectionViewCell {
    let cell =
       collectionView.dequeueReusableCell(withReuseIdentifier:
            reuseIdentifier, for: indexPath) as! MyCollectionViewCell

    cell.imageView.image = images[indexPath.row]

    return cell
}
```

69.8 Testing the Application

Compile and run the application, either on a physical iPhone device or using the iOS Simulator. Once loaded, the collection view will appear as illustrated in Figure 69-6. Clearly, each cell has been displayed at a fixed size causing the images to be compressed to fit into the containing cell. In order to improve the visual experience, some work is clearly still needed.

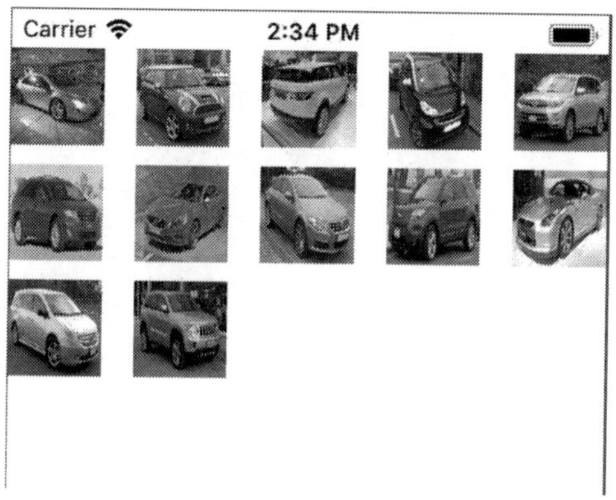

Figure 69-6

69.9 Setting Sizes for Cell Items

When the prototype cell was designed, it was set to a specific size. Unless additional steps are taken, each cell within the collection view will appear at that size. This means that images are not displayed at their original size. In actual fact, all of the car images differ in size from each other. What is needed is a way to set the size of each cell based on the size of the content it is required to display (in this instance the dimensions of the corresponding image). As outlined in the previous chapter, if a method named *sizeForItemAt* is implemented in the UICollectionViewFlowLayoutDelegate protocol class (which by default is the same class as the UICollectionViewDelegate delegate), it will be called for each cell to request size information. Clearly, by implementing this method it will be possible to have each image displayed at its own size. Remaining in *MyCollectionViewController.swift*, implement this method to identify the size of the current image and return the result to the collection view:

```
func collectionView(_ collectionView: UICollectionView,
                    layout collectionViewLayout: UICollectionViewLayout,
                    sizeForItemAt indexPath: IndexPath) -> CGSize {
    let image = images[indexPath.row]
    return image.size
}
```

Run the application once again and note that, as shown in Figure 69-7, the images are now displayed at their original sizes.

Figure 69-7

69.10 Changing Scroll Direction

As currently configured, the flow layout object assigned to the collection view is in vertical scrolling mode. As a demonstration of both one of the delegate methods for handling user interaction and the effects of horizontal scrolling, the example will now be extended to switch to horizontal scrolling when any cell in the view is selected.

When making changes to the flow layout assigned to a collection view, it is not possible to directly change properties on the layout object. Instead, and as illustrated in the following code, a new layout object must be created, configured and then set as the current layout object for the collection view. Within the *MyCollectionViewController.swift* file, implement the *didSelectItemAtIndexPath* delegate method as follows:

```
// MARK: UICollectionViewDelegate

override func collectionView(_ collectionView: UICollectionView,
didSelectItemAt indexPath: IndexPath) {
    let myLayout = UICollectionViewFlowLayout()

    myLayout.scrollDirection =
        UICollectionView.ScrollDirection.horizontal

    self.collectionView?.setCollectionViewLayout(myLayout,
                                               animated: true)
}
```

Compile and run the application and select an image once the collection view appears. Notice how the layout smoothly animates the transition from vertical to horizontal scrolling.

Note also that the layout adjusts automatically when the orientation of the device is rotated. Figure 69-8, for example shows the collection view in landscape orientation with horizontal scrolling enabled. If you are testing on a device or simulator with a large display or retina screen, try running the app on a smaller device simulator such as an iPhone 5s to fully experience the scrolling effect.

Figure 69-8

69.11 Implementing a Supplementary View

The next task in this tutorial is to demonstrate the implementation of supplementary views in the form of a header for the car image gallery. The first step is to ask Interface Builder to add a prototype header supplementary view to the UICollectionView. To do this, select the *Main.storyboard* file and click on the background of the collection view controller canvas representing the UICollectionView object. Display the Attributes Inspector in the Utilities panel, locate the *Accessories* section listed under *Collection View* and set the *Section Header* check box as illustrated in Figure 69-9.

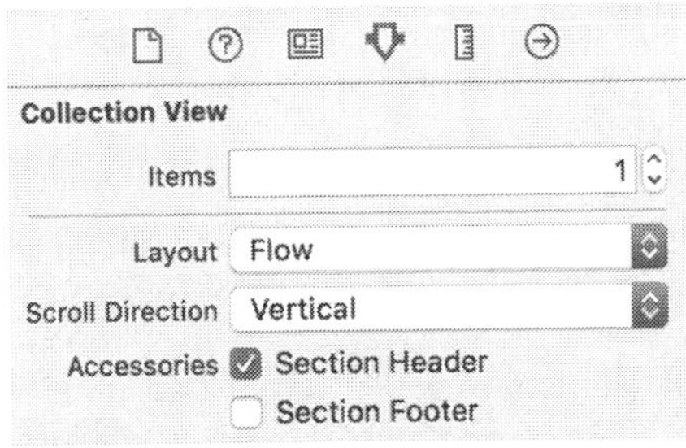

Figure 69-9

Once the header section has been enabled, a header prototype object will have been added to the storyboard view canvas. As with the prototype cell, this header can be configured using any combination of view objects from the Library panel. For this example, drag a Label object onto the prototype header and position it so the horizontal and vertical center guidelines appear. Using the Auto Layout Align menu, set constraints on the label so that it is positioned in the horizontal and vertical center of the containing view. Once completed, the layout should now resemble that of Figure 69-10.

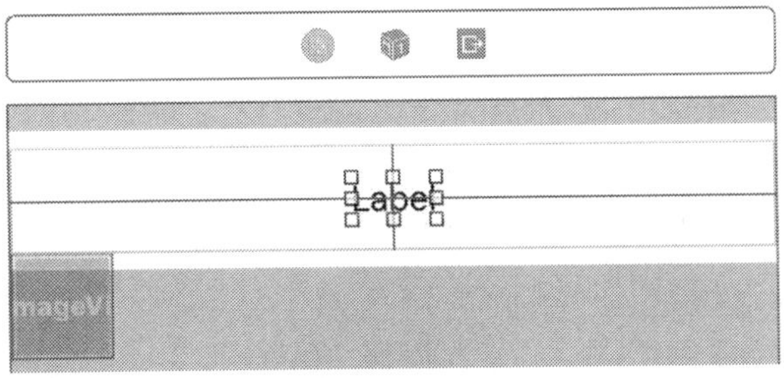

Figure 69-10

With a header prototype added to the storyboard, a new class needs to be added to the project to serve as the class for the header. Select *File -> New -> File...* and add a new iOS Cocoa Touch class named *MySupplementaryView* subclassed from UICollectionReusableView. Select the header in the storyboard and, using the Identity Inspector, change the class from UICollectionReusableView to *MySupplementaryView*.

As with cells, supplementary views are reused, so select the Attributes Inspector in the Utilities panel and enter *MyHeader* as the reuse identifier.

The text displayed on the header will be set within a data source method of the view controller. As such, an outlet to the label will be needed. Display the Assistant Editor and make sure that it is displaying the code for *MySupplementaryView.swift*. With the *MySupplementaryView.swift* file displayed in the Assistant Editor, establish an outlet connection from the label in the header and name it *headerLabel*. On completion of the connection, the content of the file should read as follows:

```
import UIKit

class MySupplementaryView: UICollectionReusableView {

    @IBOutlet weak var headerLabel: UILabel!
}
```

69.12 Implementing the Supplementary View Protocol Methods

In order for the supplementary header view to work, a data source method needs to be implemented. When the collection view is ready to display a supplementary view it will call the *viewForSupplementaryElementOfKind* method of the data source and expect, in return, a configured object ready to be displayed. Passed through as an argument to this method is a value indicating whether this is a header or footer which can be checked by the code to return the appropriate object. Note also that supplementary views use a dequeuing mechanism similar to cells. For this example, implement the *viewForSupplementaryElementOfKind* method as follows in the *MyCollectionViewController.swift* file:

```
override func collectionView(_ collectionView: UICollectionView,
 viewForSupplementaryElementOfKind kind: String, at indexPath: IndexPath) ->
  UICollectionReusableView {

    var header: MySupplementaryView?

    if kind == UICollectionView.elementKindSectionHeader  {
        header =
            collectionView.dequeueReusableSupplementaryView(ofKind: kind,
              withReuseIdentifier: "MyHeader", for: indexPath)
                 as? MySupplementaryView

        header?.headerLabel.text = "Car Image Gallery"
    }
    return header!
}
```

Compile and run the application once again and note that the header supplementary view is now visible in the collection view.

69.13 Summary

The previous chapter covered a considerable amount of ground in terms of the theory behind collection views in iOS. This chapter has put much of this theory into practice through the implementation of an example application that uses a collection view to display a gallery of images.

Chapter 70

70. Subclassing and Extending the Collection View Flow Layout

In this chapter the UICollectionViewFlowLayout class will be extended to provide custom layout behavior for the *CollectionDemo* application created in the previous chapter.

As previously described, whilst the collection view is responsible for displaying data elements in the form of cells, it is the layout object that controls how those cells are to be arranged and positioned on the screen. One of the most powerful features of collection views is the ability to switch out one layout object for another in order to change both the way in which cells are presented to the user, and the way in which that layout responds to user interaction.

In the event that the UICollectionViewFlowLayout class does not provide the necessary behavior for an application, therefore, it can be replaced with a custom layout object that does. By far the easiest way to achieve this is to subclass the UICollectionViewFlowLayout class and extend it to provide the desired layout behavior.

70.1 About the Example Layout Class

This chapter will work step-by-step through the process of creating a new collection view layout class by subclassing and extending UICollectionViewFlowLayout. The purpose of the new layout class will be to allow the user to move and stretch cells in the collection view by pinching and dragging cells. As such, the example will also demonstrate the use of gesture recognizers with collection views.

Begin by launching Xcode and loading the *CollectionDemo* project created in the previous chapter.

70.2 Subclassing the UICollectionViewFlowLayout Class

The first step is to create a new class that is itself a subclass of UICollectionViewFlowLayout. Begin, therefore, by selecting the *File -> New -> File…* menu option in Xcode and in the resulting panel, create a new iOS Cocoa Touch class file named *MyFlowLayout* that subclasses from UICollectionViewFlowLayout.

70.3 Extending the New Layout Class

The new layout class is now created and ready to be extended to add the new functionality. Since the new layout class is going to allow cells to be dragged around and resized by the user, it will need some properties to store a reference to the cell being manipulated, the scale value by which the cell is being resized and, finally, the current location of the cell on the screen. With these requirements in mind, select the *MyFlowLayout.swift* file and modify it as follows:

```
import UIKit

class MyFlowLayout: UICollectionViewFlowLayout {

    var currentCellPath: NSIndexPath?
```

```
    var currentCellCenter: CGPoint?
    var currentCellScale: CGFloat?
}
```

When the scale and center properties are changed, it will be necessary to invalidate the layout so that the collection view is updated and the cell redrawn at the new size and location on the screen. To ensure that this happens, two methods need to be implemented in the *MyFlowLayout.swift* file for the center and scale properties that invalidate the layout in addition to storing the new property values:

```
func setCurrentCellScale(scale: CGFloat)
{
    currentCellScale = scale
    self.invalidateLayout()
}

func setCurrentCellCenter(origin: CGPoint)
{
    currentCellCenter = origin
    self.invalidateLayout()
}
```

70.4 Overriding the layoutAttributesForItem(at indexPath:) Method

The collection view object makes calls to a datasource delegate object to obtain cells to be displayed within the collection, passing through an index path object to identify the cell that is required. When a cell is returned by the datasource, the collection view object then calls the layout object and expects in return a set of layout attributes in the form of a UICollectionViewLayoutAttributes object for that cell indicating how and where it is to be displayed on the screen.

The method of the layout object called by the collection view will be one of either *layoutAttributesForItem(at indexPath:)* or *layoutAttributesForElements(in rect:)*. The former method is passed the index path to the specific cell for which layout attributes are required. It is the job of this method to calculate these attributes based on internal logic and return the attributes object to the collection view.

The *layoutAttributesForElements(in rect:)* method, on the other hand, is passed a CGRect object representing a rectangular region of the device display and expects, in return, an array of attribute objects for all cells that fall within the designated region.

In order to modify the behavior of the flow layout subclass, these methods need to be overridden to apply the necessary layout attribute changes to the cell items.

The first method to be implemented in this example is the *layoutAttributesForItem(at indexPath:)* method which should be implemented in the *MyFlowLayout.swift* file as follows:

```
override func layoutAttributesForItem(at indexPath: IndexPath) ->
                        UICollectionViewLayoutAttributes? {
    let attributes =
        super.layoutAttributesForItem(at: indexPath)

    if let attributes = attributes {
        self.modifyLayoutAttributes(layoutattributes: attributes)
```

```
    }
    return attributes
}
```

Before the attributes for the requested cell can be modified, the method needs to know what those attributes would be for an unmodified UICollectionViewFlowLayout instance. Since this class is a subclass of UICollectionViewFlowLayout, we can obtain this information, as performed in the above method, via a call to the *layoutAttributesForItem* method of the superclass:

```
let attributes = super.layoutAttributesForItem(at: indexPath)
```

Having ascertained what the attributes would normally be, the method then calls a custom method named *modifyLayoutAttributes* and then returns the modified attributes to the collection view. It will be the task of the *modifyLayoutAttributes* method (which will be implemented later) to apply the resize and movement effects to the attributes of the cell over which the pinch gesture is taking place.

70.5 Overriding the layoutAttributesForElements(in rect:) Method

The *layoutAttributesForElements(in rect:)* method will need to perform a similar task to the previous method in terms of getting the attributes values for cells in the designated display region from the superclass, calling the *modifyLayoutAttributes* method and returning the results to the collection view object:

```
override func layoutAttributesForElements(in rect: CGRect) ->
        [UICollectionViewLayoutAttributes]? {

    let allAttributesInRect =
        super.layoutAttributesForElements(in: rect)

    if let allAttributesInRect = allAttributesInRect {
        for cellAttributes in allAttributesInRect {
            self.modifyLayoutAttributes(layoutattributes: cellAttributes )
        }
    }
    return allAttributesInRect
}
```

70.6 Implementing the modifyLayoutAttributes Method

By far the most interesting method to be implemented is the *modifyLayoutAttributes* method. This is where the layout attributes for the cell the user is currently manipulating on the screen are modified. This method should now be implemented as outlined in the following listing:

```
func modifyLayoutAttributes(layoutattributes:
    UICollectionViewLayoutAttributes) {

    if let currentCellPath = currentCellPath,
        let currentCellScale = currentCellScale,
        let currentCellCenter = currentCellCenter {
        if layoutattributes.indexPath == currentCellPath as IndexPath {
            layoutattributes.transform3D =
```

```
                CATransform3DMakeScale(currentCellScale,
                                       currentCellScale, 1.0)
            layoutattributes.center = currentCellCenter
            layoutattributes.zIndex = 1
        }
    }
}
```

In completing the example application, a pinch gesture recognizer will be attached to the collection view object and configured to set the *currentCellPath*, *currentCellScale* and *currentCellCenter* values of the layout object in real-time as the user pinches and moves a cell. As is evident from the above code, use is made of these settings during the attribute modification process.

Since this method will be called for each cell in the collection, it is important that the attribute modifications only be applied to the cell the user is currently moving and pinching. This cell is stored in the currentCellPath property as updated by the gesture recognizer:

```
if layoutattributes.indexPath == currentCellPath as IndexPath
```

If the cell matches that referenced by the currentCellPath property, the attributes are transformed via a call to the *CATransform3DMakeScale* function of the QuartzCore Framework, using the currentCellScale property value which is updated by the gesture recognizer during a pinching motion:

```
layoutattributes.transform3D =
    CATransform3DMakeScale(currentCellScale, currentCellScale, 1.0)
```

Finally, the center location of the cell is set to the currentCellCenter property value and the zIndex property set to 1 so that the cell appears on top of overlapping collection view contents.

The implementation of a custom collection layout is now complete. All that remains is to implement the gesture recognizer in the application code so that the flow layout knows which cell is being pinched and moved, and by how much.

70.7 Removing the Item Selection Code

The previous chapter added a *didSelectItemAt* delegate method to detect when the user selected an item in the collection view and changed the scroll direction of the layout. Since this change will conflict with the pinch recognizer, this code needs to be removed. Edit the *MyCollectionViewController.swift* file, locate the *didSelectItemAt* delegate method and remove the scroll direction code as follows:

```
override func collectionView(_ collectionView: UICollectionView,
didSelectItemAt indexPath: IndexPath) {
    let myLayout = UICollectionViewFlowLayout()

    myLayout.scrollDirection =
        UICollectionView.ScrollDirection.horizontal

    self.collectionView?.setCollectionViewLayout(myLayout,
                                        animated: true)
}
```

70.8 Adding the New Layout and Pinch Gesture Recognizer

In order to detect pinch gestures, a pinch gesture recognizer needs to be added to the collection view object. Code also needs to be added to replace the default layout object with our new custom flow layout object.

Select the *MyCollectionViewController.swift* file and modify the *viewDidLoad* method to change the layout to our new layout class and to add a pinch gesture recognizer configured to call a method named *handlePinch*:

```
override func viewDidLoad() {
    super.viewDidLoad()

    let myLayout = MyFlowLayout()

    self.collectionView?.setCollectionViewLayout(myLayout,
                                animated: true)

    let pinchRecognizer = UIPinchGestureRecognizer(target: self,
                                    action: #selector(handlePinch))

    self.collectionView?.addGestureRecognizer(pinchRecognizer)

    initialize()
}
```

70.9 Implementing the Pinch Handler

Remaining within the *MyCollectionViewController.swift* file, the last coding related task before testing the application is to write the pinch handler method, the code for which reads as follows:

```
@objc func handlePinch(gesture: UIPinchGestureRecognizer) {
    let layout = self.collectionView?.collectionViewLayout
        as! MyFlowLayout
    if gesture.state == UIGestureRecognizer.State.began
    {
        // Get the initial location of the pinch?
        let initialPinchPoint =
            gesture.location(in: self.collectionView)
        // Convert pinch location into a specific cell
        if let pinchedCellPath =
            self.collectionView?.indexPathForItem(at: initialPinchPoint) {
        // Store the indexPath to cell
            layout.currentCellPath = pinchedCellPath as NSIndexPath
        }
    }
    else if gesture.state == UIGestureRecognizer.State.changed
    {
        // Store the new center location of the selected cell
        layout.currentCellCenter =
            gesture.location(in: self.collectionView)
```

```
            // Store the scale value
            layout.setCurrentCellScale(scale: gesture.scale)
        }
        else
        {
            self.collectionView?.performBatchUpdates({
                layout.currentCellPath = nil
                layout.currentCellScale = 1.0}, completion:nil)
        }
}
```

The method begins by getting a reference to the layout object associated with the collection view:

```
let layout = self.collectionView?.collectionViewLayout as! MyFlowLayout
```

Next, it checks to find out if the gesture has just started. If so, the method will need to identify the cell over which the gesture is taking place. This is achieved by identifying the initial location of the gesture and then passing that location through to the *indexPathForItemAtPoint* method of the collection view object. The resulting indexPath is then stored in the currentCellPath property of the layout object where it can be accessed by the *modifyLayoutAttributes* method previously implemented in the MyFlowLayout class:

```
if gesture.state == UIGestureRecognizer.State.Began
{
    // Get the initial location of the pinch?
    let initialPinchPoint = gesture.locationInView(self.collectionView)

    // Convert pinch location into a specific cell
    let pinchedCellPath =
            self.collectionView?.indexPathForItemAtPoint(initialPinchPoint)

    // Store the indexPath to cell
    layout.currentCellPath = pinchedCellPath
}
```

In the event that the gesture is in progress, the current scale and location of the gesture need to be stored in the layout object:

```
else if gesture.state == UIGestureRecognizer.State.changed
{
    // Store the new center location of the selected cell
    layout.currentCellCenter =
                        gesture.locationInView(self.collectionView)
    // Store the scale value
    layout.setCurrentCellScale(gesture.scale)
}
```

Finally, if the gesture has just ended, the scale needs to be returned to 1 and the currentCellPath property reset to *nil*:

```
else
{
    self.collectionView?.performBatchUpdates({
        layout.currentCellPath = nil
        layout.currentCellScale = 1.0}, completion:nil)
}
```

This task is performed as a batch update so that the changes take place in a single animated update.

70.10 Avoiding Image Clipping

When the user pinches on a cell in the collection view and stretches the cell, the image contained therein will stretch with it. In order to avoid the enlarged image from being clipped by the containing cell when the gesture ends, a property on the MyCollectionViewCell class needs to be modified.

Within Xcode, select the *Main.storyboard* file followed by the *MyCell* entry in the Document Outline panel to the left of the storyboard canvas. Display the Attributes Inspector and, in the *Drawing* section of the panel, unset the checkbox next to *Clip to Bounds.*

70.11 Testing the Application

With a suitably provisioned iOS device attached to the development system, run the application. Once running, use pinching motions on the display to resize an image in a cell, noting that the cell can also be moved during the gesture. On ending the gesture, the cell will spring back to the original location and size. Figure 70-1 shows the collection view during the resizing of a cell.

Figure 70-1

70.12 Summary

Whilst the UICollectionViewFlowLayout class provides considerable flexibility in terms of controlling the way in which data is presented to the user, additional functionality can be added by subclassing and extending this class. In most cases the changes simply involve overriding two methods and modifying the layout attributes within those methods to implement the required layout behavior.

This chapter has worked through the implementation of a custom layout class that extends UICollectionViewFlowLayout to allow the user to move and resize the images contained in collection view cells. The chapter also looked at the use of gesture recognizers within the context of collection views.

Chapter 71

71. An Introduction to Drag and Drop in iOS 12

iOS 11 introduced a long anticipated feature in the form of drag and drop support. Drag and drop allows items in the form of views, images, files and data to be dragged and dropped either between different apps or different areas within the same app.

This chapter is intended to provide a high level overview of the way in which drag and drop works on iOS. Once these basics have been covered, subsequent chapters will explore the key aspects of drag and drop implementation in greater detail while working through the creation of two example applications.

71.1 An Overview of Drag and Drop

Drag and drop allows users to drag and drop content and data. On iPad devices, drag and drop can be performed either between apps or locally within a single app. Dragging and dropping between apps relies on the multitasking abilities of iOS on the iPad to be able to display multiple apps simultaneously. On iPhone devices, drag and drop is only supported within the local app.

A drag is initiated by performing a long press on top of the user interface element to be dragged. If drag and drop is supported, the item will appear to lift up in the form of a *preview image*. This has initiated a *drag session* (UIDragSession) which remains in effect until the drag is either cancelled or completed. The preview image is then dragged by the user to the destination. If the destination is capable of handling the item type being dragged, an indicator will appear to let the user know the item can be dropped. If a drop is attempted in a location where the drop is not supported, the drag is cancelled. Drop locations may also be configured to display a “forbidden” icon alongside the drag preview image if the data type is not supported.

Multiple items can be added to a drag session by initiating the drag and then tapping other items to be included in the session. Preview images for these additional items will appear stacked with the original preview image and an icon will appear containing the number of items contained in the session. In addition, multiple drag sessions can be performed concurrently.

When a drop is performed, the transfer of the data associated with the item is performed asynchronously so as not to impair app performance.

71.2 Drag and Drop Delegates

Drag and drop in iOS functions almost entirely through delegate methods. In order for a drag operation to work, the containing view controller must have a *drag delegate* assigned to it. Similarly, the destination view controller must be assigned a *drop delegate*. Typically a view controller will be assigned both drag and drop delegates so that the controller can act as both a drag source and drop destination.

71.3 Drag and Drop Interactions

Once the view controller has been assigned the necessary delegates, the individual views within the controller that are to support drag and drop need to have interaction objects attached. A drag source view will have a *drag interaction* (UIDragInteraction) attached, while a drop view will be assigned a *drop interaction* (UIDropInteraction). A view that is to serve both as a drag source and a drop destination must, of course, have both. These interactions have a wide range of delegate methods which, if implemented, will be called at various points during the lifecycle of the drag and drop session.

71.4 The Drag Item

Each item associated with a drag operation is represented by a *drag item* (UIDragItem) object. This object contains the preview image to be displayed during the drag and an *item provider* (UIItemProvider) instance. The item provider contains information about the item to be transferred and will be used to initiate the asynchronous data transfer when the item is dropped. Apple refers to this item provider object as a *promise* from the source app to deliver the content for the dragged item when the drop is performed.

71.5 The Drag and Drop Lifecycle

The lifecycle of a drag and drop session is handled entirely by calls to the drag and drop interaction delegate methods and the return values from those methods. A summary of the key delegate method calls are listed below in the order in which they are called during the session lifecycle.

- **itemsForBeginning** – Called when the user starts the drag with a long press on the source view. This method is mandatory and must return an array of UIDragItem objects representing the items to be dragged.
- **previewForLifting** – An optional method that is called to provide the app with the option of providing a custom preview image to be displayed for the item during the drag.
- **itemsForAddingTo** – This optional method is called when a draggable view is tapped while a drag session is already in progress. The method returns an array containing the UIDragItem objects to be added to the existing drag operation.
- **sessionDidUpdate** – Called repeatedly when the drag enters and moves within the area of potential drop destinations. This method returns a UIDropProposal object containing the operation that will be performed if the drop is made. For example, if the view cannot handle the drop it might return a *cancel* or *forbidden* operation value. Alternatively, if the drop can be handled, a *copy* or *move* value would be returned.
- **canHandle** – An optional method called when the drag session enters a potential drop destination view. This method is passed a UIDropSession object on which the *canLoadObjects* method can be called to identify if the session contains objects that the drop destination is able to handle. The method returns a Boolean value indicating whether or not the dragged item object type is supported.
- **performDrop** – This mandatory method is called when the user performs the drop and is passed UIDropInteraction and UIDropSession objects. These objects can then be used to perform the asynchronous transfer of the dragged items. When the transfer is initiated, a UIProgress object is returned which may be used within the code to track the progress of the data transfer and also to cancel the transfer before completion if necessary. When the transfer finishes, a completion handler is called allowing the app to process the data.

Note that this is a list of only the most commonly used delegate methods. Many more are available for performing tasks such as adding animation and receiving notifications at additional points along the drag and drop session timeline, some of which will be used in later chapters.

71.6 Spring Loaded Controls

Another feature available during a drag and drop session is to activate controls such as buttons by dragging over the view and holding for a brief period of time. This enables controls within the user interface to be selected without interrupting the drag session. This concept is referred to as *spring loading* and is enabled on a per control basis by setting the control's *isSpringLoaded* property to *true*.

71.7 Summary

Drag and drop support was first introduced in iOS 11 to allow users to transfer data between apps using a drag and drop paradigm. While drag and drop on iPhone devices is limited to dragging and dropping within a single app, iPad apps may also transfer data between different apps. Each drag and drop operation is represented by a drag session containing one or more drag items. Each drag item, in turn, contains an item provider. The core functionality of drag and drop is implemented using sets of drag and drop interaction delegate methods. These are called at various times during the drag and drop operation to obtain the data to be transferred, to identify whether a drop site can handle particular data types and to otherwise respond to and customize various aspects of the drag and drop session.

Chapter 72

72. An iOS 12 Drag and Drop Tutorial

With the basics of drag and drop covered in the previous chapter, this chapter will begin to demonstrate some of the key features of drag and drop within the context of an example application. Specifically, the project created in this chapter will demonstrate the use of drag and drop to allow images and text to be transferred between two separate apps. This will include the implementation of both drag and drop delegates, customizing drag animation, working with spring loaded controls and the handling of dropped content.

72.1 Creating the Drag and Drop Project

Launch Xcode and create a new iOS project named *DragAndDrop* using the Single View App template and with Swift selected as the programming language.

72.2 Designing the User Interface

Select the *Main.storyboard* file and modify the scene layout so that it contains an ImageView, TextView and a Button and matches the layout shown in Figure 72-1 (note the width of the button has been extended to the left and right margins, given a gray background and assigned text that reads "Sepia On"):

Figure 72-1

With the ImageView object selected, display the Attributes Inspector panel and change the *Content Mode* menu to *Aspect Fit*.

Display the *Resolve Auto Layout Issues* menu and select the *Reset to Suggested Constraints* option listed under *All Views in View Controller*, then delete the sample Latin text from the TextView.

Finally, display the Assistant Editor and establish an outlet connection to a variable in the *ViewController.swift* file named *imageView*. Repeat these steps for the TextView and Button, this time naming the variables *textView* and *sepiaButton* respectively. Also establish an action connection from the button to a method named *switchFilter*.

When this scene appears within the app it will be helpful to have borders displayed around the two views so that the user will know where to drop content during a drag and drop operation. Implement this now by editing the *ViewController.swift* file, adding a new method named *initialize* and calling it from the *viewDidLoad* method. Within this method, also enable spring loading on the *sepiaButton* object:

```
.
.
override func viewDidLoad() {
    super.viewDidLoad()
    initialize()
}

func initialize() {

    sepiaButton.isSpringLoaded = true

    textView.layer.borderWidth = 1
    textView.layer.borderColor = UIColor.lightGray.cgColor

    imageView.layer.borderWidth = 1
    imageView.layer.borderColor = UIColor.lightGray.cgColor
}
.
.
```

Before testing the app project so far, add a variable to store the current sepia control setting and complete the *switchFilter* action method to toggle this variable setting and change the button title to reflect the button's current mode:

```
.
.
var sepiaFilter = true
.
.
@IBAction func switchFilter(_ sender: Any) {

    sepiaFilter = sepiaFilter ? false : true
```

```
    sepiaButton.setTitle(sepiaFilter ? "Sepia On" : "Sepia Off",
                                            for: .normal)
}
```

72.3 Testing the Default Behavior

With an iPad device or simulator connected and running in landscape mode, launch the Safari browser and place it in the background. Repeat this step for the Photos app. Compile and run the DragAndDrop app and, once loaded, swipe up from the bottom of the screen to display the dock panel. From the dock, touch the Photos app icon and drag it upwards and to the right of the screen before releasing the touch so that it appears in split view mode as shown in Figure 72-2 below:

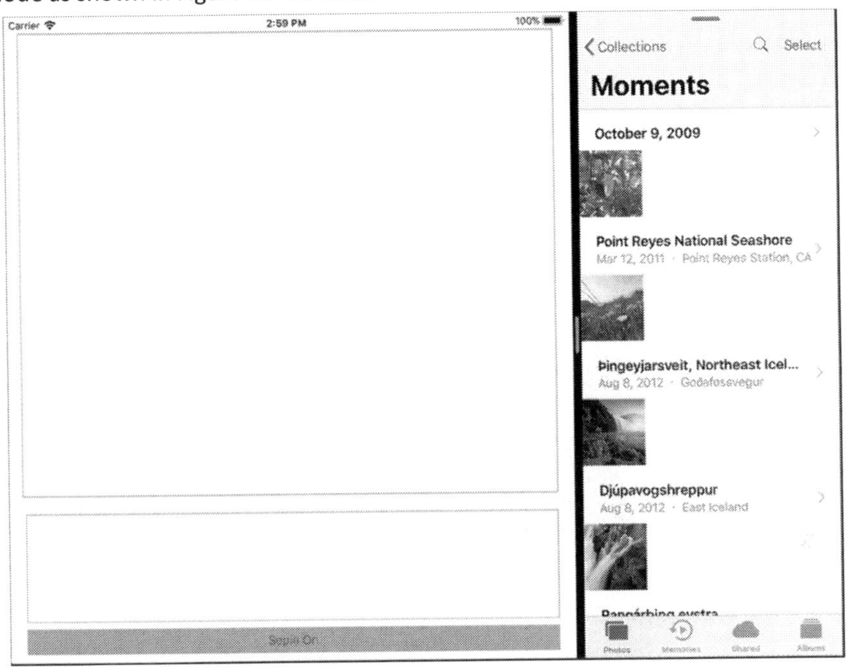

Figure 72-2

Touch and hold on one of the images in the Photos app until the image lifts up ready for dragging. Drag the lifted image preview across to the ImageView in the DragAndDrop app and attempt to drop it. Note that because the view has not been configured to handle drops, the drop is cancelled and the image preview simply disappears.

Display the dock a second time, this time dragging the Safari app icon up and to the right before dropping it onto the Photos app. Once Safari has replaced the Photo apps in the split view panel, navigate to a web page containing text and then highlight and select a section of the text using the same technique you would use if you were planning a copy and paste operation. Perform a long press over the highlighted text until the drag preview appears, then drag the text so that it hovers over the TextView in the DragAndDrop app. In this case, a green + icon appears in the top right hand corner of the drag preview image (Figure 72-3) indicating that the view will accept the drop. Releasing the drag at this point causes the dragged text to appear in the TextView widget. This is because drop support is included by default with both the TextView and TextField views.

Figure 72-3

Although drop support is built into the TextField and TextView, drag support is not. Verify this by performing a long touch on the TextView and observing that no preview image lifts from the view indicating that a drag session has started.

72.4 Adding Drop Support to the Image View

The next step in implementing drag and drop support in this project is to allow images to be dropped onto the ImageView. After the image is dropped, and before it is displayed to the user, the app will also use a sepia filter to change the appearance of the image.

For the purposes of this example, the ViewController class will serve as the drop interaction delegate so edit the *ViewController.swift* file and modify the class to make this declaration:

```
import UIKit

class ViewController: UIViewController, UIDropInteractionDelegate {
```

Remaining in the ViewController class file, modify the code in the recently added *initialize* method to attach a drop interaction instance to the image view, with the delegate set to the current view controller. Also add a line of code to enable the *isUserInteractionEnabled* on the view. By default, the ImageView class discards all forms of user interaction such as touches, focus, presses and keyboard events. In order for drag and drop to function within the image view, therefore, this property is being enabled:

```
func initialize() {

    sepiaButton.isSpringLoaded = true

    textView.layer.borderWidth = 1
    textView.layer.borderColor = UIColor.lightGray.cgColor

    imageView.layer.borderWidth = 1
    imageView.layer.borderColor = UIColor.lightGray.cgColor

    imageView.isUserInteractionEnabled = true
    imageView.addInteraction(UIDropInteraction(delegate: self))
}
```

When an image is dragged over the ImageView, the *canHandle* delegate will be called by the system to identify the types of content the view is able to handle. This method now needs to be implemented to indicate that the views in the app can potentially handle images and strings:

```
.
import MobileCoreServices
.
.
func dropInteraction(_ interaction: UIDropInteraction, canHandle session:
UIDropSession) -> Bool {
    return session.hasItemsConforming(toTypeIdentifiers:
      [kUTTypeImage as String, kUTTypeUTF8PlainText as String]) &&
                                              session.items.count == 1
}
```

The two type strings used here are from a pre-defined list of Uniform Type Identifiers defined by Apple. A full list of available identifiers can be found online at:

https://developer.apple.com/library/content/documentation/Miscellaneous/Reference/UTIRef/Articles/System-DeclaredUniformTypeIdentifiers.html

Since the ImageView can only display one image at a time, the code also checks that the drop session contains only one item. If the drop target is able to handle multiple drop items in a single operation this check would not be performed.

Next, the *sessionDidUpdate* delegate needs to be implemented to notify the drag and drop system that the ImageView will perform a copy operation on any images dropped onto the view:

```
func dropInteraction(_ interaction: UIDropInteraction, sessionDidUpdate
  session: UIDropSession) -> UIDropProposal {

    let location = session.location(in: self.view)
    let dropOperation: UIDropOperation?

    if session.canLoadObjects(ofClass: UIImage.self) {
        if  imageView.frame.contains(location) {
            dropOperation = .copy
            print("copy")
        } else {
            dropOperation = .cancel
        }
    } else {
        dropOperation = .forbidden
    }

    return UIDropProposal(operation: dropOperation!)
}
```

The code begins by identifying the location of the drop session on the screen before checking whether the session contains one or more image objects and, if so, checks that the location of the session falls within the area of the screen occupied by the *imageView* instance. If these criteria are met, a UIDropProposal object is returned by the method indicating that the view can handle the drop and will perform a copy operation on the image, otherwise the drop session is cancelled.

The final task in the process of adding drop support to the image view is to implement the *performDrop* delegate method. This method is called after the user drops the item onto the view and is responsible for handling the transfer from the drag source. It does this by calling the *loadObjects* method of the session object and processing the resulting items. In this case, since only a single image can be dropped into the view, the last image in the array is extracted, converted to sepia (if that option is selected) and displayed on the ImageView:

```
func dropInteraction(_ interaction: UIDropInteraction,
                     performDrop session: UIDropSession) {

    if session.canLoadObjects(ofClass: UIImage.self) {
        session.loadObjects(ofClass: UIImage.self) { (items) in
            if let images = items as? [UIImage] {

                if self.sepiaFilter {
                    let sepiaImage = self.convertToSepia(image: images.last!)
                    self.imageView.image = sepiaImage
                } else {
                    self.imageView.image = images.last!
                }
            }
        }
    }
}
```

Before testing the app, add the *convertToSepia* method to the ViewController class so that it reads as follows:

```
func convertToSepia(image: UIImage) -> UIImage {

    let sepiaFilter = CIFilter(name: "CISepiaTone")

    let cimage = CIImage(image: image)

    sepiaFilter?.setDefaults()
    sepiaFilter?.setValue(cimage, forKey: "inputImage")
    sepiaFilter?.setValue(NSNumber(value: 0.8 as Float),
                          forKey: "inputIntensity")

    let image = sepiaFilter?.outputImage

    let context = CIContext(options: nil)

    let cgImage = context.createCGImage(image!,
                                        from: image!.extent)

    return UIImage(cgImage: cgImage!)
```

}

72.5 Testing the Drop Behavior

Run the app and display it in a split view configuration alongside the Photos app as previously outlined in Figure 72-2. Drag an image from the Photos app and hold it over the ImageView in the DragAndDrop app. Note that this time the green + icon appears alongside the preview image indicating that the view is able to handle the image drop:

Figure 72-4

Drop the image onto the image view and wait while the image is transferred from the Photos app and converted to sepia. Once completed, the converted image will appear within the image view as shown in Figure 72-5:

Figure 72-5

Test the spring loaded button by dragging another image from the Photos app and moving it over the Sepia button. Hold the preview in position without dropping until the button flashes multiple times and the title changes to "Sepia Off". Continue dragging the preview to the image view and perform the drop. With the sepia filter turned off the image should appear unfiltered.

Next, replace the Photos app with the Safari browser, select some text and attempt to drag and drop it into the ImageView. Based on the code in the *sessionDidUpdate* method, this time the forbidden icon should appear in the top right-hand corner of the preview image indicating that this view does not accept text:

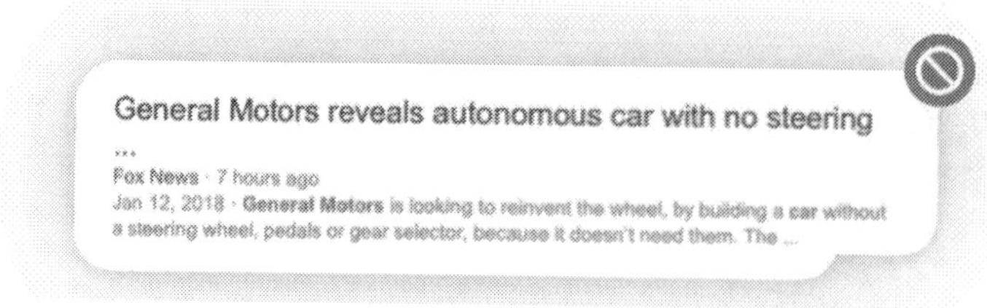

Figure 72-6

72.6 Adding Drag Support to the Views

The next phase of this project is to add drag support to both the ImageView and TextView instances within the DragAndDrop app. The first step in this process is to add a UIDragInteraction object to the views. As with the drop delegate, the view controller class will also serve as the drag delegate. Within the *ViewController.swift* file, make the following modifications to the class declaration and the *initialize* method.

```
class ViewController: UIViewController, UIDropInteractionDelegate,
        UIDragInteractionDelegate {
.
.
    func initialize() {

        textView.layer.borderWidth = 1
        textView.layer.borderColor = UIColor.lightGray.cgColor

        imageView.layer.borderWidth = 1
        imageView.layer.borderColor = UIColor.lightGray.cgColor

        imageView.isUserInteractionEnabled = true
        imageView.addInteraction(UIDropInteraction(delegate: self))

        imageView.addInteraction(UIDragInteraction(delegate: self))
        textView.addInteraction(UIDragInteraction(delegate: self))
    }
.
.
}
```

When a drag is initiated by the user, the system will make a call to the *dragInteraction(itemsForBeginning)* delegate method and will expect in return an array of UIDragItem objects containing the items to be transferred within the drag session to the drop target. Since the user interface contains two potential drag source views, code needs to be implemented within this delegate method to identify whether the drag is occurring in the ImageView or TextView instance. When called, the *dragInteraction(itemsForBeginning)* method is passed a UIDragInteraction object which, in turn, contains a copy of the view on which the drag interaction was initiated. With this knowledge, the code for the method can be implemented as follows:

```
func dragInteraction(_ interaction: UIDragInteraction, itemsForBeginning
   session: UIDragSession) -> [UIDragItem] {
    if let textView = interaction.view as? UITextView {
        let provider = NSItemProvider(object: textView.text! as NSString)
        let item = UIDragItem(itemProvider: provider)
        return [item]
    } else if let imageView = interaction.view as? UIImageView {
        guard let image = imageView.image else { return [] }
        let provider = NSItemProvider(object: image)
        let item = UIDragItem(itemProvider: provider)
        return [item]
    }
    return []
}
```

The method attempts to cast the interaction view to an ImageView and a TextView to identify the view type. If the view is an ImageView, the image is extracted from the view, placed in an NSProvider object which, in turn, is used to construct a UIDragItem instance. This is placed in an array and returned to the system. In the case of a TextView, similar steps are performed to return the text within the view.

72.7 Testing the Drag Behavior

Run the app in split panel mode with the Photos app and drag and drop an image from the Photos app onto the ImageView in the DragAndDrop app. Touch the sepia image and wait for the view to lift up indicating that the drag has started. Drag the image preview to the Photos app and drop it. The sepia image will subsequently appear in the Photos app under the *Today* section.

Replace the Photos app in the split view pane with Safari and enter the URL for a web site into the TextView of the DragAndDrop app. Touch and hold over the TextView until the preview image appears, then drag and drop it into the Safari address bar at which point the URL referenced in the text should load into the browser.

72.8 Customizing the Lift Preview Image

As currently configured, the preview image displayed during the drag is the default image. In both cases this is the snapshot of the view itself. Sometimes this is adequate but more often does not provide the best visual experience. Consider, for example, a photo in the ImageView in portrait orientation as is the case in Figure 72-7:

Figure 72-7

In this situation, the preview image includes the white space on either side of the image as shown in Figure 72-8:

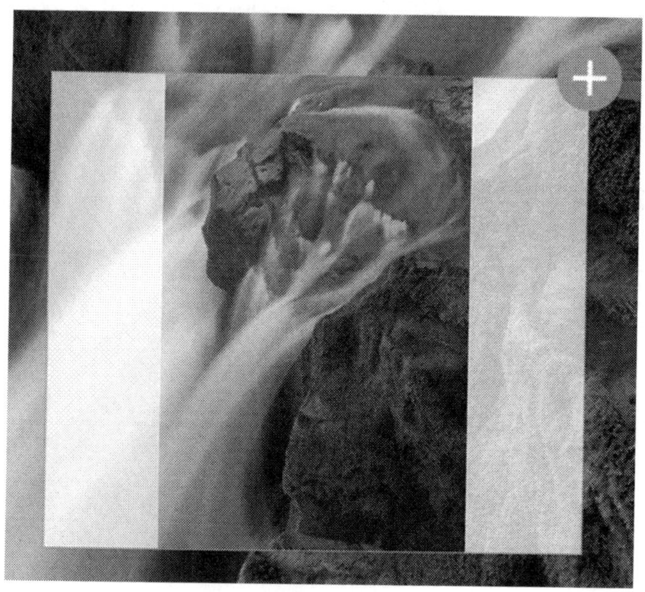

Figure 72-8

A better experience for the user would be to create the preview using only the image being transferred. This can be achieved by implementing the *previewForLifting* delegate method. Within this method, we need to once again identify if this is a text or image view. In the case of the TextView, the method will create a UITargetedDragPreview object containing a reference to the TextView. This is essentially emulating the default behavior for the preview image. In the case of the ImageView, however, the image will be extracted from the view, placed within a new UIImageView instance and used to create a custom UITargetedDragPreview object:

```
func dragInteraction(_ interaction:UIDragInteraction,
                    previewForLifting item:UIDragItem,
                              session:UIDragSession)
                               -> UITargetedDragPreview? {


        let dragView = interaction.view!
        let dragPoint = session.location(in: dragView)
        let target = UIDragPreviewTarget(container: dragView,
                            center: dragPoint)

        if (dragView as? UITextView) != nil {

            return UITargetedDragPreview(view: dragView)

        } else if let currentView = dragView as? UIImageView {

            let previewImageView = UIImageView(image: currentView.image)
            return UITargetedDragPreview(view: previewImageView,
                        parameters:UIDragPreviewParameters(),
                                        target:target)

        }
        return nil
}
```

This code requires some additional explanation. As previously stated, the objective is to return a UITargetedDragPreview object. At a minimum, this must contain a reference to the view which is to be displayed in the drag preview which is precisely the case for the TextView drag:

```
return UITargetedDragPreview(view: dragView)
```

In the case of the ImageView, the UITargetedDragPreview is created using an ImageView instance, a set of parameters in the form of a UIDragPreviewParameters object and a UIDragPreviewTarget instance:

```
return UITargetedDragPreview(view: previewImageView,
                       parameters:UIDragPreviewParameters(),
                                   target:target)
```

In this example, no specific parameters are set on the UIDragPreviewParameters object though these parameters can be useful for configuring the background color of the preview, or for specifying a rectangle or Bézier path to define custom areas of the view to be displayed in the preview.

The UIDragPreviewTarget object is constructed using a reference to the view on which the drag was initiated together with the touch point within the containing view. In the above case, the location at which the drag was initiated is used as the center value (in other words the location of the user's finger on the screen) and matches the default drag and drop behavior. Optionally, the UIDragPreviewTarget object may also be initialized with a CGAffineTransform argument which will be used to animate the preview target.

72.9 Testing the Custom Preview Image

Run the app once again, drag an image from the Photos app onto the ImageView and then initiate a drag operation on that image. Note that the image now appears without the borders. Unfortunately, a new problem has occurred in that the preview image initially appears full size and extends beyond the edges of the screen. Once the drag moves, the system scales the image down, but the initial image size also needs to be reduced considerably. To do this, the image can be scaled within the *previewForLifting* delegate method:

```
func dragInteraction(_ interaction:UIDragInteraction,
                    previewForLifting item:UIDragItem,
                              session:UIDragSession)
                                   -> UITargetedDragPreview? {

        let dragView = interaction.view!
        let dragPoint = session.location(in: dragView)
        let target = UIDragPreviewTarget(container: dragView,
                                 center: dragPoint)

        if (dragView as? UITextView) != nil {

            return UITargetedDragPreview(view: dragView)

        } else if let currentView = dragView as? UIImageView {

            let previewImageView = UIImageView(image:
                scaleImage(image: currentView.image!, width: 100))
            return UITargetedDragPreview(view: previewImageView,
                            parameters:UIDragPreviewParameters(),
                                  target:target)
        }
        return nil
}
.
.
func scaleImage (image: UIImage, width: CGFloat) -> UIImage {
    let oldWidth = image.size.width
    let scaleFactor = width / oldWidth

    let newHeight = image.size.height * scaleFactor
    let newWidth = oldWidth * scaleFactor

    UIGraphicsBeginImageContext(CGSize(width:newWidth, height:newHeight))
    image.draw(in: CGRect(x:0, y:0, width:newWidth, height:newHeight))
```

```
    let newImage = UIGraphicsGetImageFromCurrentImageContext()
    UIGraphicsEndImageContext()
    return newImage!
}
```

With these changes implemented, the preview will appear in a smaller size when the drag is first initiated.

72.10 Implementing Animation

The final task in this chapter is to implement some basic animation during the preview lifting phase. The goal will be to fade out the selected view for the duration of the drag session. This will involve changing the alpha value of the source view, and then restoring it when the drag session ends or is cancelled. This will require the addition of the following three delegate methods to the *ViewController.swift* file:

```
func dragInteraction(_ interaction: UIDragInteraction, willAnimateLiftWith
  animator: UIDragAnimating, session: UIDragSession) {
    animator.addAnimations {
        interaction.view?.alpha = 0.5
    }
}

func dragInteraction(_ interaction: UIDragInteraction, item: UIDragItem,
willAnimateCancelWith animator: UIDragAnimating) {
    animator.addAnimations {
        interaction.view?.alpha = 1.0
    }
}

func dragInteraction(_ interaction: UIDragInteraction, session:
UIDragSession, didEndWith operation: UIDropOperation) {
    interaction.view?.alpha = 1.0
}
```

Run the app one last time and verify that the source image within the DragAndDrop app fades during the drag operation and then returns to full brightness after the session ends.

72.11 Summary

This chapter has worked through the implementation of drag and drop between apps. This included the implementation of methods for both the drag and drop delegates and adding support for spring loaded controls. The app also demonstrated the steps involved in loading transferred images and text, the customization of preview images during a drag operation and some basic animation techniques.

73. An iOS 12 Collection View Drag and Drop Tutorial

The previous chapter demonstrated the use of drag and drop involving views contained in a standard view controller. Drag and drop support is also available for the TableView and CollectionView classes. Many of the concepts are the same as those used previously, though there are some differences in terms of the delegate methods. The techniques for CollectionView based drag and drop handling is largely the same as that for the TableView. This chapter will demonstrate the key drag and drop features in relation to a CollectionView example.

73.1 The Example Application

In this chapter, the CollectionDemo project created in the chapter entitled *An iOS 12 Collection View Drag and Drop Tutorial* will be extended to integrate drag and drop support. At the end of this chapter the app will allow multiple images to be selected from the collection view layout and dragged to another app. It will also be possible to drag and drop multiple images from outside the app onto the collection view. Finally, code will be added to allow an existing image within the collection view to be moved to another position in the layout using drag and drop.

Begin by locating the CollectionDemo project and loading it into Xcode. If you have yet to create this project, a pre-prepared copy can be found in the source code archive accompanying this book within the *CollectionDemo* folder.

73.2 Declaring the Drag Delegate

As with the previous chapter, the first step in implementing drop handling is to declare and implement a drop delegate class. When working with CollectionViews, the UICollectionViewDragDelegate must be implemented.

For this example, the MyCollectionViewController class will serve as both the drop and drag delegates. Since drop support will not be added until later in the chapter, only the drag delegate declaration needs to be added to the *MyCollectionViewController.swift* file as follows. Note also that code has been added to the *viewDidLoad* method to assign the class as the drag delegate:

```
.
.
class MyCollectionViewController: UICollectionViewController,
   UICollectionViewDelegateFlowLayout, UICollectionViewDragDelegate {

    var imageFiles = [String]()
    var images = [UIImage]()

    override func viewDidLoad() {
        super.viewDidLoad()
```

```
.
.
        collectionView?.dragDelegate = self
        initialize()
    }
.
.
```

73.3 Implementing Drag Support

The first delegate method that needs to be added to the class is the *itemForBeginning* method. As with the example in the previous chapter, this method returns an array of UIDragItem objects representing the items to be dragged to the destination. The *itemsForBeginning* method for the UICollectionViewDragDelegate differs slightly from the UIDragInteractionDelegate used in the previous chapter in that it is also passed an IndexPath object indicating the item within the collection view layout that is being dragged. This IndexPath instance contains both the index value of the dragged item and the section within the collection view to which it belongs. Since the layout in this example contains a single section, only the item index is needed. Implement this method now in the *MyCollectionViewController.swift* file so that it reads as follows:

```
func collectionView(_ collectionView: UICollectionView, itemsForBeginning
    session: UIDragSession, at indexPath: IndexPath) -> [UIDragItem] {

    let provider = NSItemProvider(object: images[indexPath.row])
    let dragItem = UIDragItem(itemProvider: provider)
    return [dragItem]
}
```

The code in the delegate method identifies the item being dragged, uses that value as an index into the array of car images and uses that image when creating an NSItemProvider instance. This item provider is subsequently used to create a UIDragItem instance which is returned to the drag and drop system.

Compile and run the app on a device or simulator and display the Photos app in a split view panel alongside the CollectionDemo app. Touch and hold over a car image until the preview image lifts from the screen and drag and drop it onto the Photo app where it should appear under the *Today* heading.

Now that dragging single items from the collection view layout is working, the next step is to add support for dragging multiple items.

73.4 Dragging Multiple Items

Support for adding additional items to a drag session is enabled by adding the *itemsForAddingTo* method to the delegate class. This method is called each time an item in the collection view layout is tapped while a drag session is already in progress. When called, it is passed the IndexPath for the selected item which can, in turn, be used to extract the corresponding image from the image array and to construct and return a UIDragItem object. Add this method to the *MyCollectionViewController.swift* file as follows:

```
func collectionView(_ collectionView: UICollectionView, itemsForAddingTo
  session: UIDragSession, at indexPath: IndexPath, point: CGPoint) ->
    [UIDragItem] {

    let provider = NSItemProvider(object: images[indexPath.row])
```

```
        let dragItem = UIDragItem(itemProvider: provider)
        return [dragItem]
}
```

Compile and run the app once again, start a drag session and tap other images in the layout (when using the simulator, begin the drag and then hold down the Ctrl key while selecting additional images to add to the session). As each image is tapped, the counter in the top right-hand corner of the drag preview increments and the preview images for each item are stacked together as illustrated in Figure 73-1:

Figure 73-1

With multiple images selected, drag and drop the items onto the Photos app. All of the selected images will now appear in the Photos app.

With dragging now implemented, the next step is to begin adding drop support to the project.

73.5 Adding the Drop Delegate

The first step in adding drop support is to declare and assign the UICollectionViewDropDelegate class. Remaining in the *MyCollectionViewController.swift* file, make the following changes:

```
class MyCollectionViewController: UICollectionViewController,
    UICollectionViewDelegateFlowLayout, UICollectionViewDragDelegate,
        UICollectionViewDropDelegate {

    var imageFiles = [String]()
    var images = [UIImage]()

    override func viewDidLoad() {
        super.viewDidLoad()

        let myLayout = MyFlowLayout()

        self.collectionView?.setCollectionViewLayout(myLayout,
                                                    animated: true)

        collectionView?.dragDelegate = self
        collectionView?.dropDelegate = self
        initialize()
    }
.
```

```
.
}
```

73.6 Implementing the Delegate Methods

At a minimum, the delegate class must implement the *canHandle* and *performDropWith* methods, each of which should be familiar from the previous chapter. Begin by adding the *canHandle* method to notify the system that the app can handle image drop items:

```
.
.
import MobileCoreServices
.
.
func collectionView(_ collectionView: UICollectionView, canHandle
                            session: UIDropSession) -> Bool {

    return session.hasItemsConforming(toTypeIdentifiers:
                                        [kUTTypeImage as String])
}
```

Next, add the *performDrop* method so that it reads as follows:

```
func collectionView(_ collectionView: UICollectionView, performDropWith
                        coordinator: UICollectionViewDropCoordinator) {

    let destinationIndexPath =
       coordinator.destinationIndexPath ?? IndexPath(item: 0, section: 0)

    switch coordinator.proposal.operation {
        case .copy:

            let items = coordinator.items

            for item in items {
                item.dragItem.itemProvider.loadObject(ofClass: UIImage.self,
                        completionHandler: {(newImage, error)  -> Void in

                if var image = newImage as? UIImage {
                    if image.size.width > 200 {
                        image = self.scaleImage(image: image, width: 200)
                    }

                    self.images.insert(image, at: destinationIndexPath.item)

                    DispatchQueue.main.async {
                        collectionView.insertItems(
```

```
                                at: [destinationIndexPath])
                        }
                    }
                })
            }
        default: return
    }
}
```

The *performDrop* method is called at the point at which the user drops the item or items associated with a drag operation. When called, the method is passed a drop coordinator object which contains, among other properties, the destination index path referencing the index position and section of the collection view layout at which the drop is to be performed. The method begins by obtaining this path information. If the drop was performed outside the range of items in the layout, the index path and section are both set to 0:

```
let destinationIndexPath =
      coordinator.destinationIndexPath ?? IndexPath(item: 0, section: 0)
```

The drop coordinator also includes a UIDropProposal object which, in turn, contains an operation property. This property tells the delegate method whether this is a cancel, copy or move operation. The method uses a switch statement to handle a copy operation (the switch statement will be extended later in the chapter to handle move operations):

```
switch coordinator.proposal.operation {
    case .copy:
```

Within the code for the copy case, the array of dropped items is extracted from the drop coordinator object before a *for-in* loop is used to iterate through each of the items.

```
let items = coordinator.items

                for item in items {
```

For each item, the code accesses the item provider instance via the drag item object and calls the *loadObject* method. The completion handler of the *loadObject* method is passed the image associated with the current item.

```
item.dragItem.itemProvider.loadObject(ofClass: UIImage.self,
                completionHandler: {(newImage, error)  -> Void in
```

Within the completion handler code, the image is scaled down if necessary to more closely match the size of the existing images:

```
if var image = newImage as? UIImage {
    if image.size.width > 200 {
        image = self.scaleImage(image: image, width: 200)
    }
```

Finally, the new image is added to the image array before being inserted into the collection view layout at the position defined by the destination path. Since the insertion of the image into the collection view is a user interface operation and this completion handler is running in a different thread, the insertion has to be dispatched to the main thread of the app:

```
self.images.insert(image, at: destinationIndexPath.item)

DispatchQueue.main.async {
    collectionView.insertItems(at: [destinationIndexPath])
}
```

Before testing this new code, add the *scaleImage* method to the class as follows:

```
func scaleImage (image:UIImage, width: CGFloat) -> UIImage {
    let oldWidth = image.size.width
    let scaleFactor = width / oldWidth

    let newHeight = image.size.height * scaleFactor
    let newWidth = oldWidth * scaleFactor

    UIGraphicsBeginImageContext(CGSize(width:newWidth, height:newHeight))
    image.draw(in: CGRect(x:0, y:0, width:newWidth, height:newHeight))
    let newImage = UIGraphicsGetImageFromCurrentImageContext()
    UIGraphicsEndImageContext()
    return newImage!
}
```

Compile and run the app and drag and drop an image from the Photos app onto the collection view. The dropped image should appear within the layout at the position at which it is dropped. Repeat this step, this time dragging and dropping multiple images from the Photos app onto the collection view so that all the images are inserted.

73.7 Adding Drag and Drop Animation

As currently configured, there is no animation within the collection view layout while the drag is being performed. This makes it less obvious to the user that the item will be inserted between existing cells when the drop is performed. The cells rearranging to reveal a blank space for the dropped item would provide a much improved user experience. This can be achieved with just a few lines of code via the *dropSessionDidUpdate* delegate method. This method is called each time the session updates (typically whenever the user moves the drop item over a destination) and is required to return a drop proposal object in the form of a UICollectionViewDropProposal object.

The proposal object contains values that indicate how the drop is to be handled by the destination. The first value is the operation type which, as described in the previous chapter, can be set to either *move*, *copy*, *cancel* or *forbidden*. A forbidden setting, for example, will display the forbidden icon in the drop preview indicating that the destination does not support the drop. The second setting is the intent value which must be set to one of the following options:

- **unspecified** – The default behavior. No special animation will be performed within the collection view during the drag operation
- **insertAtDestinationIndexPath** – Indicates that the dropped item will be inserted between two existing items within the layout. This causes the layout to rearrange to make space for the new item.
- **insertIntoDestinationIndexPath** – The item is placed into the item over which the drop is performed.
- **automatic** – The system will decide which intent mode to use depending on how the drop is positioned.

In this example the *insertAtDestinationIndexPath* intent will be used. Before doing that, however, it is worth exploring the *insertIntoDestinationIndexPath* intent a little more.

The *insertIntoDestinationIndexPath* intent could be used, for example, to replace an existing item with the dragged item. Alternatively, when using a TableView in which an item in the view displays a subview, this option can be used when the dropped item is to be added in some way to the subview. Consider, for example, a table view containing a list of photo categories. Selecting a category from the table view displays a collection view controller containing photos for that category. When using *insertIntoDestinationIndexPath*, dragging the item over a row in the table view will cause that cell to highlight indicating that the drop will add the photo to that category. After the item is dropped it can be added to the collection view for the corresponding category so that it appears next time the user displays it.

Within the *MyCollectionViewController.swift* file, implement the *dropSessionDidUpdate* delegate method as follows:

```
func collectionView(_ collectionView: UICollectionView, dropSessionDidUpdate
 session: UIDropSession, withDestinationIndexPath destinationIndexPath:
 IndexPath?) -> UICollectionViewDropProposal {

    if session.localDragSession != nil {
        return UICollectionViewDropProposal(operation: .forbidden,
                                   intent: .unspecified)
    } else {
        return UICollectionViewDropProposal(operation: .copy,
                                   intent: .insertAtDestinationIndexPath)
    }
}
```

The method begins by identifying if this drag originated within the local collection view, or if the drag is from an outside application. A local drag is considered a move operation, but since moving of an image has not yet been implemented in this project, the operation and intent are set to *forbidden* and *unspecified* respectively. If, on the other hand, this is an image from another app, the proposal is returned as a copy operation using the *insertAtDestinationIndexPath* intent.

After making these changes, run the app and drag an image from the Photos app over the collection. As the preview image moves, the layout will rearrange to make room for the item as shown in Figure 73-2:

Figure 73-2

Next, drag an existing image from within the collection view and note that the forbidden icon appears indicating that the item cannot be dropped and that the layout does not rearrange.

Figure 73-3

73.8 Adding the Move Behavior

The final task in this chapter is to implement the ability for the user to move items within the layout using drag and drop. The first step is to change the code in the *dropSessionDidUpdate* delegate method to indicate that moving is now supported and to select the *insertAtDestinationIndexPath* intent:

```
func collectionView(_ collectionView: UICollectionView, dropSessionDidUpdate
  session: UIDropSession, withDestinationIndexPath destinationIndexPath:
   IndexPath?) -> UICollectionViewDropProposal {

    if session.localDragSession != nil {
        return UICollectionViewDropProposal(operation: .move,
                                    intent: .insertAtDestinationIndexPath)
    } else {
        return UICollectionViewDropProposal(operation: .copy,
                                    intent: .insertAtDestinationIndexPath)
    }
}
```

Now that the *dropSessionDidUpdate* method will be returning a *move* value for local operations, the *performDrop* method needs to be updated to handle this setting in addition to the copy operation. Edit the method now to add an additional *case* construct to the switch statement:

```
func collectionView(_ collectionView: UICollectionView, performDropWith
  coordinator: UICollectionViewDropCoordinator) {


    let destinationIndexPath = coordinator.destinationIndexPath ??
IndexPath(item: 0, section: 0)

    switch coordinator.proposal.operation {
        case .copy:
.
.
.
        case .move:
```

```
            let items = coordinator.items

            for item in items {

                guard let sourceIndexPath = item.sourceIndexPath
                                                else { return }

                collectionView.performBatchUpdates({

                    let moveImage = images[sourceIndexPath.item]
                    images.remove(at: sourceIndexPath.item)
                    images.insert(moveImage, at: destinationIndexPath.item)

                    collectionView.deleteItems(at: [sourceIndexPath])
                    collectionView.insertItems(at: [destinationIndexPath])
                })
                coordinator.drop(item.dragItem,
                                toItemAt: destinationIndexPath)
            }
        default: return
    }
}
```

As was the case with the copy operation, the new code gets a reference to the items contained in the drop and iterates through each one. For each valid item, the source index path is used to extract the corresponding image from the images array. The source image is then removed from the array and inserted at the index position referenced by the destination index path. Next, the image is deleted from its old position in the collection view layout and inserted at the drop location index. Finally, the drop operation is performed via a call to the *drop* method of the coordinator instance.

Run the app one last time and verify that it is now possible to move an item within the collection view layout using drag and drop.

73.9 TableView Drag and Drop

Many of the steps and delegate methods covered in this chapter apply equally to TableView-based drag and drop with the following changes:

- TableView drag and drop uses UITableViewDragDelegate and UITableViewDropDelegate delegates.
- The performDrop coordinator is an instance of UITableViewDropCoordinator.
- The dropSessionDidUpdate method returns a UITableViewProposal object.

73.10 Summary

This chapter has demonstrated the use of drag and drop when working with collection views including support for dragging and dropping multiple items in a single session. The example created in this chapter has introduced some delegate methods that are specific to the Collection View drag and drop delegates and shown how implementing animation within the layout causes gaps to form for the dropped item. Most of the steps in this chapter also apply to the TableView class.

Chapter 74

74. Integrating Maps into iOS 12 Applications using MKMapItem

If there is one single fact about Apple that we can state with any degree of certainty, it is that the company is fanatical about retaining control of its own destiny. One glaring omission in this overriding corporate strategy has been the reliance on a competitor (in the form of Google) for mapping data in iOS. This dependency officially ended with iOS 6 through the introduction of Apple Maps.

In iOS 8, Apple Maps officially replaced the Google-based map data with data provided primarily by a company named TomTom (but also including technology from other companies, including some acquired by Apple for this purpose). Headquartered in the Netherlands, TomTom specializes in mapping and GPS systems. Of particular significance, however, is that TomTom (unlike Google) does not make smartphones, nor does it develop an operating system that competes with iOS, making it a more acceptable partner for Apple.

As part of the iOS 6 revamp of mapping, the SDK also introduced a class in the form of MKMapItem, designed solely for the purpose of easing the integration of maps and turn-by-turn directions into iOS applications. This was further enhanced in iOS 9 with the introduction of support for transit times, directions and city flyover support.

For more advanced mapping requirements, the iOS SDK also includes the original classes of the MapKit framework, details of which will be covered in later chapters.

74.1 MKMapItem and MKPlacemark Classes

The purpose of the MKMapItem class is to make it easy for applications to launch maps without having to write significant amounts of code. MKMapItem works in conjunction with the MKPlacemark class, instances of which are passed to MKMapItem to define the locations that are to be displayed in the resulting map. A range of options are also provided with MKMapItem to configure both the appearance of maps and the nature of directions that are to be displayed (i.e. whether directions are to be for driving, walking or public transit).

74.2 An Introduction to Forward and Reverse Geocoding

It is difficult to talk about mapping, in particular when dealing with the MKPlacemark class, without first venturing into the topic of geocoding. Geocoding can best be described as the process of converting a textual based geographical location (such as a street address) into geographical coordinates expressed in terms of longitude and latitude.

Within the context of iOS development, geocoding may be performed by making use of the CLGeocoder class which is used to convert a text based address string into a CLLocation object containing the coordinates corresponding to the address. The following code, for example, converts the street address of the Empire State Building in New York to longitude and latitude coordinates:

```
let addressString = "350 5th Avenue New York, NY"

CLGeocoder().geocodeAddressString(addressString,
        completionHandler: {(placemarks, error) in
```

```
    if error != nil {
        print("Geocode failed with error: \(error!.localizedDescription)")
    } else if let marks = placemarks, marks.count > 0 {
        let placemark = marks[0]
        if let location = placemark.location {
            let coords = location.coordinate

            print(coords.latitude)
            print(coords.longitude)
        }
    }
})
```

The code simply calls the *geocodeAddressString* method of a CLGeocoder instance, passing through a string object containing the street address and a completion handler to be called when the translation is complete. Passed as arguments to the handler are an array of CLPlacemark objects (one for each match for the address) together with an Error object which may be used to identify the reason for any failures.

For the purposes of this example the assumption is made that only one location matched the address string provided. The location information is then extracted from the CLPlacemark object at location 0 in the array and the coordinates displayed on the console.

The above code is an example of *forward-geocoding* in that coordinates are calculated based on a text address description. *Reverse-geocoding*, as the name suggests, involves the translation of geographical coordinates into a human readable address string. Consider, for example, the following code:

```
let newLocation = CLLocation(latitude: 40.74835, longitude: -73.984911)

CLGeocoder().reverseGeocodeLocation(newLocation, completionHandler:
{(placemarks, error) in
    if error != nil {
        print("Geocode failed with error: \(error!.localizedDescription)")
    }

    if let marks = placemarks, marks.count > 0 {
        let placemark = marks[0]
        let postalAddress = placemark.postalAddress

        if let address = postalAddress?.street,
            let city = postalAddress?.city,
            let state = postalAddress?.state,
            let zip = postalAddress?.postalCode {

                print("\(address) \(city) \(state) \(zip)")
        }
    }
```

```
})
```

In this case, a CLLocation object is initialized with longitude and latitude coordinates and then passed through to the *reverseGeocodeLocation* method of a CLGeocoder object. The method passes through to the completion handler an array of matching addresses in the form of CLPlacemark objects. Each placemark contains the address information for the matching location in the form of a CNPostalAddress object. Once again, the code assumes a single match is contained in the array and accesses and displays the address, city, state and zip properties of the postal address object on the console.

When executed, the above code results in output which reads:

```
338 5th Ave New York New York 10001
```

It should be noted that the geocoding is not actually performed on the iOS device, but rather on a server to which the device connects when a translation is required and the results subsequently returned when the translation is complete. As such, geocoding can only take place when the device has an active internet connection.

74.3 Creating MKPlacemark Instances

Each location that is to be represented when a map is displayed using the MKMapItem class must be represented by an MKPlacemark object. When MKPlacemark objects are created, they must be initialized with the geographical coordinates of the location together with an NSDictionary object containing the address property information. Continuing the example for the Empire State Building in New York, an MKPlacemark object would be created as follows:

```
import Contacts
import MapKit
.
.
let coords = CLLocationCoordinate2DMake(40.7483, -73.984911)

let address = [CNPostalAddressStreetKey: "350 5th Avenue",
               CNPostalAddressCityKey: "New York",
               CNPostalAddressStateKey: "NY",
               CNPostalAddressPostalCodeKey: "10118",
               CNPostalAddressISOCountryCodeKey: "US"]

let place = MKPlacemark(coordinate: coords, addressDictionary: address)
```

While it is possible to initialize an MKPlacemark object passing through a *nil* value for the address dictionary, this will result in the map appearing, albeit with the correct location marked, but it will be tagged as "Unknown" instead of listing the address. The coordinates are, however, mandatory when creating an MKPlacemark object. In the event that the application knows the text address but not the coordinates of a location, geocoding will need to be used to obtain the coordinates prior to creating the MKPlacemark instance.

74.4 Working with MKMapItem

Given the tasks that it is able to perform, the MKMapItem class is actually extremely simple to use. In its simplest form, it can be initialized by passing through a single MKPlacemark object as an argument, for example:

```
let mapItem = MKMapItem(placemark: place)
```

Once initialized, the *openInMaps(launchOptions:)* method will open the map positioned at the designated location with an appropriate marker as illustrated in Figure 74-1:

```
mapItem.openInMaps(launchOptions: nil)
```

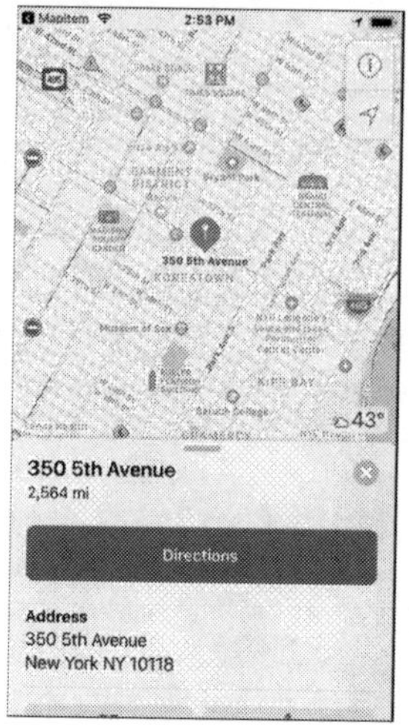

Figure 74-1

Similarly, the map may be initialized to display the current location of the user's device via a call to the MKMapItem *forCurrentLocation* method:

```
let mapItem = MKMapItem.forCurrentLocation()
```

Multiple locations may be tagged on the map by placing two or more MKMapItem objects in an array and then passing that array through to the *openMaps(with:)* class method of the MKMapItem class. For example:

```
let mapItems = [mapItem1, mapItem2, mapItem3]

MKMapItem.openMaps(with: mapItems, launchOptions: nil)
```

74.5 MKMapItem Options and Configuring Directions

In the example code fragments presented in the preceding sections, a *nil* value was passed through as the options argument to the MKMapItem methods. In actual fact, there are a number of configuration options that are available for use when opening a map. These values need to be set up within an NSDictionary object using a set of pre-defined keys and values:

- **MKLaunchOptionsDirectionsModeKey** – Controls whether directions are to be provided with the map. In the event that only one placemarker is present, directions from the current location to the placemarker will be provided. The mode for the directions should be one of either *MKLaunchOptionsDirectionsModeDriving*, *MKLaunchOptionsDirectionsModeWalking* or *MKLaunchOptionsDirectionsModeTransit*.
- **MKLaunchOptionsMapTypeKey** – Indicates whether the map should display standard, satellite, hybrid, flyover or hybrid flyover map images.
- **MKLaunchOptionsMapCenterKey** – Corresponds to a CLLocationCoordinate2D structure value containing the coordinates of the location on which the map is to be centered.

- **MKLaunchOptionsMapSpanKey** – An MKCoordinateSpan structure value designating the region that the map should display when launched.
- **MKLaunchOptionsShowsTrafficKey** – A Boolean value indicating whether or not traffic information should be superimposed over the map when it is launched.
- **MKLaunchOptionsCameraKey** – When displaying a map in 3D flyover mode, the value assigned to this key takes the form of an MKMapCamera object configured to view the map from a specified perspective.

The following code, for example, opens a map with traffic data displayed and includes turn-by-turn driving directions between two map items:

```
let mapItems = [mapItem1, mapItem2]

let options = [MKLaunchOptionsDirectionsModeKey:
                        MKLaunchOptionsDirectionsModeDriving,
                MKLaunchOptionsShowsTrafficKey: true] as [String : Any]

MKMapItem.openMaps(with: mapItems, launchOptions: options)
```

74.6 Adding Item Details to an MKMapItem

When a location is marked on a map, the address is displayed together with a blue arrow which, when selected, displays an information card for that location.

The MKMapItem class allows additional information to be added to a location through the *name*, *phoneNumber* and *url* properties. The following code, for example, adds these properties to the map item for the Empire State Building:

```
mapItem.name = "Empire State Building"
mapItem.phoneNumber = "+12127363100"
mapItem.url = URL(string: "https://esbnyc.com")

mapItem.openInMaps(launchOptions: nil)
```

When the code is executed, the map place marker displays the location name instead of the address together with the additional information:

Figure 74-2

A force touch performed on the marker displays a popover panel containing options to call the provided number or visit the website:

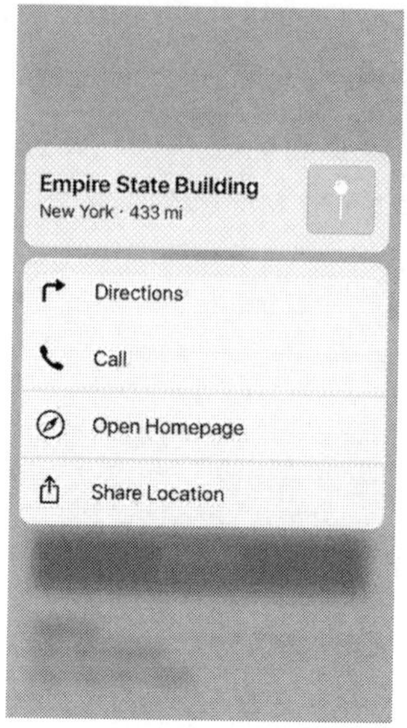

Figure 74-3

74.7 Summary

iOS 6 replaced Google Maps with maps provided by TomTom. Unlike Google Maps, which were assembled from static images, the new Apple Maps are dynamically rendered resulting in clear and smooth zooming and more precise region selections. iOS 6 also introduced the MKMapItem class, the purpose of which is to make it easy for iOS application developers to launch maps and provide turn-by-turn directions with the minimum amount of code.

Within this chapter, the basics of geocoding and the MKPlacemark and MKMapItem classes have been covered. The next chapter, entitled *An Example iOS 12 MKMapItem Application*, will work through the creation of an example application that utilizes the knowledge covered in this chapter.

Chapter 75

75. An Example iOS 12 MKMapItem Application

The objective of this chapter is to work through the creation of an example iOS application which makes use of reverse geocoding together with the MKPlacemark and MKMapItem classes. The application will consist of a screen into which the user will be required to enter destination address information. When a button is selected by the user, a map will be launched containing turn-by-turn directions from the user's current location to the specified destination.

75.1 Creating the MapItem Project

Launch Xcode and create a new project by selecting the options to create a new iOS application based on the *Single View Application* template. Enter *MapItem* as the product name and choose Swift as the programming language.

75.2 Designing the User Interface

The user interface will consist of four Text Field objects into which the destination address will be entered, together with a Button to launch the map. Select the *Main.storyboard* file in the project navigator panel and, using the Library palette, design the user interface layout such that it resembles that of Figure 75-1, taking steps to widen the Text Fields and to configure Placeholder text attributes on each one.

If you reside in a country that is not divided into States and Zip code regions, feel free to adjust the user interface accordingly.

Display the *Resolve Auto Layout Issues* menu and select the *Reset to Suggested Constraints* option listed under *All Views in View Controller*.

The next step is to connect the outlets for the text views and declare an action for the button. Select the *Street address* Text Field object, display the Assistant Editor and make sure that the editor is displaying the *ViewController.swift* file.

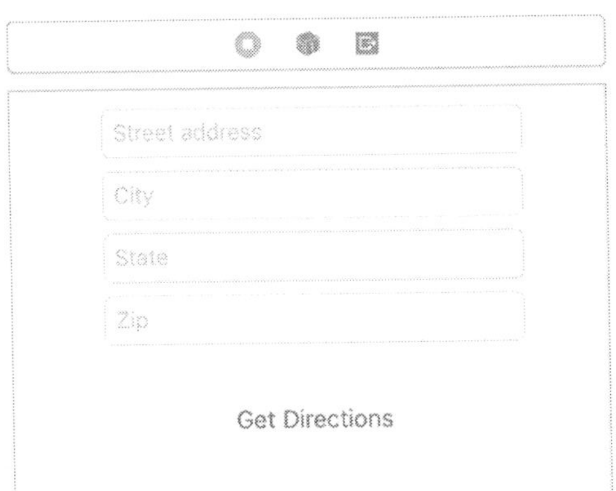

Figure 75-1

Ctrl-click on the *Street address* Text Field object and drag the resulting line to the area immediately beneath the class declaration directive in the Assistant Editor panel. Upon releasing the line, the configuration panel will appear. Configure the connection as an *Outlet* named *address* and click on the *Connect* button. Repeat these steps for the *City, State* and *Zip* text fields, connecting them to outlets named *city, state* and *zip* respectively.

Ctrl-click on the *Get Directions* button and drag the resulting line to a position beneath the new outlets declared in the Assistant Editor. In the resulting configuration panel, change the *Connection* type to *Action* and name the method *getDirections.* On completion, the beginning of the *ViewController.swift* file should read as follows:

```
import UIKit

class ViewController: UIViewController {

    @IBOutlet weak var address: UITextField!
    @IBOutlet weak var city: UITextField!
    @IBOutlet weak var state: UITextField!
    @IBOutlet weak var zip: UITextField!

    @IBAction func getDirections(_ sender: Any) {
    }
.
.
}
```

75.3 Converting the Destination using Forward Geocoding

When the user touches the button in the user interface, the *getDirections* method will be able to extract the address information from the text fields. The objective will be to create an MKPlacemark object to contain this location. As outlined in *Integrating Maps into iOS 12 Applications using MKMapItem*, an MKPlacemark instance requires the longitude and latitude of an address before it can be instantiated. The first step in the *getDirections* method is to perform a forward geocode translation of the address. Before doing so, however, it is necessary to declare a property in the *ViewController.swift* file in which to store these coordinates once they have been calculated. This will, in turn, require that the *CoreLocation* framework be imported. Now is also an opportune time to import the *MapKit* and *Contacts* frameworks, both of which will be required later in the chapter:

```
import UIKit
import Contacts
import MapKit
import CoreLocation

class ViewController: UIViewController {

    @IBOutlet weak var address: UITextField!
    @IBOutlet weak var city: UITextField!
    @IBOutlet weak var state: UITextField!
```

```
    @IBOutlet weak var zip: UITextField!
    var coords: CLLocationCoordinate2D?
.
.
}
```

Next, select the *ViewController.swift* file, locate the *getDirections* method stub and modify it to convert the address string to geographical coordinates:

```
@IBAction func getDirections(_ sender: Any) {

    if let addressString = address.text,
        let cityString = city.text,
        let stateString = state.text,
        let zipString = zip.text {

        let addressString =
            "\(addressString) \(cityString) \(stateString) \(zipString)"

        CLGeocoder().geocodeAddressString(addressString,
                    completionHandler: {(placemarks, error) in

                if error != nil {
                    print("Geocode failed: \(error!.localizedDescription)")
                } else if let marks = placemarks, marks.count > 0 {
                        let placemark = marks[0]
                        if let location = placemark.location {
                        self.coords = location.coordinate
                        self.showMap()
                    }
                }
        })
    }
}
```

The steps used to perform the geocoding translation mirror those outlined in *Integrating Maps into iOS 12 Applications using MKMapItem* with one difference in that a method named *showMap* is called in the event that a successful translation took place. All that remains, therefore, is to implement this method.

75.4 Launching the Map

With the address string and coordinates obtained, the final task is to implement the *showMap* method. This method will create a new MKPlacemark instance for the destination address, configure options for the map to request driving directions and then launch the map. Since the map will be launched with a single map item, it will default to providing directions from the current location. With the *ViewController.swift* file still selected, add the code for the *showMap* method so that it reads as follows:

```
func showMap() {
```

```
    if let addressString = address.text,
        let cityString = city.text,
        let stateString = state.text,
        let zipString = zip.text,
        let coordinates = coords {

        let addressDict =
            [CNPostalAddressStreetKey: addressString,
             CNPostalAddressCityKey: cityString,
             CNPostalAddressStateKey: stateString,
             CNPostalAddressPostalCodeKey: zipString]

        let place = MKPlacemark(coordinate: coordinates,
                        addressDictionary: addressDict)

        let mapItem = MKMapItem(placemark: place)

        let options = [MKLaunchOptionsDirectionsModeKey:
            MKLaunchOptionsDirectionsModeDriving]

        mapItem.openInMaps(launchOptions: options)
    }
}
```

The method simply creates an NSDictionary containing the contact keys and values for the destination address and then creates an MKPlacemark instance using the address dictionary and the coordinates from the forward-geocoding operation. A new MKMapItem object is created using the placemarker object before another dictionary is created and configured to request driving directions. Finally, the map is launched.

75.5 Building and Running the Application

Within the Xcode toolbar, click on the Run button to compile and run the application, either on a physical iOS device or the iOS Simulator. Once loaded, enter an address into the text fields before touching the *Get Directions* button. The map should subsequently appear together with the route between your current location and the destination address. Note that if the app is running in the simulator, the current location will likely default to Apple's headquarters in California.

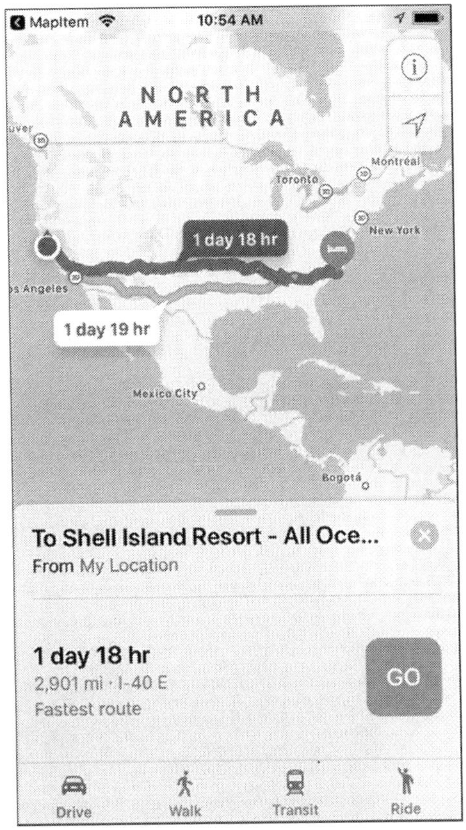

Figure 75-2

75.6 Summary

The goal of this chapter has been to work through the creation of a simple application designed to use a combination of geocoding and the MKPlacemark and MKMapItem classes. The example application created in this chapter has demonstrated the ease with which maps and directions can be integrated into iOS applications.

Chapter 76

76. Getting Location Information using the iOS 12 Core Location Framework

iOS devices are able to employ a number of different techniques for obtaining information about the current geographical location of the device. These mechanisms include GPS, cell tower triangulation and finally (and least accurately), by using the IP address of available Wi-Fi connections. The mechanism that is used by iOS to detect location information is, however, largely transparent to the application developer and the system will automatically use the most accurate solution available at any given time. In fact, all that is needed to integrate location based information into an iOS application is an understanding of how to use the Core Location Framework which, incidentally, is the subject of this chapter.

Once the basics of location tracking with Core Location have been covered in this chapter, the next chapter will provide detailed steps on how to create *An Example iOS 12 Location Application*.

76.1 The Core Location Manager

The key classes contained within the Core Location Framework are CLLocationManager and CLLocation. An instance of the CLLocationManager class can be created using the following Swift code:

```
var locationManager: CLLocationManager = CLLocationManager()
```

Once a location manager instance has been created, it must seek permission from the user to collect location information before it can begin to track data.

76.2 Requesting Location Access Authorization

Before any application can begin to track location data it must first seek permission to do so from the user. This can be achieved by making a call to one of two methods on the CLLocationManager instance depending on the specific requirement. If the application only needs to track location information when the application is in the foreground then a call should be made to the *requestWhenInUseAuthorization* method of the location manager instance. For example:

```
locationManager.requestWhenInUseAuthorization()
```

In the event that tracking is also required when the application is running in the background, the *requestAlwaysAuthorization* method should be called:

```
locationManager.requestAlwaysAuthorization()
```

If an app requires *always* authorization, the recommended path to requesting this permission is to first seek *when in use* permission and to then offer the user the opportunity to elevate this permission to *always* mode at the point that it is needed by the app. The reasoning behind this recommendation is that when seeking *always* permission, the request dialog displayed by iOS will provide the user the option of using either *when in use* or *always* location tracking. Given these choices, most users will typically select the *when in use* option. A better approach is to begin by requesting *when in use* tracking and then explain the benefits of elevating to *always* mode in a later request.

Both location authorization request method calls require that specific key-value pairs be added to the Information Property List dictionary contained within the application's *Info.plist* file. The values take the form of strings and must describe the reason why the application needs access to the user's current location. The keys associated with these values are as follows:

- **NSLocationWhenInUseUsageDescription** – A string value describing to the user why the application needs access to the current location when running in the foreground. This string is displayed when a call is made to the *requestWhenInUseAuthorization* method of the locationManager instance. The dialog displayed to the user containing this message will only provide the option to permit *when in use* location tracking. All apps built using the iOS 11 SDK or later must include this key regardless of the usage permission level being requested in order to access the device location.
- **NSLocationAlwaysAndWhenInUseUsageDesciption** – The string displayed when permission is requested for *always* authorization using the *requestAlwaysAuthorization* method. The request dialog containing this message will provide the user with the choice of selecting either *always* or *when in use* authorization. All apps built using the iOS 11 SDK or later must include this key when accessing device location information.
- **NSLocationAlwaysUsageDescription** – A string describing to the user why the application needs *always* access to the current location. This description is not used on devices running iOS 11 or later, though it should still be declared for compatibility with legacy devices.

76.3 Configuring the Desired Location Accuracy

The level of accuracy to which location information is to be tracked is specified via the *desiredAccuracy* property of the CLLocationManager object. It is important to keep in mind when configuring this property that the greater the level of accuracy selected the greater the drain on the device battery. An application should, therefore, never request a greater level of accuracy than is actually needed.

A number of predefined constant values are available for use when configuring this property:

- **kCLLocationAccuracyBestForNavigation** – Uses the highest possible level of accuracy augmented by additional sensor data. This accuracy level is intended solely for use when the device is connected to an external power supply.
- **kCLLocationAccuracyBest** – The highest recommended level of accuracy for devices running on battery power.
- **kCLLocationAccuracyNearestTenMeters** - Accurate to within 10 meters.
- **kCLLocationAccuracyHundredMeters** – Accurate to within 100 meters.
- **kCLLocationAccuracyKilometer** – Accurate to within one kilometer.
- **kCLLocationAccuracyThreeKilometers** – Accurate to within three kilometers.

The following code, for example, sets the level of accuracy for a location manager instance to "best accuracy":

```
locationManager.desiredAccuracy = kCLLocationAccuracyBest
```

76.4 Configuring the Distance Filter

The default configuration for the location manager is to report updates whenever any changes are detected in the location of the device. The *distanceFilter* property of the location manager allows applications to specify the amount of distance the device location must change before an update is triggered. If, for example, the distance filter is set to 1000 meters the application will only receive a location update when the device travels 1000 meters or more from the location of the last update. For example, to specify a distance filter of 1500 meters:

```
locationManager.distanceFilter = 1500.0
```

The distance filter may be cancelled, thereby returning to the default setting, using the *kCLDistanceFilterNone* constant:

```
locationManager.distanceFilter = kCLDistanceFilterNone
```

76.5 Continuous Background Location Updates

The location tracking options covered so far in this chapter only receive updates when the app is either in the foreground or background. As soon as the app enters the suspended state (in other words the app is still resident in memory but is no longer executing code) the updates will stop. If location updates are required even when the app is suspended (a key requirement for navigation based apps), continuous background location updates must be enabled for the app. When enabled, the app will be woken from suspension each time a location update is triggered and provided the latest location data.

Enable continuous location updates is a two-step process beginning with the addition of an entry to the project *Info.plist* file. This is most easily achieved by enabling the location updates background mode in the Xcode Capabilities panel as shown in Figure 76-1:

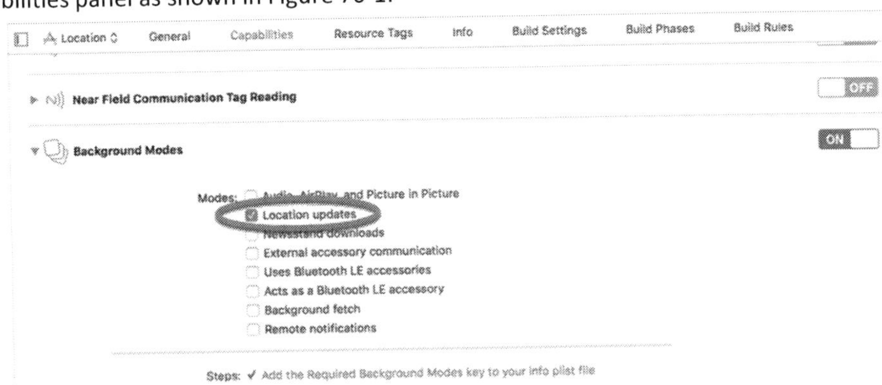

Figure 76-1

Within the app code, continuous updates are enabled by setting the *allowsBackgroundLocationUpdates* property of the location manager to *true*:

```
locationManager.allowsBackgroundLocationUpdates = true
```

To allow the location manager to temporarily suspend updates, set the *pausesLocationUpdatesAutomatically* property of the location manager to *true*.

```
locationManager.pausesLocationUpdatesAutomatically = true
```

This setting allows the location manager to extend battery life by pausing updates when it is appropriate to do so (for example when the user's location remains unchanged for a significant amount of time). When the user starts moving again, the location manager will automatically resume updates.

Continuous location background updates are available for apps for both *always* and *when in use* authorization modes. When activated for an app that only has *when in use* authorization, a blue notification bar will appear along the top of the screen, as demonstrated in Figure 76-2:

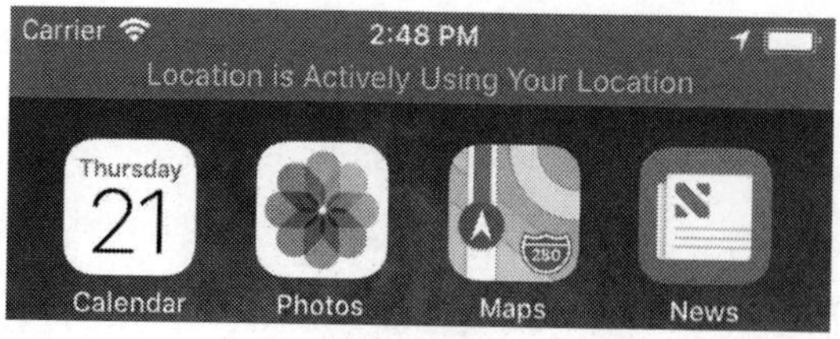

Figure 76-2

76.6 The Location Manager Delegate

Location manager updates and errors result in calls to two delegate methods defined within the CLLocationManagerDelegate protocol. Templates for the two delegate methods that must be implemented to comply with this protocol are as follows:

```
func locationManager(_ manager: CLLocationManager,
               didUpdateLocations locations: [CLLocation])
{
    // Handle location updates here
}

func locationManager(_ manager: CLLocationManager,
          didFailWithError error: Error)
{
    // Handle errors here
}
```

Each time the location changes, the *didUpdateLocations* delegate method is called and passed as an argument an array of CLLocation objects with the last object in the array containing the most recent location data.

Changes to the location tracking authorization status of an application are reported via a call to the optional *didChangeAuthorization* delegate method:

```
func locationManager(_ manager: CLLocationManager,
       didChangeAuthorization status: CLAuthorizationStatus) {

    // App may no longer be authorized to obtain location
    //information. Check status here and respond accordingly.
}
```

Once a class has been configured to act as the delegate for the location manager, that object must be assigned to the location manager instance. In most cases, the delegate will be the same view controller class in which the location manager resides, for example:

```
locationManager.delegate = self
```

76.7 Starting and Stopping Location Updates

Once suitably configured and authorized, the location manager can then be instructed to start tracking location information:

```
locationManager.startUpdatingLocation()
```

With each location update, the *didUpdateLocations* delegate method is called by the location manager and passed information about the current location.

To stop location updates, simply call the *stopUdatingLocation* method of the location manager as follows:

```
locationManager.stopUpdatingLocation()
```

76.8 Obtaining Location Information from CLLocation Objects

Location information is passed through to the *didUpdateLocation* delegate method in the form of CLLocation objects. A CLLocation object encapsulates the following data:

- Latitude
- Longitude
- Horizontal Accuracy
- Altitude
- Altitude Accuracy

76.8.1 Longitude and Latitude

Longitude and latitude values are stored as type CLLocationDegrees and may be obtained from a CLLocation object as follows:

```
let currentLatitude: CLLocationDistance =
        location.coordinate.latitude

let currentLongitude: CLLocationDistance =
        location.coordinate.longitude
```

76.8.2 Accuracy

Horizontal and vertical accuracy are stored in meters as CLLocationAccuracy values and may be accessed as follows:

```
let verticalAccuracy: CLLocationAccuracy =
        location.verticalAccuracy

let horizontalAccuracy: CLLocationAccuracy =
        location.horizontalAccuracy
```

76.8.3 Altitude

The altitude value is stored in meters as a type CLLocationDistance value and may be accessed from a CLLocation object as follows:

```
let altitude: CLLocationDistance = location.altitude
```

76.9 Getting the Current Location

If all that is required from the location manager is the user's current location without the need for continuous location updates, this can be achieved via a call to the *requestLocation* method of the location manager instance. This method will identify the current location and call the *didUpdateLocations* delegate one time passing through the current location information. Location updates are then automatically turned off:

```
locationManager.requestLocation()
```

76.10 Calculating Distances

The distance between two CLLocation points may be calculated by calling the *distance(from:)* method of the end location and passing through the start location as an argument. For example, the following code calculates the distance between the points specified by *startLocation* and *endLocation*:

```
var distance: CLLocationDistance =
        endLocation.distance(from: startLocation)
```

76.11 Summary

This chapter has provided an overview of the use of the iOS Core Location Framework to obtain location information within an iOS application. This theory will be put into practice in the next chapter entitled *An Example iOS 12 Location Application*.

Chapter 77

77. An Example iOS 12 Location Application

Having covered the basics of location management in iOS 12 applications in the previous chapter it is now time to put theory into practice and work step-by-step through an example application. The objective of this chapter is to create a simple iOS application that tracks the latitude, longitude and altitude of an iOS device. In addition, the level of location accuracy will be reported, together with the distance between a selected location and the current location of the device.

77.1 Creating the Example iOS 12 Location Project

The first step, as always, is to launch the Xcode environment and start a new project to contain the location application. Once Xcode is running, select the *File -> New -> Project…* menu option and configure a new iOS project named *Location* using the *Single View Application* template with the language set to Swift.

77.2 Designing the User Interface

The user interface for this example location app is going to consist of a number of labels and a button that will be connected to an action method. Initiate the user interface design process by selecting the *Main.storyboard* file. Once the view has loaded into the Interface Builder editing environment, create a user interface that resembles as closely as possible the view illustrated in Figure 77-1.

In the case of the five labels in the right-hand column which will display location and accuracy data, make sure that the labels are stretched to the right until the blue margin guideline appears. The data will be displayed to multiple levels of decimal points requiring space beyond the default size of the label.

Select the label object to the right of the "Current Latitude" label in the view canvas, display the Assistant Editor panel and verify that the editor is displaying the contents of the *ViewController.swift* file. Ctrl-click on the same Label object and drag to a position just below the class declaration line in the Assistant Editor. Release the line and in the resulting connection dialog establish an outlet connection named *latitude*. Repeat these steps for the remaining labels, connecting them to properties named *longitude, hAccuracy, altitude, vAccuracy* and *distance* respectively.

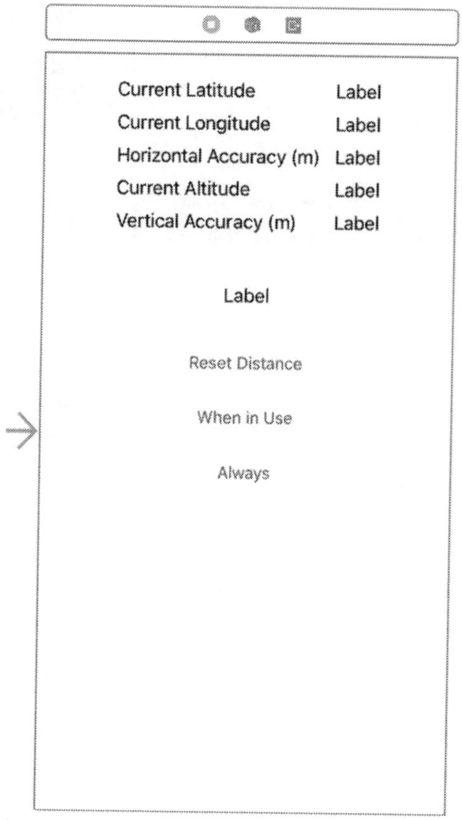

Figure 77-1

The final step of the user interface design process is to connect the button objects to action methods. Ctrl-click on the *Reset Distance* button object and drag the line to the area immediately beneath the *viewDidLoad* method in the Assistant Editor panel. Release the line and, within the resulting connection dialog, establish an Action method on the *Touch Up Inside* event configured to call a method named *resetDistance*. Repeat this step for the remaining buttons, establishing action connections to methods named *startWhenInUse* and *startAlways* respectively.

Close the Assistant Editor and add a variable to the ViewController class in which to store the start location coordinates and the location manager object. Now is also an opportune time to import the CoreLocation framework and to declare the class as implementing the CLLocationManagerDelegate protocol:

```
import UIKit
import CoreLocation

class ViewController: UIViewController, CLLocationManagerDelegate {

    @IBOutlet weak var latitude: UILabel!
    @IBOutlet weak var longitude: UILabel!
    @IBOutlet weak var hAccuracy: UILabel!
    @IBOutlet weak var altitude: UILabel!
    @IBOutlet weak var vAccuracy: UILabel!
    @IBOutlet weak var distance: UILabel!
```

```
    var locationManager: CLLocationManager = CLLocationManager()
    var startLocation: CLLocation!
.
.
}
```

77.3 Configuring the CLLocationManager Object

The next task is to configure the instance of the CLLocationManager class and to make sure that the application requests permission from the user to track the current location of the device. Since this needs to occur when the view loads, an ideal location is in the view controller's *viewDidLoad* method in the *ViewController.swift* file:

```
override func viewDidLoad() {
    super.viewDidLoad()

    locationManager.desiredAccuracy = kCLLocationAccuracyBest
    locationManager.delegate = self
    startLocation = nil
}
```

The above code changes configure the CLLocationManager object instance to use the "best accuracy" setting. The code then declares the view controller instance as the application delegate for the location manager object.

77.4 Setting up the Usage Description Keys

Within the project navigator panel, load the *Info.plist* file into the editor. As explained in the previous chapter, the two mandatory usage description key-value pairs now need to be added to the *Information Property List* dictionary. Select this entry in the list and click on the + button to add a new entry to the dictionary and, from the resulting menu, select the *Privacy – Location When in Use Usage Description* item. Once the key has been added, double-click in the corresponding value column and enter the following text:

```
The application uses this information to show you your location
```

On completion of this step, the entry should match that of Figure 77-2:

Key	Type	Value
▼ Information Property List	Dictionary	(18 items)
Privacy - Location When In Use Usage Description	String	The application uses this information to show you your location
Localization native development region	String	$(DEVELOPMENT_LANGUAGE)

Figure 77-2

Repeat this step, this time adding a *Privacy - Location Always and When In Use Usage Description* key set to the following string value:

```
Always mode is recommended for this app for improved location tracking
```

On completion of these steps, the usage description keys should appear in the property editor as follows:

Key	Type	Value
Information Property List	Dictionary	(18 items)
Privacy - Location When In Use Usage Description	String	The application uses this information to show you your location
Privacy - Location Always and When In Use Usage Desc...	String	Always mode is recommended for this app for improved location tracking

Figure 77-3

77.5 Implementing the startWhenInUse Method

This action method will request when in use permission from the user before starting location updates. Locate the method stub in the *ViewController.swift* file and modify it as follows:

```
@IBAction func startWhenInUse(_ sender: Any) {
    locationManager.requestWhenInUseAuthorization()
    locationManager.startUpdatingLocation()
}
```

77.6 Implementing the startAlways Method

The *startAlways* method is intended to demonstrate the process of persuading the user to elevate location tracking to *always* mode after already granting *when in use* permission. In this method the assumption is made that updates are already running so the first step is to stop the updates. Once updates are stopped, the permission request is made before updates are restarted:

```
@IBAction func startAlways(_ sender: Any) {
    locationManager.stopUpdatingLocation()
    locationManager.requestAlwaysAuthorization()
    locationManager.startUpdatingLocation()
}
```

77.7 Implementing the resetDistance Method

The button object in the user interface is connected to the *resetDistance* action method so the next task is to implement that action. All this method needs to do is set the *startlocation* variable to nil:

```
@IBAction func resetDistance(_ sender: Any) {
    startLocation = nil
}
```

77.8 Implementing the Application Delegate Methods

When the location manager detects a location change, it calls the *didUpdateLocations* delegate method. Since the view controller was declared as the delegate for the location manager in the *viewDidLoad* method, it is necessary to now implement this method in the *ViewController.swift* file:

```
func locationManager(_ manager: CLLocationManager,
                     didUpdateLocations locations: [CLLocation]) {

    let latestLocation: CLLocation = locations[locations.count - 1]

    latitude.text = String(format: "%.4f",
                           latestLocation.coordinate.latitude)
    longitude.text = String(format: "%.4f",
                           latestLocation.coordinate.longitude)
```

```
    hAccuracy.text = String(format: "%.4f",
                              latestLocation.horizontalAccuracy)
    altitude.text = String(format: "%.4f",
                          latestLocation.altitude)
    vAccuracy.text = String(format: "%.4f",
                             latestLocation.verticalAccuracy)

    if startLocation == nil {
        startLocation = latestLocation
    }

    let distanceBetween: CLLocationDistance =
        latestLocation.distance(from: startLocation)

    distance.text = String(format: "%.2f", distanceBetween)
}
```

When the delegate method is called it is passed an array of location objects containing the latest updates, with the last item in the array representing the most recent location information. To begin with, the delegate method extracts the last location object from the array and works through the data contained in the object. In each case, it creates a string containing the extracted value and displays it on the corresponding user interface label.

If this is the first time that the method has been called either since the application was launched or the user last pressed the *Reset Distance* button, the *startLocation* variable is set to the current location. The *distance(from:)* method of the location object is then called, passing through the *startLocation* object as an argument in order to calculate the distance between the two points. The result is then displayed on the distance label in the user interface.

The *didFailWithError* delegate method is called when an error is encountered by the location manager instance. This method should also, therefore, be implemented:

```
func locationManager(_ manager: CLLocationManager,
                     didFailWithError error: Error) {
        print(error.localizedDescription)
}
```

In this case, the error message is printed to the console. The action taken within this method is largely up to the application developer. The method, might, for example, simply display an alert to notify the user of the error.

77.9 Building and Running the Location Application

Select a suitable simulator and click on the run button located in the Xcode project window toolbar. Once the application has launched, click on the *When in Use* button at which point the request dialog shown in Figure 77-4 will appear:

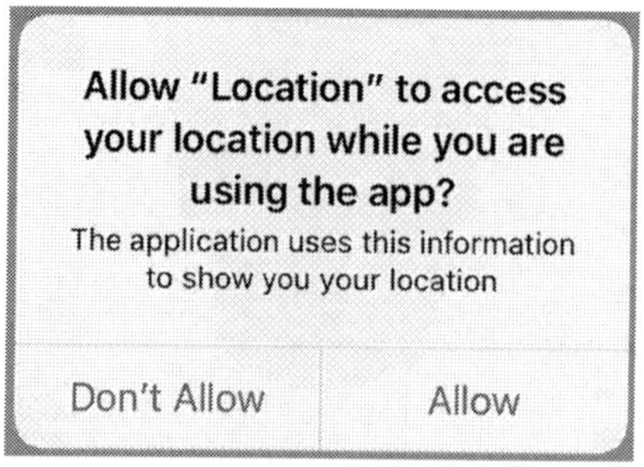

Figure 77-4

Note that this request uses the *when in use* description key and does not include the option to authorize *always* tracking. Click on the *Allow* button.

Once permission is granted, the application will begin tracking location information. By default, the iOS Simulator may be configured to have no current location causing the labels to remain unchanged. In order to simulate a location, select the iOS Simulator *Debug -> Location* menu option and select either one of the pre-defined locations or journeys (such as City Bicycle Ride), or *Custom Location...* to enter a specific latitude and longitude. The following figure shows the application running in the iOS Simulator after the *Apple* location has been selected from the menu:

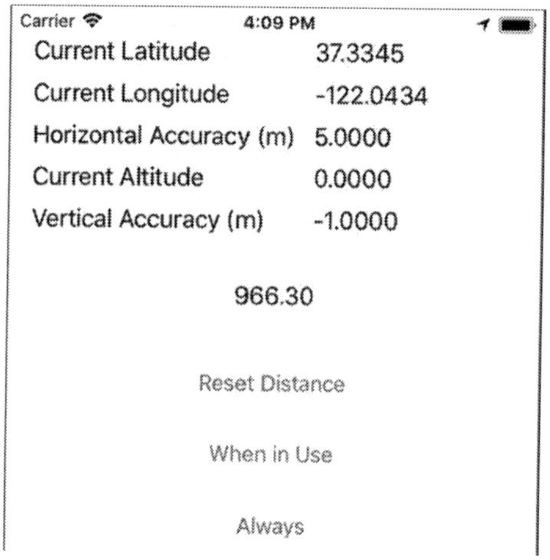

Figure 77-5

One point to note is that the distance data relates to the distance between two points, not the distance travelled. For example, if the device accompanies the user on a 10 mile trip that returns to the start location the distance will be displayed as 0 (since the start and end points are the same).

Next, click on the *Always* button to display the permission request dialog. As shown in Figure 77-6, the request dialog will appear containing the second usage description key together with options to retain the *when in use* setting or to switch to *Always* mode.

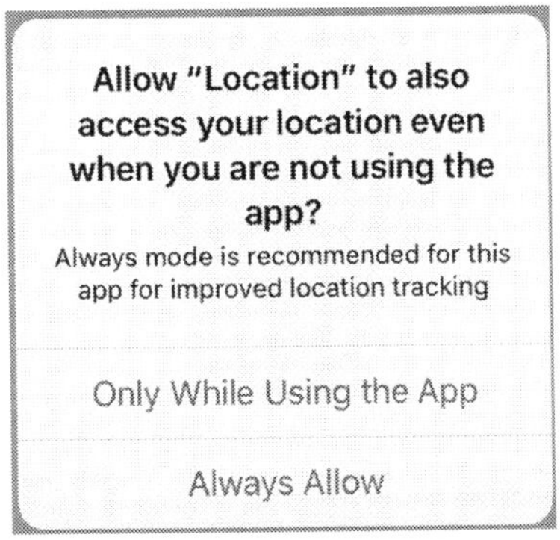

Figure 77-6

Click on the *Allow Always* button and verify that the location data continues to update.

77.10 Adding Continuous Background Location Updates

The next step is to demonstrate continuous background location updates in action. Begin by modifying the *didUpdateLocations* delegate method to print the longitude and latitude value to the Xcode console. This will allow us to verify that updating continues after the app is suspended:

```
func locationManager(_ manager: CLLocationManager,
                     didUpdateLocations locations: [CLLocation]) {
.
.
    distance.text = String(format: "%.2f", distanceBetween)

    print("Latitude = \(latestLocation.coordinate.latitude)")
    print("Longitude = \(latestLocation.coordinate.longitude)")
}
```

After making this change, run the app and click on the *When in Use* button. If necessary, select the *Freeway Drive* option from the *Debug -> Location* menu and verify that the latitude and longitude updates appear in the Xcode console panel. Click on the home button (or select the *Hardware -> Home* menu option) and note that the location updates no longer appear in the console.

Within the *ViewController.swift* file, edit the *startWhenInUse* method to enable continuous background updates:

```
@IBAction func startWhenInUse(_ sender: Any) {
    locationManager.requestWhenInUseAuthorization()
    locationManager.startUpdatingLocation()
    locationManager.allowsBackgroundLocationUpdates = true
    locationManager.pausesLocationUpdatesAutomatically = true
}
```

The project will also need to be configured to enable background location updates. Select the Location target at the top of the project navigator panel followed by the *Capabilities* tab in the main panel. Locate and enable the Background Modes capability and turn on the *Location updates* mode:

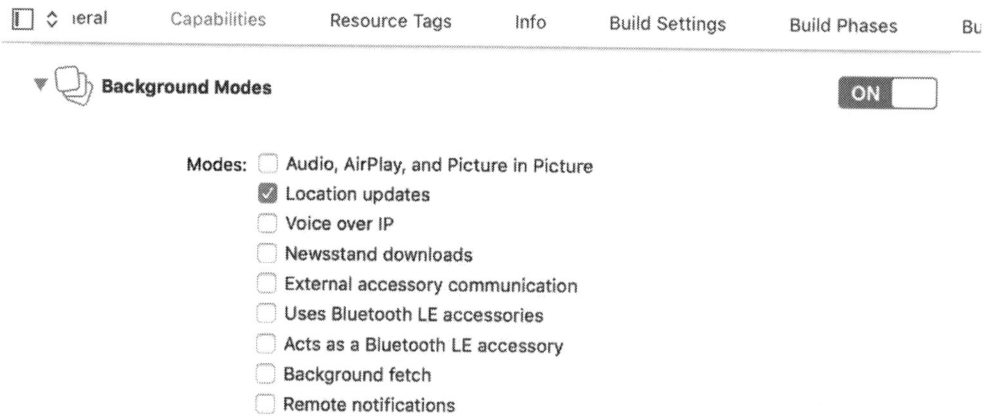

Figure 77-7

Run the app once again, click on the *When in Use* button followed by the Home button. Note that this time the location updates continue to appear in the Xcode console.

Since the app currently has *Always* authorization, the blue notification bar does not appear when the app is placed into the background. To see the notification bar in action, stop the app and delete it from the simulator to reset the location authentication settings. Once the app has been removed, install and run it again before clicking on the *When In Use* button followed by the *Allow* button in the permission request dialog. When location updates begin, clicking on the Home button should cause the updates to continue as before, but this time the blue notification bar (Figure 77-8) should be visible. Tap the notification to open the app once again.

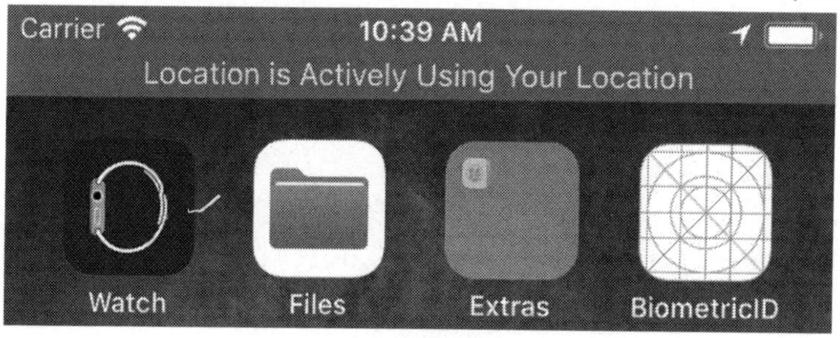

Figure 77-8

77.11 Summary

This chapter has made practical use of the features of the Core Location framework. Topics covered include the configuration of an app project to support core location updates, the differences between *always* and *when in use* location authorizations and the code necessary to initiate and handle location update events. The chapter also included a demonstration of the use of continuous background location updates.

Chapter 78

78. Working with Maps on iOS 12 with MapKit and the MKMapView Class

In the preceding chapters we spent some time looking at handling raw geographical location information in the form of longitude, latitude and altitude data. The next step is to learn about the presentation of location information to the user in the form of maps and satellite images. The goal of this chapter, therefore, is to provide an overview of the steps necessary to present the application user with location, map and satellite imagery using the MapKit Framework and, in particular, the MKMapView class. In the next chapters, this example application will be extended to make use of the Map Kit local search and directions features.

78.1 About the MapKit Framework

The MapKit Framework is based on the Apple Maps data and APIs and provides iOS developers with a simple mechanism for integrating detailed and interactive mapping capabilities into any application.

The core element of the MapKit Framework from the point of view of the app developer is the MKMapView class. This class is a subclass of UIView and provides a canvas onto which map and satellite information may be presented to the user. Information may be presented in map, satellite or hybrid (whereby the map is superimposed onto the satellite image) form. The displayed geographical region may be changed manually by the user via a process of pinching stretching and panning gestures, or programmatically from within the application code via method calls and property manipulation on the MkMapView instance. The current location of the device may also be displayed and tracked on the map view.

The MapKit Framework also includes support for adding annotations to a map. This takes the form of a pin or custom image, title and subview that may be used to mark specific locations on a map. Alternatively the annotation can take the form of a custom view controller.

Implementation of the MKMapViewDelegate protocol allows an application to receive notifications of events relating to the map view such as a change in either the location of the user or region of the map displayed or the failure of the device to identify the user's current location or to download map data.

78.2 Understanding Map Regions

The area of the map that is currently displayed to the user is referred to as the *region*. This is defined in terms of a *center location* (declared by longitude and latitude) and span of the surrounding area to be displayed. Adjusting the span has the effect of zooming in and out of the map relative to the specified center location. The region's span may be specified using either distance (in meters) or coordinate based degrees. When using degrees, one degree of latitude is equivalent to 111 km. Latitude, however, varies depending on the longitudinal distance from the equator. Given this complexity, the map view tutorial in this chapter will declare the span in terms of distance.

78.3 Getting Transit ETA Information

A MapKit feature that was introduced in iOS 9 allows the departure and arrival times and estimated travel duration to a destination using public transit to be obtained from within an iOS app. This involves the use of an MKDirections.Request object configured for travel by transit and initialized with start and end locations combined with a call to the *calculateETA(completionHandler:)* method of an appropriately configured MKDirections instance. The following method, for example, outputs the estimated arrival time for a journey by transit from the Empire State Building in New York to JFK Airport:

```
func getTransitETA() {
    let request = MKDirections.Request()
    let source = MKMapItem(placemark:
      MKPlacemark(coordinate:CLLocationCoordinate2D(latitude: 40.748384,
            longitude: -73.985479), addressDictionary: nil))
    source.name = "Empire State Building"
    request.source = source

    let destination = MKMapItem(placemark:
      MKPlacemark(coordinate:CLLocationCoordinate2D(latitude: 40.643351,
            longitude: -73.788969), addressDictionary: nil))
    destination.name = "JFK Airport"
    request.destination = destination

    request.transportType = MKDirectionsTransportType.transit

    let directions = MKDirections(request: request)
    directions.calculateETA {
        (response, error) -> Void in
        if error == nil {
            if let estimate = response {
                print("Travel time \(estimate.expectedTravelTime / 60)")
                print("Departing at \(estimate.expectedDepartureDate)")
                print("Arriving at \(estimate.expectedArrivalDate)")
            }
        }
    }
}
```

78.4 About the MKMapView Tutorial

The objective of this tutorial is to develop an iOS application designed to display a map with a marker indicating the user's current location. Buttons located in a navigation bar are provided to allow the user to zoom in on the current location and to toggle between map and satellite views. Through the implementation of the MKMapViewDelegate protocol the map will update as the user's location changes so that the current location marker is always the center point of the displayed map region.

78.5 Creating the Map Project

Begin by launching Xcode and creating a new iOS project named *MapSample* using the *Single View Application* template and the Swift programming language.

78.6 Adding the Navigation Controller

Later stages of this tutorial will require the services of a navigation controller. Since the presence of the navigation bar will have implications for the layout of the user interface of the main view, it makes sense to add the controller now. Select the *Main.storyboard* file from the project navigator panel followed by the view controller view so that it highlights in blue and use the *Editor -> Embed In -> Navigation Controller* menu option to embed a controller into the storyboard as illustrated in Figure 78-1:

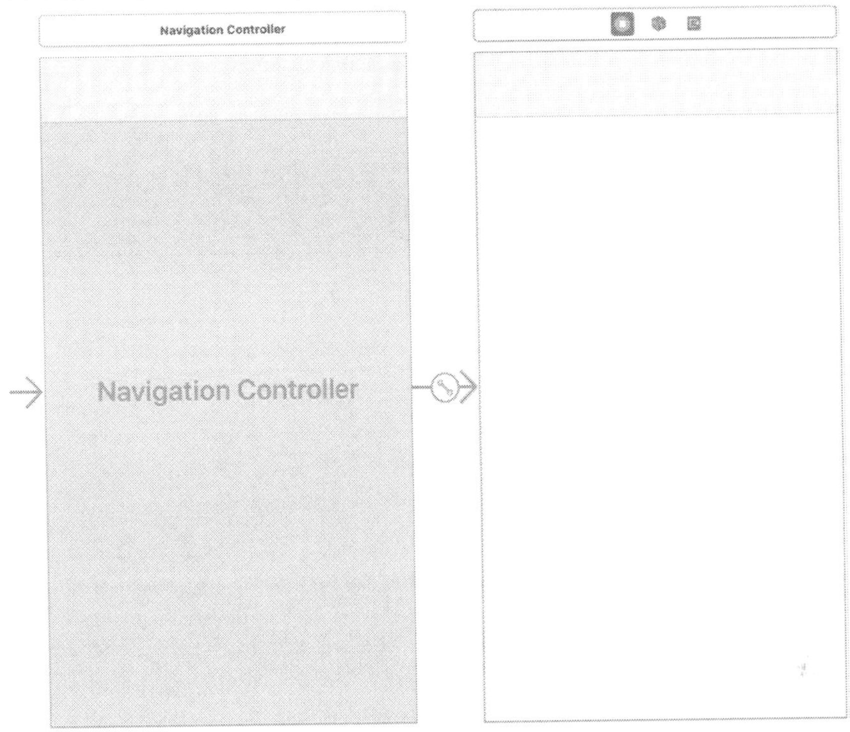

Figure 78-1

78.7 Creating the MKMapView Instance and Toolbar

The next step is to create an instance of the MKMapView class we will be using in our application and to add a toolbar instance to the user interface. Remaining in the *Main.storyboard* file, drag a *Toolbar* from the Library panel and place it at the bottom of the view canvas.

Next, drag and drop a Map Kit View object onto the canvas and resize and position it so that it takes up the remaining space in the view above the toolbar and below the navigation bar. By default the Interface Builder tool will have added a single *Bar Button Item* to the new toolbar. For the purposes of this example, however, two buttons will be required so drag and drop a second Bar Button Item from the Library panel onto the toolbar. Double-click on the toolbar button items and change the text to “Zoom” and “Type” respectively:

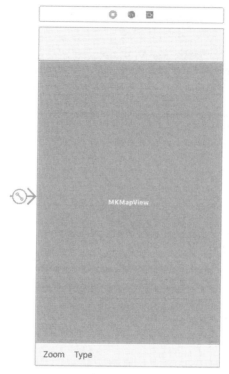

Figure 78-2

Select the MKMapView object in the scene and use the Auto Layout *Add New Constraints* menu located in the lower right-hand corner of the Interface Builder panel to configure *Spacing to nearest neighbor* constraints of 0 on all four sides of the view with the *Constrain to margins* option switched off. Once the four constraints have been added to the MKMapView object, repeat these steps with the Toolbar view selected.

Select the MKMapView object in the view canvas, display the Assistant Editor panel and verify that the editor is displaying the contents of the *ViewController.swift* file. Ctrl-click on the MKMapView object and drag to a position just below the class declaration line in the Assistant Editor. Release the line and in the resulting connection dialog establish an outlet connection named *mapView*.

Click on the "Zoom" button to select it (note that in order to select a toolbar button item it may be necessary to click on it twice since the first click selects the toolbar parent). With the button item selected, Ctrl-click on the button object and drag the line to the area immediately beneath the *viewDidLoad* method in the Assistant Editor panel. Release the line and, within the resulting connection dialog, establish an Action method on the *Touch Up Inside* event configured to call a method named *zoomIn*. Repeat this step to connect the "Type" button to a method named *changeMapType*.

Select the *ViewController.swift* file from the project navigator panel and verify that the outlets and actions have been set up correctly. Also take this opportunity to import the MapKit framework and to declare the class as implementing the MKMapViewDelegate protocol:

```
import UIKit
import MapKit

class ViewController: UIViewController, MKMapViewDelegate {
```

```
    @IBOutlet weak var mapView: MKMapView!

    override func viewDidLoad() {
        super.viewDidLoad()
    }

    @IBAction func zoomIn(_ sender: Any) {
    }


    @IBAction func changeMapType(_ sender: Any) {
    }
.
.
.
}
```

Perform a test run of the application's progress so far by clicking on the run button in the Xcode toolbar. The application should run on the iOS simulator or device as illustrated in Figure 78-3:

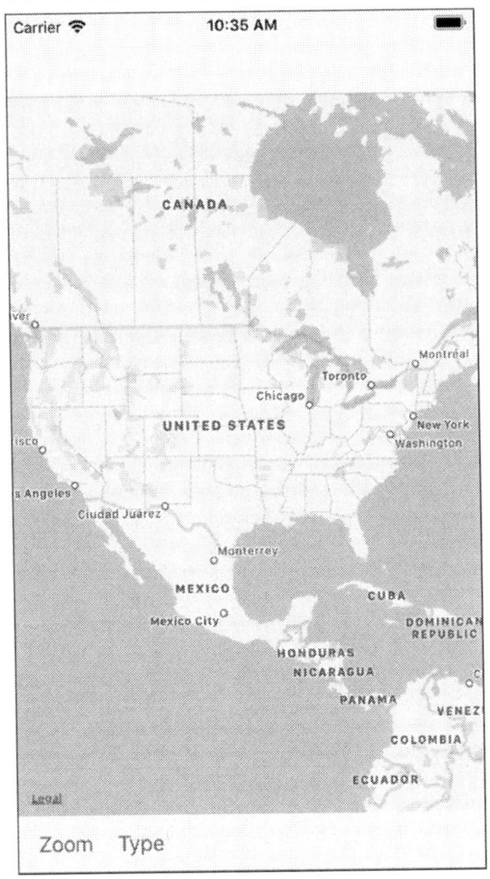

Figure 78-3

78.8 Obtaining Location Information Permission

The next task is to request permission from the user to track the current location of the device. Since this needs to occur when the application loads, an ideal location is in the application delegate *didFinishLaunchingWithOptions* method in the *AppDelegate.swift* file:

```
import UIKit
import CoreLocation

@UIApplicationMain
class AppDelegate: UIResponder, UIApplicationDelegate {

    var window: UIWindow?
    var locationManager: CLLocationManager?

    func application(_ application: UIApplication,
                didFinishLaunchingWithOptions launchOptions:
                    [UIApplicationLaunchOptionsKey: Any]?) -> Bool {

        locationManager = CLLocationManager()
        locationManager?.requestWhenInUseAuthorization()

        return true
    }
.
.
}
```

78.9 Setting up the Usage Description Keys

The above code changes included a method call to request permission from the user to track location information when the application is running in the foreground. This method call must be accompanied by the usage description strings which need to be added to the project's *Info.plist* file. Within the project navigator panel, load the *Info.plist* file into the editor. The key-value pairs need to be added to the *Information Property List* dictionary. Select this entry in the list and click on the + button to add a new entry to the dictionary and, from the resulting menu, select the *Privacy – Location When in Use Usage Description* item. Once the key has been added, double-click in the corresponding value column and enter the following text:

```
This information is required to show your current location
```

Repeat this step, this time adding a *Privacy - Location Always and When In Use Usage Description* key set to the following string value:

```
Always mode is recommended for this app for improved location tracking
```

78.10 Configuring the Map View

By default the Map View does not indicate the user's current location. By setting the *showsUserLocation* property of the MKMapView class the map is instructed to display a representation of the current location on the map in the form of a blue marker. Before user location information can be obtained, however, it is first necessary to seek permission from the user. In order to achieve these goals, select the *ViewController.swift* file and locate and modify the *viewDidLoad* method as follows:

```
override func viewDidLoad() {
    super.viewDidLoad()
    mapView.showsUserLocation = true
}
```

78.11 Changing the MapView Region

When the Zoom button is tapped by the user the map view region needs to be changed so that the user's current location is set as the center location and the region span needs to be changed to 2000 meters (analogous to zooming in to the map region). The code to implement this belongs in the *zoomIn* method which now needs to be implemented in the *ViewController.swift* file:

```
@IBAction func zoomIn(_ sender: Any) {

    if let userLocation = mapView.userLocation.location?.coordinate {

        let region = MKCoordinateRegion(
                center: userLocation, latitudinalMeters: 2000,
                                        longitudinalMeters: 2000)


        mapView.setRegion(region, animated: true)
    }
}
```

This method performs some very simple operations in order to achieve the desired effect in the mapView object. First, the user's current location coordinates are ascertained by accessing the *userLocation* property of the map view object which, in turn, contains the coordinates of the user. Next, the *MKCoordinateRegionMakeWithDistance* function is called in order to generate an MKCoordinateRegion object consisting of the user's location coordinates and a span that stretches 2000 meters both to the North and South of the current location. Finally, this region object is passed through to the *setRegion* method of the mapView object.

Now that the Zoom functionality has been implemented it is time to configure the map type switching feature of the application.

78.12 Changing the Map Type

The map type of a map view is controlled by the object's *mapType* property. Supported values for this property are MKMapType.standard, MKMapType.mutedStandard, MKMapType.satellite MKMapType.hybrid, MKMapType.satelliteFlyover and MKMapType.hybridFlyover. For the purposes of this example application the map will switch between standard and satellite modes. Within the *ViewController.swift* file modify the *changeMapType* action method connected to the Type button as follows:

```
@IBAction func changeMapType(_ sender: Any) {
    if mapView.mapType == MKMapType.standard {
        mapView.mapType = MKMapType.satellite
    } else {
        mapView.mapType = MKMapType.standard
```

```
    }
}
```

This very simple method simply toggles between the two map types when the button is tapped by the user.

78.13 Testing the MapView Application

Now that more functionality has been implemented, it is a good time to build and run the application again so click on the Xcode *Run* button to load the application into the iOS Simulator. Once the application has loaded, a blue dot should appear over Northern California. Since the application is running in the simulator environment, the location information is simulated to match either the coordinates of Apple's headquarters in Cupertino, CA, or another simulated location depending on the current setting of the *Debug -> Location* menu.

Select the Type button to display the satellite view and then zoom in to get a better look at the region:

Figure 78-4

To get real location information, load the application onto a physical iOS device.

78.14 Updating the Map View based on User Movement

Assuming that you installed the application on a physical iOS device and went somewhere with the device in your possession (or used one of the debug location settings that simulated movement) you may have noticed that the map did not update as your location changed and that the blue dot marking your current location eventually went off the screen (also assuming, of course, that you had zoomed in to a significant degree).

In order to configure the application so that the map automatically tracks the movements of the user, the first step is to make sure the application is notified when the location changes. At the start of this tutorial the view controller was declared as conforming to the MKMapViewDelegate delegate protocol. One of the methods that comprise this protocol is the *mapView(didUpdate userLocation:)* method. When implemented, this method is called by the map view object whenever the location of the device changes. We must, therefore, first specify that the MapSampleViewController class is the delegate for the mapView object, which can be performed by adding the following line to the *viewDidLoad* method located in the *ViewController.swift* file:

```
mapView.delegate = self
```

The next task involves the implementation of the *mapView(didUpdate userLocation:)* method in the *ViewController.swift* file:

```
func mapView(_ mapView: MKMapView, didUpdate
        userLocation: MKUserLocation) {
    mapView.centerCoordinate = userLocation.location!.coordinate
}
```

The delegate method is passed as an argument an MKUserLocation object containing the current location coordinates of the user. This value is simply assigned to the center coordinate property of the mapView object such that the current location remains at the center of the region. When the application is now installed and run on a device the current location will no longer move outside the displayed region as the device location changes. To experience this effect within the simulator, simply select the *Debug -> Location -> Freeway Drive* menu option and then select the Zoom button in the user interface.

78.15 Summary

This chapter has demonstrated the basics of using the MKMapView class to display map based information to the user within an iOS 12 application. The example created in the chapter also highlighted the steps involved in zooming into a region of the map, changing the map display type and configuring a map to track the user's current location.

The next chapter will explore the use of the local search feature of the MapKit Framework before extending the example application to mark all the locations of a specified business type on the map.

Chapter 79

79. Working with MapKit Local Search in iOS 12

This chapter will explore the use of the iOS MapKit MKLocalSearchRequest class to search for map locations within an iOS application. The example application created in the chapter entitled *Working with Maps on iOS 12 with MapKit and the MKMapView Class* will then be extended to demonstrate local search in action.

79.1 An Overview of iOS Local Search

Local search is implemented using the MKLocalSearch class. The purpose of this class is to allow users to search for map locations using natural language strings. Once the search has completed, the class returns a list of locations within a specified region that match the search string. A search for "Pizza", for example, will return a list of locations for any pizza restaurants within a specified area. Search requests are encapsulated in instances of the MKLocalSearchRequest class and results are returned within an MKLocalSearchResponse object which, in turn, contains an MKMapItem object for each matching location.

Local searches are performed asynchronously and a completion handler called when the search is complete. It is also important to note that the search is performed remotely on Apple's servers as opposed to locally on the device. Local search is, therefore, only available when the device has an active internet connection and is able to communicate with the search server.

The following code fragment, for example, searches for pizza locations within the currently displayed region of an MKMapView instance named *mapView*. Having performed the search, the code iterates through the results and outputs the name and phone number of each matching location to the console:

```
let request = MKLocalSearchRequest()
request.naturalLanguageQuery = "Pizza"
request.region = mapView.region

let search = MKLocalSearch(request: request)

    search.start(completionHandler: {(response, error) in

        if error != nil {
            print("Error occurred in search:
                     \(error!.localizedDescription)")
        } else if response!.mapItems.count == 0 {
            print("No matches found")
        } else {
            print("Matches found")

            for item in response!.mapItems {
```

```
                print("Name = \(item.name)")
                print("Phone = \(item.phoneNumber)")
            }
        }
})
```

The above code begins by creating an MKLocalSearchRequest request instance initialized with the search string (in this case "Pizza"). The region of the request is then set to the currently displayed region of the map view instance.

```
let request = MKLocalSearchRequest()
request.naturalLanguageQuery = "Pizza"
request.region = mapView.region
```

An MKLocalSearch instance is then created and initialized with a reference to the search request instance and the search then initiated via a call to the object's *start(completionHandler:)* method.

```
search.start(completionHandler: {(response, error) in
```

The code in the completion handler checks the response to make sure that matches were found and then accesses the *mapItems* property of the response which contains an array of mapItem instances for the matching locations. The *name* and *phoneNumber* properties of each mapItem instance are then displayed in the console:

```
if error != nil {
    print("Error occurred in search: \(error!.localizedDescription)")
} else if response!.mapItems.count == 0 {
    print("No matches found")
} else {
    print("Matches found")

    for item in response!.mapItems {
        print("Name = \(item.name)")
        print("Phone = \(item.phoneNumber)")
    }
  }
})
```

79.2 Adding Local Search to the MapSample Application

In the remainder of this chapter, the MapSample application will be extended so that the user can perform a local search. The first step in this process involves adding a text field to the first storyboard scene. Begin by launching Xcode and opening the MapSample project created in the previous chapter.

79.3 Adding the Local Search Text Field

With the project loaded into Xcode, select the *Main.storyboard* file and modify the user interface to add a Text Field object to the user interface layout (reducing the height of the map view object accordingly to make room for the new field). With the new Text Field selected, display the Attributes Inspector and enter *Local Search* into the Placeholder property field. When completed, the layout should resemble that of Figure 79-1:

Figure 79-1

Select the Map Sample view controller by clicking on the toolbar at the top of the scene so that the scene is highlighted in blue. Select the *Resolve Auto Layout Issues* menu from the toolbar in the lower right-hand corner of the storyboard canvas and select the *Reset to Suggested Constraints* menu option located beneath *All Views in View Controller*.

When the user touches the text field, the keyboard will appear. By default this will display a "Return" key. For the purposes of this application, however, a "Search" key would be more appropriate. To make this modification, select the new Text Field object, display the Attributes Inspector and change the *Return Key* setting from *Default* to *Search*.

Next, display the Assistant Editor panel and make sure that it is displaying the content of the *ViewController.swift* file. Ctrl-click on the Text Field object and drag the resulting line to the Assistant Editor panel and establish an outlet named *searchText*.

Repeat the above step, this time setting up an Action for the Text Field to call a method named *textFieldReturn* for the *Did End on Exit* event. Be sure to set the Type menu to *UITextField* as shown in Figure 79-2 before clicking on the *Connect* button:

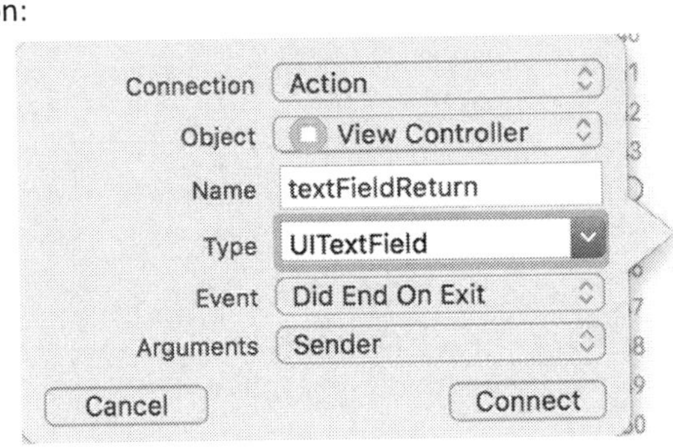

Figure 79-2

The *textFieldReturn* method will be required to perform three tasks when triggered. In the first instance it will be required to hide the keyboard from view. When matches are found for the search results, an annotation will be added to the map for each location. The second task to be performed by this method is to remove any annotations created as a result of a previous search.

Finally, the *textFieldReturn* method will initiate the search using the string entered into the text field by the user. Select the *ViewController.swift* file, locate the template *textFieldReturn* method and implement it so that it reads as follows:

```
@IBAction func textFieldReturn(_ sender: UITextField) {
    _ = sender.resignFirstResponder()
    mapView.removeAnnotations(mapView.annotations)
    self.performSearch()
}
```

79.4 Performing the Local Search

The next task is to write the code to perform the search. When the user touches the keyboard *Search* key, the above *textFieldReturn* method is called which, in turn, has been written such that it makes a call to a method named *performSearch*. Remaining within the *ViewController.swift* file, this method may now be implemented as follows:

```
func performSearch() {

    matchingItems.removeAll()
    let request = MKLocalSearch.Request()
    request.naturalLanguageQuery = searchText.text
    request.region = mapView.region

    let search = MKLocalSearch(request: request)

    search.start(completionHandler: {(response, error) in

        if let results = response {

            if let err = error {
                print("Error occurred in search:
\(err.localizedDescription)")
            } else if results.mapItems.count == 0 {
                print("No matches found")
            } else {
                print("Matches found")

                for item in results.mapItems {
                    print("Name = \(item.name ?? "No match")")
                    print("Phone = \(item.phoneNumber ?? "No Match")")

                    self.matchingItems.append(item as MKMapItem)
```

```
                    print("Matching items = \(self.matchingItems.count)")

                    let annotation = MKPointAnnotation()
                    annotation.coordinate = item.placemark.coordinate
                    annotation.title = item.name
                    self.mapView.addAnnotation(annotation)
                }
            }
        }
    })
}
```

Next, edit the *ViewController.swift* file to add the declaration for the *matchingItems* array referenced in the above method. This array is used to store the current search matches and will be used later in the tutorial:

```
import UIKit
import MapKit

class ViewController: UIViewController, MKMapViewDelegate {

    @IBOutlet weak var mapView: MKMapView!
    @IBOutlet weak var searchText: UITextField!
    var matchingItems: [MKMapItem] = [MKMapItem]()
.
.
```

The code in the *performSearch* method is largely the same as that outlined earlier in the chapter, the major difference being the addition of code to add an annotation to the map for each matching location:

```
let annotation = MKPointAnnotation()
annotation.coordinate = item.placemark.coordinate
annotation.title = item.name
self.mapView.addAnnotation(annotation)
```

Annotations are represented by instances of the MKPointAnnotation class and are, by default, represented by red pin markers on the map view (though custom icons may be specified). The coordinates of each match are obtained by accessing the placemark instance within each item. The title of the annotation is also set in the above code using the item's *name* property.

79.5 Testing the Application

Compile and run the application on an iOS device and, once running, select the zoom button before entering the name of a type of business into the local search field such as "pizza", "library" or "coffee". Touch the keyboard "Search" button and, assuming such businesses exist within the currently displayed map region, an annotation marker will appear for each matching location (Figure 79-3):

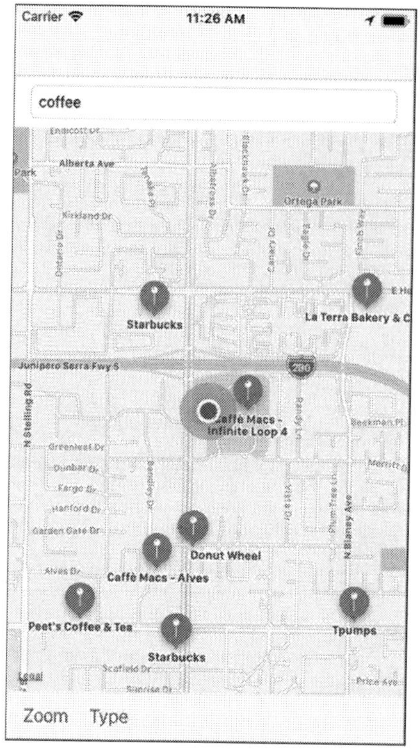

Figure 79-3

Local searches are not limited to business locations. It can also be used, for example, as an alternative to geocoding for finding local addresses.

79.6 Customized Annotation Markers

By default the annotation markers appear with a red background and a white push pin icon (referred to as the *glyph*). To change the appearance of the annotations the first step is to implement the *mapView(_:viewFor:)* delegate method within the *ViewController.swift* file. When implemented, this method will be called each time an annotation is added to the map. The method is passed the MKAnnotation object to be added and needs to return an MKMarkerAnnotationView object configured with appropriate settings ready to be displayed on the map. In the same way that the UITableView class reuses table cells, the MapView class also maintains a queue of MKMarkerAnnotationView objects ready to be used. This dramatically increases map performance when working with large volumes of annotations.

Within the *ViewController.swift* file, implement a basic form of this method as follows:

```
func mapView(_ mapView: MKMapView, viewFor annotation: MKAnnotation)
    -> MKAnnotationView? {

    let identifier = "marker"
    var view: MKMarkerAnnotationView

    if let dequeuedView = mapView.dequeueReusableAnnotationView(
                                withIdentifier: identifier)
                                    as? MKMarkerAnnotationView {
```

```
        dequeuedView.annotation = annotation
        view = dequeuedView
    } else {
        view =
          MKMarkerAnnotationView(annotation: annotation,
               reuseIdentifier: identifier)
    }
    return view
}
```

The method begins by specifying an identifier for the annotation type. If a map is to display different categories of annotation, each category will need a unique identifier. The code then checks to see if an existing annotation view with the specified identifier is available to be reused. If one is available it is returned and displayed on the map. If no reusable annotation views are available, a new one is created consisting of the annotation object passed to the method and with the identifier string.

Run the app now, zoom in on the current location and perform a search that will result in annotations appearing. Since no customizations have been made to the MKMarkerAnnotationView object, the location markers appear as before.

Modify the *mapView(_:viewFor:)* method as follows to change the color of the marker and to display text instead of the glyph icon:

```
func mapView(_ mapView: MKMapView, viewFor annotation: MKAnnotation)
  -> MKAnnotationView? {
.
.
    } else {
        view = MKMarkerAnnotationView(annotation: annotation,
                reuseIdentifier: identifier)
        view.markerTintColor = UIColor.blue
        view.glyphText = "Here"
    }
    return view
}
```

When the app is now tested, the markers appear with a blue background and display text which reads “Here” as shown in Figure 79-4:

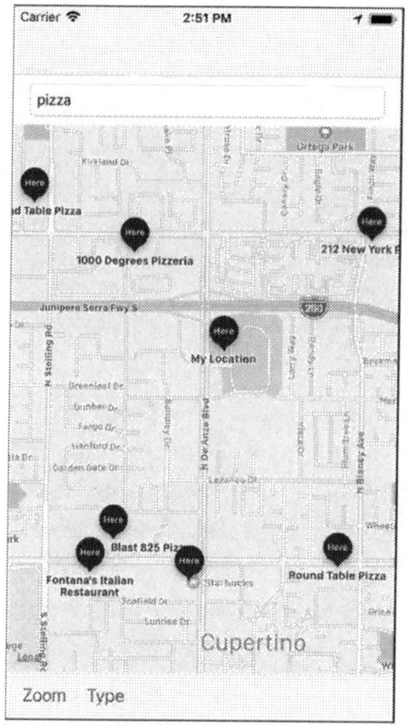

Figure 79-4

The default glyph icon may also be replaced by a different image. Ideally two images should be assigned, one sized at 20x20px to be displayed on the standard marker and a larger one (40x40px) to be displayed when the marker is selected. To try this, open a Finder window and navigate to the *map_glyphs* folder of the sample code available from the following URL:

https://www.ebookfrenzy.com/retail/ios12/

This folder contains two image files named *small-business-20.png* and *small-business-40.png*. Within Xcode, select the *Assets.xcassets* entry in the project navigator panel and drag and drop the two image files from the Finder window onto the asset panel as indicated in Figure 79-5:

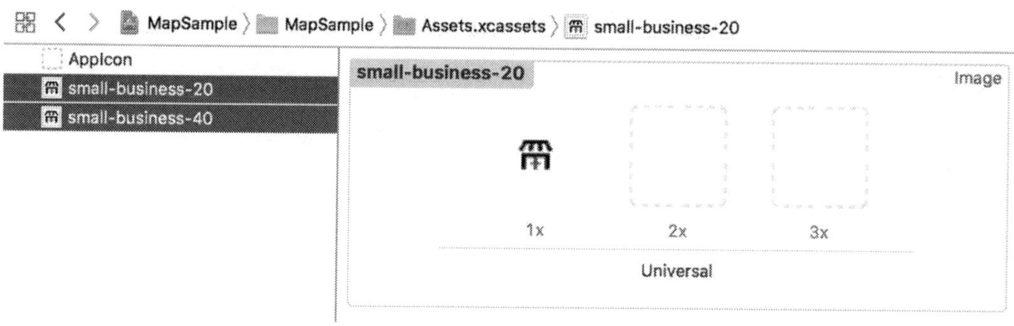

Figure 79-5

With the glyphs added, modify the code in the *mapView(_:viewFor:)* method to use these images instead of the text:

```
.
.
} else {
    view = MKMarkerAnnotationView(annotation: annotation,
```

```
                          reuseIdentifier: identifier)
    view.markerTintColor = UIColor.blue
    view.glyphText = "Here"
    view.glyphImage = UIImage(named: "small-business-20")
    view.selectedGlyphImage = UIImage(named: "small-business-40")
}
.
.
```

The markers will now display the smaller glyph when a search is performed within the app. Selecting a marker on the map will display the larger glyph image:

Figure 79-6

Another option for customizing annotation markers involves the addition of callout information which appears when a marker is selected within the app. Modify the code once again, this time adding code to add a callout to each marker:

```
} else {
    view = MKMarkerAnnotationView(annotation: annotation,
                 reuseIdentifier: identifier)
    view.markerTintColor = UIColor.blue
    view.glyphImage = UIImage(named: "small-business-20")
    view.selectedGlyphImage = UIImage(named: "small-business-40")
    view.canShowCallout = true
    view.calloutOffset = CGPoint(x: -5, y: 5)
    view.rightCalloutAccessoryView = UIButton(type: .detailDisclosure)
}
```

The new code begins by indicating that the marker is able to display a callout before specifying the position of the callout in relation to the corresponding marker. The final line of code declares a view to appear to the left of the callout text, in this case a UIButton view configured to display the standard information icon. Since UIButton is derived from UIControl, the app can receive notifications of the button being tapped by implementing the *mapView(_: calloutAccessoryControlTapped:)* delegate method. The following example implementation of this method simply outputs a message to the console when the button is tapped:

```
func mapView(_: MKMapView, annotationView:
    MKAnnotationView, calloutAccessoryControlTapped: UIControl) {
```

```
        print("Control tapped")
}
```

Run the app again, zoom in and perform a business search. When the result appears, select one of the annotations and note that the callout appears as is the case in Figure 79-7:

Figure 79-7

Click on the information button and verify that the message appears in the console window.

79.7 Annotation Marker Clustering

When too many annotations appear close together in a map it can be difficult to identify one marker from another without zooming into the area so that the markers move apart. MapKit resolves this issue by providing support for clustering of annotation markers. Clustering is enabled by assigning cluster identifiers to the MKMarkerAnnotationView objects. When a group of annotations belonging to the same cluster are grouped too closely together, a single marker appears displaying the number of annotations in the cluster.

To see clusters in action, modify the *mapView(_:viewFor:)* delegate method one last time to assign a cluster identifier to each annotation marker as follows:

```
.
.
} else {
    view = MKMarkerAnnotationView(annotation: annotation, reuseIdentifier: 
identifier)
    view.clusteringIdentifier = "myCluster"
    view.markerTintColor = UIColor.blue
.
.
```

After building and relaunching the app, enter a search term without first zooming into the map. Because the map is zoomed out the markers should be too close together to display, causing the cluster count (Figure 79-8) to appear instead:

Figure 79-8

79.8 Summary

The iOS MapKit Local Search feature allows map searches to be performed using free-form natural language strings. Once initiated, a local search will return a response containing map item objects for matching locations within a specified map region.

In this chapter the MapSample application was extended to allow the user to perform local searches and to use and customize annotations to mark matching locations on the map view in addition to marker clustering.

In the next chapter, the example will be further extended to cover the use of the Map Kit directions API, both to generate turn-by-turn directions and to draw the corresponding route on a map view.

Chapter 80

80. Using MKDirections to get iOS 12 Map Directions and Routes

This chapter will explore the use of the MapKit MKDirections class to obtain directions and route information from within an iOS application. Having covered the basics, the MapSample tutorial application will be extended to make use of these features to draw routes on a map view and display turn-by-turn driving directions.

80.1 An Overview of MKDirections

The MKDirections class was introduced into iOS as part of the iOS 7 SDK and is used to generate directions from one geographical location to another. The start and destination points for the journey are passed to an instance of the MKDirections class in the form of MKMapItem objects contained within an MKDirections.Request instance. In addition to storing the start and end points, the MKDirections.Request class also provides a number of properties that may be used to configure the request, such as indicating whether alternate route suggestions are required and specifying whether the directions should be for driving or walking.

Once directions have been requested, the MKDirections class contacts Apple's servers and awaits a response. Upon receiving a response, a completion handler is called and passed the response in the form of an MKDirections.Response object. Depending on whether or not alternate routes were requested (and assuming directions were found for the route), this object will contain one or more MKRoute objects. Each MKRoute object contains the distance, expected travel time, advisory notes and an MKPolyline object that can be used to draw the route on a map view. In addition, each MKRoute object contains an array of MKRouteStep objects, each of which contains information such as the text description of a turn-by-turn step in the route and the coordinates at which the step is to be performed. In addition, each MKRouteStep object contains a polyline object for that step and the estimated distance and travel time.

The following code fragment demonstrates an example implementation of a directions request between the user's current location and a destination location represented by an MKMapItem object named *destination*:

```
let request = MKDirections.Request()
request.source = MKMapItem.forCurrentLocation()
request.destination = destination
request.requestsAlternateRoutes = false

let directions = MKDirections(request: request)

directions.calculate(completionHandler: {(response, error) in

    if error != nil {
        print("Error getting directions")
```

```
    } else {
        self.showRoute(response)
    }
})
```

The resulting response can subsequently be used to draw the routes on a map view using the following code:

```
func showRoute(_ response: MKDirections.Response) {

    for route in response.routes {

        routeMap.add(route.polyline,
                level: MKOverlayLevel.aboveRoads)
        for step in route.steps {
            print(step.instructions)
        }
    }
}
```

The above code simply iterates through the MKRoute objects in the response and adds the polyline for each route alternate as a layer on a map view. In this instance, the overlay is configured to appear above the road names on the map.

Although the layer is added to the map view in the above code, nothing will be drawn until the *rendererFor overlay* delegate method is implemented. This method creates an instance of the MKPolylineRenderer class and then sets properties such as the line color and width:

```
func mapView(_ mapView: MKMapView, rendererFor
        overlay: MKOverlay) -> MKOverlayRenderer {

    let renderer = MKPolylineRenderer(overlay: overlay)
    renderer.strokeColor = UIColor.blue
    renderer.lineWidth = 5.0
    return renderer
}
```

Note that this method will only be called if the class in which it resides is declared as the delegate for the map view object. For example:

```
routeMap.delegate = self
```

Finally, the turn-by-turn directions for each step in the route can be accessed as follows:

```
for step in route.steps {
    print(step.instructions)
}
```

The above code simply outputs the text instructions for each step of the route. As previously discussed, additional information may also be extracted from the MKRouteStep objects as required by the application.

Having covered the basics of directions and routes in iOS, the MapSample application can be extended to put some of this theory into practice.

80.2 Adding Directions and Routes to the MapSample Application

The MapSample application will now be modified to include a *Details* button in the toolbar of the first scene. When selected, this button will display a table view listing the names and phone numbers of all locations matching the most recent local search operation. Selecting a location from the list will display another scene containing a map displaying the route from the user's current location to the selected destination.

80.3 Adding the New Classes to the Project

Load the MapSample application project into Xcode and add a new class to represent the view controller for the table view. To achieve this, select the *File -> New -> File...* menu option and create a new iOS Cocoa Touch Class file named *ResultsTableViewController* subclassed from *UITableViewController* with the *Also create XIB file* option disabled.

Since the table view will also need a class to represent the table cells, add another new class to the project named *ResultsTableCell*, this time subclassing from the UITableViewCell class.

Repeat the above steps to add a third class named *RouteViewController* subclassed from UIViewController with the *Also create XIB file* option disabled.

80.4 Configuring the Results Table View

Select the *Main.storyboard* file and drag and drop a Table View Controller object from the Library panel so that it is positioned to the right of the existing View Controller scene in the storyboard canvas (Figure 80-1):

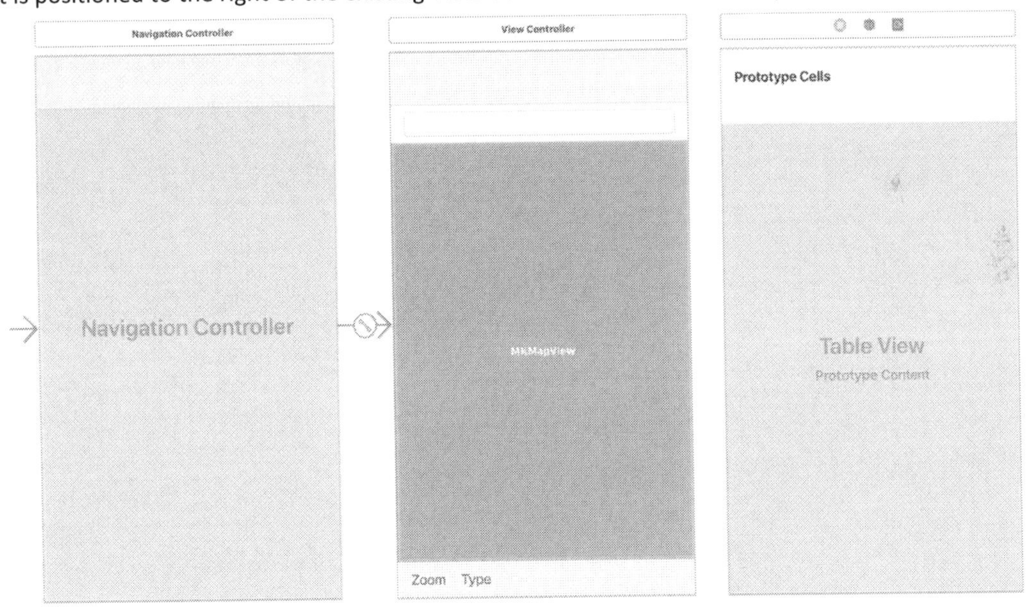

Figure 80-1

With the new controller selected, display the Identity Inspector and change the class from *UITableViewController* to *ResultsTableViewController*.

Select the prototype cell at the top of the table view and change the class setting from *UITableViewCell* to *ResultsTableCell*. With the table cell still selected, switch to the Attributes Inspector and set the *Identifier* property to *resultCell*.

Drag and drop two Label objects onto the prototype cell and position them as outlined in Figure 80-2, making sure to stretch them so that they extend to fill the width of the cell.

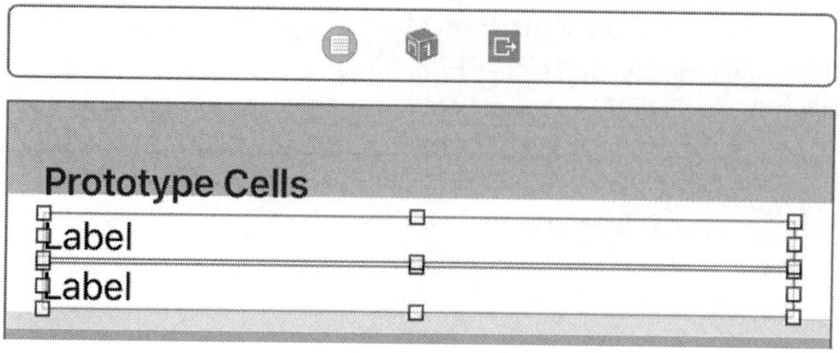

Figure 80-2

Shift-Click on the two Label views so that both are selected, display the Auto Layout *Resolve Auto Layout Issues* menu and select the *Reset to Suggested Constraints* option listed under *Selected Views.*

Display the Assistant Editor, make sure that it is displaying the *ResultsTableCell.swift* file and then establish outlets from the two labels named *nameLabel* and *phoneLabel* respectively.

Next, edit the *ResultsTableViewController.swift* file and modify it to import the MapKit Framework and to declare an array into which will be placed the MKMapItem objects representing the local search results:

```
import UIKit
import MapKit

class ResultsTableViewController: UITableViewController {

    var mapItems: [MKMapItem]?
.
.
}
```

Next, edit the file to modify the data source and delegate methods so that the table is populated with the location information when displayed (removing the #warning lines during the editing process). Note that the comment markers (/* and */) will need to be removed from around the *tableView(_:cellForRowAt:)* method:

```
override func numberOfSections(in tableView: UITableView) -> Int {
    return 1
}

override func tableView(_ tableView: UITableView, numberOfRowsInSection
section: Int) -> Int {
    return mapItems?.count ?? 0
}

override func tableView(_ tableView: UITableView, cellForRowAt indexPath:
IndexPath) -> UITableViewCell {
```

```
    let cell = tableView.dequeueReusableCell(
        withIdentifier: "resultCell", for: indexPath) as! ResultsTableCell

    // Configure the cell...
    let row = indexPath.row

    if let item = mapItems?[row] {
        cell.nameLabel.text = item.name
        cell.phoneLabel.text = item.phoneNumber
    }
    return cell
}
```

With the results table view configured, the next step is to add a segue from the first scene to this scene.

80.5 Implementing the Result Table View Segue

Select the *Main.storyboard* file and drag and drop an additional Bar Button Item from the Library panel to the toolbar in the Map Sample View Controller scene. Double-click on this new button and change the text to *Details*:

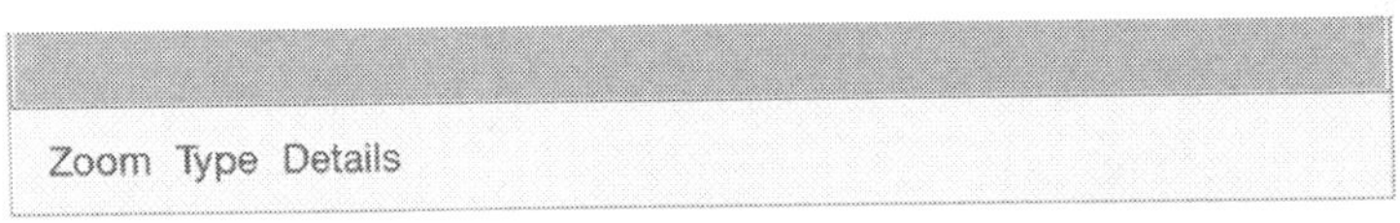

Figure 80-3

Click on the Details button to select it (it may be necessary to click twice since the first click will select the Toolbar). Establish a segue by Ctrl-clicking on the Details button and dragging to the Results Table View Controller and select *Show* from the *Action Segue* menu.

When the segue is triggered, the *mapItems* property of the ResultsTableViewController instance needs to be updated with the array of locations created by the local search. This can be performed in the *prepare(for segue:)* method which needs to be implemented in the *ViewController.swift* file as follows:

```
override func prepare(for segue: UIStoryboardSegue, sender: Any?) {

    let destination = segue.destination as!
                        ResultsTableViewController

    destination.mapItems = self.matchingItems
}
```

With the Results scene complete, compile and run the application on a device or simulator. Perform a search for a business type that returns valid results before selecting the Details toolbar button. The results table should subsequently appear (Figure 80-4) listing the names and phone numbers for the matching locations:

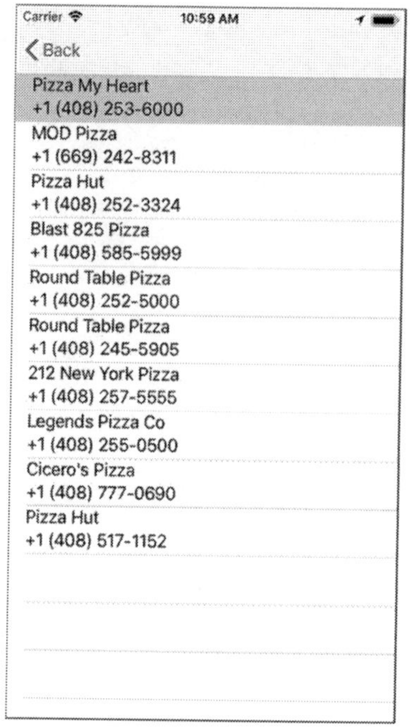

Figure 80-4

80.6 Adding the Route Scene

The last task is to display a second map view and draw on it the route from the user's current location to the location selected from the results table. The class for this scene (RouteViewController) was added earlier in the chapter so the next step is to add a scene to the storyboard and associate it with this class.

Begin by selecting the *Main.storyboard* file and dragging and dropping a View Controller item from the Library panel so that it is positioned to the right of the Results Table View Controller scene (Figure 80-5). With the new view controller scene selected (so that it appears with a blue border) display the Identity Inspector and change the class from *UIViewController* to *RouteViewController*.

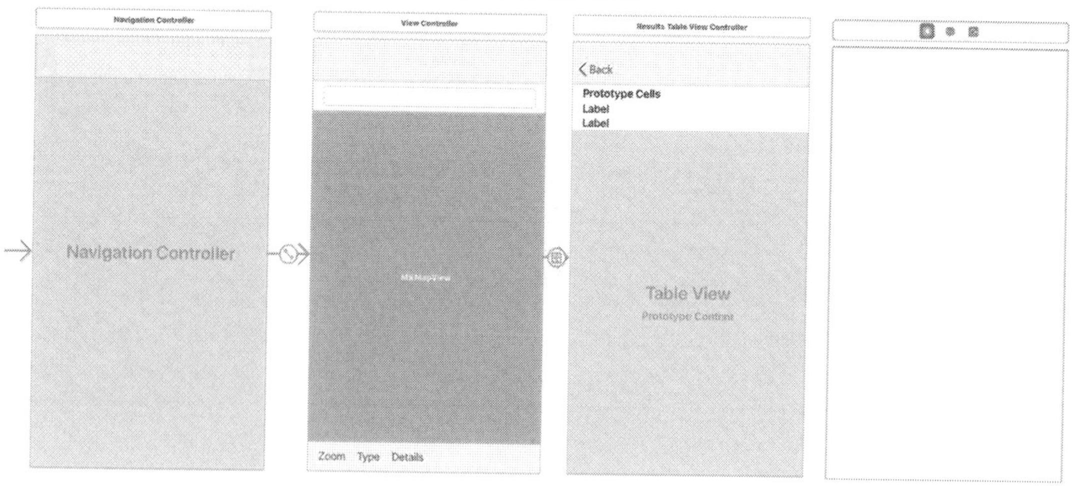

Figure 80-5

Drag and drop a MapKit View object into the new view controller scene and position it so that it occupies the entire view. Using the Auto Layout *Add New Constraints* menu, set *Spacing to nearest neighbor* constraints of 0 on all four sides of the view with the *Constrain to margins* option switched off.

Display the Assistant Editor, make sure it is displaying the content of the *RouteViewController.swift* file and then establish an outlet from the map view instance named *routeMap.* Remaining in the *RouteViewController.swift* file, add an import directive to the MapKit framework, a property into which will be stored a reference to the destination map item and a declaration that this class implements the MKMapViewDelegate protocol. With these changes implemented, the file should read as follows:

```
import UIKit
import MapKit

class RouteViewController: UIViewController {

    var destination: MKMapItem?
.
.
}
```

Now that the route scene has been added, it is time to add some code to it to establish the current location and to generate and then draw the route on the map.

80.7 Identifying the User's Current Location

Remaining within the *RouteViewController.swift* file, modify the *viewDidLoad* method to display the user's current location in the map view and set this class as the delegate for the map view:

```
override func viewDidLoad() {
     super.viewDidLoad()
     routeMap.delegate = self
     routeMap.showsUserLocation = true
}
```

The app is going to need to change the displayed map view region so that it is centered on the user's current location. One way to obtain this information would be to access the *userLocation* property of the MapView instance. The problem with this approach is that it is not possible to know when the map object has calculated the current location. This exposes the app to the risk that an attempt to set the region will be made before the location information has been identified. To avoid this problem, the *requestLocation* method of a CLLocationManager instance will instead be used. Since this method triggers a delegate call when the current location has been obtained, we can safely put the code to use the location within that delegate method.

Begin by importing the CoreLocation framework into the *RouteViewController.swift* file and declaring the class as implementing both the MKMapViewDelegate and CLLocationManagerDelegate protocols. A constant referencing a CLLocationManager object and a variable in which to store the current location also needs to be declared:

```
import UIKit
import MapKit
import CoreLocation
```

```
class RouteViewController: UIViewController, MKMapViewDelegate,
CLLocationManagerDelegate {

    var destination: MKMapItem?
    @IBOutlet weak var routeMap: MKMapView!
    var locationManager: CLLocationManager = CLLocationManager()
    var userLocation: CLLocation?
.
.
.
```

Next implement the two Core Location delegate methods:

```
func locationManager(_ manager: CLLocationManager,
       didUpdateLocations locations: [CLLocation]) {
    userLocation = locations[0]
    self.getDirections()

}

func locationManager(_ manager: CLLocationManager, didFailWithError error:
Error) {
    print(error.localizedDescription)
}
```

Next, add code to the *viewDidLoad* method to identify the current location, thereby triggering a call to the *didUpdateLocations* delegate method:

```
override func viewDidLoad() {
    super.viewDidLoad()
    routeMap.delegate = self
    routeMap.showsUserLocation = true
    locationManager.desiredAccuracy = kCLLocationAccuracyBest
    locationManager.delegate = self
    locationManager.requestLocation()
}
```

80.8 Getting the Route and Directions

Clearly, the last task performed by the Core *Location didUpdateLocations* method is to call another method named *getDirections* which now also needs to be implemented:

```
func getDirections() {

    let request = MKDirections.Request()
    request.source = MKMapItem.forCurrentLocation()

    if let destination = destination {
```

```
        request.destination = destination
    }

    request.requestsAlternateRoutes = false

    let directions = MKDirections(request: request)

    directions.calculate(completionHandler: {(response, error) in

        if let error = error {
            print(error.localizedDescription)
        } else {
            if let response = response {
                self.showRoute(response)
            }
        }
    })
}
```

This code largely matches that outlined at the start of the chapter, as is the case with the implementation of the *showRoute* method which also now needs to be implemented in the *RouteViewController.swift* file along with the corresponding *mapView rendererFor overlay* method:

```
func showRoute(_ response: MKDirections.Response) {

    for route in response.routes {

        routeMap.addOverlay(route.polyline,
                            level: MKOverlayLevel.aboveRoads)

        for step in route.steps {
            print(step.instructions)
        }
    }

    if let coordinate = userLocation?.coordinate {
        let region =
            MKCoordinateRegion(center: coordinate,
                latitudinalMeters: 2000, longitudinalMeters: 2000)
        routeMap.setRegion(region, animated: true)
    }
}

func mapView(_ mapView: MKMapView, rendererFor
        overlay: MKOverlay) -> MKOverlayRenderer {
```

```
    let renderer = MKPolylineRenderer(overlay: overlay)

    renderer.strokeColor = UIColor.blue
    renderer.lineWidth = 5.0
    return renderer
}
```

The *showRoute* method simply adds the polygon for the route as an overlay to the map view, outputs the turn-by-turn steps to the console and zooms in to the user's current location.

80.9 Establishing the Route Segue

All that remains to complete the application is to establish the segue between the results table cell and the route view. This will also require the implementation of the *prepare(for segue:)* method to pass the map item for the destination to the route scene.

Select the *Main.storyboard* file followed by the table cell in the Result Table View Controller scene (making sure the actual cell and not the view or one of the labels is selected). Ctrl-click on the prototype cell and drag the line to the Route View Controller scene. Release the line and select *Show* from the resulting menu.

Finally, edit the *ResultsTableViewController.swift* file and implement the *prepare(for segue:)* method so that the destination property matches the location associated with the selected table row:

```
override func prepare(for segue: UIStoryboardSegue, sender: Any?) {
    let routeViewController = segue.destination
        as! RouteViewController

    if let indexPath = self.tableView.indexPathForSelectedRow,
        let destination = mapItems?[indexPath.row] {
            routeViewController.destination = destination
    }
}
```

80.10 Testing the Application

Build and run the application on a suitable iOS device and perform a local search. Once search results have been returned, select the *Details* button to display the list of locations. Selecting a location from the list should now cause a second map view to appear containing the user's current location and the route from there to the selected location drawn in blue as demonstrated in Figure 80-6:

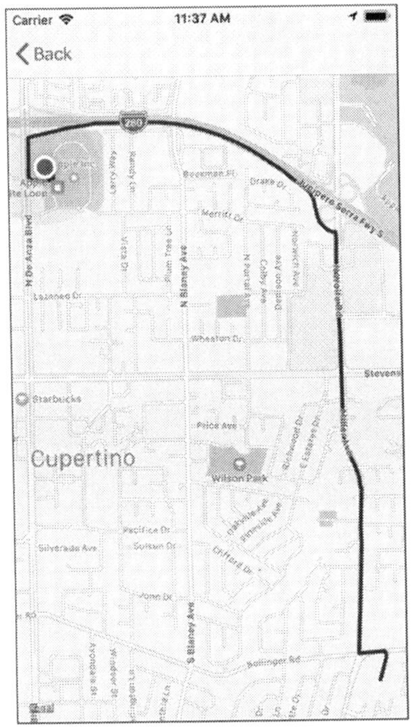

Figure 80-6

A review of the Xcode console should also reveal that the turn-by-turn directions have been output, for example:

```
Proceed to Infinite Loop
Turn right
Turn right onto Infinite Loop
Turn right onto Infinite Loop
Turn right onto N De Anza Blvd
Turn right to merge onto I-280 S
Take exit 10 onto Wolfe Road
Turn right onto N Wolfe Rd
Turn left onto Bollinger Rd
Turn right
The destination is on your left
```

80.11 Summary

The MKDirections class was added to the MapKit Framework for iOS 7 and allows directions from one location to another to be requested from Apple's mapping servers. Information returned from a request includes the text for turn-by-turn directions, the coordinates at which each step of the journey is to take place and the polygon data needed to draw the route as a map view overlay.

Chapter 81

81. An iOS 12 MapKit Flyover Tutorial

Since iOS 6, the Apple Maps app bundled with iOS has provided the ability to visually navigate photo-realistic 3D models of major cities and landmarks. This feature, referred to as "flyover" enables users to interactively pan, zoom and rotate around three-dimensional representations of key world locations when using the Maps app. From within the Maps app it is possible, for example, to navigate to, rotate around and fly-over a realistic 3D model of Paris.

Since the introduction of iOS 9, these capabilities are now available to iOS app developers as part of the MapKit framework. As will be outlined in the remainder of this chapter, the implementation of flyover behavior within a map involves the use of the MKMapView class together with the MKMapCamera class.

81.1 MKMapView Flyover Map Types

The previous chapters have explored two different map types in the form of satellite and hybrid modes. Flyover support includes two additional map types represented by *MKMapType.satelliteFlyover* and *MKMapType.hybridFlyover*. The satellite flyover mode displays pure 3D imagery while the hybrid mode includes annotations such as road names and point of interest labels. The following code, for example, configures a map view object for satellite flyover mode:

```
mapView.mapType = .satelliteFlyover
```

Figure 81-1 shows an example of an MKMapView object in satellite flyover mode showing a 3D rendering of the Statue of Liberty:

Figure 81-1

81.2 The MKMapCamera Class

The point of view from which the 3D flyover is represented to the user is controlled by assigning an MKMapCamera object to the MKMapView instance. The MKMapCamera object is configured in terms of the center coordinate of the viewed area, the distance of the camera from the center coordinate and the camera's pitch and direction in degrees relative to North as represented in Figure 81-2:

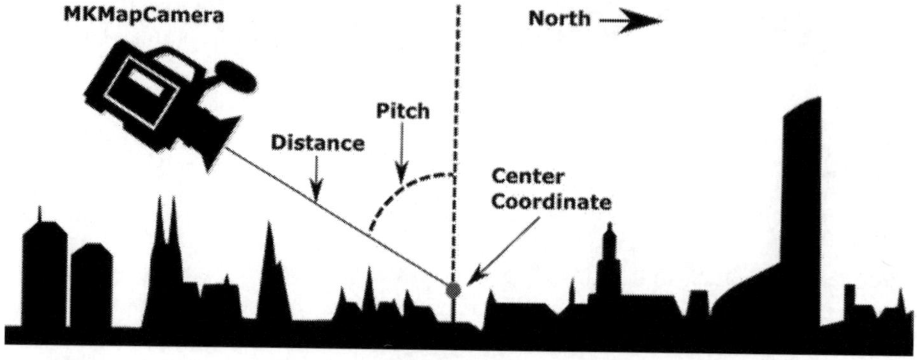

Figure 81-2

The following code, for example, configures an MKMapCamera instance located 650 meters from the Empire State Building facing East at a pitch of 30 degrees and assigns it to the camera property of a map view object named mapView:

```
let distance: CLLocationDistance = 650
let pitch: CGFloat = 30
let heading = 90.0

mapView.mapType = .satelliteFlyover

let coordinate = CLLocationCoordinate2D(latitude: 40.7484405,
                                        longitude: -73.9856644)

camera = MKMapCamera(lookingAtCenter: coordinate,
        fromDistance: distance,
        pitch: pitch,
        heading: heading)

mapView.camera = camera
```

81.3 An MKMapKit Flyover Example

The example project implemented in the remainder of this chapter will demonstrate the use of the MKMapCamera class to display a 3D Satellite Flyover rendering of the Empire State Building. The camera view will then slowly rotate around the building using an animation effect.

Begin the project by launching Xcode and creating a new iOS application project named *FlyoverDemo* using the *Single View Application* template with the Swift language option selected.

81.4 Designing the User Interface

The first step in this tutorial is to design the user interface. This is a very simple user interface consisting of an MKMapView instance and a single Button object. Select the *Main.storyboard* file and drag and drop components from the Library (*View -> Utilities -> Show Library)* onto the view. Position and size the components and set the text on the button so that the user interface resembles that shown in Figure 81-3:

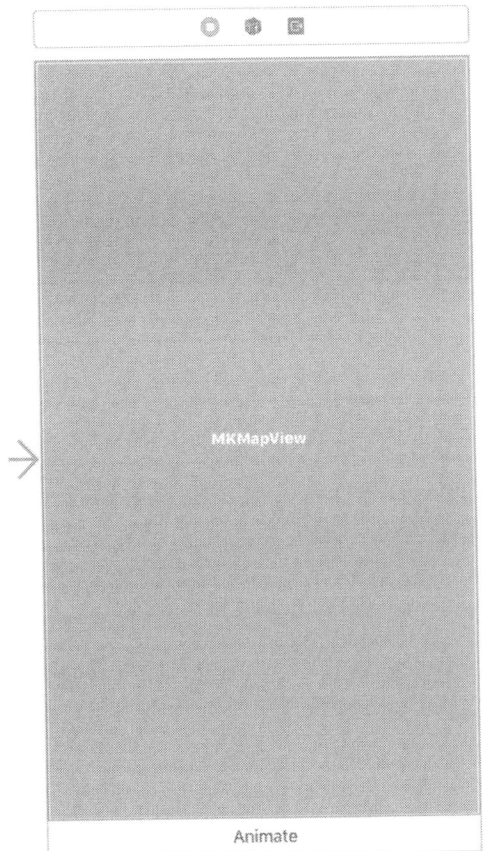

Figure 81-3

Select the Map View object in the scene layout, display the *Resolve Auto Layout Issues* menu and select the *Reset to Suggested Constraints* option listed under *All Views in View Controller.*

Display the Assistant Editor panel and establish an outlet connection from the Map View object named *mapView*. With the Assistant Editor still displayed, establish an action connection from the button object to a method named *animateCamera*.

With the connections configured, further modify the *ViewController.swift* file to import the MapKit framework as follows and to declare constants for the camera settings and a variable to contain a reference to the MKMapCamera object:

```
import UIKit
import MapKit

class ViewController: UIViewController {
```

```
    @IBOutlet weak var mapView: MKMapView!

    let distance: CLLocationDistance = 650
    let pitch: CGFloat = 65
    let heading = 0.0
    var camera: MKMapCamera?

    override func viewDidLoad() {
        super.viewDidLoad()
    }

    @IBAction func animateCamera(_ sender: Any) {
    }

    override func didReceiveMemoryWarning() {
        super.didReceiveMemoryWarning()
        // Dispose of any resources that can be recreated.
    }
}
```

81.5 Configuring the Map View and Camera

The next step is to configure the MKMapView instance to display the map in satellite flyover mode and then create and initialize the MKMapCamera object so that it is positioned above and to the side of the Empire State Building. Once the camera has been initialized it needs to be assigned to the MKMapView instance. Remaining in the *ViewController.swift* file, modify the *viewDidLoad* method to perform these tasks as follows:

```
override func viewDidLoad() {
    super.viewDidLoad()

    mapView.mapType = .satelliteFlyover

    let coordinate = CLLocationCoordinate2D(latitude: 40.7484405,
                                            longitude: -73.9856644)
    camera = MKMapCamera(lookingAtCenter: coordinate,
                         fromDistance: distance,
                         pitch: pitch,
                         heading: heading)

    if let camera = camera {
        mapView.camera = camera
    }
}
```

Compile and run the app on a physical iPhone or iPad device (at the time of writing flyover was not supported within the simulator environment). The map view should appear as illustrated in Figure 81-4:

Figure 81-4

The next step is to implement the animation sequence.

81.6 Animating Camera Changes

When the Animate button is tapped by the user the camera needs to rotate 180° around the center coordinate combined with a pitch adjustment with the changes animated over a 20 second duration. Locate the *animateCamera* method in the *ViewController.swift* file and add code as follows:

```
@IBAction func animateCamera(_ sender: Any) {

    UIView.animate(withDuration: 20.0, animations: {
        self.camera?.heading += 180
        self.camera?.pitch = 25
        if let camera = self.camera {
            self.mapView.camera = camera
        }
    })
}
```

The animation is performed using the UIView *animate(withDuration:)* method as outlined in the chapter entitled *iOS 12 Animation using UIViewPropertyAnimator*.

81.7 Testing the Map Flyover App

Compile and run the app once again and, once running, touch the Animate button. Note that the camera pans around the building in a smooth animation.

81.8 Summary

Although available to users of the Apple Maps app, the map flyover feature was not made available as a feature for use by app developers until the introduction of iOS 9. Combining an MKMapView instance with an MKMapCamera object enables photo-realistic 3D map display and navigation to be added to iOS apps. Options available for configuring an MKMapCamera view include center coordinates, distance, pitch and heading. The changes between camera views can be easily animated through the use of Core Animation features.

Chapter 82

82. Accessing the iOS 12 Camera and Photo Library

The iOS SDK provides access to both the camera device and photo library through the UIImagePickerController class. This allows videos and photographs to be taken from within an application and for existing photos and videos to be presented to the user for selection.

This chapter will cover the basics and some of the theory behind the use of the UIImagePickerController class before working through the step by step creation of an example application in *An Example iOS 12 Camera Application*.

82.1 The UIImagePickerController Class

The ultimate purpose of the UIImagePickerController class is to provide applications with either an image or video. It achieves this task by providing the user with access to the camera, camera roll and photo libraries on the device. In the case of the camera, the user is able to either take a photo or record a video depending on the capabilities of the device and the application's configuration of the UIImagePickerController object. In terms of camera roll and library access, the object provides the application with the existing image or video selected by the user. The controller also allows new photos and videos created within the application to be saved to the library.

82.2 Creating and Configuring a UIImagePickerController Instance

In order to use the UIImagePickerController, an instance of the class must first be created. In addition, properties of the instance need to be configured to control the source for the images or videos (camera, camera roll or library). Further, the types of media that are acceptable to the application must also be defined (photos, videos or both). Another configuration option defines whether the user has the option to edit a photo once it has been taken and before it is passed to the application.

The source of the media is defined by setting the *sourceType* property of the UIImagePickerController object to one of the three supported types:

- UIImagePickerController.SourceType.camera
- UIImagePickerController.SourceType.savedPhotosAlbum
- UIImagePickerController.SourceType.photoLibrary

The types of media acceptable to the application are defined by setting the *mediaTypes* property, an Array object that can be configured to support both video and images. The kUTTypeImage and kUTTypeMovie definitions contained in the MobileCoreServices Framework can be used as values when configuring this property.

Whether or not the user is permitted to perform editing before the image is passed on to the application is controlled via the *allowsEditing* Boolean property.

The following code creates a UImagePickerController instance and configures it for camera use with image support and editing disabled before displaying the controller:

```
let imagePicker = UIImagePickerController()

imagePicker.delegate = self
imagePicker.sourceType = UIImagePickerController.SourceType.photoLibrary
imagePicker.mediaTypes = [kUTTypeImage as String]
imagePicker.allowsEditing = false

self.present(imagePicker, animated: true, completion: nil)
```

It should be noted that the above code also configured the current class as the delegate for the UIImagePickerController instance. This is actually a key part of how the class works and is covered in the next section.

82.3 Configuring the UIImagePickerController Delegate

When the user is presented with the UIImagePickerController object user interface the application essentially hands control to that object. That being the case, the controller needs some way to notify the application that the user has taken a photo, recorded a video or made a library selection. It does this by calling delegate methods. The class that instantiates a UIImagePickerController instance should, therefore, declare itself as the object's delegate, conform to the UIImagePickerControllerDelegate and UINavigationControllerDelegate protocols and implement the *didFinishPickingMediaWithInfo* and *imagePickerControllerDidCancel* methods. When the user has selected or created media, the *didFinishPickingMediaWithInfo* method is called and passed an NSDictionary object containing the media and associated data. In the event that the user cancels the operation the *imagePickerControllerDidCancel* method is called. In both cases it is the responsibility of the delegate method to dismiss the view controller:

```
func imagePickerController(_ picker: UIImagePickerController,
didFinishPickingMediaWithInfo info: [UIImagePickerController.InfoKey : Any])
{
    let mediaType = info[UIImagePickerController.InfoKey.mediaType]
                                 as! NSString

    self.dismiss(animated: true, completion: nil)
}

func imagePickerControllerDidCancel(_ picker: UIImagePickerController) {
    self.dismiss(animated: true, completion: nil)
}
```

The *info* argument passed to the *didFinishPickingMediaWithInfo* method is an NSDictionary object containing the data relating to the image or video created or selected by the user. The first step is typically to identify the type of media:

```
let mediaType = info[UIImagePickerController.InfoKey.mediaType] as! NSString

if mediaType.isEqual(to: kUTTypeImage as String) {

        // Media is an image
```

```
} else if mediaType.isEqual(to: kUTTypeMovie as String) {

        // Media is a video

}
```

The original, unedited image selected or photographed by the user may be obtained from the *info* dictionary as follows:

```
let image = info[UIImagePickerController.InfoKey.originalImage] as! UIImage
```

Assuming that editing was enabled on the image picker controller object, the edited version of the image may be accessed via the *UIImagePickerControllerEditedImage* dictionary key:

```
let image = info[UIImagePickerController.InfoKey.editedImage] as! UIImage
```

If the media is a video, the URL of the recorded media may be accessed as follows:

```
let url = info[UIImagePickerController.InfoKey.mediaURL]
```

Once the image or video URL has been obtained the application can optionally save the media to the library and either display the image to the user or play the video using the AVPlayer and AVPlayerViewController classes as outlined in the chapter entitled *iOS 12 Video Playback using AVPlayer and AVPlayerViewController*.

82.4 Detecting Device Capabilities

Not all iOS devices provide the same functionality. iPhone models prior to the 3GS model, for example, do not support the recording of video. Some iPod Touch models do not have a camera so neither the camera, nor camera roll are available via the image picker controller. These differences in functionality make it important to detect the capabilities of a device when using the UIImagePickerController class. Fortunately, this may easily be achieved by a call to the *isSourceTypeAvailable* class method of the UIImagePickerController. For example, to detect the presence of a camera:

```
if UIImagePickerController.isSourceTypeAvailable(
                UIImagePickerController.SourceType.camera) {
        // Code here
}
```

Similarly, to test for access to the camera roll:

```
if UIImagePickerController.isSourceTypeAvailable(
                UIImagePickerController.SourceType.savedPhotosAlbum) {
        // Code here
}
```

Finally, to check for support for photo libraries:

```
if UIImagePickerController.isSourceTypeAvailable(
                UIImagePickerController.SourceType.photoLibrary) {
        // Code here
}
```

82.5 Saving Movies and Images

Once a video or photo created by the user using the camera is handed off to the application it is then the responsibility of the application code to save that media into the library. Photos and videos may be saved via calls to the *UIImageWriteToSavedPhotosAlbum* and *UISaveVideoAtPathToSavedPhotosAlbum* methods respectively. These methods use a *target-action* mechanism whereby the save action is initiated and the application continues to run. When the action is complete a specified method is called to notify the application of the success or otherwise of the operation.

To save an image:

```
UIImageWriteToSavedPhotosAlbum(image, self,

#selector(ViewController.image(image:didFinishSavingWithError:
                                        contextInfo:)), nil)
```

To save a video:

```
if (UIVideoAtPathIsCompatibleWithSavedPhotosAlbum(videoPath))
{
    UISaveVideoAtPathToSavedPhotosAlbum(videoPath, self,
        #selector(ViewController.image(image:didFinishSavingWithError:
                    contextInfo:)), nil)
}
```

Last, but by no means least, is the *didFinishSavingWithError* method which will be called when the action is either complete or failed due to an error:

```
func image(image: UIImage, didFinishSavingWithError
        error: NSErrorPointer, contextInfo:UnsafeRawPointer) {
    if error != nil {
        // Report error to user
    }
}
```

82.6 Summary

In this chapter we have provided an overview of the UIImagePickerController and looked at how this class can be used either to allow a user to take a picture or record video from within an iOS application or select media from the device photo libraries. Now that the theory has been covered, the next chapter entitled *An Example iOS 12 Camera Application* will work through the development of an example application designed to implement the theory covered in this chapter.

Chapter 83

83. An Example iOS 12 Camera Application

In the chapter entitled *Accessing the iOS 12 Camera and Photo Library* we looked in some detail at the steps necessary to provide access to the iOS camera and photo libraries in an iOS application. The purpose of this chapter is to build on this knowledge by working through an example iOS application designed to access the device's camera and photo libraries.

83.1 An Overview of the Application

The application user interface for this example will consist of an image view and a toolbar containing two buttons. When touched by the user, the first button will display the camera to the user and allow a photograph to be taken which will subsequently be displayed in the image view. The second button will provide access to the camera roll where the user may select an existing photo image. In the case of a new image taken with the camera, this will be saved to the camera roll.

Since we will be covering the playback of video in the next chapter (*iOS 12 Video Playback using AVPlayer and AVPlayerViewController*) the camera roll and camera will be restricted to still images in this example. The addition of video support to this application is left as an exercise for the reader.

83.2 Creating the Camera Project

Begin the project by launching Xcode and creating a new iOS application project named *Camera* using the *Single View Application* template with the Swift language option selected.

83.3 Designing the User Interface

The next step in this tutorial is to design the user interface. This is a very simple user interface consisting of an image view, a toolbar and two bar button items. Select the *Main.storyboard* file and drag and drop components from the Library (*View -> Utilities -> Show Library)* onto the view. Position and size the components and set the text on the bar button items so that the user interface resembles Figure 83-1.

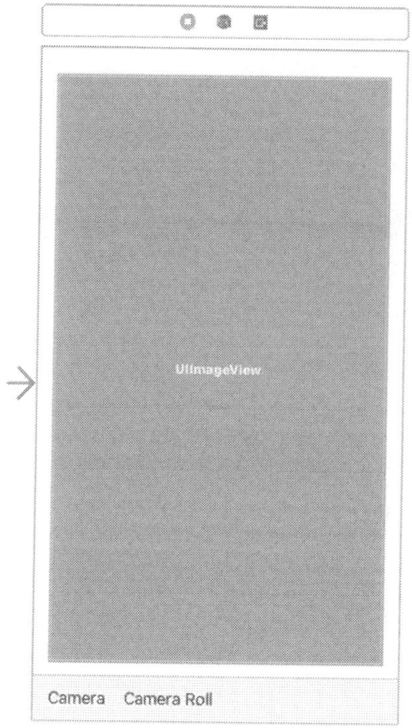

Figure 83-1

In terms of Auto Layout constraints, begin by selecting the toolbar view and clicking on the *Add New Constraints* menu in the toolbar located in the lower right-hand corner of the storyboard canvas and establish *Spacing to nearest neighbor* constraints on the bottom and two side edges of the view with the *Constrain to margins* option switched off. Also enable the height constraint option set to the current value.

Next, select the Image View object and, once again using the *Add New Constraints* menu, establish *Spacing to nearest neighbor* constraints on all four sides of the view, this time with the *Constrain to margins* option enabled.

Finally, with the Image View still selected, display the Attributes Inspector panel and change the *Content Mode* attribute to *Aspect Fit*.

Select the image view object in the view canvas and display the Assistant Editor panel. Ctrl-click on the image view object and drag to a position just below the class declaration line in the Assistant Editor. Release the line and, in the resulting connection dialog, establish an outlet connection named *imageView*.

With the Assistant Editor still visible, establish action connections for the two buttons to methods named *useCamera* and *useCameraRoll* respectively (keeping in mind that it may be necessary to click twice on each button to select it since the first click will typically select the toolbar parent object).

Close the Assistant Editor, select the *ViewController.swift* file and modify it further to add import and delegate protocol declarations together with a Boolean property declaration that will be required later in the chapter:

```
import UIKit
import MobileCoreServices

class ViewController: UIViewController, UIImagePickerControllerDelegate,
UINavigationControllerDelegate {
```

```
    @IBOutlet weak var imageView: UIImageView!
    var newMedia: Bool?
.
.
```

83.4 Implementing the Action Methods

The *useCamera* and *useCameraRoll* action methods now need to be implemented. The *useCamera* method first needs to check that the device on which the application is running has a camera. It then needs to create a UIImagePickerController instance, assign the cameraViewController as the delegate for the object and define the media source as the camera. Since we do not plan on handling videos the supported media types property is set to images only. Finally, the camera interface will be displayed. The last task is to set the *newMedia* flag to true to indicate that the image is new and is not an existing image from the camera roll. Bringing all these requirements together gives us the following *useCamera* method:

```
@IBAction func useCamera(_ sender: Any) {

    if UIImagePickerController.isSourceTypeAvailable(
                UIImagePickerController.SourceType.camera) {

        let imagePicker = UIImagePickerController()

        imagePicker.delegate = self
        imagePicker.sourceType =
                UIImagePickerController.SourceType.camera
        imagePicker.mediaTypes = [kUTTypeImage as String]
        imagePicker.allowsEditing = false

        self.present(imagePicker, animated: true,
                            completion: nil)
        newMedia = true
    }
}
```

The *useCameraRoll* method is remarkably similar to the previous method with the exception that the source of the image is declared to be UIImagePickerController.SourceType.photoLibrary and the *newMedia* flag is set to *false* (since the photo is already in the library we don't need to save it again):

```
@IBAction func useCameraRoll(_ sender: Any) {

    if UIImagePickerController.isSourceTypeAvailable(
                UIImagePickerController.SourceType.savedPhotosAlbum) {
        let imagePicker = UIImagePickerController()

        imagePicker.delegate = self
        imagePicker.sourceType =
```

```
                UIImagePickerController.SourceType.photoLibrary
        imagePicker.mediaTypes = [kUTTypeImage as String]
        imagePicker.allowsEditing = false
        self.present(imagePicker, animated: true,
                completion: nil)
        newMedia = false
    }
}
```

83.5 Writing the Delegate Methods

As described in *Accessing the iOS 12 Camera and Photo Library*, in order to fully implement an instance of the image picker controller delegate protocol it is necessary to implement some delegate methods. The most important method is *didFinishPickingMediaWithInfo* which is called when the user has finished taking or selecting an image. The code for this method in our example reads as follows:

```
func imagePickerController(_ picker: UIImagePickerController,
didFinishPickingMediaWithInfo info: [UIImagePickerController.InfoKey : Any])
{

    let mediaType = info[UIImagePickerController.InfoKey.mediaType]
                            as! NSString

    self.dismiss(animated: true, completion: nil)

    if mediaType.isEqual(to: kUTTypeImage as String) {
        let image = info[UIImagePickerController.InfoKey.originalImage]
                            as! UIImage

        imageView.image = image

        if (newMedia == true) {
            UIImageWriteToSavedPhotosAlbum(image, self,
                #selector(ViewController.image(
                    image:didFinishSavingWithError:contextInfo:)), nil)
        } else if mediaType.isEqual(to: kUTTypeMovie as String) {
                // Code to support video here
        }

    }
}

@objc func image(image: UIImage, didFinishSavingWithError error:
NSErrorPointer, contextInfo:UnsafeRawPointer) {

    if error != nil {
```

```
            let alert = UIAlertController(title: "Save Failed",
                message: "Failed to save image",
                preferredStyle: UIAlertController.Style.alert)

            let cancelAction = UIAlertAction(title: "OK",
                style: .cancel, handler: nil)

            alert.addAction(cancelAction)
            self.present(alert, animated: true,
                            completion: nil)
        }
}
```

The code in this delegate method dismisses the image picker view and identifies the type of media passed from the image picker controller. If it is an image it is displayed on the view image object of the user interface. If this is a new image it is saved to the camera roll. The *didFinishedSavingWithError* method is configured to be called when the save operation is complete. If an error occurred it is reported to the user via an alert box.

It is also necessary to implement the *imagePickerControllerDidCancel* delegate method which is called if the user cancels the image picker session without taking a picture or making an image selection. In most cases all this method needs to do is dismiss the image picker:

```
func imagePickerControllerDidCancel(_ picker: UIImagePickerController) {
    self.dismiss(animated: true, completion: nil)
}
```

83.6 Seeking Camera and Photo Library Access

Access to both the camera and the photos stored on the device require authorization from the user. This involves the declaration of three usage keys within the project *Info.plist* file.

Select the *Info.plist* file, locate the bottom entry in the list of properties and hover the mouse pointer over the item. When the plus button appears, click on it to add a new entry to the list. From within the dropdown list of available keys, locate and select the *Privacy – Camera Usage Description* option as shown in Figure 83-2:

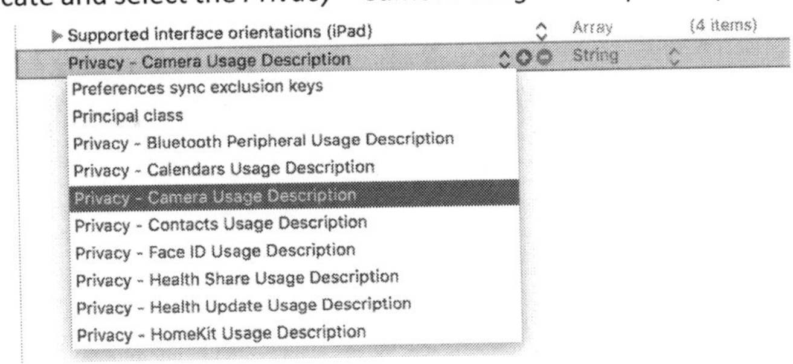

Figure 83-2

Within the value field for the property, enter a message to display to the user when requesting permission to use the camera. For example:

```
This app allows you to take photos and store them in the photo library.
```

Before closing the *Info.plist* file, now is also a convenient point to add an entry for the NSPhotoLibraryUsageDescription key, since the app will also need access to the photo library in order to search for images. Repeating the above steps, add a new entry for *Privacy – Photo Library Usage Description* with a suitable description string value. For example:

```
This app accesses your photo library to search and display photos.
```

Add another key to the list, this time selecting the *Privacy - Photo Library Additions Usage Description* option from the drop down menu. This permission is required to allow the app to add new photos to the user's photo library. Once the key has been selected, enter text similar to the following into the value field:

```
This app saves photos only to your photo library.
```

83.7 Building and Running the Application

In order to experience the full functionality of this application it will be necessary to install it on a physical iOS device with a camera.

Click on the Xcode run button to launch the application. Once the application loads, select the *Camera* button to launch the camera interface.

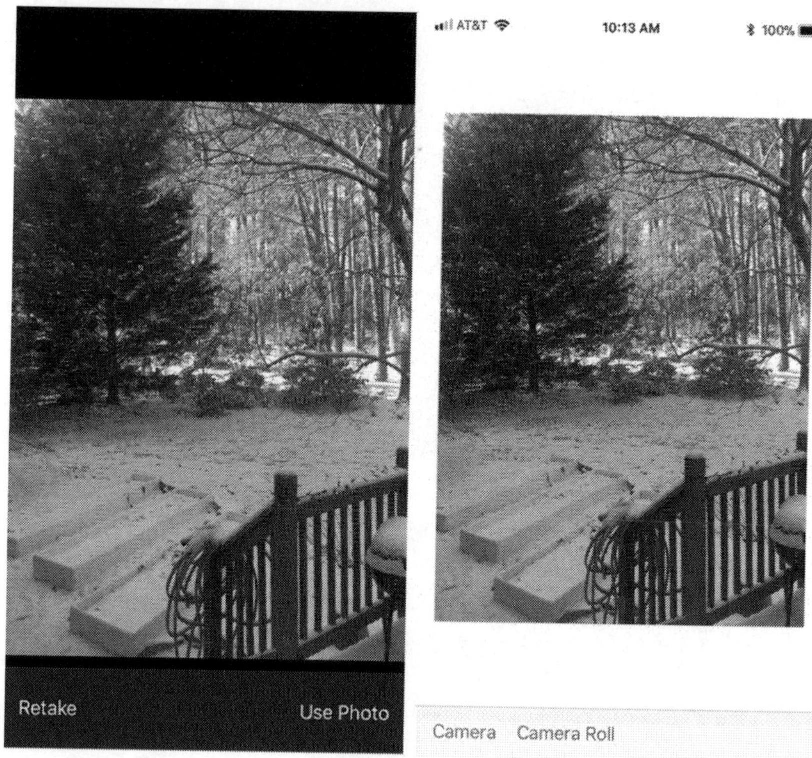

Figure 83-3

Once the picture has been taken and selected for use in the application, it will appear in the image view object of our application user interface.

Selecting the *Camera Roll* button will provide access to the camera roll and photo stream on the device where an image selection can be made:

Figure 83-4

83.8 Summary

This chapter has provided a practical example of how the UIImagePickerController class can be used to access both the camera and photo library from within an iOS app. The example also demonstrated the need to configure appropriate privacy usage keys to seek permission from the user to access the device camera and search and add images to the photo library.

Chapter 84

84. iOS 12 Video Playback using AVPlayer and AVPlayerViewController

Video playback support in iOS is provided by combining the AVFoundation AVPlayer and AVKit AVPlayerViewController classes.

This chapter presents an overview of video playback in iOS using these two classes followed by a step by step example.

84.1 The AVPlayer and AVPlayerViewController Classes

The sole purpose of the AVPlayer class is to play media content. An AVPlayer instance is initialized with the URL of the media to be played (either a path to a local file on the device or the URL of network based media). Playback can be directed to a device screen or, in the case of external playback mode, via AirPlay or an HDMI/VGA cable connection to an external screen.

The AVKit Player View Controller (AVPlayerViewController) class provides a view controller environment through which AVPlayer video is displayed to the user together with a number of controls that enable the user to manage the playback experience. Playback may also be controlled from within the application code by calling the *play* and *pause* methods of the AVPlayer instance.

84.2 The iOS Movie Player Example Application

The objective of the remainder of this chapter is to create a simple application that will play back a video when a button is pressed. The video will be streamed over the internet from a movie file located on a web server.

Begin by launching Xcode and creating a new iOS application project based on the *Single View Application* template configured for the Swift language, naming the product *AVPlayerDemo*.

84.3 Designing the User Interface

Select the *Main.storyboard* file and display the Library (*View -> Utilities -> Show Library*). Drag a single Button instance to the view window and change the text on the button to "Play Movie". With the button selected in the storyboard canvas, display the Auto Layout Align menu and add both horizontal and vertical container constraints to the view with both offset values set to 0.

From the Library panel, locate the AVKit Player View Controller object and drag and drop it onto the storyboard to the right of the existing view controller. Ctrl-click on the button in the first view controller and drag the resulting line to the AVKit Player View Controller. Release the line and select *Show* from the segue selection menu. On completion of these tasks, the storyboard should resemble that of Figure 84-1:

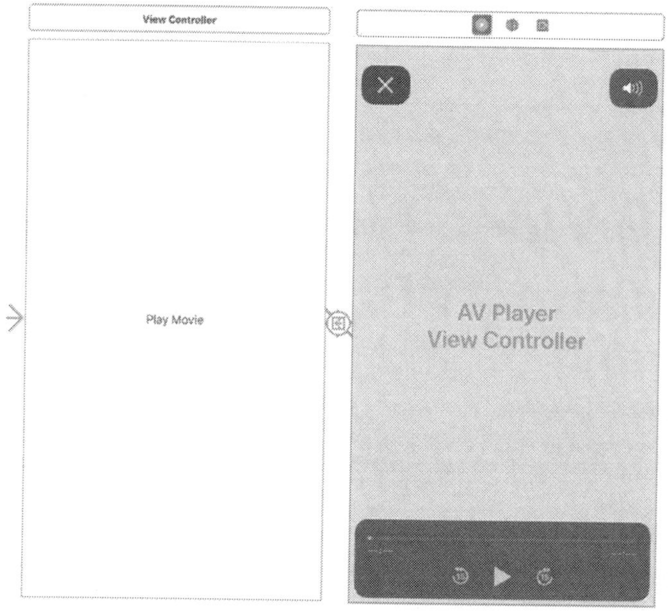

Figure 84-1

84.4 Initializing Video Playback

When the "Play Movie" button is tapped by the user the application will perform a segue to the AVPlayerViewController scene. Verify that this works by running the application and selecting the button. The AVPlayerViewController will appear and display the video playback controls but as yet no AVPlayer has been configured to play video content. This can be achieved by implementing the *prepare(for segue:)* method within the *ViewController.swift* file as follows, the code for which relies on the AVKit and AVFoundation frameworks having been imported:

```
import UIKit
import AVKit
import AVFoundation

class ViewController: UIViewController {
.
.
.
    override func prepare(for segue: UIStoryboardSegue, sender: Any?) {

        let destination = segue.destination as!
                                AVPlayerViewController
        let url = URL(string:
                "https://www.ebookfrenzy.com/ios_book/movie/movie.mov")

            if let movieURL = url {
                destination.player = AVPlayer(url: movieURL)
            }
```

```
    }
.
.
```

The code in this above method begins by obtaining a reference to the destination view controller, in this case the AVPlayerViewController instance. A URL object is then initialized with the URL of a web based video file. Finally a new AVPlayer instance is created, initialized with the video URL and assigned to the *player* property of the AVPlayerViewController object.

Running the application once again should cause the video to be available for playback within the player view controller scene.

84.5 Build and Run the Application

With the design and coding phases complete, all that remains is to build and run the application. Click on the run button located in the toolbar of the main Xcode project window. Assuming that no errors occur, the application should launch within the iOS Simulator or device. Once loaded, touching the *Play Movie* button should launch the movie player in full screen mode and playback should automatically begin:

Figure 84-2

84.6 Creating an AVPlayerViewController Instance from Code

The example shown in this chapter used storyboard scenes and a transition to display an AVPlayerViewController instance. While this is a quick approach to working with the AVPlayerViewController and AVPlayer classes, the same result may also be achieved directly by writing code within the application. The following code fragment, for example, initializes and plays video within an application using these two classes without the use of a storyboard scene:

```
let player = AVPlayer(url: url)
let playerController = AVPlayerViewController()

playerController.player = player
self.addChildViewController(playerController)
self.view.addSubview(playerController.view)
playerController.view.frame = self.view.frame

player.play()
```

84.7 Adding a Security Exception for an HTTP Connection

In iOS 9, Apple tightened the level of security for external resources such as files on remote servers. This is referred to as App Transport Security (ATS) and, by default, access to HTTP resources are now blocked within iOS apps. Wherever possible, therefore, the more secure HTTPS protocol should be used instead of HTTP. In recognition of the fact that not all servers support HTTPS it is possible to add an exception to the *Info.plist* file of the app project. This can be configured on a general basis or declared for individual domains.

To add an exception for an insecure server, locate and select the *Info.plist* file and set the properties as outlined in the figure below:

▼ App Transport Security Settings	Dictionary	(1 item)
▼ Exception Domains	Dictionary	(1 item)
▼ ebookfrenzy.com	Dictionary	(3 items)
NSIncludesSubdomains	Boolean	YES
NSTemporaryExceptionAllow...	Boolean	YES
NSTemporaryExceptionMinim...	String	TLSv1.1

Figure 84-3

Alternatively, Ctrl-click on the *Info.plist* file in the Project Navigator panel, select *Open As -> Source Code* from the resulting menu and enter the following exception settings for the ebookfrenzy.com domain:

```
<key>NSAppTransportSecurity</key>
<dict>
  <key>NSExceptionDomains</key>
  <dict>
    <key>ebookfrenzy.com</key>
    <dict>
      <key>NSIncludesSubdomains</key>
      <true/>
      <key>NSTemporaryExceptionAllowsInsecureHTTPLoads</key>
      <true/>
      <key>NSTemporaryExceptionMinimumTLSVersion</key>
      <string>TLSv1.1</string>
    </dict>
  </dict>
</dict>
```

84.8 Summary

The basic classes needed to play back video from within an iOS application are provided by the AVFoundation and AVKit frameworks. The purpose of the AVPlayer class is to facilitate the playback of video media files. The AVPlayerViewController class provides a quick and easy way to embed an AVPlayer instance into a view controller environment together with a set of standard on-screen playback controls.

Chapter 85

85. An iOS 12 Multitasking Picture in Picture Tutorial

The topic of multitasking in iOS on iPad devices was covered in some detail in the earlier chapter titled *A Guide to Multitasking in iOS 12*. An area of multitasking that was mentioned briefly in that chapter was that of Picture in Picture support. This chapter will provide a more detailed introduction to Picture in Picture multitasking before extending the *AVPlayerDemo* project created in the previous chapter to include Picture in Picture support.

85.1 An Overview of Picture in Picture Multitasking

Picture in Picture (PiP) multitasking allows the video playback within an app running on recent iPad models to appear within a floating, movable and resizable window. Figure 85-1, for example shows the upper portion of an iPad screen. In the figure, the PiP window is displayed in the top left-hand corner of the display while the user is interacting with a Safari browser session. Once displayed, the location of the PiP window can be moved by the user to any other corner of the display.

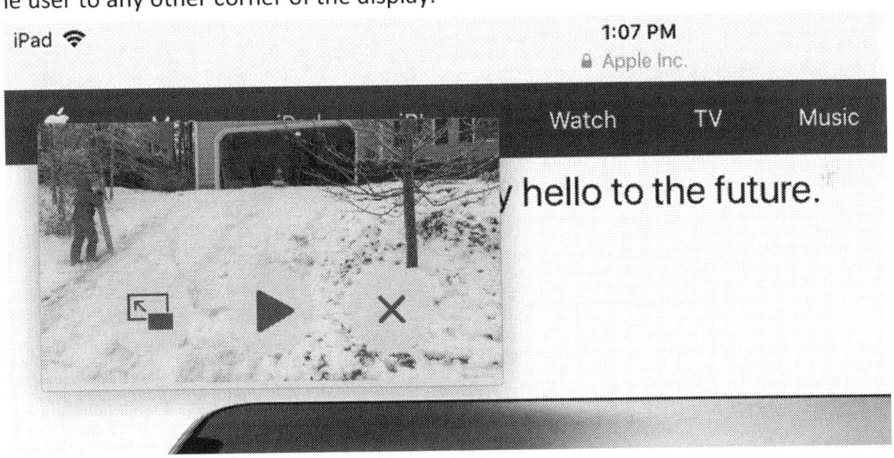

Figure 85-1

Video playback within a PiP window may only be initiated via a user action. When the user presses the Home button on the iPad device while full screen video playback is in progress, the video will be transferred to a PiP window. Alternatively, the video playback can be moved to a PiP window using a button that appears in the top left corner of the video player window as highlighted in Figure 85-2:

Figure 85-2

A set of controls is also available from within the PiP window to pause and resume playback, return to full screen viewing or exit the playback entirely.

85.2 Adding Picture in Picture Support to the AVPlayerDemo App

The remainder of this chapter will work through the steps to integrate PiP support into the AVPlayerDemo app created in the previous chapter. The first step is to enable PiP support within the project capabilities.

If the project is not already loaded, start Xcode and open the AVPlayerDemo project. In the Project Navigator panel, select the *AVPlayerDemo* project target at the top of the panel and click on the *Capabilities* tab in the main panel.

Scroll down the list of capabilities until the *Background Mode* entry comes into view. Switch Background Mode support to the *On* position and enable the checkbox next to *Audio, AirPlay and Picture in Picture* as outlined in Figure 85-3:

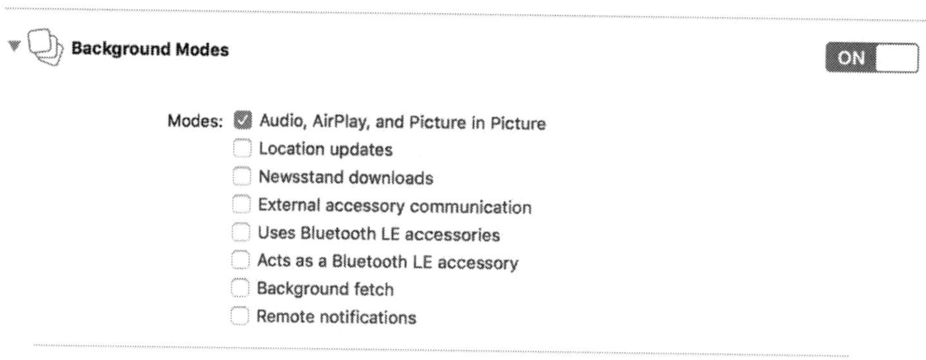

Figure 85-3

85.3 Adding the Navigation Controller

In order to better demonstrate the implementation of PiP support within an iOS app, the storyboard for the AVPlayerDemo will be adapted to include a navigation controller so that the user can navigate back to the main view controller scene from the AVKit Player scene. Within the Project Navigator panel, select the View Controller scene so that it highlights in blue and choose the Xcode *Editor -> Embed In -> Navigation Controller* menu option.

85.4 Setting the Audio Session Category

The next step is to configure the app to use an appropriate audio session category. For the purposes of this example this will be set to *AVAudioSession.Category.playback*, the code for which should now be added to the *didFinishLaunchingWithOptions* method located in the *AppDelegate.swift* file as follows:

```
.
.
import AVFoundation
.
.
func application(_ application: UIApplication, didFinishLaunchingWithOptions
launchOptions: [UIApplicationLaunchOptionsKey: Any]?) -> Bool {

    let audioSession = AVAudioSession.sharedInstance()

    do {
        try audioSession.setCategory(AVAudioSession.Category.playback,
                                         mode: .default)
    } catch {
        print("Unable to set audio session category")
    }

    return true
}
```

With these steps completed, launch the app on a physical iPad or iOS simulator session (keeping in mind that PiP support is not available on the first generation iPad Mini or any full size iPad models older than the first iPad Air). Once loaded, tap the Play Movie button and start video playback. Tap the PiP button in the video playback control bar, or use the device Home button and note that video playback is transferred to the PiP window:

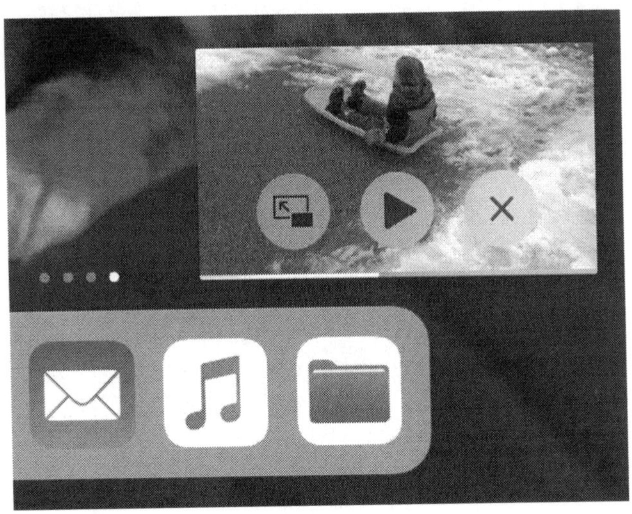

Figure 85-4

With the PiP window visible and the three control buttons displayed, tap the button to toggle back to full screen playback mode.

PiP support is now implemented with the exception of one important step. To experience the need for this additional step, run the app once again, begin movie playback and switch playback to PiP mode. Remaining within the AVPlayerDemo app, tap the *Back* button located in the navigation bar to return to the original view controller scene containing the Play Movie button. Tap the PiP button to return the movie playback to full screen at which point the movie playback window will disappear leaving just the initial view controller visible. The reason for this is that a delegate method needs to be implemented to present the full size video playback view controller in this situation.

85.5 Implementing the Delegate

The AVPlayerViewController class can have assigned to it a delegate object on which methods will be called at various points during the playback of a video. This delegate object must implement the AVPlayerViewControllerDelegate protocol. For the purposes of this example, the ViewController class will be designated as the delegate object for the class. Select the *ViewController.swift* file and modify it to declare that it now implements the AVPlayerViewControllerDelegate protocol:

```
import UIKit
import AVKit
import AVFoundation

class ViewController: UIViewController, AVPlayerViewControllerDelegate {

    override func viewDidLoad() {
        super.viewDidLoad()
        }
.
.
}
```

Having declared that the class implements the protocol, the *prepare(for segue:)* method now needs to be modified to assign the current instance of the class as the delegate for the player view controller instance:

```
override func prepare(for segue: UIStoryboardSegue, sender: Any?) {

    let destination = segue.destination as!
                            AVPlayerViewController
    let url = URL(string:
            "https://www.ebookfrenzy.com/ios_book/movie/movie.mov")

    destination.delegate = self

    if let movieURL = url {
        destination.player = AVPlayer(url: movieURL)
    }
}
```

When the user moves back from the PiP window to full screen playback mode, the *restoreUserInterfaceForPictureInPictureStopWithCompletionHandler* method is called on the delegate object. This method is passed a reference to the player view controller and a completion handler. It is the responsibility of this method to make sure that the player view controller is presented to the user before calling the completion handler with a Boolean value indicating the success or otherwise of the operation. Remaining within the *ViewController.swift* file, implement this method as follows:

```
func playerViewController(_ playerViewController: AVPlayerViewController,
  restoreUserInterfaceForPictureInPictureStopWithCompletionHandler
completionHandler: @escaping (Bool) -> Void) {

    let currentViewController =
                navigationController?.visibleViewController

    if currentViewController != playerViewController {
        if let topViewController =
                navigationController?.topViewController {

            topViewController.present(playerViewController,
                animated: true, completion: {()
                completionHandler(true)
            })
        }
    }
}
```

The delegate method is passed a reference to the player view controller instance and a completion handler. The code added to the method begins by identifying the currently visible view controller and checking if the current view controller matches the playerViewController instance. If the current view controller is not the player view controller, the navigation controller is used to obtain a reference to the top view controller which, in turn, is used to display the player view controller. The completion handler is then called and passed a true value.

If, on the other hand, the current view controller is the playerViewController, no action needs to be taken since the system will automatically display the player controller to show the movie in full screen. In fact, attempting to present the player view controller when it is already the current view controller will cause the app to crash with an error which reads as follows:

```
Application tried to present modally an active view controller
<AVPlayerViewController>
```

Run the app once again and verify that the full screen playback view now appears when the full screen button is tapped in the PiP window after navigating back to the main view controller scene.

85.6 Opting Out of Picture in Picture Support

The default behavior for the AVPlayerViewController class is to support PiP. To disable PiP support for an AVPlayerViewController instance, set the allowsPictureInPicturePlayback property on the object to false. For example:

```
playerViewController.allowsPictureInPicturePlayback = false
```

With PiP support disabled, the PiP button will no longer appear in the playback control panel of the full screen view and pressing the device Home button during video playback will no longer place the video into a PiP window.

85.7 Additional Delegate Methods

A number of other methods are supported by the AVPlayerViewControllerDelegate protocol which, if implemented in the designated delegate, will be called at various points in the life cycle of the video playback:

- **pictureInPictureControllerWillStartPictureInPicture** – Called before the transition to Picture in Picture mode is about to start.
- **pictureInPictureControllerDidStartPictureInPicture** - Called when the Picture in Picture playback has started. This method is passed a reference to the playback view controller object.
- **pictureInPictureControllerWillStopPictureInPicture** - Called when the Picture in Picture playback is about to stop. This method is passed a reference to the playback view controller object.
- **pictureInPictureControllerDidStopPictureInPicture** - Called when the Picture in Picture playback has stopped. This method is passed a reference to the playback view controller object.

85.8 Summary

Picture in Picture support leverages the multitasking capabilities of iOS to allow video playback to be placed within a floating, movable and resizable window where it continues to play as the user performs other tasks on the device. This chapter has highlighted the steps involved in implementing PiP support within an iOS app including enabling entitlements, configuring the audio session and implementing delegate methods.

Chapter 86

86. An Introduction to Extensions in iOS 12

Extensions are a feature originally introduced as part of the iOS 8 release designed to allow certain capabilities of an application to be made available for use within other applications. The developer of a photo editing application might, for example, have devised some unique image filtering capabilities and decide that those features would be particularly useful to users of the iOS Photos app. To achieve this, the developer would implement these features in a Photo Editing extension which would then appear as an option to users when editing an image within the Photos app.

Extensions fall into a variety of different categories and a number of rules and guidelines must be followed in the implementation process. While subsequent chapters will cover in detail the creation of extensions of various types, this chapter is intended to serve as a general overview and introduction to the subject of extensions in iOS.

86.1 iOS Extensions – An Overview

The sole purpose of an extension is to make a specific feature of an existing application available for access within other applications. Extensions are separate executable binaries that run independently of the corresponding application. Although extensions take the form of an individual binary, they must be supplied and installed as part of an application bundle. The application with which an extension is bundled is referred to as the *containing app*. With the exception of Message App extensions, the containing app must provide useful functionality and must not be an empty application provided solely for the purpose of delivering an extension to the user.

Once an extension has been installed, it will be accessible from other applications through a number of different techniques depending on the type of the extension. The application from which an extension is launched and used is referred to as a *host app*.

An application that translates text to a foreign language might, for example, include an extension which can be used to translate the text displayed by a host app. In such a scenario, the user would access the extension via the Share button in the user interface of the host app and the extension would display a view controller displaying the translated text. On dismissing the extension, the user is returned to the host app.

86.2 Extension Types

iOS supports a number of different extension types dictated by *extension points*. An extension point is an area of the iOS operating system which has been opened up to allow extensions to be implemented. When developing an extension, it is important to select the extension point that is most appropriate to the features of the extension. The extension types supported by iOS is constantly evolving, though the key types can be summarized as follows:

86.2.1 Today Extension

The Today extension point allows extensions to be made available within the Today view of the iOS Notification Center (the panel that appears when making a right swiping motion on the home screen of the device display as shown in Figure 86-1).

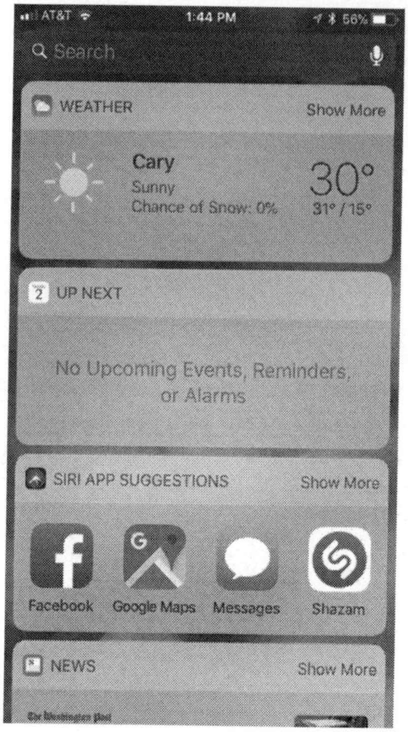

Figure 86-1

By default, the Today view displays information such as calendar appointments for the current day and prevailing stock price information.

Today extensions take the form of *widgets* that display information to the user when the Today view is displayed. Today extensions are covered in detail in the chapter entitled *An iOS 12 Today Extension Widget Tutorial.*

86.2.2 Share Extension

Share extensions provide a quick access mechanism for sharing content such as images, videos, text and web sites within a host app with social network sites or content sharing services. It is important to understand that Apple does not expect developers to write Share extensions designed to post content to destinations such as Facebook or Twitter (such sharing options are already built into iOS) but rather as a mechanism to make sharing easier for developers hosting their own sharing and social sites. Share extensions appear within the activity view controller panel which is displayed when the user taps the Share button from within a host app.

Figure 86-2, for example, shows a Share extension named "Share It" listed alongside the built-in Twitter, Facebook and Flickr share options within the activity view controller.

Figure 86-2

Share extensions can make use of the SLComposeServiceViewController class to implement the interface for posting content. This displays a view (Figure 86-3) containing a preview of the information to be posted and provides the ability to modify the content prior to posting it. For more complex requirements, a custom user interface can be designed using Interface Builder.

Figure 86-3

The actual mechanics of posting the content will be dependent on the way in which the target platform works.

86.2.3 Action Extension

The Action extension point enables extensions to be created that fall into the Action category. Action extensions allow the content within a host app to be transformed or viewed in a different way. As with Share extensions, Action extensions are accessed from the activity view controller via the Share button. Figure 86-4, for example, shows an example Action extension named "Translator" in the activity view controller of the iOS Notes app.

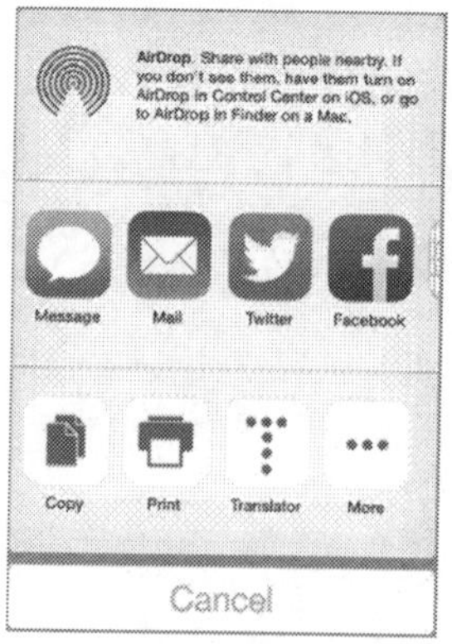

Figure 86-4

Action extensions are context sensitive in that they only appear as an option when the type of content in the host app matches one of the content types for which the extension has declared support. An Action extension that works with images, for example, will not appear in the activity view controller panel for a host app that is displaying text based content.

Action extensions are covered in detail in the chapters entitled *Creating an iOS 12 Action Extension* and *Receiving Data from an iOS 12 Action Extension*.

86.2.4 Photo Editing Extension

The Photo Editing extension point allows the photo editing capabilities of an application to be accessed from within the built-in iOS Photos app. Photo Editing extensions are displayed when the user selects an image in the Photos app, chooses the edit option and taps on the button in the top left-hand corner of the Photo editing screen. Figure 86-5 shows the Photos app displaying two Photo Editing extension options:

Figure 86-5

Photo Editing Extensions are covered in detail in the chapter entitled *Creating an iOS 12 Photo Editing Extension*.

86.2.5 Document Provider Extension

The Document Provider extension makes it possible for a containing app to act as a document repository for other applications running on the device. Depending on the level of support implemented in the extension, host apps can import, export, open, and move documents to and from the storage repository provided by the containing app. In most cases the storage repository represented by the containing app will be a third-party cloud storage service providing an alternative to Apple's iCloud service.

A Document Provider extension consists of a Document Picker View Controller extension and an optional File Provider extension. The Document Picker View Controller extension provides a user interface for the extension allowing the user to browse and select the documents available for the Document Provider extension.

The optional File Provider extension provides the host app with access to the documents residing outside of the app's sandbox and is necessary if the extension is to support move and open operations on the documents stored via the containing app.

86.2.6 Custom Keyboard Extension

The Custom Keyboard Extension, as the name suggests, provides the ability to create and install custom keyboards onto iOS devices. Keyboards developed using the Custom Keyboard extension point are available to be used by all applications on the device and, once installed, are selected from within the keyboard settings section of the Settings app on the device.

86.2.7 Audio Unit Extension

Audio Unit Extensions allow sound effects, virtual instruments and other sound based capabilities to be made available to other audio oriented host apps such as GarageBand.

86.2.8 Shared Links Extension

The Shared Links Extension provides a mechanism for an iOS app to store URL links in the Safari browser shared links list.

86.2.9 Content Blocking Extension

Content Blocking allows extensions to be added to the Safari browser to block certain types of content from appearing when users are browsing the web. This is typically used to create ad blocking solutions.

86.2.10 Sticker Pack Extension

An extension to the built-in iOS Messages App that allows packs of additional images to be provided for inclusion in message content.

86.2.11 iMessage Extension

Allows interactive content to be integrated into the Messages app. This can range from custom user interfaces to interactive games. iMessage extensions are covered in the chapters entitled *An Introduction to Building iOS 12 Message Apps* and *An iOS 12 Interactive Message App Tutorial*.

86.2.12 Intents Extension

Used when integrating an app with the SiriKit framework, these extensions are used to define the actions to be performed in response to voice commands using Siri. SiriKit integration and intents extensions are covered in the *An Introduction to SiriKit, An iOS 12 Example SiriKit Messaging Extension, An Overview of Siri Shortcut App Integration, Building Siri Shortcut Support into an iOS App* and *An iOS 12 SiriKit Photo Search Tutorial* chapters of this book.

86.3 Creating Extensions

By far the easiest approach to developing extensions is to use the extension templates provided by Xcode. Once the project for a containing app is loaded into Xcode, extensions can be added in the form of new targets by selecting the *File -> New -> Targets...* menu option. This will display the panel shown in Figure 86-6 listing a template for each of the extension types:

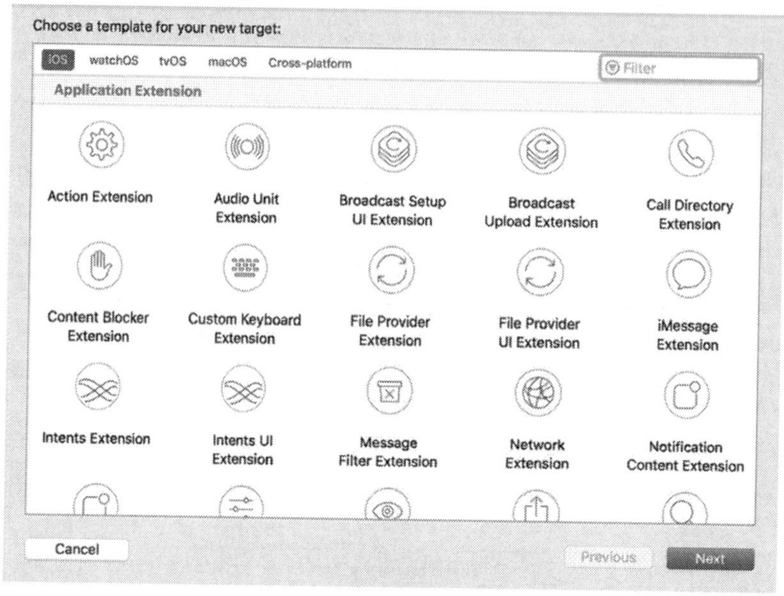

Figure 86-6

Once an extension template has been selected, simply click on *Next* to name and create the template. Once the extension has been created from the template, the steps to implement the extension will differ depending on the type of extension selected. The next few chapters will cover in detail the steps involved in implementing Today, Photo Editing, Action and Message app extensions.

86.4 Summary

Extensions in iOS provide a way for narrowly defined areas of functionality of one application to be made available from within other applications. iOS 12 currently supports a variety of extension types. It is important when developing extensions to select the most appropriate extension point before beginning development work and also to be aware that some application features may not be appropriate candidates to be placed into an extension.

Although extensions run as separate independent binaries, they are only able to be installed as part of an app bundle. The app with which an extension is bundled is called a *containing app*. An app from which an extension is launched is referred to as a *host app*.

Having covered the basics of extensions in this chapter, subsequent chapters will focus in detail on the more commonly used extension types.

Chapter 87

87. An iOS 12 Today Extension Widget Tutorial

With the basic concepts of extensions covered in the previous chapter, this chapter will work step-by-step through the creation of an example iOS 12 extension widget that will appear within the Today view of the Notifications panel. In the process of creating the example app, key areas of the Today extension implementation process will be covered in detail.

87.1 About the Example Extension Widget

The purpose of the extension created in this tutorial is to display the longitude and latitude of the user's current location within the Today view of the iOS Notification panel. The steps to achieve this will involve the addition of an extension target to an existing container app, the design of the widget user interface and the implementation of the code to obtain, display and update the appropriate location data.

As previously outlined, Apple states that the container app for a Today extension must itself perform some useful function in addition to serving as the delivery vehicle for an extension. In recognition of this requirement, the tutorial is intended to be implemented as an extension to the Location application created in the chapter of this book entitled *An Example iOS 12 Location Application*. The steps outlined in the chapter may still be followed, however, regardless of whether or not you have completed the location based chapter.

87.2 Creating the Example Project

If you previously completed the Location tutorial as outlined in the *An Example iOS 12 Location Application* chapter of this book, locate the project and load it into Xcode. If, on the other hand, you have yet to complete this tutorial, download the sample code for the examples in this book from the following URL, and locate and load the completed Location example project into Xcode:

https://www.ebookfrenzy.com/retail/ios12/

87.3 Adding the Extension to the Project

With the Location project loaded into Xcode, the next step is to add an extension target to the project using one of the extension templates provided by Xcode. From the Xcode menu, select the *File -> New -> Target...* menu option. In the resulting panel, select the *Application Extension* category listed under *iOS* in the left-hand panel, and the *Today Extension* template from the main panel as shown in Figure 87-1:

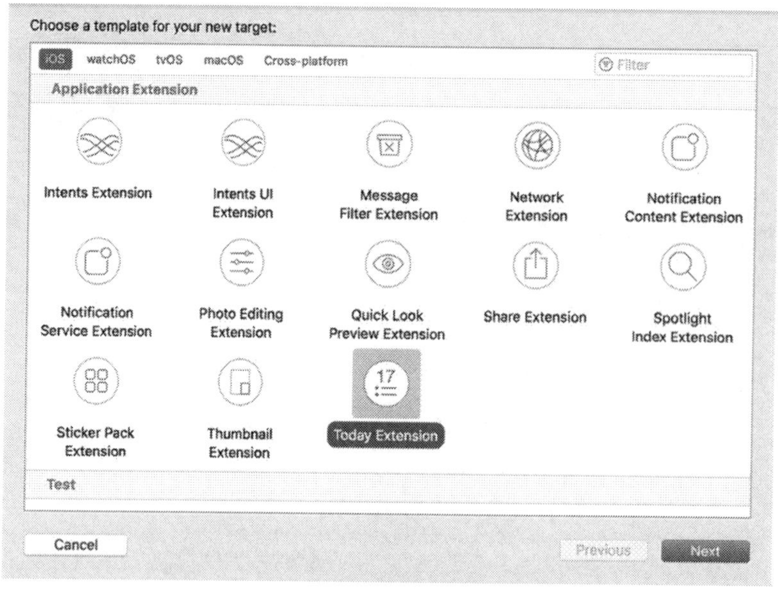

Figure 87-1

Click on the *Next* button and, on the options panel, enter *MyLocation* into the Product Name field, leaving the remaining settings unchanged from the default values provided by Xcode. Click on *Finish* to create the new extension target.

As soon as the target has been created, a new panel will appear requesting permission to activate the new scheme for the extension target. Every target within an Xcode project has associated with it a scheme which defines how that target is to be built. When an extension target is added to a project, Xcode automatically creates a corresponding scheme so that the extension can be built and run. Activate this scheme now by clicking on the *Activate* button in the request panel.

The Today extension can be tested using the default template settings simply by setting the extension scheme (MyLocation) as the active scheme from the Xcode toolbar as shown in Figure 87-2, selecting a suitable device or simulator target and clicking on the run button.

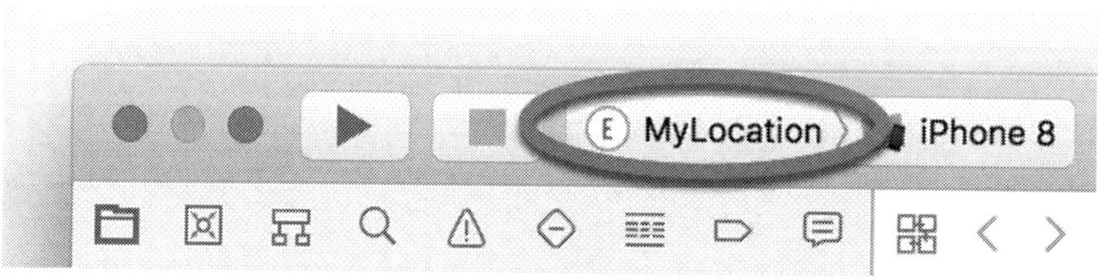

Figure 87-2

When an extension is launched it must do so within the context of a *host app*. Xcode will, therefore, automatically launch the Today app with the My Location extension loaded.

The default user interface for the Today template consists of a single label displaying text which reads "Hello World". Assuming a successful launch of the extension, the Today view will appear in the Notification panel with the widget displayed as illustrated in Figure 87-3:

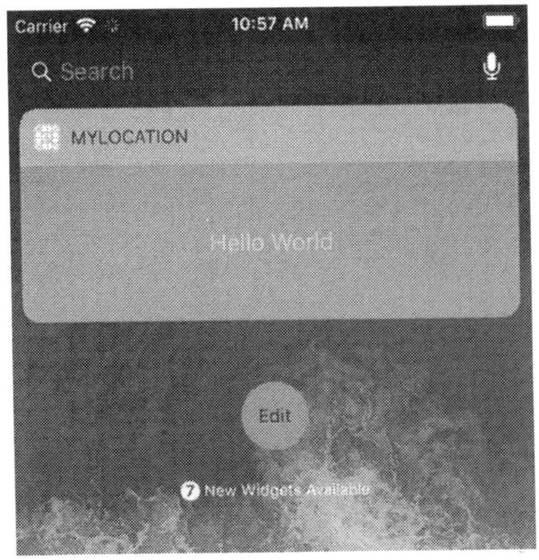

Figure 87-3

If the widget does not appear in the view, it may need to be enabled. Scroll down the Today view and select the *Edit* button when it comes into view. On the edit screen, locate the *MyLocation* widget and tap the green + button located next to it to add it to the view before selecting *Done*. If the extension is not listed, this can be resolved by stopping and relaunching it from within Xcode.

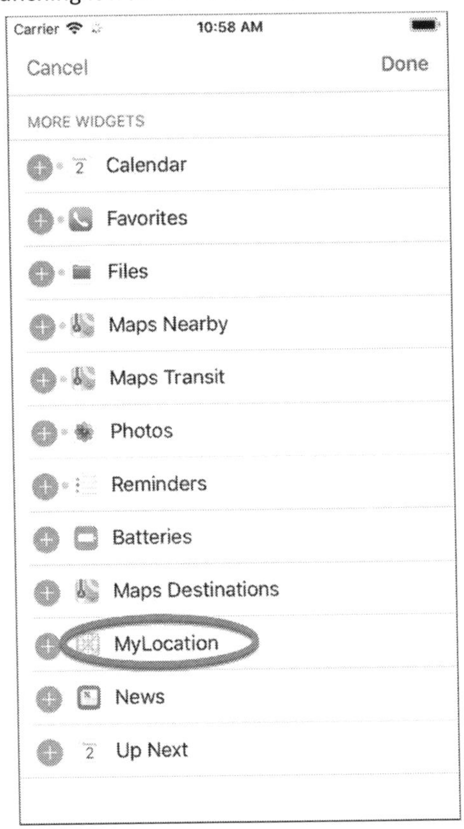

Figure 87-4

87.4 Reviewing the Extension Files

With the extension added to the project it is worth taking time to gain familiarity with the files which have been added. Within the project navigator panel a new folder will have been created entitled *MyLocation*. It is within this folder that all of the files associated with the extension are contained (Figure 87-5):

Figure 87-5

The files that make up a Today extension are as follows:

- **TodayViewController.swift** - Contains the source code for the View Controller representing the widget in the Today view.
- **MainInterface.storyboard** – The storyboard file containing the user interface of the widget as it will appear within the Today view.
- **Info.plist** – The information property list for the extension.

87.5 Designing the Widget User Interface

The Today extension template provided the project with a simple storyboard layout containing a single Label view. For the purposes of this tutorial, two labels will be required to display both the longitude and latitude of the user's current location. Within the Xcode project navigator panel, locate and select the *MyLocation -> MainInterface.storyboard* file to load it into the Interface Builder environment.

Begin by selecting and deleting the "Hello World" label from the view leaving a clean canvas on which to work (the label uses a very light shade of gray color so may not be visible within the view). By default, the template has configured the widget view with a height suitable to accommodate a single label. In order to fit two labels onto the widget this height property will need to be increased. Click on the background of the widget to select the view and display the Size Inspector. Within the inspector panel, change the *Height* property from 37 to 50 as shown in Figure 87-6:

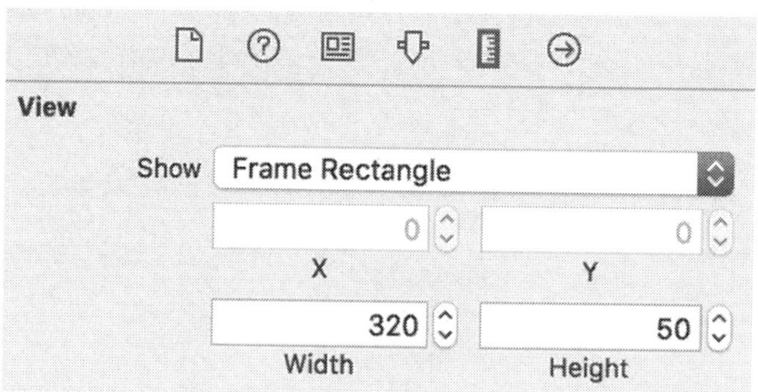

Figure 87-6

With the height increased, drag and drop two Label views from the object palette onto the view canvas so that the layout resembles that of Figure 87-7:

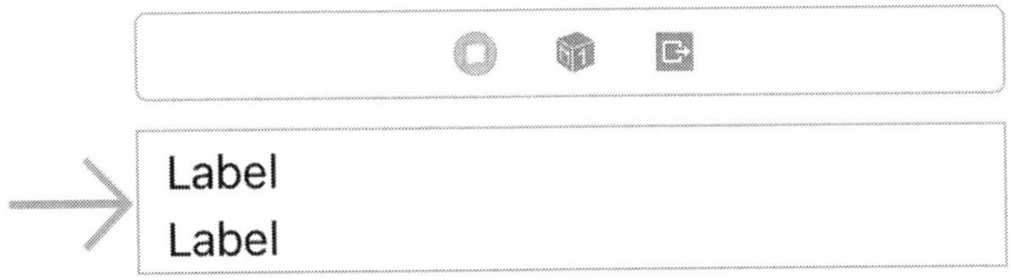

Figure 87-7

If the extension were to be launched on a device or simulator at this point, the labels would not be visible. The reason for this is that the Today view relies on Auto Layout settings within the widget layout, or specific preferred content size settings in the view controller code to decide on the size at which the widget should appear. Since no Auto Layout constraints have been configured, and no code has been added to set the preferred content size, the widget content would appear at zero height.

Select the uppermost Label and display the Auto Layout *Add New Constraints* menu (Figure 87-8). Enable the *Spacing to nearest neighbor* constraint on the top edge of the label by enabling the red constraint bar using the current value. Enable the nearest neighbor constraint on the left-hand edge of the label, once again leaving the current value unchanged. Turn off the *Constrain to margins* option, and click on the *Add 2 Constraints* button:

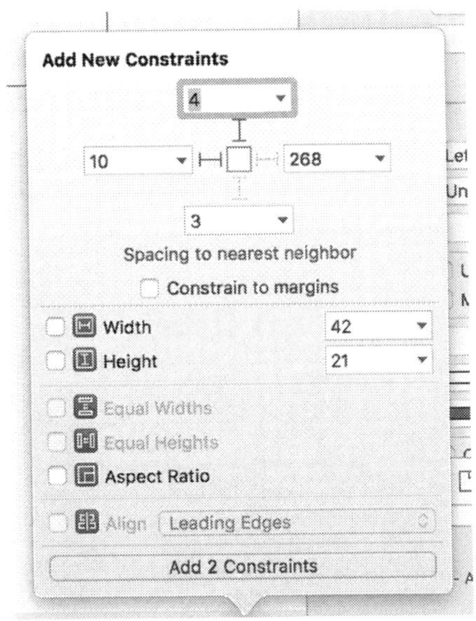

Figure 87-8

Select the bottom Label view and repeat the above steps, this time setting spacing constraints on the left and top edges of the view using the current spacing values for both constraints and once again with the *Constrain to margins* option disabled.

Run the extension and verify that the widget layout appears correctly within the Today view, returning to the storyboard file if necessary to make adjustments to the layout.

Once the layout work is complete, display the Assistant Editor panel and make sure that it is showing the source code contained in the *TodayViewController.swift* file. Ctrl-click on the upper Label view and drag the resulting line to a position beneath the class declaration line in the Assistant Editor panel. Release the line and, in the resulting connection dialog, establish an outlet connection named *latitudeLabel*. Repeat this sequence of steps for the bottom label, this time creating an outlet named *longitudeLabel*.

87.6 Setting the Preferred Content Size in Code

Although not necessary in this particular instance (since Auto Layout is being used to influence the height of the widget), it is worth noting that the height of a widget can be set in code using the *setPreferredContentSize* method of the extension view controller instance. For example, the following code changes the height of the widget to 200 before it is displayed to the user:

```
override func viewWillAppear(_ animated: Bool)
{
    var currentSize: CGSize = self.preferredContentSize
    currentSize.height = 200.0
    self.preferredContentSize = currentSize
}
```

This technique is particularly useful when it is necessary to dynamically change the size of a widget at runtime. A widget might, for example, display some initial information to the user and provide a "More" button to display more detailed information. In this scenario the "More" button would simply change the preferred content size to make additional views visible.

87.7 Modifying the Widget View Controller

The view controller class for the Today extension widget now needs to be implemented such that it obtains the user's current location and updates the labels in the widget accordingly. Select and edit the *TodayViewController.swift* file to import the CoreLocation Framework, declare an optional variable in which to store the current location and to create and initialize a location manager instance. Note also that the TodayViewController class declaration has been modified to indicate that it now implements the CLLocationManagerDelegate protocol:

```
import UIKit
import NotificationCenter
import CoreLocation

class TodayViewController: UIViewController, NCWidgetProviding, 
CLLocationManagerDelegate {

    @IBOutlet weak var latitudeLabel: UILabel!
    @IBOutlet weak var longitudeLabel: UILabel!

    var locationManager: CLLocationManager = CLLocationManager()
    var currentLocation: CLLocation?

    override func viewDidLoad() {
        super.viewDidLoad()
        locationManager.desiredAccuracy = kCLLocationAccuracyBest
        locationManager.delegate = self
        locationManager.requestLocation()
    }
.
.
```

```
.
}
```

To meet the conformance requirements of the CLLocationManagerDelegate protocol, and in order to be able to receive location update notifications, the location manager's *didUpdateLocations* delegate method now needs to be implemented along with the *didFailWithError* delegate method. The code within this method will extract the latest location information and assign it to the previously declared *currentLocation* optional variable:

```
func locationManager(_ manager: CLLocationManager, didUpdateLocations
  locations: [CLLocation]) {
    currentLocation = locations[0]
}

func locationManager(_ manager: CLLocationManager, didFailWithError error:
Error) {
    print(error.localizedDescription)
}
```

Next, a convenience function needs to be written to update the labels with the latest location data:

```
func updateWidget()
{
    if let location = currentLocation {
        let latitudeText = String(format: "Lat: %.4f",
                                  location.coordinate.latitude)

        let longitudeText = String(format: "Lon: %.4f",
                                   location.coordinate.longitude)

        latitudeLabel.text = latitudeText
        longitudeLabel.text = longitudeText
    }
}
```

This function verifies that the *currentLocation* optional variable contains a value and, if so, constructs String objects containing the current longitude and latitude values before displaying them on the corresponding widget labels.

The last modification to the widget view controller is to ensure that the *updateWidget* function is called at the appropriate times so that the user sees the latest location information each time the widget is displayed in the Today view. To make sure the function is called prior to the widget being displayed, the *viewWillAppear* method of the view controller needs to be overridden as follows:

```
override func viewWillAppear(_ animated: Bool) {
    updateWidget()
}
```

From time to time, the system will take snapshots of the widget so that information can be presented quickly to the user when the Today view is displayed. To make sure that the latest information is displayed when the system takes snapshots of the widget, it is also necessary to update the widget within the *widgetPerformUpdate(completionHandler:)* method, a template of which has been provided by Xcode in the *TodayViewController.swift* file. All that needs to be added to this method is a call to our *updateWidget* method:

```
func widgetPerformUpdate(completionHandler: ((NCUpdateResult) -> Void)) {
    updateWidget()
    completionHandler(NCUpdateResult.newData)
}
```

87.8 Testing the Extension

Compile and run the extension using the extension's scheme at which point it should appear as shown in Figure 87-9. If the labels do not update to reflect the current location, use the *Edit* button to disable and then re-enable the widget.

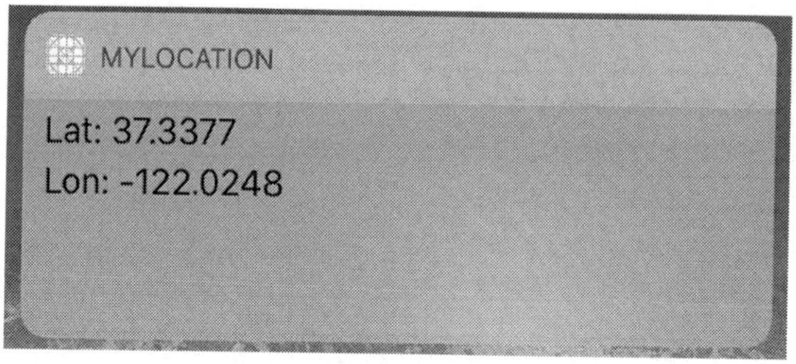

Figure 87-9

87.9 Opening the Containing App from the Extension

When developing extensions it may be useful to provide the user with the ability to open the containing application from within the extension. The MyLocation Today widget, for example, only displays a subset of the data available within the containing Location app.

Every extension has associated with it an *extension context* object, a reference to which can be accessed via the *extensionContext* property of the extension's view controller instance. Among the methods available to be called on the extension context object is the *openURL* method which can be used to launch other, suitably configured applications.

In order for an application to be launchable using the *openURL* method, the *Info.plist* file for that application must define a custom URL scheme. This essentially declares the URL name by which the application is identified (represented by the *CFBundleURLName* key and typically set using a reverse domain name identifier such as com.ebookfrenzy.location) and the schemes it supports (via an array of string values assigned to the *CFBundleURLSchemes* key).

For the purposes of this example, the *Info.plist* file for the Location application will be modified to specify a *CFBundleURLName* value of *com.ebookfrenzy.location* and a URL scheme named *location*. While this can be achieved using the Xcode property list editor, it is actually quicker in this instance to directly edit the XML source of the *Info.plist* file.

Within the project navigator panel Ctrl-click on the *Location -> Info.plist* file and select the *Open As -> Source Code* menu option. Once the file has loaded into the editor, modify it to add the URL scheme entries as follows:

```
<?xml version="1.0" encoding="UTF-8"?>
```

```
<!DOCTYPE plist PUBLIC "-//Apple//DTD PLIST 1.0//EN"
"http://www.apple.com/DTDs/PropertyList-1.0.dtd">
<plist version="1.0">
<dict>
        <key>CFBundleURLTypes</key>
        <array>
                <dict>
                        <key>CFBundleURLName</key>
                        <string>com.ebookfrenzy.location</string>
                        <key>CFBundleURLSchemes</key>
                        <array>
                                <string>location</string>
                        </array>
                </dict>
        </array>
.
.
</dict>
</plist>
```

The user interface layout for the MyLocation widget now needs to be modified to include a Button view which, when selected, will open the Location application. Select the *MainInterface.storyboard* file to load it into Interface Builder and add a Button which reads "Open" positioned as shown in Figure 87-10:

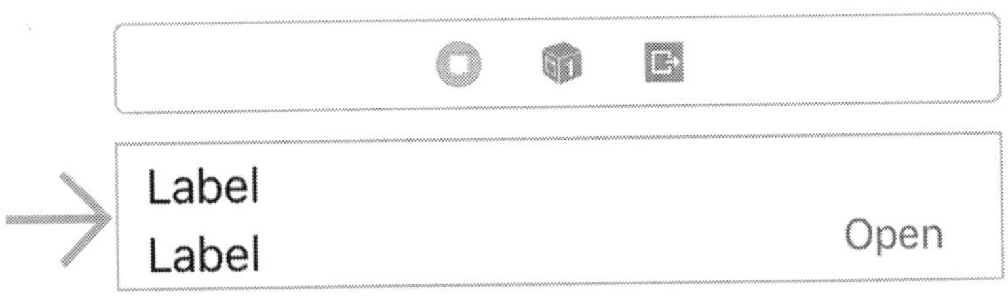

Figure 87-10

Display the Assistant Editor and verify that it is listing the source code for the *TodayViewController.swift* file. Ctrl-click and drag from the newly added Button view to the location within the Swift file where you would like the action method to be placed and release the line. In the resulting panel, change the connection type to *Action* and name the action *openApp* before clicking on the *Connect* button.

Edit the *openApp* method to construct the URL (which is referenced by the CFBundleURLSchemes *location* string) and to call the *openURL* method of the extension context:

```
@IBAction func openApp(_ sender: Any) {

    let url: URL? = URL(string: "location:")!

    if let appurl = url {
        self.extensionContext!.open(appurl,
            completionHandler: nil)
    }
```

```
}
```

In order to test this new functionality it will be necessary to build and re-install both the Location containing app and the MyLocation extension. Begin by selecting the Location scheme from the Xcode toolbar and build and run the application on the target device or simulator. Next, change the scheme to MyLocation and build and run the extension using the Today view as the host app.

Once the extension is visible in the Today view, touch the *Open* button to launch the Location container app.

87.10 **Summary**

The Today extension allows widgets to appear within the Today view of the iOS Notification panel. Today widgets are essentially view controllers with the user interface of the widget contained within a storyboard file. It is important when designing a widget to make sure that it is small and lightweight and that either Auto Layout constraints or preferred content size method calls are made to ensure that the widget is sized correctly within the Today view. The system will call the *widgetPerformUpdate(completionHandler:)* delegate method of the extension view controller at regular intervals in an effort to ensure that recent data is available to be displayed next time the view appears. A widget may provide the option to launch another app from within the Today view using the *openURL* method of the extension context instance.

Chapter 88

88. Creating an iOS 12 Photo Editing Extension

The primary purpose of the iOS Photo Editing extension is to allow the photo editing capabilities of an application to be made available from within the standard iOS Photos application. Consider, for example, a scenario where a developer has published an app that allows users to apply custom changes and special effects to videos or photos. Prior to the introduction of extensions, the only way for a user to access these capabilities would have been to launch and work within that application. By placing some of the functionality of the application into a Photo Editing extension, the user is now able to select videos or photos from within the Photos app and choose the extension from a range of editing options available on the device. Once selected, the user interface for the extension is displayed to the user so that changes can be made to the chosen image or video. Once the user has finished making the changes and exits the extension, the modified image or video is returned to the Photos app.

88.1 Creating a Photo Editing Extension

As with all extension types, by far the easiest starting point when creating a Photo Editing extension is to use the template provided by Xcode. For the purposes of this chapter, create a new Xcode project named PhotoDemo using the Single View Application template and the Swift programing language.

Once the application project has been created, a new target will need to be added for the Photo Editing extension. To achieve this, select the *File -> New -> Target…* menu option and choose the *Photo Editing Extension* template from the main panel as shown in Figure 88-1:

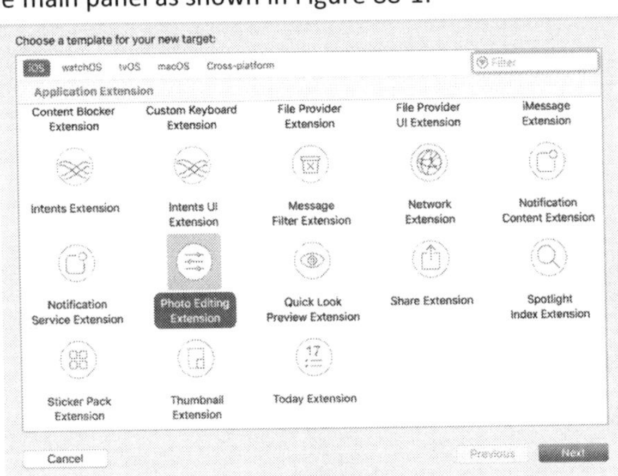

Figure 88-1

With the appropriate options selected, click on the Next button and enter *MyPhotoExt* into the Product Name field. Leave the remaining fields set to the default values and click on Finish to complete the extension creation process. When prompted, click on the *Activate* button to activate the scheme created by Xcode to enable the extension to be built and run.

Once the extension has been added, it will appear in the project navigator panel under the *MyPhotoExt* folder. This folder will contain both the Swift source code file for the extension's view controller named *PhotoEditingViewController.swift* and the corresponding user interface storyboard file named *MainInterface.storyboard*. In addition, an *Info.plist* file will be present in the sub-folder.

88.2 Accessing the Photo Editing Extension

Before beginning work on implementing the functionality of the extension, it is important to learn how to access such an extension from within the iOS Photos app. Begin by verifying that the *MyPhotoExt* build scheme is selected in the Xcode toolbar as illustrated in Figure 88-2.

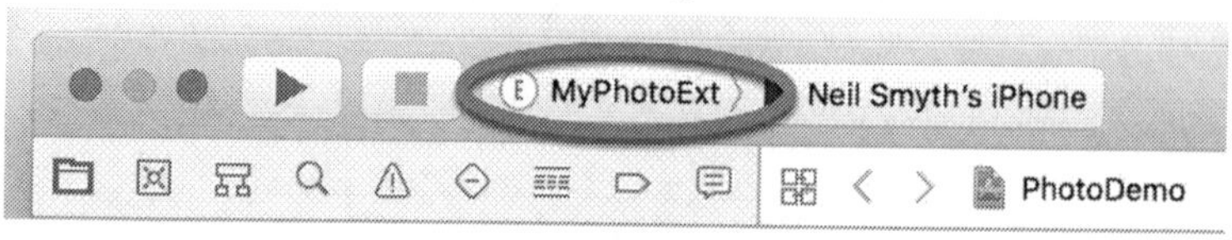

Figure 88-2

If the extension is not currently selected, click on the current scheme name and select *MyPhotoExt* from the drop down menu. Having verified that the appropriate scheme is selected, click on the toolbar run button. Since this is an extension, it can only be run within the context of a host application. As a result, Xcode will display a panel listing the applications installed on the attached device. From this list of available applications (Figure 88-3), select the *Photos* app and click on the *Run* button.

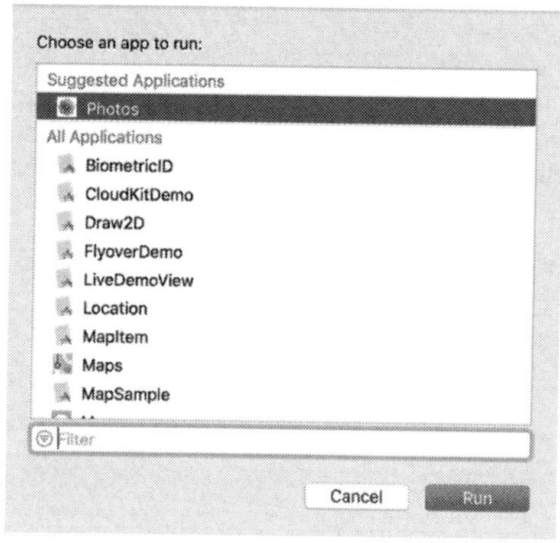

Figure 88-3

After the extension and containing application have been compiled and installed, the Photos app will automatically launch. If it does not, launch it manually from the device screen. Once the Photos app appears, select a photo from those stored on the device and, once selected, tap on the *Edit* button located in the toolbar along the top edge of the screen as illustrated in Figure 88-4 to enter the standard editing interface of the Photos app.

Figure 88-4

Within the tab bar along the bottom of the Photos editing tool is a small round button containing three dots (as highlighted in Figure 88-5):

Figure 88-5

Tapping this button will display the action panel (as shown in Figure 88-6) where Photo Editing extensions may be chosen and used to edit videos and images.

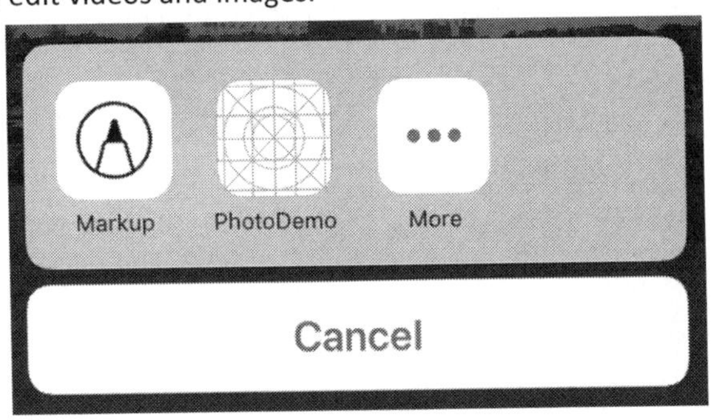

Figure 88-6

Assuming that the extension for our *PhotoDemo* application is displayed, select it and wait for the extension to launch. Once the extension has loaded it will appear in the form of the user interface as defined in the *MyPhotoExt -> MainInterface.storyboard* file.

88.3 Configuring the Info.plist File

A Photo Editing extension must declare the type of media it is able to edit. This is specified via the *PHSupportedMediaTypes* key within the *NSExtension* section of the extension's *Info.plist* file. By default, the Photo Editing template declares that the extension is capable of editing only images as follows:

```
<plist version="1.0">
.
.
.
        <key>NSExtension</key>
         <dict>
                <key>NSExtensionAttributes</key>
                <dict>
                        <key>PHSupportedMediaTypes</key>
                        <array>
                                <string>Image</string>
                        </array>
                </dict>
                <key>NSExtensionMainStoryboard</key>
                <string>MainInterface</string>
                <key>NSExtensionPointIdentifier</key>
                <string>com.apple.photo-editing</string>
        </dict>
</dict>
</plist>
```

If the extension is also able to edit video files, the *PHSupportedMediaTypes* entry within the file would be modified as follows:

```
<key>PHSupportedMediaTypes</key>
      <array>
          <string>Video</string>
          <string>Image</string>
      </array>
```

For the purposes of this example, leave the *Info.plist* file unchanged with support for images only.

88.4 Designing the User Interface

The user interface for the extension is going to consist of an Image View and a Toolbar containing three Bar Button Items. Within the Xcode project navigator panel, locate and load the *MyPhotoExt -> MainInterface.storyboard* file into Interface Builder and select and delete the "Hello World" Label view. With a clean canvas, design and configure the layout so that it consists of an Image View, Toolbar and three Toolbar Button Items as shown in Figure 88-7:

Figure 88-7

Select the Image View, display the Attributes Inspector panel and change the Content Mode setting to *Aspect Fit*.

With the Image View still selected, display the Auto Layout *Add New Constraints* menu and set *Spacing to nearest neighbor* constraints on all four sides of the view with the *Constrain to margins* option switched off.

Click to select the Toolbar view and use the Auto Layout *Add New Constraints* menu once again to apply *Spacing to nearest neighbor* constraints on the left, right and bottom edges of the view with the *Constrain to margins* option still switched off. Before adding the constraints, also enable the *Height* constraint option using the currently displayed value.

Display the Assistant Editor and verify that it is displaying the source code for the *PhotoEditingViewController.swift* file. Select the Bar Button Item displaying the "Sepia" text (note that it may be necessary to click twice since the first click will select the parent Toolbar view). With the item selected, Ctrl-click on the item and drag the resulting line to a position immediately beneath the end of the implementation of the *viewDidLoad* method in the Assistant Editor panel. Release the line and, in the connection dialog, establish an Action named *sepiaSelected*. Repeat these steps for the "Mono" and "Invert" Bar Button Items, naming the Actions *monoSelected* and *invertSelected* respectively.

Finally, Ctrl-click on the Image View and drag the resulting line to a position beneath the "class PhotoEditingViewController" declaration. Release the line and establish an Outlet for the Image View named *imageView*.

88.5 The PHContentEditingController Protocol

When Xcode created the template for the Photo Editing extension it created a View Controller class named PhotoEditingViewController and declared it as implementing the PHContentEditingController protocol. It also generated stub methods for each of the methods that must be implemented in order for the class to conform with the protocol. The remainder of implementing a Photo Editing extension primarily consists of writing the code for these methods to implement the required editing behavior. One of the first methods that will need to be implemented relates to the issue of adjustment data.

88.6 Photo Extensions and Adjustment Data

When a Photo Extension is selected by the user, a method named *canHandle(adjustmentData:)* is called on the view controller class of the extension. The method must return a true or false value depending on whether or not the extension supports adjustment data.

If an extension supports adjustment data, it is passed a copy of the original image or video together with a set of data outlining any earlier modifications made to the media during previous editing sessions. The extension then re-applies those changes to the file or video to get it back to the point where it was at the end of the last editing session. The advantage of this approach is that the extension is able to offer the user the ability to undo any previous editing operations performed within previous sessions using the extension. When editing is completed, the extension returns the modified image or video file, together with any new adjustment data reflecting edits that were performed during the current session.

If an image editing extension indicates that it does not support adjustment data, it is passed a copy of the modified image as it appeared at the end of the last editing session. This enables the user to perform additional editing tasks but does not allow previous edits to be undone. In the case of video editing extensions that do not support adjustment data, the extension will be passed the original video and previous edits will be lost. Clearly, therefore, supporting adjustment data is an important requirement for video editing.

While the example contained within this tutorial will store and return adjustment data to the Photos app allowing for future improvements to the extension it will not handle incoming adjustment data. Within the *PhotoEditingViewController.swift* file, therefore, locate and review the *canHandle(adjustmentData:)* method and verify that it is configured to return a *false* value:

```
func canHandle(_ adjustmentData: PHAdjustmentData) -> Bool {
    return false
}
```

88.7 Receiving the Content

The next method that will be called on the extension View Controller class is the *startContentEditing* method.

This method is passed as arguments a *PHContentEditingInput* object and a placeholder image. For images, this object contains a compressed version of the image suitable for displaying to the user, a URL referencing the location of the full size image, information about the orientation of the image and, in the case of extensions with adjustment data support, a set of adjustment data from previous edits.

As previously discussed, image extensions with adjustment data support implemented are passed the original image and a set of adjustments to be made to reach parity with the latest state of editing. Since it can take time to render these changes, the placeholder argument contains a snapshot of the image as it currently appears. This can be displayed to the user while the adjustment data is applied and the image rendered in the background.

For this example, the *startContentEditing* method will be implemented as follows:

```
import UIKit
import Photos
import PhotosUI

class PhotoEditingViewController: UIViewController,
PHContentEditingController {

    @IBOutlet weak var imageView: UIImageView!
```

```
    var input: PHContentEditingInput?
    var displayedImage: UIImage?
    var imageOrientation: Int32?
.
.
.
    func startContentEditing(with contentEditingInput:
          PHContentEditingInput, placeholderImage: UIImage) {

        input = contentEditingInput

        if let input = input {
            displayedImage = input.displaySizeImage
            imageOrientation = input.fullSizeImageOrientation
            imageView.image = displayedImage
        }
    }
.
.
.
}
```

The above changes declare two optional variables to contain a reference to the display sized image and the image orientation. The code in the method then assigns the display sized image from the *PHContentEditingInput* object passed to the method to the *displayedImage* variable and also stores the orientation setting in the *imageOrientation* variable. Finally, the display sized image is displayed on the Image View in the user interface so that it is visible to the user.

Compile and run the extension, selecting the Photos app as the host application, and verify that the extension displays a copy of the image in the Image View of the extension View Controller.

88.8 Implementing the Filter Actions

The actions connected to the Bar Button Items will change the image by applying Core Image sepia, monochrome and invert filters. Until the user commits the edits made in the extension, any filtering will be performed only on the display sized image to avoid the rendering delays that are likely to be incurred working on the full sized image. Having performed the filter, the modified image will be displayed on the image view instance.

Remaining within the *PhotoEditingViewController.swift* file, implement the three action methods as follows:

```
class PhotoEditingViewController: UIViewController,
 PHContentEditingController {

    @IBOutlet weak var imageView: UIImageView!

    var input: PHContentEditingInput?
    var displayedImage: UIImage?
```

```
    var imageOrientation: Int32?
    var currentFilter = "CIColorInvert"

    override func viewDidLoad() {
        super.viewDidLoad()
        // Do any additional setup after loading the view.
    }

    @IBAction func sepiaSelected(_ sender: Any) {
        currentFilter = "CISepiaTone"

        if let image = displayedImage {
            imageView.image = performFilter(image,
                                            orientation: nil)
        }
    }

    @IBAction func monoSelected(_ sender: Any) {
        currentFilter = "CIPhotoEffectMono"

        if let image = displayedImage {
            imageView.image = performFilter(image,
                                            orientation: nil)
        }
    }

    @IBAction func invertSelected(_ sender: Any) {
        currentFilter = "CIColorInvert"

        if let image = displayedImage {
            imageView.image = performFilter(image,
                                            orientation: nil)
        }
    }
.
.
.
}
```

In each case, a method named *performFilter* is called to perform the image filtering task. The next step, clearly, is to implement this method using the techniques outlined in the chapter entitled *An iOS 12 Graphics Tutorial using Core Graphics and Core Image*:

```
func performFilter(_ inputImage: UIImage, orientation: Int32?)
    -> UIImage?
```

```
{
    var resultImage: UIImage?
    var cimage: CIImage

    cimage = CIImage(image: inputImage)!

    if let orientation = orientation {
        cimage = cimage.oriented(forExifOrientation: orientation)
    }

    if let filter = CIFilter(name: currentFilter) {
        filter.setDefaults()
        filter.setValue(cimage, forKey: "inputImage")

        switch currentFilter {

            case "CISepiaTone", "CIEdges":
                filter.setValue(0.8, forKey: "inputIntensity")

            case "CIMotionBlur":
                filter.setValue(25.00, forKey:"inputRadius")
                filter.setValue(0.00, forKey:"inputAngle")

            default:
                break
        }

        if let ciFilteredImage = filter.outputImage {
            let context = CIContext(options: nil)
            if let cgImage = context.createCGImage(ciFilteredImage,
                            from: ciFilteredImage.extent) {
                resultImage = UIImage(cgImage: cgImage)
            }
        }
    }
    return resultImage
}
```

The above method takes the image passed through as a parameter, takes steps to maintain the original orientation and performs an appropriately configured filter operation on the image based on the value assigned to the *currentFilter* variable. The filtered image is then returned to the calling method.

Compile and run the extension once again, this time using the filter buttons to change the appearance of the displayed image.

88.9 Returning the Image to the Photos App

When the user has finished making changes to the image and touches the *Done* button located in the extension toolbar, the *finishContentEditing(completionHandler:)* method of the View Controller is called. This is passed a reference to a completion handler which must be called once the image has been rendered and is ready to be returned to the Photos app.

Before calling the completion handler, however, this method performs the following tasks:

1. Obtains a copy of the full size version of the image.
2. Ensures that the original orientation of the image is preserved through the rendering process.
3. Applies to the full sized image all of the editing operations previously performed on the display sized image.
4. Renders the new version of the full sized image.
5. Packages up the adjustment data outlining the edits performed during the session.

Since the above tasks (particularly the rendering phase) are likely to take time, these must be performed within a separate asynchronous thread. The code to complete this example extension can now be implemented within the template stub of the method as follows:

```
func finishContentEditing(completionHandler: @escaping
((PHContentEditingOutput?) -> Void)) {
    // Update UI to reflect that editing has finished and output is being
rendered.

    // Render and provide output on a background queue.
    DispatchQueue.global().async {
        // Create editing output from the editing input.
        if let input = self.input {
            let output = PHContentEditingOutput(contentEditingInput: input)

            let url = self.input?.fullSizeImageURL

            if let imageUrl = url,
                let fullImage = UIImage(contentsOfFile: imageUrl.path),
                let resultImage = self.performFilter(fullImage,
                                orientation: self.imageOrientation) {

                if let renderedJPEGData =
                    resultImage.jpegData(compressionQuality: 0.9)  {
                    try! renderedJPEGData.write(to:
                        output.renderedContentURL)
                }

                do {
                    let archivedData =
                     try NSKeyedArchiver.archivedData(
                            withRootObject: self.currentFilter,
                      requiringSecureCoding: true)
```

```
                let adjustmentData =
                    PHAdjustmentData(formatIdentifier:
                        "com.ebookfrenzy.photoext",
                                         formatVersion: "1.0",
                                         data: archivedData)

                output.adjustmentData = adjustmentData
            } catch {
                print("Unable to archive image data")
            }
        }
        completionHandler(output)
    }
  }
}
```

The code begins by creating a new instance of the *PHContentEditingOutput* class, initialized with the content of the input object originally passed into the extension:

```
if let input = self.input {
    let output = PHContentEditingOutput(contentEditingInput: input)
```

Next, the URL of the full sized version of the image is extracted from the original input object and the corresponding image loaded into a UIImage instance. The full sized image is then filtered via a call to the *performFilter* method:

```
if let imageUrl = url,
   let fullImage = UIImage(contentsOfFile: imageUrl.path),
   let resultImage = self.performFilter(fullImage,
                                  orientation: self.imageOrientation) {
```

With the editing operations now applied to the full sized image, it is rendered into JPEG format and written out to a location specified by the URL assigned to the *renderedContentURL* property of the previously created *PHContentEditingOutput* instance:

```
if let renderedJPEGData =
      resultImage.jpegData(compressionQuality: 0.9)  {
      try! renderedJPEGData.write(to: output.renderedContentURL)
}
```

Although the extension had previously indicated that it was not able to accept adjustment data, returning adjustment data reflecting the edits performed on the image to the Photos app is mandatory. For this tutorial, the name of the Core Image filter used to modify the image is archived into a Data instance together with a revision number and a unique identifier. This object is then packaged into a *PHAdjustmentData* instance and assigned to the *adjustmentData* property of the output object:

```
let archivedData = try NSKeyedArchiver.archivedData(
                        withRootObject: self.currentFilter,
```

```
                                requiringSecureCoding: true)
let adjustmentData =
            PHAdjustmentData(formatIdentifier:
                                    "com.ebookfrenzy.photoext",
                                formatVersion: "1.0",
                                data: archivedData)

output.adjustmentData = adjustmentData
```

If the extension were to be enhanced to handle adjustment data, code would need to be added to the *canHandle(adjustmentData:)* method to compare the *formatVersion* and *formatIdentifier* values from the incoming adjustment data with those specified in the outgoing data to verify that the data is compatible with the editing capabilities of the extension.

Finally, the completion handler is called and passed the fully configured output object. At this point, control will return to the Photos app and the modified image will appear in the Photos editing screen.

88.10 Testing the Application

Build and run the extension using the Photos app as the host and take the, by now familiar, steps to select an image and invoke the newly created Photo Editing extension. Use a toolbar button to change the appearance of the image before tapping the *Done* button. The modified image will subsequently appear within the Photos app editing screen (Figure 88-8 shows the results of the invert filter) where the changes can be committed or discarded:

Figure 88-8

88.11 Summary

The Photo Editing extension allows the image editing capabilities of a containing app to be accessed from within the standard iOS Photos app. A Photo Editing extension takes the form of a view controller which implements the PHContentEditingController protocol and the protocol's associated delegate methods.

89. Creating an iOS 12 Action Extension

As with other extension types, the purpose of the Action extension is to extend elements of functionality from one application so that it is available for use within other applications. In the case of Action extensions, this functionality generally must fit the narrow definition of enabling the user to either transform the content within a host application, or view it in a different way. An application designed to translate text into different languages might, for example, provide an extension to allow the content of other applications to be similarly translated.

This chapter will introduce the concept of Action extensions in greater detail and put theory into practice through the creation of an example application and Action extension.

89.1 An Overview of Action Extensions

Action extensions appear within the activity view controller which is the panel that appears when the user taps the Share button within a running application. Figure 89-1, for example, shows the activity view controller panel as it appears from within the Safari web browser running on an iPhone. Action extensions appear within the action area of this panel alongside the built-in actions such as printing and copying of content.

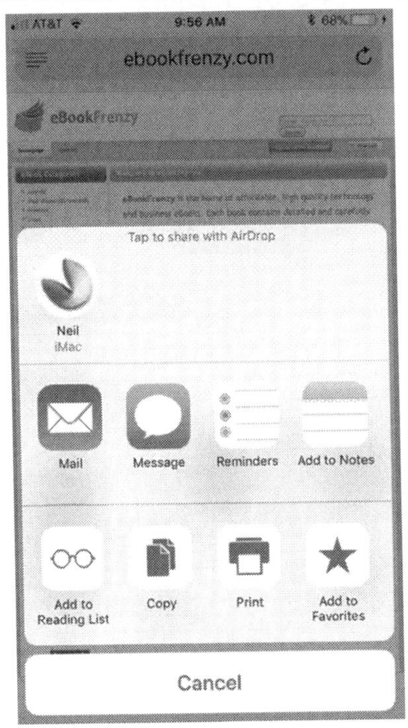

Figure 89-1

When an Action extension is created, it must declare the types of content with which it is able to work. The appearance or otherwise of the Action extension within the activity view controller is entirely context sensitive. In other words, an Action extension that is only able to work with text based content will not appear as an option in the activity view controller when the user is currently working with or viewing image or video content within a host app.

Unlike other extension types, there are two sides to an Action extension. In the first instance, there is the Action extension itself. An Action extension must be bundled with a containing application which must, in turn, provide some useful and meaningful functionality to the user. The other possibility is for host apps to be able to move beyond simply displaying the Action extension as an option within the activity view controller. With the appropriate behavior implemented, a host app can receive modified content from an Action extension and make constructive use of it on the user's behalf. In the remainder of this chapter and the next chapter, both of these concepts will be implemented through the creation of an example Action extension and host app.

89.2 About the Action Extension Example

The tutorial in the remainder of this and the next chapter is divided into two distinct phases. The initial phase involves the creation of an Action extension named "Change it Up" designed to display the text content of host apps in upper case and using a larger font so that it is easier to read. For the sake of brevity, the containing app will not provide any additional functionality beyond containing the extension, though it is important to remember that in the real world it will need to do so.

The second phase of the tutorial involves the creation of a host app that is able to receive modified content back from the Action extension and use it to replace the original content. This will be covered in the next chapter entitled *Receiving Data from an iOS 12 Action Extension*.

89.3 Creating the Action Extension Project

An Action extension is created by adding an extension target to a containing app. Begin by launching Xcode and creating a new Single View Application project named *ActionDemo* using Swift as the programming language.

89.4 Adding the Action Extension Target

With the newly created project loaded into Xcode, select the *File -> New -> Target...* menu option and, in the template panel (Figure 89-2), select the options to create an iOS Application Extension using the Action Extension template:

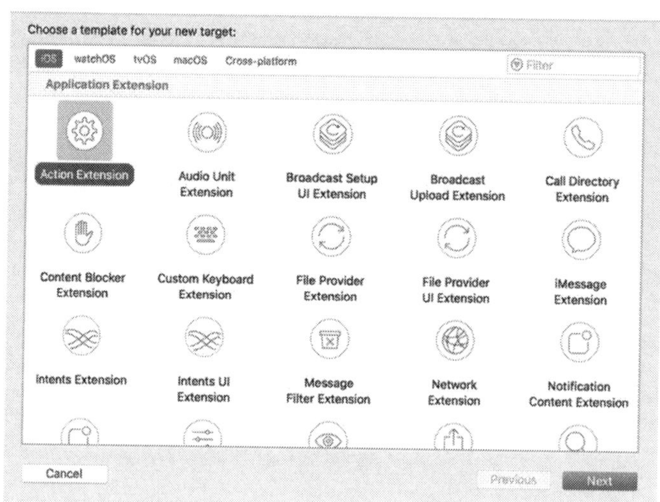

Figure 89-2

With the appropriate options selected, click on the *Next* button and enter *MyActionExt* into the Product Name field. Leave the remaining fields set to the default values and click on *Finish* to complete the extension creation process. When prompted, click on the *Activate* button to activate the scheme created by Xcode to enable the extension to be built and run.

Once the extension has been added, it will appear in the project navigator panel under the *MyActionExt* folder. This folder will contain the Swift source code file for the extension's view controller named *ActionViewController.swift*, a user interface storyboard file named *MainInterface.storyboard* and an *Info.plist* file.

89.5 Changing the Extension Display Name

An important configuration change concerns the name that will appear beneath the extension icon in the activity view controller. This is dictated by the value assigned to the *Bundle display name* key within the *Info.plist* file for the extension and currently reads "MyActionExt". Select the *Info.plist* file located under *MyActionExt* in the Project Navigator panel, locate this key and change the value so that it now reads "Change it Up".

89.6 Designing the Action Extension User Interface

The user interface for the Action extension is contained in the *MyActionExt -> MainInterface.storyboard* file. Locate this file in the project navigator panel and load it into Interface Builder.

By default, Xcode has created a template user interface consisting of a toolbar, a "Done" button and an image view. The only change necessary for the purposes of this example is to replace the image view with a text view. Select the image view in the storyboard canvas and remove it using the keyboard Delete key. From the Library panel drag and drop a Text View object onto the storyboard and position and resize it so that it fills the space previously occupied by the image view.

With the new Text View object still selected, display the *Resolve Auto Layout Issues* menu (indicated in Figure 89-3) and select the *Reset to Suggested Constraints* menu option.

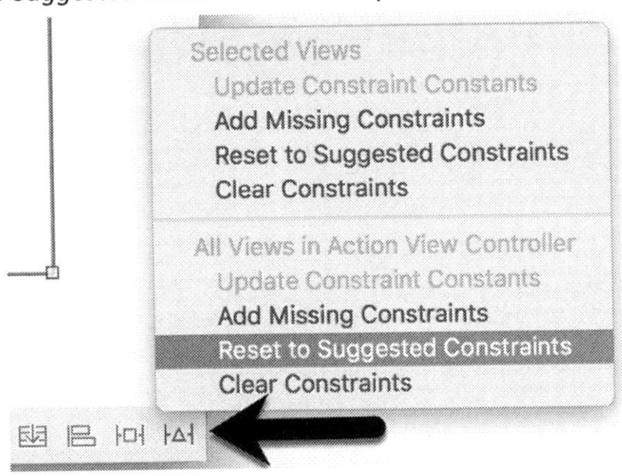

Figure 89-3

Display the Attributes Inspector for the Text View object and delete the default Latin text and, in the *Behavior* section of the panel, turn off the *Editable* option. As previously outlined, one of the features of this extension is that the content is displayed in a larger font so take this opportunity to increase the font setting in the Attribute Inspector from System 14.0 to System 39.0.

Finally, display the Assistant Editor panel and establish an outlet connection for the Text View object named *myTextView*. Remaining within the Assistant Editor, delete the line of code declaring the imageView outlet.

With these changes made, the user interface for the Action extension view controller should resemble that of Figure 89-4:

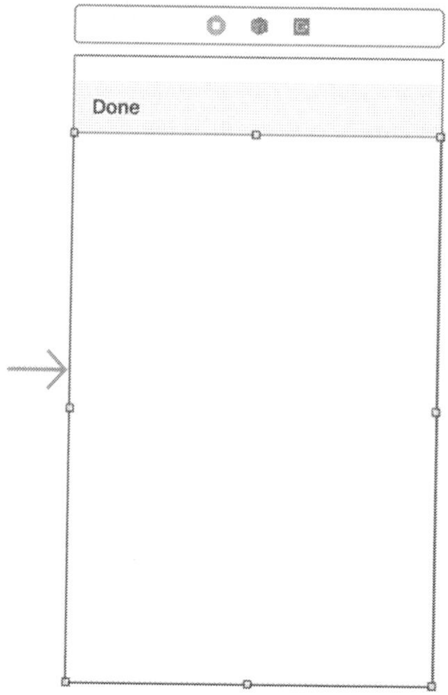

Figure 89-4

89.7 Receiving the Content

The next step in the tutorial is to add some code to receive the content from a host app when the extension is launched. All extension view controllers have an associated *extension context* in the form of an instance of the NSExtensionContext class. A reference to the extension context can be accessed via the *extensionContext* property of the view controller.

The extension context includes a property named *inputItems* in the form of an array containing objects which provide access to the content from the host app. The input items are, in turn, contained within one or more NSExtensionItem objects.

Within the *ActionViewController.swift* file, locate the *viewDidLoad* method, remove the template code added by Xcode and modify the method to obtain a reference to the first input item object:

```
override func viewDidLoad() {
    super.viewDidLoad()

    let textItem = self.extensionContext!.inputItems[0]
                        as! NSExtensionItem
}
```

Each NSExtensionItem object contains an array of *attachment* objects. These attachment objects are of type NSItemProvider and provide access to the data held by the host app. Once a reference to an attachment has been obtained, the *hasItemConformingToTypeIdentifier* method of the object can be called to verify that the host application has data of the type supported by the extension. In the case of this example, the extension supports text based content so the *kUTTypeText* uniform type identifier (UTI) is used to perform this test:

```
override func viewDidLoad() {
    super.viewDidLoad()

    let textItem = self.extensionContext!.inputItems[0]
                as! NSExtensionItem

    let textItemProvider = textItem.attachments![0]

    if textItemProvider.hasItemConformingToTypeIdentifier(
                    kUTTypeText as String) {
    }
}
```

Assuming that the host app has data of the required type, it can be loaded into the extension via a call to the *loadItem(forTypeIdentifier:)* method of the attachment provider object, once again passing through as an argument the UTI content type supported by the extension. The loading of the data from the host app is performed asynchronously so a completion handler must be specified which will be called when the data loading process is complete:

```
override func viewDidLoad() {
    super.viewDidLoad()

    let textItem = self.extensionContext!.inputItems[0]
                as! NSExtensionItem

    let textItemProvider = textItem.attachments![0]

    if textItemProvider.hasItemConformingToTypeIdentifier(
                    kUTTypeText as String) {
        textItemProvider.loadItem(forTypeIdentifier:
            kUTTypeText as String,
                        options: nil,
                         completionHandler: { (result, error) in

            })
    }
}
```

When the above code is executed, the data associated with the attachment will be loaded from the host app and the specified completion handler (in this case a closure) will be called. Clearly the next step is to implement this completion handler. Remaining within the *ActionViewController.swift* file, declare a variable named *convertString* and implement the handler code in the closure so that it reads as follows:

```
import UIKit
import MobileCoreServices

class ActionViewController: UIViewController {
```

```
    @IBOutlet weak var myTextView: UITextView!
    var convertedString: String?
.
.
.
    if textItemProvider.hasItemConformingToTypeIdentifier(
                    kUTTypeText as String) {
        textItemProvider.loadItem(forTypeIdentifier:
            kUTTypeText as String,
                        options: nil,
                        completionHandler: { (result, error) in

            self.convertedString = result as? String

            if self.convertedString != nil {
                self.convertedString = self.convertedString!.uppercased()

                DispatchQueue.main.async {
                    self.myTextView.text = self.convertedString!
                }
            }
        })
    }
```

The first parameter to the handler closure is an object that conforms to the NSSecureCoding protocol (in this case a string object containing the text loaded from the host app). Within the body of the method, this string is assigned to a new variable before being converted to upper case.

The converted text is then displayed on the Text View object in the user interface. It is important to be aware that because this is a completion handler, the code is being executed in a different thread from the main application thread. As such, any changes made to the user interface must be dispatched to the main thread, hence the *DispatchQueue* method wrapper.

89.8 Returning the Modified Data to the Host App

The final task in terms of implementing the Action extension is to return the modified content to the host app when the user taps the Done button in the extension user interface. When the Action extension template was created, Xcode connected the Done button to an action method named *done*. Locate this method in the *ActionViewController.swift* file and modify it so that it reads as follows:

```
@IBAction func done() {
    let returnProvider =
        NSItemProvider(item: convertedString as NSSecureCoding?,
                typeIdentifier: kUTTypeText as String)

    let returnItem = NSExtensionItem()
```

```
    returnItem.attachments = [returnProvider]
        self.extensionContext!.completeRequest(
            returningItems: [returnItem], completionHandler: nil)
}
```

This method essentially reverses the process of unpacking the input items. First a new NSItemProvider instance is created, configured with the modified content (represented by the string value assigned to the *convertedString* variable) and the content type identifier. Next, a new NSExtensionItem instance is created and the NSItemProvider object assigned as an attachment.

Finally, the *completeRequest(returningItems:)* method of the extension context is called, passing through the NSExtensionItem instance as an argument.

As will be outlined later in this chapter, whether the host app does anything with the returned content items is dependent upon whether or not the host app has been implemented to do so.

89.9 Testing the Extension

To test the extension, begin by making sure that the *MyExtAction* scheme (and not the *ActionDemo* containing app) is selected in the Xcode toolbar as highlighted in Figure 89-5:

Figure 89-5

With a suitable device connected to the development system, build and run the extension. As with other extension types, Xcode will prompt for a host app to work with the extension. In order for the extension to be activated, an app that works with text content must be selected. Scroll down the list of apps installed on the device to locate and select the standard Notes app (Figure 89-6). Once selected, click on the *Run* button:

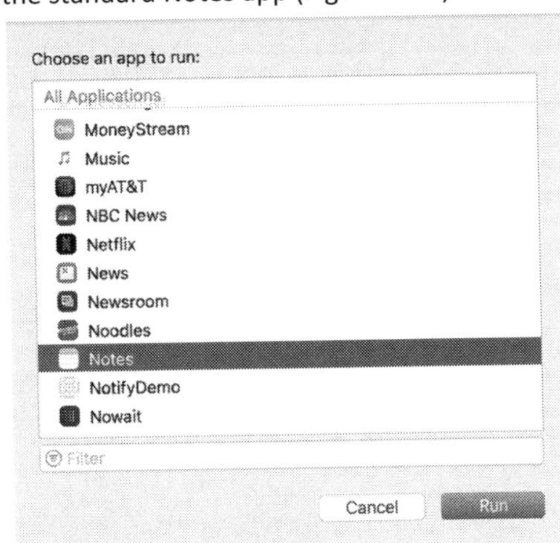

Figure 89-6

After the project has compiled and uploaded to the device, the Notes app should automatically load (manually launch it if it does not). Select an existing note within the app, or add a new one if none exist then tap the Share button located in the top toolbar. If the Action extension does not appear in the activity view controller panel, tap the *More* button and turn on the extension using the switch in the Activities list:

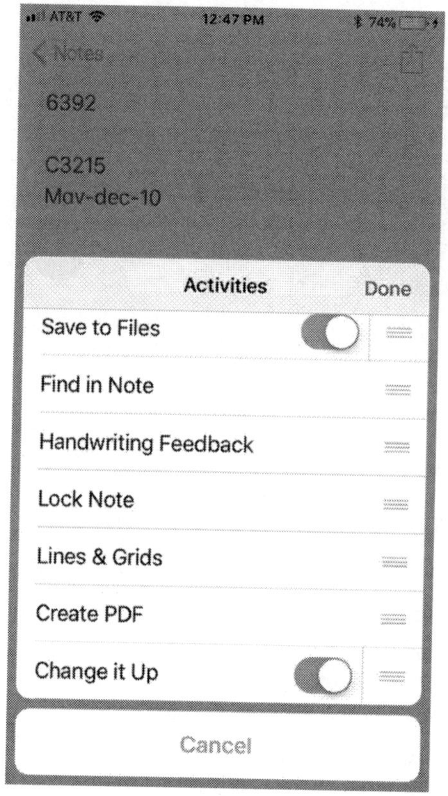

Figure 89-7

Once the extension has been enabled it should appear in the actions section of the activity view controller panel:

Figure 89-8

Once the extension is accessible, select it to launch the action, at which point the extension user interface should appear displaying the text from the note in uppercase using a larger font:

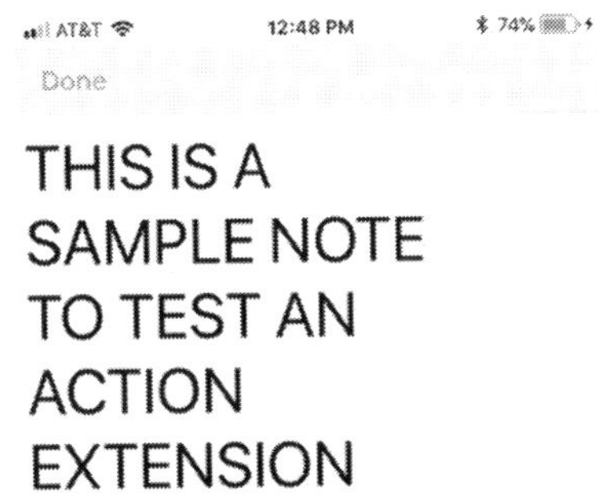

Figure 89-9

Note that there may be a delay of several seconds between selecting the Change it Up extension and the extension appearing. Having verified that the Action extension works, tap the Done button to return to the Notes app. Note that the content of the note did not change to reflect the content change to uppercase that was returned from the extension. The reason for this is that the Notes app has not implemented the functionality to accept modified content from an Action extension. As time goes by and Action extensions become more prevalent it will become more common for applications to accept modified content from Action extensions. This, of course, raises the question of how this is implemented, an area that will be covered in the next chapter entitled *Receiving Data from an iOS 12 Action Extension*.

89.10 Declaring the Supported Content Type

During creation and testing of the extension it may have come to your attention that a warning message was displayed within Xcode indicating that the embedded binary's NSExtensionRule is TRUEPREDICATE. This is because an Action extension must declare the type of content with which it is able to work. This is achieved via key-value settings located in the extension's *Info.plist* file. Select this file within the project navigator panel (MyActionExt -> Info.plist) and unfold the *NSExtension -> NSExtensionAttributes -> NSExtensionActivationRule* section of the file as shown in Figure 89-10:

▼ NSExtension	Dictionary	(3 items)
▼ NSExtensionAttributes	Dictionary	(1 item)
NSExtensionActivationRule	String	TRUEPREDICATE
NSExtensionMainStoryboard	String	MainInterface
NSExtensionPointIdentifier	String	com.apple.ui-services

Figure 89-10

The NSExtensionActivationRule defines the conditions under which the Action extension will appear as an option within the activity view controller of a host app. As currently configured, the extension will be activated under any circumstances and, as such, will cause a warning to appear during compilation indicating that the setting will need to be changed before the app will be accepted into the App Store.

Since the extension is intended to be used with text only, the rules need to be changed accordingly to remove the warning. Within the *Info.plist* properties, select the NSExtensionActivationRule line and change the value in the *Type* column from *String* to *Dictionary* as shown in Figure 89-11:

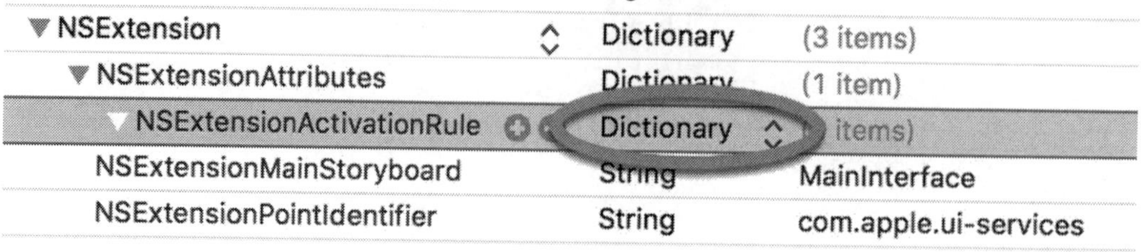

Figure 89-11

With the line still selected, click on the + button to add a new key-value pair to the rule dictionary. In the new item line, enter *NSExtensionActivationSupportsText* into the *Key* column, change the *Type* column to Boolean and select *YES* in the *Value* column. With this modification completed, the NSExtension section of the property list should match that shown in Figure 89-12:

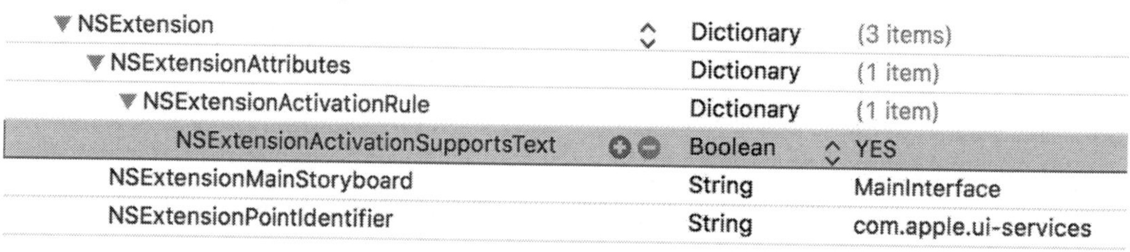

Figure 89-12

Since the Notes app requires extensions that support both images and text, the extension will no longer be available from within the Notes app once this change has been made. To continue testing in the next chapter, return the *NSExtensionActivationRule* key to a String value set once again to *TRUEPREDICATE*.

89.11 Summary

An Action extension is narrowly defined as a mechanism to transform the content in a host app or display that content to the user in a different way. An Action extension is context sensitive and must declare the type of data with which it is able to work. There are essentially three key elements to an Action extension. First, the extension must load the content data from the host app. Second, the extension displays or transforms that content in some, application specific way. Finally, the transformed data is packaged and returned to the host app. Not all host apps are able to handle data returned from an Action extension and in the next chapter we will explore the steps necessary to add such a capability.

Chapter 90

90. Receiving Data from an iOS 12 Action Extension

The previous chapter covered the steps involved in creating an Action extension in iOS that was designed to modify and display text content from a host app. In developing the extension, steps were taken to ensure that the modified content was returned to the host app when the user exited the extension. This chapter will work through the creation of an example host application that demonstrates how to receive data from an Action extension.

90.1 Creating the Example Project

Start Xcode and create a new Single View Application project named *ActionHostApp* with Swift selected as the programming language.

The finished application is going to consist of a Text View object and a toolbar containing a Share button that will provide access to the Change it Up Action extension created in the previous chapter. When the Action extension returns, the host app will receive the modified content from the extension and display it to the user.

90.2 Designing the User Interface

Locate and load the *Main.storyboard* file into the Interface Builder tool and drag and drop a Toolbar instance so that it is positioned along the bottom edge of the layout canvas. Next, drag and drop a Text View object onto the canvas and resize and position it so that it occupies the remaining space above the toolbar, stretching the view out horizontally until the blue margin guidelines appear. With the TextView object selected, display the Attributes Inspector and change the displayed text to “This is some sample text”.

Display the *Resolve Auto Layout Issues* menu and select the *Reset to Suggested Constraints* option listed under *All Views in View Controller*. At this point the layout should resemble Figure 90-1:

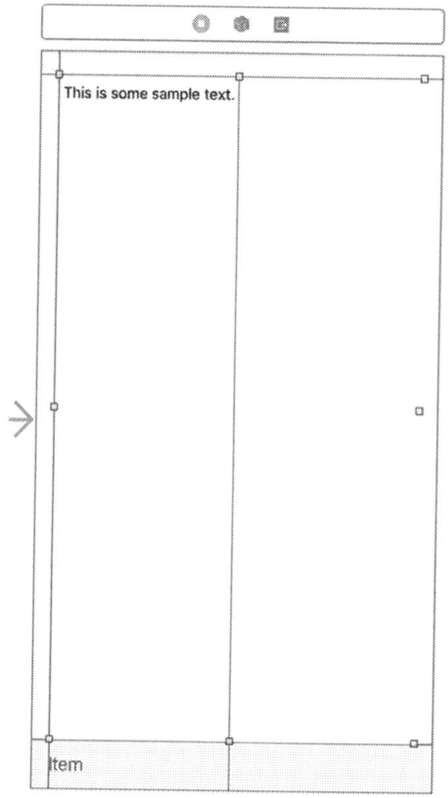

Figure 90-1

Before proceeding, display the Assistant Editor panel and establish an outlet for the Text View object named *myTextView*.

90.3 Importing the Mobile Core Services Framework

The code added to this project will make use of a definition which is declared within the Mobile Core Services framework. To avoid compilation errors, this framework must be imported into the *ViewController.swift* file as follows:

```
import UIKit
import MobileCoreServices

class ViewController: UIViewController {
.
.
.
}
```

90.4 Adding an Action Button to the Application

In order to be able to access the "Change it Up" Action extension from within this host application it will be necessary to implement an Action button. As the user interface currently stands, the toolbar contains a single button item displaying text which reads "Item". To change this to an Action button, select it in the storyboard layout (remembering that it may be necessary to click on it twice since the first click typically selects the parent toolbar rather than the button item).

With the button selected, display the Attributes Inspector and change the *System Item* menu from *Custom* to *Action*:

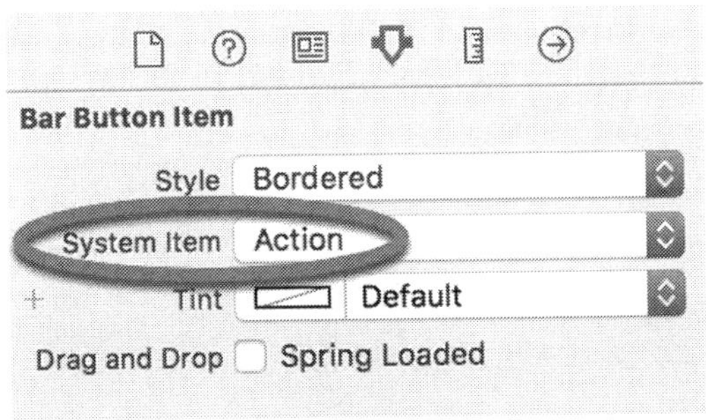

Figure 90-2

Once the change has been made, the button item should now have the standard appearance of an iOS Action button as shown in Figure 90-3:

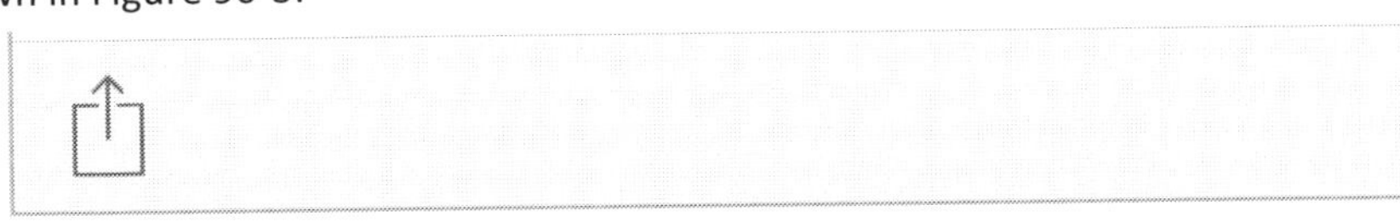

Figure 90-3

Now that the button looks like an Action button, some code needs to be added to display the activity view controller when it is tapped by the user. With the Assistant Editor displayed, Ctrl-click on the button and drag the resulting line to a suitable location within the *ViewController.swift* file. Release the line and create an Action outlet named *showActionView*. Once created, implement the code in this method so that it reads as follows:

```
@IBAction func showActionView(_ sender: Any) {
    let activityViewController =
        UIActivityViewController(activityItems:
            [myTextView.text], applicationActivities: nil)

    self.present(activityViewController,
                animated:true, completion: nil)

    activityViewController.completionWithItemsHandler =
        { (activityType, completed, returnedItems, error) in

        }
}
```

The code within the method creates a new UIActivityViewController instance initialized with the content of the Text View in the user interface. The activity view controller is then displayed to the user. Finally, a closure is assigned to act as the completion handler (the code for which will be implemented later) to be executed when the Action extension returns control to the application.

Compile and run the application and tap the Action button to test that the activity view controller appears. Select the "Change it Up" extension and verify that it displays the text extracted from the Text View. Finally, tap the Done button to return to the host app, noting that the original text content has not yet been converted to uppercase. This functionality now needs to be implemented within the completion handler method.

90.5 Receiving Data from an Extension

When the user exits from an Action extension, the completion handler assigned to the UIActivityViewController instance will be called and passed a variety of parameters. One of those parameters will be an array of NSExtensionItem objects containing NSItemProvider objects that can be used to load any data that has been returned by the extension.

Using the same techniques described in the previous chapter (*Creating an iOS 12 Action Extension*) this data can be extracted by making the following changes to the completion handler closure:

```
.
.
.
activityViewController.completionWithItemsHandler =
            { (activityType, completed, returnedItems, error) in

        if let items = returnedItems, items.count > 0 {

            let textItem: NSExtensionItem =
                items[0] as! NSExtensionItem

            let textItemProvider =
                textItem.attachments![0]

            if textItemProvider.hasItemConformingToTypeIdentifier(
                kUTTypeText as String) {

                textItemProvider.loadItem(
                    forTypeIdentifier: kUTTypeText as String,
                    options: nil,
                    completionHandler: {(string, error) -> Void in
                        let newtext = string as! String
                        DispatchQueue.main.async(execute: {
                            self.myTextView.text = newtext
                        })
                })
            }
        }
    }
}
.
.
```

.

The method obtains a reference to the item provider and verifies that at least one item has been returned from the extension. A test is then performed to make sure that it is a text item. If the item is text based, the item is loaded from the extension and a completion handler used to assign the new text to the Text View object. Note that the code to set the text on the TextView object is dispatched to the main thread for execution. This is because all user interface changes must be performed on the app's main thread and completion handler code such as this is executed in a different thread.

90.6 Testing the Application

Compile and run the application, select the Share button and launch the "Change it Up" extension. On returning to the host application the original text should now have been updated to be displayed in uppercase as modified within the extension.

90.7 Summary

In addition to providing an alternative view of the content in a host app, Action extensions can also be used to transform that content in some way. Not only can this transformation be performed and viewed within the extension, but a mechanism is also provided to return that modified content to the host app. By default, most host apps will not make use of the returned content. In reality adding this support is a relatively simple task which involves implementing a completion handler method to handle the content returned from the extension into the host app and assigning that handler method to be called when the activity view controller is displayed to the user.

Chapter 91

91. An Introduction to Building iOS 12 Message Apps

In much the same way that photo editing extensions allow custom photo editing capabilities to be added to the standard Photos app, message app extensions allow the functionality of the standard iOS Messages app to be extended and enhanced.

Message app extensions, which were introduced with iOS 10, allow app developers to provide users with creative ways to generate and send custom and interactive messages to their contacts. The possibilities offered by message apps range from simple sticker apps that allow images to be selected from sticker packs and inserted into messages, through to more advanced possibilities such as fully interactive games.

Message app extensions, once created, are made available to customers through the Messages App Store, thereby providing an additional source of potential revenue for app developers.

In this chapter, a basic overview of message app extensions will be provided, together with an outline of how the key classes and methods of the Messages framework combine to enable the creation of message apps. The next chapter, entitled *An iOS 12 Interactive Message App Tutorial*, will work through the creation of an interactive message app project.

91.1 Introducing Message Apps

Message app extensions (often referred to simply as *message apps*) are built using the standard iOS extension mechanism with the one significant difference being that a message app extension is not required to have a containing app. Users find and install message apps by browsing the Message App Store, or when they receive a message created using a message app from another user. Once a message app has been installed, it appears within the *Messages App Drawer* of the Messages app on iOS devices. This app drawer is accessed by tapping the App Store icon located in the Messages app toolbar as highlighted in Figure 91-1:

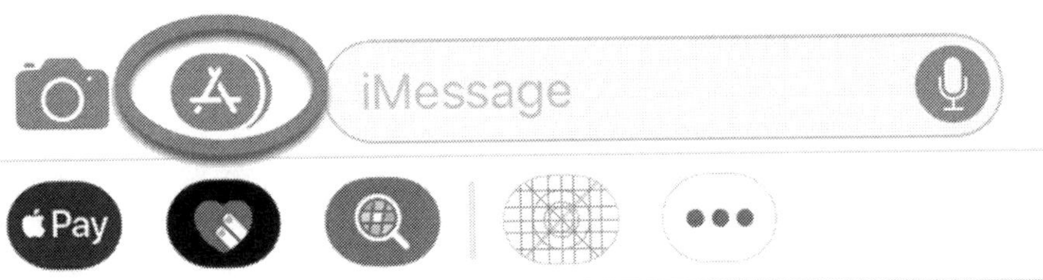

Figure 91-1

When a message app icon is tapped, the app extension is launched and displayed within the app drawer panel. When a message app is displayed, swiping left or right within the drawer scrolls through the different apps currently installed on the device. In Figure 91-2 below the app drawer is displaying a message app that allows animated images to be selected for inclusion in messages. When displayed in the app drawer, the message app is said to be using *compact presentation style*.

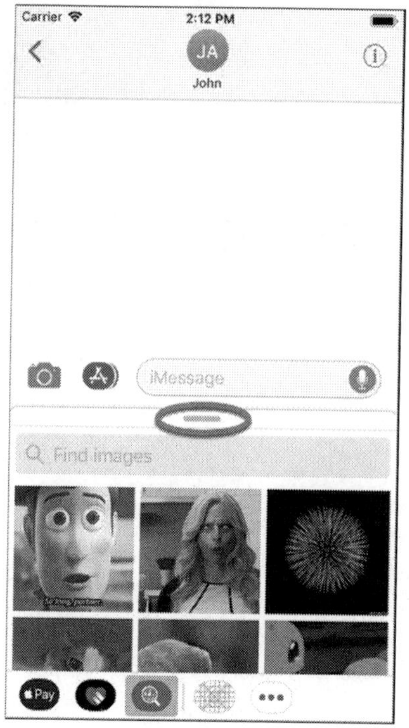

Figure 91-2

The horizontal bar (highlighted in Figure 91-2 above) switches the app to *expanded presentation style* whereby the app user interface fills the entire screen area. Tapping the down arrow in the upper right-hand corner of the expanded presentation view will switch the app back to compact style.

In addition to launching a message app from within the app drawer, selecting a message associated with a message app from the message transcript area will automatically launch the corresponding app in expanded presentation style.

If a user receives a message generated by a message app, but does not currently have that particular app installed, tapping the app icon within the message will take the user to the Messages App Store where the app may be purchased and installed. This is expected to have a viral effect in terms of selling message apps, with customers buying apps in order to be able to interact with messages received from their contacts.

91.2 Types of Message App

iOS currently supports three different types of message app extension. The first is simply a mechanism for providing collections of sticker images (referred to as *sticker packs*) for inclusion in messages sent by users. The second type of app allows a range of media content (such as text, images, web links and videos) to be inserted into messages. The third, and most powerful option, allows fully interactive message apps to be created. When developing interactive message apps, the full range of iOS frameworks and user interface controls is available when implementing the app, essentially allowing a message app of any level of richness and complexity to be created using the same approach as that taken when developing regular iOS apps.

Since interactive message apps provide the greatest flexibility and opportunities for app developers, this will be the main focus of both this chapter and the tutorial contained in the next chapter of the book.

91.3 The Key Messages Framework Classes

In the process of developing a message app, a number of classes provided by the Messages framework will need to be used. Understanding these classes and how they interact is an essential part of learning to develop message apps. In this section, a brief overview of each class and the most commonly used properties and methods of those classes will be outlined.

91.3.1 MSMessagesAppViewController

The MSMessagesAppViewController class is responsible for displaying and managing the message app in both compact and expanded presentation styles. It allows for the presentation of a user interface to the user and provides a bridge between the user interface and the underlying application logic. The class also stores information about the app status via the following properties:

- **activeConversation** – Stores the MSConversation object for the currently active conversation.
- **presentationStyle** – Contains the current presentation style for the message app (compact or expanded).

Instances of this class also receive the following lifecycle method calls:

- **willBecomeActive** – The app is about to become active within the Messages app.
- **didBecomeActive** – Called immediately after the app becomes active.
- **willResignActive** – The app is about to become inactive.
- **didResignActive** – Called after the app has become inactive.
- **willSelect** – Called after the user selects a message from the transcript but before the *selectedMessage* property of the conversation object is updated to reflect the current selection.
- **didSelect** – Called after the *selectedMessage* conversation property has been updated to reflect a message selection made by the user.
- **didReceive** – When an incoming message is received for the message app, and the message app is currently active, this method is called and passed corresponding MSMessage and MSConversation objects.
- **didStartSending** – Called when the user sends an outgoing message.
- **didCancelSending** – Called when the user cancels a message before sending it.
- **willTransition** – Called when the app is about to transition from one presentation style to another. Changes to the user interface of the message app to accommodate the presentation style change should be made here if necessary.
- **didTransition** – Called when the app has performed a transition between presentation styles.

Since MSMessagesAppViewController is a subclass of UIViewController, the class behaves in much the same way, and also receives the standard lifecycle method calls (such as *viewDidLoad*, *viewWillAppear*, *viewWillDisappear* etc.) as the UIViewController class.

91.3.2 MSConversation

The MSConversation class represents the transcript area of the Messages app when a message app extension is active. This object stores the currently selected message (in the form of an MSMessage object via the *selectedMessage* property) and provides the following API methods that may be called by the message app to insert messages into the input field of the Messages app:

- **insert** – Inserts an MSMessage object or sticker into the input field of the Messages app.
- **insertText** – Inserts text into the input field of the Messages app.
- **insertAttachment** – Inserts an attachment such as an image or video file into the Messages app input field.

Once a message has been inserted into the Messages app input field it must then be sent by the user via a tap on the send button. It is not possible for a message app to send a message directly without the user taking this step.

In addition to the methods outlined above, the MSConversation class also contains the following properties:

- **localParticipantIdentifier** – Contains the UUID of the user of the local device. Accessing the uuidString property of this item will provide the contact name of the user in a format suitable for display within the message layout.
- **remoteParticipantIdentifiers** – Contains an array of UUID objects representing the identities of remote users currently participating in the message app conversation.

91.3.3 MSMessage

The MSMessage class represents individual messages within the Messages app transcript. The key elements of an MSMessage object are as follows:

- **layout** – The layout property takes the form of an MSMessageTemplateLayout object which defines how the message is to be displayed within the so-called message bubble in the Messages app transcript area.
- **url** – The url property is used to encode the data that is to be sent along with the message. This can be a standard URL that points to a remote server where the data can be downloaded by the receiving app or, for smaller data requirements, the URL itself can be used to encode the data to be transmitted with the message. The latter approach can be achieved using the URLComponents class, a process that is covered in detail in the next chapter entitled *An iOS 12 Interactive Message App Tutorial*.
- **session** – The use of sessions in message apps allow multiple messages to be designated as being part of the same session. Session messages are presented such that only the most recent message in the session is displayed in its entirety, thereby avoiding cluttering the Messages app transcript area with the full rendering of each message.
- **accessibilityLabel** – A localized string describing the message suitable for accessibility purposes.
- **senderParticipantIdentifier** – The UUID of the user that sent the message.
- **shouldExpire** – A Boolean value indicating whether the message should expire after it has been read by the recipient.

91.3.4 MSMessageTemplateLayout

The MSMessageTemplateLayout defines how an MSMessage instance is presented to the user within the transcript area of the Messages app.

When a message contained within an MSMessage object is presented to the user it is displayed within a message bubble. Various aspects of how this message bubble appears can be defined and included within the MSMessage object.

The image, video, titles and subtitles contained within the bubble are configured using an MSMessageTemplateLayout instance which is then assigned to the *layout* property of the MSMessage instance. The diagram illustrated in Figure 91-3 provides a graphical rendering of an MSMessage-based message bubble with each of the configurable layout properties labelled accordingly:

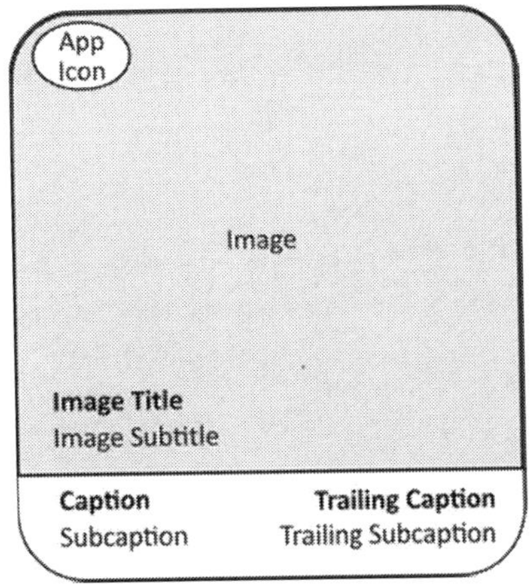

Figure 91-3

The settings in the above diagram correlate to the following properties of the MSMessageTemplateLayout class:

- **image** – The image to be displayed in the image area of the message. The recommended image size is 300pt x 300pt and the Messages framework will automatically scale the image for different display sizes. To avoid rendering issues, it is recommended that text not be included in the image.
- **mediaFileURL** – The URL of a media file to be displayed in the image (such as a video or animated image file).
- **imageTitle** – The text to display in the Image Title location.
- **imageSubtitle** – The text to appear in the Image Subtitle location.
- **caption** – Text to appear in the Caption location.
- **subCaption** – Text to appear in the Subcaption location.
- **trailingCaption** - Text to appear in the Trailing Caption location.
- **trailingSubcaption** – Text to appear in the Trailing Subcaption location.

91.4 Sending Simple Messages

To send simple text, sticker and image messages it is not necessary to create an MSMessage object. The first step is to obtain a reference to the currently active conversation. From within an MSMessagesAppViewController instance, the currently active conversation can be obtained via the *activeConversation* property:

```
let conversation = self.activeConversation
```

The next step is to make a call to the appropriate method of the active conversation instance. To send a text message, for example, the code might read as follows:

```
let conversation = self.activeConversation
conversation?.insertText("Message Text Here") { error in
        // Handle errors
}
```

Once the above code is executed, the designated text will appear in the Messages app input field ready to be sent by the user.

Similarly, an attachment may be sent using the *insertAttachment* method call, passing through a URL referencing the file to be attached to the message:

```
let conversation = self.activeConversation
conversation?.insertAttachment(myURL, withAlternateFilename: nil) { error in
        // Handle errors
}
```

91.5 Creating an MSMessage Message

In order to send an interactive message, it is necessary to use the MSMessage class. The first step, once again, is to obtain a reference to the currently active conversation:

```
let conversation = self.activeConversation
```

Next, a new MSMessage instance needs to be created within which to place the message content:

```
let message = MSMessage()
```

If the message is to be associated with a specific session, the message would be created as follows:

```
let session = MSSession()
let message = MSMessage(session: session)
```

In the above example, a newly created session object is being assigned to the message. If this message were being created in response to an incoming message that already had a session allocation, the session object from the incoming message would be used instead.

Once the message instance has been created, the layout needs to be configured using an MSMessageTemplateLayout instance. For example:

```
let layout = MSMessageTemplateLayout()
layout.imageTitle = "My Image Title"
layout.caption = "A Message Caption"
layout.subcaption = "A message subcaption"
layout.image = myImage
```

Once the layout has been defined it needs to be assigned to the MSMessage object:

```
message.layout = layout
```

Next, a url needs to be assigned containing the data to be passed along with the message, for example:

```
message.url = myUrl
```

Once the message has been configured, it can be placed in the Messages app input field using the *insert* method of the active conversation:

```
conversation?.insert(message, completionHandler: {(error) in
            // Handle error
})
```

Once the message has been inserted, it is ready to be sent by the user.

91.6 Receiving a Message

When a message is received from another instance of a message app and the message app is currently active, the *didReceive* method of the MSMessagesAppViewController instance will be called and passed both the MSMessage and MSConversation objects associated with the incoming message. When the user selects the message in the transcript, the app extension will launch, triggering a call to the *willBecomeActive* method which will, in turn, be passed a copy of the MSConversation object from which a reference to the currently selected message may also be obtained.

Because the *didReceive* method is not called unless the message app is already active, the *willBecomeActive* method is typically the best place to access the incoming MSMessage object and update the status of the app. The following sample implementation of the *willBecomeActive* method, for example, gets the selected message from the conversation object and then accesses the properties of the message to obtain the current session and the encoded URL:

```
override func willBecomeActive(with conversation: MSConversation) {
    if let message = conversation.selectedMessage? {
        let url = message.url
        let session = conversation.selectedMessage?.session
        // Decode URL and update app
    }
}
```

91.7 Supported Message App Platforms

The ability to create interactive messages using a message app extension is currently limited to devices running iOS 10 or later. Interactive messages will, however, be delivered to devices running macOS Sierra, watchOS 3 and iOS 10 in addition to older operating system versions.

When an interactive message is received on macOS Sierra, clicking on the message bubble will launch the URL contained within that message within the Safari browser. It is important to note that in this situation the web server will need to be able to decode the URL and present content within the resulting web page that relates to the message. On watchOS 3, the interactive message can be used to launch the full message app extension on a companion iOS 10 or later device.

For older versions of macOS, watchOS and iOS, an incoming interactive message is delivered in two parts. The first containing the image assigned to the message layout and the second the URL contained within the message.

91.8 Summary

Message apps are custom apps that are installed as extensions to the built-in iOS Messages app. These apps are used to create and send custom and interactive messages to other users. These extensions are made possible by the Messages framework. Message apps range in functionality from simple “sticker pack” apps through to fully interactive experiences.

This chapter has outlined the basic concepts of message apps and outlined the different classes that are typically required when developing a message app. The next chapter, entitled *An iOS 12 Interactive Message App Tutorial*, will use the information provided in this chapter to create an example interactive message app.

Chapter 92

92. An iOS 12 Interactive Message App Tutorial

The previous chapter introduced message app extensions and described the way in which the Messages framework allows custom, interactive messages to be send and received from within the standard iOS Messages app.

In this chapter, many of the concepts described in the previous chapter will be put to practical use while working through the creation of an example interactive message app extension.

92.1 About the Example Message App Project

This tutorial will create an interactive message app extension project that implements a tic-tac-toe game designed to be played by two players via the Messages app. The first player begins the game by loading the app from the message app drawer and making a selection from within the tic-tac-toe game grid. The current game status is then sent to a second player where it appears in the standard Messages app transcript area. The second player selects the message to open the message app extension where the next move can be made and sent back to the first player. This process repeats until the game is completed.

92.2 Creating the MessageApp Project

Launch Xcode and select the option to create a new Xcode project. On the template selection screen, select the *iMessage App* option as illustrated in Figure 92-1 below and click on the *Next* button:

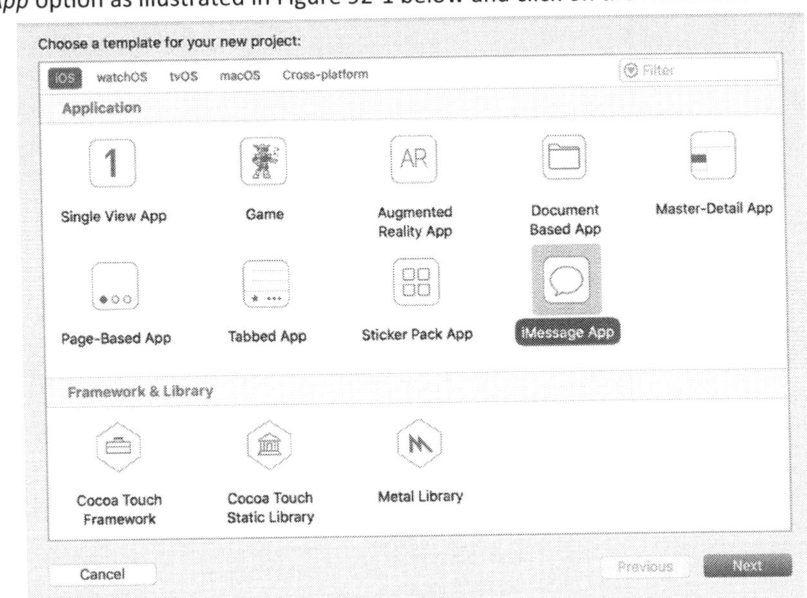

Figure 92-1

On the following screen, name the product *MessageApp* and select Swift as the language. Click the *Next* button, select a location for the project files and click the *Create* button.

A review of the project structure in the project navigator panel will reveal that both a main iOS app (named *MessageApp*) and an extension (*MessageExtension*) have been created:

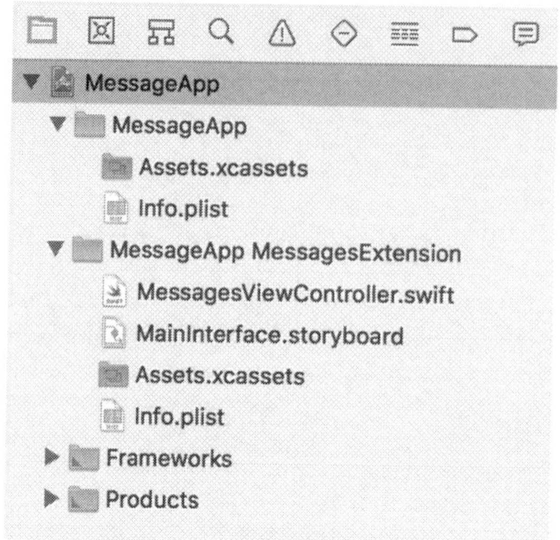

Figure 92-2

Within the MessagesExtension folder, the *MessagesViewController.swift* file contains the code for the MSMessagesAppViewController subclass while the *MainInterface.storyboard* file contains the user interface for the message app extension. By default, the layout currently consists of a Label object configured to display "Hello World".

Before making any changes to the project, run the app on an iOS simulator and note that the Message app launches and opens the app drawer containing the new message app extension:

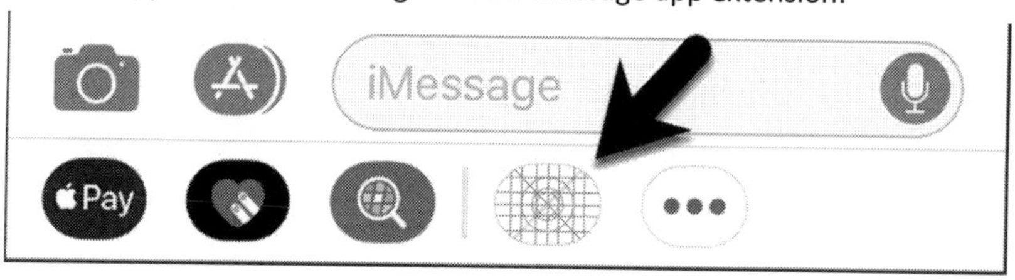

Figure 92-3

To load the extension, tap the MessageApp icon in the drawer and note that the default "Hello World" user interface appears (Figure 92-4):

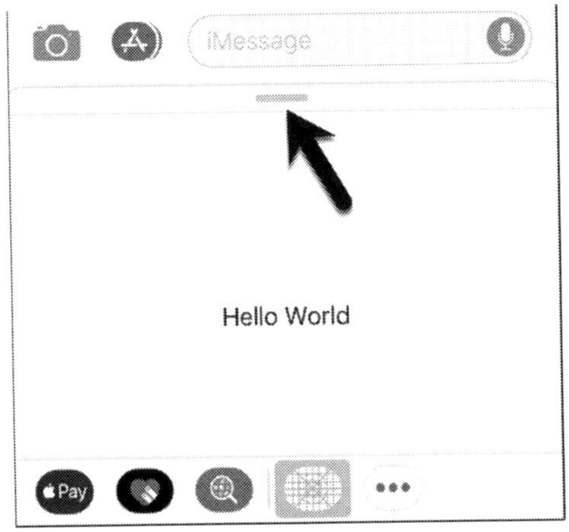

Figure 92-4

Swiping left or right over the extension app within the drawer will move between the different message apps currently installed on the device. Tapping the handle at the top of the extension panel (indicated by the arrow in the above figure) will switch the app from compact to expanded presentation style. To return to compact presentation style, tap the down arrow located at the top of the full screen view.

92.3 Designing the MessageApp User Interface

The user interface for the message app extension is going to consist of 9 Button objects arranged in a 3x3 grid using UIStackView layouts. Later in the tutorial, screenshots of the current game status will be taken and displayed in the interactive message bubbles. As a workaround for a problem with screenshots and the UIStackView class, the button collection will need to be contained within an additional UIView instance.

Begin the user interface design process by selecting the *MainInterface.storyboard* file and deleting the "Hello World" Label object. Drag and drop a View instance from the Library panel and position it so that it is centered horizontally and located along the bottom margin of the storyboard scene as illustrated in Figure 92-5:

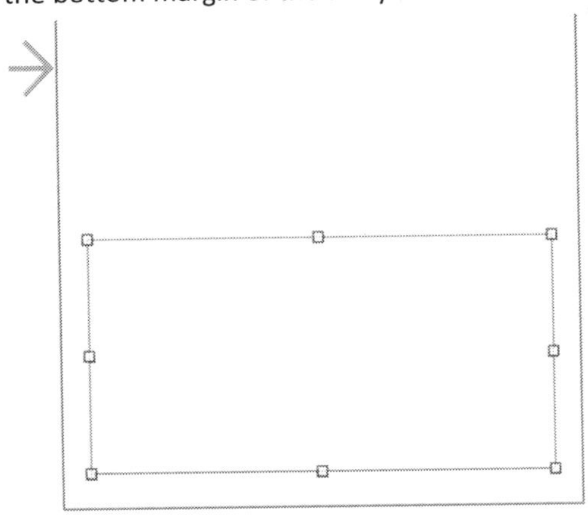

Figure 92-5

Drag a Button from the palette and place it within the newly added view. With the new button selected, display the Attributes Inspector panel and change the Background color to a light shade of gray. Double-click on the button and delete the current text so that the parent view and button match the layout shown below:

Figure 92-6

Display the Assistant Editor panel and establish an action connection from the button to a method named *buttonPressed* making sure to change the *Type* value from *Any* to *UIButton* before clicking on the *Connect* button.

Now that the first button has been added and configured it needs to be duplicated eight times. Select the button in the layout, use the Command-C keyboard shortcut to copy and Command-V to paste a duplicate. Position the new button to the right of the first button and continue pasting and moving button instances until there are three rows of three buttons:

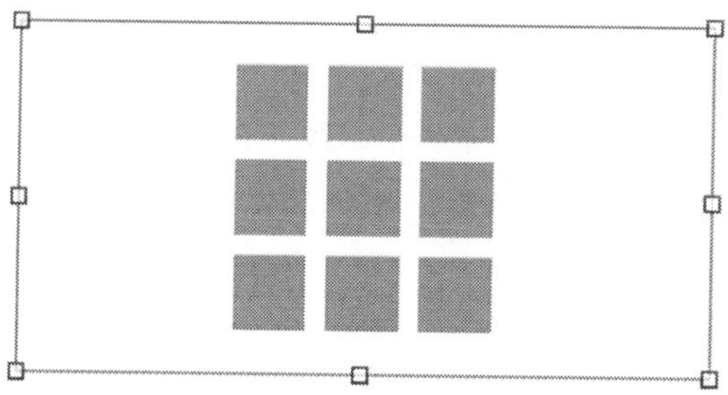

Figure 92-7

Select the first button in the top row and then hold down the shift key while selecting the remaining two buttons in that row. With all three buttons selected, click on the Embed In button (highlighted in Figure 92-8) and select the *Stack View* menu option to add the buttons to a horizontal UIStackView instance:

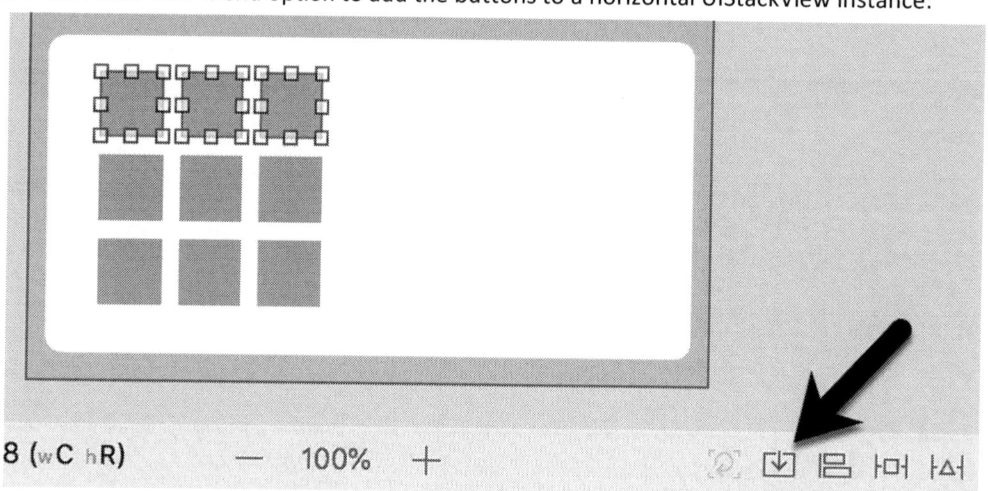

Figure 92-8

With the UIStackView instance selected, use the Attributes Inspector panel to change the Spacing attribute to 2. Repeat these steps on the two remaining rows of buttons so that each row is contained within a horizontal UIStackView.

Display the Document Outline panel, hold down the Command key and select each of the three Stack View instances:

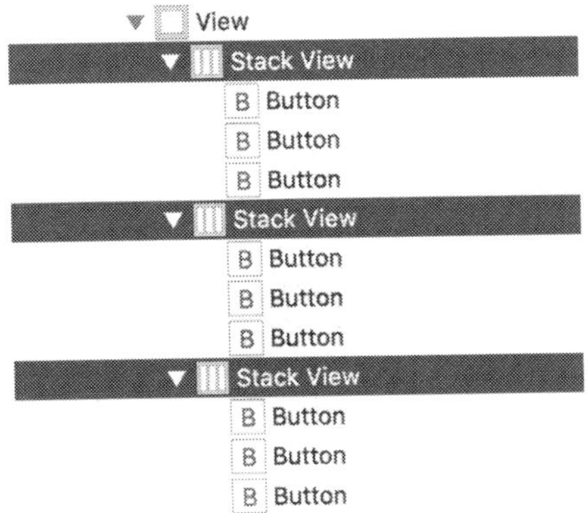

Figure 92-9

With the three Stack View entries selected, click on the Embed In button in the canvas toolbar once again to add the three horizontal stacks into a single vertical stack. Using the Attributes Inspector panel, increase the spacing property on the vertical stack view to 2.

With the vertical stack still selected, display the Auto Layout align menu and enable both the horizontal and vertical center in container options before clicking the *Add 2 Constraints* button. Reduce the width of the parent View object so that it more closely matches the size of the button grid, then use the Auto Layout *Add New Constraints* menu to set a spacing to nearest neighbor constraint on the bottom edge of the View object using with the *Constrain to margins* option enabled. Before adding the constraint, also enable the Height and Width constraint check boxes using the current values. Next, display the Auto Layout Align menu and add a constraint to center the view horizontally within the container. At this point the layout of the view and grid should match Figure 92-10. Before proceeding, display the Assistant Editor and establish an outlet connection for the View object named *gridView*:

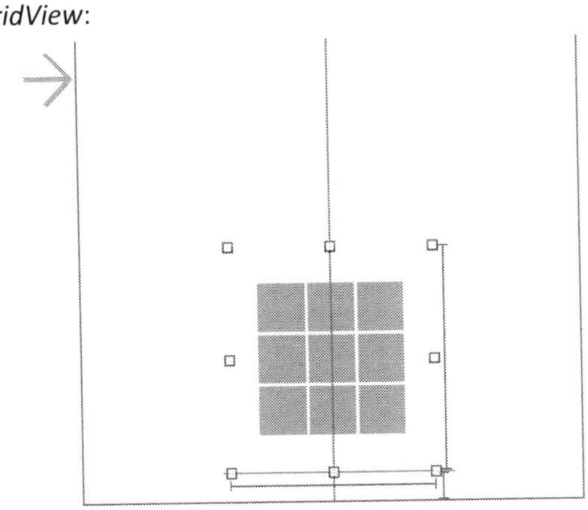

Figure 92-10

92.4 Creating the Outlet Collection

As is invariably the case, the code for the app will need to be able to access the buttons in the user interface via outlets. In this project, all of the buttons are going to be connected to the same outlet by making use of an *outlet collection*.

Where a normal outlet contains a reference to a single user interface object, an outlet collection is an array of references to multiple user interface objects. Display the Assistant Editor and select the first button on the top row of the grid (note that initial selection attempts may select the parent StackView objects so continue clicking until only the button is selected). Create the outlet collection by Ctrl-clicking on the selected button and dragging to a position beneath the class declaration line in the Assistant Editor panel. When the connection dialog appears, change the Connection menu setting from *Outlet* to *Outlet Collection* (Figure 92-11), name the connection *Buttons* and click on the *Connect* button.

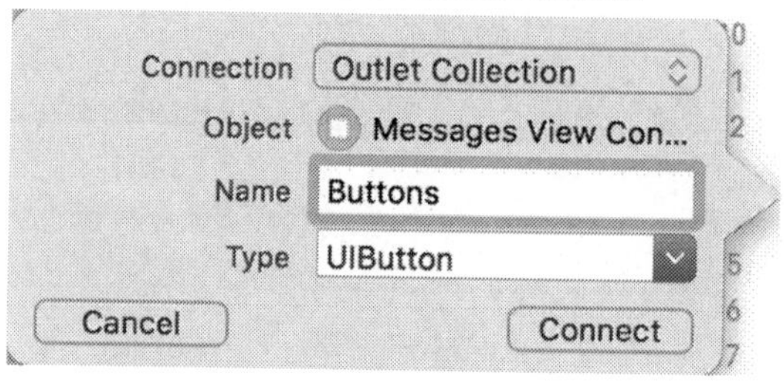

Figure 92-11

To add the second button in the first row, click on the outlet marker in the margin of the Assistant Editor panel and drag to the button as outlined in Figure 92-12:

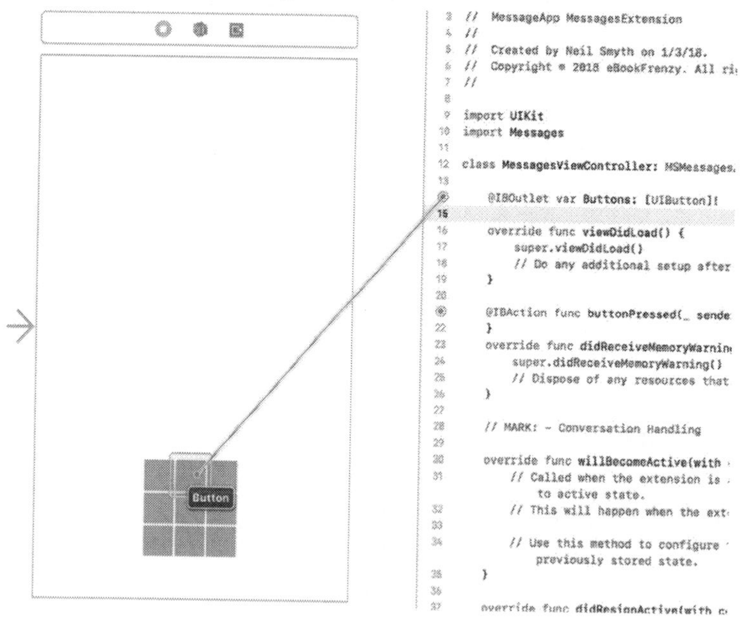

Figure 92-12

Connect the outlet collection using this technique for the remaining buttons in the grid, taking care to work from left to right and row by row (the order in which the buttons are added to the collection is important if the game is to function correctly).

Run the extension on the simulator and verify that the layout appears as designed in both compact and expanded presentation styles.

92.5 Creating the Game Model

The model for tracking the status of the game is very simple and consists of an array containing 10 string elements. The first element in the array is used to store the current player ('X' or 'O') while the remaining 9 elements contain the current settings of the corresponding buttons in the array (also 'X' or 'O'). The elements in this array are initialized with '-' characters to indicate unselected grid locations.

Open the *MessagesViewController.swift* file and add some variable declarations as follows:

```
class MessagesViewController: MSMessagesAppViewController {

    @IBOutlet weak var gridView: UIView!
    @IBOutlet var Buttons: [UIButton]!

    var gameStatus = [String](repeating: "-", count: 9)
    var currentPlayer: String = "X"
    var caption = "Want to play Tic-Tac-Toe?"
    var session: MSSession?
.
.
.
```

In addition to the array declaration, the above changes include a variable in which to temporarily store the current player setting (and which will be placed into the array when the user makes a selection), an initial setting of the message caption and a variable to store the current MSSession instance.

92.6 Responding to Button Selections

Each of the game buttons was previously configured to call a method named *buttonPressed* when tapped. This method needs to identify which button was pressed, store the current player value into the matching element of the game status array and then change the title of the button to indicate that it has been selected by the current player. Within the *MessagesViewController.swift* file, locate the template *buttonPressed* method and implement the code as follows:

```
@IBAction func buttonPressed(_ sender: UIButton) {
    for (index, button) in Buttons.enumerated() {
        if button.isEqual(sender) {

            if gameStatus[index].isEqual("-") {
                gameStatus[index] = currentPlayer
                sender.setTitle(currentPlayer, for: .normal)
            }
        }
    }
}
```

When called, this method is passed a reference to the user interface object that triggered the event. The added code iterates through the *Buttons* outlet collection until it finds the matching button. Using the index value associated with this button, the code then makes sure that the corresponding element in the gameStatus array contains a '-' character. This indicates that the button grid location has not already been selected. If the button is available, the string value representing the current player is stored at the corresponding location in the gameStatus array and also set as the button title.

Compile and run the message app on a simulator session and verify that clicking on the buttons in the game grid causes an 'X' to appear on the clicked button.

92.7 Preparing the Message URL

Once the user has selected a game move, the message needs to be prepared and inserted into the message transcript ready to be reviewed and sent by the user. Part of this message takes the form of a URL which will be used to encode the current game state so that it can be reconstructed when the second player receives the message.

For this example, the URLComponents class will be used to build a URL that contains a query item for the current player together with 9 other query items representing the status of each of the button positions in the game grid. Below is an example of how the URL might appear partway through an ongoing game:

```
https://www.ebookfrenzy.com?currentPlayer=X&position0=X&position1=O&position2
=-&position3=-&position4=-&position5=-&position6=X&position7=-&position8=-
```

The first part of the URL contains the standard HTTP scheme and domain declaration while the rest of the URL is comprised of query items. Each query item is represented by a URLQueryItem instance and contains a key-value pair. As can be seen in the example URL, the first query item contains the key "currentPlayer" which is currently assigned a value of "X". The remaining query items have keys ranging from position0 through to position8, with the value of each set to an 'X', 'O' or '-' to indicate the current status of the corresponding position in the button grid.

The code to create this URL is going to reside within a method named *prepareURL* which can now be added to the *MessagesViewController.swift* file so that it reads as follows:

```
func prepareURL() -> URL {
    var urlComponents = URLComponents()
    urlComponents.scheme = "https";
    urlComponents.host = "www.ebookfrenzy.com";
    let playerQuery = URLQueryItem(name: "currentPlayer",
                                   value: currentPlayer)

    urlComponents.queryItems = [playerQuery]

    for (index, setting) in gameStatus.enumerated() {
        let queryItem = URLQueryItem(name: "position\(index)",
                                     value: setting)
        urlComponents.queryItems?.append(queryItem)
    }
    return urlComponents.url!
}
```

The method begins by creating a URLComponents instance and configuring the scheme and host values. A new query item is then created comprising a key-value pair representing the current player information. The code then performs a looping operation through the elements of the gameStatus array. For each element, a new query item is created containing a key-value pair indicating the status of the corresponding grid position which is then appended to the urlComponent object. Finally, the encoded array is returned.

This new method now needs to be called from within the *buttonPressed* method when a valid button has been selected by the user. Now is also a good opportunity to add a call to a method named *prepareMessage* which will be created in the next section:

```
@IBAction func buttonPressed(_ sender: Any) {
    for (index, button) in Buttons.enumerated() {
        if button.isEqual(sender) {

            if gameStatus[index].isEqual("-") {
                gameStatus[index] = currentPlayer
                sender.setTitle(currentPlayer, for: .normal)
                let url = prepareURL()
                prepareMessage(url)
            }
        }
    }
}
```

92.8 Preparing and Inserting the Message

The steps to create the message to be sent will now be implemented within a method named *prepareMessage*. Add this method as follows to the *MessagesViewController.swift* file:

```
func prepareMessage(_ url: URL) {

    let message = MSMessage()

    let layout = MSMessageTemplateLayout()
    layout.caption = caption

    message.layout = layout
    message.url = url

    let conversation = self.activeConversation

    conversation?.insert(message, completionHandler: {(error) in
        if let error = error {
            print(error)
        }
    })
    self.dismiss()
}
```

The method creates a new MSMessage object and creates a template layout object with the caption set to the current value of the *caption* variable. The encoded url containing the current game status is then assigned to the url property of the message. Next, a reference to the currently active conversation is obtained before the message is inserted into the iMessage input field ready to be sent by the player. Finally, the MessagesViewController instance is dismissed from view.

Run the message app extension once again and click a button in the grid. Note that the entry now appears in the Messages app input field ready to be sent to the other player. Click on the send button (highlighted in Figure 92-13) to send the message.

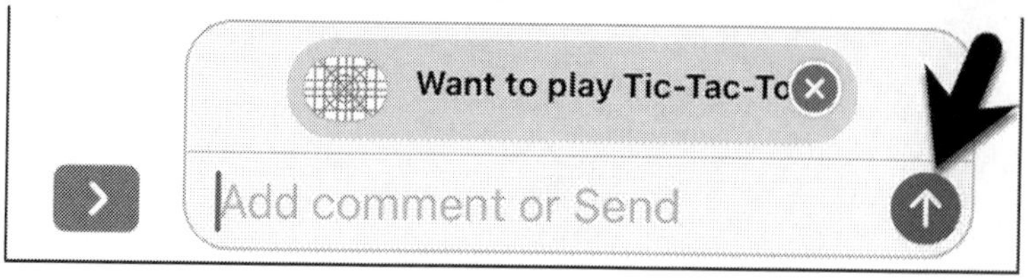

Figure 92-13

When testing messages in the simulator, the iMessage app simulates a conversation between two users named Kate Bell and John Appleseed. After the message has been sent, click the back arrow in the top left corner of the iMessage screen to move back to the conversation selection screen, select John Appleseed's conversation entry and note that the message has arrived:

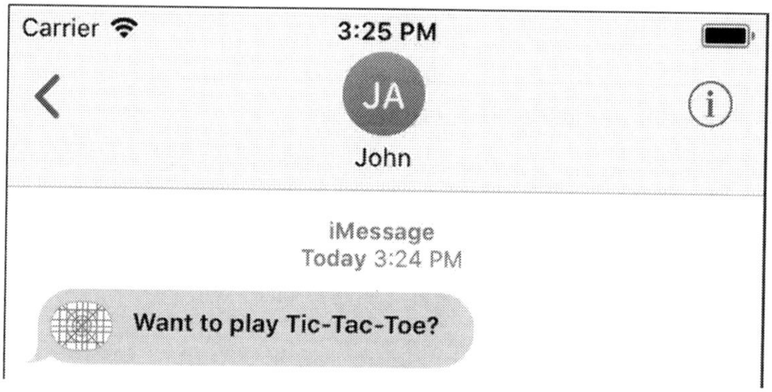

Figure 92-14

Tap the message to load the message extension where the button grid will appear. A few areas of functionality, however, have yet to be implemented. First, the current state of play is not reflected on the buttons, all of which remain blank. Also, clicking on a button causes an 'X' character to appear. Since the first player is represented by 'X', a current selection should display an 'O' on the button. Clearly some code needs to be added to handle the receipt of a message and update the game model within the message app extension.

92.9 Message Receipt Handling

The first step in handling the incoming message is to write a method to decode the incoming url and update the gameStatus array with the current status. Within the *MessagesViewController.swift* file, implement a method for this purpose named *decodeURL*:

```
func decodeURL(_ url: URL) {

    let components = URLComponents(url: url,
                        resolvingAgainstBaseURL: false)

    for (index, queryItem) in (components?.queryItems?.enumerated())! {
```

```
            if queryItem.name == "currentPlayer" {
                currentPlayer = queryItem.value == "X" ? "O" : "X"
            } else if queryItem.value != "-" {
                gameStatus[index-1] = queryItem.value!
                Buttons[index-1].setTitle(queryItem.value!, for: .normal)
            }
        }
}
```

This method essentially performs the reverse of the *prepareURL* method in that it initiates a URLComponents object from a url and then extracts the value for the current player key followed by the current setting for each of the buttons. If the status of a button is not a '-' character, then the current value (an X or O) is displayed on the corresponding button.

Next, the code to handle the incoming message needs to be implemented in the *willBecomeActive* method, a template for which has been placed within the *MessagesViewController.swift* file ready to be completed. When called by the Message framework, this method is passed an MSConversation object representing the currently active conversation. This object contains a property named *selectedMessage* referencing the MSMessage object selected by the user to launch the extension. From this object, the url containing the encoded game status data can be extracted, decoded and used to update the game status within this instance of the message app.

Locate the *willBecomeActive* method template in the *MessagesViewController.swift* file and modify it as follows:

```
override func willBecomeActive(with conversation: MSConversation) {

    if let messageURL = conversation.selectedMessage?.url {
        decodeURL(messageURL)
        caption = "It's your move!"
    }

    for (index, item) in gameStatus.enumerated() {
        if item != "-" {
            Buttons[index].setTitle(item, for: .normal)
        }
    }
}
```

The method gets the url that was embedded into the message and passes it to the *decodeURL* method for decoding and to update the internal game status model. The caption variable is then changed to indicate that this is now an ongoing game before a *for* loop updates the titles displayed on the game buttons.

Test the game again and note that the current game status is preserved between players and that Os are now displayed when the second player clicks on the grid buttons.

92.10 Setting the Message Image

At present, the message bubbles in the message transcript area contain the default app icon and the text assigned to the message caption property. A better user experience would be provided if the image property of the message bubble displayed the current status of the game.

A quick way of achieving this result is to take a screenshot of the gameView View object in which the grid layout resides. This can be achieved by adding some code to the *prepareMessage* method as follows:

```
func prepareMessage(_ url: URL) {

    let message = MSMessage()
    let layout = MSMessageTemplateLayout()
    layout.caption = caption

    UIGraphicsBeginImageContextWithOptions(gridView.bounds.size,
                gridView.isOpaque, 0);
    self.gridView.drawHierarchy(in: gridView.bounds,
                afterScreenUpdates: true)

    layout.image = UIGraphicsGetImageFromCurrentImageContext()!
    UIGraphicsEndImageContext()

    message.layout = layout
    message.url = url

    let conversation = self.activeConversation
    conversation?.insert(message, completionHandler: {(error) in
        if let error = error {
            print(error)
        }
    })
    self.dismiss()
}
```

This new code designates a graphic context covering the area of the screen containing the gridView object. A graphics rendering of the view hierarchy of which gridView is the parent is then drawn into the context. Finally an image is generated and displayed as the image property of the message layout object.

When the app is tested, the message bubbles should now contain an image showing the current status of the tic-tac-toe grid:

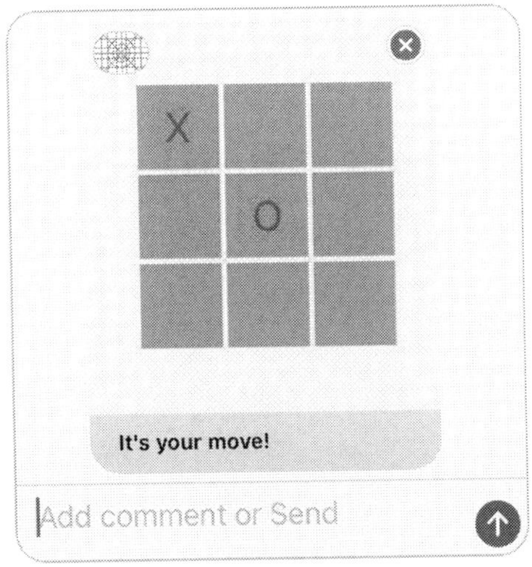

Figure 92-15

92.11 Implementing a Session

After a few messages have been sent back and forth between the players it will become clear that each entry inserted into the game appears in full within the iMessage transcript area. Since only the current state of play of the game matters at any particular time, it would be better if only the current step in the game is displayed fully in the transcript. To implement this behavior, the messages all need to be assigned to the same MSSession object. To implement this, begin by modifying the *prepareMessage* method. The method first needs to check if a session already exists, create one if it does not, and then reference the session when the MSMessage object is created:

```
func prepareMessage(_ url: URL) {

    if session == nil {
        session = MSSession()
    }

    let message = MSMessage(session: session!)

    let layout = MSMessageTemplateLayout()
    layout.caption = caption
.
.
.
}
```

Code now also needs to be added to the *willBecomeActive* method to extract the current session from the selectedMessage object within the current conversation:

```
override func willBecomeActive(with conversation: MSConversation) {

    if let messageURL = conversation.selectedMessage?.url {
        decodeURL(messageURL)
```

```
        caption = "It's your move!"
        session = conversation.selectedMessage?.session
    }
.
.
}
```

Run the app once more, play a few turns of the game with the two test user accounts and note that previous messages are represented by the app icon while only the current message is displayed with the full message bubble and image:

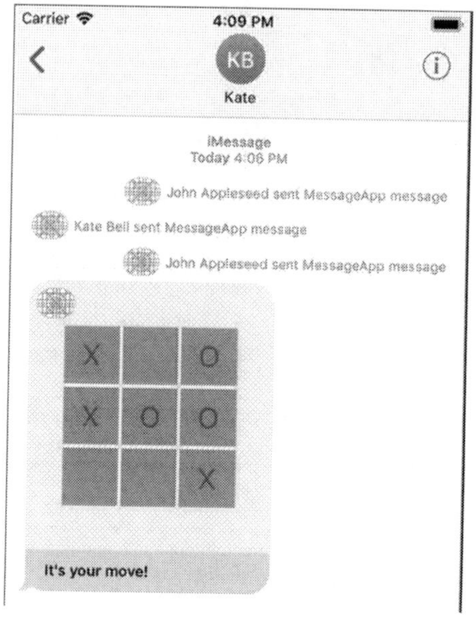

Figure 92-16

92.12 Summary

The Message framework allows message app extensions to be integrated into the standard iOS Messages app. These extensions allow interactive messages to be sent between users. This process involves obtaining a reference to the currently active conversation and the creation and configuration of an MSMessage object which is then inserted into the conversation. Data to be transferred with the message may be encoded into a URL using the URLComponents class and then assigned to the URL property of the MSMessage object. This data is then decoded when it is received by another instance of the app extension and used to restore the state of the app. To avoid cluttering the message transcript area, messages may be declared as belonging to the same session.

This chapter has worked through the creation of an example application designed to demonstrate the key steps in developing an interactive message app.

Chapter 93

93. An Introduction to SiriKit

Although Siri has been part of iOS for a number of years, it was not until the introduction of iOS 10 that some of the power of Siri has been made available to app developers through SiriKit. Initially limited to particular categories of app, SiriKit has been extended in iOS 12 to allow Siri functionality to be built into apps of any type.

The purpose of SiriKit is to allow key areas of application functionality to be accessed via voice commands through the Siri interface. An app designed to send messages, for example, may be integrated into Siri to allow messages to be composed and sent using voice commands. Similarly, a time management app might use SiriKit to allow entries to be made in the Reminders app.

This chapter will provide an overview of SiriKit and outline the ways in which apps are configured to integrate SiriKit support.

93.1 Siri and SiriKit

Most iOS users will no doubt be familiar with Siri, Apple's virtual digital assistant. Pressing and holding the home button, or saying "Hey Siri" launches Siri and allows a range of tasks to be performed by speaking in a conversational manner. Selecting the playback of a favorite song, asking for turn-by-turn directions to a location or requesting information about the weather are all examples of tasks that Siri can perform in response to voice commands.

Since the introduction of SiriKit in iOS 10, some of the capabilities of Siri are now available to iOS app developers.

When an app integrates with SiriKit, Siri handles all of the tasks associated with communicating with the user and interpreting the meaning and context of the user's words. Siri then packages up the user's request into an *intent* and passes it to the iOS app. It is then the responsibility of the iOS app to verify that enough information has been provided in the intent to perform the task and to instruct Siri to request any missing information. Once the intent contains all of the necessary data, the app performs the requested task and notifies Siri of the results. These results will be presented either by Siri or within the iOS app itself.

93.2 SiriKit Domains

When initially introduced, SiriKit could only be used with apps to perform tasks that fit into narrowly defined categories, also referred to as *domains*. With the release of iOS 10, Siri could only be used by apps when performing tasks that fit into one or more of the following domains:

- Messaging
- Notes and Lists
- Payments
- Visual Codes
- Photos
- Workouts
- Ride Booking
- CarPlay

- Car Commands
- VoIP Calling
- Restaurant Reservations

If your app fits into one of these domains then this is still the recommended approach to performing Siri integration. If, on the other hand, your app does not have a matching domain, SiriKit can now be integrated using custom Siri Shortcuts.

93.3 Siri Shortcuts

Siri Shortcuts allow frequently performed activities within an app to be stored as a shortcut and triggered via Siri using a pre-defined phrase. If a user regularly checked a specific stock price within a financial app, for example, that task could be saved as a shortcut and performed at any time via Siri voice command without the need to manually launch the app. Although lacking the power and flexibility of SiriKit domain-based integration, Siri Shortcuts provide a way for key features to be made accessible via Siri for apps that would otherwise be unable to provide any Siri integration.

An app can provide an "Add to Siri" button that allows a particular task to be configured as a shortcut. Alternatively, an app can make shortcut suggestions by *donating* actions to Siri. The user can review any shortcut suggestions within the Settings app and choose those to be added as shortcuts.

Based on user behavior patterns, Siri will also suggest shortcuts to the user in the Siri Suggestions and Search panel that appears when making a downward swiping motion on the device home screen.

Siri Shortcuts will be covered in detail in the chapters entitled *An Overview of Siri Shortcut App Integration* and *Building Siri Shortcut Support into an iOS App*. Be sure to complete this chapter before looking at the Siri Shortcut chapters. Much of the content in this chapter applies equally to SiriKit domains and Siri Shortcuts.

93.4 SiriKit Intents

Each domain allows a predefined set of tasks, or intents, to be requested by the user for fulfillment by an app. An intent represents a specific task of which Siri is aware and for which SiriKit expects an integrated iOS app to be able to perform. The Messaging domain, for example, includes intents for sending and searching for messages, while the Workout domain contains intents for choosing, starting and finishing workouts. When the user makes a request of an app via Siri, the request is placed into an intent object of the corresponding type and passed to the app for handling.

In the case of Siri Shortcuts, a SiriKit integration is implemented by using a custom intent combined with an intents definition file describing how the app will interact with Siri.

93.5 How SiriKit Integration Works

Siri integration is performed via the iOS extension mechanism (a topic covered in detail starting with the chapter entitled *An Introduction to Extensions in iOS 12*). Extensions are added as targets to the app project within Xcode in the same way as other extension types. SiriKit provides two types of extension, the key one being the Intents Extension. This extension contains an *intent handler* which is subclassed from the INExtension class of the Intents framework and contains the methods called by Siri during the process of communicating with the user. It is the responsibility of the intent handler to verify that Siri has collected all of the required information from the user, and then to execute the task defined in the intent.

The second extension type is the UI Extension. This extension is optional and comprises a storyboard file and a subclass of the IntentViewController class. When provided, Siri will use this UI when presenting information to the user. This can be useful for including additional information within the Siri user interface or for bringing the branding and theme of the main iOS app into the Siri environment.

When the user makes a request of an app via Siri, the first method to be called is the *handler(forIntent:)* method of the intent handler class contained in the Intents Extension. This method is passed the current intent object and returns a reference to the object that will serve as the intent handler. This can either be the intent handler class itself or another class that has been configured to implement one or more intent handling protocols.

The intent handler declares the types of intent it is able to handle and must then implement all of the protocol methods required to support those particular intent types. These methods are then called as part of a sequence of phases that make up the intent handling process as illustrated in Figure 93-1:

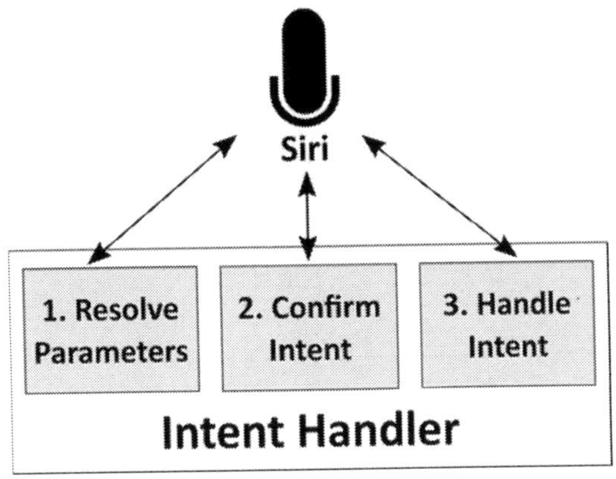

Figure 93-1

The first step after Siri calls the handler method involves calls to a series of methods to resolve the parameters associated with the intent.

93.6 Resolving Intent Parameters

Each intent domain type has associated with it a group of parameters that are used to provide details about the task to be performed by the app. While many parameters are mandatory, some are optional. The intent to send a message must, for example, contain a valid recipient parameter in order for a message to be sent. A number of parameters for a Photo search intent, on the other hand, are optional. A user might, for example, want to search for photos containing particular people, regardless of the date that the photos were taken.

When working with Siri domains, Siri knows all of the possible parameters for each intent type, and for each parameter Siri will ask the app extension's intent handler to *resolve* the parameter via a corresponding method call. If Siri already has a parameter, it will ask the intent handler to verify that the parameter is valid. If Siri does not yet have a value for a parameter it will ask the intent handler if the parameter is required. If the intent handler notifies Siri that the parameter is not required, Siri will not ask the user to provide it. If, on the other hand, the parameter is needed, Siri will ask the user to provide the information.

Consider, for example, a photo search app called CityPicSearch that displays all the photos taken in a particular city. The user might begin by saying the following:

"Hey Siri. Find photos using CityPicSearch."

From this sentence, Siri will infer that a photo search using the CityPicSearch app has been requested. Siri will know that CityPicSearch has been integrated with SiriKit and that the app has registered that it supports the InSearchForPhotosIntent intent type. Siri also knows that the InSearchForPhotosIntent intent allows photos to be searched for based on date created, people in the photo, the location of the photo and the photo album in which the photo resides. What Siri does not know, however, is which of these parameters the CityPicSearch app actually needs to perform the task. To find out this information, Siri will call the resolve method for each of these parameters on the app's intent handler. In each case the intent handler will respond indicating whether or not the parameter is required. In this case, the intent handler's *resolveLocationCreated* method will return a status indicating that the parameter is mandatory. On receiving this notification, Siri will request the missing information from the user by saying:

"Find pictures from where?"

The user will then provide a location which Siri will pass to the app by calling *resolveLocationCreated* once again, including the selection in the intent object. The app will verify the validity of the location and indicate to Siri that the parameter is valid. This process will repeat for each parameter supported by the intent type until all necessary parameter requirements have been satisfied.

Techniques are also available to assist Siri and the user clarify ambiguous parameters. The intent handler can, for example, return a list of possible options for a parameter which will then be presented to the user for selection. If the user were to ask an app to send a message to "John", the *resolveRecipients* method would be called by Siri. The method might perform a search of the contacts list and find multiple entries where the contact's first name is John. In this situation the method could return a list of contacts with the first name of John. Siri would then ask the user to clarify which "John" is the intended recipient by presenting the list of matching contacts.

Once the parameters have either been resolved or indicated as not being required, Siri will call the *confirm* method of the intent handler.

93.7 The Confirm Method

The confirm method is implemented within the extension intent handler and is called by Siri when all of the intent parameters have been resolved. This method provides the intent handler with an opportunity to make sure that it is ready to handle the intent. If the confirm method reports a ready status, Siri calls the *handle* method.

93.8 The Handle Method

The *handle* method is where the activity associated with the intent is performed. Once the task is completed, a response is passed to Siri. The form of the response will depend on the type of activity performed. For example, a photo search activity will return a count of the number of matching photos, while a send message activity will indicate whether the message was sent successfully.

The handle method may also return a *continueInApp* response. This tells Siri that the remainder of the task is to be performed within the main app. On receiving this response, Siri will launch the app, passing in an NSUserActivity object. NSUserActivity is a class that enables the status of an app to be saved and restored. In iOS 10 and later, the NSUserActivity class now has an additional property that allows an NSInteraction object to be stored along with the app state. Siri uses this *interaction* property to store the NSInteraction object for the session and pass it to the main iOS app. The interaction object, in turn, contains a copy of the intent object which the app can extract to continue processing the activity. A custom NSUserActivity object can be created by the extension and passed to the iOS app. Alternatively, if no custom object is specified, SiriKit will create one by default.

A photo search intent, for example, would need to use the *continueInApp* response and user activity object so that photos found during the search can be presented to the user (SiriKit does not currently provide a mechanism for displaying the images from a photo search intent within the Siri user interface).

It is important to note that an intent handler class may contain more than one handle method to handle different intent types. A messaging app, for example, would typically have different handler methods for send message and message search intents.

93.9 Custom Vocabulary

Clearly Siri has a broad knowledge of vocabulary in a wide range of languages. It is quite possible, however, that your app or app users might use certain words or terms which have no meaning or context for Siri. These terms can be added to your app so that they are recognized by Siri. These custom vocabulary terms are categorized as either *user-specific* or *global*.

User specific terms are terms that only apply to an individual user. This might be a photo album with an unusual name or the nicknames the user has entered for contacts in a messaging app. User specific terms are registered with Siri from within the main iOS app (not the extension) at application runtime using the *setVocabularyStrings(oftype:)* method of the NSVocabulary class and must be provided in the form of an ordered list with the most commonly used terms listed first.

User-specific custom vocabulary terms may only be specified for contact and contact group names, photo tag and album names, workout names and CarPlay car profile names. When calling the *setVocabularyStrings(oftype:)* method with the ordered list, the category type specified must be one of the following:

- contactName
- contactGroupName
- photoTag
- photoAlbumName
- workoutActivityName
- carProfileName

Global vocabulary terms are specific to your app but apply to all app users. These terms are supplied with the app bundle in the form of a property list file named *AppInventoryVocabulary.plist*. These terms are only applicable to work out and ride sharing names.

93.10 The Siri User Interface

Each SiriKit domain has a standard user interface layout that is used by default to convey information to the user during the Siri integration. The Ride Booking extension, for example, will display information such as the destination and price. These default user interfaces can be customized by adding an intent UI app extension to the project. This topic is covered in the chapter entitled *Customizing the SiriKit Intent User Interface*. In the case of a Siri Shortcut, the same technique can be used to customize the user interface that appears within Siri when the shortcut is used.

93.11 Summary

SiriKit brings some of the power of Siri to third-party apps, allowing the functionality of an app to be accessed by the user using the Siri virtual assistant interface. Siri integration was originally only available when performing tasks that fall into narrowly defined domains such as messaging, photo searching and workouts. This has now been broadened to provide support for apps of just about any type. Siri integration uses the standard iOS extensions mechanism. The Intents Extension is responsible for interacting with Siri, while the optional UI Extension provides a way to control the appearance of any results presented to the user within the Siri environment.

All of the interaction with the user is handled by Siri, with the results structured and packaged into an intent. This intent is then passed to the intent handler of the Intents Extension via a series of method calls designed to verify that all the required information has been gathered. The intent is then handled, the requested task performed and the results presented to the user either via Siri or the main iOS app.

Chapter 94

94. An iOS 12 Example SiriKit Messaging Extension

The previous chapter covered much of the theory associated with integrating Siri into an iOS app. This chapter will review the example Siri messaging extension that is created by Xcode when a new Intents Extension is added to a project. This will not only show a practical implementation of the topics covered in the previous chapter, but will also provide some more detail on how the integration works. The next chapter will cover the steps required to make use of a UI Extension within an app project.

94.1 Creating the Example Project

Begin by launching Xcode and creating a new Single View Application project named *SiriDemo* using Swift as the programming language.

94.2 Enabling the Siri Entitlement

Once the main project has been created the Siri entitlement must be enabled for the project. Select the *SiriDemo* target located at the top of the Project Navigator panel so that the main panel displays the project settings. From within this panel, select the *Capabilities* tab, locate the *Siri* entry and change the switch setting from Off to On as shown in Figure 94-1:

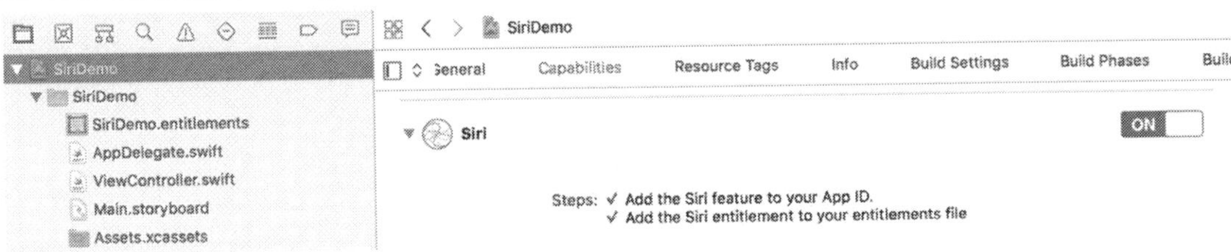

Figure 94-1

94.3 Seeking Siri Authorization

In addition to enabling the Siri entitlement, the app must also seek authorization from the user to integrate the app with Siri. This is a two-step process which begins with the addition of an entry to the *Info.plist* file of the iOS app target for the NSSiriUsageDescription key with a corresponding string value explaining how the app makes use of Siri.

Select the *Info.plist* file, locate the bottom entry in the list of properties and hover the mouse pointer over the item. When the plus button appears, click on it to add a new entry to the list. From within the dropdown list of available keys, locate and select the *Privacy – Siri Usage Description* option as shown in Figure 94-2:

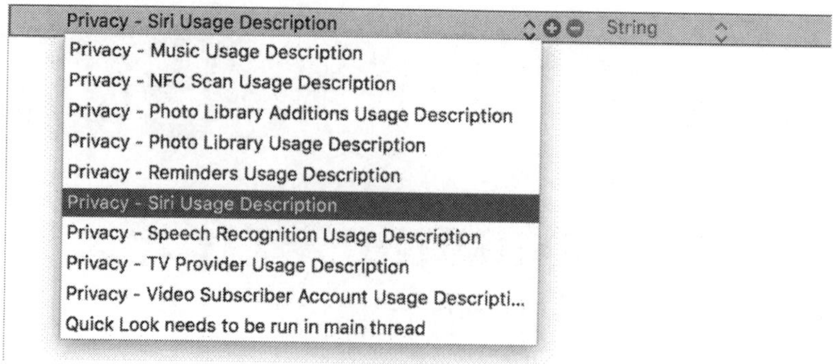

Figure 94-2

Within the value field for the property, enter a message to display to the user when requesting permission to use speech recognition. For example:

```
Siri support is used to send and review messages.
```

In addition to adding the Siri usage description key, a call also needs to be made to the *requestSiriAuthorization* class method of the INPreferences class. Ideally, this call should be made the first time that the app runs, not only so that authorization can be obtained, but also so that the user learns that the app includes Siri support. For the purposes of this project, the call will be made within the *viewDidLoad* method of the ViewController class. Edit the *ViewController.swift* file and modify it to import the Intents framework and to call the *requestSiriAuthorization* method:

```
import UIKit
import Intents

class ViewController: UIViewController {

    @IBOutlet weak var imageView: UIImageView!

    override func viewDidLoad() {
        super.viewDidLoad()

        INPreferences.requestSiriAuthorization({status in
            // Handle errors here
        })
    }
.
.
.
}
```

Before proceeding, compile and run the app on an iOS device or simulator. When the app loads, a dialog will appear requesting authorization to use Siri. Select the OK button in the dialog to provide authorization.

94.4 Adding the Extensions

The next step is to add the Intents Extension to the project ready to begin the SiriKit integration. Select the Xcode *File -> New -> Target...* menu option and add an Intents Extension to the project. Name the product

SiriDemoIntent and make sure that the *Include UI Extension* option is selected before clicking on the *Finish* button. When prompted to do so, activate the build schemes for both the Intents and UI Extensions.

94.5 Supported Intents

In order to work with Siri, an extension must specify the intent types it is able to support. These declarations are made in the *Info.plist* files of the extension folders. Within the Project Navigator panel, select the *Info.plist* file located in the *SiriDemoIntent* folder and unfold the *NSExtension -> NSExtensionAttributes* section. This will show that the *IntentsSupported* key has been assigned an array of intent class names:

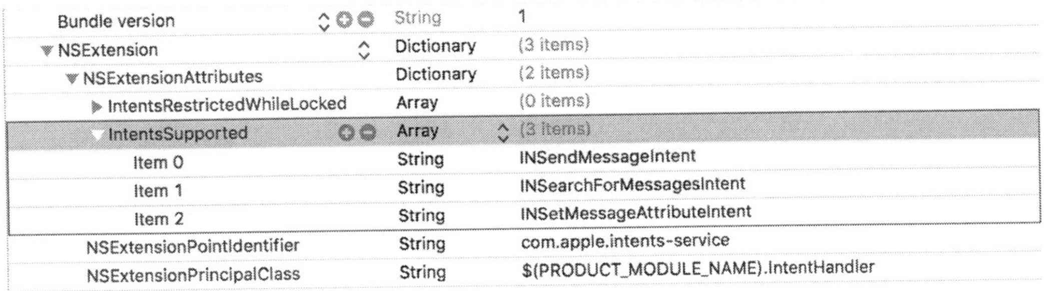

Bundle version	String	1
▼ NSExtension	Dictionary	(3 items)
▼ NSExtensionAttributes	Dictionary	(2 items)
▶ IntentsRestrictedWhileLocked	Array	(0 items)
▼ IntentsSupported	Array	(3 items)
Item 0	String	INSendMessageIntent
Item 1	String	INSearchForMessagesIntent
Item 2	String	INSetMessageAttributeIntent
NSExtensionPointIdentifier	String	com.apple.intents-service
NSExtensionPrincipalClass	String	$(PRODUCT_MODULE_NAME).IntentHandler

Figure 94-3

Note that entries are available for intents that are supported and intents that are supported but restricted when the lock screen is enabled. It might be wise, for example, for a payment based intent to be restricted when the screen is locked. As currently configured, the extension supports all of the messaging intent types without restrictions. To support a different domain, change these intents or add additional intents accordingly. For example, a photo search extension might only need to specify *INSearchForPhotosIntent* as a supported intent.

The supported intent settings are also configured in the *Info.plist* file contained in the *SiriDemoIntentUI* and will also need to be changed if the UI Extension is being used. Note that the intents supported by the Intents Extension do not necessarily have to match those of the UI Extension. This allows the UI Extension to be used only for certain intent types.

94.6 Using the Default User Interface

When this project was created at the beginning of the chapter, a UI extension was included within the Siri extension targets. As will be outlined in the next chapter, SiriKit provides a number of ways in which the user interface associated with a Siri session can be customized. At this stage, however, we only need to use the default user interface to begin testing. To allow this to happen, some changes need to be made to a method named *configureView* located in the *IntentViewController.swift* file of the *SiriDemoIntentUI* extension. Open this file now, locate the *configureView* method and modify it to read as follows:

```
func configureView(for parameters: Set<INParameter>, of interaction:
   INInteraction, interactiveBehavior: INUIInteractiveBehavior, context:
     INUIHostedViewContext, completion: @escaping (Bool, Set<INParameter>,
       CGSize) -> Void) {

    completion(true, parameters, self.desiredSize)
    if parameters.isEmpty {
        completion(false, [], CGSize.zero)
    }
}
```

In the next chapter this method, and the ways it can be used to customize the user interface will be covered in detail.

94.7 Trying the Example

Before exploring the structure of the project it is worth running the app and experiencing the Siri integration. The example simulates searching for and sending messages, so can be safely used without any messages actually being sent.

Make sure that the *SiriDemoIntent* option is selected as the run target in the toolbar as illustrated in Figure 94-4 and click on the run button.

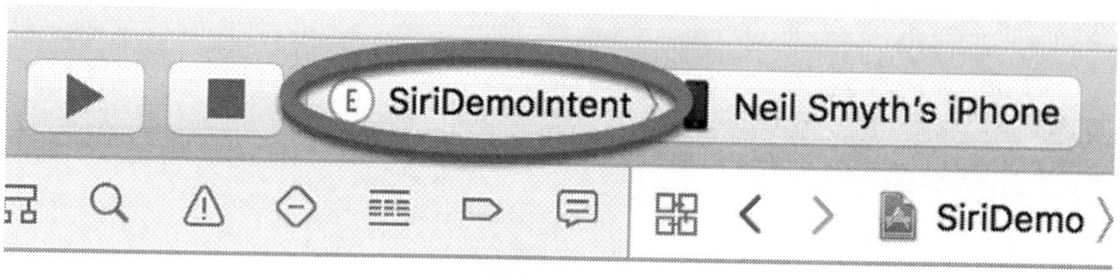

Figure 94-4

When prompted, select Siri as the app within which the extension is to run. When Siri launches experiment with phrases such as the following:

"Send a message with SiriDemo."

"Send a message to John with SiriDemo."

"Use SiriDemo to say Hello to John and Kate."

"Find Messages with SiriDemo."

If Siri indicates that SiriDemo has not yet been set up, tap the button located on the Siri screen to open the SiriDemo app. Once the app has launched, press and hold the home button to relaunch Siri and try the above phrases again.

In each case, all of the work involved in understanding the phrases and converting them into structured representations of the request is performed by Siri. All the intent handler needs to do is work with the resulting intent object.

94.8 Specifying a Default Phrase

A useful option when repeatedly testing SiriKit behavior is to configure a phrase to be passed to Siri each time the app is launched from within Xcode. This avoids having to repeatedly speak to Siri each time the app is re-launched. To specify the test phrase, select the SiriDemoIntent run target in the Xcode toolbar and select *Edit scheme…* from the resulting menu as illustrated in Figure 94-5:

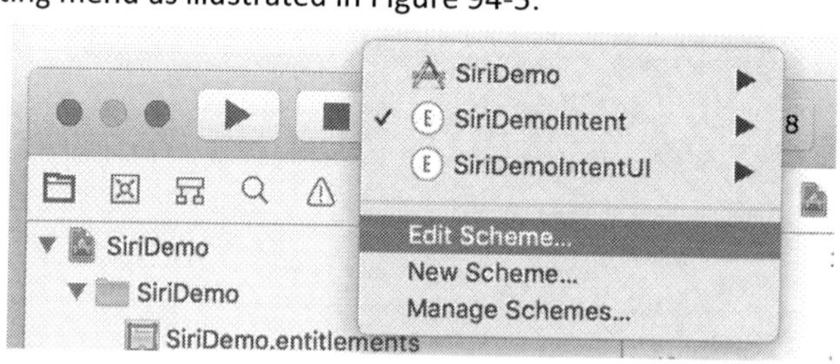

Figure 94-5

In the scheme panel, select the Run entry in the left hand panel followed by the *Info* tab in the main panel. Within the Info settings, enter a query phrase into the *Siri Intent Query* text box before closing the panel:

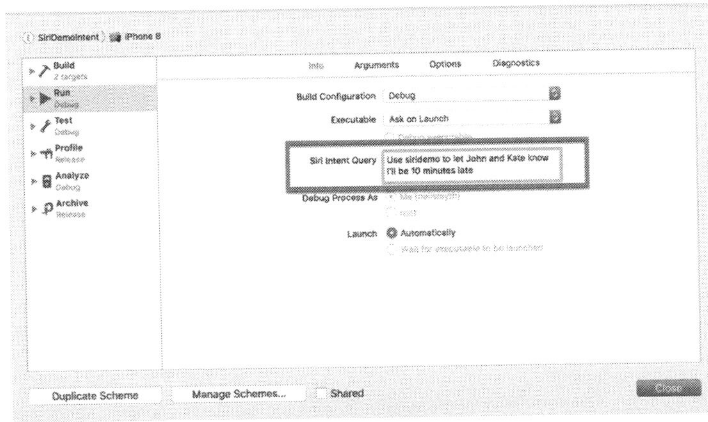

Figure 94-6

Run the extension once again and note that the phrase is automatically passed to Siri to be handled.

94.9 Reviewing the Intent Handler

The Intent Handler is declared in the *IntentHandler.swift* file in the *SiriDemoIntent* folder. Load the file into the editor and note that the class declares that it supports a range of intent handling protocols for the messaging domain:

```
class IntentHandler: INExtension, INSendMessageIntentHandling,
  INSearchForMessagesIntentHandling, INSetMessageAttributeIntentHandling {
.
.
}
```

The above declaration declares the class as supporting all three of the intents available in the messaging domain. As an alternative to listing all of the protocol names individually, the above code could have achieved the same result by referencing the *INMessagesDomainHandling* protocol which encapsulates all three protocols.

If this template were to be repurposed for a different domain, these protocol declarations would need to be replaced. For a payment extension, for example, the declaration might read as follows:

```
class IntentHandler: INExtension, INSendPaymentIntentHandling,
    INRequestPaymentIntent {
.
.
.
}
```

The class also contains the *handler* method, resolution methods for the intent parameters and the *confirm* method. The *resolveRecipients* method is of particular interest since it demonstrates the use of the resolution process to provide the user with a range of options from which to choose when a parameter is ambiguous.

The implementation also contains multiple handle methods for performing tasks for message search, message send and message attribute change intents. Take some time to review these methods before proceeding.

94.10 Summary

This chapter has provided a walk-through of the sample messaging-based extension provided by Xcode when creating a new Intents Extension. This has highlighted the steps involved in adding both Intents and UI Extensions to an existing project, and enabling and seeking SiriKit integration authorization for the project. The chapter also outlined the steps necessary for the extensions to declare supported intents and provided an opportunity to gain familiarity with the methods that make up a typical intent handler. The next chapter will outline the mechanism for implementing and configuring a UI Extension.

Chapter 95

95. Customizing the SiriKit Intent User Interface

Each SiriKit domain will default to a standard user interface layout to present information to the user during the Siri session. In the previous chapter, for example, the standard user interface was used by SiriKit to display to the user the message recipients and content to the user before sending the message. The default appearance can, however, be customized by making use of an Intent UI app extension. This UI Extension provides a way to control the appearance of information when it is displayed within the Siri interface. It also allows an extension to present additional information that would not normally be displayed by Siri or to present information using a visual style that reflects the design theme of the main app.

95.1 Modifying the UI Extension

SiriKit provides two mechanisms for performing this customization each of which involves implementing a method in the intent UI view controller class file. A simpler and less flexible option involves the use of the *configure* method. For greater control, the previously mentioned *configureView* method is available.

95.2 Using the configure Method

When the Intents Extension target was added to the SiriKitDemo project in the previous chapter, the option to also include a UI Extension was selected. The files for this extension can be found within the Project navigator panel under the *SiriDemoIntentUI* folder.

Included within the SiriDemoIntentUI extension is a storyboard file named *MainInterface.storyboard*. When loaded into Interface Builder it will become clear that this currently contains a single ViewController scene and a single UIView object. When the *configure* method is used to customize the user interface, this scene is used to display additional content which will appear directly above the standard SiriKit provided UI content. This layout is sometimes referred to as the *Siri Snippet*. For comparison purposes, consider the default UI when sending a message using SiriKit:

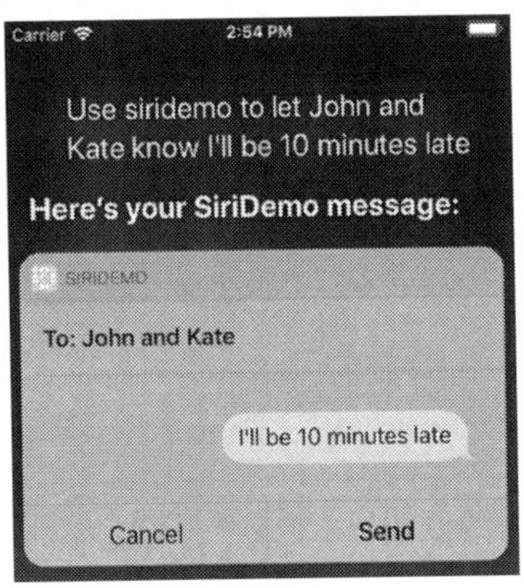

Figure 95-1

Although not visible by default, at the top of the message panel is the area represented by the UI Extension (had we not requested the UI Extension when the Intents Extension was added, this area would not be present). Specifically, this displays the scene defined in the *MainInterface.storyboard* file of the *SiriDemoIntentUI* extension folder. The lower section of the panel is the default user interface provided by Siri for this particular SiriKit domain.

To provide a custom user interface using the UI Extension, the user interface needs to be implemented in the *MainInterface.storyboard* file and the *configure* method added to the *IntentViewController.swift* file. The IntentViewController class in this file is a subclass of UIViewController and configured such that it implements the INUIHostedViewControlling protocol.

The UI Extension is only used when information is being presented to the user in relation to an intent type that has been declared as supported in the UI Extension's *Info.plist* file. When the extension is used, the *configure* method of the IntentViewController is called and passed an INInteraction object containing both the NSUserActivity and intent objects associated with the current Siri session. This allows context information about the session to be extracted and displayed to the user via the custom user interface defined in the *MainInterface.storyboard* file.

To add content above the "To:" line, therefore, we just need to implement the *configure* method and add some views to the UIView instance in the storyboard file. These views can be added either via Interface Builder or programmatically with the *configure* method.

95.3 Designing the Siri Snippet Scene

For the purposes of this example, the storyboard scene for the UI Extension will be configured to display the content of the message on a white label with a black background. Keep in mind, however, that views of any type and combination can be used in the layout, including images and maps. Select the *MainInterface.storyboard* file and drag and drop a Label object so that it is positioned in the center of the scene. Using the Auto Layout *Resolve Auto Layout Issues* menu, select the option to *Reset to Suggested Constraints*.

Select the Label object, display the Attributes Inspector panel and change the color property to white. Next, select the background view and change the background color to black. On completion of these steps, the layout should match Figure 95-2:

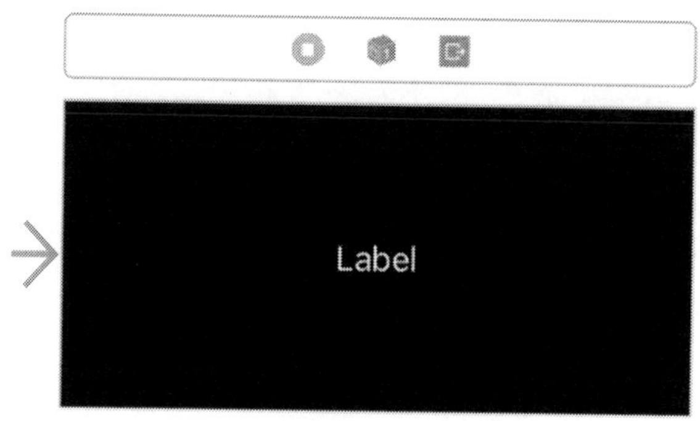

Figure 95-2

Display the Assistant Editor and establish an outlet connection from the Label object named *contentLabel* within the *IntentViewController.swift* class file.

95.4 Adding the configure Method

The *configure* method now needs to be written to detect if the current intent is a send message intent, extract the message content from the intent object and display it on the Label object within the storyboard scene. Edit the *IntentViewController.swift* file and add the *configure* method as follows:

```
func configure(with interaction: INInteraction, context:
    INUIHostedViewContext, completion: @escaping ((CGSize) -> Void)) {

    if interaction.intent is INSendMessageIntent {
        let intent = interaction.intent as! INSendMessageIntent
        self.contentLabel.text = intent.content
    }

    completion(self.desiredSize)
}
```

The added code simply checks that the intent is of type *INSendMessageIntent*, extracts the intent from the NSInteraction object and then assigns the message content contained within the intent to the text property of the Label object.

If a class contains both the *configure* and *configureView* methods, Siri will use the *configureView* method by default. To prevent this, comment out the *configureView* method as follows before testing the extension:

```
/*
func configureView(for parameters: Set<INParameter>, of interaction:
   INInteraction, interactiveBehavior: INUIInteractiveBehavior, context:
     INUIHostedViewContext, completion: @escaping (Bool, Set<INParameter>,
       CGSize) -> Void) {

    if parameters.isEmpty {
        completion(false, [], CGSize.zero)
    }
}
*/
```

Next, the *desiredSize* declaration needs to be changed so that the user interface does not use the maximum allowed size (which is much larger than is actually needed for this example):

```
var desiredSize: CGSize {
    //return self.extensionContext!.hostedViewMaximumAllowedSize
    return CGSize.init(width: 10, height: 100)
}
```

Compile and run the extension and use Siri to prepare a message so that it is ready to be sent. This time, the UI Extension section should appear as shown in Figure 95-3:

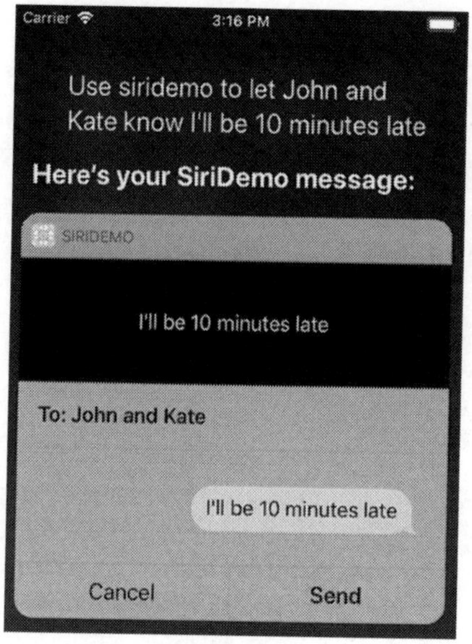

Figure 95-3

Clearly the extension user interface is working. There is, however, an issue in that the message content is now displayed twice, once by the UI Extension and once by Siri. A preferable outcome would be for the message only to appear in the UI Extension. This can be achieved using a feature referred to as *Siri override control*.

95.5 Overriding Siri Content

Siri override control defines a system whereby a UI Extension can let Siri know that it will take responsibility for displaying certain types of information, thereby avoiding duplicated content within the Siri user interface. Currently SiriKit only allows maps, message content and payment transactions to be replaced by the UI Extension.

Override control requires that the intent view controller implement the INUIHostingViewSiriProviding protocol together with the methods for the content to be overridden. Available methods are as follows:

- displaysMap
- displaysMessage
- displaysPaymentTransaction

The methods return a Boolean value indicating whether or not the Extension UI will be displaying the content.

In this case, the *displaysMessage* method needs to be added and implemented such that it returns a *true* value. Edit the *IntentViewController.swift* file and implement these changes as follows:

```
import IntentsUI

class IntentViewController: UIViewController, INUIHostedViewControlling, 
INUIHostedViewSiriProviding {
.
.
    var displaysMessage: Bool {
        return true
    }
.
```

```
.
}
```

Run the intent extension one last time, prepare a message using Siri and verify that the message content is no longer duplicated by Siri:

Figure 95-4

95.6 Using the configureView Method

Unlike the *configure* method, the *configureView* method allows each section of the default user interface to be replaced with custom content and view layout.

SiriKit considers the default layout to be a vertical stack in which each row is represented by a parameter. In Figure 95-1 above, for example, the recipients parameter is displayed in the uppermost row of the stack while the message content appears beneath it in the second row.

For each layer of the stack (starting at the top and finishing at the bottom of the layout) the *configureView* method is called, passed information about the corresponding parameters and provided the opportunity to provide a custom layout to be displayed within the corresponding stack row of the Siri user interface. The method is also passed a completion handler to be called with the appropriate configuration information to be passed back to Siri.

The parameters passed to the method take the form of INParameter instances. It is the responsibility of the *configureView* method to find out if a parameter is one for which it wants to provide a custom layout. It does this by creating local NSParameter instances of the type it is interested in and comparing these to the parameters passed to the method. Parameter instances are created by combining the intent class type with a specific key path representing the parameter (each type of intent has its own set of path keys which can be found in the documentation for that class). If the method needs to confirm that the passed parameter relates to the content of a send message intent, for example, the code would read as follows:

```
func configureView(for parameters: Set<INParameter>, of interaction:
   INInteraction, interactiveBehavior: INUIInteractiveBehavior, context:
    INUIHostedViewContext, completion: @escaping (Bool, Set<INParameter>,
      CGSize) -> Void) {

    let content = INParameter(for: INSendMessageIntent.self,
              keyPath: #keyPath(INSendMessageIntent.content))
```

```
        if parameters == [content] {
            // Configure ViewController before calling completion handler
        }
    .
    .
}
```

When creating a custom layout, it is likely that the method will need to access the data contained within the parameter. In the above code, for example, it might be useful to extract the message content from the parameter and incorporate it into the custom layout. This is achieved by calling the *parameterValue* method of the INInteraction object which is also passed to the *configureView* method. Each parameter type has associated with it a set of properties. In this case, the property for the message content is named, appropriately enough, *content* and can be accessed as follows:

```
.
.
let content = INParameter(for: INSendMessageIntent.self,
                keyPath: #keyPath(INSendMessageIntent.content))

if parameters == [content] {
    let contentString = interaction.parameterValue(for: content)
}
.
.
```

When the *configureView* method is ready to provide Siri with a custom layout, it calls the provided completion handler, passing through a Boolean *true* value, the original parameters and a CGSize object defining the size of the layout as it is to appear in the corresponding row of the Siri user interface stack, for example:

```
completion(true, parameters, size)
```

If the default Siri content is to be displayed for the specified parameters instead of a custom user interface, the completion handler is called with a *false* value and a zero CGSize object:

```
completion(false, parameters, CGSize.zero)
```

In addition to calling the *configureView* method for each parameter, Siri will first make a call to the method to request a configuration for no parameters. By default, the method should check for this condition and call the completion handler as follows:

```
if parameters.isEmpty {
    completion(false, [], CGSize.zero)
}
```

The foundation for the custom user interface for each parameter is the View contained within the intent UI *MainInterface.storyboard* file. Once the *configureView* method has identified the parameters it can dynamically add views to the layout, or make changes to existing views contained within the scene.

95.7 Implementing a configureView Custom UI

The previous section covered a considerable amount of information, much of which will become clearer by working through an example. Begin, therefore, by editing the *IntentViewController.swift* file, deleting the *configure* method added earlier in the chapter and removing the comment markers around the *configureView* method.

Next, open the *MainInterface.storyboard* file belonging to the *SiriDemoIntentUI* extension and resize the Label view so that it stretches to the left and right margin markers and move it so that it is positioned near the top of the containing View. With the Label still selected, display the Attributes Inspector and change the *Alignment* setting so that the text is left aligned, then use the *Resolve Auto Layout Issues* menu to set suggested constraints on all views. On completion of these steps, the layout should match that of Figure 95-5:

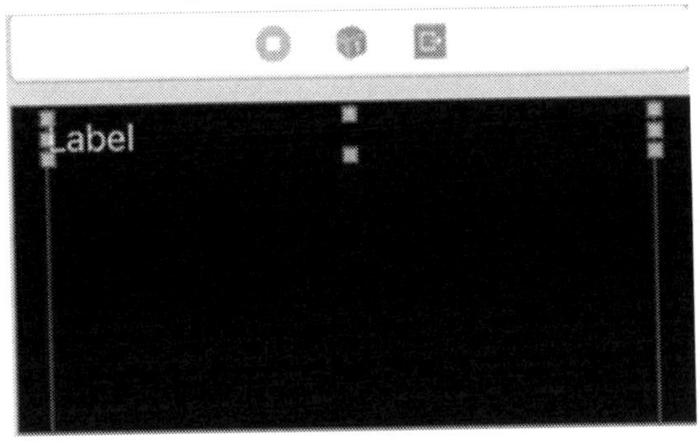

Figure 95-5

Before proceeding to the next step, establish an outlet connection from the View component to a variable in the *IntentViewController.swift* file named *contentView.*

Next, edit the *configureView* method to check for the *recipients* parameter as follows:

```
func configureView(for parameters: Set<INParameter>, of interaction:
    INInteraction, interactiveBehavior: INUIInteractiveBehavior, context:
    INUIHostedViewContext, completion: @escaping (Bool, Set<INParameter>,
     CGSize) -> Void) {

    var size = CGSize.zero

    let recipients = INParameter(for: INSendMessageIntent.self,
                         keyPath: #keyPath(INSendMessageIntent.recipients))

    if parameters == [recipients] {

        let recipientsValue = interaction.parameterValue(
                              for: recipients) as! Array<INPerson>

    } else if parameters.isEmpty {

        completion(false, [], CGSize.zero)

    }

    completion(true, parameters, size)
}
```

The recipients parameter takes the form of an array of INPerson objects, from which can be extracted the recipients' display names. Code now needs to be added to iterate through each recipient in the array, adding each name to a string to be displayed on the contentLabel view. Code will also be added to use a different font on the label and to change the background color of the view:

```
.
.
if parameters == [recipients] {
    let recipientsValue = interaction.parameterValue(
                    for: recipients) as! Array<INPerson>

    var recipientStr = "To:"
    var first = true

    for name in recipientsValue {
        let separator = first ? " " : ", "
        first = false
        recipientStr += separator + name.displayName
    }

    self.contentLabel.font = UIFont(name: "Arial-BoldItalicMT", size: 20.0)
    self.contentLabel.text = recipientStr
    self.contentView.backgroundColor = UIColor.blue
    size = CGSize(width: 100, height: 30)
} else if parameters.isEmpty {
    completion(false, [], CGSize.zero)
}

completion(true, parameters, size)
.
.
```

Compile and run the intent extension and verify that the recipient row now appears with a blue background, a 30 point height and uses a larger italic font. The content row, on the other hand, should continue to use the Siri default UI:

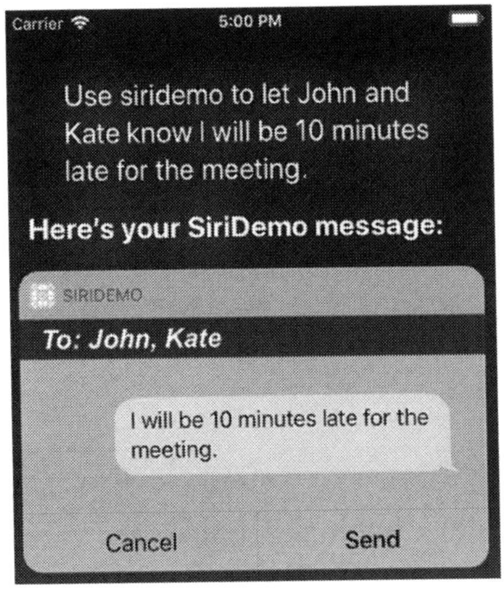

Figure 95-6

Finally, add code to the method to provide a custom UI for the content parameter:

```
.
.
let recipients = INParameter(for: INSendMessageIntent.self, keyPath:
                    #keyPath(INSendMessageIntent.recipients))

let content = INParameter(for: INSendMessageIntent.self, keyPath:
                    #keyPath(INSendMessageIntent.content))

if parameters == [recipients] {
    let recipientsValue = interaction.parameterValue(
                  for: recipients) as! Array<INPerson>

    var recipientStr = "To:"
    var first = true

    for name in recipientsValue {
        let separator = first ? " " : ", "
        first = false
        recipientStr += separator + name.displayName
    }

    self.contentLabel.font = UIFont(name: "Arial-BoldItalicMT", size: 20.0)
    self.contentLabel.text = recipientStr
    self.contentView.backgroundColor = UIColor.blue
    size = CGSize(width: 100, height: 30)
} else if parameters == [content] {
```

```
        let contentValue = interaction.parameterValue(for: content)

        self.contentLabel.text = contentValue as? String
        self.contentView.backgroundColor = UIColor.brown
        size = CGSize(width: 100, height: 70)
    } else if parameters.isEmpty {
        completion(false, [], CGSize.zero)
    }

    completion(true, parameters, size)
}
```

Run the extension one last time and verify that the content appears on the *contentLabel* view and that the view has a brown background and a 70px height:

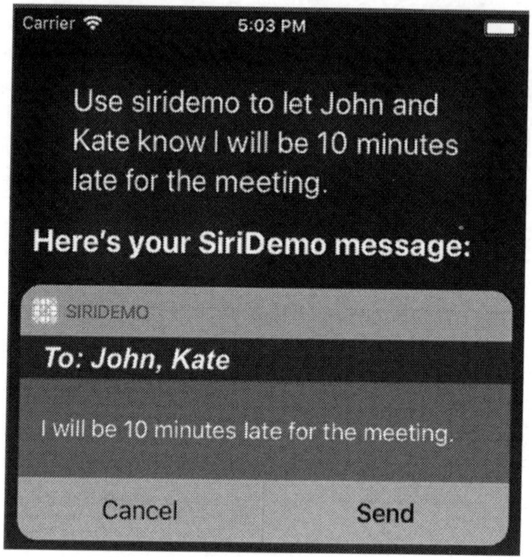

Figure 95-7

95.8 Summary

While the default user interface provided by SiriKit for the various domains will be adequate for some apps, most intent extensions will need to be customized to present information in a way that matches the style and theme of the associated app, or to provide additional information not supported by the default layout. The default UI can be replaced by adding an Intent UI extension to the app project. The UI extension provides two options for configuring the user interface presented by Siri. The simpler of the two involves the use of the *configure* method to present a custom view above the default Siri user interface layout. A more flexible approach involves the implementation of the *configureView* method. SiriKit associates each line of information displayed in the default layout with a parameter. When implemented, the *configureView* method will be called for each of these parameters and provided with the option to return a custom View containing the layout and information to be used in place of the default user interface element.

Chapter 96

96. An iOS 12 SiriKit Photo Search Tutorial

In this chapter, an example project will be created that uses the Photo domain of SiriKit to allow the user to search for and display a photo taken on a specified date using Siri. In the process of designing this app, the tutorial will also demonstrate the use of the NSUserActivity class to allow processing of the intent to be transferred from the Intents Extension to the main iOS app.

96.1 About the SiriKit Photo Search Project

As the title of this chapter suggests, the project created in this tutorial is going to take the form of an app that uses the SiriKit Photo Search domain to locate photos in the Photo library. Specifically, the app will allow the user to use Siri to search for photos taken on a specific date. In the event that photos matching the date criteria are found, the main app will be launched and used to display the first photo taken on the chosen day.

96.2 Creating the SiriPhoto Project

Begin this tutorial by launching Xcode and selecting the options to create a Single View Application named *SiriPhoto*, using Swift as the programming language.

96.3 Enabling the Siri Entitlement

Once the main project has been created, the next step is to add the Siri entitlement to the list of capabilities enabled for the project. To achieve this, select the *SiriPhoto* target located at the top of the Project Navigator panel so that the main panel displays the project settings. From within this panel, select the *Capabilities* tab, locate the *Siri* entry and change the switch setting from Off to On as shown in Figure 96-1:

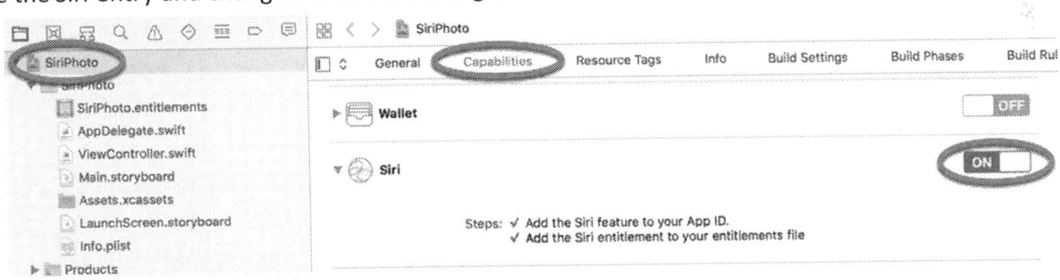

Figure 96-1

Once the Siri capability has been enabled for the project, an additional file named *SiriPhoto.entitlements* will have been added to the project.

96.4 Obtaining Siri Authorization

In addition to enabling the Siri entitlement, the app must also seek authorization from the user to integrate the app with Siri. This is a two-step process which begins with adding an entry to the *Info.plist* file for the iOS app target for the NSSiriUsageDescription key with a corresponding string value explaining how the app makes use of Siri.

Select the *Info.plist* file, locate the bottom entry in the list of properties and hover the mouse pointer over the item. When the plus button appears, click on it to add a new entry to the list. From within the dropdown list of available keys, locate and select the *Privacy – Siri Usage Description* option as shown in Figure 96-2:

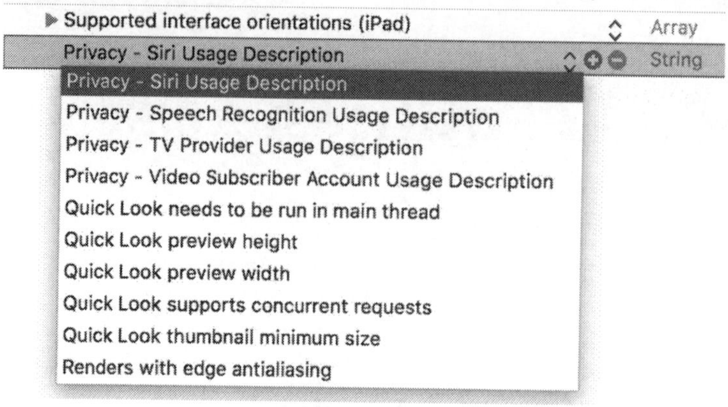

Figure 96-2

Within the value field for the property, enter a message to display to the user when requesting permission to use speech recognition. For example:

```
Siri support is used to perform photo searches.
```

Before closing the *Info.plist* file, now is also a convenient point to add an entry for the NSPhotoLibraryUsageDescription key, since the app will also need access to the photo library in order to search for images. Repeating the above steps, add a new entry for *Privacy – Photo Library Usage Description* with a suitable description string value. For example:

```
This app accesses your photo library to search and display photos.
```

In addition to adding the Siri usage description key, a call also needs to be made to the *requestSiriAuthorization* class method of the INPreferences class. The call will be made within the *viewDidLoad* method of the ViewController class. Edit the *ViewController.swift* file and modify it to import the Intents and Photos frameworks and to call the *requestSiriAuthorization* method:

```
import UIKit
import Intents
import Photos

class ViewController: UIViewController {

    @IBOutlet weak var imageView: UIImageView!

    override func viewDidLoad() {
        super.viewDidLoad()

        INPreferences.requestSiriAuthorization({status in
            // Handle errors here
        })
    }
```

```
.
.
.
}
```

Before proceeding, compile and run the app on an iOS device. When the app loads, a dialog will appear requesting authorization to use Siri. Select OK to provide authorization.

96.5 Designing the App User Interface

The user interface of the iOS app is going to consist solely of an ImageView which will be used to display the photo selected by the user. Select the *Main.storyboard* file from the Project Navigator panel and drag and drop an Image View object from the Library panel onto the scene canvas. Once added to the scene, resize the object so that it fills the entire screen (Figure 96-3):

Figure 96-3

Display the Auto Layout *Resolve Auto Layout Issues* menu and select the *Reset to Suggested Constraints* menu option located under the *All Views in View Controller* menu subheading. With the ImageView object selected, display the Attributes Inspector panel and change the *Content Mode* property to *Aspect Fit*.

In order to be able to assign an image to the Image View an outlet will be required. Display the Assistant Editor panel and establish an outlet connection from the Image View object named *imageView*.

96.6 Adding the Intents Extension to the Project

With some of the initial work on the iOS app complete, it is now time to add the Intents Extension to the project. Select Xcode's *File -> New -> Target...* menu option to display the template selection screen. From the range of available templates, select the *Intents Extension* option as shown in Figure 96-4:

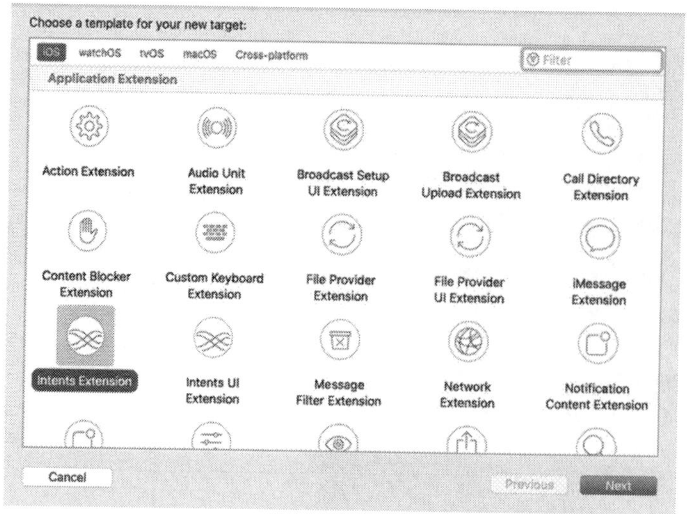

Figure 96-4

With the Intents Extension template selected, click on the *Next* button and enter *SiriPhotoIntent* into the Product Name field. Before clicking on the *Finish* button, turn off the *Include UI Extension* option (the UI Extension is not supported by the SiriKit Photo domain). When prompted to do so, enable the build scheme for the Intents Extension by clicking on the *Activate* button in the resulting panel.

96.7 Reviewing the Default Intents Extension

The files for the Intents Extension are located in the *SiriPhotoIntent* folder which will now be accessible from within the Project Navigator panel. Within this folder are an *Info.plist* file and a file named *IntentHandler.swift*. The *IntentHandler.swift* file contains the IntentHandler class declaration and has been preconfigured with the basic functionality for the example SiriKit message domain extension as covered in the previous chapter.

96.8 Modifying the Supported Intents

Currently we have an app which is intended to search for photos but is currently configured to send messages. Clearly some changes need to be made to implement the required functionality.

The first step is to configure the *Info.plist* file for the SiriPhotoIntent extension. Select this file and unfold the NSExtension settings until the *IntentsSupported* array is visible:

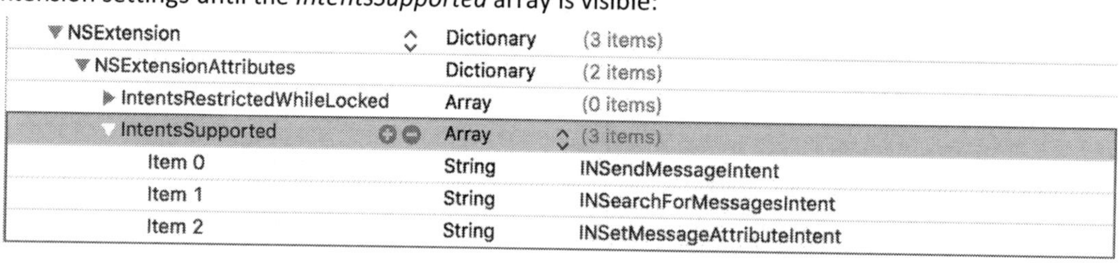

Figure 96-5

A review of the current values for this key will reveal that the extension is currently configured to handle intents associated with the SiriKit messages domain. This needs to be modified to support photo search intents. Change the string assigned to *Item 0* to *INSearchForPhotosIntent* and then delete items 1 and 2. On completion of these steps the array should match that shown in Figure 96-6:

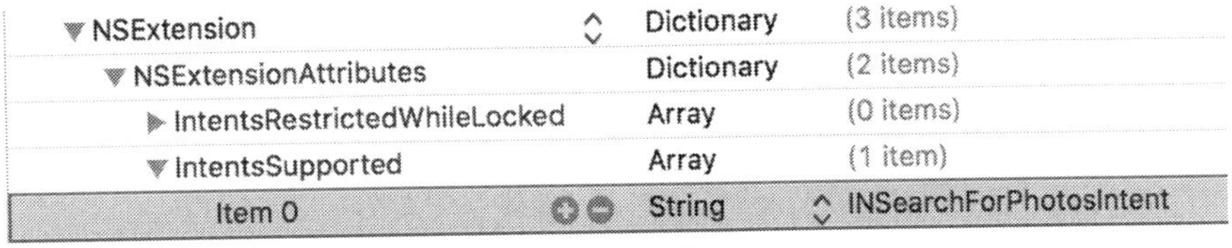

Figure 96-6

96.9 Modifying the IntentHandler Implementation

The IntentHandler class in the *IntentHandler.swift* file is currently declared as implementing message intent handling protocols. This now needs to be changed to indicate that the class is implementing photo search intent handling and to import the Photos framework. Edit the *IntentHandler.swift* file and change the class declaration so it reads as follows:

```
import Intents
import Photos

class IntentHandler: INExtension, INSearchForPhotosIntentHandling {
.
.
}
```

The only method currently implemented within the *IntentHandler.swift* file which can be reused for a Photo Search extension is the *handler* method. All of the other methods are specific to message handling and can be deleted from the file before continuing. On completion of this task, the file should read as follows:

```
import Intents
import Photos

class IntentHandler: INExtension, INSearchForPhotosIntentHandling {

    override func handler(for intent: INIntent) -> Any {
        return self
    }
}
```

The handler method is the entry point into the extension and is called by SiriKit when the user indicates that the SiriPhoto app is to be used to perform a task. When calling this method, SiriKit expects in return a reference to the object responsible for handling the intent. Since this will be the responsibility of the IntentHandler class, the handler method simply returns a reference to itself.

96.10 Implementing the Resolve Methods

SiriKit is aware of a range of parameters which can be used to specify photo search criteria. These parameters consist of the photo creation date, the geographical location where the photo was taken, the people in the photo and album in which it resides. For each of these parameters, SiriKit will call a specific resolve method on the IntentHandler instance. Each method is passed the current intent object and is required to notify Siri whether or not the parameter is required and, if so, whether the intent contains a valid property value. The methods are also passed a completion handler reference which must be called to notify Siri of the response.

The first method called by Siri is the *resolveDateCreated* method which should now be implemented in the *IntentHandler.swift* file as follows:

```
func resolveDateCreated(for
    intent: INSearchForPhotosIntent,
    with completion: @escaping
        (INDateComponentsRangeResolutionResult) -> Void) {

    if let dateCreated = intent.dateCreated {
        completion(INDateComponentsRangeResolutionResult.success(
            with: dateCreated))
    } else {
        completion(INDateComponentsRangeResolutionResult.needsValue())
    }
}
```

The method verifies that the dateCreated property of the intent object contains a value. In the event that it does, the completion handler is called indicating to Siri that the date requirement has been successfully met within the intent. In this situation, Siri will call the next resolve method in the sequence.

If no date has been provided the completion handler is called indicating the property is still needed. On receiving this response, Siri will ask the user to provide a date for the photo search. This process will repeat until either a date is provided or the user abandons the Siri session.

The SiriPhoto app is only able to search for photos by date. The remaining resolver methods can, therefore, be implemented simply to return *notRequired* results to Siri. This will let Siri know that values for these parameters do not need to be obtained from the user. Remaining within the *IntentHandler.swift* file, implement these methods as follows:

```
func resolveAlbumName(for intent: INSearchForPhotosIntent,
    with completion: @escaping (INStringResolutionResult) -> Void) {
    completion(INStringResolutionResult.notRequired())
}

func resolvePeopleInPhoto(for intent:
     INSearchForPhotosIntent, with completion: @escaping
([INPersonResolutionResult]) -> Void) {
    completion([INPersonResolutionResult.notRequired()])
}

func resolveLocationCreated(for intent:
    INSearchForPhotosIntent, with completion: @escaping
(INPlacemarkResolutionResult) -> Void) {
        completion(INPlacemarkResolutionResult.notRequired())
}
```

With these methods implemented, the resolution phase of the intent handling process is now complete.

96.11 Implementing the Confirmation Method

When Siri has gathered the necessary information for the user, a call is made to the *confirm* method of the intent handler instance. The purpose of this call is to provide the handler with an opportunity to check that everything is ready to handle the intent. In the case of the SiriPhoto app, there are no special requirements so the method can be implemented to reply with a *ready* status:

```
func confirm(intent: INSearchForPhotosIntent,
    completion: @escaping (INSearchForPhotosIntentResponse) -> Void)
{
    let response = INSearchForPhotosIntentResponse(code: .ready,
        userActivity: nil)
    completion(response)
}
```

96.12 Handling the Intent

The last step in implementing the extension is to handle the intent. After the confirm method indicates that the extension is ready, Siri calls the *handle* method. This method is, once again, passed the intent object and a completion handler to be called when the intent has been handled by the extension. Implement this method now so that it reads as follows:

```
func handle(intent: INSearchForPhotosIntent, completion: @escaping
    (INSearchForPhotosIntentResponse) -> Void) {

    let response = INSearchForPhotosIntentResponse(code:
        INSearchForPhotosIntentResponseCode.continueInApp,
            userActivity: nil)

    if intent.dateCreated != nil {
        let calendar = Calendar(identifier: .gregorian)

        if let startComponents = intent.dateCreated?.startDateComponents,
            let endComponents = intent.dateCreated?.endDateComponents {

            if let startDate = calendar.date(from:
                startComponents),
              let endDate = calendar.date(from:
                  endComponents) {

            response.searchResultsCount = photoSearchFrom(startDate,
                                         to: endDate)

            }
        }
    }
    completion(response)
}
```

The above code requires some explanation. The method begins by creating a new intent response instance and configures it with a code to let Siri know that the intent handling will be continued within the main SiriPhoto app. The userActivity argument to the method is set to nil, instructing SiriKit to create an NSUserActivity object on our behalf:

```
let response = INSearchForPhotosIntentResponse(code:
                    INSearchForPhotosIntentResponseCode.continueInApp,
                          userActivity: nil)
```

Next, the code converts the start and end dates from DateComponents objects to Date objects and calls a method named *photoSearchFrom(to:)* to confirm that photo matches are available for the specified date range. The *photoSearchFrom(to:)* method (which will be implemented next) returns a count of the matching photos. This count is then assigned to the searchResultsCount property of the response object, which is then returned to Siri via the completion handler:

```
    if let startComponents = intent.dateCreated?.startDateComponents,
        let endComponents = intent.dateCreated?.endDateComponents {

        if let startDate = calendar.date(from:
            startComponents),
          let endDate = calendar.date(from:
              endComponents) {

        response.searchResultsCount = photoSearchFrom(startDate,
                                    to: endDate)
        }
    }
}
completion(response)
```

If the extension returns a zero count via the searchResultsCount property of the response object, Siri will notify the user that no photos matched the search criteria. If one or more photo matches were found, Siri will launch the main SiriPhoto app and pass it the NSUserActivity object.

The final step in implementing the extension is to add the *photoSearchFrom(to:)* method to the *IntentHandler.swift* file:

```
func photoSearchFrom(_ startDate: Date, to endDate: Date) -> Int {

    let fetchOptions = PHFetchOptions()

    fetchOptions.predicate = NSPredicate(format: "creationDate > %@ AND 
creationDate < %@", startDate as CVarArg, endDate as CVarArg)
    let fetchResult = PHAsset.fetchAssets(with: PHAssetMediaType.image,
                            options: fetchOptions)
    return fetchResult.count
}
```

The method makes use of the standard iOS Photos framework to perform a search of the Photo library. It begins by creating a PHFetchOptions object. A predicate is then initialized and assigned to the fetchOptions instance specifying that the search is looking for photos taken between the start and end dates.

Finally, the search for matching images is initiated, and the resulting count of matches returned.

96.13 Testing the App

Though there is still some work to be completed for the main SiriPhoto app, the Siri extension functionality is now ready to be tested. Within Xcode, make sure that SiriPhotoIntent is selected as the current target and click on the run button. When prompted for a host app, select Siri and click the run button.

When Siri has started listening, say the following:

"Find a photo with SiriPhoto"

Siri will respond by seeking the day for which you would like to find a photo. After you specify a date, Siri will either launch the SiriPhoto app if photos exist for that day, or state that no photos could be found. Note that the first time a photo is requested the privacy dialog will appear seeking permission to access the photo library. Provide permission when prompted and then repeat the photo search request.

96.14 Handling the NSUserActivity Object

The intent handler in the extension has instructed Siri to continue the intent handling process by launching the main SiriPhoto app. When the app is launched by Siri it will be provided the NSUserActivity object for the session containing the intent object. When an app is launched and passed an NSUserActivity object, the *continue userActivity* method of the app delegate is called and passed the activity object.

Edit the *AppDelegate.swift* file for the SiriPhoto target and implement this method so that it reads as follows:

```
func application(_ application: UIApplication,
        continue userActivity: NSUserActivity,
        restorationHandler: @escaping ([UIUserActivityRestoring]?)
                  -> Void) -> Bool {

    let viewController =
                self.window?.rootViewController as! ViewController
    viewController.handleActivity(userActivity)
    return true
}
```

The method obtains a reference to the root view controller of the app and then calls a method named *handleActivity* on that controller, passing through the user activity object as an argument. Select the *ViewController.swift* file and implement the *handleActivity* method as follows:

```
func handleActivity(_ userActivity: NSUserActivity) {

    let intent = userActivity.interaction?.intent
                        as! INSearchForPhotosIntent

    if (intent.dateCreated?.startDateComponents) != nil {
        let calendar = Calendar(identifier: .gregorian)
        let startDate = calendar.date(from:
                (intent.dateCreated?.startDateComponents)!)
```

```
        let endDate = calendar.date(from:
                (intent.dateCreated?.endDateComponents)!)
        displayPhoto(startDate!, endDate!)
    }
}
```

The *handleActivity* method extracts the intent from the user activity object and then converts the start and end dates to Date objects. These dates are then passed to the *displayPhoto* method which now also needs to be added to the *ViewController.swift* file:

```
func displayPhoto(_ startDate: Date, _ endDate: Date) {

    let fetchOptions = PHFetchOptions()

    fetchOptions.predicate = NSPredicate(format: "creationDate > %@ AND
creationDate < %@", startDate as CVarArg, endDate as CVarArg)
    let fetchResult = PHAsset.fetchAssets(with:
                PHAssetMediaType.image, options: fetchOptions)

    let imgManager = PHImageManager.default()

    imgManager.requestImage(for: fetchResult.firstObject! as PHAsset,
                targetSize: view.frame.size,
                contentMode: PHImageContentMode.aspectFill,
                options: nil,
                resultHandler: { (image, _) in
        self.imageView.image = image
    })
}
```

The *displayPhoto* method performs the same steps used by the intent handler to search the Photo library based on the search date parameters. Once the search results have returned, however, the PHImageManager instance is used to retrieve the image from the library and display it on the Image View object.

96.15 Testing the Completed App

Run the SiriPhotoIntent extension, perform a photo search and, assuming photos are available for the selected day, wait for the main SiriPhoto app to load. When the app has loaded, the first photo taken on the specified date should appear within the Image View.

96.16 Summary

This chapter has worked through the creation of a simple app designed to use SiriKit to locate a photo taken on a particular date. The example has demonstrated the creation of an Intents Extension and the implementation of the intent handler methods necessary to interact with the Siri environment, including resolving missing parameters in the Siri intent. The project also explored the use of the NSUserActivity class to transfer the intent from the extension to the main iOS app.

Chapter 97

97. An Overview of Siri Shortcut App Integration

When SiriKit was first introduced with iOS 10, an app had to fit neatly into one of the SiriKit domains covered in the chapter entitled *An Introduction to SiriKit* in order to integrate with Siri. With the introduction of iOS 12, however, SiriKit has been extended to allow an app of any type to make key features available for access via Siri voice commands, otherwise known as Siri Shortcuts. This chapter will provide a high level overview of Siri Shortcuts and the steps involved in turning app features into Siri Shortcuts.

97.1 An Overview of Siri Shortcuts

A Siri shortcut is essentially a commonly used feature of an app that can be invoked by the user via a chosen phrase. The app for a fast-food restaurant might, for example, allow the user to order a favorite lunch item by simply using the phrase "Order Lunch" from within Siri. Once a shortcut has been configured, iOS learns the usage patterns of the shortcut and will begin to place that shortcut in the Siri Suggestions area on the device at appropriate times of the day. If the user uses the lunch ordering shortcut at lunch times on weekdays, the system will suggest the shortcut at that time of day.

A shortcut can be configured within an app by providing the user with an Add to Siri button at appropriate places in the app. Our hypothetical restaurant app might, for example, include an Add to Siri button on the order confirmation page which, when selected, will allow the user to add that order as a shortcut and provide a phrase to Siri with which to launch the shortcut in future.

An app may also suggest (a concept referred to as *donating*) a feature or user activity as a possible shortcut candidate which the user can then turn into a shortcut via the *Siri & Search* section of the Settings app.

As with the SiriKit domains, the key element of a Siri Shortcut is an intent extension. Unlike domain based extensions such as messaging and photo search which strictly define the parameters and behavior of the intent, Siri shortcut intents are customizable to meet the specific requirements of the app. A restaurant app, for example would include a custom shortcut intent designed to handle information such as the menu items ordered, the method of payment and the pick-up or delivery location. Unlike SiriKit domain extensions, however, the parameters for the intent are stored when the shortcut is created and are not requested from the user by Siri when the shortcut is invoked. A shortcut to order the user's usual morning coffee, for example, will already be configured with the coffee item and pickup location, both of which will be passed to the intent handler by Siri when the shortcut is triggered.

The intent will also need to be configured with custom responses such as notifying the user through Siri that the shortcut was successfully completed, a particular item in an order is currently unavailable or that the pickup location is currently closed.

The key component of a Siri Shortcut in terms of specifying the parameters and responses is the *SiriKit Intent Definition* file.

97.2 An Introduction to the Intent Definition File

When a SiriKit extension such as a Messaging Extension is added to an iOS project, it makes use of a pre-defined *system intent* provided by SiriKit (in the case of a Messaging extension, for example, this might involve the INSendMessageIntent). In the case of Siri shortcuts, however, a custom intent is created and configured to fit with the requirements of the app. The key to creating a custom intent lies within the Intent Definition file.

An Intent Definition file can be added to an Xcode project by selecting the Xcode *File -> New -> File...* menu option and choosing the *SiriKit Intent Definition File* from the *Resource* section of the template selection dialog.

Once created, Xcode provides an editor specifically for adding and configuring custom intents (in fact the editor may also be used to create customized variations of the system intents such as the Messaging, Workout and Payment intents). New intents are added by clicking on the + button in the lower left corner of the editor window and making a selection from the menu:

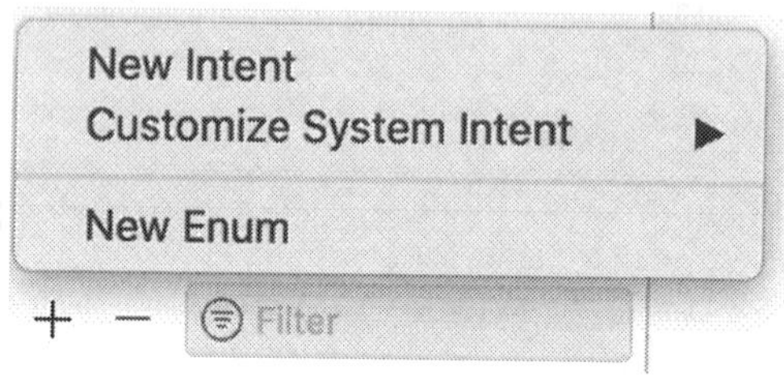

Figure 97-1

Selecting the *Customize System Intent* option will provide a list of system intents from which to choose while the *New Intent* option creates an entirely new intent with no pre-existing configuration settings. Once a new custom intent has been created, it appears in the editor as shown in Figure 97-2:

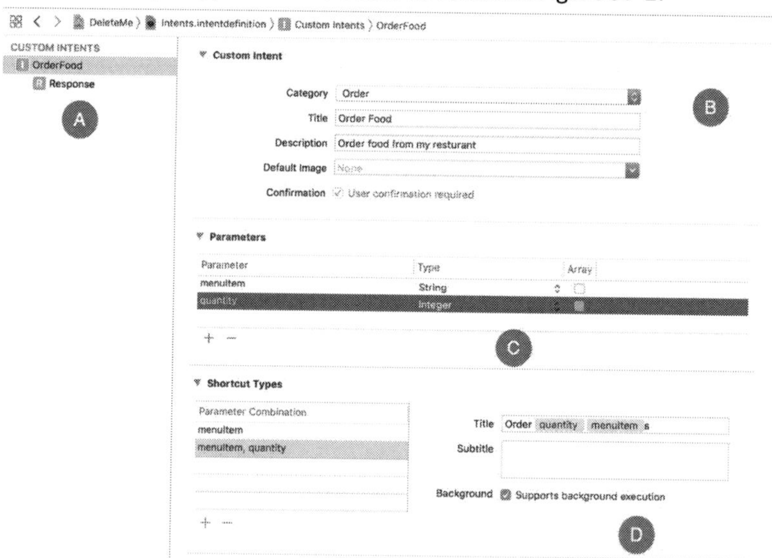

Figure 97-2

The section marked A in the above figure lists the custom intents contained within the file. The Custom Intent section (B) is where the category of the intent is selected from a list of options including categories such as order, buy, do, open, search etc. Since this example is an intent for ordering food, the category is set to Order.

This section also includes the title of the intent, a description and an optional image to include with the shortcut. A checkbox is also provided to require Siri to seek confirmation from the user before completing the shortcut. For some intent categories such as buying and ordering this option is mandatory.

The parameters section (C) allows the parameters that will be passed to the intent to be declared. If the custom intent is based on an existing SiriKit system intent, this area will be populated with all of parameters the intent is already configured to handle and the settings cannot be changed. For a new custom intent, as many parameters as necessary may be declared as configured in terms of name, type and whether or not the parameter is an array.

Finally, the Shortcut Types section (D) allows different variations of the shortcut to be configured. A shortcut type is defined by the combination of parameters used within the shortcut. For each combination of parameters that the shortcut needs to support, settings are configured including the title of the shortcut and whether or not the host app can perform the associated task in the background without presenting a view controller to the user. Each intent can have as many parameter combinations as necessary to provide a flexible user shortcut experience.

The Custom Intents panel (A) also lists a Response entry under the custom intent name. When selected, the editor displays the screen shown in Figure 97-3:

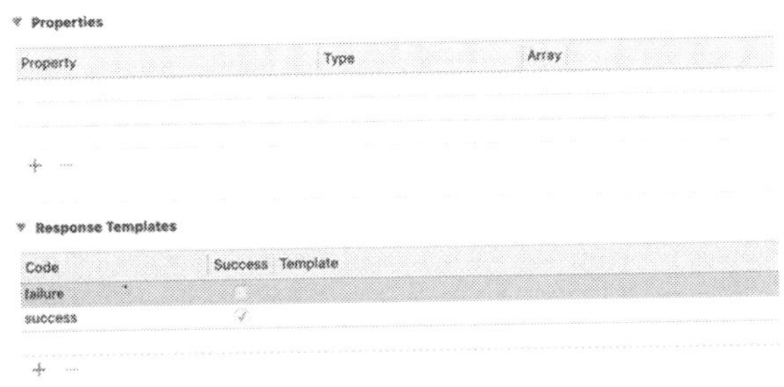

Figure 97-3

Keep in mind that a Siri shortcut involves a two-way interaction between Siri and the user and that to maintain this interaction Siri needs to know how to respond to the user based on the results of the intent execution. This is defined through a range of *response templates* which define the phrases to be spoken by Siri when the intent returns specific codes. These response settings also allow parameters to be configured for inclusion in the response phrases. A restaurant app might, for example, have a response code named *failureStoreClosed* which results in Siri responding with the phrase "We are sorry, we cannot complete your cheeseburger order because the store is closed.", and a success response code with the phase "Your order of two coffees will be ready for pickup in 20 minutes".

Once the Intent Definition file has been configured, Xcode will automatically generate a set of class files ready for use within the intent handler code of the extension.

97.3 Automatically Generated Classes

The purpose of the Intent Definition file is to allow Xcode to generate a set of classes that will be used when implementing the shortcut extension. Assuming that a custom intent named OrderFood was added to the definition file, the following classes would be automatically generated by Xcode:

- **OrderFoodIntent** – The intent object that encapsulates all of the parameters declared in the definition file. An instance of this class will be passed by Siri to the *handler()*, *handle()* and *confirm()* methods of the extension intent handler configured with the appropriate parameter values for the current shortcut.

- **OrderIntentHandling** – Defines the protocol to which the intent handler must conform in order to be able to fully handle food ordering intents.
- **OrderIntentResponse** – A class encapsulating the response codes, templates and parameters declared for the intent in the Intent Definition file. The intent handler will use this class to return response codes and parameter values to Siri so that the appropriate response can be communicated to the user.

Use of these classes within the intent handler will be covered in the next chapter entitled *Building Siri Shortcut Support into an iOS App*.

97.4 Donating Shortcuts

An app typically donates a shortcut when a common action is performed by the user. This donation does not automatically turn the activity into a shortcut, but includes it as a suggested shortcut within the Settings app. A donation is made by calling the *donate()* method of an INInteraction instance which has been initialized with a shortcut intent object. For example:

```
let intent = OrderFoodIntent()

intent.menuItem = "Cheeseburger"
intent.quantity = 1
intent.suggestedInvocationPhrase = "Order Lunch"

let interaction = INInteraction(intent: intent, response: nil)

interaction.donate { (error) in
    if error != nil {
        // Handle donation failure
    }
}
```

97.5 The Add to Siri Button

The Add to Siri button allows a shortcut to be added to Siri directly from within an app. This involves writing code to create an INUIAddVoiceShortcutButton instance, initializing it with a shortcut intent object with shortcut parameters configured and then adding it to a user interface view. A target method is then added to the button to be called when the button is clicked:

```
shortcutIntent = OrderFoodIntent()

shortcutIntent.quantity = 1
shortcutIntent.menuItem = "Cheeseburger"
shortcutIntent?.suggestedInvocationPhrase = "Order Lunch")"

let shortcutButton = INUIAddVoiceShortcutButton(style: .whiteOutline)
shortcutButton.translatesAutoresizingMaskIntoConstraints = false
shortcutButton.shortcut = INShortcut(intent: shortcutIntent)

view.addSubview(shortcutButton)

shortcutButton.addTarget(self, action: #selector(addToSiri(_:)),
```

```
                        for: .touchUpInside)
```

The last line of code in the above example configures the button to call a method named *addToSiri()*. It is the responsibility of this method to display an INUIAddVoiceShortcutViewController instance to the user where the shortcut setup (including recording the voice phrase) will be completed. The code for this method could be implemented as follows:

```
@objc
func addToSiri(_ sender: Any) {

    if let intent = shortcutIntent {
        if let shortcut = INShortcut(intent: intent) {
            let viewController =
                   INUIAddVoiceShortcutViewController(shortcut: shortcut)
            viewController.modalPresentationStyle = .formSheet
            viewController.delegate = self
            present(viewController, animated: true, completion: nil)
        }
    }
}
```

This method takes the previously configured shortcut intent and uses it to initialize an INShortcut object which, in turn, is used in the creation of the INUIAddVoiceShortcutViewController instance. A delegate is declared and the view controller displayed to the user. The class declared as the delegate must conform to the INUIAddVoiceShortcutViewControllerDelegate protocol and, at a minimum, implement the following two delegate methods, both of which are needed to dismiss the voice shortcut view controller:

```
func addVoiceShortcutViewController(_ controller:
 INUIAddVoiceShortcutViewController, didFinishWith voiceShortcut:
  INVoiceShortcut?, error: Error?) {
    controller.dismiss(animated: true, completion: nil)
}

func addVoiceShortcutViewControllerDidCancel(_ controller:
  INUIAddVoiceShortcutViewController) {
    controller.dismiss(animated: true, completion: nil)
}
```

97.6 Summary

Siri shortcuts allow commonly performed tasks within apps to be invoked using Siri via a user provided phrase. When added, a shortcut contains all of the parameter values needed to complete the task within the app together with templates defining how Siri should respond based on the status reported by the intent handler. A shortcut is implemented by creating a custom intent extension and configuring an Intent Definition file containing all of the information regarding the intent, parameters and responses. From this information, Xcode generates all of the class files necessary to implement the shortcut. Shortcuts can be added to Siri either via an Add to Siri button within the host app, or by the app donating suggested shortcuts. A list of donated shortcuts can be found in the Siri & Search section of the iOS Settings App.

Chapter 98

98. Building Siri Shortcut Support into an iOS App

As previously discussed, the purpose of Siri Shortcuts is to allow key features of an app to be invoked by the user via Siri by speaking custom phrases. This chapter will demonstrate how to integrate shortcut support into an existing iOS app, including the creation of a custom intent and intent UI, the configuration of an Intent Definition file and outline the code necessary to handle the intents, provide responses, donate shortcuts to Siri and, finally, implement an Add to Siri button.

98.1 About the Example App

The app used as the basis for this tutorial is a simple app that simulates the purchasing of financial stocks and shares. The app is named ShortcutDemo and can be found in the sample code download available at the following URL:

https://www.ebookfrenzy.com/retail/ios12/

The app consists of a "buy" screen into which the stock symbol and quantity are entered and the purchase initiated and a "history" screen consisting of a table view listing all previous transactions. Selecting an entry in the transaction history displays a third screen displaying details about the corresponding stock purchase.

98.2 App Groups and UserDefaults

Much about the way in which the app has been constructed will be familiar from techniques outlined in previous chapters of the book. The project does, however, use two iOS SDK features not previously addressed.

To provide a simple way to persistently store previous transaction data, the ShortcutDemo app makes use of a feature referred to as UserDefaults. Primarily provided as a way for apps to access and store default user preferences (such as language preferences or color choices), UserDefaults can also be used to store small amounts of data needed by the app in the form of key-value pairs. In the case of the ShortcutDemo app, UserDefaults is used to store three arrays containing the symbol, quantity and time stamp data for all stock purchase transactions. Since this is a test app that needs to store minimal amounts of data, UserDefaults is more than adequate. In a real-world environment, however, a storage system capable of handling larger volumes of data such as SQLite, CoreData or iCloud storage would need to be used.

In order to share the UserDefaults data between the app and the intents extension, the project also makes use of *app groups*. App groups allow apps to share data with other apps and targets within the same app group. App groups are assigned a name (typically similar to group.com.mydomain.myapp) and are enabled and configured within the Xcode project capabilities screen.

98.3 Preparing the Project

Once the ShortcutDemo project has been downloaded and opened within Xcode, some configuration changes need to be made before the app can be compiled and run. Begin by selecting the ShortcutDemo target at the top of the project navigator panel and, within the *General* screen, select your developer ID from the Team menu in the Signing section.

Next, select the Capabilities tab and locate the App Group section. Click on the + button located beneath the list of App Groups (as indicated in Figure 98-1):

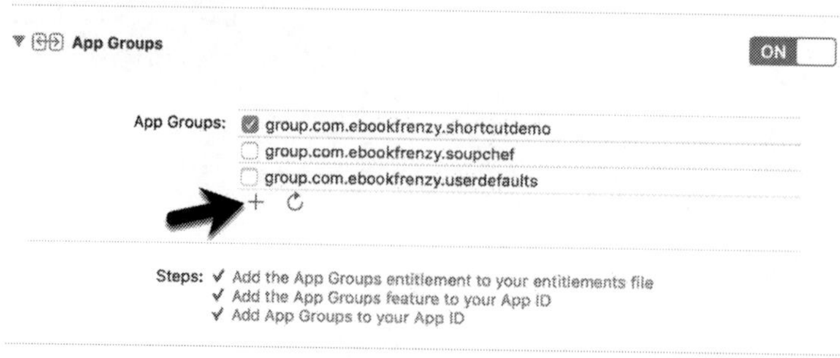

Figure 98-1

In the resulting panel, provide a name for the app group container that will be unique to your project (for example group.com.<your name>.shortcutdemo). Once a container name has been entered, click on the OK button to add it to the project entitlements file (*ShortcutDemo.entitlements*).

Now that the container has been created, the container name needs to be referenced in the project code. Edit the *BuyViewController.swift* file and replace the container name in the following line of code with your own container name:

```
let defaults = UserDefaults(suiteName: "YOUR CONTAINER NAME HERE")
```

Repeat this step once more within the *HistoryTableViewController.swift* file.

With the changes made, compile and run the app on a device or emulator and enter a stock symbol and quantity (for example 100 shares of TSLA stock and 20 GE shares) and click on the *Buy Stock* button. Assuming the transaction is successful, select the *Purchase History* tab at the bottom of the screen and confirm that the transaction appears in the list as shown in Figure 98-2:

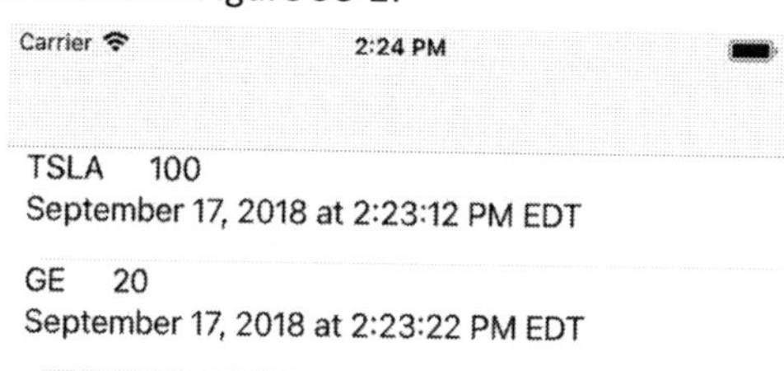

Figure 98-2

Select one of the transactions to display the Detail screen for that purchase:

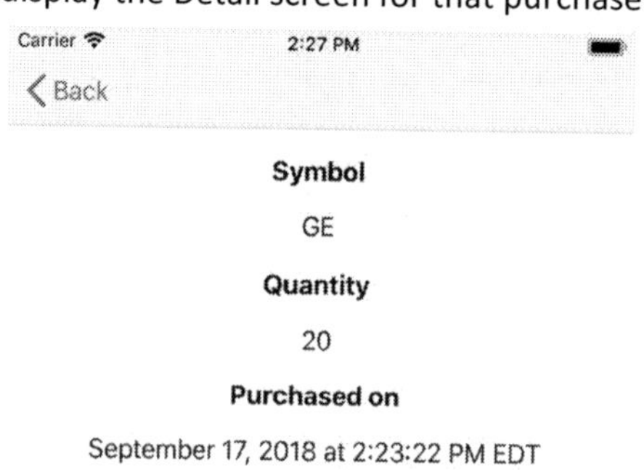

Figure 98-3

With the app installed, configured and running, the next step is to begin integrating shortcut support into the project.

98.4 Enabling Siri Support

The first step in adding Siri shortcuts to the project is to enable the Siri capability. Once again, select the ShortcutDemo target at the top of the project navigator panel followed by the *Capabilities* tab, then locate and enable Siri:

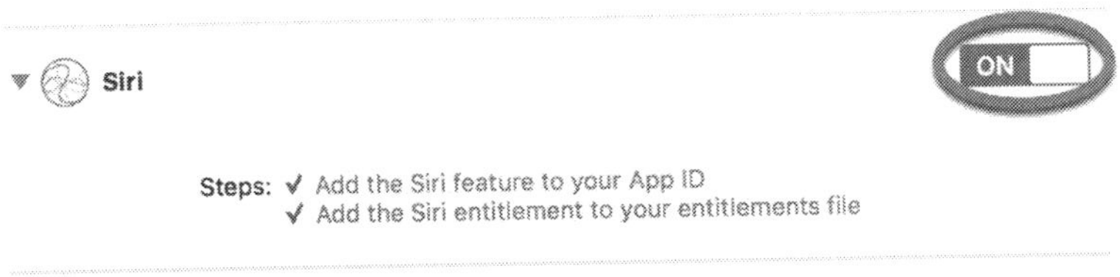

Figure 98-4

98.5 Adding the Intents Extension

As with the extension types covered in the previous chapters, a intents extension will be needed for the Siri shortcuts associated with this app. Select the *File -> New -> Target...* menu option, followed by the Intents Extension option and click on the Next button. On the options screen, enter *ShortcutDemoIntent* into the product name field and make sure that the *Include UI Extension* option is enabled before clicking on the Finish button.

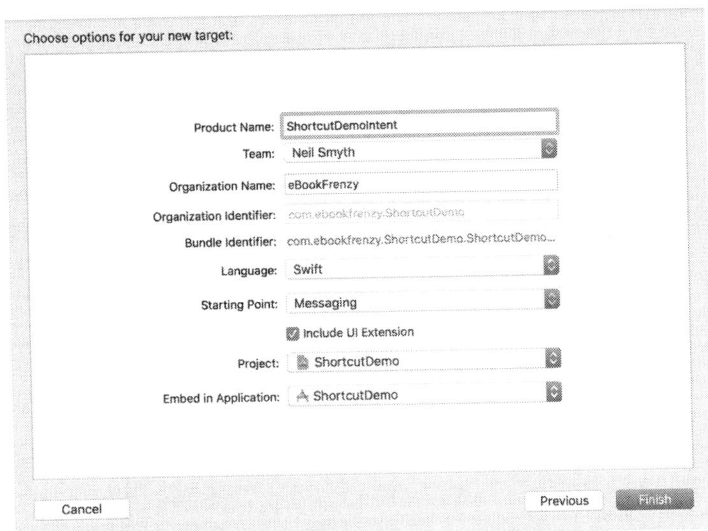

Figure 98-5

When prompted to do so, activate both the ShortcutDemoIntent and ShortcutDemoIngtentUI target schemes.

By default, the intents extension will have been configured as a messaging extension. Since this project requires a custom extension for handling shortcuts, much of the template code provided by Xcode can be removed so edit the *ShortcutDemoIntent -> IntentHander.swift* file so that it reads as follows:

```
class IntentHandler: INExtension {

    override func handler(for intent: INIntent) -> Any {
```

```
            return self
        }
}
```

98.6 Adding the SiriKit Intent Definition File

Now that the intent extension has been added to the project, the SiriKit Intent Definition file needs to be added so that the intent can be configured. Select the *File -> New -> File...* menu option, scroll down to the *Resource* section and select the *SiriKit Intent Definition File* template followed by the Next button:

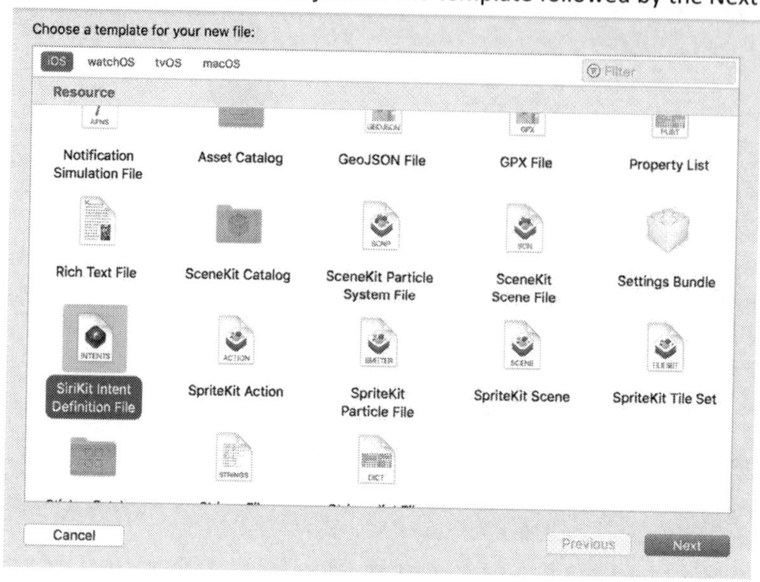

Figure 98-6

Keep the default name of *Intents* in the Save As: field, but make sure that the file is generated into the *ShortCutDemo* folder of the project and is available to all of the targets in the project by selecting all three options in the Targets section of the dialog before clicking on the Create button:

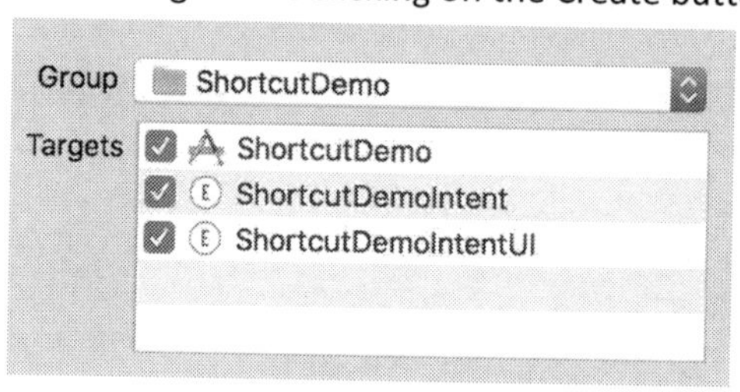

Figure 98-7

In order to be able to share the UserDefaults data stored by the main app, the ShortcutDemoIntent extension will need to be made a member of the same app group as the ShortcutDemo app. To set this up, select the ShortcutDemo target at the top of the Project navigator panel and, in the Capabilities panel, change the menu highlighted in Figure 98-8 from ShortcutDemo to ShortcutDemoIntent, turn on the App Group capability and enable the checkbox next to the app group used by the main app:

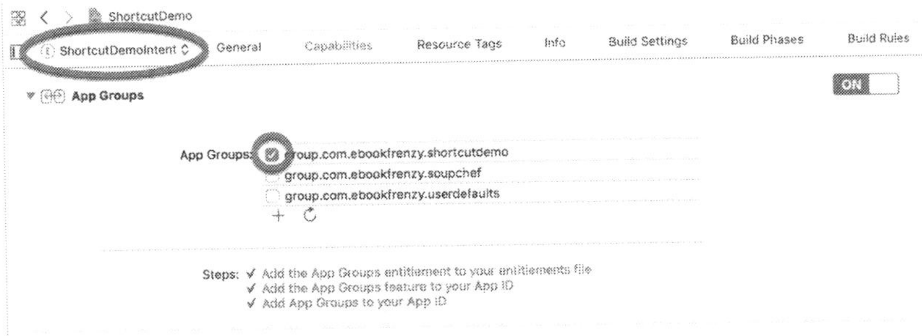

Figure 98-8

98.7 Configuring the SiriKit Intent Definition File

Locate the *Intents.intentdefinition* file and select it to load it into the editor. The file is currently empty, so add a new intent by clicking on the + button in the lower left-hand corner of the editor panel and selecting the *New Intent* menu option:

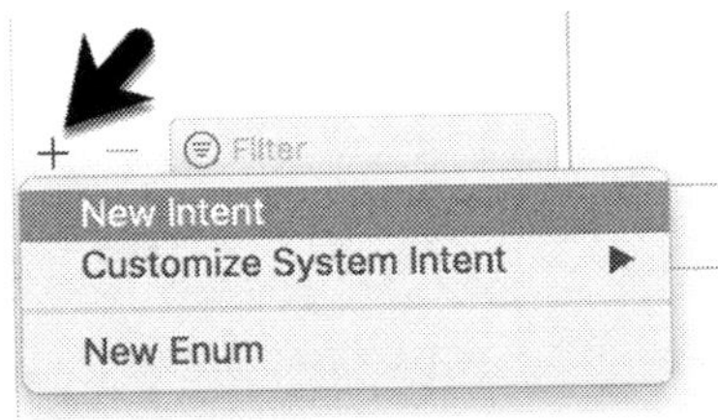

Figure 98-9

In the Custom Intents panel, rename the new intent to *BuyStock* as shown in Figure 98-10:

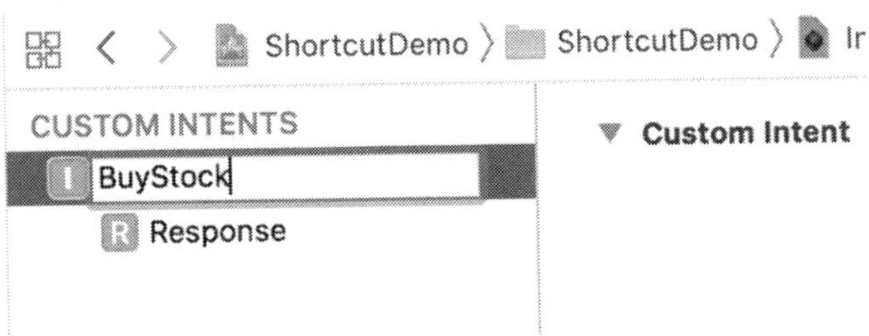

Figure 98-10

Next, change the Category setting in the Custom Intent section of the editor from "Do" to "Buy" and enter "Buy Stocks" and "Buy stocks and shares" into the *Title* and *Description* fields respectively. Since this is a buy category intent, the *User confirmation required* option is enabled by default and cannot be disabled:

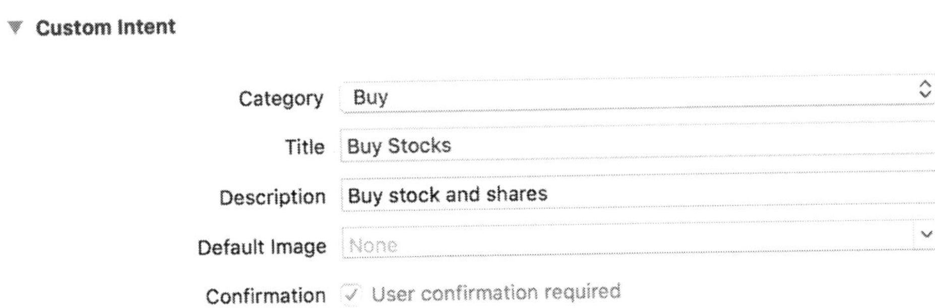

Figure 98-11

98.8 Adding Intent Parameters

In order to complete a purchase, the intent is going to need two parameters in the form of the stock symbol and quantity. Remaining within the Intent Definition editor, use the '+' button located beneath the Parameters section to add parameters named *symbol* and *quantity* with both configured as String type with the Array option disabled:

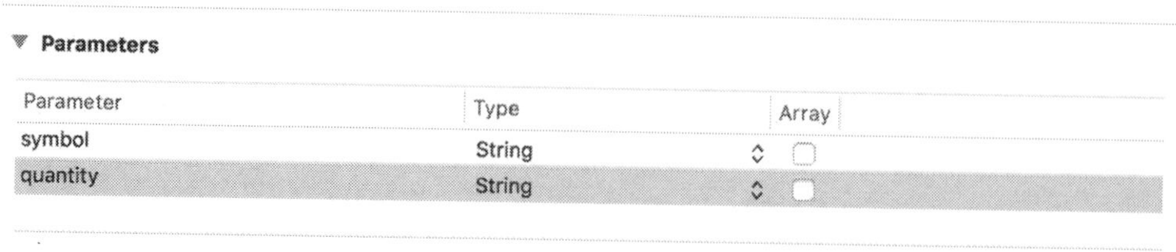

Figure 98-12

98.9 Declaring Shortcut Types

A shortcut intent can be configured to handle different combinations of intent parameters. Each unique combination of parameters defines a *shortcut type*. For each shortcut type, the intent needs to know the phrase that Siri will speak when interacting with the user together with an optional subtitle, each of which can contain embedded parameters. For this example, the only combination required involves both the symbol and quantity so click on the '+' button in the Shortcut Types section of the editor and select both parameters from the resulting dialog before clicking on the *Add Shortcut Type* button:

Figure 98-13

Select the newly added parameter combination and begin typing into the Title field. Type the word "Buy" followed by the first few letters of the word "quantity". Xcode will notice that this could be a reference to the quantity parameter name and suggests it as an option to embed the parameter into the phrase as shown in Figure 98-14:

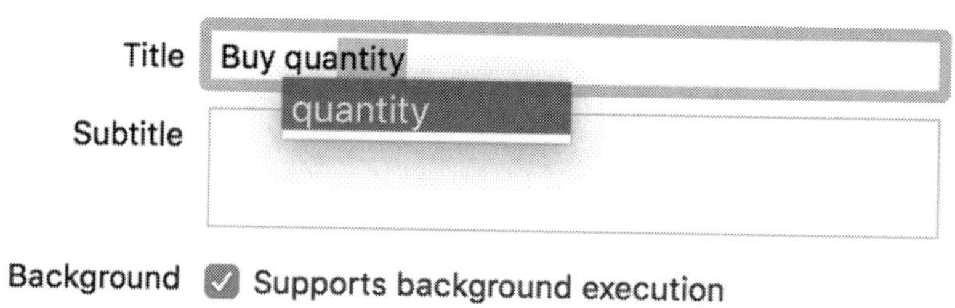

Figure 98-14

Select the parameter from the suggestion to embed it into the phrase, then continue typing so that the message reads "Buy quantity shares of symbol" where "symbol" is also an embedded parameter:

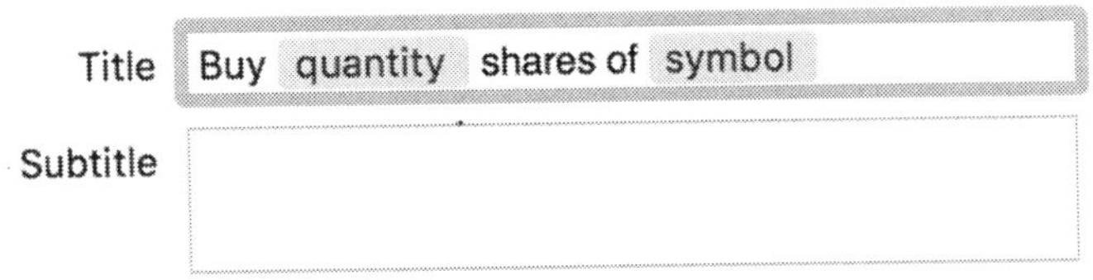

Figure 98-15

The *Supports background execution* option defines whether or not the app can handle the shortcut type in the background without having to be presented to the user for additional input. Make sure this option is enabled for this shortcut type.

98.10 Configuring the Intent Response

The final area to be addressed within the Intent Definition file is the response handling. To view these settings, select the *Response* entry located beneath the *BuyStock* intent in the Custom Intents panel:

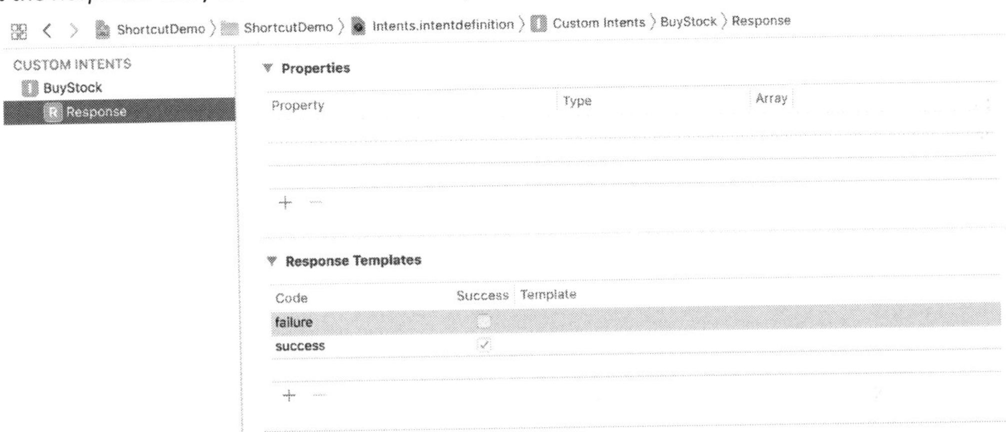

Figure 98-16

The first task is to declare the parameters that will be included in the response phrases. As with the intent configuration, add both the symbol and quantity parameters configured as Strings.

Next, double-click in the Template column of the failure row of the Response Template section and enter the following text, taking care to ensure that the parameters are embedded into the text:

```
Sorry, could not purchase quantity shares of symbol
```

Repeat this step to add the following template text to the success code:

```
Successfully purchased quantity symbol shares
```

Finally, add a new template with the code limitExceeded, the Success option switched off and the template text set to the following:

```
Please use the app to buy more than 100 symbol shares
```

This final response will be used later in the tutorial to force the user to use the app when trying to purchase more than 100 shares when using a shortcut. On completion of these steps the response templates should match those in Figure 98-17:

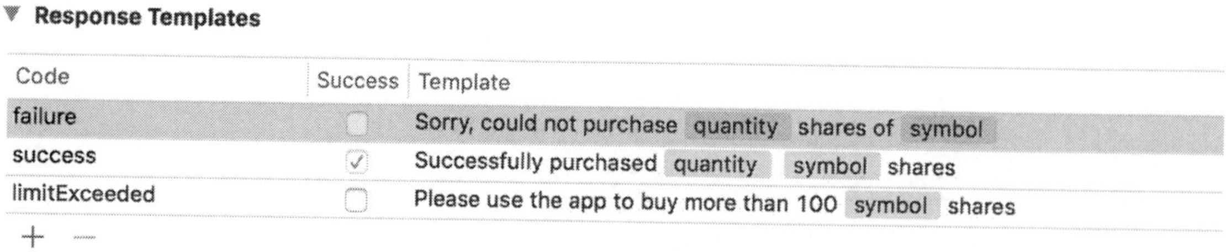

Code	Success	Template
failure		Sorry, could not purchase quantity shares of symbol
success	✓	Successfully purchased quantity symbol shares
limitExceeded		Please use the app to buy more than 100 symbol shares

Figure 98-17

Behind the scenes, Xcode will take the information provided within the Intent Definition file and automatically generate new classes named BuyStockIntentHandling, BuyStockIntent and BuyStockIntentReponse, all of which will be used in the intent handling code. To make sure these file are generated before editing the code, select the ShortcutDemo target in the toolbar and run the app on a device or simulator.

98.11 Configuring Target Membership

Many of the classes and targets in the project are interdependent and need to be accessible to each other during both compilation and execution. To allow this access, a number of classes and files within the project need specific target membership settings. While some of these settings will have set up correctly by default, others may need to be set up manually before testing the app. Begin by selecting the *BuyViewController.swift* file in the project navigator panel and display the File Inspector (*View -> Inspectors -> Show File Inspector*). In the file inspector, locate the Target Membership section and make sure that the ShortcutDemo, ShortcutDemoIntent and ShortcutDemoIntentUI targets are all enabled as shown in Figure 98-18:

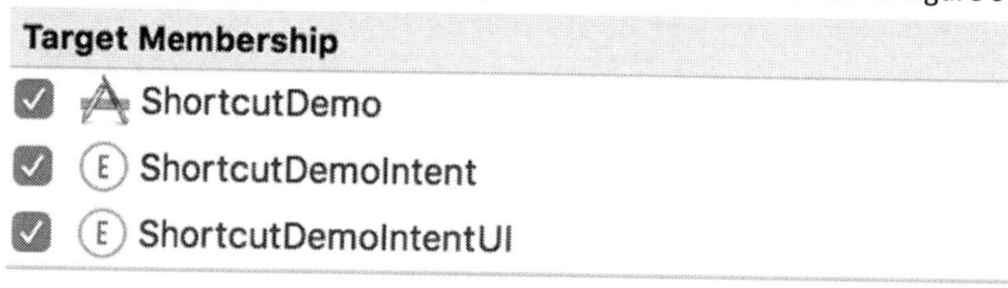

Figure 98-18

Repeat these steps for the *IntentHandler.swift* and *IntentViewController.swift* files.

98.12 Modifying the Intent Handler Code

Now that the intent definition is complete and the classes have been auto-generated by Xcode, the intent handler needs to be modified to implement the BuyStockIntentHandling protocol.

Edit the *IntentHandler.swift* file and make the following changes:

```
import Intents

class IntentHandler: INExtension, BuyStockIntentHandling {

    override func handler(for intent: INIntent) -> Any {

        guard intent is BuyStockIntent else {
            fatalError("Unknown intent type: \(intent)")
        }
```

```
        return self
    }

    func handle(intent: BuyStockIntent,
        completion: @escaping (BuyStockIntentResponse) -> Void) {

    }
}
```

The *handler()* method simply checks that the intent type is recognized and, if so, returns itself as the intent handler.

Code now needs to be added to the *handle()* method to perform the stock purchase:

```
func handle(intent: BuyStockIntent, completion:
                @escaping (BuyStockIntentResponse) -> Void) {

    let viewController = BuyViewController()

    guard let symbol = intent.symbol,
        let quantity = intent.quantity
        else {
            completion(BuyStockIntentResponse(code: .failure,
                                     userActivity: nil))
            return
    }

    let result = viewController.makePurchase(symbol: symbol,
                                      quantity: quantity)

    if result {
        completion(BuyStockIntentResponse.success(quantity: quantity,
                                          symbol: symbol))
    } else {
        completion(BuyStockIntentResponse.limitExceeded(symbol: symbol))
    }
}
```

When called, the method is passed a BuyStockIntent intent instance and completion handler to be called when the purchase is completed. The method begins by creating a BuyViewController instance before extracting the symbol and quantity parameter values from the intent object:

```
let viewController = BuyViewController()

guard let symbol = intent.symbol,
    let quantity = intent.quantity else {
        completion(BuyStockIntentResponse(code: .failure
```

```
                                                    userActivity: nil))
            return
        }
```

These values are then passed through to the *makePurchase()* method of the view controller to perform the purchase transaction. Finally, the result returned by the *makePurchase()* method is used to select the appropriate response to be passed to the completion handler. In each case, the appropriate parameters are passed to the completion handler for inclusion in the response template:

```
let result = viewController.makePurchase(symbol: symbol, quantity: quantity)

if result {
    completion(BuyStockIntentResponse.success(quantity: quantity,
                                               symbol: symbol))
} else {
    completion(BuyStockIntentResponse.limitExceeded(symbol: symbol))
}
```

98.13 Adding the Confirm Method

To fully conform with the BuyStockIntentHandling protocol, the IntentHandler class also needs to contain a *confirm()* method. As outlined in the SiriKit introductory chapter, this method is called by Siri to check that the handler is ready to handle the intent. All that is needed for this example is for the *confirm()* method to provide Siri with a ready status as follows:

```
public func confirm(intent: BuyStockIntent,
        completion: @escaping (BuyStockIntentResponse) -> Void) {

    completion(BuyStockIntentResponse(code: .ready, userActivity: nil))
}
```

98.14 Donating Shortcuts to Siri

Each time the user completes a stock purchase within the main app the action needs to be donated to Siri as a potential shortcut. The code to make these donations should now be added to the *BuyViewController.swift* file in a method named *makeDonation()*, which also requires that the Intents framework be imported:

```
.
.
import Intents
.
.
func makeDonation(symbol: String, quantity: String) {
    let intent = BuyStockIntent()

    intent.quantity = quantity
    intent.symbol = symbol
    intent.suggestedInvocationPhrase = "Buy \(quantity) \(symbol)"
```

```
    let interaction = INInteraction(intent: intent, response: nil)

    interaction.donate { (error) in
        if error != nil {
            if let error = error as NSError? {
                print("Donation failed: %@" + error.localizedDescription)
            }
        } else {
            print("Successfully donated interaction")
        }
    }
}
```

The method is passed string values representing the stock and quantity of the purchase. A new BuyStockIntent instance is then created and populated with both these values and a suggested activation phrase containing both the quantity and symbol. Next, an INInteraction object is created using the BuyStockIntent instance and the *donate()* method of the object called to make the donation. The success or otherwise of the donation is then output to the console for diagnostic purposes.

The donation will only be made after a successful purchase has been completed, so add the call to *makeDonation()* after the *saveTransaction()* call in the *buyStock()* action method:

```
@IBAction func buyStock(_ sender: Any) {
    if let symbol = stockSymbol.text, let quantity = stockQuantity.text {
        if ((!symbol.isEmpty) || (!quantity.isEmpty)) {
            saveTransaction(symbol: symbol, quantity: quantity)
            makeDonation(symbol: symbol, quantity: quantity)
            statusLabel.text = "Transaction completed"
            stockSymbol.text = ""
            stockQuantity.text = ""
        } else {
            statusLabel.text = "Enter a symbol and quantity"
        }
    }
}
```

98.15 Testing the Shortcuts

Before running and testing the app, some settings on the target device or simulator need to be changed in order to be able to fully test the shortcut functionality. To enable these settings, open the Settings app on the device or simulator on which you intend to test the app, select the Developer option and locate and enable the *Display Recent Shortcuts* and *Display Donations on Lock Screen* options as shown in Figure 98-19:

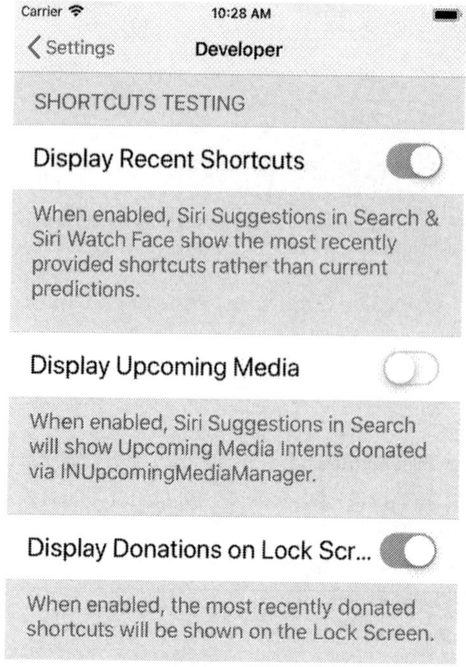

Figure 98-19

These settings will ensure that newly donated shortcuts always appear in Siri search and on the lock screen rather than relying on Siri to predict when the shortcuts should be suggested to the user.

With the settings changed, run the app and make a stock purchase (for example buy 75 IBM shares). After the purchase is complete, check the Xcode console to verify that the "Successfully donated interaction" message appears.

Next, open the Settings app, select the Siri & Search option and verify that the shortcut is now listed as a suggestion:

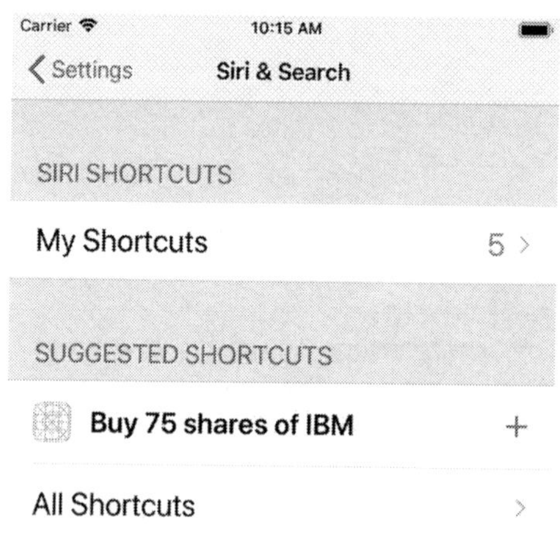

Figure 98-20

Click on the '+' button to the right of the shortcut title to display the Add to Siri screen (Figure 98-21) followed by the record button and speak a phrase to be associated with the shortcut. Note that "Buy 75 IBM" is suggested as configured when the donation was made in the *makeDonation()* method.

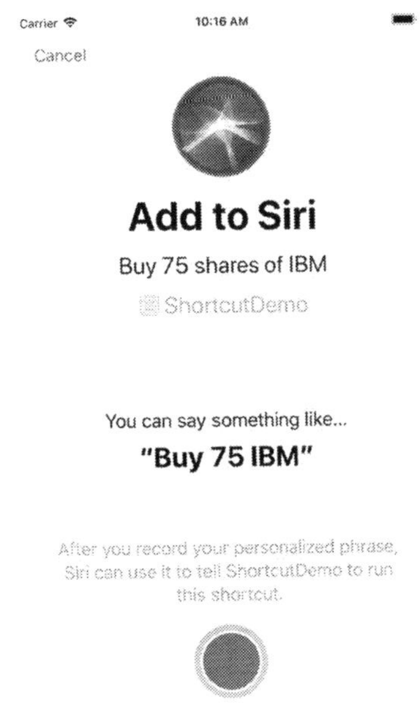

Figure 98-21

After the recording is finished, click the Done button to display the "My Shortcuts" screen within which the new shortcut will be listed.

Press and hold the Home button to launch Siri and speak the shortcut phrase. Siri will seek confirmation that the purchase is to be made. After completing the purchase, Siri will use the success response template declared in the Intent Definition file to confirm that the transaction was successful.

After making a purchase using the shortcut, open the ShortcutDemo app and verify that the transaction appears in the transaction history.

98.16 Designing the Intent UI

When the shortcut was tested, the intent UI will have appeared as a large empty space. Clearly some additional steps are required before the shortcut is complete. Select the *MainInterface.storyboard* file located in the ShortcutDemoIntentUI folder in the project navigator and drag and drop a Label from the Library so that it is positioned within the top and left margins. Stretch the label so that it extends to the right-hand margin, then use the *Add Auto Layout Constraints* menu to add constraints on the left, top and right hand edges of the label with the *Constraint to Margins* option enabled. The completed layout should match Figure 98-22 below:

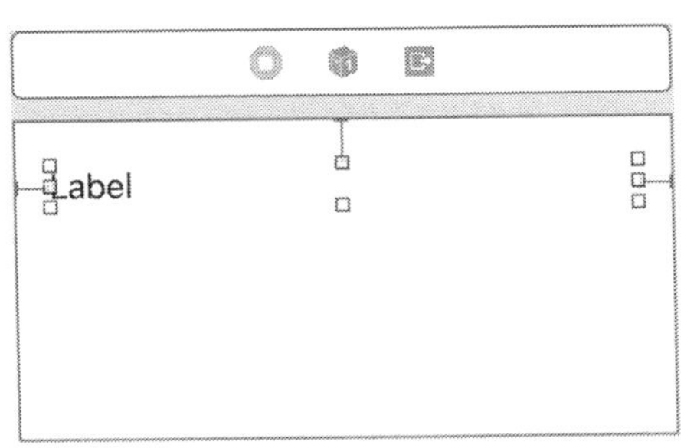

Figure 98-22

Display the Assistant Editor, make sure that it is displaying the *IntentViewController.swift* file and establish an outlet connection for the Label named *confirmLabel*. Edit the *IntentViewController.swift* file and modify the *configureView()* method and *declaredSize* variable so that the code reads as follows:

```
func configureView(for parameters: Set<INParameter>,
  of interaction: INInteraction,
  interactiveBehavior: INUIInteractiveBehavior,
  context: INUIHostedViewContext,
  completion: @escaping (Bool, Set<INParameter>, CGSize) -> Void) {

    guard let intent = interaction.intent as? BuyStockIntent else {
        completion(false, Set(), .zero)
        return
    }

    if let symbol = intent.symbol, let quantity = intent.quantity {
        self.confirmLabel.text = "Buy \(quantity) \(symbol) shares?"
    }

    completion(true, parameters, self.desiredSize)
}

var desiredSize: CGSize {
    return CGSize.init(width: 10, height: 100)
}
```

Re-build and run the app, then use Siri to trigger the shortcut. This time the intent UI will contain text describing the purchase to be made:

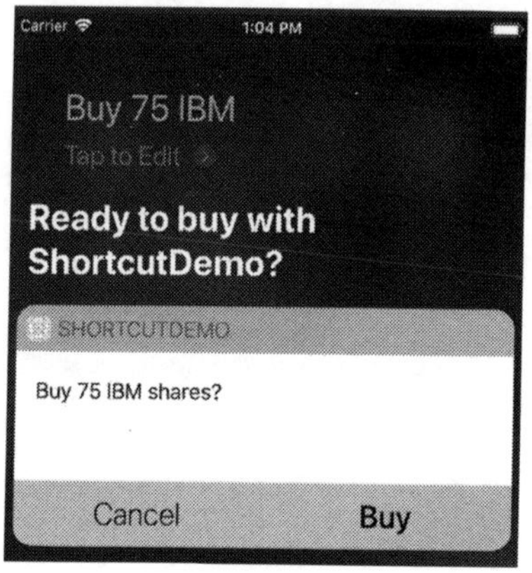

Figure 98-23

98.17 Passing Control to the Host App

Earlier in the chapter, a response was included in the Intent Definition file, the purpose of which was to report a failure in the event that the user exceeded a purchase of more than 100 shares using a shortcut. The objective here is to have Siri explain the problem and provide the user with the option to launch the

ShortcutDemo app and make the purchase manually. When the app launches, the purchase screen needs to be pre-populated with the symbol and quantity requested by the user.

Open the *IntentHandler.swift* file and note that the *handle()* method is already designed to handle a failure result from the main app and pass a limitExceeded response back to Siri:

```
if result {
    completion(BuyStockIntentResponse.success(quantity: quantity,
                                               symbol: symbol))
} else {
    completion(BuyStockIntentResponse.limitExceeded(symbol: symbol))
}
```

Some code now needs to be added to the *makePurchase()* method in the *BuyViewController.swift* file to return a false value if more than 100 shares are being purchased:

```
func makePurchase(symbol: String, quantity: String) -> Bool {

    if let count = Int(quantity) {
        if count > 100 {
            return false
        }
    }

    saveTransaction(symbol: symbol, quantity: quantity)
    return true
}
```

When Siri receives the limitExceeded failure response it will provide the user with the option to launch the host app to complete the transaction. When the app launches under these conditions, the *continue userActivity* method within the AppDelegate class will be called and passed a UserActivity object containing the shortcut intent object. Within the *AppDelegate.swift* file, add this method as follows:

```
func application(_ application: UIApplication,
  continue userActivity: NSUserActivity,
  restorationHandler: @escaping ([UIUserActivityRestoring]?) -> Void) -> Bool
{

    guard userActivity.interaction?.intent is BuyStockIntent else {
        return false
    }

    let rootViewController =
           window?.rootViewController as? UITabBarController
    let firstVC =
           rootViewController?.viewControllers?[0] as! BuyViewController
    rootViewController?.selectedIndex = 0
    let intent = userActivity.interaction?.intent as! BuyStockIntent
```

```
    firstVC.stockSymbol.text = intent.symbol
    firstVC.stockQuantity.text = intent.quantity

    return true
}
```

The method begins by checking that this is our stock purchasing intent before obtaining a reference to the first view controller within the tab bar controller (which corresponds to an instance of BuyViewController). Next, the intent is extracted from the UserActivity object and the symbol and quantity displayed within the two text fields in the view controller so that all the user has to do is tap the buy button to complete the transaction.

Compile and run the app and make a purchase of 200 IBM shares. Repeat the steps previously outlined to make a shortcut from the transaction and then use Siri to attempt to repeat the purchase. After receiving confirmation that the purchase is to continue, Siri will report that it is not possible to purchase more than 100 shares without opening the app:

Figure 98-24

Tap the button to open the app and verify that the symbol and quantity fields on the buy screen are populated with the correct symbol and quantity. Complete the purchase within the app and confirm that it is listed in the transaction history.

98.18 Adding an Add to Siri Button

The tutorial so far has relied entirely on creating shortcuts based on donation suggestions made within the app. It is also possible to include Add to Siri buttons within an app to directly create a shortcut without having to go through the shortcut suggestion process. This involves adding INUIAddVoiceShortcutButton instances to user interface layouts, implementing some delegate methods and displaying an INUIAddVoiceShortcutViewController to the user to complete the shortcut setup.

In terms of the ShortcutDemo app, the transaction detail screen is an ideal place to include a Siri button to turn a previous purchase into a Siri shortcut. Within Xcode, edit the *DetailViewController.swift* file to import the IntentsUI framework, declare the class as implementing the voice shortcut protocol and to add a variable to store the intent to be added to Siri:

```
import UIKit
import IntentsUI

class DetailViewController: UIViewController,
        INUIAddVoiceShortcutViewControllerDelegate {
```

```
.
.
    var shortcutIntent: BuyStockIntent?
.
.
```

Next, add the following method to the class and call it from the *viewDidLoad()* method:

```
.
.
override func viewDidLoad() {
    super.viewDidLoad()

    symbolLabel.text = symbol
    quantityLabel.text = quantity
    timestampLabel.text = timeStamp

    addShortcutButton()
}

func addShortcutButton() {

    shortcutIntent = BuyStockIntent()

    shortcutIntent?.quantity = quantity
    shortcutIntent?.symbol = symbol

    shortcutIntent?.suggestedInvocationPhrase = "Buy \(symbol ?? "Stock")"

    if let intent = shortcutIntent {

        let shortcutButton = INUIAddVoiceShortcutButton(style: .whiteOutline)
        shortcutButton.translatesAutoresizingMaskIntoConstraints = false
        shortcutButton.shortcut = INShortcut(intent: intent)

        view.addSubview(shortcutButton)

        view.centerXAnchor.constraint(
                equalTo: shortcutButton.centerXAnchor).isActive = true
        view.centerYAnchor.constraint(equalTo:
                shortcutButton.centerYAnchor).isActive = true

        shortcutButton.addTarget(self, action: #selector(addToSiri(_:)),
                                          for: .touchUpInside)
    }
```

```
}
.
.
```

The method begins by creating a BuyStockIntent instance and configuring it with the symbol and quantity from the transaction currently displayed on the detail screen. A new voice shortcut button instance is then created and initialized with the shortcut intent before being added to the view and constrained to the center of the scene. Finally the *addTarget()* method of the voice shortcut button object is called and passed a reference to a method named *addToSiri()* which now needs to be implemented:

```
@objc
func addToSiri(_ sender: Any) {

    if let intent = shortcutIntent {

        if let shortcut = INShortcut(intent: intent) {
            let viewController =
                INUIAddVoiceShortcutViewController(shortcut: shortcut)
            viewController.modalPresentationStyle = .formSheet
            viewController.delegate = self
            present(viewController, animated: true, completion: nil)
        }
    }
}
```

This method creates an INShortcut instance containing the shortcut intent, generates an INUIAddVoiceShortcutViewController instance, designates the current class as the delegate and then presents the view controller to the user.

The final task before testing the button is to add some delegate methods. Remaining in the *DetailViewController.swift* file, add the following methods to dismiss the view controller when the operation is either completed or cancelled:

```
func addVoiceShortcutViewController(_ controller:
 INUIAddVoiceShortcutViewController, didFinishWith voiceShortcut:
  INVoiceShortcut?, error: Error?) {
    controller.dismiss(animated: true, completion: nil)
}

func addVoiceShortcutViewControllerDidCancel(_ controller:
  INUIAddVoiceShortcutViewController) {
    controller.dismiss(animated: true, completion: nil)
}
```

98.19 Testing the Add to Siri Button

Run the app once more and make a purchase that has not previously been configured as a shortcut. Once the purchase has been made, select the transaction in the purchase history screen so that it appears in the detail screen where the Add to Siri button should now be present:

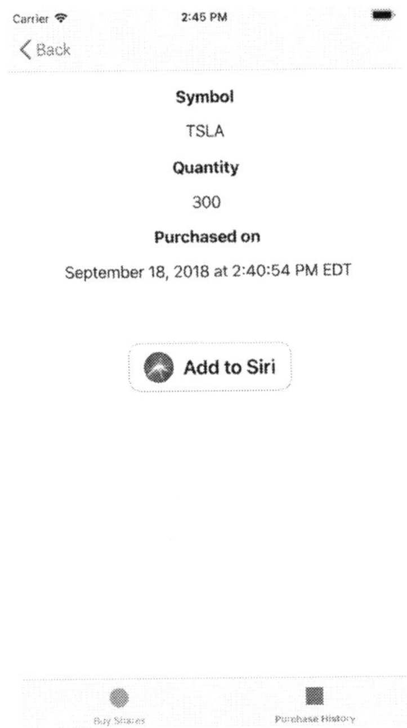

Figure 98-25

Tap the button and complete the shortcut setup in the voice shortcut view controller:

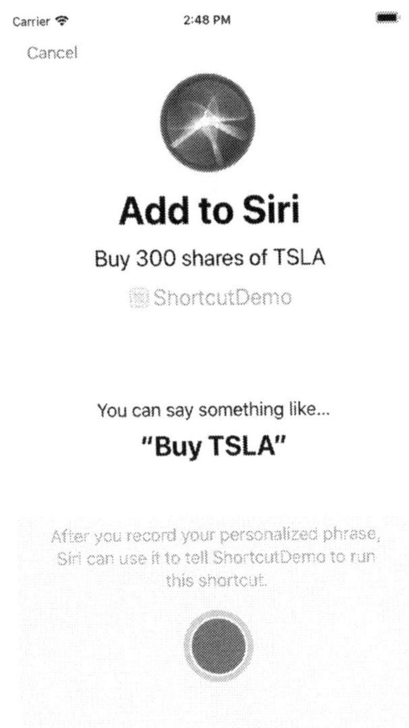

Figure 98-26

Record a phrase and click the Done button to return to the details screen where the button will now indicate that the shortcut has been added:

Figure 98-27

As a final test launch Siri and verify that the new shortcut works.

98.20 Summary

This chapter has provided a practical demonstration of how to integrate Siri shortcut support into an iOS app. This included the creation and configuration of an Intent Definition file, the addition of a custom intent extension and the implementation of intent handling code. The example project also demonstrated transferring of control from the intent to the host app and the implementation of an Add to Siri button.

Chapter 99

99. An Introduction to Machine Learning on iOS

Machine learning is one of the key components of artificial intelligence and involves the use of data analysis to teach software to perform tasks without specifically being programmed to do so. Machine learning is being used in a wide range of fields and industries to perform tasks such as identifying spam email, detecting people and objects in images, fraud detection and in financial trading systems to name but a few examples.

Apple first introduced machine learning capabilities for iOS and macOS in 2017 with the introduction of the Core ML framework and has continued to add improvements in iOS 12 with the release of Create ML.

Machine learning is a large and complex technology area so the goal of this and subsequent chapters is to provide an overview of the basics of this topic to get up to speed quickly and provide a knowledge basis on which to build more advanced machine learning skills.

99.1 Datasets and Machine Learning Models

Machine learning begins with the gathering of datasets to be used to train and create a learning model. To create a model that can detect happy or sad sentiments expressed in text messages, for example, the model would to be trained with a dataset containing both types of message with each message labelled to indicate whether the message is happy or sad. Similarly, a model intended to identify a particular car model from photos would need to be trained with images of the model of car in a variety of colors taken from multiple angles and distances.

The model will be built by iterating through the training dataset and learning how to categorize similar data. Once the training is complete, the model is tested by applying it to a dataset containing data not previously included during training. The results of the training can then be analyzed to check for accuracy and the model improved if necessary by providing additional training data and increasing the number of iterations performed during the training phase.

Once a model is complete, it is referred to as a *trained model* and is ready to be used in real-world situations.

99.2 Machine Learning in Xcode and iOS

The first step in implementing machine learning within an iOS app is to create the model. Once a complex and time consuming task, this is now made easier through the introduction of Create ML. Create ML (in the form of the CreateMLUI class) can be used from within an Xcode playground to visually create a model by writing a few lines of code, dragging and dropping training and testing datasets into the Assistant Editor and viewing the results. Alternatively, models may also be created programmatically from within an app by making use of the CreateML class.

Training a model to identify whether an image contains a picture of a dog or cat, for example, can be as simple as creating a training folder containing one subfolder of cat images and another containing dog images. All that is necessary to train the model is to drag the training folder and drop it onto the model builder in the Xcode playground window.

Alternatively, the training dataset can consist of CSV or JSON data containing the training data. The following JSON excerpt, for example, is used to teach a model to distinguish between legitimate and spam email message titles:

```
[
    {
        "text": "Congratulations, you've won $1000!",
        "label": "spam"
    }, {
        "text": "Meeting reminder",
        "label": "not spam"
    }, {
        "text": "Lose 20lb in one month",
        "label": "spam"
    } ...
]
```

When dividing data into training and testing sets, the general recommendation is to use 80% of the data for training and 20% for testing.

Once the model has been sufficiently trained, it can be saved to a file and added to an Xcode app project simply by dragging and dropping the file onto the project navigator panel where it is ready to be used in the app code.

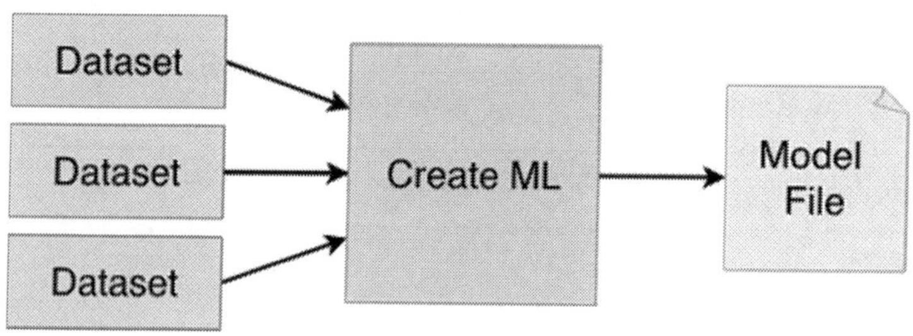

Figure 99-1

99.3 iOS Machine Learning Frameworks

When a trained model has been added to an app project, the classes of the Core ML framework are used to create and initiate requests to be performed using the model. In addition to Core ML, iOS also includes frameworks specifically for working with images (Vision framework), text and natural language (NaturalLangauge framework) and game playing (GameplayKit framework).

In a testament to the power contained in a device the size of an iPhone, machine learning operations run locally on the device using both the CPU and, for more intensive tasks, the GPU, maintaining privacy of user data and avoiding reliance on a network connection.

99.4 Summary

This chapter has provided a basic introduction to machine learning in iOS, covered the creation of machine learning models using Create ML and outlined the frameworks available for implementing machine learning within an iOS app. The next chapter will demonstrate the use of Create ML to build a machine learning model for image analysis which will then be used in an iOS app in the chapter entitled *An iOS Vision and CoreML Image Classification Tutorial*.

Chapter 100

100. Using Create ML to Build an Image Classification Model

This chapter will demonstrate the use of Create ML to build an image classification model trained to classify images based on whether the image contains one of four specific items (an apple, banana, cat or a mixture of fruits).

The tutorial will include the training and testing of an image recognition machine learning model using an Xcode playground. In the next chapter this model will be integrated into an app and used to perform image classifications when a user takes a photo or selects an image from the photo library.

100.1 About the Dataset

As explained in the previous chapter, an image classification model is trained by providing it with a range of images that have already been categorized. Once the training process has been performed, the model is then tested using a set of images that were not previously used in the training process. Once the testing achieves a high enough level of validation, the model is ready to be integrated into an app project.

For this example, a dataset containing images of apples, bananas, mixed fruit and cats will be used for training. The dataset is contained within a folder named *CreateML_dataset* which is included with the source code download available at the following URL:

https://www.ebookfrenzy.com/retail/ios12/

The dataset includes a *Training* folder containing images divided into four subfolders organized as shown in Figure 100-1:

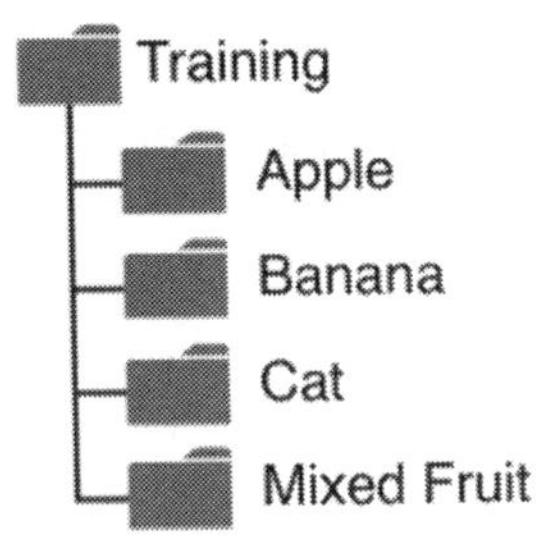

Figure 100-1

The dataset also includes a *Testing* folder containing images for each classification, none of which were used during the training session. Once the dataset has been downloaded, take some time to browse the folders and images to get an understanding of the structure of the data.

100.2 Creating the Machine Learning Model

With the dataset prepared, the next step is to create the model. This will be achieved from within an Xcode playground so launch Xcode and select the option to create a new blank playground. When prompted, select the options to create a blank *macOS* playground named *CreateML* (the CreateML Image Classifier Builder is not available within iOS playgrounds).

Once a blank macOS playground has been created, remove all of the default code from the editing panel and replace it with the following:

```
import CreateMLUI

let builder = MLImageClassifierBuilder()
builder.showInLiveView()
```

When the code is run, it will create an image classifier builder instance and display it in the Assistant Editor. If the Assistant Editor is not yet visible, display it using the button indicated by the arrow in Figure 100-2:

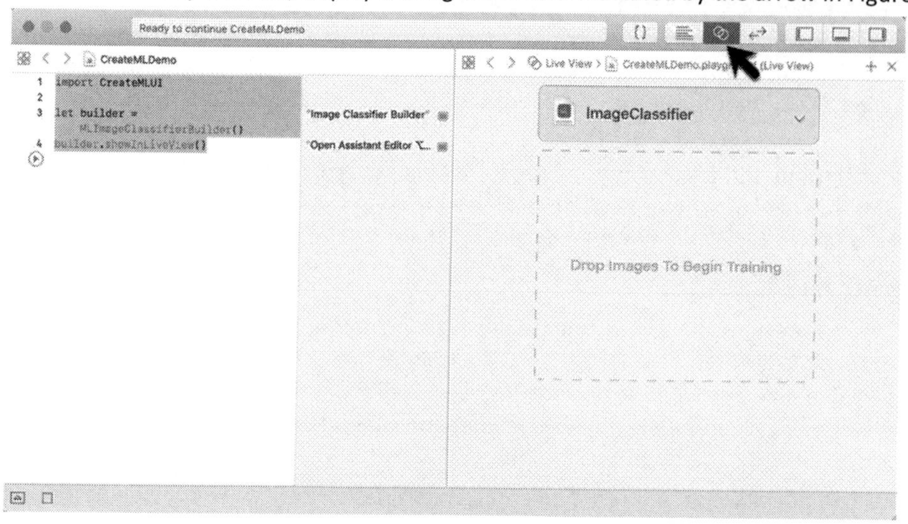

Figure 100-2

Open a Finder window, navigate to the dataset Training folder and drag and drop it onto the drop box labeled "Drop Images To Begin Training". The builder will work through each image file and then generate a validation set. The results of the process will appear both in the console panel and within the builder window:

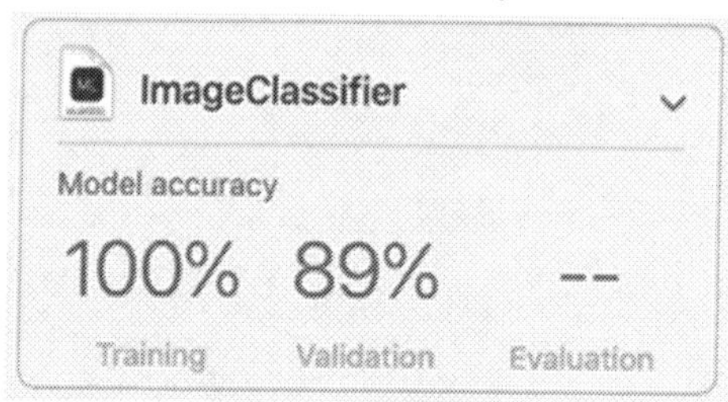

Figure 100-3

By default the builder will perform 10 validation iterations. Accuracy can be improved by increasing the number of iterations. To achieve this, stop the playground using the stop button in the lower left corner of the main playground panel and click on the down arrow in the title area of the builder. In the resulting panel increase the number of iterations before repeating the training:

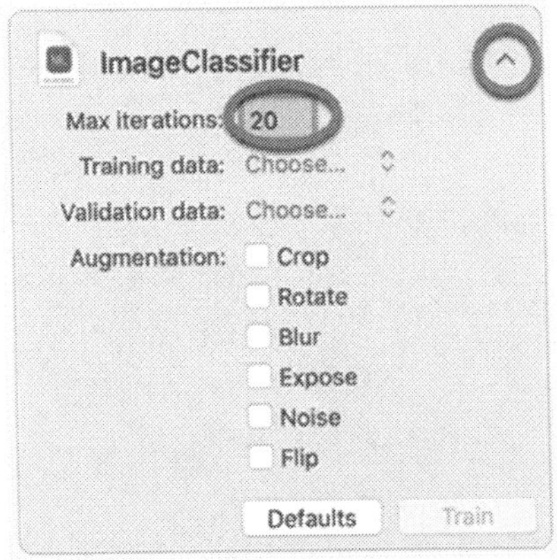

Figure 100-4

Once a high level of accuracy has been achieved, drag the Testing folder from the Finder window onto the drop box area and wait while the model categorizes the test images. Scroll through the results to review the accuracy of the training session.

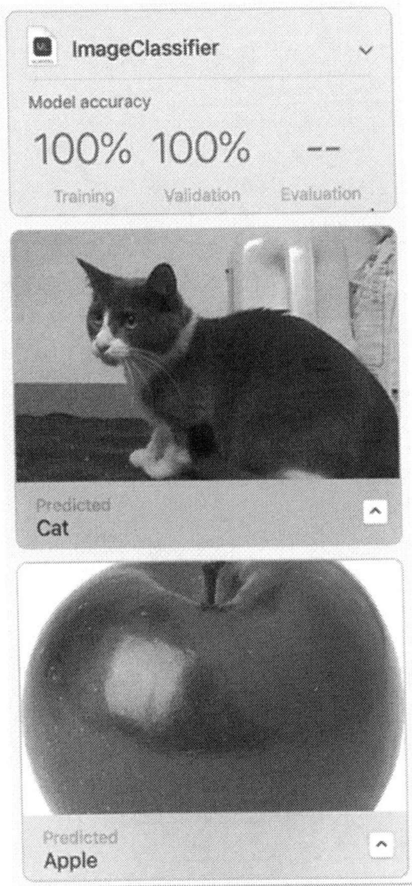

Figure 100-5

Double-click on the ImageClassifier title in the builder and change the name of the model to *MyImageClassifier*, click the down arrow to the right of the title and provide an author name, description and file location before clicking on the Save button.

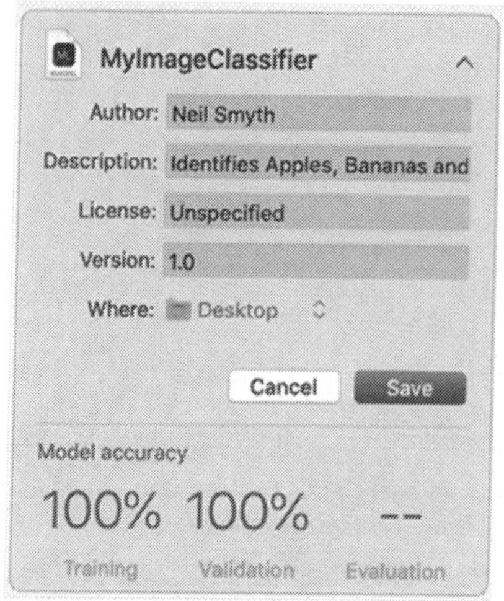

Figure 100-6

Once the model has been saved, it is ready to be used with in an app.

100.3 Summary

A key component of any machine learning implementation is a well trained model and the accuracy of that model is dependent on the dataset used during the model training. Once comprehensive training data has been gathered, Create ML makes it easy to create and test machine learning models from within an Xcode playground. This involves the use of the Create ML classifier builder. This chapter demonstrated the use of the Image classifier builder to create and save a model designed to identify a number of different object types within images. In the next chapter, this model will be put to use to perform image identification within an existing iOS app.

Chapter 101

101. An iOS Vision and Core ML Image Classification Tutorial

Having created an image classification machine learning model in the previous chapter, this chapter will take that model and use it in conjunction with the iOS Core ML and Vision frameworks to build image classification features into an iOS app.

101.1 Preparing the Project

The project used as the basis for this tutorial is the Camera app created previously in the chapter entitled *An Example iOS 12 Camera Application*. If you have not already completed the Camera tutorial, a completed copy of the project can be found in the source code archive download.

Using a Finder window, duplicate the Camera project folder, naming the copy Camera_ML and load it into Xcode.

101.2 Adding the Model

Using the Finder window once again, locate the *MyImageClassifier.mlmodel* file created in the previous chapter and drag and drop it on the Xcode Project navigator panel, accepting the defaults in the confirmation panel:

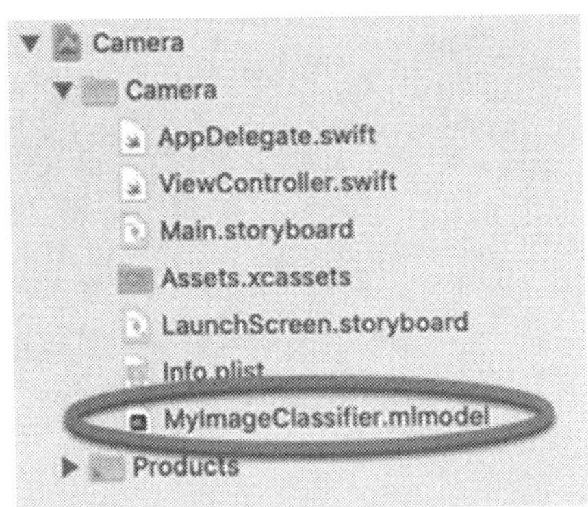

Figure 101-1

101.3 Modifying the User Interface

The existing user interface layout for the Camera app will need an additional Label view to be added so that the results of the classification can be presented to the user. Within Xcode, select the *Main.storyboard* file, display the Library panel and drag and drop a Label onto the toolbar so that it is positioned as shown in Figure 101-2:

Figure 101-2

With the Label selected use the *Add New Constraints* menu to add constraints to the left, right and bottom edges of the Label with the *Constrain to Margins* option enabled.

Finally, display the Assistant Editor panel and establish an outlet connection from the Label to a variable named *identityLabel*.

101.4 Initializing the Core ML Request

When the user either takes or selects a photo, the app will need to pass a request to an instance of the VNImageRequestHandler class to perform the classification. This request takes the form of a VNCoreMLRequest instance initialized with the machine learning model to be used. This model is provided in the form of a VNCoreMLModel object which, in turn, must be initialized with the machine learning model (in this case the model contained within the *MyImageClassifier.mlmodel* file).

The VNCoreMLRequest object also provides the option to specify a completion handler method to be called once the request has been processed. This method will be passed a VNRequest object from which the results of the classification can be checked and appropriate action taken.

Within the *ViewController.swift* file, add a method named *buildRequest()* to create a VNCoreMLRequest object, configure it with the MyImageClassifier model and assign a method named *checkResults()* as the completion handler to be called when the classification process finishes. This *buildRequest()* method will be called later in the tutorial when the VNImageRequestHandler instance is created:

```
.
.
import UIKit
import MobileCoreServices
import CoreML
import Vision
.
.
func buildRequest() -> VNCoreMLRequest {

    do {
        let model = try VNCoreMLModel(for: MyImageClassifier().model)

        let request = VNCoreMLRequest(model: model, completionHandler: {
            [weak self] request, error in
                self?.checkResults(for: request, error: error)
        })
        request.imageCropAndScaleOption = .centerCrop
        return request
    } catch {
        fatalError("Failed to load ML model: \(error)")
```

```
    }
}
.
.
```

101.5 Handling the Results of the Core ML Request

The completion handler for the above classification request is configured to call a method named *checkResults()* when the image analysis is completed. This method now needs to be added to the *ViewController.swift* file as follows:

```
func checkResults(for request: VNRequest, error: Error?) {
    DispatchQueue.main.async {
        guard let results = request.results else {
            self.identityLabel.text =
               "Unable to classify image.\n\(error!.localizedDescription)"
            return
        }

        let classifications = results as! [VNClassificationObservation]

        if classifications.isEmpty {
            self.identityLabel.text = "Nothing recognized."
        } else {
            let bestClassifications = classifications.prefix(1)

            let bestMatch = bestClassifications[0]

            if bestMatch.confidence < 0.60 {
                self.identityLabel.text = "No Match"
            } else {
                self.identityLabel.text = bestMatch.identifier
            }
        }
    }
}
```

The code begins by dispatching the result handling activities to a separate thread so that the code in the method is run asynchronously from the rest of the app:

```
func performClassification(for request: VNRequest, error: Error?) {
    DispatchQueue.main.async {
```

The method has been passed a VNRequest object which contains the results of the classification in the form of an array of VNClassificationObservation objects. The items in the array are positioned in order of best match to worst match. The method checks that the request object contains results and then extracts the array of observations.

```
let classifications = results as! [VNClassificationObservation]
```

The code notifies the user if no matches were found, otherwise the best match is taken from the results:

```
  if classifications.isEmpty {
      self.identityLabel.text = "Nothing recognized."
} else {
    let bestClassifications = classifications.prefix(1)

    let bestMatch = bestClassifications[0]
```

Having identified the closest match, the confidence value of the match is tested to make sure that the match was made with a greater than 70% degree of certainty. If the confidence level is high enough, the identifier for the match (in this case "Apple", "Banana", "Cat" or "Mixed") is displayed on the Label view. Otherwise "No match" is displayed:

```
if bestMatch.confidence < 0.70 {
    self.identityLabel.text = "No Match"
} else {
    self.identityLabel.text = bestMatch.identifier
}
```

101.6 Making the Classification Request

When the user either takes a picture or selects a photo library the image picker delegate methods will need a way to make the Core ML classification request. Begin implementing this behavior by adding another method to the *ViewController.swift* file:

```
func startClassification(for image: UIImage) {

    if let orientation =
                CGImagePropertyOrientation(rawValue:
                        UInt32(image.imageOrientation.rawValue)) {

        guard let ciImage = CIImage(image: image) else
            { fatalError("Unable to create \(CIImage.self) from \(image).") }

        DispatchQueue.global(qos: .userInitiated).async {
            let handler = VNImageRequestHandler(ciImage: ciImage,
                        orientation: orientation)
            do {
                let request = self.buildRequest()
                try handler.perform([request])
            } catch {
                print("Classification failed: \(error.localizedDescription)")
            }
        }
    }
}
```

The method is passed a UIImage object from which the current orientation is obtained before being converted to a CIImage instance. On a separate thread, a VNImageRequestHandler instance is created and initialized with the image object and orientation value. Next, the *buildRequest()* method created at the beginning of this chapter is called to obtain a VNCoreMLRequest object initialized with the trained model.

Finally, the request object is placed in an array (the VNImageRequestHandler class can handle multiple requests simultaneously) and passed to the *perform()* method of the handler. This will initiate a chain of events starting with the image classification analysis and ending with the resulting call to the *checkResults()* method which, in turn, updates the Label view.

The last step before testing the app is to make sure the *startClassification()* method gets called from the *didFinishPickingMediaWithInfo* image picker delegate method:

```
func imagePickerController(_ picker: UIImagePickerController,
didFinishPickingMediaWithInfo info: [UIImagePickerController.InfoKey : Any])
{

    let mediaType =
          info[UIImagePickerController.InfoKey.mediaType] as! NSString

    self.dismiss(animated: true, completion: nil)

    if mediaType.isEqual(to: kUTTypeImage as String) {
        let image = info[UIImagePickerController.InfoKey.originalImage]
            as! UIImage

        imageView.image = image

        startClassification(for: image)
.
.
}
```

101.7 Testing the App

Compile and run the app on a simulator and click on the Camera Roll button. When the image picker appears, open a Finder window and drag and drop some images onto the simulator screen (try both dataset images and images downloaded from the internet) to add them to the library. Select one of these images to return to the Camera app and verify that the label updates with the correct identification:

Figure 101-3

Repeat this step a few times, including selecting images that do not result in a match. Once the app has been tested on a simulator, install it on a physical device and test it by taking real life photos.

101.8 **Summary**

This chapter has demonstrated how a machine learning model can be used within an app to perform image classification tasks using classes from the Core ML and Vision frameworks together with a minimal amount of coding. The tutorial included both the creation and initiation of a machine learning request object and the handling of results from a completed classification request.

Chapter 102

102. Preparing and Submitting an iOS 12 Application to the App Store

Having developed an iOS application the final step is to submit it to Apple's App Store. Preparing and submitting an application is a multistep process details of which will be covered in this chapter.

102.1 Verifying the iOS Distribution Certificate

The chapter entitled *Joining the Apple Developer Program* covered the steps involved in generating signing certificates. In that chapter, both a development and distribution certificate were generated. Up until this point in the book, applications have been signed using the development certificate so that testing could be performed on physical iOS devices. Before an application can be submitted to the App Store, however, it must be signed using the distribution certificate. The presence of the distribution certificate may be verified from within the Xcode 10 *Preferences* settings.

With Xcode running, select the *Xcode -> Preferences...* menu option and select the *Accounts* category from the toolbar of the resulting window. Assuming that Apple IDs have been configured as outlined in *Joining the Apple Developer Program*, a list of one or more Apple IDs will be shown in the accounts panel as illustrated in Figure 102-1:

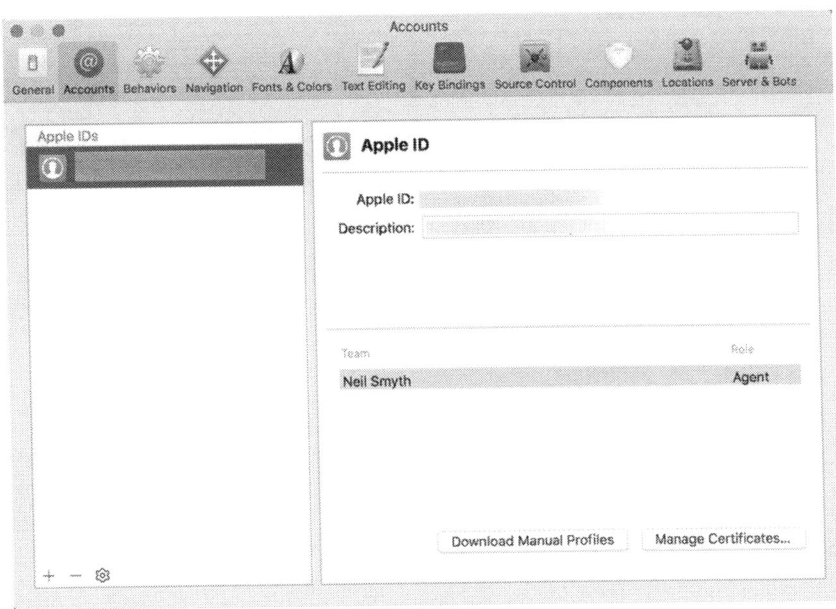

Figure 102-1

Select the Apple ID to be used to sign the application and click on the *Manage Certificates...* button to display the list of signing identities and provisioning profiles associated with that ID:

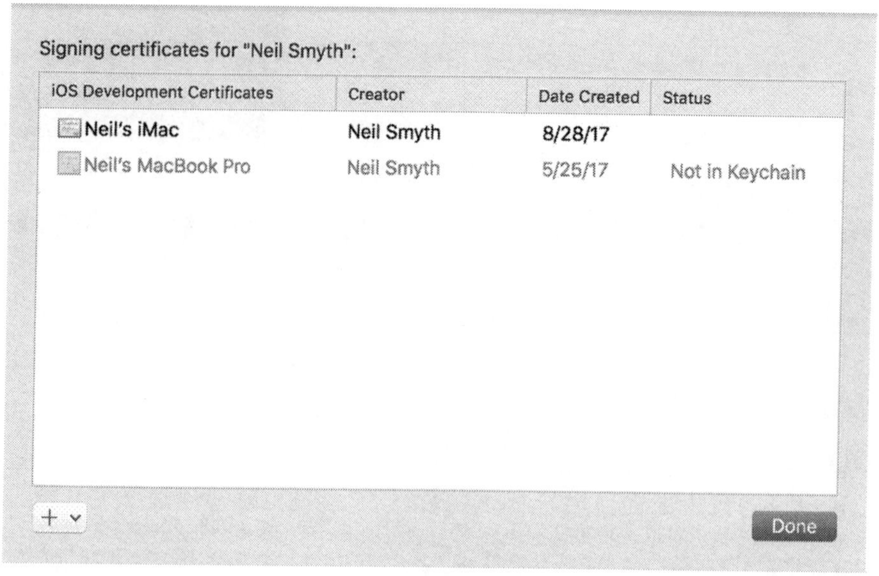

Figure 102-2

If no iOS distribution certificate is listed, use the menu highlighted in Figure 102-3 to generate one:

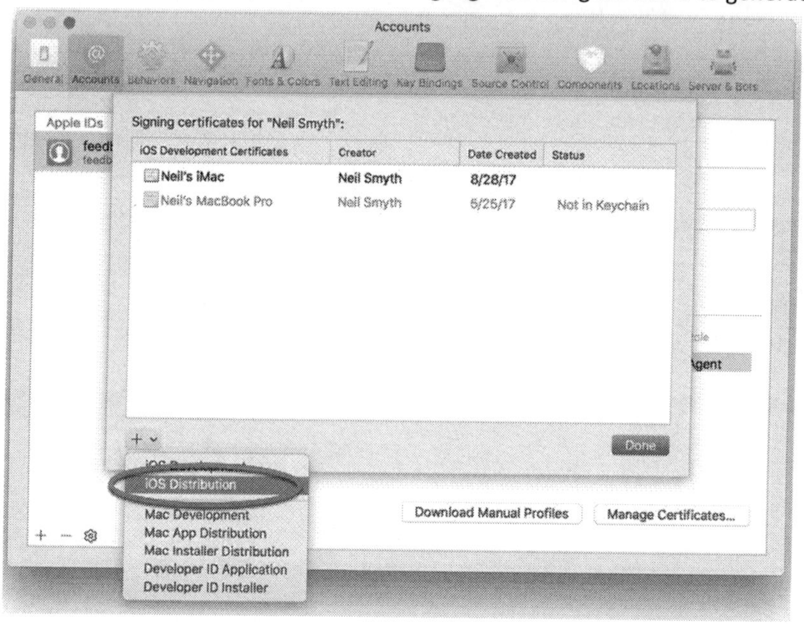

Figure 102-3

Xcode will then contact the developer portal and generate and download a new signing certificate suitable for use when signing applications for submission to the App Store. Once the signing identity has been generated, the certificate will appear in the list as shown in Figure 102-4:

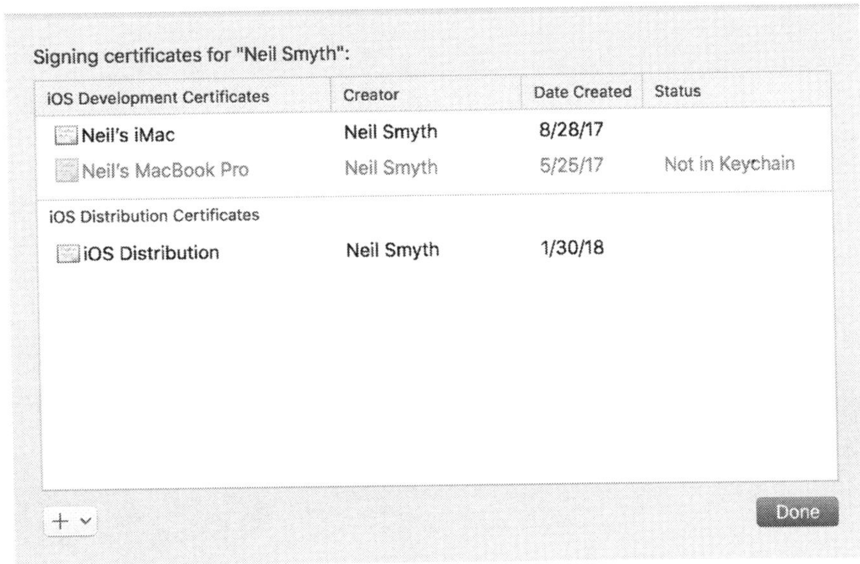

Figure 102-4

102.2 Adding App Icons

Before rebuilding the application for distribution it is important to ensure that app icons have been added to the application. The app icons are used to represent your application on the home screen, settings panel and search results on the device. Each of these categories requires a suitable icon in PNG format and formatted for a number of different dimensions. In addition, different variants of the icons will need to be added for retina and non-retina displays and depending on whether the application is for the iPhone or iPad (or both).

App icons are added using the project settings screen of the application project within Xcode. To view these settings, load the project into Xcode and select the application target at the top of the project navigator panel. In the main panel, select the *General* tab and scroll down to the App Icons and Launch Images sections. By default, Xcode will look for the App icon images within an asset catalog named *AppIcon* located in the *Assets.xcassets* asset catalog. Next to the *App Icons Source* menu is a small arrow (as indicated in Figure 102-5) which, when clicked, will provide access to the asset catalog of the App icons.

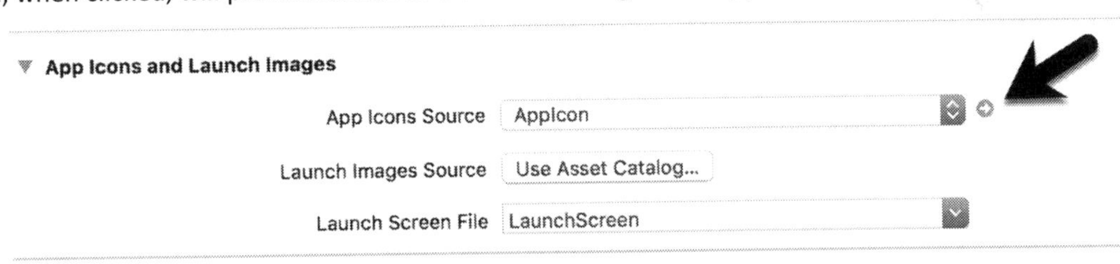

Figure 102-5

When selected, the AppIcon asset catalog screen will display showing placeholders for each icon size:

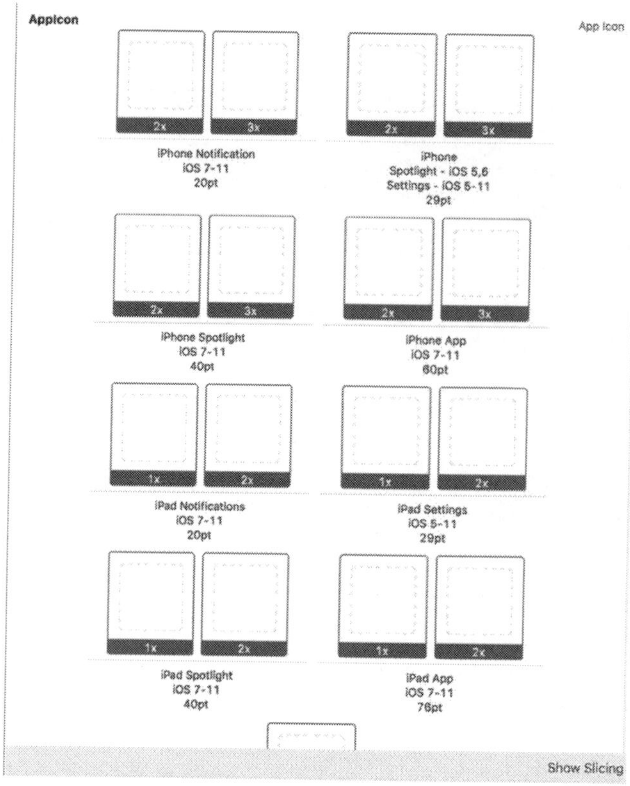

Figure 102-6

To add images, simply drag and drop the missing PNG format image files from a Finder window onto the corresponding placeholders in the asset catalog, or Ctrl-click on the catalog and select *Import* from the menu to import multiple files.

102.3 Designing the Launch Screen

The launch screen contains the content that appears when the application is starting up. The design for this screen is contained in the *LaunchScreen.storyboard* file which will have been generated automatically during the project creation process.

Load the file into Interface Builder and modify it to meet your requirements, including adding any images that may be required and keeping in mind that the layout must use Auto Layout and Size Classes to ensure that the layout appears correctly on all screen sizes. Note also that the layout is limited to UIKit classes and cannot include a WKWebView object.

102.4 Assign the Project to a Team

As part of the submission process, the project must be associated with a development team to ensure that the correct signing credentials are used. In the project navigator panel, select the project name to display the project settings panel. Click the General tab and within the Identity section, select a team from the menu as shown in Figure 102-7:

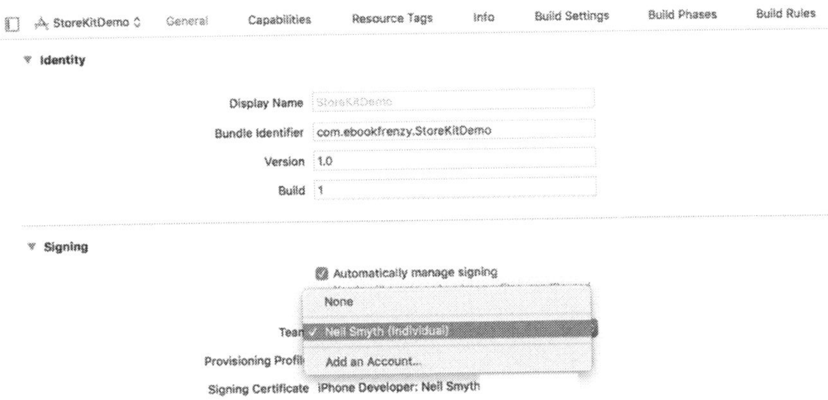

Figure 102-7

102.5 Archiving the Application for Distribution

The application must now be rebuilt using the previously installed distribution profile. To generate the archive, select the Xcode *Product -> Archive* menu option. Note that if the Archive menu is disabled this is most likely because a simulator option is currently selected as the run target in the Xcode toolbar. Changing this menu either to a connected device, or the generic *iOS Device* target option should enable the Archive option in the Product menu.

Xcode will proceed to archive the application ready for submission. Once the process is complete the archive will be displayed in the Archive screen of the Organizer dialog ready for upload and distribution:

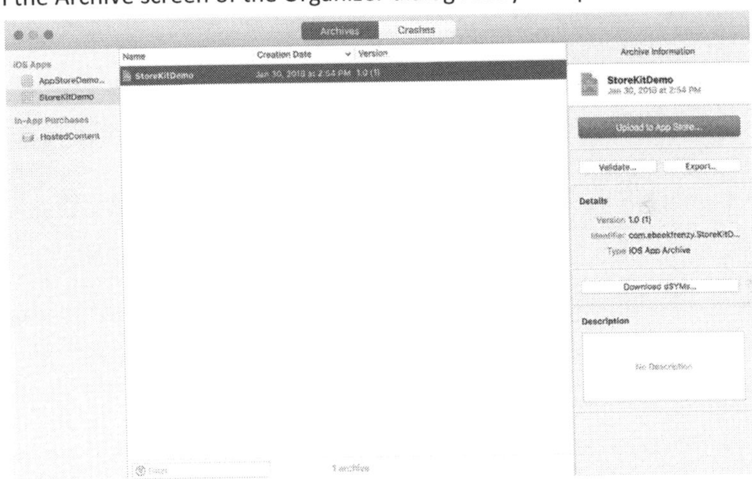

Figure 102-8

102.6 Configuring the Application in iTunes Connect

Before an application can be submitted to the App Store for review it must first be configured in iTunes Connect. Enrollment in the Apple Developer program automatically results in the creation of an iTunes Connect account using the same login credentials. iTunes Connect is a portal where developers enter tax and payment information, input details about applications and track the status of those applications in terms of sales and revenues.

Access iTunes Connect by navigating to *https://itunesconnect.apple.com* in a web browser and entering your Apple Developer program login and password details.

First time users should click on the *Agreements, Tax, and Banking* option and work through the various tasks to accept Apple's terms and conditions and to input appropriate tax and banking information for the receipt of sales revenue.

Once the administrative tasks are complete, select the *My Apps* option and click on the + button followed by *New App* to enter information about the application. Begin by selecting the *iOS* checkbox and entering a name for the application together with an SKU of your own creation. Also select or enter the bundle ID that matches the application that has been prepared for upload in Xcode:

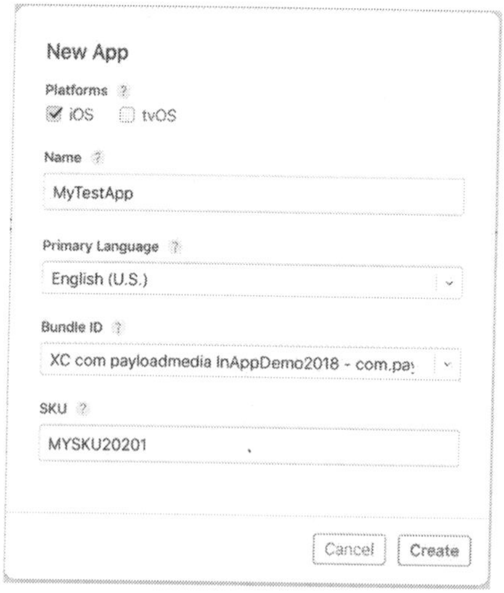

Figure 102-9

Once the application has been added it will appear within the My Apps screen listed as *Prepare for submission*:

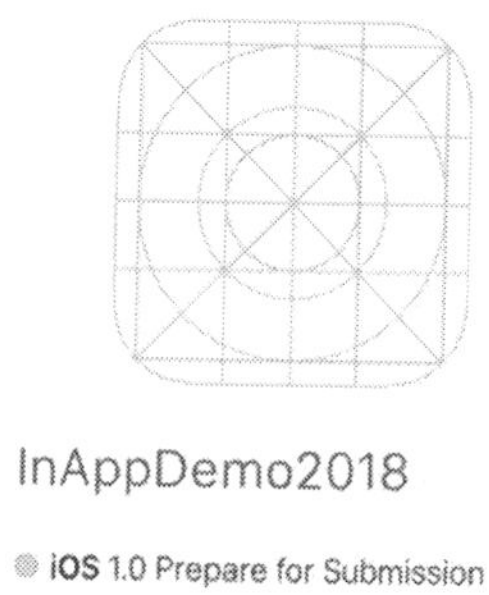

Figure 102-10

102.7 Validating and Submitting the Application

To validate the application, return to the Xcode archives window, make sure the application archive is selected and click on the *Validate...* button. Enter your iOS Developer program login credentials when prompted to do so. If more than one signing identity is configured within Xcode, select the desired identity from the menu.

Xcode will connect to the iTunes Connect service, locate the matching app entry added in the previous step and display the summary screen shown in Figure 102-11:

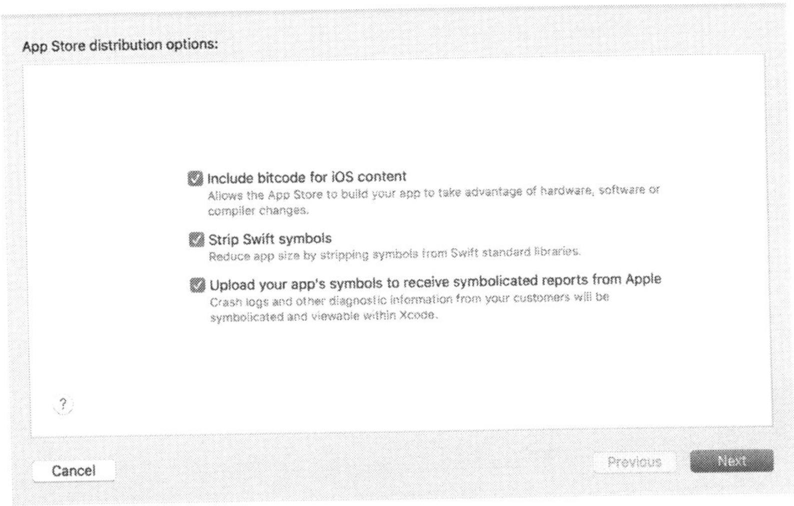
App Store distribution options:
Include bitcode for iOS content
Allows the App Store to build your app to take advantage of hardware, software or compiler changes.
Strip Swift symbols
Reduce app size by stripping symbols from Swift standard libraries.
Upload your app's symbols to receive symbolicated reports from Apple
Crash logs and other diagnostic information from your customers will be symbolicated and viewable within Xcode.
?
Cancel
Previous
Next

Figure 102-11

This screen includes the following options for selection:

- **Include bitcode for iOS content** – Bitcode is an intermediate binary format introduced with iOS 9. By including the app in bitcode format, it can be compiled by Apple so that it is optimized for the full range of target iOS devices and to take advantage of future hardware and software advances. Selection of this option is recommended.
- **Strip Swift Symbols** – Reduces the size of the app by removing symbol data from the Swift libraries linked with the app.
- **Upload your app's symbols** – If selected, Apple will include symbol information for the app. This information, which includes function and method names, source code line numbers and file paths, will be included in the crash logs provided to you by Apple in the event that your app crashes when in use by a customer. Selection of this option is recommended.

The next screen will provide the option to allow Xcode to automatically manage signing for the app, or to allow you to make manual certificate selections. Unless you are part of a team that uses multiple distribution certificates, automatic signing is usually a good choice:

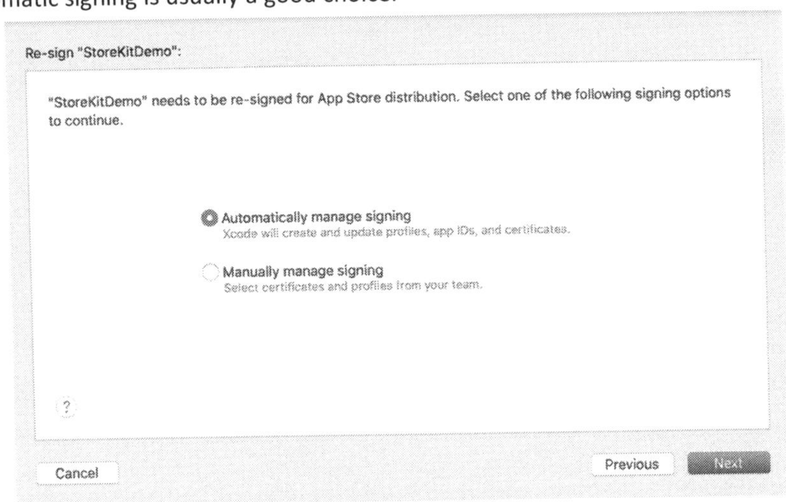
Re-sign "StoreKitDemo":
"StoreKitDemo" needs to be re-signed for App Store distribution. Select one of the following signing options to continue.
Automatically manage signing
Xcode will create and update profiles, app IDs, and certificates.
Manually manage signing
Select certificates and profiles from your team.
?
Cancel
Previous
Next

Figure 102-12

The final screen summarizes the certificate, profile and entitlements associated with the app:

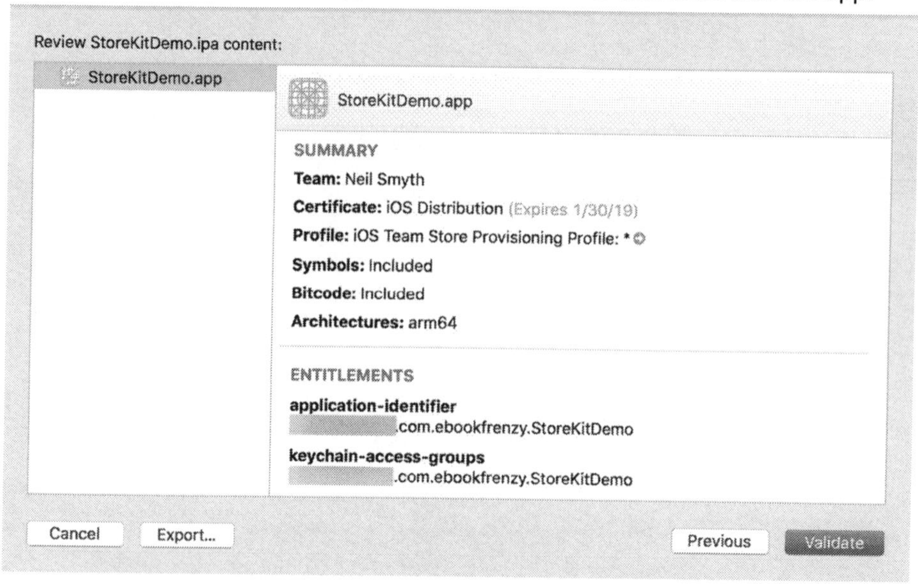

Figure 102-13

Click the *Validate* button to perform the validation and correct any problems that are reported. Once validation has passed, click on the *Done* button to dismiss the panel:

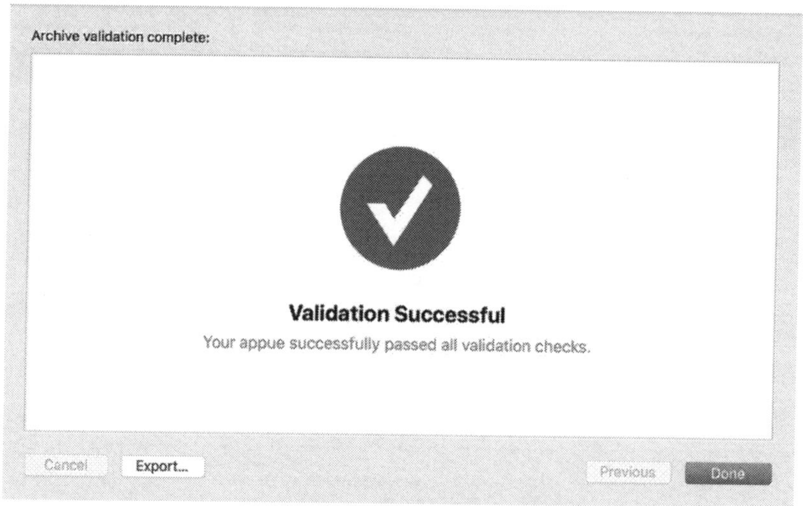

Figure 102-14

The application is now ready to be uploaded for App Store review.

Make sure the application archive is still selected and click on the *Upload to App Store...* button. Enter your developer program login credentials when prompted and review the summary information before clicking on the *Upload* button. Wait for the upload process to complete at which point a message should appear indicating that the submission was successful:

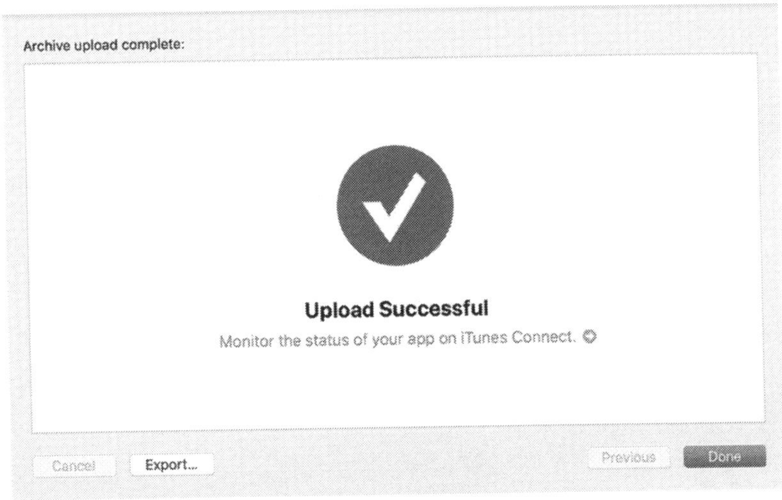

Figure 102-15

102.8 Configuring and Submitting the App for Review

On the My Apps screen of the iTunes Connect portal, select the new app entry to display the configuration screen where options are available to set up pre-release test users, designate pricing, enter product descriptions and upload screenshots and preview videos. Once this information has been entered and saved and the app is ready for submission to the App Store, select the *Prepare for Submission* option (marked A in Figure 102-16) followed by the *Submit for Review* button (marked B):

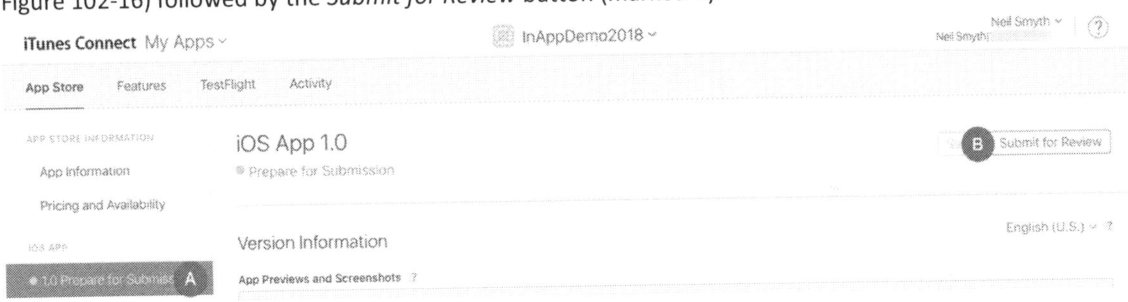

Figure 102-16

Once Apple has completed the review process an email will arrive stating whether the application has been accepted or not. In the event that the application has been rejected, reasons for the rejection will be stated and the application may be resubmitted once these issues have been addressed.

Index

B

C

D

E

F

G

H

I

K

L

M

N

O

P

Q

R

S

T

U

V

W

X

49825904R00443

Made in the USA
Columbia, SC
27 January 2019